Vegetables on the Side

The Complete Guide to Buying and Cooking

Sallie Y. Williams

Macmillan • USA

For Jerry

MACMILLAN
A Simon & Schuster Macmillan Company
1633 Broadway
New York, NY 10019-6785

Macmillan Publishing books may be purchased for business or sales promotional use. For information please write: Special Markets Department, Macmillan Publishing USA, 1633 Broadway, New York, NY 10019.

Copyright © 1995 by Sallie Y. Williams
Paperback edition © 1998 by Sallie Y. Williams

Library of Congress Cataloging-in-Publication Data

Williams, Sallie Y.
Vegetables on the side : the complete guide to buying and cooking vegetables / by Sallie Y. Williams.
p. cm.
Includes index.
ISBN 0-02-862336-3
1. Cookery (Vegetables) 2. Side dishes (Cookery) 3. Marketing (Home economics) I. Title.
TX801.W52   1995   94-43366
641.6'5—dc20   CIP

Manufactured in the United States of America
10 9 8 7 6 5 4 3 2 1

Acknowledgments

It is impossible here to thank everyone who has helped me with the preparation of this book. Without the good offices of Susan Lescher, however, it would never have become a reality, and I will be forever in her debt. Pam Hoenig, who had the confidence in me to suggest such a big undertaking, was extremely understanding when illness delayed everything. To all those people, including my ever-willing parents, whose patience I tried with unending requests to "taste this," I can only say I am especially grateful for their forbearance. I would also like to express my great appreciation to Jane Sigal, my editor. It is due to her skilled and patient efforts that my initial manuscript became a finished work.

Contents

Introduction

Is there anything more appealing in a supermarket or greengrocer than the colorful display of fresh produce? Never again will the home cook have to wonder how to choose or prepare the freshest of vegetables available in the market. This book will help you when it comes to selecting produce, and also gives advice on storing, cleaning, and preparing it for cooking. And it gives clear recipes for its use.

When fresh produce is not an option, there is advice on preparing frozen, dried (as in the case of mushrooms, peas, and beans), or even, sometimes, canned vegetables to present them in their best possible light.

With this book in hand, even the novice cook should no longer cringe at the thought of a sink full of fresh mustard greens or wonder what is the simplest method of cooking just-picked corn or how to prepare that funny, bumpy-looking bulb of celery root. And the experienced cook will want to keep this book nearby for helpful tips and ideas on preparing that bumper crop of zucchini or eggplant.

For many cooks, the chore of deciding how to prepare the requisite "two (or more) vegetables" to serve with the main course is the worst part of cooking. This book is meant to make that job easier. While there are a few vegetable soups and salads, sauces and condiments in among the rightful side dishes and while some of the recipes could make a light lunch or dinner by themselves, all the recipes were conceived as accompaniments, not as the centerpiece of a meal.

Pick your vegetable, either one you have on hand, or one that is at its peak in the market, and you are bound to find in these pages a way to serve it that will suit your menu. Though there are no main-course dishes here, each recipe is introduced with suggestions of what it might best accompany.

Vegetables have been getting a lot of good press in the last few years. It is no longer just a question of choking down spinach in order to have muscles like Popeye; it's now a matter of preventing disease and possibly extending life as well as adding interest to meals.

Of course, not everyone is going to love, or even like, every kind of vegetable, but there is certainly such a variety available these days that many vegetables will satisfy even the finickiest tastes. Start children young—most of them get used to the basics from little jars even before they are off the bottle, but once they start chewing we often seem to cut vegetables, especially fresh ones, from their menu. Try simple preparations at first, and then branch out to more complicated fare. There are plenty of each to experiment with here.

Why not sample a new vegetable every few weeks? Keep serving those you enjoy and skip on to something else when you find one that doesn't seem to please. Branch out and experiment, eliminating the mystique and apprehension that seem to surround fresh vegetables.

I hope this book has a place in every kitchen—right next to the stove.

Artichokes, Globe

This thistle relative, native to the Mediterranean, has been cultivated as a vegetable for more than a thousand years. Well known to the Greeks and Romans, artichokes were a rich man's vegetable, imaginatively prepared and often served at elaborate dinners and banquets to impress jaded diners.

Today, artichokes are an integral part of the cuisines of Italy, France, and Spain—and are certainly not restricted to special occasions. They are served in nearly every way imaginable, from simply boiled or steamed to fried or mixed into complex pasta and meat dishes—all wonderful. During the great wave of European immigration, our forebears brought their beloved vegetable with them to the New World, where it has been grown commercially ever since, almost exclusively around Castroville, California—which bills itself as the "artichoke capital of the world."

The globe artichoke we eat in this country is only one of many varieties, most of which are grown in Italy and Spain. There you will find tiny tender buds, artichokes with purple leaves, and long pointed buds as well as the large round vegetable we know.

Artichokes are actually the unopened flower buds of the plant, which, if left on the stem, would turn into large, purple, thistlelike blossoms. While some varieties of artichoke produce only tiny buds, the large vegetable grown here actually produces several sizes on the same plant, depending on where the bud appears on the stem. The lower, more shaded buds, are generally smaller and may be marketed as "baby" artichokes, but they are just as mature as the large ones on the upper branches.

There is often confusion about the difference between artichoke hearts and bottoms, which, for the purposes of this book, are not interchangeable. Hearts generally come from whole small artichokes whose tops have been cut off and outer leaves removed; they're usually blanched. They are often frozen or canned.

These can be halved or quartered and are used in antipasto, cooked dishes, or salads. The choke part of these little artichokes is so tender it can be eaten right along with the rest.

Artichoke bottoms are the meaty part of the artichoke left after all the leaves and choke are removed. These are usually filled with something or cut up in salads; they're served hot or cold.

Artichokes contain a substance called cynarin, which makes anything you eat with, or after, artichokes taste sweet. This same substance also makes wine taste metallic, and for that reason, wine is often not served with artichoke dishes. A liqueur maker has taken advantage of this natural sweetness and created a potent digestif from artichokes called Cynar, an acquired taste for some.

When served whole, the artichoke is one food that can be eaten out of hand, even in the most elegant surroundings. After the artichoke is served, though, I suggest that you pass small bowls of warm water, with a slice of lemon in each one, so everyone can rinse his or her fingers before tackling the rest of the meal.

Artichokes are high in fiber, provide potassium and vitamins A and C, and are low in fat.

Selection: Truly fresh artichokes can be hard to find, especially in supermarkets. Buy the tightest buds you can, regardless of the size. Once the leaves begin to open, the vegetable can be dry and tough and may have lost much of its flavor. The stem should look moist and not shriveled or woody. Avoid any buds that have bruises or dark spots that might be mold. A slight bronzish color just means the artichokes have been touched by frost, and, if the bud looks in otherwise good condition, this will not affect the taste or quality.

Whether your recipe calls for hearts or bottoms, baby or large artichokes, select ones of the same size to ensure they will all be cooked at the same time.

Frozen artichokes are fine for recipes calling for little Italian chokes. Just treat them as if they have been parboiled. Canned hearts and bottoms are also acceptable in a pinch, but they should be well rinsed to remove the canning liquid and some of the salt used in the preserving process. Even though it seems wasteful, I suggest that, if at all possible, you trim your own hearts and bottoms from whole artichokes for a more flavorful finished product.

Peak season lasts from March to June, but artichokes are in the market all year. Count on one large artichoke per person, or two or three if buds are small. If you will be serving only the hearts or bottoms, you will need two per person, unless they are very large.

Storage and Preparation: Artichokes should be stored at home for only a day or two. Keep them in a plastic bag in the vegetable crisper and prepare as soon as possible. Steamed or boiled artichokes can be wrapped in plastic wrap or sealed in plastic bags and kept up to two days in the refrigerator before serving. To bake artichokes after precooking them, remove them from the refrigerator, stuff them or finish the recipe, bake, and serve.

To serve whole precooked artichokes cold as an appetizer or salad, bring them to room temperature or microwave on high until they are no longer chilled, about $1\frac{1}{2}$ minutes. It is best not to put them into a conventional oven to warm up, as they can easily become overcooked.

Rinse raw artichokes well and remove any small, hard, or discolored leaves. Cut the stem off even with the base (or bang the stem sharply down onto the counter and then twist off the stem to remove it entirely, along with any stringy fibers) so the choke can stand straight up in a pan, and cut about one-third off the top to remove most of the spines. Rub all cut surfaces with half a lemon to prevent discoloring. If you like, use kitchen shears to cut the spiny tops off the remaining leaves, taking about $\frac{1}{2}$ inch off each leaf and remembering to rub the cuts with lemon juice.

When hearts or bottoms are called for, there are two ways to prepare them. The simplest way is to cook the whole artichoke by any one of the methods mentioned below and then, for hearts, cut off the tops and outer leaves or, for bottoms, carefully remove all the leaves and bristly choke, trimming the base until round and evenly shaped.

Professional chefs often like to trim the bottoms before cooking to make them all as uniform as possible. To do this, remove all the heavy outer leaves and, using a large, very sharp knife, cut off the pale remaining leaves about $\frac{1}{2}$ inch above the choke. With the knife, cut around the base, trimming it into an even shape. As soon as the base is finished, rub it with a cut lemon and then drop it into a bowl of 1 quart of water to which 2 tablespoons of lemon juice have been added. Once all the bottoms have been prepared, simmer them in acidulated water (water with lemon juice in it) until tender, but not falling apart. Cool them until easy to handle and pull out the choke. The bottoms are ready to fill or sauce as you like.

If you have only large artichokes when babies are called for, prepare them this way: Use a sharp knife to cut off the top third of the artichoke. Trim any remaining spines and cut the stem even with the base. Halve the artichoke lengthwise and remove the choke with a sharp spoon (a grapefruit spoon is perfect for this). Slice the halves lengthwise into thin wedges and then simmer in acidulated water to cover until tender, about 20 minutes. They are ready to be sautéed, braised, or otherwise used in the recipe. Or prepare the artichoke but leave it whole. Boil or steam it until tender, then halve, remove the choke, and slice.

Boiled Artichokes

Place the prepared whole artichokes in a kettle just large enough to hold all the artichokes standing upright in one layer. Pour in enough water to come about one-third the way up the chokes, cover, and simmer until you can insert a fork easily into the bottom of the largest choke, 30 to 45 minutes. Drain the cooked artichokes upside down.

At this point it is very easy to spread the leaves open from the top and use a spoon to scrape out the fuzzy, inedible choke at the bottom. Serve warm or at room temperature.

Steamed Artichokes

Artichokes can be steamed in a steamer basket or a colander, covered, over simmering water until tender, 45 to 60 minutes, depending on the size.

Microwaved Artichokes

Artichokes tend to keep more of their green color when they are microwaved than when they are boiled or steamed. So if color is important, you can microwave artichokes upside down in a single layer in a shallow dish. Cover loosely with microwave wrap and vent. For 1 artichoke, pour about $\frac{1}{4}$ cup water into the dish and microwave on high for 6 to 8 minutes, or a little longer if it is very large. For 3 or 4 artichokes, use $\frac{1}{2}$ cup water and count 10 to 15 minutes (or more), depending on size. Let the chokes stand 5 minutes and then drain before serving or continuing with the recipe.

Artichoke Salad

This salad always brings back memories of hot summer days along the Italian coast, good food, and great company. Serve it alongside chicken, veal, or fish, and accompany it with focaccia, an Italian flat bread found in many specialty bakeries.

Makes 6 servings

12 very small fresh artichokes, trimmed and
    boiled, steamed, or microwaved until very
    tender, halved lengthwise, chokes removed
    if necessary; or one 9-ounce package frozen
    artichoke hearts, thawed and halved length-
    wise; or 2 large artichokes, prepared as
    described on page 3
1 cup cooked chickpeas, canned, drained and
    rinsed, or freshly made (page 38)
½ cup oil-cured olives
1 small green bell pepper, seeded and cut into
    1-inch pieces
2 bunches (12 to 16) green onions (scallions),
    white and light green parts only, cut into
    ½-inch lengths
1 cup smallest cherry tomatoes
1 clove garlic, minced
Salt and freshly ground black pepper to taste
1 tablespoon fresh lemon juice
¼ cup red wine vinegar
½ cup extra-virgin olive oil, the fruitier the
    better
2 tablespoons chopped fresh oregano, plus sprigs
    for garnishing
1 head Bibb or Boston lettuce
4 ounces feta cheese, crumbled (1 cup)

In a large bowl, toss together the artichokes, chickpeas, olives, bell pepper, green onions, and tomatoes.

In a small bowl, beat together garlic, salt, pepper, lemon juice, vinegar, olive oil, and chopped oregano. Pour this dressing over the vegetables and toss well. Refrigerate, covered, at least 1 hour.

To serve, mound the vegetables on the lettuce leaves. Sprinkle with the feta and garnish with the oregano sprigs.

Artichoke and Spinach Gratin

Artichokes belong in all manner of dishes besides being served whole. Combine them with spinach and cheese and you have a delicious new addition to your table.

Makes 6 servings

2 tablespoons butter
½ medium-size onion, thinly sliced
½ pound large mushrooms, stems trimmed, sliced
One 3-ounce package cream cheese, softened
½ cup heavy cream
½ teaspoon dried oregano
Salt and freshly ground black pepper to taste
2 pounds spinach, stemmed, cut crosswise into
    strips, cooked in the water that clings to
    the leaves after washing until it wilts,
    and drained
4 large artichokes, trimmed, top one-third cut
    off, halved lengthwise, chokes removed, cut
    lengthwise into thin wedges, and boiled or
    steamed until very tender
¼ cup freshly grated Parmesan cheese

Preheat the oven to 325°F.

Melt the butter in a small skillet over medium heat. Add the onions and the mushrooms and cook, stirring, until just turning golden brown, about 10 minutes.

Butter a medium-size gratin dish. In a medium-size bowl, beat together the cream cheese and heavy cream. Beat in the oregano, salt, and pepper.

Stir the spinach into the mushroom mixture. Spread one-third of the mixture in the bottom of the prepared dish. Top with half of the artichokes. Dot with the cream cheese mixture. Repeat the layers of mushroom mixture, artichoke, and cream cheese mixture. Finish with the rest of the mushroom mixture. Dot with the remaining cream cheese mixture. Cover with aluminum foil and bake for 20 minutes. Remove the foil, sprinkle with the Parmesan cheese and bake until golden brown and bubbling, 15 minutes longer. Serve very hot.

Summer Stuffed Artichoke Bottoms

Serve this alongside cold poached fish or with grilled poultry. One artichoke bottom is enough for a side dish, but if you are planning artichoke bottoms as a luncheon main dish, two make a better meal.

Makes 6 servings

One 15-ounce container skim-milk ricotta
2 bunches (12 to 16) green onions (scallions),
    white part only, thinly sliced
2 cloves garlic, minced
$\frac{1}{3}$ cup chopped fresh parsley
Salt and freshly ground black pepper to taste
Hot pepper sauce to taste
$\frac{1}{2}$ large ripe tomato, peeled, seeded,
    and finely diced
1 head leaf lettuce
12 medium-size fresh artichoke bottoms, trimmed
    and boiled, steamed, or microwaved until
    tender, chokes removed, or canned artichoke
    bottoms, well rinsed
1 small red bell pepper, roasted (page 258),
    peeled, and cut into $\frac{1}{4}$-inch strips

In a small bowl, beat together the ricotta, green onions, garlic, parsley, salt, pepper, and hot pepper sauce. Refrigerate the mixture 30 minutes or more. Gently stir in the tomato.

Arrange the lettuce leaves on chilled plates. Set the artichoke bottoms on the lettuce, using 2 per serving. Spoon the cheese mixture into the bottoms. Serve cool, but not overchilled, garnished with the red pepper strips.

Variation: *Use the cheese mixture to fill the cavities of 6 cooled, cooked artichokes from which the chokes have been removed. Serve at room temperature.*

Artichoke Hearts and Tomato Gratin

This hearty dish will satisfy even the most ravenous appetites. Served with a tossed salad and lots of crusty bread, it could be a meal in itself.

Makes 6 servings

4 tablespoons ($\frac{1}{2}$ stick) butter, plus additional
    for buttering
2 medium-size Russet potatoes, peeled and
    thinly sliced
Salt and freshly ground black pepper
    to taste
1 large onion, thinly sliced
12 very small artichokes, trimmed, halved or
    quartered lengthwise, depending on size,
    and chokes removed if necessary
3 large tomatoes, thickly sliced
2 tablespoons chopped fresh oregano
$\frac{3}{4}$ cup chicken stock
$\frac{1}{4}$ cup dry white wine
$\frac{1}{3}$ cup plain dried bread crumbs

Preheat the oven to 350° F.

Generously butter a medium-size heavy gratin dish. Arrange the potatoes in 1 layer in the bottom of the dish. Dot with some of the 4 tablespoons butter and season with salt and pepper.

Layer the onion, artichoke hearts, and tomatoes, dotting each layer with additional butter and seasoning with salt and pepper. Sprinkle the oregano over the tomatoes. Pour in the stock and wine. Cover with aluminum foil and bake for 45 minutes.

Remove the foil, sprinkle with the bread crumbs, and bake until the crumbs are a rich golden brown, about 30 minutes longer. Serve very hot, or at room temperature.

Sautéed Baby Artichokes and Vegetables

Serve this wonderful dish with a grilled steak, and dinner is all done. If Italian baby artichokes are available, use them. Otherwise choose very small globe artichokes.

Makes 6 servings

3 tablespoons good-quality olive oil
1 large green bell pepper, seeded and cut into
    2-inch pieces
1 clove garlic, minced
12 fresh baby artichokes, trimmed, halved
    lengthwise, and boiled, steamed, or
    microwaved until very tender, chokes
    removed if necessary; or one 9-ounce
    package frozen hearts, thawed and halved
    lengthwise
6 small red potatoes, quartered and steamed until
    tender, about 20 minutes
½ pint boiling onions, boiled in water to cover
    for 1 minute, drained, peeled, and steamed
    for 5 minutes
1 teaspoon chopped fresh thyme
¼ cup dry white wine
Salt and freshly ground black pepper to taste

Heat the olive oil in a large heavy skillet over medium heat. Add the bell pepper and cook, stirring, until just tender, about 5 minutes. Stir in the garlic and cook 1 minute. Add the remaining vegetables. Toss until they are coated with the oil. Add the thyme. Stir in the wine, cover, and cook over low heat for 5 minutes. Season well with salt and pepper. Serve very hot, or at room temperature.

Braised Artichokes with Little Onions and Bacon

This is similar to Barigoule, but has its own definite personality.

Makes 6 servings

12 small or 6 large artichokes, trimmed, halved
    lengthwise, and chokes removed if necessary
1 pint boiling onions, boiled in water to cover
    for 1 minute, drained, and peeled; or one
    16-ounce package frozen baby onions,
    thawed
½ pound slab bacon, cut into thick chunks, fried
    until beginning to crisp, and drained on
    paper towels (page 42)
1 large ripe tomato, seeded and coarsely chopped
2 tablespoons good-quality olive oil
1 cup dry white wine
1 scant teaspoon dried Italian herbs, such as
    oregano, marjoram, rosemary, and thyme,
    or a prepared mix
Salt and freshly ground black pepper to taste

Combine all the ingredients in a large heavy saucepan. Cover and simmer over low heat until the artichokes are very tender, 40 to 45 minutes. Remove the cover and boil for a short time to reduce the sauce slightly. Serve warm, or at room temperature with the sauce spooned over.

Stuffed Artichokes

These are wonderful as a first course or as the accompaniment to plain herb-grilled fish.

Makes 6 servings (see Note)

2 tablespoons butter
⅓ cup good-quality olive oil, plus additional for
    drizzling
1 large onion, halved and thinly sliced
2 large cloves garlic, minced, or to taste
1 teaspoon dried Italian herbs, such as oregano,
    marjoram, rosemary, and thyme, or a
    prepared mix
1 large ripe tomato, peeled, seeded, and chopped
About ¾ cup plain dried bread crumbs

½ cup chopped fresh parsley
⅔ cup freshly grated Parmesan cheese
6 large artichokes, trimmed and boiled, steamed,
    or microwaved until tender, chokes removed

Preheat the oven to 325°F.

Heat the butter and the ⅓ cup of olive oil in a medium-size heavy skillet over low heat. Add the onion and cook, stirring, until translucent, about 10 minutes. Add the garlic and cook 30 seconds longer. Stir in the herbs and tomato. Continue cooking 1 minute more.

Stir in enough bread crumbs (up to ¾ cup) to hold the mixture lightly together. Mix together the parsley and cheese and stir into the crumb mixture.

Stuff the crumb mixture into the center and between the leaves of the cooked chokes. Arrange the artichokes, standing up, in a shallow glass or other baking dish just large enough to hold them in a single layer. Drizzle with just a little olive oil and bake, covered with foil, for 30 minutes. Remove the foil and bake until the artichokes are very tender and the crumb mixture is golden brown, about 15 minutes longer. Serve very hot or warm.

Note: *If a whole artichoke is too big for dinnertime appetites, halve all the ingredients. Cut the cooked artichokes in half lengthwise, remove the chokes, and stuff the centers with the crumb mixture. Spoon some between the leaves as well. Arrange, cut side down, in the baking dish and continue with the recipe. Serve each person an artichoke half.*

Steamed Artichokes with Pesto Mayonnaise

Plain mayonnaise, Hollandaise sauce, melted butter, or vinaigrette dressing is often served with cooked artichokes. Somehow the addition of pesto to homemade mayonnaise turns an ordinary presentation into something very special.

Makes 6 servings

3 large artichokes, trimmed and boiled, steamed,
    or microwaved until tender, halved length-
    wise, chokes removed, and cooled to room
    temperature
⅓ cup pesto, prepared or homemade
    (recipe follows)
⅔ cup mayonnaise, prepared or homemade
    (page 13)
3 tablespoons chopped fresh parsley

Arrange the artichokes, cut side up, on dinner plates. Beat the pesto into the mayonnaise. Spoon the sauce into the center of each artichoke. Garnish with the parsley. Pass the remaining pesto-mayonnaise in a separate dish.

Pesto

Proportions for this sauce vary all over the lot. I prefer a very nutty flavor and add more pine nuts than some. But fresh basil is a must. Dried basil will not work.

Makes about 1½ cups

2 cups fresh basil leaves
3 cloves garlic
½ cup freshly grated Parmesan cheese
½ cup olive oil
¼ cup pine nuts
Salt and freshly ground black pepper to taste
1 teaspoon butter, softened (optional)

Place all the ingredients, except the butter, in a food processor. Process until smooth, stopping occasionally to scrape down the sides of the bowl.

Using a rubber spatula, scrape the pesto into a small bowl. If a creamier consistency is desired, beat in the butter. The addition of the butter is traditional in parts of Italy but is purely a matter of taste.

Artichokes à la Barigoule

This is my variation of an old and very popular Provençal dish. In fact there are a multitude of versions, but the theme is always the same. This dish can be served very hot, warm, or at room temperature. Serve with crusty bread alongside cold roast chicken.

Makes 6 servings

3 tablespoons good-quality olive oil
3 ounces slab bacon, cut into $\frac{1}{4}$-inch dice
2 small onions, chopped
2 large carrots, peeled and chopped
12 small fresh artichokes, outer leaves removed,
    tops trimmed, quartered lengthwise, chokes
    removed if necessary; or one 9-ounce
    package frozen hearts, thawed and halved or
    quartered lengthwise
Salt and freshly ground black pepper to taste
$\frac{1}{4}$ pound tiny button mushrooms or large
    mushrooms (quartered), stems trimmed
2 cloves garlic, minced
$\frac{1}{3}$ cup chopped fresh parsley
1 cup dry white wine
$\frac{1}{2}$ cup well-flavored chicken stock

In a medium-size heavy saucepan with a tight-fitting lid, combine the oil, bacon, onions, carrots, and artichokes. Cook, covered, over very low heat, stirring from time to time, until the onions begin to turn golden brown, about 20 minutes. Season well with salt and pepper.

Stir in the mushrooms, garlic, and parsley. Add the wine and stock. Cover and simmer over very low heat until the artichokes are very tender but not falling apart, about 45 minutes. Remove the cover and boil hard to reduce the liquid by about one-quarter.

Season again with salt and pepper if needed. Serve in shallow soup plates.

Artichoke Ratatouille

Add this to your summer repertoire. Or, in deepest February when summer seems years away, cook up a batch of this, substituting one $14\frac{1}{2}$-ounce can of diced tomatoes for the fresh ones. I like this with whole grilled fish, such as snapper.

Makes 6 servings

3 tablespoons good-quality olive oil
2 large onions, halved and thinly sliced
2 cloves garlic, sliced
2 large red or green bell peppers, seeded and cut
    into 1-inch pieces
6 small fresh artichokes, trimmed, quartered
    lengthwise, and chokes removed if necessary;
    or one-half 9-ounce package frozen hearts,
    thawed and quartered lengthwise
2 to 3 large ripe tomatoes, cut into chunks
Salt and freshly ground black pepper to taste
1 tablespoon chopped fresh thyme;
    or 1 teaspoon dried
$\frac{1}{2}$ cup dry white wine

Heat the oil in a medium-size heavy kettle over low heat. Add the onion, garlic, and bell peppers and cook, stirring from time to time, until crisply tender, 5 or 6 minutes. Add the remaining ingredients in the order listed. Do not stir.

Cover and simmer until the vegetables are tender, about 20 minutes. Just before serving, stir gently, being careful not to break up the vegetables. Serve hot, warm, or at room temperature.

Artichokes, Jerusalem

Despite their name, these delicious little tubers bear no relationship whatsoever to artichokes, and rather than coming from the Middle East, they are native North Americans. While they were loved by Native Americans even when the first colonists arrived on these shores and are enthusiastically eaten in Europe, they have not gained the popularity here they probably deserve.

Actually, Jerusalem artichokes are underground tubers produced by a relative of the sunflower, which in Italy are called *girasole*, literally meaning "turning toward the sun," as sunflowers do. Jerusalem may be an English-language corruption of the Italian. The artichoke part is easier to understand as they do have a somewhat nutty flavor recalling cooked artichokes.

Some people call these tubers topinambours, perhaps for the Native American tribe of the same name that may have introduced them to the colonists. Frequently, you will see them on French menus and in French markets under this name.

Lately, greengrocers have begun selling this vegetable as sunchokes, which is probably a much more appropriate name given its relationship to sunflowers.

Jerusalem artichokes can be eaten both raw and cooked. Raw, they are crisp and delicious on crudité platters, in salads, and as part of an antipasto. They can also be cooked in almost any imaginable way: boiled, steamed, braised, sautéed, stir-fried, baked, fried, or pureed. In fact, anything you can do with a potato—with or without other ingredients—you can do to or with a Jerusalem artichoke.

One word of warning, though. Jerusalem artichokes contain a sugar that can be hard for some people to digest and can cause gastric distress. As a precaution, sample them sparingly the first time, and then enjoy them to their fullest when you know they agree with you.

If you have trouble finding these artichokes in your supermarket or greengrocer's, don't give up. They are frequently stocked by organic grocers and health-food stores that specialize in fresh produce.

Jerusalem artichokes are high in iron and natural fiber and are a good source of potassium.

Selection: Choose the plumpest tubers possible, with clear beige skins. Avoid any that are shriveled, have black spots, or show any signs of mold. If you can find ones that are nearly smooth and not too knobby, they will be easier to prepare.

Fresh Jerusalem artichokes are often in the market all year long, though they are generally at their best during the winter: October through April.

No matter what the preparation, count on at least ¼ pound per person.

Storage and Preparation: Store unwashed Jerusalem artichokes in a closed plastic bag in the vegetable bin of the refrigerator. If they are very fresh, they should keep at least a week. The new perforated vegetable bags are best at eliminating sweating and helping to prevent mold.

Wash the artichokes thoroughly, scrubbing to remove any dirt that might be clinging in the crevices. Most cooks like to peel them before eating, although it really isn't necessary. After the artichokes are cooked, the skin slips right off, but they can be peeled with a vegetable peeler if you plan to eat them raw. Once they have been peeled or cut, Jerusalem artichokes turn an unpleasant gray color, unless dropped quickly into acidulated water (1 to 2 tablespoons

lemon juice or vinegar to 1 quart of water). If slicing, dicing, or cutting the peeled chokes into other shapes, be sure to return the pieces to the acidulated water until they are ready to be cooked. Drain and dry the pieces before continuing with the recipe.

Boiled Jerusalem Artichokes

Cover the peeled artichokes with water and salt lightly. Bring to a boil over high heat, then reduce the heat to medium so the water just simmers, and cook until the chokes are tender, 12 to 15 minutes. Drain. When overcooked, these chokes almost seem to collapse, and they do it suddenly—so it is a good idea to stick them with a sharp knife from time to time and to remove them from the heat the minute they are tender. If you like, boil the artichokes in their skins, then cool slightly and slip off the skins before continuing. If you are going to cook the artichokes in oil or butter or add them to a dish that will be cooked further, just parboil them for 3 minutes, drain them, peel, and continue with the recipe. If parboiled, they do not need to be put into the acidulated water.

Microwaved Jerusalem Artichokes

Place the peeled artichokes in a microwave dish with 2 tablespoons water. Cover, vent, and microwave on high for about 5 minutes. (Be careful here. It may be better to cook them 1 or 2 minutes at a time, testing for doneness each time, so that they do not overcook.) Let stand 5 minutes and then drain before continuing with the recipe.

Gingered Jerusalem Artichokes

I think this is delicious with roast lamb. Try it the next time you barbecue a butterflied leg of lamb. The crisply tender artichokes absorb the gingery flavor of the sauce.

Makes 6 to 8 servings

2 tablespoons mild vegetable oil, preferably peanut

3 green onions (scallions), white and light green parts only, sliced, plus additional for garnishing

2 pounds Jerusalem artichokes, peeled, steamed until crisply tender, about 15 minutes, cooled, and sliced

1 tablespoon minced fresh ginger

1 tablespoon light soy sauce, or teriyaki sauce

2 tablespoons chicken stock

3 tablespoons dry white wine

Heat the oil in a wok or large heavy skillet over high heat. Add the 3 green onions and stir-fry for 30 seconds. Stir in the artichokes and ginger. Cook, tossing or stirring, for 1 to 2 minutes. Mix together the soy sauce, stock, and wine in a small bowl and pour over the vegetables. Cook, tossing to coat the vegetables, for 30 seconds. Serve very hot, garnished with the additional green onion.

Jerusalem Artichoke and Mushroom Sauté

The anise taste of the tarragon makes this a perfect accompaniment to baked or roasted chicken or turkey. Why not try it with a crisply roasted duck?

Makes 6 servings

2 tablespoons butter

½ pound white mushrooms, stems trimmed, halved or quartered

1½ pounds Jerusalem artichokes, peeled, thickly sliced, rubbed with lemon juice, and steamed until crisply tender, about 15 minutes

Salt and freshly ground black pepper to taste

2 tablespoons chopped fresh tarragon

Melt the butter in a heavy skillet over medium-high heat. Cook the mushrooms, tossing, until they just turn golden brown, 4 to 5 minutes. Add the artichokes. Season well with salt and pepper. Cook, tossing or stirring, until the artichokes are fork tender, 5 to 6 minutes. Sprinkle with the tarragon and serve very hot.

Variation: *For a more unctuous dish, stir in a few tablespoons of heavy cream when the artichokes are just tender and heat through.*

Jerusalem Artichoke Puree

It isn't necessary to add potatoes to the artichokes in the puree, but I think the flavor of the combined vegetables is special. Try serving this with roast goose!

Makes 6 servings

1 pound Jerusalem artichokes, boiled in salted water to cover until very tender, drained and peeled

1 large Russet potato, peeled, cut into chunks, boiled in salted water to cover until tender, about 10 minutes, and drained

1 clove garlic, pressed

1 tablespoon chopped fresh parsley

1 tablespoon butter

Salt and freshly ground black pepper to taste

2 tablespoons heavy cream (optional)

In a medium-size bowl, mash the artichokes and potato together or put through a ricer. In a medium-size saucepan, stir together the mashed artichokes and potato. Beat in the garlic, parsley, and butter. Season well with salt and pepper.

If needed, stir in the cream to make a smooth puree. Heat over very low heat until very hot.

Braised Jerusalem Artichokes

These little nuggets have a very delicate taste and will take on the flavors of whatever they are cooked with. This dish lets the natural flavor shine as much as possible. Serve them with roast poultry or grilled veal.

Makes 4 to 6 servings

1½ pounds Jerusalem artichokes, peeled, sliced
    ¼ inch thick and soaked in acidulated water
    (2 tablespoons lemon juice in 1 quart water)
2 tablespoons butter
3 green onions (scallions), white and light green
    parts only, cut into 1-inch lengths
½ cup well-flavored chicken stock
Salt and freshly ground black pepper to taste
1 tablespoon chopped fresh oregano, plus
    additional for garnishing

Drain the artichokes well and dry on a kitchen towel. Melt the butter in a medium-size heavy skillet over medium heat. Add the green onions and the drained artichokes and cook, tossing, for 3 to 4 minutes. Stir in the stock, salt, pepper, and the 1 tablespoon oregano. Simmer, uncovered, over medium heat until the artichokes are just tender and most of the liquid is evaporated, 8 to 10 minutes.

Serve very hot, garnished with plenty of freshly ground pepper and the additional oregano.

Braised Jerusalem Artichokes with Peas and Pancetta

This is a delicious accompaniment to grilled pork chops or tuna steaks. The pancetta and peas add their own flavor to the delicate tubers.

Makes 6 servings

¼ pound pancetta, coarsely chopped
1 teaspoon butter
1 pound Jerusalem artichokes, peeled if you like,
    soaked in acidulated water (2 tablespoons
    lemon juice in 1 quart water), halved or
    quartered, and dried on a kitchen towel
½ cup chicken stock
¼ cup dry white wine
1 cup shelled fresh or thawed frozen peas
Salt and freshly ground black pepper to taste
2 tablespoons chopped fresh parsley

In a medium-size heavy skillet, cook the pancetta over medium heat until the fat becomes translucent, about 2 minutes. Remove the pancetta from the skillet with a slotted spoon and drain on paper towels. Melt the butter in the same skillet, still over medium heat. Add the artichokes and cook, turning or tossing, for 2 minutes. Pour in the stock and wine. Simmer, covered, until the artichokes are just beginning to be tender, about 10 minutes. Stir in the peas and reserved pancetta. Simmer over low heat, covered, until the peas are tender, about 8 minutes, or a little longer depending on the age of the peas.

Uncover and cook, still over low heat, to reduce the pan juices. Season well with salt and freshly ground pepper. Stir in the parsley and serve hot.
Variation: *Try serving this over cooked spaghetti, with freshly grated Parmesan cheese on the side.*

Jerusalem Artichoke Rémoulade

This variation on the theme of Céleri Rémoulade, a traditional French salad of celeriac (celery root) and mayonnaise, is equally delicious. In fact, you can substitute 1 cup of celeriac cut into matchstick strips for half of the Jerusalem artichoke to produce a totally new flavor. This is the classic French rémoulade, not the rémoulade that is popular in New Orleans. Serve this with a buffet of cold meats and fish.

Makes 6 servings

¾ pound Jerusalem artichokes, peeled, sliced
    lengthwise, cut into matchstick strips, and
    soaked in acidulated water (2 tablespoons
    lemon juice in 1 quart water)
2 large carrots, peeled and cut into matchstick
    strips
1 bunch (6 to 8) green onions (scallions), white
    and light green parts only, thinly sliced
½ teaspoon celery seed
1 cup mayonnaise, prepared or homemade (recipe
    follows)
2 tablespoons Dijon-style mustard
Salt and freshly ground black pepper to taste
1 head leaf lettuce
Chopped fresh parsley

Drain the artichokes and dry on a kitchen towel. In
a medium-size bowl, toss them with the carrots, green
onions, and celery seed. Combine the mayonnaise
and mustard in a small bowl. Pour this sauce over the
vegetables, toss, and season well with salt and
pepper.

Cover and refrigerate for several hours. Serve
chilled on a bed of lettuce, garnished with the
parsley.

Homemade Mayonnaise

Makes about 1 cup

2 large egg yolks
1 teaspoon Dijon-style mustard
About 1 teaspoon fresh lemon juice
Salt and freshly ground black pepper to taste
1 cup olive oil, mild vegetable oil, or a mixture
    of both

In a medium-size bowl, beat together the egg yolks,
mustard, lemon juice, salt, and pepper with a whisk.
Whisk in the oil, a teaspoon at a time, until the mixture thickens and begins to look like mayonnaise.
Then whisk in the remaining oil in a thin stream.
Add a little more lemon juice if the mixture is too
thick. Serve cold or at room temperature.

Note: *While almost all the outbreaks of salmonellosis involving eggs have occurred in the food-service sector, there's no reason for home cooks to flout egg safety rules. The only way to guarantee a safe egg is to cook it thoroughly. But if, like me, you still eat poached, fried, and boiled eggs with runny yolks and still make your own mayonnaise, at least take care to use only the freshest eggs. Never use cracked raw eggs and always keeps eggs refrigerated. Place cold eggs in either a hot frying pan or in boiling water. Don't keep cooked eggs warm for too long—eat them as soon as you have prepared everyone's portion.*

Roasted Jerusalem Artichokes

The nutty flavor of these artichokes is deliciously evident when they are prepared this way. Grilled fish and freshly cooked spinach go very well with these roasted nuggets.

Makes 6 servings

1½ pounds Jerusalem artichokes, scrubbed
    and dried
2 tablespoons good-quality olive oil
1 teaspoon dried Italian herbs, such as
    oregano, marjoram, rosemary, and thyme,
    or a prepared mix
Seasoned pepper, such as Mrs. Dash, to taste
Salt to taste

Preheat the oven to 375°F.

In a medium-size bowl, toss the artichokes with
the olive oil and spread in a small baking pan. Season with the herbs and pepper. Roast until tender
but not collapsed, about 45 minutes. Salt generously
and serve very hot.

Artichokes, Chinese or Japanese (Crosnes)

This is another artichoke that is not an artichoke. These little curlicue tubers have a taste that does somewhat resemble that of a cooked globe artichoke and, even more so, that of Jerusalem artichokes. These are Asian in origin, Chinese by way of Japan and then brought to Europe in the late nineteenth century.

First grown in the Western world in Crosne (pronounced *crone*), France, the name of the town stuck to the new vegetable. For a while crosnes were very popular, especially in France where you can still find them in many specialty vegetable shops, but for the most part they have more or less gone out of style. This may be because they are difficult to keep fresh during transport from farm to market and are somewhat labor intensive to prepare for cooking.

These delicate tubers are hard to find in American markets, but if you ever come across them, I think they are worth a small effort to prepare.

Crosnes can be eaten raw or pickled as part of a crudité platter or antipasto, but they are generally served cooked. I have eaten them braised, boiled, sauced, roasted, and pureed, and I think they are best when served as an accompaniment to roasted meat or grilled steak.

Selection: Fresh crosnes are nearly white or pale beige. They are knotted, twisted little tubers, 1 to 3 inches in length. Choose them about 2 inches long if you have a selection. Pick the firmest and crispest available. Do not buy them if they are the least bit spongy, spotted, or show any signs of mold.

Crosnes are best after the first freeze and are generally available all winter. Count on 1 pound serving four to six people.

Storage and Preparation: Crosnes are fairly fragile and do not keep well. They can be stored in the vegetable bin of the refrigerator for two to three days, wrapped in paper towels inside a plastic bag or sealed in a perforated plastic vegetable bag. If, by chance, you or someone you know grows them, leave them in the ground until just before cooking time. They seem to last longest this way and can be dug even after the first frost.

The twisted shape makes these tubers hard to wash, and they should be scrubbed with a brush before cooking to remove all the dirt that may be embedded in the cracks.

The easiest way to peel crosnes is to parboil them for 3 or 4 minutes and to rub off the thin skin. Traditionally, the French place the raw, washed tubers in a clean kitchen towel with some coarse salt and then toss and rub the vegetable until most of the skin comes off. They must then be well rinsed to remove excess salt before proceeding with any recipe. I find it easier just to leave the skins on since they do not seem to hinder any preparation. Nor do the skins harm the taste of the cooked vegetable.

Boiled Crosnes

Boil the scrubbed and, if you like, peeled crosnes in salted water to cover until tender but not mushy, about 15 minutes, then drain. The smaller the tuber, the less time they will need to cook. Crosnes are like Jerusalem artichokes in that they tend to collapse if they are overcooked. It is a good idea to test them with the point of a sharp knife from time to time and to remove them from the heat once they are just tender. They will continue to cook a little even after being taken off the heat.

Steamed Crosnes

Arrange the scrubbed and, if you like, peeled crosnes in a single layer in a steamer basket or colander. Steam over simmering water until tender but not mushy, 15 to 20 minutes, testing with the point of a sharp knife so that they do not overcook.

Crosnes in Mornay Sauce

For a richer dish, and one that will stretch just a little further if crosnes are at a premium, try incorporating them in a cheese sauce. Serve this with roast or grilled chicken.

Makes 4 to 6 servings

1 tablespoon butter
1 tablespoon all-purpose flour
1 cup milk, whole or skim
1 cup grated Gruyère, Cheddar, or fontina cheese
Pinch ground red (cayenne) pepper
1 pound crosnes, scrubbed, trimmed if necessary,
    and steamed or boiled in salted water to
    cover until just tender, drained
Salt and freshly ground black pepper to taste

Melt the butter in a medium-size heavy saucepan over low heat. Stir in the flour and cook, stirring, until bubbling but not browned, about 3 minutes. Stir in the milk all at once, whisking until smooth. Increase the heat to medium and cook, stirring occasionally, until the mixture thickens.

Stir in the cheese and cook, stirring constantly, until the cheese melts. Season with cayenne, salt, and black pepper. Stir in the crosnes, and heat through, but do not boil. Serve very hot.

Crosnes with Butter and Garlic

I think this is the best way to prepare crosnes. I like to serve them this way with roast lamb whenever I find them.

Makes 6 servings

2 tablespoons butter
1 pound crosnes, scrubbed, trimmed if necessary,
    and steamed or boiled in salted water to
    cover until tender, drained

2 cloves garlic, minced
2 tablespoons chopped fresh parsley
Salt and freshly ground black pepper to taste

Melt the butter in a small skillet or in a medium-size heavy saucepan over medium heat. Add the crosnes and toss to coat with the butter. Add the garlic and parsley, and cook, tossing, until the garlic is soft but not burned, about 1 minute. Season well with salt and pepper and serve very hot.

Note: *The crosnes can be boiled or steamed in advance, and reheated in boiling water to cover, or microwaved for 1 minute, before continuing with the recipe.*

Fried Crosnes

It is difficult to stop eating these crisp little morsels: they are almost as addictive as peanuts. Serve them as an appetizer, or pass a bowl of hot fried crosnes with a glass of white wine while the rest of the dinner is being put on the table.

Makes 4 to 6 servings

1 pound crosnes, scrubbed, trimmed if necessary,
    boiled in salted water to cover until tender,
    and drained
Mild vegetable oil for deep-frying
Beer Batter (recipe follows)
Salt

Dry the crosnes on a kitchen towel.

Heat the oil to 375°F. in a deep-fat fryer.

Whisk the Beer Batter well. Dip the dried crosnes into the batter. Fry the crosnes in batches in the hot oil until golden brown and crisp, 2 to 3 minutes per batch. Drain well on paper towels and season with salt. Serve very hot.

Beer Batter

This batter is a delicious basic batter for deep-frying many kinds of vegetables.

Makes about 2 cups

1½ cups beer
1 cup all-purpose flour
1 tablespoon salt
Freshly ground black pepper to taste

In a large bowl, whisk together the beer and flour. Whisk in the salt and season with the pepper. The batter should be light. If not using immediately, be sure to whisk the batter well just before coating the vegetables with it.

Note: *The batter can be made up to 1 hour ahead of time and kept at room temperature.*

Asparagus

A true harbinger of spring, asparagus has been known, eaten, and cultivated for more than two thousand years. The Greeks and Romans not only enjoyed pencil-thin wild asparagus, which, it seems, they cooked very quickly and ate crisp, but they also knew how to grow thick domesticated spears, which they served with pride and which they felt had other than nutritional properties.

In Germany, the love of fresh asparagus has resulted in a spring *Spargelfest* that pits chefs against one another as they try to create entire menus featuring the vegetable. Each day during this six-week-long festival, the menus offer a selection of new and different dishes, including such concoctions as asparagus ice cream.

Often, in fine restaurants in France, asparagus spears are wrapped in a white napkin to be eaten with a special pair of silver tongs. If tongs are not available, it is one of the very few foods that Europeans will eat with their fingers. Here is an instance when small bowls of warm water containing a little lemon juice or a lemon slice would be welcome to let diners rinse their fingers before attacking the rest of the meal.

Asparagus can be cooked and eaten hot, warm, or chilled. When served chilled, they are often treated as if they were a salad. Eaten hot, or at least warm, asparagus can be a wonderful first course or an excellent side dish. If you are serving them with a Hollandaise or Maltaise sauce, don't have them boiling hot when you put the sauce on. These delicate emulsified butter sauces are meant to be eaten warm, not very hot, and they may separate if put on a vegetable that is too hot.

Asparagus are a good source of vitamins A and C and potassium. They are low in sodium and calories: 1 cup has only about thirty-five calories.

Selection: Fresh asparagus must be bright green, plump, and crisp with tight buds that have not begun to spread and sprout. Even pencil-thin spears should not be limp. Well-kept asparagus has been refrigerated from field to market. Within hours of being left at room temperature, asparagus loses much of its inherent sugar, and that robs it of the fresh, clean taste we love. And there is nothing that compares with going out to the garden and cutting the asparagus for dinner just before cooking it.

Regardless of what type you like best, pencil thin, extra thick, in between, or white, be sure to select all the spears of the same thickness so that they will cook uniformly.

Asparagus are at their peak in the spring through the month of June. Count on 2 pounds for six servings.

Storage and Preparation: Use a vegetable peeler to peel the stems of asparagus that are thick or have a heavy skin. Otherwise simply wash the asparagus very well to remove any silt or sand caught in the buds. If not using asparagus immediately, cut off a half inch of the stem and stand the asparagus upright in a container of water in the refrigerator—like a bunch of flowers.

Just before cooking, cut all the spears to the same length so they will all be cooked at the same time. (Length, as well as thickness, affects cooking time.) Many authorities advocate bending the asparagus and letting them snap in two where they will. The theory is that they break where they become tender, leaving the woody, tough part behind. This is fine in principle, but leaves you with some spears several inches longer than others, making them cook at different times. The presentation is less attractive, too. If the last inch or so of some of the spears you have cut seems to be a little tough, simply peel it with a vegetable peeler or sharp knife.

Tip: *When serving plain steamed or boiled asparagus hot, there is a simple way to avoid overcooking. Up to several hours ahead of time, simmer or steam the asparagus until crisply tender. Cool quickly in cold water, drain, and set aside. Just before serving, plunge the precooked asparagus into boiling water to cover until very hot, just 30 to 60 seconds, depending on the thickness of the spears. Then drain the asparagus and serve it at once, accompanied by your favorite sauce.*

Steamed Asparagus

If the recipe calls for the asparagus to be cut up, steaming is often the best way to prepare them. Simply place the prepared asparagus in a steamer basket or colander over simmering water and steam, covered, until tender, about 5 minutes. Test with the point of a sharp knife, and continue cooking if needed. Whole asparagus can also be steamed and will retain more nutrients, but cooking time is slightly longer than boiling. If preparing the asparagus in advance, be sure to chill them quickly in cold water so that they do not continue to cook as they cool.

Microwaved Asparagus

Arrange the prepared asparagus in a microwave dish with the tips as close to the center as possible. (Most microwave ovens have a nearly dead spot in the center where food cooks less quickly than it does at the outer perimeter, so the tips will not be overdone before the stalks are finished cooking.) Pour in about $1/4$ cup water, cover with plastic microwave wrap, being sure to leave a steam vent, and microwave on high until tender, 4 to 5 minutes. Test, being careful of the steam, and microwave 1 minute more if necessary. Let stand 3 minutes before serving.

Boiled Asparagus

There are special, expensive asparagus cookers, narrow upright pots with a basket that fits inside, but I find them difficult to use unless you tie the spears in bundles before putting them into the basket. You fill this pot with water to come about halfway up the spears, cover, and bring to a boil. The boiling water cooks the tougher stalks at the same time that steam cooks the tender tops. I find, however, that bundling the spears makes the outer asparagus cook more quickly than the interior ones, so that some are overcooked while others are not cooked quite enough.

A simpler method is to cook the prepared asparagus in 1 layer in a large skillet or sauté pan in boiling water to cover until tender, 6 to 8 minutes, then drain. Asparagus cook quickly this way and all are available to test with a sharp pointed knife so that they do not become overdone. If cooking ahead, remove the spears one or two at a time, when they become crisply tender, and chill quickly in cold water, then drain on a kitchen towel. They can be reheated when you are ready to serve them.

Asparagus with Ham and Hollandaise

The addition of ham to a simple dish of asparagus and Hollandaise sauce gives this recipe a very German flavor. It is perfect for a more substantial first course or when serving the asparagus as part of a spring supper buffet.

Makes 6 to 8 servings

2 pounds asparagus, trimmed, cut to the same length, steamed or boiled in water to cover until crisply tender, and drained
$1/4$ pounds very thinly sliced Westphalian, Parma, or salty Virginia ham
$1/2$ cup blender Hollandaise (below)
Freshly ground black pepper to taste

Wrap several asparagus spears in each ham slice. Arrange these rolls on a serving platter, or place 2 or 3 rolls on salad or dinner plates. Spoon warm blender Hollandaise sauce over the middle of the asparagus bundles. Grind the pepper over the top. Serve while the asparagus are still warm but not hot.

Asparagus with Blender Hollandaise

Classic handmade Hollandaise is delicious but fills many cooks with dread. This easy blender version can be made at the last minute and never fails to please. I like it with just a drop or two of hot pepper sauce added, giving the finished sauce just a bit more character. Serve these asparagus with almost anything or on their own as an appetizer.

Makes 6 servings

2 pounds asparagus, trimmed and cut to the same length
2 large egg yolks
1 whole large egg

1 tablespoon fresh lemon juice, or white wine
   vinegar
Salt and freshly ground white pepper to taste
Hot pepper sauce (optional)
8 tablespoons (1 stick) butter, melted, very hot
   but not boiling

Steam the asparagus in a steamer basket or a colander, covered, over simmering water until crisply
tender, 6 to 8 minutes; the time will depend on the
thickness of the spears. Keep warm, but do not cook
further.

Just before serving, prepare the blender
Hollandaise sauce. Combine the egg yolks and whole
egg with the lemon juice and salt and pepper in the
container of a blender. If desired, add a drop or two
of hot pepper sauce. Blend on high until well combined, about 30 seconds. With the blender running,
pour in the butter in a thin stream. The sauce will
thicken as the butter is added. Turn off the blender.

Arrange the asparagus on a serving dish or dinner
plates. Spoon some of the sauce over the asparagus
tips. Serve while still warm. Pass the remaining sauce
in a separate dish.

Note: *The hot butter in the blender Hollandaise
sauce cooks the eggs enough to thicken the yolks
and destroy any bacteria without scrambling
them. Never let the sauce sit around, even in a
water bath. Serve it as soon as it's made. See
page 13 for more discussion of egg safety.*

Asparagus with Parmesan Cheese

*While this is a very simple dish, it is extremely satisfying.
Because it is so simple, it requires the freshest asparagus
available. Olive oil may easily be substituted for the
butter, but use extra-virgin for the most flavor. Serve
with roast lamb or chicken or alongside veal Marsala or
piccata.*

Makes 6 servings

2 pounds asparagus, trimmed, cut to the same
   length, steamed or boiled in water to cover
   until just tender, and drained
2 tablespoons butter, melted, or extra-virgin
   olive oil
1/3 cup freshly grated Parmesan cheese
Freshly ground black pepper to taste

Arrange the hot asparagus on a heated serving platter. Drizzle with butter or olive oil. Sprinkle the tips
generously with the cheese and grind the pepper over
the top.

Asparagus Mimosa

*The garnish in this recipe resembles the feathery blossoms
of the mimosa tree. Not only is it an attractive presentation, it is a delicious way to serve asparagus when everyone is ready for something new.*

Makes 6 servings

2 pounds asparagus, trimmed, steamed or boiled
   in water to cover until just tender, drained,
   and kept warm
2 hard-cooked large eggs, peeled and chopped
1/2 bunch (3 or 4) green onions (scallions), white
   and light green parts only, minced
1/2 teaspoon ground cumin
1 heaping tablespoon chopped fresh parsley
1 tablespoon red wine vinegar
3 tablespoons extra-virgin olive oil
Salt and freshly ground black pepper to taste

Arrange the cooked asparagus on warm, but not hot,
serving plates.

In a small bowl, toss together the eggs, green
onions, cumin, and parsley. In another small bowl,
beat together the vinegar, olive oil, and salt and pepper. Drizzle the olive oil mixture over the asparagus.
Spoon the egg mixture over the asparagus tops. Serve
warm, but not hot.

Asparagus and Cauliflower Salad

Here winter and spring come together in a colorful and refreshing salad. I like to have the vegetables relatively crisp, but if you like more tender morsels, cook them a little longer. Serve this alongside cold meats, or with grilled fish, or even with the first charcoal-grilled hamburgers of the season.

Makes 6 servings

1 head leaf lettuce, chilled
1 small head very white cauliflower, separated into flowerets, steamed until barely tender, 5 to 8 minutes, and cooled
1 pound asparagus, trimmed, cut to 6-inch lengths, steamed or boiled in water to cover until crisply tender, drained, and cooled
3 tablespoons chopped fresh parsley
1 tablespoon Dijon-style mustard
1 cup mayonnaise, prepared or homemade (page 13)
½ cup plain low-fat yogurt
2 tablespoons chopped fresh tarragon

Arrange the lettuce on a serving plate. Arrange the cauliflower and asparagus on the bed of lettuce. Garnish with the parsley.

In a small bowl, beat the mustard into the mayonnaise. Beat in the yogurt and then fold in the tarragon. Serve this sauce cool but not chilled, in a separate sauce boat.

Sautéed Asparagus and Peppers

This very easy to prepare yet elegant dish is a perfect accompaniment to grilled chicken or lamb, and it is ideal when served with a poached fillet of salmon.

Makes 6 servings

2 tablespoons olive oil
3 large bell peppers, any color (red, yellow, or orange is especially attractive), seeded and cut into ¼-inch strips
1½ pounds asparagus, trimmed, cut to 6-inch lengths, steamed or boiled in water to cover until crisply tender, and drained
¼ cup dry white wine
2 tablespoons cold butter, cut into pieces
Salt and freshly black ground pepper to taste

Heat the oil in a large heavy skillet over medium heat. Add the bell pepper strips and cook, stirring occasionally, until just tender and lightly browned around the edges, 7 to 10 minutes. Add the asparagus and wine. Cook over high heat until all but about 2 tablespoons of the wine has evaporated, 3 to 4 minutes.

Remove the skillet from the heat. Add the butter, a piece at a time, and shake the skillet until the sauce becomes thick and frothy, but the butter does not melt completely. Season well with salt and pepper and serve at once.

Note: *The secret to this sauce is to add very cold butter and to shake the skillet until the butter is creamy colored and frothy. Do not return the skillet to the heat.*

Asparagus with Raita

Raita, or rayta, is of Indian origin, although similar condiments exist in many Middle Eastern countries. Aside from yogurt, which is the base, it can include many different ingredients, but the combination of mint and onion is almost a classic. While the garlic can be omitted if you like, it gives great flavor to the finished sauce. Often served along with blazing hot curries, this is delicious with many other dishes, such as cold roast lamb.

Makes 6 servings

1 cup best-quality plain yogurt
2 tablespoons chopped fresh mint, plus sprigs
      for garnishing
1 clove garlic, minced
2 tablespoons minced onion
Salt to taste
2 pounds asparagus, trimmed, cut to the same
      length, steamed or boiled in water to cover
      until crisply tender, drained, and cooled to
      room temperature
Fresh mint sprigs

Beat together the yogurt, the chopped mint, the garlic, and onion in a small bowl. Season well with salt.
Refrigerate for at least 1 hour.

Arrange the asparagus on a serving platter. Spoon
a little of the sauce over the tops. Garnish with the
mint sprigs. Pass any remaining sauce in a separate
dish.

Asparagus with New Potatoes and Peas

*If spring could be represented by just one dish, this would
certainly fit the bill. Served with pink roast lamb, this
should become a staple of your Easter menu. Anytime
that you can find fresh peas in the pod, this will be the
ideal way to accompany almost any roast poultry or beef.*

Makes 6 servings

1 pound smallest new red potatoes, unpeeled,
      cut into quarters
2 bunches (12 to 16) green onions (scallions),
      white and light green parts only, cut into
      3-inch lengths,
1 cup shelled fresh peas
1 pound thin asparagus, trimmed, cut into 3-inch
      lengths, and steamed until just tender
Salt and freshly ground black pepper to taste
2 tablespoons chopped fresh parsley
2 tablespoons chopped fresh basil
2 tablespoons butter

In a large deep skillet over medium heat, simmer the
potatoes and green onions in water to cover until
just tender, 5 to 7 minutes.

Stir in the peas and simmer 3 to 4 minutes longer.
Drain off the liquid. Stir in the asparagus, salt, pepper, herbs, and butter. Toss over low heat until very
hot and the vegetables are well coated with the
butter, 2 to 3 minutes.

Variations: *When truly fresh peas in the pod are not
available but sugar snap peas are in the market, substitute $1/4$ pound of sugar snap peas for the shelled peas.
Steam them in a steamer basket or a colander, covered,
over simmering water until crisply tender, about 4 minutes, and add them to the dish at the same time as the
asparagus. You can also substitute any variety of the small
new potatoes that may be available in your market for
the red potatoes.*

Roasted Asparagus

*These roasted asparagus, combined with roasted pota-
toes or rutabagas and tiny roasted carrots, make a great
vegetable accompaniment for any kind of grilled meat or
firm-fleshed fish.*

Makes 6 servings

2 pounds asparagus, trimmed and cut to
      the same length
Good-quality olive oil
Salt and freshly ground black pepper to taste

Preheat the oven to 400°F.

Brush the asparagus with olive oil. Arrange them
in a single layer in a medium-size baking pan and
season well with salt and pepper.

Roast the asparagus until tender, about 15 minutes. Serve very hot.

Note: *If roasting potatoes and carrots at the
same time, add the asparagus for the last 15
minutes of cooking.*

Crustless Asparagus Quiche

Lighter than a classic quiche, this is a great side dish with roast ham, cold meats of any kind, or with a mixed salad for lunch or Sunday supper.

Makes 6 servings

1 tablespoon butter
1 tablespoon all-purpose flour
Salt and freshly ground black pepper to taste
1½ cups milk, hot
2 large whole eggs
¼ cup freshly grated Parmesan cheese
1½ pounds fresh asparagus, trimmed, cut into 2-inch lengths, boiled in water to cover for 1 minute, and drained; or two 10-ounce packages frozen asparagus spears, thawed and cut into 2-inch lengths
1 small onion, very thinly sliced
2 tablespoons snipped fresh chives

Preheat the oven to 350°F.

In a medium-size heavy saucepan, melt the butter over low heat and stir in the flour. Cook until bubbling but not browned, about 3 minutes. Season with salt and pepper. Stir in the milk all at once, whisking well to make a smooth sauce. Cook, stirring, until the sauce thickens, about 3 minutes. Remove the saucepan from the heat and cool slightly. Beat in the eggs, 1 at a time. Stir in the cheese.

Arrange the asparagus in a 9-inch quiche plate or glass pie plate. Arrange the onion on top. Pour the egg mixture over the asparagus and bake until set, about 45 minutes. Serve hot, or warm, cut into wedges and garnished with the chives.

Warm Asparagus and New Potato Salad

Take this outside to serve with the first outdoor meal of the season. I think it goes very well with any cold meat or poultry, but it's really great with cold poached fish.

Makes 6 servings

1 pound asparagus, trimmed, cut into 2-inch lengths, and steamed until just tender
1 pound smallest new potatoes (red or brown), unpeeled, boiled in salted water to cover until just tender, about 10 minutes, drained, and halved or quartered depending on size
1 bunch (6 to 8) green onions (scallions), white and light green parts only, sliced
Salt and freshly ground black pepper to taste
⅓ cup chopped fresh parsley
½ cup extra-virgin olive oil
2 tablespoons balsamic vinegar
½ cup crumbled blue cheese

In a large bowl, toss together the asparagus, potatoes, and green onions. Season well with salt and pepper.

In a small bowl, beat together the parsley, oil, and vinegar. Toss some of this dressing with the vegetables. Continue to add dressing until the salad is well moistened. Serve just warm, topped with the cheese.

Variation: *For a different taste using the same ingredients, quarter the potatoes and roast at 375°F. until tender inside and golden outside, 30 to 40 minutes. Continue with the recipe.*

Stir-fried Asparagus with Black Bean–Garlic Sauce

In a Chinese menu, this would be just one of many dishes. For Western meals, it will accompany roast lamb, pork, or poultry very well, along with plenty of freshly steamed rice, whether white or brown.

Makes 6 servings

2 tablespoons mild vegetable oil, preferably peanut
1 bunch (6 to 8) green onions (scallions), white and light green parts only, cut on the diagonal into 1-inch lengths
1½ pounds asparagus, trimmed and cut on the diagonal into 2-inch lengths

1 clove garlic, minced
2 tablespoons dry white wine
3 tablespoons chicken stock
1 tablespoon light soy sauce
2 tablespoons Chinese black bean sauce

Heat the oil in a heavy wok or large slope-sided frying pan over high heat, until shimmering, about 1 minute. Add the green onions and stir-fry for 2 minutes. Add the asparagus and stir-fry for 2 minutes longer. Stir in the garlic. Add the wine and stock. Cover and cook over medium heat until the asparagus is crisply tender, 3 to 4 minutes. Stir in the soy sauce and black bean sauce. Heat through. Serve at once, very hot.

Braised Asparagus with Three Onions

The key to this delicious dish is to cook the leeks and green onions until tender while not overcooking the asparagus. They should remain crisply tender. Serve this dish with pork roast, grilled pork chops, or spareribs.

Makes 6 servings

4 tablespoons (1/2 stick) butter
2 large leeks, including 1 inch of light green, halved lengthwise, and thinly sliced
4 bunches (at least 24) green onions (scallions), white and light green parts only, sliced
1 1/2 pounds asparagus, trimmed and cut into 2-inch lengths
1 cup shredded Savoy cabbage
1/2 cup well-flavored chicken stock
3 tablespoons snipped fresh chives
Salt and freshly ground black pepper to taste
Hot pepper sauce to taste (optional)

Melt the butter in a large heavy skillet over low heat. Stir in the leeks and green onions and cook, stirring occasionally, until tender, about 10 minutes. Do not hurry the cooking or they will burn. Add the asparagus and cabbage and pour in the stock. Cover and cook until the cabbage and asparagus are tender, 5 to 6 minutes.

Remove the cover, increase the heat to medium, and boil to reduce the liquid to a few spoonfuls of thick, shiny sauce, 4 to 5 minutes. Stir in the chives and season with salt and pepper. Stir in the hot pepper sauce if using. Serve very hot.

Asparagus and Fresh Vegetable Salsa

The addition of a vegetable salsa makes an entire salad out of the asparagus. There is no hot pepper in this salsa, although you can add it to your heart's content. Try serving these asparagus with a thick grilled steak or tuna.

Makes 6 servings

1 large ripe tomato, seeded and finely chopped
1/4 small cucumber, peeled, halved lengthwise, seeded, and finely chopped
1/4 medium-size green or red bell pepper, seeded and finely chopped
2 green onions (scallions), white and light green parts only, thinly sliced
1 clove garlic, minced (optional)
2 tablespoons fresh lime juice
2 tablespoons very fruity olive oil
2 tablespoons chopped fresh cilantro, plus additional for garnishing
Salt and freshly ground black pepper to taste
1 pound asparagus, trimmed, cut to the same length, steamed or boiled in water to cover until crisply tender, and drained

Combine all the ingredients, except the asparagus and additional cilantro for garnishing, in a medium-size bowl. Refrigerate 3 or 4 hours and up to overnight.

Just before serving, reheat the asparagus in boiling water to cover for 1 minute. Drain.

Arrange the asparagus on serving plates. Spoon cold salsa over the hot asparagus. Garnish with the additional cilantro and serve.

Nursery-style Asparagus

Here is an old-fashioned dish, wonderful for lunch or light supper with a tossed salad and good crusty bread. Children love it because not only can they eat it with their fingers, they can dunk to their hearts' content. For very small children, count only one egg apiece.

Makes 4 servings

1 pound asparagus, trimmed, steamed or boiled in water to cover until tender, drained, and kept warm
8 large eggs, soft-cooked (about 5 minutes), hot, in the shell
Salt and freshly ground black pepper to taste

Arrange the eggs in egg cups, set on plates, allowing 2 eggs per person. Divide the asparagus among the serving plates.

To serve, cut the tops off the hot eggs. Season the yolk with salt and freshly ground pepper. The asparagus should be dipped into the yolk and eaten out of hand. The remaining egg is eaten with a spoon.

Note: *Cooking eggs until the yolks begin to thicken but are not hard, 4 to 5 minutes, raises the internal temperature high enough to destroy any bacteria that may be present. See page 13 for more discussion on egg safety.*

Asparagus Mushroom Ragout

The better the mushrooms, the better this dish will be. There is plenty of character here, enough to stand up to marinated lamb shanks, grilled tuna, or roast beef.

Makes 6 servings

3 tablespoons butter
1 small onion, minced
1/2 pound mushrooms, such as shiitake (stems discarded), oyster, cloud ear, or a mixture, stems trimmed, sliced
1/2 cup chicken stock
1/4 cup dry white wine
1/2 teaspoon ground cumin
1 1/2 pounds asparagus, trimmed and cut into 2-inch lengths
Salt and freshly ground black pepper to taste
1/3 cup heavy cream
1 tablespoon snipped fresh chives

Melt the butter in a medium-size heavy skillet over medium heat. Cook the onion, stirring occasionally, for 2 minutes. Stir in the mushrooms and cook, stirring, until the mushrooms are golden and the onions are tender, 8 to 10 minutes. Stir in the stock, wine, and cumin. Add the asparagus and season well with salt and pepper. Simmer until the asparagus are just tender, about 5 minutes. Increase the heat to high and simmer the sauce until it reduces to about 2 tablespoons, 2 to 3 minutes. Stir in the cream and boil hard until the sauce thickens and coats the vegetables, 1 to 2 minutes. Serve very hot, garnished with the chives.

Sweet-and-Sour Asparagus

Serve this with skinless chicken breasts, baked until just tender, or with plainly baked white-fleshed fish.

Makes 6 servings

2 pounds asparagus, trimmed and cut on the diagonal into 1/2-inch pieces, keeping the tips about 2 inches long
1/2 cup water
1 tablespoon sugar
Salt and freshly ground black pepper to taste
1/4 large green or red bell pepper, seeded and chopped

3 tablespoons red wine vinegar
1 tablespoon butter or extra-virgin olive oil
Hot pepper sauce to taste

Place the asparagus in a heavy wok or a large skillet. Add the water and sugar and season well with salt and pepper. Cover and cook over medium heat, until crisply tender, about 4 minutes. Add the bell pepper. Stir in the vinegar and cook, uncovered, over high heat until most of the liquid evaporates, about 1 minute. Add the butter or olive oil and hot pepper sauce. Toss or stir until the butter melts and the asparagus is coated with sauce. Serve very hot.

Cream of Asparagus Soup with Tomato

Asparagus season deserves at least one soup, and this one deserves your attention. If desire attacks when fresh asparagus are not available, use best-quality frozen spears, defrosted, but do not use canned asparagus.

Makes about 6 servings

1 pound asparagus, trimmed, cut into 1-inch
   lengths, tips reserved
½ small onion, chopped
1 small Russet potato, peeled and cut into
   ¼-inch dice
1 quart well-flavored chicken stock
½ cup heavy cream
Salt and freshly ground black pepper to taste
1 tablespoon olive oil
2 medium-size or 1 very large ripe tomato,
   peeled, seeded, and chopped
1 tablespoon chopped fresh basil

Steam the asparagus tips in a steamer basket or a colander, covered, over simmering water until tender. Set aside.

In a heavy medium-size saucepan, combine the remaining asparagus, the onion, potato, and stock. Simmer over medium heat until the vegetables are very tender, 20 to 30 minutes. Puree this mixture in a food processor. Pour the pureed soup through a sieve or strainer back into the saucepan to remove any fibers. Stir in the cream and season well with salt and pepper. Heat through, but do not boil.

Heat the oil in a small skillet or sauté pan over medium-high heat and cook the tomatoes, stirring, until soft and the liquid they give off has evaporated, about 5 minutes. Season with salt and pepper.

To serve, place a large spoonful of tomatoes in each bowl. Ladle in the soup and garnish with the reserved asparagus tips and the basil. Serve very hot.
Variation: *Chill the asparagus soup for several hours. Do not cook the tomatoes, but garnish the chilled soup with chopped ripe tomato and cold asparagus tops. A sprinkling of ground cumin can be added if desired.*

Warm Asparagus with Orange Mayonnaise

My mother still prefers asparagus with mayonnaise, a dish often served in her southern home. Flavoring the mayonnaise with orange juice turns a simple vegetable into a very special first course or side dish for any roast meat.

Makes 6 servings

1 cup mayonnaise, prepared or homemade
   (page 13)
½ teaspoon ground ginger
3 tablespoons fresh orange juice
Grated zest of 1 orange
2 pounds asparagus, trimmed, cut to the same
   length, steamed or boiled in water to cover
   until crisply tender, and drained
Sweet Hungarian paprika

In a small bowl, beat together the mayonnaise, ginger, orange juice, and zest. Refrigerate at least 1 hour and up to overnight.

Arrange the asparagus on serving plates. Spoon the mayonnaise sauce over the tips and garnish with a sprinkling of paprika. Serve at once.

Oven-fried Asparagus

This oven preparation is very much like the Roasted Asparagus but with a crispy crust.

Makes 6 servings

1/3 cup plain dried bread crumbs
1 tablespoon freshly grated Parmesan cheese
Salt and seasoned pepper, such as Mrs. Dash, to taste
2 pounds asparagus, trimmed and cut to the same length
2 tablespoons good-quality olive oil

Preheat the oven to 475°F.

Place the bread crumbs, cheese, salt, and pepper in a large plastic bag. In a large bowl, toss the asparagus with the oil and place the spears in the bag of crumbs and cheese. Shake to coat. Arrange the coated asparagus in a single layer on a baking sheet.

Bake the asparagus until the coating is browned and crisp, 10 to 15 minutes. Serve very hot.

Asparagus-Mushroom Risotto

There is an affinity between asparagus and mushrooms that should be maximized. The creamy goodness of a fine risotto is the perfect showcase for these two stars. Put this alongside veal of any kind, baked red snapper, or even Cajun-style catfish.

Makes 6 servings

1 tablespoon butter
1/4 pound shiitake mushrooms, stems discarded, sliced
2 tablespoons olive oil
1/2 small onion, minced
1 1/2 cups arborio rice (or another round or short-grained rice)
4 to 4 1/2 cups well-flavored chicken stock, boiling
1/4 cup freshly grated Parmesan cheese, plus additional for serving
1 pound asparagus, trimmed, cut into 1 1/2-inch lengths, steamed until crisply tender, tips reserved
Salt and freshly ground black pepper to taste
Chopped fresh parsley

Melt the butter in a small skillet over medium heat. Cook the mushrooms, stirring occasionally, until just tender, 6 to 7 minutes.

In a large heavy saucepan, heat the olive oil over low heat and cook the onion, stirring, until translucent, 4 to 5 minutes. Stir in the rice and cook, stirring, until the rice has turned translucent and is coated with oil, about 3 minutes; the time will vary with the type of rice used.

Increase the heat slightly to medium-low and stir in 1/2 cup of the boiling stock. Cook, stirring gently with a wooden spoon, until the liquid is almost absorbed. Stir in the remaining stock, 1/2 cup at a time, and cook after each addition, stirring, until almost absorbed. This will take 20 to 25 minutes in all. The rice should be tender, creamy, and not dry. When the rice has absorbed as much stock as it will (perhaps not all 4 1/2 cups), stir in the cheese, asparagus, and mushrooms. If the rice becomes too dry, stir in a little more stock. Season well with salt and pepper.

Serve very hot, garnished with the asparagus tips and parsley. Pass more cheese and the pepper mill.

Note: *Risotto is a last-minute dish that requires constant attention. The end result should be creamy, not soupy, but not fluffy dry either. It is a good idea to have the rest of the meal ready to go, the table completely set, and the diners waiting with bated breath and a glass of wine before you start the rice. The asparagus and mushrooms can be prepared ahead of time, which will save some time. No matter how labor intensive, however, a good risotto is worth every minute of effort.*

Asparagus Maltaise in Pastry

Add orange juice and zest to Hollandaise sauce, and voilà—Maltaise sauce. Here I use the blender method (as I do for Hollandaise sauce). This Maltaise sauce tastes delicious and is pretty much hassle free, since it can be made in 1 or 2 minutes just before serving the dish. It's wonderful as a showy appetizer but goes very well with plain broiled or grilled salmon and tuna.

Makes 6 servings

One 17¼-ounce package frozen puff-pastry dough, defrosted
1 large egg yolk, beaten with a pinch of salt

Maltaise Sauce

3 tablespoons fresh orange juice
1 tablespoon grated orange zest
1 cup blender Hollandaise (page 20), very warm but not hot
Freshly ground black pepper to taste
1½ pounds asparagus, trimmed, cut to the same length, steamed or boiled in water to cover until crisply tender, drained, and cooled

Preheat the oven to the temperature suggested on the package of puff-pastry dough.

Unroll the dough and cut it into 4 × 2½-inch rectangles. Lay the rectangles on an ungreased baking sheet that has been lightly sprinkled with water. Brush the tops of the rectangles with a little of the beaten egg yolk. Bake until golden brown and puffed, about 20 minutes. Remove the baking sheet from the oven, loosen the pastries with a spatula, cool them on a rack, and split horizontally.

In a small warmed bowl, beat the orange juice and zest into the warm blender Hollandaise sauce.

Just before serving, reheat the asparagus in boiling water to cover for 1 minute, and drain.

Arrange the bottom halves of the pastry on warmed plates. Divide the hot asparagus among the plates and arrange on top of the pastry. Spoon some of the warm sauce over the asparagus. Place the pastry lids on top of the asparagus at an angle, or prop them against the bottoms.

Serve as soon as possible with the remaining sauce in a separate dish. Pass a pepper mill.

Avocados

Technically, avocados are a fruit, but they are so often served with savory preparations, from shrimp salad to fiery Southwestern concoctions, that they really should be included here.

Avocados are a New World native, and our name seems to be a derivative of the Aztec word *ahuacatl*. They require a hot climate to ripen properly, so they are most popular in near-tropical areas and are used in many recipes in Mexico and South America as well as in Florida and Southern California. Spain, Israel, and North Africa also incorporate avocados into a variety of dishes.

The principal drawback of this delicately flavored fruit is its fat content. Since an avocado can contain up to 25 percent fat, dieters often steer clear of any dish that features it, which is a shame, as it contains no cholesterol and has a high potassium content—even higher than an equal amount of that old standby, the banana.

There are many varieties of avocados grown throughout the world, but the majority of those found in American markets are either Haas or Florida. The dark, almost black, rough-skinned

Haas is a relatively small avocado with a rich, delicious taste. It is a creamy golden color inside, generally with a bright green edge near the skin. Florida avocados are much larger, bright green, and smooth-skinned, with a blander flavor and less unctuous, more watery flesh.

Most recipes call for using avocados raw, but it would be a mistake to miss out on one or two hot preparations. They can be filled and baked or stirred into stews and soups at the last minute. They should be only just heated through, however, because they tend to become bitter if they are overcooked, and it is important to keep a watchful eye.

Selection: Avocados do not ripen on the tree, so they are picked while "green" and shipped still rock hard. They generally arrive in the market very firm or just beginning to ripen. Choose the plumpest fruit available and avoid any that are the least bit shriveled or bruised. If they are not stiff firm, the fruit should just yield to a gentle overall pressure. Do not try to push a thumb into the flesh and avoid any that are very soft. Occasionally, a ripe avocado will rattle when shaken, because the seed will sometimes separate from the flesh. But this doesn't happen often and isn't a good test.

Because they are grown in warm climates, avocados are available all year round, though they are best, and often cheapest, between April and August.

One large avocado, about ¾ to 1 cup of pulp, will serve two. If they are small, it is best to allow one whole avocado per person. If part of a salad, one good-size avocado will serve four.

Storage and Preparation: Once an avocado is refrigerated, it will not ripen further. Ripening at home can be hastened by putting the avocado in a brown paper bag at room temperature. If there is time, just leave the fruit uncovered at room temperature for several days. Be sure to check every day so it doesn't ripen too far. Once ripe, store it in the refrigerator for a day or two at the longest.

After it is cut, the flesh of an avocado quickly turns an ugly dark gray or black color. The best way to prevent this darkening is to moisten the cut surface with fresh lemon or lime juice. Some people suggest that leaving the seed in the cut half, or pressing it into guacamole or another avocado dish will prevent darkening, but my nonscientific studies of this method don't seem to bear out this theory. The only part that doesn't turn dark seems to be the part touched by the seed. A sheet of plastic wrap pressed directly on the surface seems to do just as well. A little lemon juice, salad dressing, or vinegar and an airtight covering of plastic wrap are, in my experience, the most effective methods of maintaining an appetizing creamy color. To be absolutely certain of a good color, prepare avacodo dishes at the last moment.

Tip: *Here is an easy trick for removing the seed of a cut avocado. Cut the avocado in half lengthwise, following the outline of the seed. Hold the half containing the seed in the palm of your left hand (if you are right-handed). Take a heavy-bladed knife and strike the seed, imbedding the blade in it. Twist the knife, almost like opening a jar, and the seed will come loose. Hit the seed with the handle of a heavy wooden spoon to remove it from the knife. The halves are then ready to fill, to peel for slicing or chopping, or to scoop out for a puree.*

Cold Avocado Mousse

Serve this delicious mousse alongside thin slices of smoked salmon or with smoked trout fillets, or add to any summer buffet table.

Makes 6 to 8 servings

2 medium-size ripe Haas avocados, halved, seed removed, flesh scooped out with a spoon
2 tablespoons fresh lime juice
1 heaping tablespoon grated onion
¼ teaspoon salt, or more to taste
6 drops hot pepper sauce, or more to taste
1 cup heavy cream, beaten until stiff
2 tablespoons chopped fresh cilantro
1 small ripe tomato, peeled, seeded, and finely diced
1 bunch (6 to 8) green onions (scallions), white part only, thinly sliced

In a medium-size bowl, mash the avocado with the lime juice. Stir in the grated onion, salt, and hot pepper sauce. Gently fold in the whipped cream and cilantro.

Spoon the mousse into a chilled serving dish. Cover and chill for several hours. Serve by spoonfuls, garnished with tomato and green onion.

Avocados au Gratín

This hot preparation may well change your attitude toward avocados. No longer just a salad component, avocados can accompany roast chicken or turkey, too.

Makes 6 servings as a side dish; 3 servings as a luncheon main course

2 tablespoons very fruity extra-virgin olive oil
¼ large green bell pepper, seeded and
   finely chopped
6 green onions (scallions), white and light green
   parts only, thinly sliced
1 clove garlic, minced
2 small ripe tomatoes, peeled, seeded,
   and chopped
1 tablespoon chopped fresh thyme
Salt and freshly ground black pepper to taste
2 tablespoons butter
2 tablespoons all-purpose flour
1 cup milk, hot
4 ounces Gruyère or Cheddar cheese, grated
   (1 cup)
3 large ripe Haas avocados, halved, seed removed,
   and moistened with lemon juice

Preheat the oven to 450°F.

Heat the olive oil in a small skillet over medium heat. Cook the bell pepper, stirring occasionally, until just translucent, about 5 minutes or more. Add the green onions and garlic and cook, stirring, 2 minutes longer. Stir in the tomatoes, season with the thyme, salt, and pepper, and cook about 3 minutes. Set aside.

Melt the butter in a medium-size heavy saucepan over low heat. Stir in the flour. Cook, stirring, until bubbling but not browned, about 3 minutes. Stir in the hot milk all at once, whisking until smooth. Cook 3 minutes. Stir in three-quarters of the cheese, cook, still over low heat, just until the cheese melts, about 1 minute. Remove the pan from the heat. Stir in the tomato mixture.

Pile the mixture into the avocado halves, mounding it slightly. Sprinkle with the remaining cheese.

Arrange the filled halves on an ungreased baking sheet. Bake only until the filling is bubbling and cheese is lightly browned, about 15 minutes. Take care not to overcook the avocado, as it can become bitter. Remove from the oven and serve at once.

> Note: *For a more substantial dish, stir 1 cup of fresh crabmeat or chopped cooked shrimp into the filling before piling it into the avocado halves.*

Avocado Salsa

Adding diced avocado to a fresh uncooked salsa turns it into something very special. I think this salsa is wonderful with grilled fish of any kind.

Makes about 2 cups

2 large ripe tomatoes, seeded and chopped
½ small cucumber, peeled, halved lengthwise,
   seeded, and chopped
½ small green bell pepper, seeded and chopped
½ small onion, minced
1 clove garlic, minced
3 tablespoons fresh lime juice
1 teaspoon ground cumin
3 tablespoons olive oil
Salt and freshly ground black pepper to taste
Hot pepper sauce to taste
3 tablespoons chopped fresh cilantro, plus
   additional for garnishing
1 large ripe Haas avocado

Combine all the ingredients, except the avocado and the additional cilantro for garnishing, in a medium-size glass or other bowl. Be sure to season well with salt, pepper, cumin, and hot pepper sauce. Chill, covered, for several hours or overnight.

Just before serving, peel the avocado, remove the seed, and cut the flesh into ¼-inch dice. Stir gently into the salsa. Garnish with the additional cilantro. Serve at once.

Bloody Mary Aspic with Avocado

Often served at "ladies' luncheons," the aspic is an old-fashioned dish that deserves a wider audience. This tangy variation will work itself into more and more of your summer menus. It is a natural with cold poached fish such as bluefish, red snapper, or salmon, or add it to a summer salad plate.

Makes 6 to 8 servings

2 envelopes unflavored gelatin
3½ cups well-flavored prepared Bloody Mary mix, as spicy as desired
1 tablespoon prepared white horseradish (grated horseradish in vinegar, not a mayonnaise-based horseradish sauce)
½ cup sliced green onions (scallions), white and light green parts only
⅓ cup minced celery
¼ cup minced green bell pepper
1 small ripe Haas avocado, halved, seed removed, peeled, cut into ¼-inch dice, and tossed with 1 tablespoon fresh lemon juice
1 small head leaf lettuce
Light sour cream or mayonnaise, prepared or homemade (page 13), or plain yogurt

Soften the gelatin in 1 cup of the Bloody Mary mix in a microwave oven on high, for about 1 minute. Stir well to dissolve. Pour the mixture into a large bowl and stir in the remaining Bloody Mary mix and the horseradish. Refrigerate until the mixture begins to thicken and sets lightly. (The mixture should mound up slightly in a spoon but not set completely.) Gently fold in the green onion, celery, bell pepper, and avocado.

Spoon the mixture into a lightly oiled 1-quart mold. Cover the mold with plastic wrap and refrigerate until firmly set, at least 4 hours.

To serve, unmold the aspic onto a lightly moistened serving platter lined with a bed of leaf lettuce and garnish with a little sour cream, mayonnaise, or plain yogurt.

Avocado, Grapefruit, Red Onion, and Feta Salad

The very rich texture of ripe avocado is the perfect foil for the refreshing taste of citrus fruit. Add onion, the sharpness of feta cheese, and peppery arugula for a great salad to serve with grilled fish or even thick grilled pork chops.

Makes 6 servings

1 large bunch arugula
1 large or 2 small ripe Haas avocados, halved, seed removed, peeled, sliced lengthwise, and lightly moistened with lemon juice
1 large red or pink grapefruit, peeled and sectioned, any juice reserved
1 medium-size red onion, or Vidalia if available, very thinly sliced, separated into rings, soaked 1 hour in ice water, and well drained
2 ounces feta cheese, crumbled (about ½ cup)
½ cup best-quality plain yogurt
2 tablespoons honey
¼ cup fresh orange juice
2 tablespoons reserved grapefruit juice
1 teaspoon minced candied ginger (packed in sugar syrup)
Freshly ground black pepper to taste

Arrange the arugula in the bottom of a large glass or other salad bowl. Arrange the avocado in 1 layer over the greens.

Arrange the grapefruit sections over the avocado and then top with the onion rings. Sprinkle all with the cheese.

In a medium-size bowl, beat together the yogurt, honey, orange and grapefruit juices, and candied ginger. Just before serving, spoon some of this dressing over the salad. Season the salad with freshly ground pepper. Pass any remaining dressing in a separate bowl.

Note: *Soaking the onion rings in ice water not only crisps them but makes them milder tasting.*

Avocado Pudding

While this is not really a pudding, it is a delicious example of a sweet avocado dish made with a fully ripe avocado. Serve as a dessert or as part of a cold buffet with cold roast pork or ham.

Makes 6 to 8 servings

2 large ripe Haas avocados, halved, seed removed, flesh scooped out with a spoon
Juice of 2 small fresh limes (about $1/4$ cup)
$1/3$ cup confectioners' sugar
2 cups best-quality plain yogurt, whole milk or low-fat
6 very thin slices of fresh lime

In a food processor, puree the avocado with the lime juice and sugar. Stir this mixture into the yogurt. Sweeten with more sugar if desired.

Spoon the mixture into custard cups or small ramekins and garnish each with 1 thin slice of lime.

Avocado Butter

While not exactly a side dish, this avocado preparation is an easy, delicious instant sauce to serve with vegetables, grilled fish, or hot pasta. The contrast between the cold sauce and hot dish is a welcome change of pace. Serve with cold poached salmon or striped bass, too.

Makes about 1 cup

1 small ripe Haas avocado, halved, seed removed, flesh scooped out with a spoon
8 tablespoons (1 stick) butter, softened
$1/4$ cup chopped fresh parsley
2 tablespoons chopped fresh tarragon
1 tablespoon fresh lemon juice
$1/2$ small clove garlic, pressed (optional)
6 drops hot pepper sauce, or to taste
Salt to taste (optional)

Puree all the ingredients in a food processor until just smooth. Mound in a small serving bowl. Serve at room temperature or refrigerate 1 hour.

Yogurt Avocado Toss

This fresh-flavored mixture is a welcome addition to any menu that centers around a curry.

Makes about 2 cups

2 large ripe Haas avocados, halved, seed removed, peeled, cut into large dice, and tossed with 1 tablespoon fresh lemon juice
1 small onion, cut into $1/4$-inch dice
1 large ripe tomato, peeled, seeded, and cut into $1/4$-inch dice
1 large cucumber, peeled, halved lengthwise, seeded, and cut into $1/4$-inch-thick slices
1 large clove garlic, pressed
3 tablespoons chopped fresh mint, plus additional for garnishing
$1 1/2$ cups best-quality plain yogurt, whole milk or low fat
Salt and freshly ground black pepper to taste
6 drops hot pepper sauce

In a large bowl, toss the avocado, onion, tomato, and cucumber.

In a small bowl, stir together the garlic, the 3 tablespoons of mint, and the yogurt. Season well with the salt, pepper, and hot pepper sauce. Stir into the avocado mixture. Mound the mixture in a glass serving bowl and garnish with the additional mint.

Stuffed Avocados

Ripe avocado halves can be filled with all sorts of things. The following list is just a beginning. Many of the fillings are found elsewhere in this book, or use your imagination to create your own inventions.

1. Chili without beans (hot)
2. Sloppy Joe mixture (hot)
3. Chiles con Queso (page 265)
4. Shrimp salad (cold)
5. Russian Salad (cold) (page 103)
6. Chicken salad (cold)
7. Tuna salad (cold)
8. Classic Céleri Rémoulade (cold) (page 115)
9. German Potato Salad (warm) (page 292)
10. Ragout of Mushrooms (hot) (page 216)
11. Cottage cheese mixed with sliced green onions (cold)
12. Hot chicken hash
13. Homemade corned beef hash (hot)

Beans

Ah, the lowly bean. Fresh or dried, it has played an enormous role in the history of food. Legumes—including peas, beans, and lentils—probably still nourish more people and animals in the world than any other food. Sometimes praised, sometimes denigrated as the commonest form of nutrition available, beans have sustained virtually every society at one time or another.

Beans grown for drying were one of the very first crops cultivated by man. Some variety of legume, dried and used for food, is grown in literally every country of the world. The variety is staggering (nearly twelve thousand kinds are known) and the wholesome, nourishing dishes traditionally prepared are frequently as delicious as they are life sustaining.

Fresh beans, such as green beans, tiny French haricots verts, wax beans, Chinese yard-long beans, and Italian flat beans, are eaten pod and all. Other fresh beans, lima beans and fava beans for example, along with all dried beans, are shelled, and the pod is often fed to animals as fodder. Dried beans are basically the same vegetable as many of the fresh varieties we eat. They have simply been left on the vine to wither and

dry completely before being harvested. They are a naturally dehydrated food that must be soaked or simmered to restore the water content.

Dried beans have much to recommend them. Pound for pound they pack more energy and nutritional value than almost any other food. They keep well for long periods of time, are easy to carry or ship, are inexpensive, and lend themselves to even the most rudimentary cooking conditions. If all else fails, they can simply be boiled over a small fire and flavored with almost anything at hand, even if that is only a pinch of salt. For these reasons travelers of all kinds have relied on them during long voyages, whether they were conquering armies, trading expeditions, or our own settlers migrating west. More has been accomplished on a stomachful of beans than can possibly be imagined. And what we don't eat we feed to our animals.

Full of complex carbohydrates, including sugars, and high in fiber, beans are slow to digest—what your grandmother used to call a "stick-to-the-ribs" food. In fact, it is precisely these complex sugars that lead to the one unfortunate aspect of beans (and some other vegetables, such as broccoli, peppers, and cucumbers as well). Many people lack the specific enzyme that breaks down these complex sugars into simpler ones that can be more easily and completely digested. The result is that the residual sugars ferment in the digestive tract, creating gases that can be uncomfortable for the consumer and unpleasant for his or her neighbors.

There have been many solutions proffered over the years, and there have even been government studies that seemed to indicate that continued consumption of beans or other ultra-high fiber foods would acclimate the body after a period of time. While this may be true for some, the majority of people who lack the enzyme continue to suffer the effects of this gas-producing process to some degree or other. There is hope now, however. In the last year or two a product called Beano® has been developed that can safely provide this enzyme (alpha galactosidase)—in the form of a tablet or drops. People who have never before been able to digest beans (and some other vegetables, such as broccoli, cabbage, peppers, and cucumbers) in a socially acceptable manner can now indulge to their hearts' content without the worry of unpleasant after effects. And I have it on good authority that this product has saved at least one marriage!

Fresh Beans

Selection: As with so many other vegetables, the best way to enjoy fresh beans is to pick them from the garden immediately before they are cooked. Fresh picked beans are so sweet that they are almost an entirely different vegetable from the supermarket specimens. If you are not lucky enough to grow your own, and there is no farm stand nearby, it might be better to buy frozen beans than "fresh" ones that have languished too long between vine and cooking pot.

And I would strongly suggest never buying preshelled beans unless they are frozen. It has been my experience that packaged, preshelled beans are tough and dry—and no amount of simmering will restore their texture and taste. In fact, if at all possible, shell beans should be left in the pod until just before cooking.

Green beans, wax beans, haricots verts, Chinese yard-long beans, and Italian flat beans should all be as moist and snappy as possible. They should have a clear, bright green (or yellow if choosing wax beans) color, without any brown or shriveled spots. If the stem is still attached, it should also be green and not dark and dry. Two pounds of fresh green beans will serve six to eight.

Fresh shell beans, such as limas, black-eyed peas, pigeon peas, purple beans, fava beans, and French flageolets (a small green kidney-shaped bean) should also be as plump and crisp as possible. Choose only those that are bright colored, also with no brown spots or hint of mold. If the shells do not pop open easily, they are probably old and will not be tender and sweet. If less-than-fresh beans are the only kind you can find, it is better to choose something else or to buy the frozen variety.

Most shell beans have a lot of waste, and it will require at least 4 pounds in the shell to produce enough for six servings. Fava beans are much heavier, however, and you will need 7 to 8 pounds of whole beans to serve six.

Storage and Preparation: The quicker fresh beans, whole or shelled, are prepared, the better. If they are to be stored, place them, unwashed, in a perforated plastic bag in the crisper drawer of the refrigerator and prepare them within a day or two. The longer they are stored, the more sugar will be converted to starch, resulting in a less lively vegetable. Some people suggest rinsing the beans before refrigerating to keep them hydrated, but I find this leads them to develop mold quickly.

Modern varieties of whole beans, including wax beans, are bred to be stringless and will need to have only the stem end removed. But if you happen on stringy beans, any strings can be removed by carefully drawing the stem along the seam. Very large green beans may have to have both ends removed, or topped and tailed, removing strings along both sides. Wash trimmed beans, drain, and then continue with the recipe.

Shell beans should be prepared just before serving. Open the shell by pressing a thumbnail along the seam—it should pop open easily. Run a thumb along the inside of the shell to loosen the beans and drop them into a bowl. Once all the beans have been shelled, pick them over to remove any that are brown or shriveled. Rinse the shelled beans and drain them before continuing with the cooking.

> Tip: *Do not add lemon juice, vinegar, wine, or other acidic dressing to green beans until just before serving. The acid will leach the color and turn them an unappetizing gray color.*

Dried Beans

Selection: Most dried beans in this country are sold in bags, boxes, or plastic packages. Look for clean, fresh-looking packages, without any holes in them. If bulk beans are available, look for those that are hard, shiny, and bright colored. When buying in bulk, avoid beans that are separated or shriveled.

A good rule of thumb is to count on 1 cup of dried beans to result in 2 cups cooked. About ¼ cup dried or ½ cup cooked beans serves one person. Dried beans are generally low in fat and high in fiber and, depending on the variety, contain 250 to 300 calories per cup when cooked.

Preparation: Almost all dried peas, beans, and legumes need to be soaked to rehydrate before cooking. Several exceptions include split peas, lentils, and black-eyed peas. If time isn't a problem, wash and pick over the beans, removing any little stones (they get scooped up when the beans are prepared—and add a little gratuitous weight to the packages), separated or shriveled beans, and any other extraneous material that may have come along for the ride. Place the washed beans in a large bowl and add enough water to cover them by several inches. Soak the beans at least 8 hours or overnight if possible. The beans will swell quite a lot. When you are ready to cook, drain the beans, rinse again (to remove some of the gas-producing sugars) and turn them into the cooking pot.

If time is of the essence, the "quick-soak" method produces nearly the same succulent bean. Wash and pick over the beans. Place them in a large saucepan and add enough water to cover them by several inches. Bring the beans to a boil over medium heat and boil for 2 minutes. Remove the saucepan from the heat, cover and let stand 1 hour before draining, rinsing, and continuing with the recipe.

Tip: *Dried beans become tough-skinned and sometimes remain irrevocably hard if they are cooked with salt or acidic ingredients such as tomatoes or lemon juice. The beans should be simmered until nearly fully cooked before adding tomatoes, vinegar, or lemon juice. Season the beans with salt in the last 30 minutes of cooking. This will ensure that they will be tender and reduces the risk of oversalting.*

Boiled Green Beans

Drop 1 pound topped and tailed green beans in rapidly boiling water to cover. Boil until crisply tender, about 4 minutes. Drain. If you are planning to use them cold, refresh them under cold running water immediately after draining. Very thin green beans, especially haricots verts, will take only 2 to 3 minutes to be crisply tender. Be careful not to overcook.

Steamed Green Beans

Arrange 1 pound topped and tailed green beans in a colander or steamer basket. Steam, covered, over simmering water until crisply tender, 4 to 5 minutes. Very thin green beans will take only 3 to 4 minutes. Be careful not to overcook. If not serving the beans at once, or if they are to be served cold, refresh them under cold running water to preserve the green color.

Microwaved Green Beans

Arrange 1 pound topped and tailed green beans evenly in a microwaveable dish. Add 2 tablespoons water. Cover and vent. Microwave on high 5 to 6 minutes. Let stand 3 minutes before removing the cover.

Three-Bean Salad

While this salad may be old hat, it continues to sustain many a group of summer picnickers and has earned its place on buffet tables all over the country. It is so popular that you can buy it already prepared in jars, and in a pinch can mix it together from canned beans (being sure to rinse them thoroughly to remove as much salt as possible). But making it fresh is by far the best method.

Makes 6 to 8 servings

½ pound wax beans, topped, tailed, and strung if necessary, cut into 2-inch lengths, and steamed until crisply tender
2 cups dried kidney beans, picked over, soaked overnight, simmered until tender, and drained
⅓ cup white wine vinegar or cider vinegar
¼ teaspoon dry mustard
1 tablespoon sugar
Salt and freshly ground black pepper to taste
½ cup mild vegetable oil, preferably peanut
⅓ cup chopped fresh parsley
1 pound thinnest green beans, topped, tailed, strung if necessary, cut into 2-inch lengths (optional), and steamed until crisply tender

In a large bowl, toss together the wax beans and kidney beans.

In a small bowl, beat together the vinegar, mustard, and sugar. Season well with salt and pepper. Beat in the oil. Stir in the parsley. Pour this dressing over the beans. Toss. Cover and refrigerate for several hours or overnight. Just before serving, toss in the green beans and check the seasoning. Add more salt and pepper if desired.

Note: *The green beans may be added at the same time as the wax beans, but they will not keep their bright green color. Their taste and texture will not be affected, however, and they will absorb more of the flavor of the dressing.*

Green Bean Casserole

This is a fresh version of that old standby mushroom-soup-and-green-bean casserole, a childhood pantry dish unfortunately full of salt and fat. Serve this often and enjoy a childhood favorite in an up-to-date form. I like to pair this with a classic Thanksgiving stuffed turkey.

Makes 6 servings

6 tablespoons (¾ stick) butter
½ small onion, very thinly sliced
1 clove garlic, minced
¼ pound white mushrooms, stems
   trimmed, sliced
¼ cup dry white wine
2 tablespoons all-purpose flour
Salt and freshly ground black pepper to taste
1 cup milk
1½ pounds fresh green beans, topped, tailed,
   strung if necessary, cut into 2-inch lengths,
   steamed or boiled in water to cover until just
   tender, and drained; or two 10-ounce
   packages frozen cut green beans, thawed
⅔ cup plain dried bread crumbs

Preheat the oven to 350°F.

Melt 2 tablespoons of the butter in a medium-size heavy skillet over medium heat. Cook the onion, stirring occasionally, just until translucent, 5 or 6 minutes. Stir in the garlic and cook 1 minute longer. Add the mushrooms and cook until most of the moisture is evaporated, 5 to 8 minutes. Stir in the wine, increase the heat and boil 1 minute. Remove the skillet from the heat and set aside.

In a small saucepan, melt 1 tablespoon of the butter over low heat. Stir in the flour, season well with salt and pepper and cook gently, without browning, for 3 minutes. Stir in the milk all at once, whisking constantly to avoid lumps. Cook, still over low heat, until thickened, about 3 minutes.

Remove the saucepan from the heat. Stir in the green beans and then the mushroom mixture. Spoon into a medium-size gratin dish.

In a small saucepan, melt the 3 remaining tablespoons of butter over low heat and then stir in the bread crumbs. Spread the buttered crumbs over the green bean and mushroom mixture. Bake until hot and bubbling and the crumbs are crisp and golden brown, about 25 minutes. Serve very hot.

Variation: *For a zippier dish, add hot pepper sauce to taste to the sauce before stirring in the beans and mushrooms.*

Italian-style Green Beans

These are delicious with lamb or pork. If flat Italian green beans are available, substitute them in the recipe.

Makes 6 servings

2 tablespoons good-quality olive oil
1 to 2 cloves garlic, minced
2 pounds thinnest green beans, topped and tailed
1 cup chicken stock; or 1 cup water
Salt and freshly ground black pepper to taste
1 tablespoon chopped fresh oregano, plus
   additional for garnishing

Heat the oil in a large heavy saucepan over medium heat. Add the garlic and cook, being careful not to burn it, for 1 minute. Stir in the beans and toss to coat with the oil. Stir in the stock. Season with salt, pepper, and the 1 tablespoon of oregano. Simmer, still over medium heat, until the beans are barely tender and most of the liquid is evaporated, 5 to 7 minutes. Serve very hot, garnished with the additional oregano.

Green Bean Salad

Add this delicious salad to any cold buffet, antipasto platter, or summer salad plate.

Makes 6 to 8 servings

6 tablespoons extra-virgin olive oil
2 tablespoons red wine vinegar
1 tablespoon Dijon-style mustard
Salt and freshly ground black pepper to taste
3 green onions (scallions), white and light green
    parts only, very thinly sliced
1 tablespoon chopped fresh parsley
1½ pounds green beans, topped, tailed, strung
    if necessary, steamed until crisply tender,
    and chilled
1 large hard-cooked egg, peeled and chopped

In a small bowl, beat together the oil, vinegar, and mustard. Season with salt and pepper. Stir the green onions and parsley into this vinaigrette. In a large bowl, toss the beans with the vinaigrette. Serve the salad in a bowl, garnished with the egg.

Green Bean Salade Folle

In French this means "crazy salad." Originally prepared with a generous slice or two of foie gras, it might well have been crazy to use such an expensive ingredient in a salad. I have substituted much more reasonably priced chicken livers and I think this makes a very satisfying first course salad or as the principal dish in a summer luncheon menu.

Makes 6 to 8 servings

1 quart torn mixed salad greens, such as leaf
    lettuce, watercress, endive, and arugula
2 tablespoons extra-virgin olive oil
2 tablespoons plus 2 teaspoons red wine vinegar
2 tablespoons chopped fresh oregano
½ pound thinnest fresh green beans, topped,
    tailed, steamed until crisply tender, tossed
    with 1 tablespoon olive oil, and cooled; or
    one half 16-ounce package thinnest frozen
    green beans, thawed and tossed with the oil
3 tablespoons butter
¾ cup chicken livers, trimmed and cut into
    bite-size pieces

1 clove garlic, minced
3 green onions (scallions), white and light green
    parts only, thinly sliced
Salt and freshly ground black pepper to taste
2 tablespoons chopped fresh parsley
Nasturtium flowers

In a large bowl, toss together the greens. Pour in the olive oil and 2 teaspoons of the vinegar. Add the oregano and toss to coat the greens lightly. Arrange the greens on chilled salad plates. Divide the green beans among the salad plates.

Melt the butter in a large heavy skillet over medium-high heat. Cook the chicken livers, stirring, until browned but still a little pink inside, about 4 minutes. Add the garlic and green onions and cook about 30 seconds longer, shaking the skillet to move the chicken livers around. Stir in the remaining 2 tablespoons of vinegar. Cook 30 seconds and then season well with salt and pepper.

Spoon the hot livers onto the salads. Divide the sauce evenly. Garnish the salads with the parsley and nasturtium flowers. Serve at once.

Green Beans with Tarragon Butter

Enjoy these delicious beans with pan-sautéed salmon.

Makes 6 servings

4 tablespoons (½ stick) butter, softened
2 tablespoons chopped fresh tarragon
1 teaspoon minced green onion (scallion)
1 teaspoon light soy sauce
1½ pounds green beans, topped, tailed,
    strung if necessary, and steamed until
    crisply tender

In a small bowl, beat together the butter, tarragon, green onion, and soy sauce. Toss 2 tablespoons of this prepared butter with the hot beans. Pass the remaining butter in a small bowl. Serve very hot.

Green Beans and Pears in Tarragon

There is something about the anise flavor of tarragon that goes extremely well with green beans. The sweet, unusual addition of fresh pears makes this the perfect company vegetable. I like it served with pork, ham, or better yet, crisply roasted duck.

Makes 6 servings

1 tablespoon butter
1½ pounds thinnest green beans, topped and tailed
1 large crisply ripe Bosc (or other) pear, peeled, cored, quartered lengthwise, and thinly sliced lengthwise
¼ cup dry white wine
¼ cup water
Salt and freshly ground black pepper to taste
1½ tablespoons chopped fresh tarragon
½ cup heavy cream

Heat the butter in a medium-size heavy saucepan over medium heat. Add the beans and pear and toss to coat. Stir in the wine and water. Cover partially and cook over low heat until the pear is very tender, 4 to 5 minutes. Remove the cover and season with the salt, pepper, and tarragon. Stir in the cream. Cook over high heat until the cream begins to evaporate and the sauce thickens and begins to coat the beans, about 4 minutes. The pears will melt into the sauce and cling to the cooked beans. Serve very hot.

Green Beans and Bacon

In the old days, the bacon would be cooked with the beans for a long slow infusion of taste. Today, with changing tastes, the two are cooked separately, both remaining crisp; the flavors combine but are still individually distinct. I serve this with chicken or veal.

Makes 6 servings

5 thick slices bacon
1 small onion, very thinly sliced
1 teaspoon sugar
2 tablespoons red wine vinegar
1½ pounds green beans, topped, tailed, strung if necessary, and steamed until just tender
Salt and freshly ground black pepper to taste
½ teaspoon dried thyme

In a medium-size skillet, cook the bacon over medium heat until crisp, about 10 minutes. Drain the bacon on paper towels, leaving the fat in the skillet. Crumble the bacon and set aside.

In the fat in the same skillet, cook the onion over medium heat until translucent, about 5 minutes. Drain. Stir the sugar and vinegar into the hot skillet, cooking over medium heat just until dissolved. Add the beans and reserved bacon. Heat through, tossing to coat with the vinegar. Season well with salt, pepper, and thyme. Serve very hot.

Old-fashioned Southern Green Beans

I feel compelled to include one of the primary southern dishes of my childhood. There are many philosophies about the salt pork. Some cooks will only use ham hocks or the bone from a country-cured ham instead of salt pork. Some cook the salt pork in the beans, some render the salt pork first and use only the fat, discarding the pork. Some add the fried salt pork at the end. I like to cook the two together. Serve with fried chicken, roast turkey, ham, or pork roast.

Makes 6 to 8 servings

2 pounds good-size green beans, topped, tailed, and strung
¼ pound salt pork, thickly sliced; or streak-of-lean (see Note); or 1 smoked ham hock or ham bone
¼ teaspoon crushed red pepper (optional)
Salt and freshly ground black pepper to taste

Place the beans in a large heavy kettle. Add the salt pork. Pour in enough water to cover the beans and add the crushed red pepper (if using) salt, and pepper.

Simmer very gently over low heat until the beans are very tender, about 2 hours. If using a ham hock or bone, remove it and take the meat off the bone. Stir the meat into the beans. Serve very hot. Add a slice of salt pork to each serving if desired.

Note: *Streak-of-lean is salt pork with a large strip of meat in the middle rather than what we call fat back, which is salt pork with no marbled meat in it.*

Green Beans with Mushrooms and Little Onions

This combination goes well with almost any entrée, but is especially good with veal.

Makes 6 to 8 servings

2 tablespoons butter
½ pound medium-size white mushrooms, stems trimmed, quartered
2 pounds green beans, topped, tailed, strung if necessary, and steamed until crisply tender
1 pint boiling onions, boiled in water for 1 minute, drained, peeled, and steamed until tender, about 5 minutes; or one half 16-ounce package frozen baby onions, thawed
Salt and freshly ground black pepper to taste
1 teaspoon dried Italian herbs, such as oregano, marjoram, rosemary, and thyme; or a prepared mix

Melt the butter in a large heavy skillet over medium heat. Cook the mushrooms, stirring occasionally, until

golden, about 5 minutes. Add the green beans and onions and toss until very hot. Season with salt, pepper, and herbs. Serve very hot.

Green Beans and Tomatoes Provençale

Garlic, olive oil, and fresh herbs are inextricably associated with the Provençal region of southern France. Add some tomatoes and an onion, and these green beans become the perfect accompaniment to a whole grilled fish, roast leg of lamb, or roast chicken.

Makes 6 to 8 servings

2 tablespoons good-quality olive oil
½ small onion, thinly sliced
1 clove garlic, minced
2 large ripe tomatoes, peeled, seeded, and chopped
Salt and freshly ground black pepper to taste
1 tablespoon chopped fresh oregano, plus additional for garnishing
2 pounds thinnest fresh green beans, topped, tailed, strung if necessary, steamed until crisply tender, refreshed in cold water, and drained; or one 16-ounce package thinnest frozen green beans, thawed

Heat the oil in a medium-size heavy saucepan over low heat. Cook the onion, stirring occasionally, until just translucent, 5 to 6 minutes. Stir in the garlic. Cook gently 1 minute. Stir in the tomatoes and season with salt, pepper, and the 1 tablespoon of oregano. Cook, stirring occasionally, until the tomatoes are wilted, but not too soft, 4 to 5 minutes. Stir in the beans and heat through. Serve the beans very hot, garnished with the additional oregano.

Oven-roasted Green Beans and Red Peppers

Roasting gives these beans a very special character. For the best results, use large fresh Blue Lake beans. Serve them next to a perfectly grilled steak or a large chunk of grilled tuna.

Makes 6 to 8 servings

1½ pounds green beans, topped, tailed, and
    strung if necessary
1 large red bell pepper, seeded and cut into long
    ¼-inch strips
2 tablespoons olive oil
½ teaspoon dried thyme, or more to taste
Salt and freshly ground black pepper to taste
Chopped fresh thyme

Preheat the oven to 450°F.

Toss the beans and bell pepper in a medium-size bowl with the oil. Spread them in a shallow roasting pan large enough to hold the beans in a single layer. Sprinkle with the dried thyme. Roast, tossing with a spatula once or twice, until tender, about 10 minutes. It is fine for them to have golden brown ends.

Season well with salt and pepper, and serve hot, garnished with the fresh thyme.

Green Beans and Sugar Snap Peas with Hot Pepper Relish

Served hot, these beans are delicious with grilled tuna or swordfish—or halibut, if you are lucky enough to find it fresh. For lunch, try this snappy bean mixture together with a cheese omelet. I also like to add them to a cold buffet, along with cold poached fish and cold roast lamb, beef, or chicken.

Makes 6 to 8 servings

2 tablespoons chopped fresh cilantro
2 tablespoons chopped green bell pepper
2 tablespoons minced onion
1 small jalapeño pepper, seeded and minced;
    or 1 teaspoon minced habañero pepper
1 small clove garlic, minced
2 tablespoons fresh lemon or lime juice
Salt and freshly ground black pepper to taste
2 tablespoons extra-virgin olive oil
1 pound thinnest fresh green beans, topped
    and tailed; or one 16-ounce package frozen
    thinnest green beans, thawed
1 pound sugar snap peas, topped and strung;
    or one 16-ounce package frozen sugar snap
    peas, thawed
1 tablespoon butter, melted

In a large bowl, combine the cilantro, bell pepper, onion, jalapeño pepper, and garlic. Stir in the lemon juice, salt, pepper, and olive oil. Set aside.

Steam the beans and peas, separately, in a steamer basket or a colander, covered, over simmering water until crisply tender. Toss with the melted butter. Serve the beans and snap peas hot, or at room temperature, with the cold relish spooned over them.

Field Peas and Snaps

Field peas are another name for black-eyed peas. This combination is a classic and is delicious when served with barbecued pork or grilled fish.

Makes 6 servings

2 cups shelled fresh black-eyed peas; or 1 cup
    dried black-eyed peas, picked over, soaked
    overnight, and drained; or one 15-ounce can
    black-eyed peas, drained (do not cook again
    before adding the green beans)
1 cup chicken stock
1 clove garlic, crushed
½ jalapeño pepper, stemmed, seeded and minced
1 pound thinnest green beans, topped and tailed
1 tablespoon butter

Salt and freshly ground black pepper to taste
1 tablespoon chopped fresh parsley

Place the black-eyed peas in a medium-size kettle. Add the stock, garlic, and jalapeño pepper. Simmer over medium-low heat until just barely tender, 30 minutes or more, depending on the freshness of the peas. Add the green beans and simmer until they are just tender, 5 to 6 minutes. Drain. Stir the butter into the beans. Season well with salt and pepper. Serve hot, garnished with the parsley.

Black-eyed Pea and Spinach Fricassee

To fricassee something is almost the same as to braise it; that is, cooking food in a small amount of liquid. This delicious combination of fresh black-eyed peas and spinach is a welcome addition to any home-style meal.

Makes 6 servings

2 cups shelled fresh black-eyed peas; or 1 cup dried black-eyed peas, picked over, soaked overnight, and drained
1 small onion, chopped
1 clove garlic, minced
2 tablespoons butter
2 pounds spinach, stemmed and shredded
1 medium-size tomato, peeled, seeded, and chopped
1/4 cup dry white wine
Salt and freshly ground black pepper to taste
3 thick slices bacon, fried until crisp, drained on paper towels, and crumbled (page 42)

In a large kettle, combine the peas, onion, and garlic. Add water to cover the peas by 2 inches. Simmer over low heat until the peas are tender, 30 to 60 minutes. The time will depend on the freshness of the peas. Drain the beans and keep warm.

Melt the butter in a large kettle over medium heat. Add the spinach and cook in the water that clings to the leaves after washing just until the spinach is wilted, 3 to 4 minutes. Add tomato, wine, and the reserved black-eyed peas. Simmer, uncovered, stirring, until very hot and the tomato is beginning to just soften, 3 to 4 minutes. Season well with salt and pepper. Serve very hot, garnished with the bacon.

Black-eyed Peas with Texas Relish

Sometimes a similar dish is called Texas caviar. It is a delicious way to eat black-eyed peas. Plan to serve them with grilled steak.

Makes 6 servings

3 cups shelled fresh black-eyed peas
1 large onion, chopped
1 clove garlic, minced
1 quart water or chicken stock
Salt and freshly ground black pepper to taste
Texas Relish (recipe follows)

In a large saucepan, combine the black-eyed peas, onion, garlic, and water. Simmer over low heat until the peas are tender, 30 to 60 minutes. The time will depend entirely on the freshness of the peas. Season well with salt and pepper.

Drain the peas and serve hot. Pass Texas Relish on the side for diners to spoon on top.

Texas Relish

1 large tomato, peeled, seeded, and chopped
1/2 medium-size onion, minced
1 poblano or New Mexico chile, seeded and minced
1 small clove garlic, minced
1/4 cup distilled white vinegar or cider vinegar
2 tablespoons extra-virgin olive oil
Salt and freshly ground black pepper to taste

Combine all ingredients in a medium-size bowl and let stand at least 1 hour.

Refried Black-eyed Peas

This was a favorite dish during my childhood, one we asked for over and over again. I still like it, especially with barbecued beef.

Makes 6 to 8 servings

1 pound (about 3 cups) dried black-eyed peas, picked over, soaked overnight, and drained
4 thick slices bacon
2 tablespoons minced onion
1 small jalapeño pepper, seeded and minced
Salt and freshly ground black pepper to taste
Hot pepper sauce to taste (optional)

Place the beans in a large kettle. Add water to cover them by 2 inches. Simmer over low heat until tender, about 1 hour. Drain.

Meanwhile, in a medium-size skillet, cook the bacon over medium heat until crisp, about 10 minutes. Drain the bacon on paper towels, leaving the fat in the skillet. Crumble the bacon and set aside.

Pour off all but 2 to 3 tablespoons bacon fat from the skillet and reserve it. Add the onion to the fat left in the skillet and cook over medium heat for 2 minutes. Add the drained peas and mash with a potato masher or heavy fork. Add the jalapeño pepper and season with salt and pepper. Cook over medium-high heat, turning once or twice with a spatula, until thick, hot, and beginning to brown, about 15 minutes.

Add a little of the reserved bacon fat if the mixture begins to stick to the skillet. Add hot pepper sauce if you like. Serve very hot, garnished with the crumbled bacon.

Variation: *For added flavor, stir ½ cup grated Monterey Jack cheese into the peas after they're mashed and heat, turning, just until melted.*

Note: *In a pinch, substitute two 15-ounce cans black-eyed peas, drained and rinsed, for the cooked peas.*

Baby Lima Bean Combo

Choose the tiniest limas you can find for this vegetable combination. They should be quite tender when cooked. Serve with roast lamb or grilled butterflied lamb.

Makes 6 servings

2 tablespoons good-quality olive oil
1 pound baby limas in the pod, shelled (about 1½ cups shelled fresh lima beans)
1 pound fresh green peas in the pod, shelled; or 1 cup thawed frozen green peas
1 cup boiling onions, boiled in water to cover for 1 minute, drained, and peeled; or 1 cup thawed frozen baby onions
¼ pound green beans, topped, tailed, strung if necessary, and cut on the diagonal into 1-inch lengths
1 teaspoon sugar
Salt and freshly ground black pepper to taste
½ cup chicken stock
2 tablespoon chopped fresh mint

Heat the oil in a large saucepan over medium heat. Add all the vegetables and stir to coat with the oil. Sprinkle with the sugar and season well with salt and pepper. Stir in the stock. Cover and simmer over low heat until tender, about 20 minutes.

Uncover and stir in the mint. Raise the heat to medium and cook just until the liquid is almost all gone, about 5 minutes longer. Serve very hot.
Variation: *Pass a bowl of regular or light sour cream with this dish, letting each diner spoon a little on top of his or her serving.*

Creamed Lima Beans

There is only a short time in early July when really good fresh limas are in the market. Take advantage of the season and prepare them often. I like this simple dish as an alternative to fresh succotash, and serve it with grilled fish, such as orange roughy or red snapper, or even bluefish. If you like, it can be substituted for French fla-geolet beans as an accompaniment to rare roast lamb.

Makes 6 servings

**4 pounds fresh limas in the pod, shelled
(3 to 3½ cups shelled fresh limas)
1 cup heavy cream
Salt and freshly ground black pepper to taste
2 tablespoons chopped fresh parsley**

Place the beans in a large kettle. Add water to cover the beans by 2 inches and simmer over low heat until the beans are tender, about 20 minutes. Drain.

Meanwhile, in a small saucepan, simmer the cream over medium heat until it reduces by half, 5 to 10 minutes. Drain.

Stir the reduced cream into the cooked beans and cook, stirring, over low heat until very hot. Season with salt and pepper to taste and stir in the parsley. Serve very hot.

Variation: *This can be garnished with 3 or 4 slices of bacon, fried until crisp, drained on paper towels, and crumbled (page 42). Or sprinkle the beans with 2 green onions (scallions), white and 2 inches of dark green only, sliced.*

Scintillating Succotash

A combination of corn and beans was a staple of the Native American diet when the first European settlers arrived on the scene. Over the years the duo has become an American classic. The variations are almost endless, are often geographic, and can be as complex as Brunswick stew (which was originally fortified with squirrel, but now incorporates chicken). This simple version of succotash seems to satisfy even confirmed lima bean haters.

Makes 6 servings

**1 pound fresh lima beans in the pod, shelled
(about 1½ cups shelled fresh lima beans); or
1½ cups thawed frozen large or baby limas
2 cups well-flavored chicken stock**

**2 cups fresh corn kernels cut from the cob
(3 or 4 ears); or 2 cups thawed frozen corn
kernels, yellow or shoepeg; or, in a pinch,
2 cups drained canned corn
3 tablespoons butter
½ small onion, very thinly sliced
½ pound green beans, topped, tailed, strung if
necessary, cut into 2-inch lengths, and
steamed until crisply tender
¼ cup heavy cream
Salt and freshly ground black pepper to taste
Hot pepper sauce to taste (optional)
2 tablespoons chopped fresh parsley**

In a medium-size saucepan, simmer the limas over low heat in the stock until very tender, 15 minutes or longer, depending on the age of the beans. Add the corn and cook over medium heat for 2 minutes longer. Drain.

Melt the butter in a large heavy saucepan over medium heat. Cook the onion, stirring occasionally, until translucent, about 4 minutes. Stir in the green beans and the cooked limas and corn. Cook 1 minute longer. Stir in the cream. Season well with salt and pepper, and add hot pepper sauce if using. Simmer 2 to 3 minutes longer. Serve very hot, garnished with the parsley.

Variation: *On another occasion, add 1 ripe tomato, peeled, seeded, and chopped, to the onion before adding the beans and corn.*

Fava Chili

Chili is delicious made from many kinds of beans. The classic is pinto, but black beans, kidney beans, and even fava beans make wonderful eating.

Makes 6 to 8 servings

2 cups shelled fresh or thawed frozen fava beans;
    or 1 cup dried lima beans, picked over,
    soaked overnight, and drained (dried fava
    beans need to be soaked and skinned,
    a time-consuming proposition)
6 cloves garlic, chopped
1 large onion, chopped
Two 14½-ounce cans chopped tomatoes; or
    4 large tomatoes, peeled, seeded, and
    chopped
1 tablespoon olive oil
1 medium-size green bell pepper, seeded
    and chopped
2 jalapeño peppers, seeded and minced
Salt and freshly ground black pepper to taste
2 tablespoons ground cumin
2 tablespoons well-flavored chili powder
1 bunch (6 to 8) green onions (scallions), white
    and light green parts only, sliced
1 cup grated Cheddar or Monterey Jack cheese
Sour cream, regular or light
1 small ripe tomato, peeled, seeded, and chopped

Place the beans in a large kettle. Cover with water by 2 inches. Stir in the garlic and three-quarters of the chopped onion. Simmer over low heat until the beans are tender, 30 to 45 minutes. Drain the beans and stir in the tomato. Simmer over low heat for 15 minutes, stirring gently from time to time.

Heat the olive oil in a small skillet over medium heat. Cook the remaining onion, stirring occasionally, until tender, 5 to 6 minutes. Stir in the peppers and season well with salt and pepper. Stir this mixture into the beans and simmer over medium-low heat for 10 minutes. Stir in the cumin and chili powder. Cook 2 minutes longer. Serve very hot. Pass the green onions, cheese, sour cream, and chopped tomato.

Note: *A little guacamole goes very well as a condiment with this chili.*

Favas and Tomatoes

If fresh fava beans are not available, use fresh lima beans. The flavor will not be quite the same, but the combination is still delicious.

Makes 6 servings

2 tablespoons olive oil, plus additional for serving
2 cups shelled fresh or thawed frozen fava beans
1 bunch (6 to 8) green onions (scallions), white
    and light green parts only, sliced
1 clove garlic, minced
½ cup chicken stock
2 large ripe tomatoes, peeled, seeded,
    and chopped
1 tablespoon chopped fresh oregano;
    or 1 teaspoon dried
Salt and freshly ground black pepper to taste

Heat the olive oil in a large heavy saucepan over medium heat. Add the beans and cook, stirring, for 2 to 3 minutes. Add the green onions and garlic. Cook 1 minute longer. Stir in the stock, cover, and simmer over low heat until the beans are tender, up to 30 minutes.

Stir in the tomatoes and oregano. Simmer over low heat, until the tomatoes are just tender, 5 to 10 minutes. Season well with salt and pepper. Serve very hot or at room temperature. If serving at room temperature, be sure there is enough salt, along with an extra drizzle of olive oil.

Note: *Cooling or chilling dulls the flavor of any seasoning. For this reason, any salad, cold soup, or cold vegetable dish needs to be liberally seasoned before serving.*

Note: *One word of caution. Fava beans, which were the bean most often cultivated in Europe and the Middle East until other varieties were imported, are a special case. Not only do mature beans have to be peeled individually after shelling (this is easy to do once they are cooked) because the skin becomes tough with age, but some people with a Mediterranean heritage suffer from favism and can be poisoned by eating favas, though small quantities from time to time generally will not affect anyone badly.*

Beer Beans

These savory beans are delicious with any outdoor barbecue, but especially with ribs.

Makes 8 servings

1 pound (about 3 cups) dried beans, such as black beans or red kidney beans, picked over, soaked overnight, and drained
2 tablespoons good-quality olive oil
1 small onion, minced
2 cloves garlic, minced
1 teaspoon salt
1 teaspoon ground cumin
One 12-ounce can beer, regular or light
$1/3$ cup chopped fresh cilantro
1 bunch (6 to 8) green onions (scallions), white part only, thinly sliced
Sour cream, regular or light

Place the beans in a large kettle. Add enough water to cover the beans by about 2 inches. Simmer gently over medium-low heat, uncovered, until tender, $1\frac{1}{2}$ to 2 hours.

In a small skillet, heat the olive oil over medium heat. Cook the onion, stirring occasionally, until just translucent, about 5 minutes. Add the garlic and cook over low heat, without burning, for 1 minute longer. Stir the onions and garlic into the beans. Stir in the salt, cumin, and beer. Simmer over low heat 30 minutes longer. Just before serving, stir in the cilantro. Garnish with the green onions and sour cream.

Black Bean Salsa

Salsas add so much to so many meals. Add them to outdoor barbecues and cold buffets or serve them with any grilled meat or fish. This salsa is substantial and goes well with Cajun blackened catfish. You can replace the water for cooking the beans with unsalted chicken stock if you like.

Makes about 3 cups; 6 to 8 servings

1 cup dried black beans, picked over, soaked overnight, and drained
4 cloves garlic, 2 crushed and 2 minced
1 large onion, halved
2 bunches (12 to 16) green onions (scallions), white and half the green part only, sliced
1 large tomato, cut into $1/4$-inch dice
$1/2$ medium-size green bell pepper, seeded and cut into $1/4$-inch dice
1 jalapeño pepper, seeded and minced
2 tablespoons fresh lime juice
Salt and freshly ground black pepper to taste
$1/4$ cup very fruity olive oil
3 tablespoons chopped fresh cilantro

Place the beans in a medium-size heavy saucepan. Pour in enough water to cover the beans by 2 inches. Add the 2 crushed garlic cloves and the onion halves. Simmer over low heat until tender, 1 to $1\frac{1}{2}$ hours. Drain and remove the onion and garlic. Cool.

In a large bowl, combine the cooked beans with all the remaining ingredients. Chill 2 to 3 hours. Serve cool but not directly from the refrigerator.

Moros y Blancos

Many cultures combine beans with rice or another grain that can create a complete protein and eliminate the need for any animal protein at all. The ingredients are inexpensive and practically universally available.

With the addition of onion, bell pepper, garlic, and tomato, this is an especially tasty version of beans and rice, and I think it goes very well with pork or poultry. For another version, see Red Beans and Rice on page 52.

Makes 6 to 8 servings

1 cup dried black beans, picked over, soaked
    overnight, and drained
3 tablespoons good-quality olive oil
1 small onion, chopped
½ medium-size green bell pepper, seeded
    and chopped
2 cloves garlic, minced
1 large ripe tomato, chopped
½ cup dry white wine
1 teaspoon ground cumin
Salt and freshly ground black pepper to taste
3 tablespoons chopped fresh parsley
4 cups freshly cooked rice, hot (about 1⅓ cups
    raw rice)

Place the beans in a large kettle. Add water to cover them by 2 inches. Simmer over low heat until just beginning to soften, 45 to 60 minutes.

Heat the oil in a medium-size heavy skillet over low heat. Stir in the onion, pepper, and garlic. Cook, stirring occasionally, until translucent about 5 minutes. Stir in the tomatoes and wine. Increase the heat to medium-high and cook, stirring, until the wine reduces by half, about 10 minutes. Stir in the seasonings and parsley. Simmer 1 minute longer. Stir the vegetable mixture into the beans and continue to cook over low heat until the beans are very tender and most, but not all, of the liquid is absorbed, 30 minutes or longer.

To serve, mound the cooked rice on a heated serving platter, or in a large bowl. Spoon the bean mixture over the rice.

Note: *The beans should have a little liquid with them to create a small amount of sauce that will moisten the rice.*

Kidney Bean and Beet Salad

This is a substantial salad that is especially good in the summertime. Take it along on a picnic or serve it with barbecued anything, from hot dogs to sirloin steak or fish.

Makes 6 to 8 servings

4 medium-size new potatoes, unpeeled, boiled in
    salted water to cover until tender, about
    15 minutes, drained, and cut into large cubes
¾ cup dried red kidney beans, picked over,
    soaked overnight, drained, and simmered in
    water to cover until tender
3 medium-size beets, trimmed and baked in a
    325°F. oven until tender, 1 to 1½ hours, or
    boiled in water to cover until tender, about
    30 minutes, peeled, and cut into large cubes
1 sweet onion, preferably Vidalia, Maui, or Walla
    Walla, finely diced
½ cup mayonnaise, prepared or homemade
    (page 13)
¼ cup sour cream, regular or light
1 teaspoon celery seed
Salt and freshly ground black pepper to taste
¼ cup chopped fresh parsley, plus sprigs
    for garnishing
1 small head leaf lettuce

In a large bowl, toss together potatoes, beans, beets, and onion. In a small bowl, beat together the mayonnaise, sour cream, celery seed, salt, pepper, and chopped parsley. Toss this dressing gently with the vegetables. Chill for 1 hour or longer.

To serve, arrange the lettuce on a serving platter. Mound the salad on the lettuce and garnish with the parsley sprigs.

Variation: *I like to add several minced anchovy fillets to this salad for a Scandinavian touch.*

Barbecue Beans

Don't hesitate to serve these along with classic Texas barbecue beef, pork ribs, and chicken.

Makes 6 to 8 servings

1 pound (about 3 cups) dried beans, preferably
    pink beans, pinto beans, or kidney beans,
    picked over, soaked overnight, and drained
2 smoked ham hocks
1 large onion, quartered
3 cloves garlic, crushed
2 teaspoons well-flavored chili powder, or more
    to taste
3 large ripe tomatoes, chopped
Salt and freshly ground black pepper to taste
Sour cream, regular or light
2 tablespoons chopped fresh cilantro

Place the beans in a medium-size heavy kettle. Add the ham hocks, onion, garlic, and chili powder. Stir in enough water to cover the beans by 2 inches. Cover and simmer over low heat until the beans are just tender, about 2 hours. Stir in the tomatoes and cook 30 minutes longer. Season well with salt and pepper and add more chili powder if you like. Heat 5 minutes longer. Remove the ham hocks and strip the meat from the bones. Return the meat to the beans. Serve very hot in bowls, garnished with the sour cream and cilantro.

Note: *Do not add the tomatoes or salt until the beans are already tender. The acid in the tomatoes slows the softening of the beans, as does the salt.*

Refried Beans

These are a classic accompaniment for a Tex-Mex meal, but I find them delicious with any barbecued pork or beef

dish. Often these beans are served simply mashed and hot, without being refried. Serve them refried or not, whatever suits your fancy. Obviously, they will be less caloric if not refried.

Makes 6 servings

2 cups cooked dried beans, such as pinto or
    pink kidney beans, picked over, soaked
    overnight, drained, simmered until tender,
    and drained again
1 teaspoon salt
3 to 4 tablespoons bacon fat (or, traditionally,
    lard), plus 2 optional tablespoons for frying
2 tablespoons butter, plus 2 tablespoons for
    frying (both optional)
Freshly ground black pepper to taste (optional)
1 teaspoon minced jalapeño or other hot chile
    (optional)
2 ounces (½ cup) freshly grated Monterey Jack
    or Cheddar cheese (optional)

Mash the beans with the salt, 3 to 4 tablespoons of the bacon fat, and 2 tablespoons of the butter if using. If desired, stir in the ground pepper, jalapeño pepper, and/or cheese. Serve hot.

Alternatively, heat the remaining 2 tablespoons of bacon fat or butter in a large skillet. Add the mashed beans and fry, turning occasionally, until hot and beginning to brown, about 10 minutes. It isn't necessary to fry this in one large cake.

Variation: *For another presentation, chill the mashed bean mixture until firm. Form the chilled mixture into cakes 2 to 3 inches in diameter and fry them in the remaining bacon fat or butter, turning once, until crisp on the outside, 3 to 4 minutes per side. Serve very hot.*

Note: *You can also use canned beans here instead of soaking and simmering dried beans. Drain and rinse the canned beans before using.*

Red Beans and Rice

The satisfying combination of meaty kidney beans and rice can be as down-home as boiled beans and boiled rice or as upscale as the spicy mixture presented here. Good with pork of all kinds, especially spicy grilled Cajun andouille sausage.

Makes 8 to 10 servings

1 pound (3 to 3½ cups) dried red kidney beans, picked over, soaked overnight, and drained
1 large onion, chopped
2 large cloves garlic, minced
1 tablespoon chopped fresh thyme, or 1 teaspoon dried
6 ounces salt pork or streak-of-lean (page 43), sliced, soaked in water to cover for 1 hour, and drained
Freshly ground black pepper to taste
¼ teaspoon crushed red pepper
Salt to taste
Hot pepper sauce to taste
4 cups freshly cooked rice, hot (about 1⅓ cups raw)
Chopped fresh parsley

Place the beans, onion, garlic, thyme, salt pork, black pepper, and red pepper in a medium-size kettle. Add water to cover the beans by 2 inches. Cover and simmer over low heat until the beans are tender, about 2 hours. Remove the cover and season with salt and hot pepper sauce. Simmer until the beans are very tender but not dry—there should be enough liquid to serve as a bit of sauce—about 10 minutes.

To serve, mound the rice on serving plates or in bowls. Spoon the beans generously over the rice and garnish with the parsley.

Pinto Beans in Goulash

Add a salad and some full-flavored rye bread for a complete Sunday-night supper. As a side dish, it goes very well with barbecued ribs.

Makes 8 to 10 servings

1 pound (about 3½ cups) dried pinto beans, picked over, soaked overnight, and drained
6 cups unsalted beef stock, more or less
3 tablespoons butter
2 large onions, chopped
1 large Russet potato, peeled and cut into ¼-inch dice
2 large ripe tomatoes, chopped
1 teaspoon salt
1 tablespoon hot Hungarian paprika
3 tablespoons chopped fresh parsley
Sour cream, regular or light

Place the beans in a medium-size heavy kettle. Add enough stock to cover by 2 inches. Bring to a simmer over medium heat.

Melt the butter in a small skillet over medium heat. Cook the onions, stirring, until golden, 7 to 8 minutes. Stir the onions into the beans. Simmer, covered, over low heat, for 30 minutes. Add a little more stock if necessary, and simmer until the beans are just tender, at least 1 hour more. Stir in the potato and tomatoes. Season with salt and paprika. Simmer until the beans are very tender but not mushy, 20 to 30 minutes. Stir in the parsley.

Serve the beans very hot in bowls, with a spoonful of sour cream on top of each serving.

Old-fashioned New England Baked Beans

Traditionally, these beans were put together on Saturday night, slid into the damped oven or buried in the coals of the banked fire on the kitchen hearth, and cooked slowly all night. Then the pot was pulled out to serve with brown bread or another homemade bread as a work-free Sabbath meal. I still like them as part of a cold-weather, Sunday-night dinner, the cooking beans filling the kitchen with wonderful smells of what is to come. Serve the beans with brown bread or crusty sourdough bread and butter.

Makes 8 to 10 servings

1 pound (about 3 cups) dried navy beans, picked
over, soaked overnight, and drained
2 medium-size onions, chopped
$\frac{1}{3}$ cup packed dark brown sugar
$\frac{1}{4}$ cup molasses
$1\frac{1}{2}$ teaspoons dry mustard
2 cups water or chicken stock, boiling
Salt and freshly ground black pepper to taste
6 ounces salt pork, slab bacon, or hog jowl
(see Note), traditionally left in one piece,
but cubed if preferred

Preheat the oven to 250°F.

Place the beans in a large kettle. Add water to
cover the beans by 2 inches. Simmer the beans
uncovered over low heat until barely tender, 30 to
45 minutes. The skins will just begin to pop when
you blow on a spoonful of the beans. Drain.

In a large bowl, mix together all the remaining
ingredients, including the salt pork if cubed. Stir in
the beans. Pour into a medium-size bean pot or covered flameproof casserole.

If cooking the salt pork in one piece, use a sharp
knife to make cuts, about $\frac{1}{4}$-inch apart through the
piece to about $\frac{1}{4}$ inch from the bottom. Bend the
piece, fanning out the slices. Push the pork down into
the beans until totally covered.

Cover the pot and bake 8 to 10 hours. Uncover
the pot for the last hour to dry out the surface slightly.

Note: *Hog jowl is a smoked product made from
the cheeks of hogs. It is much leaner and thinner than bacon and makes great seasoning meat,
but it's available only in some country markets.*

Pasta e Fagioli Salad

*Pasta and bean soup, brought to the New World by our
Italian ancestors, is a very rewarding, substantial cold-
weather meal. Surprisingly, the same combination lends
itself very well to the cold salads that are so welcome during the summer months. Add this to your next outdoor
meal, along with cold roast chicken, for a real treat.*

Makes 6 servings

1 cup dried beans, such as cannellini, navy, or
Great Northern, picked over, soaked overnight, simmered until tender, and drained,
cooled to room temperature
2 cups cooked pasta shapes, such as small elbows,
bow ties, or rotini, drained, cooled to room
temperature
$\frac{1}{4}$ pound thinnest green beans, topped, tailed,
and steamed until crisply tender; or 1 cup
thawed frozen thinnest green beans, at room
temperature
2 large ripe tomatoes, peeled, seeded,
and chopped
2 cloves garlic, minced
$\frac{1}{2}$ small red onion, thinly sliced
2 tablespoons red wine vinegar
$\frac{1}{3}$ cup extra-virgin olive oil, plus additional
to taste
Salt and freshly ground black pepper to taste
3 to 4 tablespoons chopped fresh basil
Freshly grated Parmesan cheese

In a large bowl, toss together the drained beans and
pasta. Add the green beans, tomatoes, garlic, and
onion, and toss. In a small bowl, mix together the
vinegar, olive oil, salt, and pepper. Pour this dressing
over the vegetables. Toss to coat. Chill at least 1 hour.
Serve at room temperature, tossed at the last minute
with the basil and more olive oil if needed. Pass the
cheese and a pepper mill separately.

Note: *You can also use 2 cups canned beans
here instead of soaking and simmering dried
beans. Drain and rinse the canned beans before
adding them to the recipe.*

Marinated Chickpeas with Little Onions and Peppers

The chickpea, or garbanzo, is not a universally appreciated bean, but I think this combination might change a few skeptical minds. It will go very well alongside a platter of barbecued chicken or pork, or serve with grilled butterflied leg of lamb.

Makes 6 to 8 servings

1 cup dried chickpeas, picked over, soaked
    overnight, and drained; or 2 cups canned
    chickpeas, drained and rinsed—do not cook
1 pint smallest boiling onions, boiled in water
    to cover for 1 minute, drained, peeled,
    simmered in salted water to cover until
    tender, and drained; or 1½ cups frozen baby
    onions, thawed, simmered in salted water to
    cover for 5 minutes and drained
2 tablespoons pure olive oil
1 small red bell pepper, seeded and cut into
    1-inch pieces
½ small green bell pepper, seeded and cut into
    1-inch pieces
2 cloves garlic, minced
¼ cup fresh lemon juice (1 large lemon)
½ cup extra-virgin olive oil
Salt and freshly ground black pepper to taste
3 to 4 tablespoons chopped fresh parsley, plus
    additional for garnishing
Hot pepper sauce to taste

Place the chickpeas in a medium-size heavy saucepan. Add water to cover by 2 inches. Simmer over low heat until very tender, 2 or more hours. Drain well. Place the chickpeas in a large glass or other nonreactive bowl. Stir in the onions.

Heat the pure olive oil in a medium-size heavy skillet over medium heat. Cook the bell peppers, stirring occasionally, until just beginning to be translucent and tender, 4 to 5 minutes. Stir the cooked peppers into the chickpeas.

In a small bowl, combine the garlic, lemon juice, extra-virgin olive oil, salt, pepper, and parsley. Pour this dressing over the chickpeas and toss well. Add the hot pepper sauce. Marinate overnight.

Serve at room temperature, garnished with the additional parsley.

Note: *Remember that chilling will dull the seasoning, so be generous with the salt and pepper.*

Pureed Chickpeas with Garlic and Pepper

Once you have everyone enjoying chickpeas, add this to a dinner where lamb or grilled chicken holds the spotlight. A grilled whole fish, seasoned with fennel, will also go very well.

Makes 6 servings

2 cups dried chickpeas, picked over, soaked
    overnight, and drained; or 4 cups canned
    chickpeas, drained, rinsed and cooked until
    very tender
¼ to ½ cup cold water, if needed
2 tablespoons pure olive oil
1 large onion, halved and thinly sliced
1 large red bell pepper, seeded and thinly sliced
2 cloves garlic, minced
Salt and freshly ground black pepper to taste
½ teaspoon ground cumin
2 tablespoons chopped fresh cilantro

Place the soaked chickpeas in a medium-size kettle. Add water to cover by about 2 inches. Cover and simmer over low heat until very tender, 2 hours or longer. Drain the chickpeas and puree them or the canned variety in a blender or food processor. If the puree is too thick, add the cold water, 1 tablespoon at a time, to thin it.

Heat the olive oil in a medium-size heavy skillet over low heat. Cook the onion, bell pepper, and garlic, stirring occasionally, until the onions are golden and the peppers are very soft, 15 minutes or more.

Stir the chickpea puree into the skillet. Season well with salt, pepper, and cumin. Heat thoroughly. Serve the puree very hot, garnished with the cilantro. Or cool the puree to room temperature and serve as part of an antipasto buffet.

Felafel

These little fried cakes are as popular in Israel as hot dogs are in America, though Israeli felafel tend to have a great deal more garlic in them than this recipe calls for. Traditionally several of these hot garlicky cakes are served in warm pita bread as a sandwich, garnished with chopped cucumber, lettuce, tomato, and green onion. They also make a delicious appetizer when served with hot pepper sauce or a fiery salsa, and I think they go well alongside hamburgers hot off the grill with hot (spicy) ketchup!

Makes 6 to 8 servings

2 cups dried chickpeas, picked over, soaked
    overnight, and drained (do not use canned)
2 tablespoons water
3 or 4 large cloves garlic
½ small onion, coarsely chopped
3 tablespoons chopped fresh parsley
3 tablespoons chopped fresh cilantro
1 tablespoon ground cumin, or more to taste
1 teaspoon salt
Freshly ground black pepper to taste
1 cup plain dried bread crumbs made from stale
    home-style white bread
Mild vegetable oil for deep-frying
Hot sauce to taste

Place the chickpeas, water, garlic, and onion in a food processor. Process until pureed. Add the parsley, cilantro, and cumin, and season generously with salt and pepper. Process until well mixed. Turn the chickpea mixture into a medium-size bowl. Stir in the bread crumbs, mixing well. A spoon is not nearly as effective as using your hands to mix in the crumbs.

Form the chickpea mixture into balls, using about 1 heaping tablespoon for each and shaping with your hands. If the mixture sticks to your hands, wet them before shaping the balls.

Heat the oil to 350°F. in a deep-fat fryer. (The oil should not be too hot.) Fry the balls, several at a time, until they are a nice golden brown and crisp on the outside, 2 to 3 minutes per batch. Drain the crisp balls on paper towels and keep warm until all the felafel are fried. Serve as hot as possible and pass the hot pepper sauce separately.

Variation: *For a spicier treat, add 1 teaspoon crushed red pepper to the mixture at the same time you stir in the bread crumbs, before shaping the balls.*

Hummus bi Tahini

Some sort of chickpea paste is served throughout the Middle East. This is a delicious dip or spread for toasted pita bread. But it also has a place on an antipasto buffet or as part of a cold supper.

Makes about 2 cups

1 cup dried chickpeas, picked over, soaked overnight, and drained; or 2½ cups canned chickpeas, drained and rinsed—do not cook further
2 cloves garlic, peeled, or more to taste
½ cup cold water, or more if needed
¼ cup fresh lemon juice (1 large lemon)
⅓ cup tahini (see Note)
Salt and freshly ground black pepper to taste
Hot pepper sauce, or hot red (cayenne) pepper, to taste (optional)
Extra-virgin olive oil for serving
1½ tablespoons chopped fresh parsley

Place the soaked chickpeas in a medium-size kettle and add water to cover by 2 inches. Cover the kettle and simmer over low heat until very tender, at least 2 hours. Drain well. Cool.

In a food processor, process the garlic, water, and lemon juice until almost smooth. Add the cooled or canned chickpeas and process until smooth. If the mixture is too thick, add more water, 1 tablespoon at a time, until the puree is thick, but smooth.

Transfer the chickpea puree to a medium-size bowl. Stir in the tahini and season well with salt, pepper and, if using, the hot pepper sauce. The mixture should be smooth, the consistency of a thick dip.

For a traditional Middle Eastern presentation, serve this puree spread in a deep plate or shallow bowl, drizzled with olive oil and garnished with parsley. Or spoon it into a bowl, make a little well in the surface, fill with olive oil, and garnish with the parsley.

Variation: For a more colorful, but not authentic, presentation, increase the parsley to 3 tablespoons and stir it into the puree just before serving.

Note: *Tahini is sesame seed paste, which is sold commercially in many supermarkets and in most health-food stores. The paste is available in both cans and jars. Once opened, the paste can be kept in the refrigerator almost indefinitely, at the very least for several months. If you buy tahini in a can, after opening remove any remaining paste and store in a clean jar with a tightfitting lid. I like to cover the surface of the paste with a very thin layer of sesame seed oil to eliminate any chance of discoloration.*

Beets

Even though beets have been cultivated for more than a thousand years, they were originally grown primarily for their green tops, and probably did not have the swollen root of today's vegetable. A relative of Swiss chard, very fresh beet greens are tender and sweet, almost like spinach, when cooked. Old beet greens are somewhat tough and strong tasting but are still good in combination with other vegetables. It may also be that the original beets cultivated for their roots were white or yellow, much like sugar beets, and were likely not at all tender—or sweet, even when just pulled.

Modern beets appeared in Europe sometime during the sixteenth century and their popularity spread slowly, for the most part through Eastern Europe, Scandinavia, and on into Russia. While Western Europeans had little imagination when cooking beets, in Russia, beets came into their own. There, at least, soups and stews as well as salads were prepared with red or orange beets.

In Europe, most beets are still sold precooked, often baked. Before ovens were common in homes, beets were frequently put into bakers' large ovens when they were cooling after the day's bread baking was finished. Depending on their size, beets can take up to several hours to bake, and the dwindling heat of the bread ovens was perfect.

These precooked beets, sold cold, were generally sliced, diced, or cut into matchstick strips and served as part of a crudité platter. Once in a while the slices were reheated, with a little butter and perhaps a little vinegar, but for a long time that was the extent of European beet cuisine. In France, today, cooked beets are available in refrigerated Cryovac packaging, whole or cut up, all ready for saucing, hot or cold. And innovative French chefs are especially fond of the beet for its flamboyant, deep scarlet color.

American chefs seem to have rediscovered beets, too, especially the exotic colored ones: candy striped red and white, orange, pink, dark red, and even yellowish white varieties are available to home gardeners and can also be found in some specialty greengrocers. They are extremely attractive in salads and are deliciously decorative additions to any menu.

Beets are one of the few canned vegetables, along with beans, corn, hominy, and sauerkraut, that are, in my estimation, good enough for more than emergency fare. Treat them as already cooked, ready to be sauced or garnished any way you like. I save the juice from the can, add an equal amount of cider vinegar, and use it to pickle peeled, hard-cooked eggs.

While I have never seen commercially frozen beets, home-cooked beets freeze very well. Just cook; drain, if necessary; peel, slice, dice, etc.; and freeze in small airtight plastic freezer bags. Plan to use them within a month or two.

Low in fat and calories—4 ounces contain about fifty calories—beets are also a good source of vitamin C, potassium, and iron.

Selection: Like most root vegetables, it is essential to choose the freshest beets available. Once you have tasted beets that were pulled just before cooking you will be spoiled forever. While even canned beets are sweet, just-pulled ones are almost like candy.

The smaller they are, the more tender and sweet the beets will be. Look for beets with the leaves still on. If the leaves are crisp and green without yellow, wilted edges, the beets should be fresh. Some supermarkets sell beets that have already had the leaves cut off, called "clipped top." These can still be acceptable, but they are never as fresh and may be out of cold storage. Watch out for shriveled, dried-out beets—they tend to be woody. And avoid any that are spongy feeling or show signs of mold.

If you have access to a specialty greengrocer or farmers' market, look for some of the more colorful varieties that are available now. The red-and-white whorled ones, along with those that are a red-orange color, bleed less than traditional red or purple beets and are wonderful for adding to salads or serving on their own without coloring everything they touch.

Beets are frequently in the market all year round, but they are at their best from late May until the weather gets very hot. Later beets can be somewhat tough. Count on 2 pounds of untrimmed beets for six servings.

Storage and Preparation: Fresh beets should be stored, unwashed, in the crisper drawer of the refrigerator. Cut off the leaves about 2 inches from the beet and do not trim the roots. This will prevent them from bleeding profusely when they are cooked. While they will remain fresh for three or four days in a perforated vegetable bag, I think beets should be prepared as soon as possible after they are pulled.

Leave the skins on to prevent bleeding, whether baking, boiling, or steaming. They are easily peeled when hot. Scrub fresh beets well just before cooking, taking care not to break or cut the skin.

Beets, especially baby ones, are perfect for cooking several hours ahead and chilling. Cut medium-size or large beets into chunks and then reheat in the microwave or boiling water to cover for 1 or 2 minutes before peeling, saucing, and serving.

Boiled Beets

Place the trimmed whole beets in a large saucepan. Add water to cover and 2 tablespoons lemon juice or vinegar to discourage the beets from bleeding into the water and help keep them brightly colored. (This is known as acidulated water.) Simmer over medium heat until tender, 25 to 60 minutes, depending on the age and size of the beets. Refresh in cold water until easy to handle, 2 to 3 minutes. Peel and leave whole or cut up, depending on the recipe.

Baked Beets

If you have time, I believe that baking beets retains more of their sweetness and nutritional value than any other cooking method. Lightly oil the trimmed beets (or not if you prefer) and place them, uncovered, in one layer in a baking pan. Bake the beets in a preheated 325°F. oven for 1 to 2 hours. Again, the time depends on the age and size of the beets. If you are baking very tiny, new beets, the cooking time may be as little as 30 minutes, but it is difficult to find these little gems, so count on at least 1 hour. Large ones will definitely take longer, up to 2 hours or more. Some cooks wrap beets in aluminum foil before baking, but I think it is unnecessary and this method actually steams them instead. Cool the baked beets, peel them, and continue with the recipe.

Steamed Beets

Place trimmed whole beets in a steamer basket or a colander over simmering water. Cover and steam until tender, 45 minutes to 1½ hours. Remove from the steamer, cool slightly, and peel.

Microwaved Beets

Arrange 1 pound trimmed whole medium-size beets in a microwave dish, pour in about ½ cup water, cover with plastic microwave wrap, and vent. Microwave on high, turning the beets over several times, until tender, 15 to 18 minutes. (Be careful to vent the steam before turning the beets.) I have also had good luck with large beets, wrapping each in a microwaveable paper towel and microwaving on high about 20 minutes. This seems to avoid a hard spot on the bottom. The cooking time, of course, will vary, depending on the size and age of the beets. Cool the cooked beets and peel before continuing with the recipe.

Beets with Orange Juice and Zest

Beets just seem to naturally go with orange juice and this variation of a classic sweet-and-sour dish contains just enough to enhance the sweet flavor of the vegetable.

Makes 6 servings

2 tablespoons butter
1/3 cup fresh orange juice
1 tablespoon fresh lemon juice
1 tablespoon grated orange zest
1 tablespoon orange liqueur, such as Grand Marnier or Triple Sec
2 pounds beets, trimmed, baked or boiled in acidulated water (page 59) to cover until tender, drained, peeled, and sliced
Salt and freshly ground black pepper to taste
1 tablespoon chopped fresh parsley

Melt the butter in a heavy saucepan over high heat. Add the orange juice, lemon juice, zest, and liqueur. Boil for 1 minute. Add the beets and season well with salt and pepper. Simmer over very low heat, tossing from time to time to coat the beets well, about 10 minutes. Serve very hot, garnished with the chopped parsley.

Apple and Beet Compote

The rosy color of this delicious sweet-and-savory compote makes it a lovely addition to a dinner plate. Add it to any menu containing roast pork, spareribs, ham, even grilled fish.

Makes 6 to 8 servings

1 pound beets, trimmed, boiled in acidulated water (page 59) to cover, and drained, or baked until tender, peeled, and cut into 1/4-inch dice
1 small red onion, halved and thinly sliced
2 medium-size Granny Smith apples, peeled, cored, and chopped
1/2 cup not-too-dry white wine, apple cider, or apple juice
Salt and freshly ground black pepper to taste
1/2 teaspoon ground cardamom
2 tablespoons butter

Combine the beets, onion, and apples in a medium-size heavy saucepan. Add the wine, and season with salt, pepper, and cardamom. Cover and simmer over low heat until the apples and beets begin to fall apart, 15 to 20 minutes. Beat in the butter, breaking up the beets and apples. The mixture should be lumpy rather than smooth. Serve the compote very hot, warm, or at room temperature.

Beet Custards

Prepare these ahead of time and bake them at the last minute. The texture is a nice combination of smooth custard with luscious morsels of beet. They are delicious served hot alongside grilled fish and add a colorful touch to any menu.

Makes 6 servings

2 tablespoons butter, plus additional, melted, for buttering
Plain dried bread crumbs
2 tablespoons all-purpose flour
Salt and freshly ground black pepper to taste
1 cup milk
2 large eggs, beaten
2 tablespoons orange zest
1 pound beets, trimmed, baked or steamed until tender, peeled, and minced
Fresh parsley sprigs

Preheat the oven to 375°F. Brush six 5-ounce ramekins or dariole molds with the melted butter. Coat the inside lightly with the bread crumbs.

Melt the 2 tablespoons of butter over low heat in a small heavy saucepan. Stir in the flour and cook, stirring so it doesn't brown, for 3 minutes. Season with salt and pepper. Stir in the milk all at once. Cook over medium-low heat, stirring until smooth and the sauce thickens, 3 to 10 minutes. Remove the saucepan from the heat and beat in the egg.

Stir in the orange zest and beets. Spoon the mixture into the prepared molds. Place the filled molds in a baking pan and pour in boiling water until it reaches halfway up the sides of the molds. Bake until set, about 30 minutes. Remove the molds from the pan and cool on a rack for 5 minutes.

To unmold, run a thin knife around the outside of the custards. Invert 1 ramekin onto a wide spatula. Rap sharply on the counter to release the custard. Slide the custard onto the dinner or serving plate. Repeat with the remaining custards. Serve the custards hot, garnished with the parsley sprigs.

Note: *For a more deeply colored custard, boil the unpeeled beets until tender and substitute ½ cup of the beet cooking liquid for ½ cup of the milk.*

Beet Salad

Add this salad to a summer cold buffet or serve it alongside a platter of cold cuts.

Makes 6 servings

2 pounds beets, trimmed, boiled in acidulated water (page 59) to cover and drained or baked until tender, peeled, and thinly sliced
1 bunch (about 10 medium) radishes, thinly sliced
1 bunch (6 to 8) green onions (scallions), white part only, thinly sliced
½ teaspoon caraway seeds, crushed
Salt and freshly ground black pepper to taste
2 tablespoons cider vinegar
⅓ cup mild vegetable oil
1 tablespoon heavy cream

1 small head leaf lettuce
2 large hard-cooked eggs, peeled and quartered lengthwise or sliced
1 tablespoon chopped fresh parsley

In a medium-size bowl, toss together the beets, radishes, and green onions. Season with the caraway seeds, salt, and pepper. In a small bowl, beat together the vinegar, oil, and cream. Pour over the salad and toss all gently.

Serve the salad on a bed of leaf lettuce. Garnish with the eggs and parsley.

Beets with Mushrooms and Green Onions

The contrast of textures is what makes this a delightful dish. Serve it with almost any main course.

Makes 6 servings

2 tablespoons butter
1 clove garlic, minced (optional)
1 bunch (6 to 8) green onions (scallions), white and light green parts only, sliced
¼ pound shiitake (stems discarded) or portabella mushrooms, stems trimmed, cut up or sliced
¼ cup dry white wine
1 pound beets, trimmed, boiled in acidulated water (page 59) to cover until tender, drained, peeled, and sliced
½ cup heavy cream
3 tablespoons chopped fresh parsley

Melt the butter in a medium-size heavy saucepan over low heat. Cook the garlic, if using, and green onions, stirring occasionally, for 1 minute.

Stir in the mushrooms and cook until just beginning to turn golden, 3 to 5 minutes. Stir in the wine and cook until it is nearly evaporated, about 3 minutes.

Stir in the beets and cream. Simmer over medium heat until thickened, about 4 minutes. Stir in the parsley and serve very hot.

Creamed Beets

Like creamed potatoes, this is an old-fashioned dish that deserves a place on modern menus.

Makes 6 servings

1 cup heavy cream
1 tablespoon butter
1 bunch (6 to 8) green onions (scallions), white part only, thinly sliced
2 pounds beets, trimmed, baked until tender, peeled, and cut into ¼-inch dice
Salt and freshly ground black pepper to taste
2 tablespoons snipped fresh chives

In a medium-size heavy saucepan, simmer the cream over medium heat until reduced by half, 5 to 7 minutes; keep warm.

Melt the butter in another medium-size heavy saucepan over low heat. Cook the green onions, stirring occasionally, for 1 minute. Stir in the beets and reduced cream. Season well with salt and freshly ground pepper. Heat through. Serve very hot garnished with the chives.

Beet Salad with Snow Peas and New Potatoes

Choose the smallest new potatoes, the crispest snow peas, and crisp tiny beets for a truly delicious accompaniment to roast chicken.

Makes 6 to 8 servings

2 pounds smallest beets, trimmed, boiled in acidulated water (page 59) to cover and drained or baked until tender, peeled, sliced, or, if really small, halved
1½ pounds smallest new potatoes, boiled in salted water to cover until tender, drained, cooled, and cut into wedges
1 large sweet onion, or red onion, thinly sliced
¼ pound snow peas, or sugar snap peas, topped, strung, and steamed until crisply tender
¼ cup white wine vinegar
1 tablespoon sugar
⅓ cup extra-virgin olive oil, or mild vegetable oil, preferably peanut
Salt and freshly ground black pepper to taste
1 tablespoon capers, drained, rinsed, and coarsely chopped
2 large hard-cooked eggs, peeled and quartered lengthwise
Sour cream, regular or light
3 tablespoons chopped fresh parsley

In a large bowl, toss together the beets, potatoes, onion, and peas.

In a small bowl, beat together the vinegar, sugar, olive oil, salt, pepper, and capers. Toss this dressing with the vegetables. Chill for at least 1 hour.

Arrange the salad in a glass or other serving bowl. Garnish with the eggs and sour cream. Dust with the parsley and serve.

Beet and Fennel Salad

The anise flavor of fresh fennel goes very well with the sweetness of beets. Serve this with poached salmon, striped bass, or baked chicken.

Makes 6 to 8 servings

1 head leaf lettuce
3 large beets, trimmed, boiled in acidulated water (page 59) to cover and drained or baked until tender, peeled, sliced, and cut into matchstick strips
1 small bulb fennel, base trimmed, top cut off, and cut into matchstick strips
1 small sweet onion, thinly sliced and separated into rings
1 large hard-cooked egg, peeled and finely chopped

1 tablespoon malt vinegar or rice vinegar
⅓ cup mild vegetable oil, such as peanut
    or canola
1 tablespoon fresh orange juice
1 tablespoon chopped fresh dill
Salt and freshly ground black pepper to taste

Line a glass or other salad bowl with lettuce leaves. Arrange the beets on the lettuce. Strew with the fennel, then the onion. Top with the egg.

In a small bowl, beat together the vinegar, oil, and orange juice. Season well with dill, salt, and pepper. Just before serving, pour this dressing over the salad. Toss and serve at once.

Old-fashioned Spicy Pickled Beets

I like to serve these with any kind of cold buffet, but they are terrific on a Thanksgiving Day table, too.

Makes 4 or 5 half-pint jars (depending on size of beets)

4 pounds smallest beets, trimmed, boiled in
    acidulated water (page 59) to cover until just
    tender, drained, peeled, and, if large, cut into
    quarters
3 cups cider vinegar
1 cup water
½ cup granulated sugar
½ cup packed light brown sugar
1 teaspoon whole allspice
1 teaspoon whole cloves
One 3-inch cinnamon stick, broken into
    several pieces
Salt to taste

Place the beets in a large nonreactive saucepan. Add the remaining ingredients and simmer over medium heat about 15 minutes.

Remove the pan from heat and pack the cooked beets in hot, sterilized half-pint jars. Strain the cooking liquid over the beets, leaving ¼ to ½ inch head space. Seal and process in a boiling water bath for 20 to 30 minutes. Cool and store in a dark place, or refrigerate any that do not seal correctly. Let these pickles mature at least three weeks before serving.

Belgian Endive

There are several apocryphal stories that try to explain how this delightful vegetable came into being. Most of them center around accidental occurrences. One suggests that a farmer, interrupted by the trials of the Belgian revolution in 1830, left some of his chicory roots in a darkened cellar. He had been about to dry the roots to roast and grind for ersatz coffee when he was called away. Returning a few weeks later he found that the roots had sprouted small, tight white heads that did not at all resemble the curly green chicory he was used to. He tasted them, thoroughly enjoyed the slightly bitter taste, and the endive was on its way to stardom.

Actually "Capuchin's Beard," an early name for the same second, forced growth of the chicory plant, is known to have been cultivated even before 1751. It was then, and is now, an extremely labor-intensive crop. The chicory (a relative of our curly endive) is grown in fields. The roots are dug up, the first-growth leaves cut, and the sheared roots laid out in hydroponic bins. The bins are stored in huge racks that are rolled into totally dark buildings the size of small hangers. The second-growth heads of endive (or *witloof*, which is Flemish for "white leaf") are harvested by hand, wrapped in blue tissue, and hand-packed into boxes for shipment. Some artisanal farmers still grow small crops by simply mounding earth over the roots after cutting the first leaves. They must watch the shoots carefully and continue to cover them with earth or they will not maintain their creamy white color. This small, chancy production generally remains in its own neighborhood.

Virtually all the endive sold in America is grown in Belgium and imported, although there is some experimental growth beginning here. In

Europe endive is in every market and priced within almost any budget. In America we generally buy it one head at a time, and purchasing enough for serving as a vegetable can be an expensive undertaking. It is truly worthwhile treating yourself from time to time, though, to the very special taste of this delicious "white gold from Belgium."

Selection: Look for very crisp, compact heads that are creamy white with the leaf tops just barely pale green. The finest endive have pale yellow tops with no green at all. Avoid any heads with leaves that have begun to splay outward from the tight core. Small heads are more delicately flavored, but large heads, up to 5 inches in length, are very good when used in salads, or braised to accompany a main course.

Be careful to avoid heads that are limp, have brown spots, or show any mold, especially on the root end.

Endive is available year round. It has almost no nutritional value. Count on two to three heads per person.

Storage and Preparation: Store fresh Belgian endive wrapped in the blue paper it comes in if you find it that way. Otherwise, endive will remain crisp and fresh for a week or two if stored, unwashed, in the vegetable bin of the refrigerator, wrapped in paper towels, sealed in a perforated vegetable bag.

Endive simply need to be wiped clean, and the root end trimmed. If braising, they can be halved lengthwise. If using in a salad, cut them across in slices of any thickness you prefer. The leaves are easy to separate. Whole leaves are very attractive as a garnish on salad plates, or they may be filled with all sorts of spreads, dips, and salsas for almost instant hors d'oeuvres. One of my favorites is cream cheese mixed with smoked salmon garnished with salmon eggs and fresh dill—quick and elegant.

Stuffed Braised Endive

Enjoy these hot with roast chicken or duck.

Makes 6 servings

6 largest heads endive, trimmed
2 tablespoons ground walnuts
2 ounces blue cheese, crumbled (about ½ cup)
3 tablespoons butter, softened
1 teaspoon fresh lemon juice
2 tablespoons chopped fresh parsley
Pinch ground red (cayenne) pepper
½ cup well-flavored chicken stock, hot
Salt and freshly ground pepper to taste

Using a sharp pointed knife, hollow out the core of each head of endive, leaving a thin shell to hold the head together. Reserve the core for another use.

In a small bowl, beat together the walnuts, blue cheese, 1 tablespoon of the butter, the lemon juice, parsley, and cayenne. Using a small spoon, or a pastry bag fitted with a plain tip, force the cheese mixture into the endive.

Melt the remaining 2 tablespoons of butter over low heat in a heavy skillet large enough to hold the endives in a single layer. Arrange the filled endives in the skillet and turn to coat them with butter. Pour in the hot stock, cover, and cook, basting from time to time, until the endives are crisply tender, 15 to 20 minutes. Remove the cover and raise the heat to medium-high to evaporate any remaining liquid. Season well with salt and pepper and serve very hot.

Note: *These may also be served at room temperature alongside cold poached fish or any leftover cold roast meats.*

Endive and Ham Ramekins

What an elegant way to present this deliciously different vegetable. Poached or baked skinless chicken breasts are the perfect accompaniment.

Makes 6 servings

2 tablespoons butter, plus additional, melted,
    for buttering
Finely ground plain dried bread crumbs
6 medium-size heads endive, trimmed
    and chopped
¼ cup dry white wine
5 large eggs, beaten
2 cups heavy cream
½ cup finely chopped smoked ham
1 tablespoon freshly grated Parmesan cheese
Salt and freshly ground black pepper to taste
Fresh parsley sprigs

Lightly butter six 1-cup ramekins. Dust with the bread crumbs, knocking out any excess.

Melt the 2 tablespoons of butter in a small skillet over low heat. Add the endive and wine. Cover and simmer until the endive is very tender, about 20 minutes. Drain the endive in a colander, pressing out any excess liquid.

Preheat the oven to 325°F.

In a medium-size bowl, beat together the eggs and cream until light. Stir in the well-drained endive and the ham. Stir in the cheese and season the mixture well with salt and pepper. Divide the mixture among the prepared ramekins. Arrange the filled ramekins in a baking pan. Pour in boiling water until it is halfway up the sides of the ramekins. Cover with aluminum foil.

Bake until the custards are set and a knife inserted in the center of one of the custards comes out clean, about 40 minutes. Remove the pan from the oven and the ramekins from the pan. Cool on a rack for 5 minutes.

To serve, unmold by running a sharp knife carefully around the edge of each custard. Invert each ramekin onto a lightly moistened wide spatula and rap the two gently against the counter to loosen. Slide the custards onto a serving plate or onto individual dinner plates. Garnish with the parsley. Serve hot or at room temperature.

Note: *These are also very pretty when garnished with a few blades of chives and a chive blossom or with a colorful nasturtium blossom.*

Endive, Walnut, and Gorgonzola Salad

This is a classic French salad, which I love to serve at lunch with cold meats and cheese; but it goes equally well with more substantial dinner entrées such as pot roast.

Makes about 6 servings

3 heads endive, trimmed, cut across into 1-inch
    slices, separated
½ cup walnut halves, toasted (see Note)
3 ounces Gorgonzola or another crumbly blue-
    veined cheese, crumbled (about ¾ cup)
1 teaspoon Dijon-style mustard
Salt and freshly ground black pepper to taste
1 tablespoon red wine vinegar
¼ to ⅓ cup extra-virgin olive oil

Place the endive in a medium-size salad bowl. Sprinkle the walnuts and then the cheese on top.

In a small bowl, beat together the mustard, seasonings, and vinegar. Beat in the oil a little at a time until the dressing is thick. Just before serving, pour this dressing over the salad and toss.

Note: *To toast walnuts, or any nuts, spread them on a baking sheet. Toast in a preheated 375°F. oven until fragrant, 3 to 4 minutes. Remove the baking sheet from the oven and cool the nuts completely.*

Variation: Add 1 bunch (6 to 8) green onions (scallions), white and light green parts only, thinly sliced, to the salad before tossing with the dressing.

Braised Endive

The slightly tart flavor of cooked endive is evident in this deliciously simple dish. Serve it with grilled swordfish; roast pork; or game birds such as partridge, pheasant, or in a pinch, a crisply roasted duck.

Makes 6 servings

**12 to 18 heads endive trimmed, halved
   lengthwise if very large
3 tablespoons butter, cut up, or more to taste
¹/₂ cup dry white wine
¹/₂ cup well-flavored chicken stock
Salt and freshly ground black pepper to taste**

Arrange the endive in one layer in a large heavy skillet. Dot with the butter and pour in the wine and stock. Season well with salt and pepper. Cover and cook over very low heat, turning once, until very tender, 20 to 25 minutes. Remove the cover and raise the heat to medium-high to evaporate most of the liquid. Cook until the edges of the endive are golden brown. Serve very hot.

Note: *A little freshly grated Parmesan cheese can be sprinkled over the tips of the endive just before serving if desired.*

Cream-braised Endive

This variation of braised endive is wonderful with grilled veal chops and goes marvelously well with baked or poached salmon.

Makes 6 servings

**2 tablespoons butter
6 to 12 heads endive, trimmed and halved
   lengthwise, unless very small
1 cup well-flavored chicken stock
¹/₂ cup heavy cream
¹/₂ teaspoon ground cumin
Salt and freshly ground black pepper to taste**

Preheat the oven to 400°F. Generously butter a shallow baking dish or gratin dish large enough to hold the endive halves snugly in a single layer. Fit the endives into the prepared dish.

In a small saucepan, combine the stock, cream, and cumin. Bring to a boil, stirring to dilute the cumin. Pour over the endives. Season with salt. Cover the dish with aluminum foil and cook in the preheated oven until the endives are just tender, about 20 minutes. Remove the foil and continue cooking, basting the endives with the creamy mixture once or twice, until the sauce is thick and almost caramelized, about 10 minutes.

Remove the dish from the oven and season the endives generously with pepper. Serve very hot with the sauce spooned over.

Broccoli

If George Bush's mother made him eat mounds of broccoli as a child, she had either spent a lot of time in Italy or was a very up-to-date homemaker. Broccoli is a relative newcomer to the American scene, brought here by our Italian ancestors during the great immigration at the beginning of this century. They, of course, had known and loved broccoli for at least a hundred years, and in the 1920s, enterprising new citizens grew fields of it in California, shipping it east to the more sophisticated markets.

The Chinese have long enjoyed a form of broccoli that is grown mostly for its stalk and leaves and has very few flower buds. It has a lovely, slightly bitter taste that more closely resembles that of broccoli raab than our familiar, much milder sprouting broccoli. American broccoli can be substituted for Chinese broccoli in any recipe.

One of the so-called cruciferous vegetables and a close relative of cauliflower—and cabbage—broccoli, it turns out, may be one of the most beneficial vegetables we eat. Not only does it provide ample quantities of calcium and vitamins A and C, it is high in beta-carotene,

an antioxidant that may help prevent certain types of cancer. In addition to all the other health benefits that broccoli offers, the calcium it contains is readily absorbable. All of which does you no good at all if you share our former president's aversion. Given half a chance, however, and when well prepared, broccoli can be as delicious as it is good for you.

Broccoli is extremely versatile. It can be eaten cooked or raw, hot, warm, or cold. Excellent when steamed until just tender and sauced with only a little lemon butter, it also lends itself to much more complex dishes incorporating many other ingredients. It can be boiled, baked, pureed, cut up in stir-fries, added to salads or served up on its own, to dip or sauce any way you choose.

Broccoli can really be two vegetables in one. The flowerets, a beautiful dark green color and relatively delicate in flavor, are best if cooked until crisply tender. The stems, when peeled and sliced into any manner of shapes, are excellent raw, in salads or as part of a crudité platter, or cooked and served as a separate vegetable—alone or in combination with other things.

Selection: Broccoli stores well if treated with respect. Look for bright green crisp stems and leaves, topped by deep green, tightly closed flowerets. The leaves should not be limp or yellowed, and you should avoid any bunches that show open or yellowing flowerets. The stem ends should be moist and pale green, not hard or tinged with brown.

Look for the new purple-headed broccoli; the taste is the same, but it makes a delightfully colorful addition to any menu when cooked until crisply tender. (If overcooked it turns green.) An even, deep purple color on the flowerets and a crisp, green stem indicate freshness.

When broccoli is old, it will be limp and, when cooked, strong smelling—with an odor much like cabbage. Then it becomes the vegetable that makes all children balk at the prospect of eating it—no matter how much melted cheese you pour on top.

One of the few vegetables available truly fresh all year, broccoli is at its best during the winter. A good cold-weather choice, it is abundant and inexpensive during the long months from November to April.

Count on 2 pounds of trimmed heads—or about 4 pounds untrimmed—for six servings.

Storage and Preparation: Broccoli keeps well in the vegetable drawer of the refrigerator. Place the unwashed bunches in a regular plastic bag or a perforated vegetable bag, and close. Store up to four days. Or if the broccoli is very fresh, cut about 1 inch off the bottom of the stems and stand upright in a container of water. Cover loosely with a plastic bag and refrigerate up to four or five days.

Preparation varies. Wash the heads well, trimming the leaves and the stem ends. If using the whole heads, cut the stems to about 4 inches in length. Peel them just before cooking if they are very thick. To use only the flowerets, separate the head from the stem, and break or cut it into individual flowerets. The size will depend on the use, but they should be uniform to ensure even cooking. If using the stems alone, for salad, soup, or another vegetable preparation, peel them with a sharp knife; the thick skin strips off easily. Then slice them into matchstick strips, rounds, or another shape.

Like asparagus, broccoli can be cooked until crisply tender several hours before serving. Refresh it immediately in cold water, drain, and refrigerate, or hold 1 or 2 hours at room temperature. Reheat in boiling water for about 1 minute or microwave on high for 1 to $1\frac{1}{2}$ minutes before saucing or continuing with the recipe.

Steamed Broccoli

This is the way I like to cook broccoli, especially small flowerets. Arrange the flowerets in a steamer basket or colander and steam, covered, over simmering water for about 5 minutes. Whole stems with flowerets will need 8 to 10 minutes. Serve at once, or refresh in cold water and drain well.

Boiled Broccoli

Broccoli can be boiled quickly in a large quantity of salted water. Separate into flowerets and drop into the boiling water until tender, 3 to 4 minutes. Whole stems with flowerets will take 7 to 10 minutes. Check with a fork for doneness and do not overcook. Drain and serve at once.

When boiling them, I prefer to cook the broccoli flowerets in only 1 or 2 inches of water. Cook over medium heat, covered, for 3 to 4 minutes. Cook whole stems with flowerets for 6 to 8 minutes. Drain and serve.

Microwaved Broccoli

Microwaving is the method that best retains the dark green color of the flowerets. Arrange the flowerets in a single layer in a microwave dish. Add about ¼ cup water, cover with plastic microwave wrap, vent, and microwave on high for about 7 minutes. Let stand 2 minutes before uncovering.

If cooking the whole heads, arrange them, stem beside stem, flowerets on the outside, add water, cover, and vent, then microwave on high until the point of a sharp knife easily pierces the stem, about 10 minutes. Let stand 5 minutes, uncover, drain, and serve.

Steamed Broccoli with Soy-Sesame Sauce

The Chinese have long had a vegetable somewhat like broccoli raab, and they have combined it with many other

ingredients, including beef and pork. This slightly less bitter version can be served with grilled seafood of any kind, including large, peeled shrimp.

Makes 6 to 8 servings

3 tablespoons soy sauce
1 tablespoon toasted sesame oil
1 tablespoon grated fresh ginger
1 small clove garlic, minced
2 pounds broccoli, stems removed and reserved for another use, heads separated into flowerets, steamed until crisply tender, kept hot
1 tablespoon sesame seeds, toasted (see Note)

Combine soy sauce, sesame oil, ginger, and garlic in a small saucepan. Cook over low heat until just hot, 1 to 2 minutes.

To serve, arrange the broccoli in a serving dish. Pour the sauce over the broccoli and toss gently. Sprinkle with the sesame seeds and serve very hot.

> Note: *To toast sesame seeds, spread them on a small baking sheet and bake in a preheated 375°F. toaster oven or a regular oven for 3 to 4 minutes. Cool completely.*

Variation: *Heat 2 tablespoons butter in a small skillet. Stir in 2 tablespoons sesame seeds and cook over medium-high heat until golden brown, about 2 minutes. Stir in 1 tablespoon teriyaki sauce and hot pepper sauce to taste. Heat through and pour over the hot steamed broccoli. Serve very hot.*

Broccoli and Cauliflower au Gratin

This colorful, old-fashioned dish is delicious with baked fish, roast pork, or poultry.

Makes 6 servings

3 tablespoons butter, melted, plus additional
   for buttering
1 small cauliflower, cored, head separated into
   flowerets, steamed or boiled in salted water
   to cover until just tender, and drained
1 pound broccoli, stem removed and reserved for
   another use, head separated into flowerets,
   steamed or boiled in salted water to cover
   until just tender, and drained
Salt and freshly ground black pepper to taste
½ cup heavy cream
⅓ cup plain dried bread crumbs

Preheat the oven to 450°F.

Generously butter a medium-size gratin dish. Toss the cauliflower and broccoli together and arrange in the prepared dish. Season well with salt and pepper. Pour in the cream.

In a small bowl, combine the 3 tablespoons of butter and the bread crumbs. Spread over the vegetables. Bake until bubbling, the crumbs are golden brown, and the vegetables are very hot, 15 to 20 minutes.

Broccoli and Roasted Potatoes

The contrast of the crisp, roasted potatoes and tender broccoli is the attraction of this dish. It goes very well with roast pork or, in fact, pork of any kind, including grilled Italian sausages.

Makes 6 servings

4 large Russet potatoes, unpeeled, cut into
   wedges
1 tablespoon olive oil
1 clove garlic, minced
Salt to taste
Seasoned pepper, such as Mrs. Dash, to taste
1 pound broccoli, stem removed and reserved for
   another use, head separated into flowerets
   and steamed until crisply tender
Freshly ground Parmesan cheese (optional)

Preheat the oven to 375°F.

In a large bowl, toss together the potatoes, olive oil, garlic, salt, and seasoned pepper. Spread on a baking sheet. Roast in the preheated oven, turning once or twice, until well browned and crisp, 40 to 50 minutes.

Remove the baking sheet from the oven and toss the broccoli with the potatoes. Return the vegetables to the baking sheet and roast, turning once, 5 to 7 minutes longer. Serve very hot, sprinkled with the cheese if desired.

Broccoli Puree

No matter how often I serve this it seems to be a new dish for someone at the table. As a discovery, it is usually a very happy one. I like it with roast chicken.

Makes 6 to 8 servings

2 pounds broccoli, stems removed and reserved
   for another use, heads separated into
   flowerets
2 tablespoons butter
Salt and freshly ground black pepper to taste
Pinch nutmeg
2 to 3 tablespoons heavy cream, hot
1 tablespoon chopped fresh parsley

Steam or boil the broccoli in salted water to cover until very tender, but still very green. Refresh under cold water to stop it from cooking further and to set the color, drain, and then puree in a food processor or food mill until smooth.

Turn the puree into a medium-size saucepan and cook over very low heat, stirring, to evaporate any remaining water and dry out the puree. The puree should be thick enough to mound up in a spoon. Stir in the butter. Season well with salt, pepper, and nutmeg.

Just before serving, stir in the cream, 1 tablespoon at a time, until the puree is of the desired consistency. It should be creamy but not exude liquid. Serve very hot, garnished with the parsley.

Broccoli Soufflé

Like any other soufflé, this one needs to be served the minute it is cooked, piping hot and fragrant. Everyone should be seated before it is ready to come out of the oven. This is excellent with a traditional roast turkey but can also be the main course, along with a salad, for a light lunch or late supper.

Makes 6 servings

2 tablespoons butter, plus additional for buttering
Freshly grated Parmesan cheese
2 tablespoons all-purpose flour
Salt and freshly ground black pepper to taste
1½ cups milk
1 tablespoon Dijon-style mustard
5 large eggs, separated, whites beaten until stiff
1 pound broccoli, stem removed and reserved for
    another use, head separated into flowerets
    and steamed and chopped to make 1¼ to
    1½ cups

Preheat the oven to 375°F.

Generously butter a 1½-quart soufflé dish. Dust the inside with cheese, knocking the dish gently to dislodge any excess.

Melt the 2 tablespoons of butter in a small heavy saucepan over low heat. Stir in the flour and cook without browning for 3 minutes. Season well with salt and pepper. Stir in the milk all at once, whisking until smooth. Cook, stirring, over low heat until thick, 3 to 5 minutes. Remove the saucepan from the heat. Beat in the mustard. Beat in the egg yolks 1 at a time. Stir in the broccoli. Cool for 10 minutes. Stir in one-third of the egg whites to lighten the mixture. Gently fold in the remaining egg whites.

Spoon the soufflé mixture into the prepared dish and bake until the soufflé rises well above the edge of the dish and the top is lightly browned, 30 to 35 minutes. Serve at once, very hot.

Variation: *Remove the soufflé from the oven and allow it to cool completely in the dish. It will fall as it cools. Invert the cooled soufflé onto a serving plate. Dust with freshly grated Parmesan cheese. Serve in wedges as part of a cold buffet lunch or dinner. Pass hot pepper sauce, or your favorite salsa, for extra flavor.*

Note: *Once the soufflé mixture has been spread in the soufflé dish, it can stand at room temperature, tightly covered with plastic wrap, for 1 hour before cooking. This trick lets you prepare the mixture a little ahead of time and reduces the amount of last-minute kitchen work always associated with soufflés.*

Broccoli Rounds with Onions and Mushrooms

Here is a good way to use leftover stems. These little rounds remind me of the carrot "coins" my mother used to serve us when we were children. With the broccoli, serve grilled steak.

Makes 6 servings

2 tablespoons butter, or pure olive oil
1 small onion, thinly sliced
4 or 5 cups thinly sliced rounds of peeled
    broccoli stems
¼ pound white mushrooms, stems
    trimmed, sliced
1 clove garlic, minced
1 tablespoon fresh lemon juice
Salt and freshly ground black pepper to taste
2 teaspoons chopped fresh thyme

Melt the butter or heat the oil in a large heavy skillet over medium heat. Cook the onion, stirring occasionally, for about 5 minutes. Do not brown. Stir in the broccoli, mushrooms, and garlic. Cook, still over medium heat, stirring from time to time, until tender, about 6 minutes.

Stir in the lemon juice and season well with salt, pepper, and thyme. Cook, tossing, 1 minute and serve very hot.

Variation: *Instead of using lemon juice, stir in ⅓ cup heavy cream. Season well with salt, pepper, and thyme, and heat through.*

Broccoli and Cauliflower Custard

In France, a similar sort of dish is called a *pain*, or "bread," perhaps because like bread dough the mixture takes the shape of its mold. It goes very well with grilled steak or fish.

Makes 6 servings

1 tablespoon butter, plus additional for buttering
1 small onion, halved and thinly sliced
3 cups small cauliflower flowerets, steamed until just tender
3 cups small broccoli flowerets, steamed until just tender
2 large eggs, beaten
1 cup milk, or half-and-half if a more unctuous dish is desired
1 tablespoon Dijon-style mustard
Salt and freshly ground white pepper to taste
2 tablespoons chopped fresh parsley
2 tablespoons freshly grated Parmesan cheese, plus additional for serving

Melt the butter in a small skillet over low heat. Cook the onion, stirring occasionally, until translucent, about 10 minutes.

Preheat the oven to 325°F.

Generously butter a 2-quart deep baking dish. In a large bowl, toss together the cauliflower, broccoli, and onion. Pile the mixture into the prepared dish.

In a medium-size bowl, beat together the eggs, milk, mustard, salt, pepper, and parsley. Pour this mixture over the vegetables.

Bake 25 minutes. Sprinkle with the 2 tablespoons of cheese and bake until the top is browned and the custard is set, or when a sharp knife inserted into the center comes out clean, 5 to 10 minutes longer.

To serve, run a sharp knife around the inside edge of the dish. Invert the dish onto a heated serving platter. Serve very hot, cut into wedges, with the additional cheese.

Stir-fried Broccoli with Water Chestnuts and Mushrooms

Here's another Western version of an Asian combination. Serve this with a grilled T-bone steak or a thick tuna steak, grilled until crusty on the outside, just done inside.

Makes 6 servings

1 pound broccoli, stem removed, peeled, and sliced ¼ inch thick, head separated into flowerets
2 tablespoons mild vegetable oil, preferably peanut
½ pound shiitake mushrooms, stems discarded, sliced
One 8-ounce can water chestnuts, drained and sliced
3 green onions (scallions), white and light green parts only, sliced on the diagonal
¼ cup chicken stock
1 tablespoon cornstarch
2 tablespoons dry sherry
2 tablespoons soy sauce
1 tablespoon teriyaki sauce
1 clove garlic, minced
2 tablespoons grated fresh ginger
¼ teaspoon hot pepper sauce, or to taste

Steam or boil the broccoli in salted water to cover until just tender, drain, refresh in cold water, and dry on paper towels.

Heat the oil in a wok or large heavy skillet over very high heat. Add the mushrooms and cook, stirring, for 3 minutes. Stir in the water chestnuts, broccoli, and green onions and cook, stirring, until very hot, about 3 minutes more. The vegetables do not need much more cooking but should be very hot.

In a medium-size bowl, combine the remaining ingredients and add them to the wok. Cook, stirring, until thick and hot, about 1 minute. Serve immediately, very hot.

Broccoli Polonaise

Polonaise *refers to the topping on the broccoli in this recipe. The same combination of chopped egg, parsley, butter, and crumbs is delicious on other vegetables, such as green beans, cauliflower, and even fresh peas.*

Makes 6 servings

2 pounds whole broccoli heads, stems peeled,
    trimmed to about 4 inches in length
3 large hard-cooked eggs, peeled and mashed
    or minced
¼ cup chopped fresh parsley
¼ cup plain dried bread crumbs
3 tablespoons butter
Salt and freshly ground black pepper to taste

Steam the broccoli, whole, in a steamer basket or colander, covered, over simmering water until just tender, 6 to 10 minutes. Keep hot.

Combine the eggs and parsley in a small bowl.

While the broccoli is steaming, combine the bread crumbs and butter in a small skillet. Cook over medium-high heat until golden brown, 2 to 3 minutes. Be careful not to burn them.

To serve, arrange the hot broccoli on a heated serving platter or in a shallow serving bowl. Sprinkle the egg and parsley mixture over the hot broccoli. Pour the hot buttered crumbs over all. Season well with salt and pepper and serve immediately.

Broccoli Pesto Salad

Most broccoli recipes use the flowerets. Some use the flowerets and some of the stem. This one uses only all those stems that seem to be left over. Once they are peeled, raw broccoli stems are surprisingly tender and are delicious on their own. I like to add this to a cookout menu, along with potato salad and cold meats.

Makes 6 to 8 servings

¼ cup pesto, prepared or homemade (page 7),
    at room temperature
⅔ cup mayonnaise, prepared or homemade
    (page 13)
3 cups fine matchstick strips of peeled
    broccoli stems
1 bunch (6 to 8) green onions (scallions), white
    and light green parts only, thinly sliced
1 medium-size carrot, peeled and grated
1 head leaf lettuce
Chopped fresh basil

In a small bowl, beat the pesto into the mayonnaise to make a dressing.

Toss the broccoli, green onions, and carrot together in a medium-size bowl. Pour the dressing over the vegetables and toss to coat thoroughly. Refrigerate, covered, for at least 2 hours.

To serve, heap the salad on a bed of fresh lettuce. Garnish with the basil.

Broccoli Raab

Broccoli raab (or rabe, or rapini) is one of those vegetables like Belgian endive: It is either an instant favorite, or you will never want to sample it more than once. For me, it has a delicious, pleasantly bitter taste that is both earthy and satisfying. It is actually a cross between cabbage and turnip, though the root is not eaten.

Broccoli raab has thin, branching stems with narrow, dark green leaves and tiny bunches of flowerets. Sometimes a few of the flowerets are open, showing a brilliant yellow color. One variety of this vegetable is called rape, or colsa. During World War II it was extensively grown for the oil in the seeds, and much cooking oil and margarine was made from it. In early summer you can still see fields and fields of the magnificent yellow flowers spread like enormous, lush carpets in the French and Swiss country-side. Rape has one of the shortest growing periods of any cash crop. For this reason it is grown in Alaska and northern Canada where six to eight weeks is the extent of the commercial farming season. It is often used as animal fodder as well as a source of cooking and lubricating oil.

Broccoli raab can be eaten raw or cooked. It can be substituted for Chinese broccoli in any recipe and has much the same taste, texture, and appearance.

Broccoli raab is rich in vitamin C, calcium, and like most other cruciferous vegetables, beta-carotene.

Selection: Look for long, thin, green stalks with crisp dark leaves. A few yellow flowers are fine, but most of the buds should be tightly closed and dark green. Avoid any stems that are limp or have faded yellow leaves.

You can sometimes find broccoli raab during the winter, but it is in early spring, late March and April, that is at its freshest. Look for it in markets with a large Italian clientele. Enjoy it often during the short season, like asparagus.

Count on 1½ pounds of untrimmed broccoli raab to serve six.

Storage and Preparation: Broccoli raab is not as hardy as sprouting broccoli and should be eaten as fresh as possible. If you cannot prepare it the day you buy it, store it, unwashed, wrapped in paper towels in a plastic bag, or in a perforated vegetable bag, and use it within one or two days.

To prepare it, cut off the lower stem and remove any of the larger, tough leaves, or any that show signs of yellow. Some cooks like to peel the stem, sort of like tough asparagus, which they say removes the strings. Unless the stems are very thick and seem to be somewhat woody, I think peeling is unnecessary.

The stems and tops can be cooked whole, like asparagus, or can be cut up or chopped.

Hot Spicy Broccoli Raab

The lovely green color of this dish makes it the perfect plate mate for grilled orange roughy or savory baked chicken breasts.

Makes 6 servings

3 tablespoons mild vegetable oil, preferably peanut
1 teaspoon Chinese hot oil
2 cloves garlic, minced
1 jalapeño pepper, seeded and minced
1½ pounds broccoli raab, trimmed and cut into 2- to 3-inch lengths
2 teaspoons soy sauce, or to taste

Heat the oils in a large heavy skillet or wok over high heat. Stir-fry the garlic and pepper for 30 seconds. Add the broccoli raab and cook, stirring, until crisply tender and very hot, 3 to 4 minutes. Remove the skillet or wok from the heat. Stir in the soy sauce and toss well to season all the broccoli raab. Serve hot or warm.

Roman-style Broccoli Raab

I think this variation of the classic Italian method of cooking broccoli raab is especially good because the stalks are left 6 to 7 inches in length, like asparagus. Cooked this way it is a very attractive, distinctively flavored vegetable. Try it with roast spring lamb.

Makes 6 servings

2 tablespoons olive oil
2 cloves garlic, minced
1½ pounds broccoli raab, trimmed
½ cup dry white wine
Salt and freshly ground black pepper to taste
3 tablespoons freshly grated Parmesan cheese

Heat the olive oil in a large heavy skillet over medium heat. Cook the garlic no more than 1 minute, being careful not to burn it. Add the broccoli raab in one layer and cook, turning the stems to coat with the oil, for 2 minutes.

Pour in the wine. Season with the salt and pepper. Cover the skillet, reduce the heat to medium-low, and cook until the stems are tender but still crisp and very green, 4 to 6 minutes. Remove the cover, increase the heat to high, and cook, taking care not to burn the broccoli, until the liquid reduces to 1 tablespoon. Serve the broccoli very hot, with the cheese sprinkled over the buds.

Variation: *Cut the trimmed broccoli raab into 2-inch lengths. Once the broccoli raab has cooked, remove the cover, pour in ½ cup heavy cream, and boil to reduce the sauce by half. Season with salt and pepper and toss with 1 pound vermicelli or angel-hair pasta that has been cooked until just al dente and drained. Garnish with freshly grated Parmesan cheese. This amount makes a first course for six at dinner or a main course for four to six at lunch when accompanied by a salad.*

Note: *Substitute small, thin spears of sprouting broccoli if broccoli raab is not available, but the vegetable flavor will be more delicate.*

Brussels Sprouts

Perhaps the most maligned of all vegetables, Brussels sprouts don't have to be the mushy, strong-smelling little nuggets we remember from school cafeteria steam tables.

These tiny little cabbage relatives offer many of the same nutritional qualities that their larger cousins contain. Not only are Brussels sprouts one of the cruciferous vegetables, along with cauliflower and broccoli, they have the advantage of being quick to prepare and relatively versatile. Almost anything you can do to or with cabbage is also appropriate for Brussels sprouts. Full of beta-carotene and vitamin C, they provide the same antioxidant qualities as the other members of this family.

It is likely that this vegetable was developed near the northern European city of Brussels about five hundred years ago, which makes it a relatively young vegetable. It probably wasn't brought to America until the early years of the twentieth century, and even then it was really only popular with the new immigrants who were already familiar with it.

One of the reasons for its lack of universal acceptance may be the fact that old, poorly treated Brussels sprouts are often yellowed, tough, woody, strong smelling, and vile tasting. Then they are truly the nightmare vegetable that all children, and many adults, tend to gag over.

To enjoy this delightful addition to your vegetable repertoire, you must find a supply of succulent, young, tender, really fresh sprouts. Of course the best way is to grow them yourself. They are a good bet to grow at home, for the more you pick, the more they produce—through frost and snow. In fact it was once thought that sprouts needed a frost to reach their peak. New varieties are milder and more tender. The next best thing to homegrown is to find a market that sells the sprouts still attached to the tall upright stalk on which they grow. Pick them off as you need them and you will be astonished at the difference in taste—it may change your whole attitude toward this dreaded vegetable.

Why not try serving these little morsels in unexpected ways? Parboil sprouts in water to cover for 3 minutes, drain, and add to skewers of shish-kabobs, especially if you are grilling pork cubes. Or brush parboiled sprouts with olive oil and then grill in a fish grid (so they won't fall out) over hot coals (turning at least once), until browned outside and crisply tender, about 15 minutes. Or add crisp tiny sprouts to your next crudité platter.

Like many members of the cabbage family, Brussels sprouts may produce uncomfortable gastric problems for those who lack certain enzymes. The same product now on the market that allows almost everyone to enjoy beans (see page 37) is often very effective against the gassy quality of broccoli and Brussels sprouts as well as peppers, cucumbers, and other troublesome vegetables. Just a few drops or a tablet or two of Beano® just before eating the sprouts provides the enzyme (alpha galactosidase) necessary to break down the simple sugars that create this unfortunate phenomenon.

Selection: If at all possible, buy sprouts that are sold still on the stem. They are generally fresher and more tender than loose or packaged sprouts. If they are not available on the stem, loose sprouts are your best bet. Shuffle through them, looking for the smallest, greenest, most succulent sprouts, choosing them all the same size. Personally, I think the smaller the better. Avoid any sprouts that look dry, yellowed, or have brown stems. If there are any signs of mold, black spots, leaf holes or if the sprouts are spongy to the touch, it is best simply to pick another vegetable. It is especially important for Brussels sprouts to be as fresh as possible.

Still, if your heart is set on sprouts and the produce department does not have any that meet the fresh criteria, there are frozen sprouts that are very acceptable. Choose the tiny variety, let them thaw, and treat them as if they were parboiled. While they cannot be used as if they were raw, they are delicious in most cooked dishes.

Brussels sprouts are available all year, but I think they are at their best from late fall until the end of January.

Count on ½ cup frozen sprouts or ¼ pound fresh per person. That means about three servings per packed pint.

Storage and Preparation: If you are not going to use Brussels sprouts the day you buy them, loose sprouts should be placed unwashed in a plastic bag or a perforated vegetable bag and refrigerated. They will keep three or four days. Prepacked sprouts, in cellophane-wrapped pint containers, need to be picked over as soon as you get them home. Empty the packages, toss out any that look old, brown, or dry or that have spots, brown stems, or leaf holes, which might mean worms inside. Store the rest as if they were loose fresh.

To prepare Brussels sprouts, trim just a small slice off the stem end. Pull off only those outer leaves that are very dry or discolored. Wash them well in cold water. There is some debate about the old-fashioned habit of cutting an X in the stem end to ensure even cooking. While tiny sprouts probably don't need it, I still cut an X in the stems of larger ones. In my opinion, the secret to successful sprouts is quick cooking and I think the X allows the heat to penetrate the stem faster. It may be my imagination, but I don't think so. You want the finished vegetable to be bright green, tender, and not mushy.

Steamed Brussels Sprouts

Steam trimmed Brussels sprouts in a steamer basket or a colander, covered, over simmering water until tender, 6 to 12 minutes. To speed cooking time, halve the sprouts lengthwise.

Boiled Brussels Sprouts

In a medium-size saucepan, boil 1 pound of trimmed Brussels sprouts in salted water or chicken stock to cover until tender, 5 to 10 minutes; the time depends on the age and size of the sprouts. The sprouts are ready when they can be easily pierced with the point of a sharp knife or the tines of a cooking fork. Drain and toss with a little butter. Season well with salt and pepper.

Microwaved Brussels Sprouts

Arrange 1 pound of trimmed Brussels sprouts in a microwave dish. Add $1/4$ cup water, cover with plastic microwave wrap, and vent. Microwave small whole sprouts on high for 6 to 7 minutes. Large, halved sprouts will take 6 to 8 minutes.

Nutty Sprouts

If ever Brussels sprouts can be called irresistible, it's when they are prepared this way. The sweet crispness of the pecans is a great addition to the assertive flavor of the little buds. Serve this with braised beef.

Makes 6 to 8 servings

4 thick slices bacon, chopped
1 small onion, halved and sliced
2 pints (about $1^1/2$ pounds) small Brussels sprouts, trimmed, an X cut into the stems, boiled in salted water to cover until just tender, and drained

Salt and freshly ground black pepper to taste
2 tablespoons dry white wine
$1/2$ cup pecan pieces, toasted (page 70)
1 tablespoon chopped fresh parsley

In a large heavy skillet over medium heat, fry the bacon until crisp, about 10 minutes, remove it, and drain on paper towels. Pour off all but 2 tablespoons of the fat.

Cook the onion in the same skillet over medium heat until just translucent, 7 or 8 minutes. Add the Brussels sprouts and toss until heated through. Season well with salt and pepper. Stir in the wine. Remove the skillet from the heat, and stir in the pecans. Serve very hot, with the bacon and parsley.

Holiday Sprouts

Why not add this to your repertoire of dishes for Christmas, especially for a menu that includes roast goose? It is equally good with grilled tuna.

Makes 6 servings

2 pints (about $1^1/2$ pounds) small Brussels sprouts, trimmed and halved lengthwise
2 tablespoons butter
$1/4$ cup fresh orange juice
1 tablespoon grated fresh ginger
1 teaspoon sugar
1 teaspoon Canton ginger liqueur (optional)
Salt and freshly ground black pepper to taste
Chopped fresh parsley

Steam the sprouts in a steamer basket or colander over simmering water, covered, until tender, 6 to 7 minutes.

While the sprouts are cooking, melt the butter in a small saucepan over medium heat. Stir in the orange juice, ginger, sugar, and, if using, the liqueur. Simmer until thick, about 5 minutes. Stir in the hot sprouts. Season well with salt and pepper.

To serve, spoon the sprouts into a heated serving dish and garnish with the parsley.

Brussels Sprouts with Chestnuts and Pearl Onions

The English have long enjoyed Brussels sprouts, though they are often cooked into an insuperably mushy mass. When the sprouts are still crisply tender, this combination is delicious, and is especially good with game birds and roast duck.

Makes 6 servings

2 tablespoons butter
1 pound fresh chestnuts, peeled, simmered in
    salted water or chicken stock to cover until
    tender, and drained
2 pints (1½ pounds) smallest Brussels sprouts,
    trimmed, boiled in salted water to cover until
    crisply tender, and drained
1 cup small pearl (boiling) onions, boiled in water
    to cover for 1 minute, drained, peeled, and
    steamed until just tender
1 teaspoon ground cumin
Salt and freshly ground black pepper to taste
2 tablespoons chopped fresh parsley

Melt the butter in a large saucepan over medium heat. Add the chestnuts, sprouts, and onions. Season well with cumin, salt, and pepper. Cook, tossing gently, until all the vegetables are heated through, 3 to 5 minutes. Serve the vegetables very hot, garnished with the parsley.

Chopped Brussels Sprouts with Olives and Dill

Chopped Brussels sprouts have a delightful texture. Be careful not to overcook them; they should retain a certain crispness. Serve this with pork or roast poultry.

Makes 6 servings

2 tablespoons butter
2 pints (about 1½ pounds) Brussels sprouts,
    trimmed and coarsely chopped

½ cup chicken stock
¼ cup dry white wine
1 ounce (one-third of a 3-ounce package)
    cream cheese
Salt and freshly ground black pepper to taste
½ cup oil-cured green olives, boiled in water to
    cover for 3 minutes, drained, pit removed,
    and halved
1 tablespoon chopped fresh dill

Melt the butter in a medium-size heavy skillet over medium heat. Cook the sprouts in the butter, tossing or stirring to prevent them from burning, for 3 minutes. Stir in the stock, wine, and cream cheese. Season well with salt and pepper. Stir in the olives and increase the heat to medium-high. Cook, stirring, until the sauce is thickened, about 2 minutes. Do not overcook. Serve very hot, garnished with the dill.

Stir-fried Brussels Sprouts with Mushrooms, Sesame, and Broccoli

Grilled tuna is the perfect accompaniment for this colorful dish.

Makes 6 servings

1 tablespoon mild vegetable oil, preferably peanut
1 tablespoon toasted sesame oil
¼ pound white button mushrooms,
    stems trimmed
2 cloves garlic, minced
1 pint (about ¾ pound) smallest fresh Brussels
    sprouts, trimmed and steamed 2 minutes; or
    1½ cups thawed frozen tiny Brussels sprouts
2 cups broccoli flowerets, steamed until
    crisply tender
¼ cup chicken stock
2 tablespoons soy sauce
1 teaspoon cornstarch
2 tablespoons dry white wine
1 tablespoon sesame seeds, toasted (page 70)

Heat the oils in a wok or large heavy skillet over high heat. Add the mushrooms and cook, stirring, about 2 minutes. Add the garlic and Brussels sprouts, and cook 1 minute. Stir in the broccoli and cook, stirring, 2 minutes longer.

Mix together the stock, soy sauce, cornstarch, and wine. Stir into the vegetables and cook, tossing, until the sauce is thickened, about 2 minutes. Serve very hot, garnished with the sesame seeds.

Creamed Brussels Sprouts with Chives

I wish children were not repelled by Brussels sprouts. These miniature cabbages are too cute not to like, and when they are prepared like this, they are delightful. Roast turkey seems to me the perfect entrée to serve with these morsels.

Makes 6 servings

2 pints (about 1½ pounds) Brussels sprouts, trimmed and halved lengthwise
2 tablespoons butter
2 tablespoons all-purpose flour
Salt and freshly ground black pepper to taste
1 cup milk, or half-and-half, hot
3 tablespoons snipped fresh chives

In a large saucepan, simmer the halved sprouts in salted water to cover until crisply tender, 4 or 5 minutes (fresh Brussels sprouts cook very quickly.) Drain and keep warm.

Melt the butter in a small saucepan over medium heat. Stir in the flour and cook, stirring, for about 3 minutes, being careful not to let the mixture brown. Season well with salt and pepper. Stir in the hot milk, whisking until smooth. Cook over low heat, stirring from time to time, until thickened, at least 3 minutes.

Pour the sauce over the drained sprouts and heat through. Serve very hot, garnished with the chives.
Variations: *Simmer 1 cup small peeled boiling onions in salted water to cover until tender, about 10 minutes. Drain*

and stir into the cream sauce along with the Brussels sprouts.

Or cook ¼ pound sliced white mushrooms in 1 tablespoon butter over medium heat until barely golden, about 5 minutes. Stir them into the cream sauce along with the Brussels sprouts.

Brussels Sprouts with Avgolemono

Avgolemono is a Greek egg-and-lemon sauce that goes very well with the flavor of Brussels sprouts. The sauce must be made at the last minute and should be well seasoned with salt and pepper.

Makes 6 servings

2 pints (about 1½ pounds) small Brussels sprouts, trimmed and an X cut in the stem ends
3 large egg yolks
¼ cup fresh lemon juice
1 cup well-flavored chicken stock, hot but not boiling
Salt and freshly ground white pepper to taste

Boil the Brussels sprouts in salted water to cover or steam them, covered, in a steamer basket or a colander over simmering water until tender, 8 to 10 minutes, depending on size, and drain. Keep hot.

In a medium-size double boiler or saucepan set over simmering but not boiling water, beat the egg yolks with a whisk over until light yellow and thick, 2 to 3 minutes. Beat in the lemon juice. The mixture should be frothy. Beat in the stock, a little at a time until the sauce is thick and airy. Be careful to keep the water underneath the pan at a bare simmer or you could end up with scrambled eggs instead of a frothy sauce. Season with salt and pepper. Serve the sauce at once, poured over the hot Brussels sprouts.

Puree of Brussels Sprouts

Sort of a variation of the old Irish dish colcannon, this is great served with a tasty variety of grilled sausages.

Makes 6 servings

2 pints (about 1½ pounds) Brussels sprouts, trimmed and chopped
1 large Russet potato, peeled, cut into 1-inch cubes, boiled in salted water to cover until very tender, and drained
1 tablespoon chopped fresh tarragon
2 tablespoons butter
¼ to ½ cup heavy cream
Salt and freshly ground black pepper to taste

Boil the Brussels sprouts in salted water to cover, or steam them, covered, in a steamer basket or a colander over simmering water until very tender but still very green, 5 to 7 minutes, depending on size, and drain well. Puree the Brussels sprouts in a food processor or food mill until smooth.

Push the potato through a ricer into a medium-size saucepan and beat until smooth. Beat the sprout puree into the potatoes. Beat in the tarragon and butter. Add the cream, a little at a time and beat until the mixture is smooth and very thick but not too stiff. Season well with salt and pepper.

Reheat this puree over medium heat, stirring, until very hot. Do not burn. Serve very hot.

> Note: *This mixture can be made ahead and reheated, covered and vented, in the microwave on high for 1 to 1½ minutes.*

Variation: *If there is any puree left over, beat 1 egg into 1 to 1½ cups of the mixture. Stir in enough plain dried bread crumbs (about ¼ cup) to hold the mixture together. Spoon onto a hot greased griddle or skillet and fry until golden brown on both sides. These are wonderful with a dollop of sour cream or half-and-half on the side.*

Caraway Sprouts and Potatoes

I like to serve this dish with roast pork or roast fresh ham. Bake it right alongside the roast for an easy, no-last-minute-work dinner.

Makes 6 servings

4 tablespoons (½ stick) butter
4 large Russet potatoes, unpeeled, sliced about ¼ inch thick
1 large onion, thinly sliced
2 pints (1½ pounds) Brussels sprouts, trimmed and halved lengthwise
2 teaspoons caraway seeds
Salt and freshly ground black pepper to taste
2 cups well-flavored chicken stock
½ cup dry white wine
½ cup plain dried bread crumbs

Preheat the oven to 375°F. Generously butter a 2-quart covered shallow ovenproof casserole or baking dish with 2 tablespoons of the butter.

Spread half the potato slices in the bottom of the prepared dish. Top with half the onion and half the Brussels sprouts. Dot with ½ tablespoon of the butter, sprinkle with half the caraway seeds and season well with salt and pepper. Repeat the layers. Pour the stock and wine over the vegetables. Cover and bake for 1 hour.

In a small saucepan, melt the remaining 1 tablespoon butter over medium heat. Stir in the crumbs and remove the pan from the heat. Remove the cover of the casserole and spread the buttered crumbs on top of the vegetables. Return the dish to the oven and bake until golden brown and bubbling, another 20 to 30 minutes. Serve very hot.

> Note: *This has a definite caraway flavor. If a more subdued taste is desired, cut the caraway seeds to 1 teaspoon.*

Cabbage

If Brussels sprouts are relative newcomers to the vegetable scene, cabbage is their ancient ancestor. A variety of leaf cabbage has grown wild in parts of Europe for thousands of years, and it is probably the source that farmers used during the Middle Ages to develop the heading cabbages we know today. Even before these heading cabbages came on the scene some eight hundred years ago, ancient Greeks and Romans were mad about cabbage. We know they ate it both raw and cooked, as a sort of salad, maybe as a kind of pickle or relish, and as a vegetable. Later, the big, heavy cabbages we now enjoy became an easy-to-grow, versatile staple of man's winter diet.

In fact, in many parts of Europe even today, cabbage is such a large part of the winter diet that huge fields of cabbage are cultivated for late harvest. I have often driven on country roads on crisp fall nights surrounded by the fragrance of the gases given off by ripening cabbage—a distinct and not unpleasant aroma.

There are many cabbage varieties, but the few we find most often in the market are green, red, Savoy, bok choy, and napa. They are often interchangeable, but each has its own character.

Green cabbage is a tight, heavy head of pale green, almost white leaves. It must be cooked a relatively short time to avoid the smelly steam-table limpness we all dislike.

Red cabbage is also a tight, heavy head with somewhat coarser leaves. It can stand long cooking, but requires the addition of an acid, such as lemon juice or red wine, to keep its rich red color from turning an unappealing blue. It is also delicious raw and can be combined with green or Savoy cabbage to make wonderful salads.

Savoy cabbage has a less dense head than green cabbage, with tender, curly, light green leaves, and is at its best in late summer and early fall, though it is also available during the winter. The flavor is more delicate than green cabbage, and I prefer it in cooked dishes.

Bok choy is a loose-headed cabbage with thick white ribs. It somewhat resembles a head of romaine lettuce. It can be eaten raw, in salads, or cooked. The stems alone can be used in stir-fries or eaten like celery, or they can be cooked with the leaves, which are delicious when they are prepared like spinach.

Napa cabbage can be substituted for green cabbage in almost any recipe. It forms a compact, but not tight, heavy head, and its leaves are crinkly, a little like Savoy. It is delicious raw in salads, and I like it in baked dishes and soups.

Cabbage has become so universally popular that, in some cultures, it is preserved so that it can be enjoyed all year long. Cabbage tends to ferment when salted and aged, and this sour characteristic seems to appeal to many. Shredded and salted, cabbage becomes sauerkraut. An Asian counterpart is also salted and pickled with fermented fish sauce and hot peppers to become kimchi in Korea, a dinner-table standby and all-around sought-after treat. This Korean condiment is an acquired taste for some Westerners.

All cabbages offer the health benefits of their cruciferous brethren, at least to one degree or another. Red cabbage, for instance, has more vitamin C than green cabbage, and Savoy contains a substantial amount of beta-carotene; red and green do not. All cabbages are low in calories and provide a moderate source of fiber.

The age-old problem of digesting cabbage without having its gaseous aftereffects is easily prevented by using Beano® (see page 37).

Selection: The rules of thumb are basically the same for all cabbages. The heavier the head relative to its companions in the bin, the better. The leaves should be crisp and light colored, without any brown or discolored areas. Avoid any heads that are light in weight, limp leafed, spongy, or show any sign of mold on the stem and lower leaves. Holes in the leaves might mean worms inside the head.

Green and red cabbage are available all year long, though they are at their best in the fall and early winter. Savoy cabbage is at its best from October to early winter.

A large head of green or red cabbage will serve six to eight people, cooked, and up to twelve when made into coleslaw or other salad. A large head of Savoy makes up to six servings cooked, and one head of bok choy is enough for four to six. A good-sized head of napa serves four to six people when cooked and eight to ten, raw.

Storage and Preparation: Do not wash cabbage until you are ready to prepare it. Wrap the whole head in plastic wrap or enclose it in a locking plastic bag or perforated vegetable bag. An uncut cabbage can be held in the refrigerator up to two weeks. Once cut, the unused portion of the cabbage should be tightly wrapped, to be prepared and eaten as soon as possible.

Cabbage can be washed just before preparing. Be sure to dry it well. Unlike lettuce, I think the tightly closed inner leaves are generally clean, but if there are any blemishes, it is probably best to rinse and drain it well.

Do not use carbon-steel knives to cut either red or green cabbage. They will discolor the cut surfaces and give the cabbage a metallic taste.

Before cooking a head of cabbage whole, remove any limp outer leaves. Use a sharp knife to core the head. Rinse it, drain, cored side down, and then proceed with the recipe.

To serve cabbage in wedges, remove any limp outer leaves, then quarter the head from top to core. Cut out most of the solid hard core, but leave enough to hold the leaves together. Cut the quarters into wedges, rinse, drain, and cook according to the recipe.

To shred or grate cabbage, remove any limp outer leaves, cut the head in half from top to core, then in quarters. Cut out the solid core from each quarter, then lay it on its cut side and thinly slice or shred, cutting across the quarter. The quarters can also be cut into smaller wedges and then shredded or sliced with the slicing disk of a food processor.

To prepare bok choy, cut off the end of the stem and cut the leaves from the center stems. Cut the stems into pieces of the desired length. Rinse the cut stems well and drain before continuing with the recipe. The leaves can be cooked whole, cut across into thick slices, or thinly sliced for shreds. Rinse the leaves well and drain. If using in salads, dry the leaves in a salad spinner.

Napa cabbage can be cut across the head into thick slices or shredded. The leaves will separate easily. Rinse them well and drain or dry in a salad spinner. If you are going to steam the leaves, leave the water that clings to them. To use whole leaves, separate them from the base of the head and cut out the thick center stem. The stem can be eaten raw or sliced and added to stir-fries, soups, or salads.

Basically, the secret of wonderful cooked cabbage lies in not overcooking it. Overcooking makes cabbage mushy, strong smelling, and unpleasant tasting.

Steamed Cabbage

Steaming produces a much less watery finished vegetable. I prefer it, except when parboiling cabbage for stuffing or adding to a baked dish. Drain the steamed cabbage well before continuing. (Sometimes even steamed vegetables can become slightly watery and often need to be drained for 1 or 2 minutes.)

A steamer basket or colander set over simmering water or stock is perfect for steaming cabbage. A rack in a wok also works very well, as do the bamboo steamers that fit on top of kettles and woks. I usually arrange the cut cabbage—wedges or shreds—in the basket or colander and then place over the already boiling liquid. This is a great method for cooking both bok choy and napa—the color remains bright and the vegetable retains much of its flavor and nutritional value.

Wedges and quarters (if they will fit into the steamer) will take from 12 to 20 minutes, depending on their size.

Cut-up or shredded cabbage will take 5 to 8 minutes total, and the pieces should be gently stirred or tossed once or twice, depending on the amount being steamed.

Microwaved Cabbage

While wedges of cabbage can be microwaved, I think they are better if steamed. However, cut-up or shredded cabbage does very well in the microwave if it is stirred once or twice during the cooking time. Three cups shredded cabbage can be placed in a deep microwave dish. Add 1/4 cup water (or well-flavored chicken stock), cover loosely, and vent. Microwave on high for 2 minutes. Uncover carefully, stir, recover, and microwave 4 more minutes, in 2-minute intervals. Let stand 4 minutes and serve or continue with the recipe.

Boiled Cabbage

Boiling cabbage really does not need to perfume the whole neighborhood. The short cooking time that produces the best cabbage will generally not produce the sulfurous odor that lingers for hours, if not days. Use plenty of water and do not cover the pot.

Cabbage leaves that will be used for stuffing can be boiled in salted water to cover for 3 minutes. Drain and spread out to wrap around the filling.

Cut-up or shredded cabbage should also be boiled in salted water to cover until just wilted, 5 to 6 minutes. Drain and serve, or continue with the recipe.

Wedges and quarters can be boiled gently until a fork can be easily inserted into the thickest part of the wedge, 12 to 15 minutes, depending on the size and age of the cabbage. Drain well, serve very hot, and pass a good mustard along with plenty of salt and pepper. If calories are not a problem, I like to drizzle a little melted butter over the hot cabbage.

Wilted Cabbage with Walnuts and Blue Cheese

Once you try this with corned beef, you will never go back to plain boiled cabbage.

Makes 6 servings

3 tablespoons butter
1/2 medium-size onion, thinly sliced
1 small head Savoy cabbage, shredded
1/4 cup chicken stock
Freshly ground black pepper to taste
1/3 cup crumbled blue cheese
1/4 cup walnut or pecan pieces, toasted (page 70)

Melt the butter in a large heavy skillet over medium heat. Cook the onion, stirring occasionally, until just translucent, 7 or 8 minutes.

Stir in the cabbage and stock, and season well with pepper. Cook over medium heat, stirring from time to time, until the cabbage is wilted and tender, 15 minutes or more. Raise the heat to high and cook the cabbage, tossing, until the liquid is evaporated, 2 to 3 minutes. Serve warm or hot, garnished with the blue cheese and walnut pieces. Toss just before serving.

Cabbage Soufflé

I think this is a surprisingly delicate dish. It is a delicious cold-weather menu addition, especially with game, roast duck, goose, or even a slow-cooked pot roast of beef.

Makes 6 to 8 servings

4 tablespoons (1/2 stick) butter, plus additional for buttering
1/4 cup freshly grated Parmesan cheese, plus additional for dusting
3 green onions (scallions), white and light green parts only, minced
1/2 small head Savoy cabbage, shredded, steamed until just tender, kept warm
Salt and freshly ground black pepper to taste
3 tablespoons all-purpose flour
1 cup milk, heated until bubbles appear around the edge
4 large eggs, separated, whites beaten until stiff

Preheat the oven to 375°F. Generously butter a 1½-quart soufflé dish. Dust with cheese, knocking out any excess.

Melt 1 tablespoon of the butter in a small saucepan over medium heat. Cook the green onions, stirring occasionally, until tender, 3 to 4 minutes

Place the cabbage in a medium-size bowl. Add the cooked green onions and mash them into the cabbage, beating until the mixture is almost smooth. Season well with salt and pepper. Cool.

Melt the remaining 3 tablespoons of butter in a large heavy saucepan over medium heat. Add the flour and cook, stirring, for 3 minutes. Beat in the milk all at once, whisking until smooth. Cook over low heat until thick, about 3 minutes. Beat in the egg yolks, one at a time. Season well with salt and pepper. Stir in the cheese. Stir in the cabbage mixture. Cool slightly. Fold in the egg whites.

Spoon the soufflé mixture into the prepared dish and bake until puffed and golden brown, about 30 minutes. Serve at once.

Bubble and Squeak

While this version is not quite traditional, the idea of the combination is an English standard. Named for the little noises the dish makes while it cooks, bubble and squeak has long been a favorite food for millions. While my recipe is lighter than the classic, it may be a little heavy for a side dish, unless everyone has a good appetite. It is, however, delicious for cold-weather lunches with a glass of beer. And it is definitely divine for a comfort Sunday supper with a big salad. If serving as a side dish, why not put it alongside a good garlicky beef sausage, such as kosher kielbasa, thuringer, or summer sausage.

Makes 6 servings

3 tablespoons butter
1 small onion, sliced
2 1/4-inch thick slices leftover rare roast beef, cut
    into cubes
2 cups chopped leftover cooked green cabbage,
    or chopped cabbage, steamed over boiling
    water until just tender, about 5 minutes
3 large Russet potatoes, boiled in salted water
    to cover and drained, or baked until tender,
    peeled, halved, and sliced
Salt and freshly ground black pepper to taste

Melt the butter in a large heavy skillet over medium heat. Cook the onion, stirring occasionally, until just translucent, about 5 minutes. Add the roast beef, cabbage, and potatoes. Cook, turning the mixture over from time to time, until well browned, 15 to 20 minutes. Season well with salt and pepper. Use the flat side of a wide spatula to mash all the ingredients into a large, lumpy pancake. Continue to cook until the cake is crisp on the bottom, 6 to 8 minutes. Loosen the cake from the pan with a spatula and invert it onto a heated serving plate. Cut into wedges to serve.

Note: *Each serving can be garnished with a spoonful or two of sour cream, regular or light, and a sprinkling of snipped chives.*

Grilled Cabbage

Add this to a platter of grilled vegetables and serve it alongside any grilled fish.

Makes 8 servings

1 tablespoon soy sauce
2 tablespoons teriyaki sauce
1 small clove garlic, pressed
1 tablespoon dry white wine or sherry
1/2 teaspoon ground cumin
3 tablespoons mild vegetable oil, preferably
    peanut or canola
1 large head green cabbage, cored, halved, and
    cut into 8 wedges

Prepare a hot fire in a barbecue grill or preheat a gas or electric grill. Oil the grill rack.

In a small bowl, beat together all the ingredients, except the cabbage. Brush the cabbage wedges well with the basting sauce. Place the cabbage on the grill rack about 4 inches from the heat and cook, basting several times, until well browned, about 5 minutes on each side. Serve hot.

Note: *I don't suggest broiling the cabbage instead of grilling it. You won't get the same crusty result.*

Cabbage and Tomato Bake

Definitely winter dinner fare, serve this with baked spareribs or smothered pork chops, an old southern dish. The pork chops are browned (sometimes dusted with flour) and a little liquid is added, then covered and cooked until tender.

Makes 6 to 8 servings

2 tablespoons olive oil
1 small onion, halved and thinly sliced
1 small head green or Savoy cabbage, halved, cored, and thickly sliced
Salt and freshly ground black pepper to taste
½ cup dry white wine, or chicken stock
2 medium-size ripe tomatoes, sliced; or one 14½-ounce can sliced tomatoes, drained
1 cup grated Monterey Jack cheese
½ teaspoon dried Italian herbs, such as oregano, marjoram, rosemary, and thyme, or a prepared mix

Heat the oil in a large heavy skillet over medium heat. Cook the onion, stirring, for 1 minute. Stir in the cabbage and continue to cook, stirring, until the cabbage is limp, 4 to 5 minutes. Season well with salt and pepper and pour in the wine.

Preheat the oven to 350°F. Lightly butter a 2-quart deep ovenproof casserole.

Layer the cabbage mixture with the tomatoes and cheese, ending with cheese. Season each layer of tomatoes with a little of the Italian herbs. Bake until the cheese is golden brown and the casserole is bubbling, about 30 minutes.

Virginia Cabbage Bake

Here is a dish that can accompany nearly anything in your repertoire. Wonderful with fried oysters, it is equally good with plain grilled fish—grouper, orange roughy, or even catfish fillets.

Makes 6 to 8 servings

1 tablespoon butter, plus additional for buttering
1 tablespoon all-purpose flour
1 cup well-flavored chicken stock, boiling
½ cup heavy cream
1 medium-size head green or Savoy cabbage, shredded, steamed over boiling water, until tender, about 10 minutes
1 bunch (6 to 8) green onions (scallions), white and light green parts only, thinly sliced
½ cup diced Virginia ham
Salt and freshly ground black pepper to taste
¾ cup grated Monterey Jack or fontina cheese
¼ cup plain dried bread crumbs

Preheat the oven to 325 to 350°F. Generously butter a medium-size deep ovenproof casserole.

Melt 1 tablespoon of butter in a medium-size heavy saucepan over medium heat. Stir in the flour and cook, stirring, for 3 minutes without browning. Pour in the stock and cream, stirring, and cook over low heat until thick, 3 to 4 minutes. Remove the pan from the heat.

Stir the cabbage into the sauce, along with the green onions and the ham. Season well with pepper and add salt if needed. Stir in the cheese.

Pile the mixture into the buttered casserole. Sprinkle with the bread crumbs. Bake until well browned and bubbling, about 30 minutes.

Gratin of Cabbage

This is delicious with grilled sausages or pork chops. I also like it with roast duck and baked ham.

Makes 6 to 8 servings

2 tablespoons butter, plus 1 tablespoon (optional) for dotting
1 small onion, cut into ¼-inch dice
½ medium-size red bell pepper, seeded and cut into ¼-inch dice

3 medium-size waxy white potatoes, boiled in
salted water to cover until just tender,
drained, peeled, and cut into ¼-inch dice
1 small head green cabbage, coarsely chopped and
steamed until just tender, about 5 minutes
Salt and freshly ground black pepper to taste
½ cup heavy cream
3 tablespoons plain dried bread crumbs
3 tablespoons freshly grated Parmesan cheese

Preheat the oven to 400°F.

Melt 2 tablespoons of butter in a large heavy
skillet over medium heat. Cook the onion and bell
pepper, stirring occasionally, until very tender, about
15 minutes. Toss the mixture with the potatoes and
cabbage. Season well with salt and pepper.

Spoon the mixture into a medium-size gratin dish.
Pour in the cream and dot with the remaining 1 tablespoon butter, if desired. In a small bowl, mix the bread
crumbs with the cheese and sprinkle the mixture over
the cabbage. Bake until bubbling and the top is golden
brown, about 20 minutes. Serve very hot.

Note: *For a change of texture, thinly slice the
onion, pepper, and potatoes, and shred the cabbage. Follow the recipe. Spread the mixture in
the gratin dish. Finish as above.*

Red Cabbage with Bacon

*Serve this with grilled turkey sausages and mashed pota-
toes for an old-fashioned sort of supper. It is a perfect
après-ski menu or for after a long day putting the garden
to bed for the winter.*

Makes 6 servings

5 slices thick-cut bacon, cut across into
½-inch pieces
1 very small (about 1½ pounds) head red
cabbage, shredded

½ cup dry red wine
Salt and freshly ground black pepper to taste
2 green onions (scallions), white and light green
parts only, sliced

Fry the bacon in a large heavy skillet over medium
heat until almost crisp, 5 to 7 minutes. Remove with
a slotted spoon and drain on paper towels. Drain all
but about 3 tablespoons of the fat.

Stir the cabbage into the same skillet with the
reserved bacon fat and cook, tossing, for 2 minutes.
Stir in the wine and season well with salt and pepper. Simmer over medium heat, tossing from time to
time, until the liquid is evaporated and the cabbage
is tender, about 15 minutes. Do not overcook the
cabbage. Stir in the bacon. Serve very hot, garnished
with the scallions.

Caraway Creamed Cabbage

*This is very good with roast poultry and goes well with
duck or rare roast beef.*

Makes 6 servings

2 tablespoons butter
1 small onion, thinly sliced
1 head Savoy cabbage, shredded
1 teaspoon caraway seeds, crushed or ground
¼ cup dry white wine
One 3-ounce package cream cheese, softened
3 tablespoons milk
Salt and freshly ground black pepper to taste

Melt the butter in a large heavy saucepan over
medium heat. Cook the onion, stirring occasionally,
until just limp, about 5 minutes. Stir in the cabbage,
caraway seeds, and wine. Cover and cook until the
cabbage is tender, 10 to 15 minutes.

In a medium-size bowl, beat together the cream
cheese and milk. Stir the cheese mixture into the
cabbage. Heat through, but do not boil. Season well
with salt and pepper. Serve very hot.

Sweet-and-Sour Red Cabbage

A classic combination that is a natural with sauerbraten or braised beef, this is also wonderful with roast goose or duck and is even fine with grilled tuna.

Serves 6 to 8

2 tablespoons butter
2 tablespoons mild vegetable oil, preferably peanut
1 medium-size onion, halved and thinly sliced
1 small (less than 2 pounds) head red cabbage, shredded or thinly sliced
$\frac{1}{3}$ cup red wine vinegar
1 large Granny Smith apple, peeled, quartered, cored, and thinly sliced
1 tablespoon sugar
1 cup good, hearty beef stock
Salt and freshly ground pepper to taste

Melt the butter in the oil in a large heavy sauté pan or frying pan over medium heat. Cook the onion, stirring occasionally, until translucent, 8 to 10 minutes. Add the cabbage and cook, stirring occasionally, until the cabbage begins to wilt, 3 to 5 minutes. Stir in the vinegar and toss to coat the cabbage. Stir in the apple and sugar. Stir in the stock. Cover and simmer over low heat until the apple is quite tender, 15 to 20 minutes. Uncover, season well with salt and pepper. Simmer over medium-low heat, stirring from time to time, until most of the liquid is evaporated, another 10 to 15 minutes. Serve very hot.

Bok Choy with Sesame Seeds

The delicate flavor of bok choy makes this dish a nice accompaniment for grilled fish, though I also like it with steamed Chinese sausages and rice.

Makes 6 servings

2 tablespoons mild vegetable oil, preferably peanut
1 tablespoon toasted sesame oil
1 to $1\frac{1}{2}$ pounds bok choy, greens stripped from the white stem, stem cut into 1-inch lengths, and leaves chopped
1 teaspoon salt
Pinch sugar
$\frac{1}{4}$ cup water
$\frac{1}{4}$ teaspoon Chinese chili paste (optional, but recommended)
1 tablespoon sesame seeds, toasted (page 70)

Heat the oils until very hot in a wok or large heavy skillet over high heat. Stir in the stem pieces of the bok choy and cook, stirring, for 1 minute. Add the leaves and cook, stirring, 1 minute longer. Season with salt and sugar and add water and, if desired, chili paste. Toss to mix well. Cover, reduce the heat slightly to medium-high, and cook until the stems are crisply tender and the leaves are wilted but still bright green, 4 to 5 minutes. Serve very hot, garnished with the sesame seeds.

Note: *You may substitute $\frac{1}{2}$ teaspoon soy sauce for the salt, but the color will not be as bright.*

Smothered Cabbage

Cabbage seems to mean comfort food. While I love it cold in salads in the heat of summer, I think there are many wonderful, and wonderfully easy, hot dishes that are substantial enough to stand up to even the coldest weather. This dish is as good with a roast pheasant as it is with a large ring of kielbasa or other garlicky sausage.

Makes 6 to 8 serving

1 tablespoon butter
1 large green bell pepper, seeded and sliced
1 large head green or Savoy cabbage, trimmed, halved, and cored
Salt and freshly ground black pepper to taste

½ cup beer
¼ cup heavy cream
1 tablespoon chopped fresh parsley

Melt the butter in a large heavy sauté pan or flame-proof casserole over medium heat. Cook the bell pepper, stirring from time to time, until tender, about 10 minutes. Arrange the cabbage, cut side down, on top of the bell pepper. Season well with salt and pepper and pour in the beer. Cover the pan and simmer over low heat until the cabbage is just tender, do not overcook. The time will vary, but begin checking after about 15 minutes.

Remove the cabbage to a heated serving platter and keep warm. Stir the cream into the bell pepper, raise the heat to medium and cook until the sauce begins to thicken, 2 to 3 minutes. To serve, spoon the bell pepper and sauce over the cabbage and garnish with the parsley.

Note: *I like to use Le Creuset or other enameled cast-iron cookware for this recipe.*

Curly Cabbage with Onions and Bacon

I think this is delicious when served with grilled shrimp or a dish of garlicky scampi.

Makes 6 to 8 servings

4 thick slices bacon, cut into 1-inch pieces
2 large onions, thickly sliced
½ green bell pepper, seeded and thinly sliced
1 small head Savoy cabbage, thickly shredded
1 teaspoon caraway seeds
2 tablespoons cider vinegar
1 teaspoon sugar
Salt and seasoned pepper, such as Mrs. Dash,
    to taste
Hot pepper sauce to taste (optional)

Cook the bacon in a medium-size heavy skillet over medium heat until almost crisp, 5 to 7 minutes. Remove the bacon from the skillet and drain on paper towels, leaving the fat in the skillet.

Cook the onions and bell pepper in the bacon fat that remains in the skillet over medium heat, stirring occasionally, until the vegetables are just translucent, about 10 minutes. Stir in the cabbage and caraway seeds. Cook, stirring, until the cabbage wilts and becomes tender but not mushy, 6 to 7 minutes. Stir in the vinegar and sugar and cook over medium heat for 2 minutes. Stir in the reserved bacon and season well with salt and seasoned pepper. Serve hot and pass the hot pepper sauce on the side.

Apple Cabbage Slaw

Add this very colorful salad to your next picnic menu and watch it disappear.

Makes 6 to 8 servings

1 small head red cabbage, finely grated or
    thinly sliced
1 large Granny Smith apple, unpeeled, quartered,
    cored, and thinly sliced
1 small sweet onion, halved and very thinly sliced
¼ cup fresh lemon juice
⅓ cup chopped fresh parsley
½ cup mayonnaise, prepared or homemade
    (page 13)
½ cup plain yogurt
Freshly ground black pepper to taste
2 ounces blue cheese, crumbled (½ cup)

Toss the cabbage, apple, and onion with the lemon juice in a large bowl. In a medium-size bowl, beat together the parsley, mayonnaise, and yogurt. Toss with the cabbage mixture. Season well with freshly ground pepper. Garnish with the blue cheese. Refrigerate for 2 to 3 hours.

Note: *For an added fillip, garnish with 2 tablespoons of toasted walnut pieces.*

Bok Choy and Sweet Pepper Stir-Fry

If you add ¹/₂ pound peeled raw shrimp to this and toss the mixture for 2 to 3 minutes, you have a great main course for three or four friends. Otherwise, serve it with a grilled tuna steak or red snapper fillet.

Makes 6 servings

3 tablespoons mild vegetable oil, preferably peanut
¹/₂ red bell pepper, cut into 1-inch pieces
¹/₂ green bell pepper, cut into 1-inch pieces
1¹/₂ pounds bok choy, greens stripped from stems, stems cut into 1-inch lengths, and leaves chopped
¹/₂ cup chicken stock
1 tablespoon dry sherry
Salt and freshly ground black pepper to taste
Pinch sugar

Heat the oil until very hot in a wok or large heavy skillet over high heat. Add the bell peppers and cook, stirring, 3 minutes. Add bok choy stems and cook, stirring for 2 minutes. Stir in the leaves and toss for 1 minute. Add the stock, sherry, salt, pepper, and sugar. Cover and cook over low heat for 5 minutes. Remove the cover, raise the heat to high and evaporate most of the liquid, tossing the vegetables so they will not scorch. Serve very hot.

> **Note:** *For a dish with more bite, add a pinch of crushed red pepper along with the salt, pepper, and sugar.*

Cabbage Tortilla Rolls

Almost like individual cabbage strudels, these rolls make a good accompaniment for roast pork. Two of them make a main-course serving for Saturday lunch or Sunday supper.

Makes 12 rolls

Twelve 8-inch flour tortillas
3 slices bacon, chopped
1 tablespoon butter
2 medium-size onions, very thinly sliced
¹/₂ small head green cabbage, shredded or finely chopped
Salt and freshly ground black pepper to taste
¹/₂ teaspoon caraway seeds, crushed
Sour cream, regular or light
Freshly snipped chives (optional)

Wrap the tortillas in aluminum foil and warm them in a 275°F. oven, about 30 minutes. Or wrap the tortillas in paper towels and microwave them on high for 30 to 60 seconds. Wrap them in a kitchen towel and keep them warm.

Cook the bacon in a small heavy skillet over medium heat until almost crisp, about 5 minutes. Remove the bacon from the skillet and drain on paper towels, leaving the fat in the skillet.

Melt the butter in the bacon fat in the skillet over medium heat. Add the onions and cook, stirring occasionally, until tender and golden, about 10 minutes. Stir in the cabbage. Season well with salt and plenty of ground pepper. (The filling should be highly seasoned with pepper.) Stir in the caraway seeds. Cook, stirring, until the cabbage is very tender, 12 to 15 minutes. Stir in the bacon.

To serve, spoon some of the cabbage mixture on one edge of each warm tortilla, and roll up the tortilla. Arrange the rolls on a heated ovenproof serving platter, cover with aluminum foil, and keep warm in a 200°F. oven until all are made.

Serve hot, garnished with a dollop of sour cream and, if desired, a sprinkling of chives.

Stuffed Savoy Cabbage

Not nearly as substantial as most stuffed cabbages, I like this with grilled pork tenderloin or plain grilled chicken.

Makes 6 to 8 servings

2 tablespoons butter, plus additional for buttering
½ medium-size onion, minced
1 rib celery, minced
¼ medium-size green bell pepper, minced
¼ small red bell pepper, minced
2 cloves garlic, minced
2 cups cooked (about ⅔ cup raw) rice, hot
3 tablespoons chopped fresh parsley
1 large egg, beaten
Salt and freshly ground black pepper to taste
1 medium-size head Savoy cabbage, core
    trimmed, boiled whole in salted water
    to cover for 10 minutes, and drained
¼ cup plain dried bread crumbs

Preheat the oven to 325°F. Lightly butter a medium-size, shallow, round, ovenproof casserole.

Melt 2 tablespoons of butter in a small skillet over medium heat. Add the onion, celery, bell peppers, and garlic, and cook, stirring occasionally, until translucent, 10 to 12 minutes. Remove the skillet from the heat. Stir in the rice, parsley, and egg. Season well with salt and pepper.

Carefully separate the leaves of the cabbage from the top until there is a large opening in the middle. If necessary, remove some of the innermost leaves and reserve for another use. Fill the hollow with the rice mixture. Re-form the cabbage, pressing the leaves tightly around the filling.

Arrange the filled cabbage, core side down, in the buttered casserole. Spread the bread crumbs on top. Bake until the crumbs are well browned, about 45 minutes. Serve the stuffed cabbage hot, cut into wedges.

Summer Slaw

I cannot tell you how many times I have made this slaw for family meals, for parties, and for friends. Added to a buffet table with sliced ripe tomatoes, cold fried chicken, and hot corn on the cob, it becomes part of one of the South's quintessential al fresco meals.

Makes 6 to 8 generous servings

1 small head green or Savoy cabbage, very finely
    shredded or thinly sliced
1 sweet onion, very thinly sliced
1 teaspoon celery seed
1 cup mayonnaise, prepared or homemade
    (page 13)
½ cup sour cream, regular or light
1 tablespoon dry mustard
Salt and freshly ground black pepper to taste
3 tablespoons chopped fresh parsley, plus
    additional for garnishing

In a large bowl, toss together the cabbage, onion, and celery seed. In a small bowl, beat together the mayonnaise, sour cream, and mustard. Season well with salt and freshly ground pepper. Stir in 3 tablespoons parsley. Toss this dressing with the cabbage and onion mixture. Refrigerate for several hours or overnight. Serve, garnished with the additional parsley. *Variation: For added color and flavor, toss ¼ of a large red bell pepper, very thinly sliced, into the cabbage and onion mixture. Continue with the rest of the recipe.*

Note: *It is important to chill this salad so the flavor will develop. That makes it a perfect make-ahead dish.*

Cardoons

Cardoons, in the thistle family, are hard to find in American markets, but they are well worth trying if you happen to stumble across them or know someone who grows the vegetable. It is the long prickly stalks of the cardoon that are eaten, not the flowers, in contrast to their cousin the globe artichoke, although cardoon flower buds are edible and can be prepared like artichokes. Unless you grow cardoons, though, it is unlikely that you will ever find the buds.

Long a winter favorite in southern Europe, cardoons were probably brought to America from Piedmont by the Italian immigrants who came in the early years of this century. Recipes do not abound, but in Italy, France, and Switzerland you will find cardoons in soups, gratins, and other down-to-earth dishes. I have often eaten cardoon gratins in the mountains of Switzerland.

The plant looks like a large bunch of celery with pale green, or grayish green, fuzzy stalks. Some small farmers blanch their plants, tying up the stalks and mounding the earth up the leaves. This makes them very white and gives them a sweeter flavor. They have a delicate taste, a little bit like a globe artichoke.

Cardoons can be eaten raw as well as cooked. They are crisply tender when peeled and strung, with a texture somewhat like celery. The classic Piemontese preparation is Bagna Cauda (page 96), a hot olive oil, butter, garlic, and anchovy dip (or "bath") for crisp raw cardoons and other vegetables. It is the type of communal meal that tends to bring out the best in the participants.

Cardoons are low in calories and high in sodium and magnesium.

Selection: Choose the smallest, crispest, inner stalks available, bypassing any that feel limp or spongy. The ribs should be pale green or grayish white, plump, and covered with prickly fuzz. Avoid any that have signs of mold or brown spots. While you may be lucky to stumble on this interesting vegetable, it doesn't make any sense to buy it if it is in poor condition.

Occasionally, you can find in the market fresh cardoons that have had their stalks separated, allowing you to buy only what you need. Cardoons are generally available from early November until the heavy cold of January.

You will need about 2 pounds of untrimmed cardoon stalks for six servings.

Storage and Preparation: It is best to prepare any cardoons you come across as quickly as possible. If it is absolutely necessary to store them, put them, unwashed, into a perforated plastic vegetable bag and refrigerate for a day or two at the most.

Like artichokes, cardoons will turn an unappealing gray once they are peeled or cut. Have a large bowl of water handy, to which you have added 2 tablespoons lemon juice or vinegar (acidulated water). Remove any leaves from the stalks. Use a vegetable parer to strip off the fuzz and any spines you may find. Cut the stalks into desired lengths, removing any fibrous strings, just as you would with celery. Drop the prepared pieces into the acidulated water as soon as you finish each one.

If the dish calls for cooked cardoons, boil them in the acidulated water for 3 to 4 minutes and drain before continuing with the recipe. If serving raw, leave them in the cold acidulated water until just before serving. Drain and serve—they will be crisp and unblemished.

Boiled or Braised Cardoons

Arrange prepared cardoons in a nonreactive skillet or sauté pan. Pour in enough acidulated water (see above), chicken stock, or veal stock to barely cover. Cover the skillet and simmer the cardoons over low heat until very tender but not mushy, 30 to 40 minutes.

Cardoons can also be cooked *à blanc*: Combine 2 tablespoons lemon juice or vinegar with 2 tablespoons flour. Stir this mixture into a large saucepan filled with 2 quarts of cold water until dissolved. Add the prepared cardoons, place the pan over medium heat and bring to a boil. Reduce the heat and simmer the cardoons until very tender. The lemon juice and flour will maintain the vegetable's white color.

Steamed Cardoons

Steam prepared cardoons in a steamer basket or colander, covered, over simmering water until very tender but not mushy, 45 to 60 minutes. Check from time to time so they do not overcook.

Braised Cardoons and Onions

Serve this with a roast chicken or add it to your favorite turkey dinner.

Makes 6 servings

2½ pounds cardoons, leaves removed, stalks
    trimmed and strung, cut into 3-inch pieces
2 tablespoons fresh lemon juice
3 tablespoons butter
2 cups boiling onions, boiled in water to cover
    for 1 minute, drained, and peeled; or one
    16-ounce bag frozen baby onions, thawed
⅓ cup heavy cream
Salt and freshly ground black pepper to taste
3 tablespoons chopped fresh parsley

Toss the cardoons with the lemon juice. Boil the cardoons in salted water to cover for 5 minutes. Drain.

In a large heavy skillet, melt the butter over low heat and cook the cardoons and onions, covered, until tender, 25 to 30 minutes. Pour in the cream, season well with salt and pepper, and cook, tossing the vegetables to coat with the sauce, 3 to 4 minutes longer. Serve it very hot, garnished with the parsley.

Gratin of Cardoons with Bacon

This could also be a main course for a light workday supper, along with a tossed salad and good crisp bread. But, it is truly delicious with roast veal or grilled veal chops.

Makes 6 to 8 servings

2 tablespoons butter, plus additional for buttering
2½ pounds cardoons, leaves removed, stalks
    trimmed and strung, cut into 3-inch pieces,
    and simmered in chicken stock to cover for
    30 minutes, drained, stock reserved

2 tablespoons all-purpose flour
1½ cups reserved chicken stock, hot
Salt and freshly ground black pepper to taste
2 tablespoons chopped fresh parsley
½ cup grated Gruyère cheese
½ pound slab bacon, cut lengthwise into ¼-inch
    slices and then crosswise into ½-inch pieces,
    fried until golden and just beginning to crisp,
    drained on paper towels (page 42)

Preheat the oven to 400°F.

Generously butter a medium-size shallow glass or other nonreactive baking dish. Arrange the cardoons in the prepared dish.

Melt 2 tablespoons of butter in a small or medium-size heavy saucepan over medium heat. Stir in the flour and cook gently without browning, stirring, for 3 minutes. Stir in the stock all at once, whisking until smooth. Cook, stirring, over medium heat, until thick, 3 or 4 minutes. Season well with salt and pepper and stir in the parsley.

Pour the sauce over the cardoons. Spread the cheese over the sauce. Spread the bacon over the surface and bake until golden brown and bubbling, about 25 minutes.

Bagna Cauda

Bagna cauda means "hot bath" in Italian, and this is the nicest way I know to "bathe" fresh vegetables. Serve this with all sorts of fresh vegetables cut into sticks as a "hand" salad, as part of an informal cold lunch, or on a cocktail buffet table.

Makes about 1½ cups sauce

4 tablespoons (½ stick) butter
½ cup good-quality fruity olive oil
    (not necessarily extra-virgin)
3 to 4 cloves garlic, minced
4 to 6 anchovy fillets, or to taste, drained
    and minced
1 tablespoon chopped fresh parsley, or more
    to taste (optional)

Assorted vegetables, cut into 3- to 4-inch
lengths, such as cardoons (leaves removed),
Belgian endive leaves, fennel bulbs, green
peppers, carrots, cucumbers, Jerusalem
artichokes, jicama, broccoli stems, and
green onions

Melt the butter over very low heat in a small saucepan that can be set over a warmer. Add the olive oil
and then the garlic. Heat gently until quite warm,
but do not cook the garlic. Add the anchovies, stirring until they dissolve and the mixture begins to
bubble very gently. Add the parsley. Serve the sauce
very warm, set over a liquid fuel burner, candle, or
spirit lamp. Pass the vegetables separately.

> Note: *Some like to cook the tougher vegetables
> briefly, but I think the real attraction of this dish
> is the contrast between the unctuous warm sauce
> and the cold crispness of the vegetables.*
>
> *Add the anchovies to suit your taste—for
> some people more is better. You can easily double
> the quantity, but do not double the garlic, and
> add more anchovy fillets one at a time to avoid
> overwhelming the sauce.*

Variation: *Around Turin, cream is sometimes substituted for the olive oil and minced white truffles are added.
I like the more rustic version better, and white truffles are
not only extremely hard to find but cost a fortune.*

Cardoons au Gratin

This is a traditional way to serve cardoons, especially in
the mountains of Switzerland. In fact, the Swiss have a
very acceptable canned cardoon that they can use when
pressed for time. Serve with thick-cut veal chops, preferably grilled over charcoal or, better yet, a wood fire.

Makes 6 to 8 servings

4 tablespoons all-purpose flour
2 tablespoons fresh lemon juice
2 pounds cardoons, leaves removed and
discarded, stalks strung and cut into
3- to 4-inch lengths
3 tablespoons butter, plus additional for buttering
1 cup milk, hot
Salt and freshly ground black pepper to taste
Pinch nutmeg
4 ounces Gruyère (or Comté or Swiss) cheese,
grated (1 cup)

In a small bowl, mix 2 tablespoons of the flour and
the lemon juice with enough water to dissolve the
mixture. Beat this *blanc* into a large kettle with
enough cold, salted water to cover the cardoons. Add
the cardoons and bring to a boil. (The *blanc* mixture
will keep the cardoons from turning an unappetizing
gray color.) Simmer over low until tender, 30 to
45 minutes. Drain well.

Preheat the oven to 400°F. Generously butter a
1½-quart ovenproof casserole.

Melt 3 tablespoons of butter in a medium-size
heavy saucepan over medium heat. Stir in the
remaining 2 tablespoons of flour and cook, stirring,
for 3 minutes. Do not brown. Beat in the milk with a
whisk and cook, whisking constantly, until thickened,
at least 3 minutes. Season with salt and pepper and
add the nutmeg. Stir in three-quarters of the cheese.

Arrange the drained cardoons in the prepared casserole. Pour the cheese sauce over them and spread
the remaining cheese on top. Bake until golden brown
and bubbling, 20 to 25 minutes. Serve hot.

Carrots

Even though today's familiar bright orange carrot bears little resemblance to its ancient ancestor, some variety or other of carrot has been cultivated for more than two thousand years. It wasn't until about three hundred years ago, however, that the long-rooted, sweet, orange carrot was developed. Maybe it is just that sweet crunchiness that has made the carrot so universally popular. In fact carrots do contain more sugar than any other vegetable, except beets—and they have the advantage of not bleeding color all over the plate.

If you have ever tasted a crisp young carrot, just pulled from the earth and washed at a garden spigot, you have an idea of exactly how sweet carrots can be—a far cry from the big, dry, sometimes woody vegetable packed into ingeniously striped plastic bags.

Carrots crop up in cuisines from one end of the world to the other. They are often used raw in salads or as crudités and are delicious when cooked. From simple boiled carrots, seasoned with salt and pepper, to complex vegetable dishes like soufflés, gratins, and stir-fries, this vegetable lends itself to many different culinary styles and tastes. In addition to savory dishes, the sweetness of carrots makes them easy to incorporate in dessert confections, such as puddings, custards, and moist, delicious carrot cake. I occasionally make a grated carrot tart sweetened with honey.

Raw carrot sticks are a dieter's mainstay and untold millions of schoolchildren find them packed in the lunches they bring from home. And what cocktail party buffet is complete without raw carrots and something for dipping?

Not only are carrots easy to keep and prepare, they offer some very important health benefits. They are low in fat and calories and very high in the antioxidant beta-carotene. They also provide some vitamin C and a fair amount of potassium. Whether or not they can help you see in the dark is still up for debate, however; and they do not have any effect at all on the curliness of hair.

Selection: The best, sweetest carrots in the market—other than those that have just been pulled from the ground—are the ones sold in bunches with the tops still intact. It only takes a glance to see if the tops are crisp, bright green, and fresh or if they are yellowed and limp. If the tops are fresh, it is a good bet that the carrots will be sweet and crunchy. A little dirt clinging to the roots is fine, too, since commercial washing processes can break the thin skin and destroy much of their vitamin content. If the tops have wilted, many markets will clip them to about 2 inches above the carrot. If they are still bright orange and plumply juicy looking without appearing limp, they are probably fairly fresh.

If bunch carrots are not available, choose the best-looking carrots you can find prepacked in plastic bags, avoiding any that have moisture on the inside of the bag. Pass up any that are limp, look tired, show any signs of mold, or have black spots on them. The best carrots will have been refrigerated continuously from farm to market.

The size of carrots to buy depends on what you want to do with them. Tiny baby carrots are good for eating raw or cooking whole. Medium-size carrots are perfect for cooking, cut into rounds, chunks, or matchstick strips; and large carrots can be cut into even lengths and turned or pared into any shape desired. Large ones are also good grated or shredded for salads, purees, and pastries. Large old carrots, however can be woody, with hard cores. These are great for horses, but if nothing else is available, you will probably have to cut them into lengths, quarter them lengthwise, and remove the tough core before cooking.

Frozen carrots are a good substitute for fresh when you are cooking them. They can be glazed, braised, or added to soups and stews. They should be thawed and then treated as if they were parboiled. These are too soft-textured to serve

"raw," and I personally do not like to use frozen carrots in stir-fries or sautés.

Carrots are available all year, but local farm products are at their peak quality in late June and early July.

You will need about 1½ pounds of carrots for six servings.

Storage and Preparation: If you have bought carrots with the tops on and intend to store them, cut the tops off to about 2 inches above the carrots. If you do not cut them, the stems will continue to pull moisture out of the carrots and the roots will not remain crisp. Place the clipped carrots, unwashed, in a perforated plastic vegetable bag and refrigerate as soon as possible. They will keep up to two weeks, but check them from time to time to be sure they have no mold or decayed spots.

I like to rewrap bagged carrots, sorting out any that are spotted or less than fresh and putting the good ones in a clean perforated vegetable bag before refrigerating them.

Small carrots should be well washed, but not roughly scrubbed or peeled. Most of the nutrients lie very close to the skin and you want to preserve as many as possible. Older carrots should be well washed and peeled before cooking or cutting to serve them raw. If they will be added to soups, stews, stocks, or braising liquids, just wash them well and cut into desired size or shape. They do not need to be peeled. Try to make all the pieces the same size, no matter what the shape, so that they will cook evenly. Even if cutting them into pieces, all carrots should have the stem end trimmed. The tip can also be trimmed if discolored or misshapen.

Tip: Carrots can be precooked, refreshed in cold water, drained, and then reheated in the microwave on high for 1 to 2 minutes before serving.

Boiled Carrots

Prepared small whole carrots should be boiled in salted water to cover until tender, 6 to 10 minutes, and drained. Better yet, add only 1/4 inch water, stock, or other liquid to the saucepan, cover, and cook them about the same length of time, shaking once or twice to keep the carrots from sticking.

Cut-up carrots can be cooked the same way, but for 5 to 6 minutes, depending on their size and age.

Steamed Carrots

Place the prepared carrots in a steamer basket or colander over simmering water and steam, covered, until tender when pierced with the point of a sharp knife, about 10 minutes for small whole carrots and 4 to 6 minutes for cut-up or "turned" carrots (page 99).

Microwaved Carrots

Arrange 1 pound of prepared baby carrots or about 3 cups cut-up carrots in a microwave dish. Add 1/4 cup liquid, cover with plastic microwave wrap, and vent. Microwave on high for 4 to 5 minutes, and let stand 4 to 5 minutes before serving.

Vichy Carrots

Vichy is a town in central France that has long been a health spa. The local spring water is slightly carbonated naturally and is reputed to have all sorts of healthful qualities. For a healthful combination, try these carrots with steamed or broiled fish.

Makes 6 to 8 servings

2 tablespoons butter
2 pounds baby carrots, trimmed
3 cups (more or less), water, or carbonated mineral water (classically Vichy water)
Pinch sugar
Salt and freshly ground black pepper to taste
Chopped fresh parsley

Combine the butter and carrots in a large saucepan. Add enough water to cover and bring to a boil over medium-high. Stir in the sugar. Simmer over medium heat until all the water is evaporated and the carrots are tender and coated with the butter that remains in the pan, up to 30 minutes. Season well with salt and pepper. Serve the carrots very hot, garnished with the parsley.

Note: *Vichy carrots is a traditional French dish of boiled, glazed carrots, but the basic recipe can be used with onions, potatoes, mushrooms, turnips, and other vegetables. Use seltzer water or club soda in place of mineral water if you like, but watch out when adding salt as some carbonated waters have a fairly high sodium content.*

Variation: *For a little different taste, substitute 1 teaspoon of honey for the sugar.*

Carrot, Potato, and Onion Gratin

I like to serve this delightful vegetable combination with a grilled steak, but it also goes very well with roast beef, pot roast, or a whole baked striped bass.

Makes 6 to 8 servings

4 tablespoons (1/2 stick) butter, plus additional for buttering

2 large Russet potatoes, unpeeled, thinly sliced
2 large onions, thinly sliced
1 pound carrots, peeled and cut on the diagonal
    into long thin slices
Salt and freshly ground black pepper to taste
1 cup well-flavored chicken stock
½ cup freshly grated Parmesan cheese

Preheat the oven to 350°F. Generously butter a medium-size gratin dish.

Make a layer of one-third of the potato slices in the bottom of the prepared gratin dish. Add a layer of half the onions and then half the carrots. Dot with 2 tablespoons of the butter and season well with salt and pepper. Repeat the layers and finish with the remaining one-third of the potato slices. Dot with the remaining 2 tablespoons of butter and season with salt and pepper. Pour in the stock.

Cover with aluminum foil and bake until the vegetables are tender, about 45 minutes. Uncover and sprinkle with the cheese. Bake 10 minutes longer, until the cheese is golden brown. Serve very hot.

Wine-braised Carrots

Serve this with roast lamb or grilled lamb chops.

Makes 6 servings

1½ pounds carrots, peeled and cut on the
    diagonal into thick slices
½ small onion, minced
2 tablespoons butter, cut into 8 pieces
Salt and freshly ground black pepper to taste
1 teaspoon ground ginger
⅓ cup water
⅓ cup dry white wine
1 teaspoon chopped fresh parsley

Preheat the oven to 350°F.

Spread the carrots in a medium-size shallow baking dish. Sprinkle the onion on top. Dot with butter and season well with salt, pepper, and ginger. Pour in the water and wine. Cover with aluminum foil and bake until the carrots are very tender but not falling

apart, about 30 minutes. Remove the foil and bake 5 minutes longer until the carrots are barely golden. Serve very hot, garnished with the parsley.

Variation: Substitute 1 tablespoon minced candied ginger for the ground ginger.

All-American Grated Carrot Salad

The addition of raisins to carrot salad seems, as far as I can tell, to be strictly American. Many European countries have some version of grated carrot salad, often with a simple vinaigrette dressing. In Sweden they might add apple. The island of Mauritius, which has a large Hindu population, is home to a grated carrot salad containing thinly sliced onions and tiny fiery hot red peppers called birds' tongues, which is usually served with equally hot curries. I think this tamer American version is a good summer salad, especially as part of a cold lunch or dinner alongside cold roast meat or poultry.

Makes 6 to 8 servings

5 large carrots, peeled and grated
1 tablespoon fresh lemon juice
½ cup raisins (Muscat are fine if you like),
    plumped in boiling water to cover
    and drained
½ to ¾ cup mayonnaise, prepared or homemade
    (page 13)
Salt and freshly ground black pepper to taste
3 tablespoons chopped fresh parsley
1 head leaf lettuce
¼ cup pecan pieces, toasted (page 70)

In a large bowl, toss the carrots with the lemon juice. Stir in the raisins and mayonnaise. Season well with salt and pepper. Stir in the parsley. Serve on a bed of lettuce leaves, garnished with the pecans.

Variations: For classic French carottes rapées, eliminate the raisins and pecans, and substitute ⅓ cup of classic vinaigrette for the mayonnaise.

Or, substitute ⅓ cup dried cherries, plumped in boiling water to cover and drained, for the raisins.

Herb-glazed Carrots

This is similar to Vichy carrots but has a more robust flavor and can easily stand up to grilled red snapper or veal chops.

Makes 6 to 8 servings

2 pounds medium-size carrots, peeled and sliced,
    or baby carrots, trimmed and left whole
1 cup chicken stock
2 tablespoons butter
1 tablespoon chopped fresh parsley
1 tablespoon chopped fresh tarragon
1 tablespoon chopped fresh chives
Salt and freshly ground black pepper to taste

Combine the carrots, stock, and butter in a medium-size saucepan. Cook over medium heat until the stock is almost evaporated and the carrots are tender, 15 to 20 minutes. Stir in the herbs and season well with salt and pepper. Toss to coat the carrots with butter and herbs. Serve very hot.

Creamed Carrots and Baby Onions

An old-fashioned dish, this combination is wonderful with grilled fish or chicken.

Makes 6 to 8 servings

1 pound carrots, peeled and cut on the diagonal
    into $1/2$-inch slices
1 pint boiling onions, boiled in water to cover for
    1 minute, drained, and peeled; or 2 cups
    thawed frozen baby onions
2 cups heavy cream
Salt and freshly ground black pepper to taste
2 tablespoons snipped fresh chives

Boil the carrots and onions in salted water to cover until tender, but not mushy, about 15 minutes.

Frozen onions will take less time, 6 to 8 minutes. Drain well.

Meanwhile, in a medium-size heavy saucepan, simmer the cream over high heat until it reduces to 1 cup, 6 to 8 minutes.

In a medium-size saucepan, combine the reduced cream and the vegetables, and cook over high heat, stirring, until the cream is thick and coats the vegetables, about 5 minutes. Season well with salt and pepper. Serve very hot, garnished with the chives.

Variation: *Just before serving, add 1 cup fresh peas, boiled in salted water to cover and drained, or steamed until just tender, 8 to 10 minutes. The three-vegetable combination will easily serve eight.*

Gingered Carrot Soufflé

A very elegant way to serve carrots, this soufflé is easy to make and delicious with poached fish, especially turbot, or with paper-thin veal scaloppine.

Makes 6 to 8 servings

2 tablespoons butter, plus additional for buttering
2 tablespoons all-purpose flour
1 cup milk
1 teaspoon ground ginger
Salt and freshly ground white pepper to taste
2 cups carrots, coarsely chopped, steamed or
    boiled in salted water to cover until tender,
    drained, and pureed
3 large eggs, separated, whites beaten until stiff
3 tablespoons chopped fresh parsley

Preheat the oven to 375°F. Generously butter a $1\frac{1}{2}$-quart soufflé dish.

Melt 2 tablespoons of butter in a medium-size saucepan over medium heat. Stir in the flour and cook, stirring, for 3 minutes. Do not brown. Stir in the milk, all at once, whisking until smooth. Cook 3 minutes.

Remove the saucepan from the heat. Season with the ginger, salt, and pepper. Stir in the carrot puree. Beat in the egg yolks, one at a time. Cool slightly.

Fold in the egg whites. Fold in the chopped parsley.

Spoon the mixture into the prepared soufflé dish. Bake until puffed and golden brown on top, about 30 minutes. Serve at once.

Russian Salad

The French love this salad and it is available in every traiteur, or prepared-food shop, as well as most bistros. Often it is served as an appetizer, a small mound of it topped by half a hard-cooked egg covered with more mayonnaise. I think it is a delicious salad to serve with cold roast meats, cold poached salmon, or steamed shrimp.

Makes 6 to 8 servings

½ cup diced carrots, boiled in salted water
    to cover until tender, about 5 minutes,
    and drained
½ cup shelled peas, steamed until tender, about
    6 minutes
2 medium-size waxy white potatoes, peeled,
    cut into ¼-inch dice, and boiled in salted
    water to cover until tender, about 6 minutes,
    and drained
½ cup diced celery
½ cup diced white turnip, boiled in salted
    water to cover until tender, about 5 minutes,
    and drained
1 cup ¼-inch pieces green beans, boiled in salted
    water to cover until tender, about 3 minutes,
    and drained
2 tablespoons minced red onion
2 tablespoons fresh lemon juice
½ to ¾ cup mayonnaise, prepared or homemade
    (page 13)
1 tablespoon Dijon-style mustard
2 tablespoons heavy cream, or light sour cream
    if preferred
3 tablespoons chopped fresh parsley, plus
    additional for garnishing
Salt and freshly ground black pepper to taste
4 hard-cooked large eggs, peeled
    and quartered

Combine the vegetables in a large bowl. Toss with the lemon juice. In a medium-size bowl, beat together the mayonnaise, mustard, and cream. Stir in the parsley. Gently mix this dressing with the vegetables. Season well with salt and pepper. Refrigerate the mixture for several hours.

Serve chilled garnished with the quartered eggs and the additional parsley.

Note: *The secret to this salad is to have all the vegetables cut into uniform dice about the size of large fresh peas.*

Dilly Marinated Carrot Slices

Add these pickled carrots to any picnic or buffet table for just the right touch. They also go perfectly with cold meats, such as roast beef or ham.

Makes about 4 cups; about 8 servings as a side dish, 12 or more as relish

2 cloves garlic, halved and thinly sliced
¾ cup olive oil
1 tablespoon Dijon-style mustard
¼ cup white wine vinegar
2 tablespoons chopped fresh parsley
¼ cup chopped fresh dill, plus sprigs
    for garnishing
1 pound carrots, peeled, cut on the diagonal
    into ½-inch slices, steamed or boiled in
    salted water to cover until crisply tender,
    and drained
Salt and freshly ground black pepper to taste

In a medium-size bowl, stir together the garlic, olive oil, mustard, vinegar, parsley, and chopped dill.

Put the hot carrots in a medium-size bowl. Pour the dressing over the carrots. Season with salt and pepper. Add the dill sprigs. Cover and marinate, refrigerated, at least 24 hours, turning occasionally. Serve cold, or at room temperature.

Gingered Carrot Puree

Even recalcitrant children love this puree, and it is sophisticated enough to serve with poached fillets of sole or other delicate fish.

Makes 6 to 8 servings

1½ pounds carrots, peeled and cut into chunks
¾ cup well-seasoned chicken stock
2 tablespoons grated fresh ginger
2 tablespoons butter
2 tablespoons heavy cream
Salt and freshly ground white pepper to taste

In a large covered saucepan, simmer the carrots in the stock over medium heat until tender, 20 to 25 minutes; drain, reserving the stock. Puree the carrots in a food processor or blender, adding a little of the reserved stock if the puree is too thick. Beat in the ginger, butter, and cream, and season well with salt and pepper.

Return the puree to the saucepan and cook, stirring, over low heat to dry it out, but be careful not to burn it. The puree should be thick enough to mound up in the spoon and not weep on the plate. Serve hot. Garnish with a grind of pepper.

Carrot Pancakes with Dill and Parsley

These crisp little cakes go well with almost anything but are great with wine-baked chicken breasts.

Makes 6 servings

2 cups grated carrots
½ small onion, thinly sliced
⅓ cup chopped fresh parsley
3 tablespoons snipped fresh chives
¼ cup plain dried bread crumbs
1 large egg, beaten
¼ cup milk

Salt and freshly ground black pepper to taste
Butter
Sour cream, regular or light

In a medium-size bowl, stir together the carrots, onion, parsley, chives, bread crumbs, egg, and milk. Season very well with salt and pepper.

Heat 1 tablespoon of butter in a large heavy skillet or a large griddle over medium-high heat. Drop the carrot mixture by large tablespoonfuls into the heated skillet, spacing well apart. Flatten slightly with a wide spatula. Fry the cakes until golden on the bottom, 3 to 4 minutes. Turn and brown the second side, about 2 minutes. They should be crisp on the outside, soft inside. Remove the cakes, drain on paper towels, and keep warm. Repeat with the remaining mixture, adding more butter as needed. Serve very hot with the sour cream on the side.

Note: *If you prefer very crisp cakes, use the spatula to flatten the carrot mixture into very thin rounds in the hot skillet.*

Roasted Carrots, Parsnips, and Scallions

Roasting brings out the innate sweetness of these root vegetables. Put them together with a good roast beef or serve them alongside grilled chops—lamb, pork, or veal.

Makes 6 to 8 servings

1 pound baby carrots, trimmed
1 pound smallest early parsnips, peeled, halved
    lengthwise, cored if tough, and cut into
    4-inch lengths
1 tablespoon olive oil
Seasoned pepper, such as Mrs. Dash, to taste
2 bunches (12 to 16) green onions (scallions),
    cut into 6-inch lengths and steamed
    5 minutes

Salt to taste
1 tablespoon chopped fresh parsley

Preheat the oven to 375°F.

In a large bowl, toss the carrots and parsnips with the oil. Transfer the vegetables to a shallow roasting pan large enough to hold the vegetables in a single layer, leaving any excess oil in the bowl. Arrange the vegetables in one layer. Season them with pepper. Roast, turning once or twice, for 30 minutes. Toss the green onions in the remaining oil and add to the roasting pan. Roast until all the vegetables are well browned, 15 to 20 minutes longer. Season with salt. Serve very hot, garnished with the parsley.

Cauliflower

The original "cabbage flower" was probably developed in Asia and could be almost as old as its relative the green cabbage. It seems to have made its way west with the help of sea and land traders, until it arrived in modern Europe sometime in the sixteenth century. There are sources, however, that believe the ancient Romans knew cauliflower, and it has definitely been very popular in Italy in more recent times.

Cauliflower is a "blanched vegetable," one that is covered to guard it from the sun and keep it from making chlorophyll, thus maintaining a milky white color. Modern varieties are self-blanching, meaning that the leaves fold naturally over the developing flower, or curd. Old-time farmers often had to tie the leaves over the immature curd to keep out the sun.

Today's cauliflower can be white, light green (almost chartreuse), or purple. The green variety is actually a hybrid of cauliflower and broccoli and is available in some markets under the name "broccoflower." This variety is not blanched and is easier to cultivate. It is less aggressive in flavor and has a tendency to cook more quickly than the white. The purple head is delicious in crudité platters, salads, bagna cauda, or other recipes in which it will be used raw, since the purple color disappears if it is cooked, and the flowerets turn dark green.

This is one of those vegetables that has been in American markets only about a hundred years. For some it is an acquired taste, one that becomes palatable only if it is masked with a sauce, most commonly cheese. You rarely see a whole boiled or steamed curd anymore. They were popular twenty-five years ago, especially when topped with buttered bread crumbs or a brown butter sauce. A whole cooked cauliflower is still an impressive presentation.

106

Cauliflower is a member of the cruciferous family, and it offers several health benefits. Low in sodium and calories, cauliflower contains large amounts of vitamin C and potassium. It is also a good source of absorbable calcium and can bolster the calcium intake of people who avoid dairy products.

Selection: Choose the heaviest most compact heads available with very tightly spaced, snow white flowerets. The curd should not show any signs of brown or yellow. Avoid any curds that are cream colored or have the grainy texture of rice. The surrounding leaves should be bright light green, not wilted. Examine the stem end of the head for any signs of mold or decay.

If you are buying cauliflower that has already been trimmed and separated into flowerets, look for those that are the whitest possible and do not have any moisture on the inside of the bag. Cauliflower is so easy to prepare, though, that I would buy a whole head unless you want only a small amount.

A medium-size head of cauliflower— 2½ to 3 pounds—will serve six to eight people when it is cooked. One head, separated into flowerets and served raw, will feed eight to ten, or more.

Storage and Preparation: A very fresh head of cauliflower should be left unwashed, loosely wrapped or enclosed in a perforated vegetable bag and can be stored in the refrigerator vegetable drawer for three or four days. Prepared flowerets, again unwashed to prevent mold, can be enclosed in a perforated vegetable bag for a day or two.

To prepare a whole head, turn it upside down and, with a sharp knife, remove much of the heavy core. Leave just enough to hold the curd together. Remove any little leaves from around and in between the flowerets. Rinse well and turn cut side down to drain. The core can be sliced or cut into matchstick strips and combined with broccoli stems cut into coins, strips of carrot, and sliced onions, served either raw in a vinaigrette or mayonnaise dressing, or simmered 5 to 6 minutes, drained, and tossed in an aromatic butter sauce.

To prepare flowerets, remove the core, and with a sharp knife cut the curd into small flowerets, following the stems in the head. If the flowerets are to be cooked, try to make them all about the same size so they will cook evenly. Rinse them well and drain. If serving raw, I suggest drying them in a kitchen towel before arranging them on the crudité platter or in the salad bowl.

No matter how you serve cauliflower, whole head or in flowerets, it is important not to overcook it. Long cooking intensifies the flavor and can make it very unpleasant. Cooked cauliflower should be eaten as soon as it is crisply tender, or as soon as the dish is removed from the oven. Day-old cauliflower not only leaves an odor in the refrigerator but can taste obnoxiously strong. Quick cooking also lessens the chance that the whole house will smell like cauliflower. Some old-time cooks used to cook a piece of bread with the cauliflower to eliminate the odor, but I find odor isn't much of a problem if the cooking time is short.

Steamed Cauliflower

Steam a whole cauliflower head, cored, in a steamer basket or a colander, covered, over simmering water for 20 to 25 minutes, depending on the size and age of the head. Flowerets will take 5 to 6 minutes.

Boiled Cauliflower

Although very few people boil a whole head of cauliflower these days, it is still an impressive way to serve it. Place a whole head, cored, in a kettle, cover with water, and lightly salt. To preserve the white color, add $\frac{1}{4}$ cup milk or 2 tablespoons lemon juice or vinegar to the water. Bring to a boil and simmer over medium heat until the core is just tender when pierced with a fork, 15 to 18 minutes. Drain and serve on a heated platter topped with buttered bread crumbs, browned butter with 1 tablespoon lemon juice added, or with a cheese sauce. Blue cheese is very good with cauliflower. Flowerets can be prepared in the same manner, but should be simmered for only about 5 minutes to avoid overcooking.

Microwaved Cauliflower

Place a whole cauliflower head, cored, in a microwave dish. Pour in $\frac{1}{4}$ cup water. Cover loosely with plastic microwave wrap, vent, and microwave on high about 10 minutes, turning once about halfway through. (I usually put the head core side up for 5 minutes, vent, open, and turn the head over so the core is down for the last 5 minutes.) Let stand 4 or 5 minutes before serving.

Flowerets should be arranged in a microwave dish with 2 tablespoons water. Cover with plastic microwave wrap and vent. Microwave on high for 5 to 6 minutes, vent, and continue with the recipe or serve, tossed in a little butter or olive oil.

Fried Cauliflower with Hot Pepper Mayonnaise

Almost like snacking on popcorn, it is difficult to eat just a few pieces of this. An appetizer on its own, I think it is also a nice side dish with veal or pork cutlets.

Makes 6 to 8 servings

Hot Pepper Mayonnaise

$\frac{1}{2}$ cup mayonnaise, prepared or homemade (page 13)
$\frac{1}{4}$ teaspoon crushed red pepper
3 large green onions (scallions), white and light green parts only, thinly sliced
2 tablespoons chopped fresh cilantro
Hot pepper sauce to taste

Beer Batter (page 17) (see Note)
Oil for deep-frying
1 medium-size head cauliflower or broccoflower, cored, separated into flowerets, and steamed until tender, and patted dry with paper towels
Salt

To make the hot pepper mayonnaise, in a small bowl, beat together the mayonnaise, crushed red pepper, and green onions. Stir in the cilantro and hot pepper sauce. Refrigerate 1 hour or longer to blend the flavors. Serve cool, but not chilled.

In a deep-fat fryer or deep heavy skillet, heat the oil to 370°F. Whisk the beer batter until frothy. Dredge the cauliflower flowerets in the batter. Drop them one by one into the hot fat. Fry in batches until golden brown, about 2 minutes per batch. Remove with a slotted spoon and drain on paper towels. Dust lightly with salt. Serve hot with the hot pepper mayonnaise for dipping.

Variation: *Substitute a pinch ground red (cayenne) pepper for the freshly ground black pepper for Beer Batter in this recipe.*

Note: *If it is necessary to fry them in batches, keep the fritters hot in a 300°F. oven until all are fried.*

Curried Cauliflower and Broccoli

I think this fragrant dish goes very well with lamb—grilled, roasted, or braised.

Makes 6 to 8 servings

4 tablespoons olive oil
2 medium-size onions, cut stem to root into
      thin wedges
1 tablespoon grated fresh ginger
2 cloves garlic, minced
1 tablespoon hot curry powder, or more to taste
1 teaspoon ground cumin
Salt to taste
1/4 teaspoon crushed red pepper
2 cups cauliflower flowerets
2 cups broccoli flowerets
1 large Russet potato, unpeeled, cut into
      1-inch cubes
1/2 cup chicken stock, or water
1 tablespoon chopped fresh parsley (optional)

Heat 2 tablespoons of the olive oil in a medium-size heavy skillet over medium-high heat. Cook the onions, stirring occasionally, until golden, about 15 minutes. Stir in the ginger, garlic, curry powder, and cumin. Cook over medium heat, stirring, until the spices begin to give off their fragrance, about 2 minutes. Season the mixture well with salt and

the crushed red pepper. Remove the skillet from the heat and keep warm.

Heat the remaining oil in another large heavy skillet over medium heat. Add the cauliflower, broccoli, and potato, and cook, stirring or tossing often, for about 5 minutes. Add the stock. Cover and simmer over low heat until the potatoes are tender, 5 to 6 minutes longer. Remove the cover and increase the heat to high. Cook until most of the liquid is evaporated, about 2 minutes. Stir in the onion mixture and heat through. Serve alongside hot steamed rice.

Cauliflower à la Grecque

This same method can be used to prepare button mushrooms or baby carrots. Serve as part of a cold buffet spread.

Makes 6 to 8 servings

1 cup dry white wine
1/4 cup fresh lemon juice
1 tablespoon chopped fresh thyme,
      or 1 teaspoon dried
1 bay leaf
1/2 teaspoon coriander seeds, crushed
1/2 teaspoon black peppercorns
1/3 cup olive oil
Salt and freshly ground black pepper to taste
1/2 cup water, or well-flavored chicken stock
1 medium-size whole cauliflower, cored,
      separated into flowerets, steamed or
      boiled in salted water to cover until
      just tender, and drained
2 tablespoons chopped fresh parsley

In a medium-size saucepan, combine all the ingredients, except the cauliflower and parsley. Boil over medium heat for 10 minutes.

Place the cauliflower in a medium-size nonreactive heatproof bowl. Pour the hot wine mixture over the cauliflower and let stand until cool. Cover and refrigerate several hours or up to two days.

To serve, bring the cauliflower to room temperature. Garnish with the parsley.

Italian Cauliflower Sauté

Olive oil, garlic, and parsley raise plain cauliflower to a higher plane. Serve it with grilled veal chops or scaloppine or grilled red snapper.

Makes 4 to 6 servings

2 tablespoons olive oil
2 cloves garlic, minced
3 tablespoons chopped fresh parsley
1 small head cauliflower, cored, separated into
    flowerets, boiled in salted water to cover
    until just tender, 4 to 5 minutes, and drained
½ large ripe tomato, halved, seeded, and chopped
¼ cup dry white wine
Salt and freshly ground black pepper to taste
¼ cup freshly grated Parmesan cheese

Heat the oil in a large heavy skillet over medium heat. Cook the garlic and parsley, stirring, being careful not to burn the garlic, for 1 minute. Add the cauliflower and cook, tossing or stirring, until beginning to turn golden, 3 to 4 minutes. Stir in the tomato and wine and season with salt and pepper. Cook, tossing, 2 minutes longer. Serve very hot, garnished with the cheese.

Roquefort Cauliflower Bake

The rich, salty taste of Roquefort cheese makes this dish a great accompaniment for the perfectly grilled steak or for a very crisp roast duck.

Makes 6 to 8 servings

4 tablespoons (½ stick) butter, plus more for
    greasing casserole
2 tablespoons all-purpose flour
Salt and freshly ground black pepper to taste
1½ cups milk, hot
4 ounces Roquefort cheese, or Maytag blue
    cheese, crumbled (1 cup)

2 large leeks, white and light green parts only,
    thinly sliced and steamed until very tender
2 small heads cauliflower, cored, separated into
    flowerets, and steamed until just tender
5 tablespoons plain dried bread crumbs

Preheat the oven to 400°F. Lightly grease a shallow 2-quart ovenproof casserole.

Melt 2 tablespoons of the butter in a medium-size saucepan over low heat. Add the flour and cook, stirring, for 3 minutes. Do not brown. Season well with salt and pepper. Whisk in the hot milk, all at once. Simmer over low heat, stirring occasionally, until the mixture is thick, about 3 minutes. Add the cheese and stir until it is melted. Stir in the leeks, then the cauliflower, and spoon this mixture into the prepared casserole.

Melt the remaining 2 tablespoons of butter in a small saucepan over medium heat. Remove the pan from the heat and stir in the bread crumbs. Spoon this mixture evenly over the cauliflower. Bake until bubbling and the crumbs are well browned, about 20 minutes. Serve hot.

Cauliflower Sauté with Broccoli and Mushrooms

I like to serve this with any roast meat, but it is also delicious with broiled swordfish or tuna. Any fresh mushrooms will do here, but this is much better with shiitake or other full-flavored mushrooms.

Makes 6 servings

2 tablespoons olive oil
1 tablespoon butter
½ pound full-flavored mushrooms, stems
    trimmed, halved
½ small head cauliflower, cored and separated
    into flowerets, boiled in salted water to cover
    until crisply tender, and drained
1 pound broccoli, stemmed, head separated into
    flowerets, boiled in salted water to cover
    until crisply tender, and drained

1 tablespoon soy sauce
¼ cup dry white wine
Freshly ground black pepper to taste
2 to 3 tablespoons chopped fresh parsley

Heat the oil and butter in a large heavy sauté pan or skillet over high heat. Add the mushrooms and cook, stirring occasionally, until the moisture evaporates and the mushrooms begin to turn golden, about 5 minutes. Add the cauliflower and broccoli and cook, tossing, until the vegetables are tender, about 3 minutes.

Stir in the soy sauce and wine and season well with pepper. Cook 30 seconds. Serve very hot, garnished with the parsley.

Cauliflower Flan with Cheddar Pepper Sauce

If cauliflower is ever a company dish, this preparation qualifies. Serve it with Cajun grilled or blackened fish for a delightful combination.

Makes 6 servings

2 tablespoons butter, plus additional for buttering
Plain dried bread crumbs
½ medium-size head cauliflower, cored, separated into tiny flowerets, boiled in salted water to cover until very tender, and drained
Salt and freshly ground black pepper to taste
Pinch ground red (cayenne) pepper
3 large eggs, beaten
1 cup milk, hot
½ cup fresh bread crumbs
Cheddar Pepper Sauce (recipe follows)

Preheat the oven to 375°F. Generously butter an 8-inch flan mold or round cake pan. Coat with the dried bread crumbs, knocking out any excess.

Toss the cauliflower with 2 tablespoons of the butter. Season well with salt, black pepper, and red pepper. In a large bowl, beat together the eggs, milk, and fresh bread crumbs. Stir in the cauliflower. Pour the mixture into the prepared mold.

Place the mold in a larger shallow baking pan and pour in boiling water to reach about halfway up the mold. Bake until the center is set, about 30 minutes. Remove the mold from the water bath and unmold onto a heated serving platter. Serve with the cheddar pepper sauce.

Variation: *Substitute an equal amount of broccoli for the cauliflower.*

Cheddar Pepper Sauce

Makes about 1 cup

1 tablespoon olive oil
One 6-ounce can chopped green chiles
1 jalapeño pepper, seeded and minced
½ medium-size onion, very thinly sliced
1 clove garlic, minced
2 tablespoons dry white wine
Hot pepper sauce to taste
8 ounces mild Cheddar cheese, grated (2 cups); or 8 ounces processed pasteurized cheese, such as Velveeta, cubed

Preheat the oven to 325°F.

In a small saucepan, heat the olive oil over low heat. Stir in the chiles, jalapeño pepper, onion, garlic, and wine. Cover and cook, stirring from time to time, over very low heat until soft, about 20 minutes. Stir in the hot pepper sauce.

Spoon the pepper mixture into a small deep ovenproof casserole. Spread the cheese on top. Bake the casserole until the cheese is melted and the mixture is bubbling, about 20 minutes. Stir to combine peppers and cheese. Spoon over the Cauliflower Flan, or serve with crisp tortilla chips.

Note: *A faster version of this sauce can be made by spooning the cooked-pepper mixture into a small microwave dish. Add the pasteurized cheese cubes (grated Cheddar doesn't melt very well in the microwave), and microwave on high for 4 minutes. Remove from the microwave and stir well before proceeding.*

Cauliflower Vegetable Fritters

This is an excellent way to use leftover vegetables. I like to spoon a little mustard mayonnaise sauce on top and serve the fritters as an appetizer or put them alongside grilled chicken breasts.

Makes 6 to 8 servings

Mustard Mayonnaise Sauce

½ cup mayonnaise, prepared or homemade
  (page 13)
¼ cup sour cream, regular or light
2 tablespoons Dijon-style mustard
1 tablespoon fresh lemon juice

Fritters

1 cup cooked cauliflower flowerets, mashed
1 cup cooked mashed potatoes
1 cup cooked chopped carrots, mashed
2 tablespoons minced onion
1 clove garlic, minced (optional but
  recommended)
2 large eggs, beaten
¼ cup all-purpose flour
½ teaspoon baking powder
¼ cup chopped fresh parsley
Salt and freshly ground black pepper to taste
Oil for deep-frying

To make the mustard mayonnaise sauce, in a small bowl beat together the mayonnaise, sour cream, mustard, and lemon juice. Refrigerate several hours.

In a large bowl, combine the mashed cauliflower, potatoes, and carrots. Stir in the onion and garlic. Beat in the eggs and then the flour that has been mixed with the baking powder. Stir in the parsley. Season well with salt and pepper.

In a deep-fat fryer or deep heavy skillet, heat the oil to 375°F.

Drop the vegetable mixture by tablespoonfuls into the hot fat. Fry in batches until golden brown, about 2 minutes per batch. Remove with a slotted spoon and drain on paper towels. Dust lightly with salt. Serve very hot, garnished with a little of the mustard mayonnaise sauce. Pass the remaining mustard mayonnaise sauce separately.

Note: *If it is necessary to fry in batches, keep warm in a 300°F. oven until all are fried. Serve at once.*

Quick Italian-style Cauliflower

This homey version of Italian-style cauliflower is delicious with grilled chicken.

Makes 4 to 6 servings

¼ cup olive oil
1 clove garlic, minced
3 tablespoons chopped fresh parsley
1 tablespoon balsamic vinegar
Salt and freshly ground black pepper to taste
1 small head cauliflower, cored, separated into
  flowerets, steamed or boiled in salted water
  to cover until just tender, 5 to 6 minutes,
  drained, and kept warm in a deep heated
  serving dish
Freshly grated Parmesan cheese

Heat the oil in a small saucepan over low heat. Cook the garlic, stirring, for 1 minute. Do not let it burn. Stir in the parsley and vinegar. Season well with salt and pepper. Heat through. Pour the hot sauce over the cauliflower. Toss to coat all the flowerets. Serve immediately, lightly dusted with the cheese.

Celeriac
(Celery Root)

If you have never tried this European favorite vegetable, you are in for a treat. Winter menus in France, Italy, and Holland—as well as in some parts of Switzerland and Germany—feature salads, soups, purees, and other dishes made from this crisp refreshing root. The flavor is much like branch celery, which is reasonable since they are members of the same family.

The large, rounded root is just about the same size as a grapefruit. Outwardly it can somewhat resemble a jicama, but the inside is distinctly flavorful.

While every bistro and traiteur (prepared-food shop) as well as many upscale restaurants in France serve celeriac as céleri rémoulade (crisp matchsticks of celeriac in a mustardy mayonnaise dressing), this versatile vegetable deserves to be presented in other ways. Added to soups and stews, purees and sautés, it give a definite celery taste with a smooth, rich texture. It also blends

beautifully with other vegetables such as carrots and potatoes.

Celeriac is low in calories and high in vitamin C and potassium.

Selection: Modern varieties of celeriac are usually firm and crisp inside, without the woody pith of earlier ones. Choose the heaviest, plumpest roots in the market. While they are almost always sold without the tops, if you find them with tops attached, choose one that has fresh, crisp leaves that have not begun to yellow and turn limp. Avoid any roots that have soft spots; show any signs of mold; or have damp, slippery patches that might indicate poor storage and decay. Watch out for knife or spade cuts in the skin. There are natural folds in the exterior of celeriac, but they are not breaks in the skin, which can cause interior decay. Look for roots that are 3 to 4 inches in diameter. Larger ones can be less tender.

Celeriac is at its best in the fall, but I have often found it in the market up until Easter.

You will need about ¼ pound of prepared celeriac per person. Because there is abundant waste in preparation, add about 25 percent more to the total weight. If you are serving six, count on nearly 2 pounds of celeriac.

Storage and Preparation: When you find fresh celeriac, prepare it as soon as possible. If you must store it for several days, keep the root, uncovered, in the vegetable bin of the refrigerator. Avoid putting it in a plastic bag.

Because celeriac has a very knobby, rough exterior, it must be peeled deep. First scrub the roots well, paying attention to the dents and folds. Once cut, celeriac tends to turn a rusty brown if not placed in acidulated water (water to which vinegar or lemon juice has been added—see page 59). As with cabbage, use a stainless-steel knife to avoid discoloration.

The easiest way to peel celeriac is the same way you would peel a grapefruit using a knife. Cut a slice off the top and the bottom, then cut off strips from the top to the bottom, turning the root after each strip. This allows you to cut deeply enough to remove any folds of the skin.

If using for a salad, slice the peeled root into ¼-inch slices and then cut into thin matchstick strips or grate the root into acidulated water. When preparing for use in purees, soups, or stews, slice the peeled root into ½- to 1-inch slices and then cut into dice. Drop into acidulated water or toss with 2 tablespoons lemon juice and then proceed with the recipe.

Braised or Parboiled Celeriac

To braise, place diced or sliced celeriac in a heavy saucepan or skillet. Add about ¼ inch water or chicken stock to the pan. Cover and simmer over low heat until the celeriac is tender, 15 to 20 minutes. Test with the point of a knife. Drain and serve with butter, salt, pepper, and a dusting of chopped fresh parsley.

To parboil, place diced or sliced celeriac in a heavy saucepan. Add 2 tablespoons lemon juice and enough water to cover the vegetable. Cover loosely and bring to a boil over medium heat. Reduce the heat to low and simmer 3 to 5 minutes. Drain and continue with the recipe.

Two-Celery Puree

Combine the flavors of both stalk celery and celery root for a delicious puree that fits especially well into game menus. I like it with venison, duck, and pheasant. Out of game season, serve this with lamb chops or roast rack of lamb.

Makes 6 to 8 servings

1 small celeriac, peeled and cut into large dice
1 tablespoon fresh lemon juice
6 ribs celery, strung and coarsely chopped
1 cup chicken stock
1 large Russet potato, peeled and cut into large dice
2 to 3 tablespoons butter
¼ cup heavy cream, or more to taste
Salt and freshly ground white pepper to taste
Chopped fresh parsley

In a medium-size saucepan, boil the celeriac in salted water to cover and the lemon juice over medium heat, until very tender, about 15 minutes. Drain and put it through a ricer.

In a medium-size saucepan, cook the chopped celery in the stock over low heat until tender, 10 to 15 minutes. Drain well and puree in a blender or food processor. Pour the puree into a colander or sieve and allow it to drain for 10 minutes.

Simmer the potato in salted water to cover over medium-low heat until very tender, about 15 minutes. Drain well and put the potatoes through a ricer.

Combine the three purees in a large heavy saucepan. Beat in the butter and the cream. Cook over low heat until very thick and creamy. Season very well with salt and pepper. If the puree becomes too stiff, add more cream, 1 teaspoon at a time, until the consistency is like creamy mashed potatoes, it should not weep on the plate. Serve very hot, garnished with the parsley.

Celeriac Hash Browns

The fresh celery taste makes these hash browns a great addition to any hearty breakfast, but I also serve them with grilled turkey burgers for a rustic busy-night supper.

Makes 6 servings

1 large celeriac, peeled and cut into ½-inch cubes
2 tablespoons fresh lemon juice
3 tablespoons olive oil
1 large onion, halved and thinly sliced
½ small green bell pepper, thinly sliced or minced (optional)
2 large Russet potatoes, peeled, cut into ½-inch cubes, boiled in salted water to cover until just tender, about 12 to 15 minutes, and drained
Salt and freshly ground black pepper to taste
1 tablespoon chopped fresh parsley

In a medium-size saucepan over low heat, simmer the celeriac in salted water to cover with the lemon juice until just tender enough to pierce with a fork, about 10 minutes. Drain well.

Heat the oil in a large heavy skillet over medium heat. Stir in the onion and, if using, the bell pepper and cook, stirring, for 2 minutes. Stir in the drained celeriac and potatoes. Season well with salt and pepper. Fry over medium heat, turning frequently with a spatula, until well browned and crisp, 15 to 20 minutes. Do not burn. Serve very hot garnished with the parsley.

Classic Céleri Rémoulade

In France every bistro worth its salt serves this simple dish as an appetizer. It is so popular that some version is sold in every traiteur, or prepared-food shop, and can even be bought in jars, in supermarkets, and at take-away salad bars. Serve it as part of an appetizer plate, along with carrot salad, vinegared cucumber salad, vinegared beets, etc. It also goes very well with cold roast meats such as chicken, veal, and lamb.

Makes 6 to 8 servings

1 large celeriac, peeled, sliced thin, cut into matchstick strips or shredded
2 tablespoons fresh lemon juice
1 cup mayonnaise, prepared or homemade (page 13)
2 tablespoons Dijon-style mustard
Salt and freshly ground black pepper
1 tablespoon chopped fresh parsley

In a large nonreactive bowl, quickly toss the celeriac with the lemon juice. In a smaller bowl, combine the mayonnaise and mustard. Toss this dressing with the celeriac. Season well with salt and pepper.

Chill the salad, covered, for at least 1 hour. Serve garnished with the parsley.

Variations: *Add 1 small garlic clove, minced, to the shredded celeriac before tossing with the lemon juice, then chill the salad overnight. I also like to add about 3 tablespoons of finely chopped fresh parsley to the salad to give it a little color. Garnish at serving time with a little more chopped parsley.*

Glazed Celeriac

This is wonderful with grilled grouper or chicken breasts.

Makes 6 servings

2 tablespoons butter
2 medium-size or 1 large celeriac, peeled,
    sliced, cut into matchstick strips, boiled
    in acidulated, salted water (water to which
    2 tablespoons lemon juice has been added)
    to cover for 3 to 4 minutes, and drained
1 teaspoon sugar
Salt and freshly ground black pepper to taste
1 teaspoon dried Italian herbs, such as oregano,
    marjoram, rosemary, and thyme, or a pre-
    pared mix; or 1 tablespoon chopped fresh
    tarragon
1/4 cup heavy cream
1 tablespoon chopped fresh parsley

Melt the butter in a large heavy skillet over medium
heat. Stir in the celeriac and sugar. Toss to coat the
celeriac with the butter. Cover and cook over low
heat until tender, about 10 minutes. Season well with
salt, pepper, and herbs. Pour in the cream, raise the
heat to medium and cook, tossing, for 2 to 3 minutes
longer. The sauce should coat the vegetable. Serve
very hot, garnished with the parsley.

Variation: *Add 1 large carrot, peeled and cut into
2 1/2-inch matchstick strips, to the boiled and drained
celeriac. Continue with the recipe. Increase the heavy
cream by 1 to 2 tablespoons.*

Louisiana-style Céleri Rémoulade

*I love this Creole version of the classic French salad. It
has enough character to stand alongside spicy fillets of
Cajun grilled catfish.*

Makes 6 to 8 servings

1 large celeriac, peeled, thinly sliced, and cut into
    matchstick strips or shredded
2 tablespoons fresh lemon juice
2 tablespoons capers, drained and chopped
2 hard-cooked eggs, peeled and chopped
    (optional)
1 teaspoon chopped fresh tarragon
1 tablespoon chopped fresh chervil
1 tablespoon snipped fresh chives
1/4 cup chopped fresh parsley, or fresh cilantro,
    plus 1 tablespoon for garnishing
1 tablespoon Dijon-style mustard
1 1/2 cups mayonnaise, prepared or homemade
    (page 13)
Salt and freshly ground black pepper to taste
Hot pepper sauce to taste (optional)

In a medium-size nonreactive bowl, toss the celeriac
with the lemon juice.

In a small bowl, beat together the remaining
ingredients, seasoning well with salt, pepper, and
hot pepper sauce. Stir enough of this sauce into the
celeriac to make a creamy salad, about the same
consistency as coleslaw. Taste and season again with
salt and pepper if needed. Chill several hours. Serve
cold, garnished with the parsley. Pass any remaining
sauce in a separate dish.

Variation: *For a different salad and flavor, stir in 2 teaspoons sweet Hungarian paprika.*

Gratin of Celeriac and Potatoes

*There is almost nothing better with a grilled steak than
this home-style gratin.*

Makes 6 to 8 servings

1 large celeriac peeled and thinly sliced
1 tablespoon fresh lemon juice
Salt and freshly ground black pepper to taste
2 tablespoons butter, plus additional for buttering
4 ounces Gruyère cheese, grated (1 cup)

2 large Russet potatoes, unpeeled, thinly sliced, boiled in salted water to cover until tender, and drained

1 cup heavy cream

$\frac{1}{2}$ cup plain dried bread crumbs

Preheat the oven to 375°F. Generously butter a medium-size gratin dish.

In a large saucepan, toss the celeriac with the lemon juice, add salted water to just cover. Simmer over low heat until just tender, 5 to 6 minutes. Drain.

In the prepared dish, make a layer of half of the celeriac. Dot with $\frac{1}{2}$ tablespoon of the butter. Sprinkle with $\frac{1}{4}$ cup of the cheese and season with salt and pepper. Top with half of the potatoes, dot with $\frac{1}{2}$ tablespoon more butter, sprinkle with $\frac{1}{4}$ cup cheese, and season with salt and pepper. Repeat the layers. Pour in the cream and spread the bread crumbs on top.

Bake in the preheated oven until bubbling hot and golden brown, about 30 minutes. Serve very hot.

Celery

The sixteenth century in Europe was a time of great advances in agriculture. Many hitherto wild vegetables were developed for cultivation, and vegetables known in other parts of the world were introduced to the European market. Bunch celery was one of the wild varieties first brought into cultivation around that time, even though the Romans had enjoyed its wild ancestor. Many experiments later we have the large bunching heads of several kinds of crisp celery, ranging in color from milky white to dark green. All of the varieties grown in America are referred to as Pascal.

Some of the very dark green celery on the market can be somewhat bitter and stringier than the lighter varieties. Some modern dark green celery, however, is just as sweet as the whiter or light green varieties. Often it is just chance that determines what you find at the market.

There is some confusion about how to refer to celery. The head, or bunch, is really called a stalk. Individual stems are called ribs. In this book, I always use the word *rib* to mean an individual stem, including in some cases the leaves at the top.

Celery hearts are the smallest, center-most, lightest-color ribs in each stalk. You can make true celery hearts by breaking off the darker outer ribs of each stalk, trimming the base to remove the tough stem, and cutting off the tops. Supermarkets often sell plastic packages containing 2 or 3 celery "hearts," but these are generally simply whole stalks that have been trimmed of most of their leaves.

The whole stalk is usable. Even tough, stringy outer ribs can be cut up and added to stocks. The leaves are wonderful in soups and stews. In fact, celery leaves can be dried for several hours in a 200°F. oven, cooled, and crumbled. Store them in a glass jar with a tight-fitting lid and add them to soups, stews, sauces, and salads for a delicious celery flavor. To microwave, put a single layer of washed and dried celery leaves on a double layer of paper towels and microwave on high for 2 minutes.

Raw celery is a delicious ingredient in many salads and makes a wonderful addition to a crudité platter. The ribs can be stuffed with cheese or other fillings, including peanut butter, for snacks or cocktail party nibbles.

Because celery has a very high water content, it is extremely low in calories. For this reason celery sticks are usually a large part of a dieter's snack time fare. The crunchy texture is very satisfying. Braised celery is also a delicious low-fat, low-calorie vegetable. Celery contains folic acid and some vitamin C.

Selection: The stalk should be crisp and tight, with bright light green leaves that are not at all yellowed or limp. Avoid any stalks that have browned spots, cracked ribs, or brown slippery leaves. If there is a choice between stalks with light green and dark green ribs, I would generally choose the lightest ones. While some dark green varieties are sweet, usually the older, more developed stalks have more fibers and can sometimes be unpleasantly bitter.

Most of the celery sold in America is grown in California, and is available year round. Its fresh taste and crunchy texture make it a welcome addition to monotonous winter menus.

When cooking celery as a vegetable on its own, count on about ¼ pound raw per person.

Storage and Preparation: Fresh, crisp celery stalks will keep in the refrigerator up to two weeks. I like to store them in perforated vegetable bags. Limp celery can sometimes be made crisp again by soaking the ribs in ice water for about 30 minutes.

To prepare celery, wash very well, trim the end of the stalk, remove the ribs and cut into desired lengths. If eating it raw, keep the celery covered in the refrigerator until ready to serve.

Braised or Boiled Celery

Arrange the prepared celery in a heavy skillet or kettle. Pour in water or chicken stock—mixed with about ¼ cup white wine, if desired—to a depth of about ½ inch. Bring to a boil over medium heat. Cover, reduce the heat to medium-low, and simmer until tender when pierced with the point of a sharp knife, 10 to 15 minutes. Drain. Season and serve.

Steamed Celery

Steaming preserves most of the delicate celery taste. Arrange cut-up celery in a steamer basket or colander over simmering water. Cover loosely and steam until the pieces are tender when pierced with the point of a sharp knife, 10 to 15 minutes. Serve very hot, or continue with the recipe.

Microwaved Celery

Arrange about 1 pound of cut-up celery in one layer in a microwave dish. Add ¼ cup water and cover with plastic microwave wrap. Vent. Microwave on high for 10 minutes. Let stand 3 to 4 minutes, open, and serve.

Fresh Celery and Tomato Casserole

Good recipes for cooked celery are hard to come by. This fresh-tasting combination makes a welcome addition to any summer cookout. It goes especially well with grilled fish or shellfish, and complements roast or grilled lamb almost as well as a ratatouille.

Makes 6 to 8 servings

1 whole stalk celery, separated into ribs, trimmed, and cut into 3-inch pieces including any leaves
2 large ripe tomatoes, seeded and cut into large dice
1 clove garlic, minced
1 large onion, halved and sliced
1 green bell pepper, seeded and cut into ½-inch pieces
½ cup well-flavored chicken stock
¼ cup dry white wine
Salt and freshly ground black pepper to taste
1 tablespoon chopped fresh thyme, or 1 teaspoon dried
Pinch ground red (cayenne) pepper

Preheat the oven to 375°F.

Arrange the celery in the bottom of a 2-quart ovenproof casserole. Top with the tomatoes. Sprinkle with the garlic. Add the onion and bell pepper. Pour in the stock and wine. Season well with the salt, black pepper, and thyme. Sprinkle with the red pepper. Cover and bake for 30 minutes. Uncover the casserole, stir the vegetables gently, and bake until much of the liquid is evaporated, about 15 minutes longer. Serve very hot.

Cheesy Baked Celery

I like to serve this with veal, especially thick grilled chops topped with a garnish of chopped tomato, green onion, and lettuce.

Makes 6 servings

1 stalk celery, separated into ribs, trimmed, and cut into ½-inch slices
1 cup water
Salt and freshly ground black pepper to taste
½ cup heavy cream
½ cup freshly grated Parmesan cheese

Preheat the oven to 400°F.

Place the celery in a large skillet. Pour in the water and simmer, covered, over low heat until tender when pierced with a knife, about 15 minutes. Drain thoroughly.

Arrange the cooked celery in a medium-size shallow baking dish. Season well with salt and pepper. Pour in the cream. Spread the cheese over the top and bake until bubbling hot and the cheese is golden brown, 10 to 15 minutes. Serve very hot.

Variation: Stir the cooked celery into 1½ cups white sauce made with 2 tablespoons butter, 2 tablespoons all-purpose flour, salt, pepper, and 1½ cups chicken stock or milk (see page 110). Spread the mixture in a buttered medium-size shallow baking dish and top with ½ to ¾ cup grated Cheddar cheese. Bake until bubbling and golden, 15 to 20 minutes. Serve very hot.

Creamy Two-Celery Salad

Serve this with a cookout menu of hamburgers, hot dogs, or any other favorite barbecue feature.

Makes 6 servings

6 ribs celery, trimmed, strung, and cut into large dice
1 bunch (6 to 8) green onions (scallions), white and light green parts only, thinly sliced
½ large red bell pepper, seeded and cut into ¼-inch dice
½ small celeriac (celery root), peeled and finely diced
½ cup mayonnaise, prepared or homemade (page 13)

½ cup light sour cream
¼ cup chopped fresh cilantro, plus additional for
    garnishing
2 tablespoons Dijon-style mustard
1 teaspoon celery seed
Salt and freshly ground black pepper to taste
Hot pepper sauce to taste (optional)
1 head leaf lettuce

In a medium-size bowl, toss the vegetables together. In a small bowl, beat together the mayonnaise, sour cream, cilantro, mustard, and celery seed. Season with salt and pepper and, if using, the hot pepper sauce. Add this dressing to the vegetables, a little at a time, until the salad is the consistency of coleslaw or whatever the consistency you like—I find I like it a little wetter than some people do. Chill 2 to 3 hours. Serve on a bed of lettuce, garnished with the additional cilantro.

Wine-braised Celery and Fennel

I like this more upscale version of braised celery, too. The lovely anise flavor of the fennel makes this a perfect dish to serve with grilled or pan-broiled tuna or salmon.

Makes 6 to 8 servings

8 large ribs celery, trimmed and cut into
    3-inch lengths
1 large bulb fennel, stem and stalks trimmed,
    halved vertically and sliced lengthwise
    ¼ inch thick
2 tablespoons butter
½ cup dry white wine
½ teaspoon dried chervil
Salt and freshly ground black pepper to taste

Arrange the celery and fennel in a large skillet. Dot with the butter. Pour in the wine and season well with the chervil, salt, and pepper. Bring to a boil over medium heat. Cover partially and simmer over low heat until the fennel is tender when pierced with a

fork, about 20 minutes. Remove the cover, raise the heat to medium and boil until only 3 tablespoons of liquid remain, 3 to 4 minutes. Serve very hot, spooning the sauce over the vegetables.

Variation: For more of an anise flavor, add 1 teaspoon anisette or Sambucca liqueur to the pan when the cover is removed to reduce the sauce.

Old-fashioned Waldorf Salad

There may well be fifty "authentic" Waldorf salads. Some are even made with frozen topping and marshmallows! This one, though, is one I have made for years and is delicious with holiday dinners.

Makes 6 to 8 servings

3 medium-size ribs celery thinly sliced
3 large, very crisp red Delicious or Gala apples,
    unpeeled, quartered, cored, and cut into
    ¼-inch dice
½ cup raisins, preferably Muscat, plumped
    10 minutes in boiling water to cover
    and drained
½ cup walnut or pecan pieces, toasted (page 70)
¾ cup mayonnaise, prepared or homemade
    (page 13)
½ teaspoon celery seed
Salt and freshly ground black pepper to taste
1 head leaf lettuce
1 tablespoon chopped toasted walnuts or pecans
    for garnish

In a large bowl, toss together the celery, apple, raisins, and nut pieces. In a smaller bowl, stir together the mayonnaise and the celery seed. Stir this dressing into the salad, adding it in several batches, until the salad is well moistened but the ingredients still retain their individual character. Season well with salt and pepper. Refrigerate 1 hour.

To serve, arrange the lettuce in a salad bowl or on a serving platter. Pile the chilled salad on top and garnish with the chopped nuts.

Celery-Cucumber Salad

Take this along on your next summer picnic or add it to the Sunday night cookout menu. It will disappear in a hurry. The recipe doubles easily.

Makes 6 to 8 servings

4 ribs celery, strung if necessary and thinly sliced
½ English cucumber, halved lengthwise, seeded, and thinly sliced
2 bunches (12 to 16) green onions (scallions), white and light green parts only, thinly sliced; or 1 small sweet onion, halved and thinly sliced
½ red bell pepper, seeded and minced or very thinly sliced
¼ cup chopped fresh parsley, plus 1 tablespoon for garnishing
1 tablespoon Dijon-style mustard
½ teaspoon ground cumin
Salt and freshly ground black pepper to taste
2 tablespoons white wine vinegar
½ cup salad or extra-virgin olive oil

In a medium-size bowl, toss together the celery, cucumber, and onions. Add the bell pepper and the ¼ cup of parsley. In a small bowl, whisk together the mustard, cumin, salt pepper, and vinegar. Slowly whisk in the oil until the dressing is thick.

Just before serving, toss half the dressing with the vegetables. Add more dressing if the salad appears too dry. Pass the remaining dressing in a small bowl. Serve the salad chilled, garnished with the additional parsley.

Classic Braised Celery

One of life's comfort foods, braised celery seems to taste good even when nothing else will tempt. (Cooking mellows the strong taste of raw celery.) Add it to any menu up to and maybe even including scrambled eggs.

Makes 6 to 8 servings

1 tablespoon butter, softened
1 whole stalk celery, trimmed, separated into ribs and cut into 2- or 3-inch lengths
1 cup well-flavored chicken stock
½ cup dry white wine
1 teaspoon dried Italian herbs, such as oregano, marjoram, rosemary, and thyme, or a prepared mix (optional, but recommended)
Salt and freshly ground black pepper to taste
Freshly grated Parmesan cheese (optional)

Melt the butter in a large heavy saucepan or deep skillet. Arrange the celery in the pan. Pour in the stock and wine. Season well with herbs, salt, and pepper. Bring to a boil over medium heat. Simmer gently, partially covered, over low heat until the celery is tender, about 20 minutes. Drain. Serve very hot, garnished with the cheese if desired.

Chard, Swiss

S wiss chard, a member of the beet family, has no bulbous root, consequently only the leaves and stems are eaten. There are primarily two varieties of chard found in American markets. Ruby red or "rhubarb chard," which has thin, very red stems and deep green leaves, and green chard, which has much thicker, more succulent white stems and bright green leaves. Both varieties have a deliciously delicate flavor—much finer than beet greens.

Chard has long been popular in Europe, especially along the Mediterranean coast where it grows wild. The thick stems of green chard are sometimes separated from the leaves and then steamed or boiled like asparagus. Any of the recipes for asparagus in this book can be prepared with chard stems. In fact, Swiss chard is really two vegetables in one. The stems and leaves are often cooked separately and then combined in a finished dish or served separately. Chard leaves can be substituted for spinach in most recipes.

In Italy you will find soups, pasta fillings, and gratins made from chard, and I have even eaten a sweet tart—or *tourte*—made with chard leaves and apples when I was on the Mediterranean coast of France near Nice.

Swiss chard is easy to grow and is prolific if regularly picked. As with many other vegetables, once you have eaten chard that has just been brought in from the garden it will be hard to go back to supermarket produce.

Chard is low in calories, a good source of absorbable iron and calcium, and contains vitamins C and A.

Selection: Look for crisp, fresh-looking leaves and plump, tender stalks. Red stalks tend to be a bit more fibrous than the white variety and may require longer cooking. I suggest avoiding any chard with stalks larger than 1 inch in width, as they can be too stringy to eat and the leaves may taste somewhat strong or have a bitter edge. Do not buy chard that is limp or yellowed or that has dried-out, brown-spotted stalks.

Sometimes chard is available all summer, but the best is in the markets from late summer to the first frost.

If using it plain as you would spinach, you will need about ½ pound of fresh chard per person.

Storage and Preparation: Chard wilts quickly and is best when cooked as fresh as possible. If for some reason you cannot prepare it the day it is bought, place the unwashed chard in a perforated vegetable bag in the vegetable bin of the refrigerator and plan to eat it within a day, or two at the most.

Chard should be thoroughly washed like spinach, and then the stems should be stripped from the leaves. The easiest way to strip the stems is to hold the leaf in the left hand. Fold the leaf over so that the stem is on the right side. Grasp the bottom of the stem and pull up (or down)—it should separate from the leaf. If the leaves are a little tough, fold the leaf so the stem is on the right side, lay it on a board, and use a sharp knife to cut the stem away from the leaf.

Once cut, green chard stems will turn brown quickly. To prevent discoloring, add 2 tablespoons lemon juice to a bowl filled with 1 quart of water and drop in the stems as soon as they are prepared. Trim the stems, cut into the desired length, and drop them into the acidulated water. If parboiling the stems, cook them in the acidulated water.

Basic Swiss Chard

Chard leaves are best when cooked like spinach, in the water that clings to the leaves after washing. Simply pile the leaves in a large kettle or skillet set over medium heat and cook them, stirring occasionally, until the leaves wilt and seem to melt into themselves. The cooking time will depend on the size and freshness of the leaves but will only be a matter of a few minutes. Stir with a fork and serve or continue with the recipe. The leaves can also be boiled for 2 to 3 minutes in a large kettle of salted water to cover and drained. This is a good way to cook the leaves if you want them whole for stuffing. The leaves can be left whole, cut into strips or chopped, depending on the dish you are making.

Gratinéed Swiss Chard

Two vegetables in one, Swiss chard is a terrific change of pace from spinach or other greens. Try this with roast chicken or baked fish fillets.

Makes 6 servings

2 pounds Swiss chard, leaves stripped from stems
2 tablespoons butter
2 tablespoons all-purpose flour
Salt and freshly ground black pepper to taste
1 cup milk, skim milk, cream, or chicken stock, depending on richness desired
Pinch nutmeg
½ to ¾ cup (2 to 3 ounces) grated Gruyère or other Swiss-type cheese

Preheat the oven to 475°F.

Cut the chard stems into 2-inch lengths and boil in acidulated water (see page 124) to cover until tender. The time will depend on the thickness of the stems. Drain and keep warm.

Cut the chard leaves into large pieces. Place them in a kettle and cook them over low heat in the water that clings to them after washing just until the leaves wilt, about 2 minutes. Drain and stir into the stems.

Melt the butter in a medium-size saucepan over medium heat. Stir in the flour and cook, stirring occasionally, until just beginning to turn a very light golden color, about 3 minutes. Do not brown. Season with salt and pepper. Stir in the milk and simmer over low heat until thick, at least 3 minutes. Stir in the nutmeg. Fold in all the chard. Spoon into a medium-size gratin dish. Spread the cheese on top.

Bake in the hot oven until the dish is bubbling and the cheese is melted and golden brown, 15 to 20 minutes. Serve very hot.

Swiss Chard with Garlic and Olive Oil

Here is chard with an Italian accent, to serve with roast veal or chicken.

Makes about 6 servings

2 pounds Swiss chard, leaves stripped from stems and sliced into 1-inch strips, stems cut into 2-inch lengths
3 tablespoons olive oil
2 cloves garlic, minced
Salt and freshly ground black pepper to taste
Hot pepper sauce

In a medium-size saucepan, boil the Swiss chard stems in acidulated water (see page 124) to cover, for 5 minutes. Drain well. Place the leaves in a medium-size kettle and cook them over low heat in the water that clings to them after washing just until they wilt, 2 to 3 minutes. Drain.

Heat the oil in a medium-size heavy skillet over medium heat, add the stems and cook, stirring, until tender, 5 to 6 minutes. Stir in the garlic and cook

30 to 60 seconds, being careful not to burn it. Stir in the wilted leaves, season well with salt and pepper and toss or stir until heated through. Serve very hot. Pass the hot pepper sauce separately.

Variations: For a Spanish flavor, stir ½ cup golden raisins, plumped in boiling water to cover and drained, and ¼ cup toasted pine nuts into the stems in the skillet just before adding the leaves.

For a different Italian flavor, and a more substantial dish, try increasing the garlic by 1 clove and then stir 1½ cups cooked, drained navy beans or cannellini beans (or drained and rinsed canned cannellini beans) into the garlic and oil before adding the chard leaves. Heat thoroughly, tossing to coat the beans with oil. Stir in the chard leaves, and season with salt and pepper. Serve very hot with hot pepper sauce. Or serve warm or at room temperature with a little more olive oil drizzled over the top. Freshly grated Parmesan cheese on the side goes well with this.

Swiss Chard with Garlic and Feta Cheese

Try this with grilled whole fish, such as sea bass or red snapper. You will think you are in Greece.

Makes 6 servings

2 tablespoons olive oil
3 small cloves garlic, minced, or more to taste)
2 pounds Swiss chard, stemmed (stems reserved for another use)
Salt and freshly ground black pepper to taste
2 ounces feta cheese, crumbled (½ cup)

Heat the olive oil in a large heavy skillet over medium heat. Cook the garlic, stirring, for 1 minute. Do not burn it. Remove from the skillet and set aside. Add the chard leaves to the skillet and cook, stirring occasionally, over medium heat, in the water that clings to the leaves after washing just until wilted and tender, 3 to 5 minutes. Stir in the reserved garlic and season well with salt and pepper. To serve, pile chard into a heated vegetable dish and sprinkle the cheese over the top. Serve at once.

Steamed Swiss Chard

While this has a more assertive flavor than spinach, it is equally delicious with all sorts of entrées, from roast lamb to fillet of sole.

Makes 6 servings

2 tablespoons mild vegetable oil, preferably
    peanut
½ small onion, thinly sliced
2 cloves garlic, minced
2 pounds Swiss chard, stems reserved for another
    use, leaves torn into pieces
2 tablespoons dry white wine, or dry sherry
Salt and freshly ground black pepper to taste

Heat the oil in a wok over high heat until very hot. Add the onion and garlic and cook, stirring occasionally, for 2 minutes. Add the chard leaves and stir to coat, cover, and cook over medium heat until the leaves are soft and tender, about 5 minutes. Stir in the wine and cook, tossing or stirring occasionally, for 2 more minutes. Season well with salt and pepper. Serve very hot.

Variation: Sprinkle 4 slices of thick-cut bacon, fried until crisp, drained on paper towels, and crumbled (page 42), on top of the hot chard.

Swiss Chard Pie

This makes not only a delightful main course for a light lunch but a great addition to any menu that includes grilled chicken or fish. The cottage cheese gives the filling a delicious tangy taste.

Makes 6 to 8 servings

Pastry dough for a 1-crust 9-inch pie, prepared or
    homemade (recipe follows)
1 tablespoon butter
2 pounds Swiss chard, stemmed (stems reserved
    for another use), leaves chopped

½ cup grated Gruyère cheese
½ cup cottage cheese, or skim-milk ricotta
3 large eggs, beaten
1 cup half-and-half
Pinch nutmeg
Salt and freshly ground black pepper to taste

Preheat the oven to 450°F.

Roll out the pastry dough and line a 9-inch pie plate, making a fluted rim. Bake the pie shell lined with parchment paper and weighted with dried beans for 6 minutes. Remove the paper and beans and cool the shell.

Melt the butter in a medium-size kettle over medium heat. Add the chard leaves and cook, stirring occasionally, until wilted, 2 to 3 minutes. Remove the kettle from the heat and cool.

Spread the grated cheese over the bottom of the partially baked pie shell. In a blender, combine the cottage cheese, eggs, half-and-half, and nutmeg. Blend just until well mixed, and season well with salt and pepper. Stir the cottage cheese mixture into the cooked chard and pour this mixture into the pie shell.

Bake for 15 minutes, reduce the oven temperature to 350°F. Bake until the center is set and a knife inserted into the middle comes out clean, about 15 minutes longer. Cool 5 minutes. Cut into wedges to serve.

Basic Pie Pastry Dough

The amount of ingredients is given for both one-crust and two-crust pies. The method for this simple basic pastry dough remains the same. Do not knead or overwork the dough. The more pie pastry dough is handled the tougher and less flaky the crust will be.

Makes one 9-inch pie crust

1½ cups unbleached, all-purpose flour
½ teaspoon salt
½ cup shortening (vegetable shortening, lard,
    butter, or a combination of any two), chilled
4 to 5 tablespoons ice water

Makes one 9-inch two-crust pie

2 cups unbleached, all-purpose flour
3/4 teaspoon salt
2/3 cup shortening (vegetable shortening, lard,
     butter, or a combination of any two), chilled
5 to 7 tablespoons ice water

In a large bowl, stir or sift together the flour and salt.
Using a pastry cutter or two knives, cut in the shortening until the lumps are about the same size as small
peas, or slightly smaller.

   Sprinkle the minimum amount of ice water over
the mixture and stir gently with a fork until the dough
holds together. If the dough is still too dry, add the
remaining ice water, 1 tablespoon at a time, until it
does hold together when you pinch it.

   Turn the dough out onto a lightly floured work
surface and gather it into a ball. Or divide it into
2 equal balls for a 2-crust pie. Flatten slightly. Chill
the dough for an hour if you like. Roll out on a lightly
floured work surface and proceed with the recipe.

Food Processor Pie Pastry Dough

*This is a quick and easy pastry, but it is important to
process the ingredients as little as possible.*

Makes one 9-inch 2-crust pie

1 1/2 cups unbleached, all-purpose flour
1/2 teaspoon salt
1/2 cup less 1 tablespoon vegetable shortening,
     very cold or frozen, cut into 8 pieces
     (see Note)
1 tablespoon butter, frozen
6 to 8 tablespoons ice water
1 teaspoon lemon juice, iced

Place the flour and salt in a food processor. Pulse to
mix well. Remove the cover and arrange the shortening and butter evenly in the flour mixture. Replace
the cover and pulse once or twice until the shortening and flour resemble very coarse meal. Remove the
cover and sprinkle 6 tablespoons of the ice water and
the lemon juice over the flour mixture. Replace the
cover and process several seconds, just until the mixture begins to form a ball. If it appears too dry, add
the remaining ice water, 1 tablespoon at a time. Do
not overprocess.

   Once it begins to form a ball, remove the dough
from the processor and place it on a lightly floured
work surface. Form it into 2 rounds, flatten slightly,
and chill at least 1 hour. Roll out on a lightly floured
work surface and proceed with the recipe.

Note: *The new vegetable shortening sticks make
it very easy to measure this quantity. Also, they
can easily be chilled or frozen.*

Chayote

How is it that such a mild-mannered vegetable has come to be known by so many different names? In the southwestern United States it is chayote (*sha-yo-tay*) or cho cho, in New Orleans it is Christophene or mirliton, other places know it as a vegetable pear. Regardless of what it is called, though, chayote is a pleasantly delicate squash relative.

Chayote is a native Latin American, well known to the Aztecs (our word may be derived from the Aztec word *chayotl*), and was certainly popular with the native inhabitants by the time the conquistadors arrived. The vine is relatively easy to grow, and the vegetable is long lasting and versatile. The plant is now established in many parts of the world, including China and Australia, where chayote is nearly as popular as in Mexico, South America, and the Caribbean. Generally, Americans eat only the vegetable part of the plant, but the vine shoots can be cooked like asparagus, and in some countries the roots are often prepared like large sweet potatoes.

The delicate, somewhat cucumber-like flavor of the chayote lends itself to combinations featuring more dominant tastes. The halves can be stuffed with all manner of ingredients. Once parboiled, it can be cut into sticks or chunks and deep fried like potatoes, or it can be marinated in oil and vinegar for a crisply tender salad. Add it to soups, stews, and casseroles like any other summer squash. Feature it in stir-fries or vegetable curries. It can be thinly sliced and eaten raw in salads, but I prefer it parboiled several minutes before chilling and dressing. In the Caribbean and western Africa, it is even used in sweet desserts.

Chayote is low in calories and relatively high in vitamin C and potassium.

Unfortunately, in many areas chayote is absurdly expensive, a fact that is difficult to understand given the vines' tendency toward prolific growth.

Selection: This pale green, convoluted pear-shaped vegetable is becoming more and more popular. Look for those that are about the size of a large Bartlett pear, are hard, have an even pale green color all over, and show no signs of yellowing. There is a western variety, however, that is dark green when ripe. Just be sure there are no soft spots if this is the type you find in your market. Avoid any that have brown spots or are soft to the touch. The chayote should be as crisp and crunchy as a cucumber. The skin can be nearly smooth and only slightly convoluted, but some varieties are deeply grooved; and the skin can be hairy or even spiny.

Chayote is a winter vegetable. Prices and quality will be best between October and early spring.

You will need to count on one chayote for every two diners, unless the vegetables are very large, when one for three should do. If the recipe calls for stuffing the halves, count on one-half per person.

Storage and Preparation: Chayote is a hardy vegetable if it is handled properly. Store the pears, unwashed, in the refrigerator in a perforated plastic vegetable bag for up to two weeks.

Wash them just before preparing. Chayote have very tough skins and need to be peeled, even if they are going to be incorporated into stews or casseroles. Peeling them raw can be a little unpleasant as they exude a slimy liquid that can sting the skin of your fingers. If the recipe calls for peeling them raw, do it with a vegetable peeler under running water or in a basin of cool water to cover. The easiest way to peel chayote, however, is to parboil them in water to cover for 3 to 5 minutes. Cool slightly and the skin should just slip right off.

There is one large, soft edible seed in the center of the vegetable, which is often discarded. In some areas, the seed is eaten if the chayote is not too large, and the seed is still tender.

Boiled Chayote

Parboiling chayote makes them easier to peel. They can be boiled whole in water to cover for 3 to 5 minutes, drained, and peeled. If parboiling for stuffing, boil whole in water to cover for 25 to 40 minutes, depending on the size of the vegetable, and drain. Halve the chayote lengthwise and remove the seed. Continue with the recipe.

Parboiling chayote to eat cold in salads makes the vegetable absorb more of the flavor of the dressing. They can be peeled and sliced, cubed, or cut into strips, boiled in water to cover for 3 minutes, drained, and chilled before continuing with the salad. Or halve the squash lengthwise, boil in water to cover for 5 to 6 minutes, drain, peel, and cut into desired shape.

Mirlitons Creole

Cajun and Creole have long lived side by side in Louisiana. Creole often draws on the best of a French and Spanish cooking heritage for dishes of exquisite delicacy. Serve these delicious stuffed chayote with poached fish and a side dish of freshly steamed rice.

Makes 6 servings

3 tablespoons butter, plus additional for buttering and dotting
1 small onion, minced
2 cloves garlic, minced
3 medium-size mirlitons (chayote), boiled whole in salted water to cover until tender and drained
½ pound tiny peeled cooked shrimp, chopped
Salt and freshly ground black pepper to taste
¼ cup chopped fresh parsley
1 tablespoon chopped fresh thyme, or ½ to 1 teaspoon dried
½ to 1 cup fresh bread crumbs
Hot pepper sauce to taste (optional, but recommended)

Preheat the oven to 375°F. Generously butter a shallow baking dish large enough to hold the chayote halves in a single layer.

Melt 3 tablespoons of butter in a medium-size heavy skillet over medium heat. Cook the onion and garlic, stirring occasionally, until tender, 8 to 10 minutes.

While the onion and garlic are cooking, cut the chayote in half lengthwise and remove the seeds. Scoop out most of the flesh, leaving about ¼ inch around the inside of the shell. Mash the flesh with a fork. Stir the mashed flesh into the skillet with the onion and garlic and cook over medium heat, stirring, until most of the liquid is evaporated, 4 to 5 minutes. Stir in the shrimp. Stir in the salt, pepper, parsley, and thyme. Stir in enough bread crumbs to make this filling hold its shape when spooned into the shells. Season with hot pepper sauce if desired.

Fill the chayote shells with the shrimp mixture. Dot each with butter. Arrange the filled shells in the prepared baking dish. Bake until the filling is very hot and the tops are golden brown, about 30 minutes.

Variation: *For a heartier luncheon or supper dish, add ¼ pound smoked ham, minced, to the stuffing at the same time as the shrimp.*

Chayote with Red Peppers and Onions

The addition of hot chiles to this delicately flavored squash brings out the best in its character. This is a truly all-purpose dish to be served hot with grilled fish, warm with grilled chicken, or at room temperature with cold meats, or as part of an antipasto platter.

Makes 6 servings

3 tablespoons olive oil
2 medium-size onions, thinly sliced
2 red bell peppers, seeded and thinly sliced
1 small New Mexico chile, seeded and minced
2 small cloves, garlic, thinly sliced
3 medium-size chayote, peeled and thinly sliced
1 tablespoon chopped fresh oregano, or 1 teaspoon dried
½ to 1 cup well-flavored chicken stock
Salt and freshly ground black pepper to taste
2 tablespoons chopped fresh parsley

Heat the oil in a large heavy skillet over medium heat. Add the onions, bell peppers, and chile and cook, stirring, until just translucent, 10 to 12 minutes. Stir in the garlic, chayote, and oregano. Cook over low heat, stirring or tossing until the chayote begins to turn translucent, 3 to 4 minutes. Stir in ½ cup of the stock and season well with salt and pepper. Simmer the mixture over low heat until the chayote is very tender and most of the liquid is evaporated, 15 to 20 minutes. Serve the chayote hot, warm, or at room temperature, garnished with the parsley.

Ginger-baked Stuffed Chayote

I really like to serve this with broiled or grilled tuna steaks that have been marinated in a mixture of olive oil, soy sauce, garlic, and sherry.

Makes 6 servings

Butter
3 small chayote, halved lengthwise, seeds removed, boiled in salted water to cover until tender, drained, and cooled.
1 bunch (6 to 8) green onions (scallions), white and light green parts only, minced
1 tablespoon grated fresh ginger
1 large egg, beaten
1/2 cup half-and-half
1/2 cup fresh bread crumbs
Salt and freshly ground black pepper to taste

Preheat the oven to 325°F. Generously butter a shallow baking dish large enough to hold the chayote halves in a single layer.

Scoop the flesh out of the skins, leaving about 1/4 inch around the inside of the shell. Mash the removed chayote, place it in a colander, and press out as much liquid as possible.

Turn the drained pulp into a medium-size bowl. Beat in the green onions, ginger, egg, and half-and-half. Stir in enough of the bread crumbs to make the filling hold its shape when placed in the shells.

Stuff the mixture into the shells and dot each with butter. Arrange them in the prepared baking dish. Bake until slightly puffed and golden brown, 45 to 60 minutes. Serve very hot.

Cheese-stuffed Chayote

Chayote classically lends itself to stuffing, and this cheesy variation makes a perfect accompaniment to roast chicken or turkey.

Makes 6 servings

2 tablespoons butter, plus additional for buttering
3 medium-size chayote, boiled in salted water to cover until tender and drained
1/2 small onion, minced
1/4 medium-size green bell pepper, seeded and minced
1 1/2 teaspoons chopped fresh thyme, or 1/2 teaspoon dried
Salt and freshly ground black pepper to taste
1 tablespoon mayonnaise, prepared or homemade (page 13)
3/4 cup grated Monterey Jack cheese
6 slices bacon, fried until crisp, drained, and crumbled (page 42)
1/2 cup plain dried bread crumbs
Freshly grated Parmesan cheese
Hot pepper sauce (optional)

Preheat the oven to 400°F. Generously butter a shallow baking dish large enough to hold the chayote halves in a single layer.

Halve the chayote lengthwise. Remove the seeds and scrape out the flesh, leaving about 1/4 inch all around the inside of the shell. Mash the removed flesh and place it in a colander over a bowl to drain, pressing out as much liquid as possible.

Melt 2 tablespoons of butter in a medium-size heavy skillet over medium heat. Cook the onion and bell pepper, stirring occasionally, until translucent, about 10 minutes. Mix in the drained chayote and cook, stirring, until the mixture is fairly dry but not browned, about 5 minutes longer. Remove the skillet from the heat and stir in the thyme. Season well with salt and pepper. Stir in the mayonnaise, Monterey Jack cheese, and bacon. Add enough bread crumbs, 1 tablespoon at a time, up to 1/2 cup, so the mixture will hold its shape in the chayote shells.

Mound the filling in the 6 shells. Sprinkle the filling generously with Parmesan cheese. Arrange the stuffed squash in one layer in the prepared baking dish. Bake until the filling is bubbling hot and golden brown, 20 to 25 minutes. Serve very hot, with hot pepper sauce on the side if you like.

Cajun Stuffed Chayote

Cajun is the cooking style developed by the descendants of the Acadian French who were banished from Canada in the mid-1700s and migrated to Louisiana. Cajun cooking makes something wonderful out of the most mundane ingredients. Along with a salad, this substantial vegetable dish makes a light luncheon or workaday dinner. For a heartier dinner menu, serve it on a plate alongside roast pork or even smothered pork chops.

Makes 6 servings

Butter
2 tablespoons olive oil
1 large onion, chopped
1/2 medium-size green bell pepper, seeded
    and chopped
2 medium-size ripe tomatoes, peeled, seeded,
    and chopped
1 teaspoon dried sage
1/4 pound hot pork sausage, crumbled, fried,
    and drained
3 medium-size chayote, halved lengthwise, seeds
    removed, boiled in salted water to cover until
    tender, and drained
Hot pepper sauce to taste

Preheat the oven to 375°F. Generously butter a shallow baking dish large enough to hold the chayote halves in one layer.

Heat the oil in a medium-size heavy skillet over medium heat. Cook the onion and bell pepper, stirring occasionally, until translucent, about 10 minutes. Stir in the tomatoes and sage. Cook about 5 minutes more. Stir in the drained sausage.

Scoop out the flesh of the chayote, leaving about 1/4 inch all around the inside of the shell. Chop (do not mash) the removed flesh—there should be distinct lumps—and add it to the sausage mixture.

Fill the shells with the stuffing. Arrange the filled shells in the prepared baking dish. Bake until bubbling hot, 30 to 40 minutes. Serve very hot with the hot pepper sauce on the side.

Stewed Chayote

Here is a savory combination to serve with grilled, marinated shrimp or other shellfish.

Makes 6 servings

2 tablespoons olive oil
3 small chayote, halved lengthwise, seeded,
    peeled, and cut into 1-inch chunks
1 small onion, cut into 1/4-inch dice
1/2 small green bell pepper, seeded and cut into
    1/4-inch dice
1/2 cup golden raisins, plumped in boiling water
    to cover and drained
Salt and freshly ground black pepper to taste
1/2 cup well-flavored chicken stock
2 ripe tomatoes, peeled, seeded, and chopped
2 tablespoons chopped fresh oregano, or 1 1/2 to
    2 teaspoons dried

Heat the olive oil in a large heavy saucepan over medium heat. Cook the chayote, onion, and bell pepper in the oil, tossing or stirring, for 3 minutes. Stir in the raisins. Season well with salt and pepper. Stir in the stock, cover, and simmer over low heat for 20 minutes.

Stir in the tomatoes and oregano, checking the salt and pepper. Add salt if needed. Simmer, uncovered, for 10 to 15 minutes, until much of the liquid has evaporated and the chayote is tender. Serve very hot.

Collards

Green leafy vegetables are abundant in the southern part of the United States. One of the South's favorite "greens" is the collard. A member of the cruciferous family, along with cabbage and broccoli, collards should be considered just as healthful as their renowned cousins.

Collards have been cultivated since ancient times, were widely known throughout Africa, and might even have been brought to America by the black slaves. Their popularity is finally beginning to spread to other parts of the country, as they are good for you, easy to grow, can withstand extreme heat and will survive into the first cold months.

In the past, greens, especially collards, have been cooked to within an inch of their lives— a long, slow boiling, usually with bacon, ham bones or hock, or salt pork. A little experimenting has revealed that they can, and should, be treated more like spinach. While the flavor is more pronounced than spinach, it is not as strong as kale or mustard greens. The larger, more mature leaves should be steamed or simply wilted in the water that clings to the leaves after washing. Smaller, more delicate leaves can be added raw to green salads for a delicious taste, reminiscent of cabbage.

Home gardeners love collards. The greens grow on straight, tall stalks, each leaf separate. Picking is done from the bottom of the stalk up and can continue until the final hard frost kills the plant. In the fall, and in some places right through Christmas, you can often see kitchen gardens with tall stalks standing, plucked up to the final delicate leaves that are being saved for that last "mess" of fresh greens before winter takes over.

Collards are low in calories and are rich in beta-carotene, vitamin C, and absorbable calcium.

Selection: Don't be put off by the unfamiliar aspect of collards if you have never tried them.

133

Look for leaves that have a rich, deep blue-green color and that are crisp, succulent, and not at all wilted. Avoid any that are strong smelling, have yellowed edges, or dried up stems. If the leaves are torn or show brown spots, they have been badly handled and should be left where they are.

While collards are hardier than spinach, like all greens they should be cooked as quickly as possible after picking. Of course, the best collards are picked, washed, and cooked within about 30 minutes, but those that have been treated well once they have left the field should still be full of flavor and vitamins when they reach the market. Most greens arrive in the supermarket two to three days after they have been picked. If they have been refrigerated, another day or two will not hurt them, but a good rule of thumb is to prepare greens—of any kind—the same day they are purchased, or the next day at the outside.

Collards are in the markets from late July until October or later.

Collards, like other fresh greens, diminish considerably during cooking. You will need at least ¼ pound of fresh collards per person.

Storage and Preparation: If collards cannot be prepared the day they are bought, they can be kept refrigerated a day or two at home. There is a small controversy about storing collards and other greens. One group suggests washing them in several changes of cold water, shaking them nearly dry, and then storing one to two days in a paper or perforated vegetable bag in the vegetable section of the refrigerator. I have done this, and it works well if the greens are spun in a salad dryer first. I have also found that leaving too much water on the leaves tends to turn them a little slimy very quickly. If you will be preparing the greens within 24 hours of buying them, store them, unwashed, in a plastic bag in the vegetable section of the refrigerator.

Collards must be thoroughly washed, though they will not be as gritty as spinach, kale, or mustard greens. Generally I wash them in two to three changes of water, swishing them well in each change and lifting them out of each "bath" to leave the sand and grit behind.

If the leaves are very large and the stems have thickened, remove the stems by holding each leaf in your left hand, folding the leaf so that the stem is on the right, and pulling the stem up to strip it off the leaf. The thick stems should be discarded. Large leaves can be sliced or chopped for a finer presentation.

Very small leaves should be left whole. If using small leaves for a salad, spin them in a salad spinner to dry them before adding to the salad mixture.

Steamed Collards

There are two ways to steam collards and other greens. Just as for spinach, they can be wilted in the water that clings to the leaves after they have been washed and drained. Simply pile the clean leaves in a large kettle and cook over high heat, stirring from time to time, until they collapse in on themselves and are tender, about 3 minutes. Remove the kettle from the heat, season the collards with salt and pepper and stir in a little butter, or drizzle with olive oil or vinegar. Steaming retains a maximum amount of color and nutrients.

If you prefer, the clean leaves can be piled in a steamer basket or colander and steamed, covered, over simmering water or stock until wilted and tender, 5 to 6 minutes. Season with salt and pepper and serve.

Boiled Collards

There are at least two schools of thought about boiling collards. The quick-cook method is to plunge the clean leaves into boiling stock or salted water to cover, simmer until tender, 5 to 10 minutes, drain, and season. The stock or water can be saved and used as a base for soups, stews, and sauces.

The southern method is the slow-cook variation. Place the clean leaves in a large kettle. Add enough salted water to cover and a little bacon, ham, salt pork, or other meaty flavoring (bacon fat is used if that is all there is). Cover and simmer up to 3 hours or more. Drain, season, and serve. The cooking liquid can be used for soups and sauces, or drunk either hot or cold.

Collards with Garlic and Olive Oil

Here is what we might consider a very American vegetable served in a decidedly Mediterranean style. Since collards were known to the Romans, this is probably a more ancient way of preparing them than our boiled classic. Add it to a menu that features a broiled steak or maybe double-thick lamb chops.

Makes 6 servings

3 tablespoons olive oil
3 cloves garlic, minced
2 pounds collards, stemmed, chopped, cooked in the water that clings to the leaves after washing until just wilted, and drained
Salt and freshly ground black pepper to taste

Heat the oil in a large heavy skillet over low heat. Add the garlic and cook, stirring, about 1 minute. Be careful not to burn it. Stir in the collards and cook, stirring, until tender, 2 to 3 minutes. Season well with salt and pepper. Serve hot.

Note: *It isn't traditional, but I like a few drops of hot pepper sauce on these greens.*

Italian Braised Collards

This is a good way to introduce collards to those who have never tasted them. I like to pair this with veal scaloppine or poached fish fillets, but it would be equally good with any kind of grilled fish.

Makes 6 servings

3 tablespoons pure olive oil
2 medium-size shallots, minced; or ½ small onion, minced
1 large tomato, peeled, seeded, and chopped
1 clove garlic, minced
2 pounds collards, stemmed and very coarsely chopped
½ cup dry white wine
½ teaspoon dried Italian herbs, such as oregano, marjoram, rosemary, and thyme, or a prepared mix; or 2 teaspoons chopped fresh oregano
Salt and freshly ground black pepper to taste
Extra-virgin olive oil (optional)

Heat the pure olive oil in a large heavy kettle over low heat. Cook the shallots, tomato, and garlic, stirring occasionally, for 5 minutes. Stir in the collards, tossing to coat them with the oil. Stir in the wine and herbs. Season well with salt and pepper. Cover and simmer over low heat until the collards are tender, stirring from time to time. This will take about 15 minutes, depending on the age of the collards. Serve very hot, drizzled with a little extra-virgin olive oil, if desired.

Old-fashioned Long-cook Collards and Salt Pork

Growing up in Virginia was a wondrous experience. Collards were always cooked this way, and the cooking liquid (the pot "likker") was always saved and drunk cold or used as a soup base. This dish goes awfully well with baked chicken breasts, baked ham, smothered pork chops, or pan-fried fish fillets—catfish in particular.

Makes 6 servings

¼ pound salt pork (streak-of-lean—see
    page 43), thickly sliced
2 pounds collards, stemmed and, if you like,
    leaves chopped
Freshly ground black pepper to taste
Salt if necessary
Cider vinegar or hot pepper sauce to taste
    (optional)

Place the salt pork in a large kettle. Cover with water and simmer over low heat for 30 minutes. Add the collards and more water to cover all and simmer very gently over low heat until tender, 30 minutes more, or longer—3 hours or more if you want *very* tender greens. Drain and season with salt if necessary and freshly ground pepper. Serve very hot with the salt pork alongside, and pass vinegar and/or hot pepper sauce if you like.

Vinegared Collards

I think this quick-to-make "mess of greens" is delicious with any kind of roast or grilled poultry.

Makes 6 servings

2 pounds collards, stemmed and chopped
½ cup water
Salt and freshly ground black pepper to taste
1 tablespoon malt vinegar, or more to taste

Pile the collards in a large kettle. Add the water and season well with salt and pepper. Cover and cook over medium heat until the greens are just tender, about 5 minutes. Uncover the pot and add the vinegar. Cook until most of the liquid is evaporated and the collards are tender, but not too soft, 2 to 3 minutes longer. Add salt and pepper if necessary. Serve very hot.

Corn

Corn may well be the most famous of all the New World vegetables. Cultivated by native Americans for thousands of years before the first Europeans sailed west, corn was introduced to the newcomers by the local tribes. If the first reaction was not overwhelmingly favorable, the colonists learned to love it, since it literally kept them alive once their wheat and barley crops failed to thrive.

From the American Indians, the settlers learned to make corn into hominy, and then ate it like a cereal. They ground it into meal and then even finer into flour. They made puddings and breads from it as well as soups, stews, and mushes.

In fact corn was a basic all-purpose crop. Not only did it feed the colonists but it nourished their animals, filled their mattresses, insulated their cabins, and warmed their hearths.

When the colonists finally became acclimated to this strange, thoroughly American grain, corn was no longer new in the Old Country. It had already been carried home by the great explorers, first to Spain, then to the rest of Europe. Later the Portuguese took it with them on their routes to Asia, as well as Africa, where it is known as mealies. Until recently in Europe, however, this foreign grain was thought fit only to feed to animals, and the American habit of eating it right off the cob gave credence to the image of the American as barbarian. Once it was accepted as food for humans, it was often used cold in salads and relishes or ground into meal and boiled like polenta in Italy or mamaliga in Romania, to be sauced and enhanced by adding butter, cheese, tomatoes, and other savory combinations.

It is still difficult in Europe to find corn that is fresh enough to eat off the cob. And more than once I have taken packets of various sweet corn seeds to my European friends who developed a taste for corn on the cob while in America and who longed to grow it in their own gardens.

This very ancient grain was known in virtually every part of the New World. In some areas of what is now Central and South America, it was the only cultivated grain crop. While hybrids were not unknown, the original corn varieties grown were much coarser than the sweet corn we love. It was much more like the field corn we feed to animals and poultry.

Today, there are many varieties of sweet corn, some white, some yellow, and even some with both colors on the same cob. All are delicious if they are fresh. Like many other vegetables, corn definitely is better the shorter the time between garden or field and the plate. As soon as the cob is picked the sugars in the kernels begin to turn to starch, the corn begins to toughen and to lose that candy-sweet flavor we love. If you asked old-time farmers what was the best way to cook corn, they would tell you to build a fire in the field and not pick the corn, much less husk it, until the water was boiling.

If you ever have the opportunity to grow your own sweet corn, put a pot of boiling water on the stove, send the kids out to pick and husk the ears, and drop them right into the boiling water. Remove the pot from the heat. Cover and let stand for 5 to 8 minutes, depending on the size of the ears. Serve it very hot with butter and salt, or brush it with a mixture of olive oil and chopped fresh herbs. You will never be satisfied with corn from the supermarket again.

In most places, corn is truly only a summer crop. The first of the local crop is generally in the markets around the Fourth of July and lasts until the end of August. In our house it is a part of almost every menu while it lasts. Fortunately, corn can be preserved in many ways. Frozen corn, both ears and kernels cut from the cob, is delicious. Simply thaw it and use it as if it has been cooked. To my way of thinking, canned corn is one of the few vegetables that is not ruined by the canning process. I suggest draining it and

rinsing to remove some of the salt that has been added during the preserving process, but it can be eaten as is, or heated and incorporated as is into cooked dishes.

Selection: Corn on the cob should be as fresh as possible. If it is not home grown, "U-pick-it" is the next best guarantee of freshness. While refrigeration will slow down the sugar-to-starch conversion process, it will not stop it, and freshness diminishes each hour that passes from field to table. A good farm stand or farmer's market can be the best commercial source for fresh corn, but beware of corn that is picked the afternoon before sale or is picked early in the morning and allowed to languish in the sun until you buy it. It would be better in that case to buy supermarket corn that has been refrigerated or at least handled in cool surroundings. During the high season most farmers pick more than once a day and will be glad to tell you when they are bringing in freshly picked corn.

If you are relegated to supermarket corn, choose the greenest, most moist ears you can find, with silks that are as clear and yellow as possible. Dried up stem ends and coarse, dark brown tassels indicate corn that is old or has been long off the stalk.

I get very upset with people who go into a market or vegetable stall and pull down the husks of every ear they pick up. Normally, they jab a fingernail into a kernel, discard the ear, never pulling the husk up again, thereby letting the ear dry out. Hefting the ear, running your fingers up the outside of the husk will often tell you if it is fresh or dried out. If you feel you cannot choose without pulling back the husk, pull back only about 1 inch and feel the kernels. If they feel plump and do not look shriveled or dry, the corn is probably fresh. Should you feel compelled to jab a fingernail into a kernel, look for a very liquid, milky juice. And when you reject an ear, smooth the husk back as much as possible to preserve any moisture that may remain. The only time I feel it might be wise to pull the husks back farther than about 1 inch is at the end of the season when corn worms may have invaded the crop. But you can usually tell from the tassel end—you will see the trails made by the worms as they work down into the cob—or from holes in the husks themselves if the ear is harboring visitors.

Corn is low in calories and is a good source of vitamin C and fiber. As a life-sustaining grain, however, unlike wheat, oats, and barley, it lacks niacin; and any diet that doesn't contain another source of protein or niacin as well as other vitamins will be insufficient and can lead to a condition called pellagra.

You will need one to two ears of corn per person. Depending on the size of the ears, one ear will yield $\frac{1}{3}$ to $\frac{1}{2}$ cup corn cut from the cob.

Storage and Preparation: Store corn in the husk in the refrigerator until ready to prepare it. And corn should definitely be prepared the day you buy it. If plans change and you must wait 24 hours, place the unhusked corn in a perforated vegetable bag and store in the vegetable section of the refrigerator. Use as quickly as possible. If all else fails and you cannot serve the corn right away, husk the ears, boil them in water to cover for 5 minutes, cool, and cut the corn from the cob. It can then be refrigerated for another day or two or put into freezer bags or containers and frozen.

Much has been made about removing corn silk before cooking. If the ears are to be boiled, obviously the husks must be removed and the silk stripped off. A damp paper towel often makes it easier to remove the silk and keeps it from flying all around. In fact, as a child, it was my job to husk the corn—outdoors—just before dinner, thereby keeping the silk out of the kitchen. But, if the corn is to be cooked in the husk, either roasted on a grill, in the coals, or in the microwave, I can see no earthly reason for going through the exercise of pulling back the husks and removing all that pesky silk. As far as I can determine, cooking corn with the silk on has no adverse effect on the eater, and once the corn is cooked, the silk pulls right off with the husk, in one smooth motion.

If the recipe calls for corn cut from the cob, you can use leftover corn that has been cooked on the cob or fresh uncooked corn. In either case, husk the corn, remove the silk, and rinse. Stand the ear on end, holding it at the top. Use a very sharp knife and cut down from top to bottom to remove the kernels, as close to the cob as possible. I find it convenient to stand the ears in a wide bowl so that the kernels do not scatter everywhere.

If you are making creamed corn and the recipe calls for slitting the kernels, slice down the middle of each row of kernels on the cob with the point of a sharp knife before pressing the back of a knife down the cob to push out as much of the inside of the kernels as possible. This method releases the milky liquid inside the kernels which will thicken the final dish slightly.

Tip: *Adding salt to the water in which corn is cooked will toughen the kernels. Some cooks suggest stirring a pinch (up to 1 teaspoon) of sugar into the water before adding the ears of corn. I am not convinced the sugar adds anything—if the corn is very fresh it will be very sweet; if it isn't, it won't be as sweet, even with sugar added.*

Boiled Corn

Drop the husked ears of corn into a kettle of rapidly boiling water to cover. Cover the pot, bring to a boil again, and cook 3 minutes. Remove the kettle from the heat and let stand, covered, for 5 minutes (see page 138 for just-picked corn). Drain and serve very hot. Any leftover corn can be reheated by dropping it into boiling water to cover for about 1 minute.

Microwaved Corn

Place the unhusked corn in a single layer on the turntable of a microwave oven, alternating tips and stem ends. Microwave on high, 5 minutes for 2 ears, 8 minutes for 3 or 4 ears. Let the corn stand 5 minutes before husking. Be careful when pulling the husks back as they will be very hot and the corn will be steaming.

Roasted or Grilled Corn

Soak the unhusked corn in cold water to cover for 30 minutes. Drain. Roast the corn in a 400°F. oven, turning it at least once, for 20 minutes. Or place the soaked corn on the barbecue grill over medium-hot coals. Grill, turning the corn from time to time, 20 to 25 minutes. Serve hot. Be careful when pulling the husks back, as they will be very hot and the corn will be steaming.

Home-style Creamed Corn

Some recipes for creamed corn call for slitting each row of kernels to release the milky liquid they contain. I prefer to leave the kernels whole; either method will work here. Serve this with any grilled meat and thick slices of garden-ripened tomatoes.

Makes 6 servings

2 tablespoons butter
2 teaspoons minced onion
2 cups cooked fresh corn kernels, cut from the cob (4 to 5 ears), or thawed frozen corn kernels
2 tablespoons all-purpose flour
1 cup half-and-half, heated until bubbles appear around the edge and hot
1 tablespoon sugar
Salt and freshly ground black pepper to taste
2 tablespoons chopped fresh parsley

Melt the butter in a medium-size heavy saucepan over low heat. Stir in the onion and cook, stirring, for 2 minutes. Add the corn. Cook, stirring to coat with the butter, for 2 to 3 minutes. Sprinkle the flour over the corn and toss with a spoon. Stir in the half-and-half, along with the sugar. Stir well. Simmer, stirring from time to time, over low heat until thickened, at least 3 to 4 minutes. Season well with salt and pepper. Stir in the parsley and serve very hot.

Corn Pudding

If you live in the southern part of the United States, this has been a summertime tradition all your life. If you do not, it is time to learn about this wonderful way to enjoy corn cut from the cob. Serve this with a grilled steak or perhaps barbecued chicken.

Makes 6 to 8 servings

3 tablespoons butter, melted but not boiling hot, plus additional for buttering

4 large eggs, separated, whites beaten until stiff
1 teaspoon sugar
1 teaspoon salt, or to taste
Pinch nutmeg
2 cups milk
2 cups fresh corn kernels, cut from the cob (4 to
     5 ears), or 2 cups thawed frozen corn kernels
Freshly ground pepper to taste
Hot pepper sauce to taste

Preheat the oven to 350°F. Generously butter a 2-quart deep baking dish, ovenproof casserole, or soufflé dish.

In a large bowl, beat together the melted butter, egg yolks, sugar, salt, and nutmeg. Stir in the milk and then the corn. Season well with pepper and pepper sauce. Gently fold in the egg whites. Pour the batter into the prepared baking dish and bake until the custard is set in the middle, 45 to 60 minutes. Serve at once.

Variations: *Stir the white part of 1 bunch (6 to 8) green onions (scallions), minced, into the corn before seasoning. Or add ¼ cup freshly grated Parmesan cheese just before folding in the egg whites.*

Cheese Creamed Corn

I like this variation on plain creamed corn. It will be a welcome addition to your corn repertoire. It is delightful with a grilled steak or with a succulent roast chicken.

Makes 6 servings

2 tablespoon butter
2 cups cooked fresh corn kernels, cut from the
     cob (4 to 5 ears), or 2 cups thawed frozen
     corn kernels
1 bunch (6 to 8) green onions (scallions), white
     and light green parts only, thinly sliced
1 tablespoon chopped fresh oregano, or
     1 teaspoon dried
2 ounces cream cheese, cut up
½ cup half-and-half
Salt and freshly ground black pepper to taste
Chopped fresh parsley

Melt the butter in a medium-size heavy saucepan over low heat. Stir in the corn and heat for 1 minute. Stir in the green onions and oregano. Cook over medium heat for 1 minute. Stir in the cream cheese and half-and-half. Stir until the cheese is melted and the corn is hot, 3 to 4 minutes. Season with salt and pepper. Serve very hot, garnished with the parsley.

Note: *If you would like a more pronounced cheese flavor, substitute 1 cup grated Gruyère or fontina cheese for the cream cheese.*

Scalloped Corn

I remember this dish as a late summer standby when everyone was tiring of corn on the cob. It was also served a lot during the summer that I had large gaps in my front teeth and couldn't manage corn on the cob. This is delicious with baked ham.

Makes 6 servings

3 tablespoons butter, plus additional for buttering
3 cups fresh corn kernels, cut from the cob (6 to
     8 ears), or 3 cups thawed frozen corn kernels
1 bunch (6 to 8) large green onions (scallions),
     white and light green parts only, thinly sliced
Salt and freshly ground white pepper to taste
¾ cup heavy cream
¾ cup cracker crumbs, or dry bread crumbs

Preheat the oven to 350°F. Generously butter a 1½-quart deep baking dish.

In a medium-size bowl, combine the corn and green onions. Spoon the mixture into the prepared baking dish. Season well with salt and pepper. Pour in the cream.

Combine the crumbs with the melted butter. Spread over the corn. Bake until bubbling hot and golden brown on top, 35 to 40 minutes.

Variations: *Add hot pepper sauce to taste if you like. Or stir 3 tablespoons minced red bell pepper into the corn and green onion mixture.*

Stir-fried Corn with Snow Peas and Shiitake Mushrooms

The secret here is to have everything ready before you begin cooking. There is no better accompaniment to grilled fish.

Makes 6 servings

2 tablespoons mild vegetable oil, preferably peanut
½ pound shiitake mushrooms, stems discarded, cut into large pieces
¼ pound snow peas, topped, tailed, and strung; or 1 cup thawed frozen snow peas
2 cups cooked fresh corn kernels, cut from the cob (4 to 5 ears), or 2 cups thawed frozen corn kernels
2 tablespoons dry sherry or rice wine
1 tablespoon soy sauce
2 tablespoons chicken stock
1 teaspoon cornstarch
1 tablespoon sliced green onions (scallions)

Heat the oil in a wok over high heat. Cook the mushrooms, stirring, for 2 minutes. Add the snow peas and cook, stirring, 2 more minutes. Stir in the corn.

In a small bowl, mix together the sherry, soy sauce, stock, and cornstarch. Stir into the vegetables and cook, stirring, until the sauce thickens, 1 to 3 minutes. Serve very hot, garnished with the green onions.

Fresh Corn Soufflé

This is a more sophisticated dish than Corn Pudding, and it is a delicious addition to any company meal. Grilled salmon, Braised Fennel, and this corn soufflé make a terrific summer dinner party menu.

Makes 6 to 8 servings

3 tablespoons butter, plus additional, for buttering
¼ cup freshly grated Parmesan cheese, plus additional for dusting
2 large green onions (scallions), white part only, very thinly sliced
2 tablespoons all-purpose flour
Salt and freshly ground black pepper to taste
Pinch ground red (cayenne) pepper
1 cup milk
3 large eggs, separated, whites beaten until stiff
½ cup fresh corn kernels, cut from the cob (1 to 2 ears), or ½ cup thawed frozen corn kernels

Preheat the oven to 375°F. Generously butter a 1½-quart soufflé dish and dust the inside with cheese, knocking out any excess.

Melt 3 tablespoons of butter in a medium saucepan over low heat. Cook the green onions, stirring, for 1 minute. Stir in the flour and cook, stirring, for 1 minute. Take care not to brown the flour. Season well with salt, black pepper, and red pepper. Whisk in the milk, beating until smooth. Simmer over low heat, stirring, until thick, about 3 minutes. Stir in the cheese and continue to cook just until it melts.

Remove the saucepan from the heat. Beat in the egg yolks, one at a time. Stir in the corn. Cool slightly, and gently fold in the beaten egg whites.

Spoon the mixture into the prepared soufflé dish. Bake until just set, about 30 minutes. Serve at once, very hot, dusted with more cheese.

Corn Fritters with Spicy Orange Dipping Sauce

These crisp little golden morsels make a wonderful summertime appetizer or cocktail nibble. They will also go very well with cold roast chicken.

Makes 6 to 8 servings

2 large eggs, beaten
¾ cup milk
1 teaspoon ground cumin

2 cups unbleached all-purpose flour
Salt and freshly ground black pepper to taste
2 cups cooked fresh corn kernels, cut from the
    cob (4 to 5 ears), or 2 cups thawed frozen
    corn kernels
3 tablespoons chopped fresh parsley
Oil for deep-frying
Spicy Orange Sauce (recipe follows)

In a medium-size bowl, beat together the eggs and milk. In another medium-size bowl, stir the cumin into the flour. Season well with salt and pepper. Beat the egg mixture into the flour with a whisk. Stir in the corn and parsley.

Heat the oil to 375°F. in deep-fat fryer. Drop the corn mixture by tablespoons into the hot fat without crowding the pan. Fry, turning once, until golden brown, about 3 minutes per batch. Remove from the oil with a slotted spoon and drain on paper towels. Serve hot, with a bowl of Spicy Orange Sauce.

Spicy Orange Sauce

Makes about ⅔ cup

½ cup orange marmalade
¼ cup fresh orange juice
1 tablespoon fresh lemon juice
1 tablespoon grated fresh ginger
½ teaspoon ground cumin
1 teaspoon Dijon-style mustard
Hot pepper sauce to taste

Combine the marmalade, orange and lemon juices, ginger, cumin, and mustard in a blender. Blend until smooth. Pour into a serving bowl and stir in the hot pepper sauce.

Confetti Summer Salad

Summer picnics are some of my most favorite meals. But I do get tired of the same old potato salad and coleslaw.

This colorful combination of garden fresh vegetables and beans is not only delicious but nutritious. Serve it with fried chicken, barbecued ribs, or even hot dogs and hamburgers, and watch it disappear. Make plenty—it will be good the next day, too.

Makes 6 to 8 servings

2 cups cooked fresh corn kernels, cut from
    the cob (4 to 5 ears), or thawed frozen
    corn kernels
3 cups cooked beans, such as lima, navy, or
    black, or a mixture of two or three kinds
1 bunch (6 to 8) green onions (scallions), white
    and light green parts only, sliced
1 green or red bell pepper, seeded and cut into
    ¼-inch dice
2 small carrots, peeled and cut into ¼-inch dice
⅓ cup sliced green olives
1 small onion, minced
1 large tomato, seeded and cut into ¼-inch dice
2 tablespoons soy sauce
2 tablespoons rice wine (or white wine, or
    champagne) vinegar
1 tablespoon grated fresh ginger
1 clove garlic, minced (optional,
    but recommended)
3 to 4 tablespoons chopped fresh parsley, plus
    additional for garnishing
Freshly ground black pepper to taste
½ cup olive oil
Leaf lettuce

In a large bowl, gently toss together the corn, beans, green onions, bell pepper, carrots, olives, onion, and tomato.

Beat together the remaining ingredients, except the leaf lettuce, in a small bowl, or shake them in a tightly covered jar. Pour this dressing over the salad. Toss and refrigerate for 1 hour.

Line a salad bowl with the leaf lettuce. Mound the salad in the dish and garnish with the additional chopped parsley.

Variation: *Add 1 seeded, minced jalapeño pepper to the vegetables if you like a more aggressive salad.*

Fresh Corn with Rice

This variation on the traditional beans and rice combination is delicious with roast poultry, especially Cornish hens.

Makes 6 servings

2 tablespoons butter
1 bunch (6 to 8) green onions (scallions), white part only, thinly sliced
2 cups fresh corn kernels, cut from the cob (4 to 5 ears), or 2 cups thawed frozen corn kernels
Salt and freshly ground black pepper to taste
½ teaspoon ground cumin
¼ cup chicken stock
2 cups cooked long-grain rice (about ⅔ cup raw rice), hot
Chopped fresh parsley

Melt the butter in a medium skillet over medium heat. Add the green onions and cook 1 minute. Stir in the corn and cook over medium heat for 2 minutes. Season with salt, pepper, and cumin. Stir in the stock and cook until almost all the liquid is evaporated, 2 to 3 minutes. Stir the rice into the corn and heat through. Serve very hot, garnished with the chopped parsley.
Variation: *Stir 2 cups shredded fresh spinach into the corn mixture before adding the stock. Cook 2 minutes, stirring. Add the stock and continue with the recipe. This will serve 6 to 8 people*

Fried Corn with Green Onions

What a wonderful way to use leftover cooked corn on the cob. Fresh corn is one of those seasonal treats that sometimes seems to overwhelm us. There are lots of ways to enjoy it other than plain steamed, boiled, or microwaved. Serve this with almost any main course, from grilled shrimp to hamburgers.

Makes 6 servings

2 tablespoons butter
¼ medium-size green bell pepper, seeded and minced; or 1 small jalapeño pepper, seeded and minced
1 bunch (6 to 8) green onions (scallions), white part only, thinly sliced
2 cups cooked fresh corn kernels, cut from the cob (4 or 5 ears), or 2 cups thawed frozen corn kernels
Salt and freshly ground black pepper
3 tablespoons chopped fresh cilantro, or parsley

Melt the butter in a small skillet over low heat. Stir in the bell or jalapeño pepper and green onions and cook, stirring occasionally, for 2 minutes. Stir in the corn and cook, stirring, over medium heat for 5 minutes. Season well with salt and pepper. Stir in the cilantro. Serve very hot.
Variation: *Stir 2 cups shredded bitter greens, such as escarole or mustard greens, into the corn mixture. Add ¼ cup chicken stock. Cook 3 to 4 minutes longer, until the greens are just wilted. Serve very hot with hot pepper sauce on the side.*

Corn Cakes

I like to garnish these savory cakes with Black Bean Salsa (page 49), partnered with a grilled fresh tuna steak.

Makes 6 servings

2 cups cooked fresh corn kernels, cut from the cob (4 or 5 ears), or 2 cups thawed frozen corn kernels; or 2 cups drained canned corn kernels
1 large egg
½ cup milk
1 clove garlic, pressed (optional)
1 cup fresh bread crumbs
Salt and freshly ground black pepper to taste
¼ cup chopped fresh parsley
5 tablespoons butter, melted

Puree half of the corn in a blender. Add the egg, milk, garlic, and the bread crumbs. Puree until very smooth. Pour the mixture into a medium-size bowl. Season well with salt and pepper. Stir in the remaining corn and the parsley. Chill for 1 hour.

Melt 1 tablespoon of the butter in a large heavy skillet set over medium-high heat. Pour in the batter by tablespoonfuls to form 2½-inch pancakes, spacing well apart. Fry, turning once, until golden brown on both sides, 2 to 3 minutes per side. Remove the finished cakes from the skillet and keep warm. Continue with the remaining batter, adding the butter, 1 tablespoon at a time before spooning in the batter. Serve very hot.

Maque Choux

Here is a classic Cajun dish that would go very well with some fried alligator, but if none is available, why not serve it with grilled fish or chicken?

Makes 6 servings

3 slices bacon
1 small onion, chopped
1 small green bell pepper, seeded and cut into
    ¼-inch dice
4 cups fresh corn kernels, cut from the cob
    (about 8 ears), or thawed frozen corn kernels
Salt and freshly ground black pepper to taste
½ teaspoon dried thyme
1 tablespoon chopped fresh parsley
2 large tomatoes, peeled, seeded, and chopped
½ teaspoon hot pepper sauce, or more to taste
¼ cup heavy cream

Cook the bacon in a medium-size heavy skillet over medium heat until almost crisp, 8 to 10 minutes. Remove the bacon from the skillet and drain on paper towels, leaving the fat in the skillet. Crumble the bacon.

Cook the onion and bell pepper in the bacon fat in the skillet over medium heat, stirring, until just translucent, about 5 minutes. Stir in the corn and season well with salt, pepper, and thyme. Cook for another 5 minutes.

Stir in the parsley, tomatoes, hot sauce, and cream. Cover and simmer about 5 minutes. Serve very hot, garnished with the crumbled bacon.

Note: *For a change of pace, replace the corn with two 15-ounce cans of yellow hominy that have been well drained, rinsed, and simmered in boiling water to cover for 30 minutes, then drained again.*

Cucumbers

One of my most pleasant memories of childhood was the first cucumber sandwich of the summer. My mother gloried in them, and it was a very special treat when she made them for us. She would spread mayonnaise on thin slices of white bread (with the crusts cut off if we were being good) and then pile on very thin slices of peeled cucumber. A little salt and lots of freshly ground pepper were all the seasoning needed. She had to make us at least two whole sandwiches apiece, because we devoured them.

Cucumbers are an ancient pleasure. They have been cultivated for well over three thousand years. This member of the gourd family probably was first grown in, or around, India and was brought west by the very early traders. We know that the ancient Egyptians enjoyed them as did the Romans, who even seem to have grown them in protected areas so they would be available all year long. Cucumbers were so popular in Europe that the early explorers brought them to the New World on their first voyages. The native population took to them at once and cultivation spread quickly.

Cucumbers are easy to grow, are nearly 96 percent water, and should be crisp and refreshing to eat. They are much more versatile than many cooks give them credit for and are as delicious cooked as they are incorporated into salads, cold dishes, and pickles.

Cucumbers are a dieter's dream. They are low in everything—fat, calories, sodium. But they are only a moderate source of fiber.

They can, however, cause intestinal distress in some people. I have found, though, that if the seeds are removed, cucumbers are not nearly as gas producing as when the seeds are left in. For those who continue to have problems, but thoroughly enjoy eating cucumbers, try Beano® (see page 37).

Selection: There are several types of cucumbers generally available in the market. The medium-size very dark green cucumbers that are

146

commonly sold are usually waxed to help retain moisture and increase shelf life. They must be peeled before eating, and if left on the vine too long before picking, they tend to be all seed and very little flesh. The long lighter green English, or European, cucumbers (often sold in a plastic shrink wrap) are generally not waxed, can be eaten skin and all, and have many fewer and smaller seeds than the common varieties. These are often called "burpless" cucumbers and frequently give sensitive people less gastric problems. Kirby cucumbers, sometimes called pickling cucumbers, vary in color from medium green to almost lemon yellow. These can be substituted for garden cucumbers in salads and other cold dishes, but they sometimes have a slightly bitter taste and large seeds. Because they are not waxed, Kirby cucumbers can be eaten unpeeled, but the skin is tougher than that of garden cucumbers.

No matter which variety you choose, look for plump, heavy cucumbers, with no soft spots, bruises, or shriveled ends. The color should be good and clear, the darker green the better, and except for Kirby cucumbers, there should be no yellow showing.

June to September is the high season for locally grown cucumbers, but they ship well, once they are waxed, and are available all year long.

The amount of cucumber per serving varies considerably depending on the recipe.

Storage and Preparation: Cucumbers should not be washed until just before they will be used. They can be stored, wrapped tightly in a plastic bag or plastic wrap, in the vegetable compartment of the refrigerator, up to several days. Once the cucumber has been cut, the remainder should be tightly wrapped in plastic wrap and used as soon as possible. Cut cucumbers quickly become soft and slimy. Cucumbers should never be frozen; they turn to mush when defrosted.

All cucumbers should be thoroughly washed before using. English cucumbers and the smaller Kirby variety do not need to be peeled but can be scored with the tines of a fork or peeled in alternating strips for an attractive appearance. Waxed cucumbers should be peeled.

Older varieties of cucumbers were often a little bitter and many recipes (including some in this book) call for salting the cut pieces and allowing them to drain. Bitterness is not generally a problem now, but the great amount of moisture in cucumbers sometimes makes them weep after they have been cut. Salting can keep creamy dressings from becoming too thin and diluted. Be sure, however, to rinse the cucumbers thoroughly after they have drained for 30 minutes or so, so that the final preparation is not overly salty and unpleasant.

> Tip: *Seeding cucumbers is a quick, easy job. Peel (or not, depending on the use and variety you are using) the cucumber and halve it lengthwise with a sharp knife. Run the tip of a sharp teaspoon down the center of the cucumber half. The seeds should come right out, leaving a hollow shell that can be cut into lengths, sticks, matchstick strips, or slices of any thickness.*

Raita

Raitas are yogurt-based condiments served with curries of all kinds. This is very definitely the most classic of all the combinations.

Makes about 1½ cups

1 large common cucumber, peeled, halved
   lengthwise, seeded, and grated, chopped, or
   very thinly sliced; or ½ English cucumber,
   unpeeled if you like, prepared in the same
   manner
1 cup best-quality plain yogurt
3 tablespoons chopped fresh mint, or more
   to taste
Salt and freshly ground black pepper to taste

Stir together all the ingredients. Chill for several hours or overnight.
Variations: *Stir 3 tablespoons finely minced red or green bell pepper into the mixture. Alternatively, add ¼ cup thinly sliced green onions (scallions). Or add both bell peppers and onions.*

Cucumber and Yogurt Salad

Serve this refreshing salad with roast lamb—or goat if you can get it.

Makes 6 servings

1 large English cucumber, unpeeled, halved
   lengthwise, seeded, and sliced ¼ inch thick;
   or 2 common cucumbers, peeled, and
   prepared in the same manner.
Salt
3 to 4 garlic cloves, minced or pressed
½ small onion, minced or thinly sliced
1½ cups best-quality plain yogurt
¼ cup chopped fresh parsley, or mint, plus
   additional for garnishing
Freshly ground black pepper to taste

Place the cucumber slices in a colander. Sprinkle well with salt and let drain 30 to 60 minutes. Rinse well and press out as much liquid as possible.
   Roll up the cucumbers into a dry kitchen towel and twist the ends to squeeze out as much liquid as possible. Place the cucumbers in a medium-size bowl. Beat together the garlic, onion, yogurt, and parsley. Season well with pepper. Combine the dressing with the cucumbers and refrigerate for 30 to 35 minutes. Serve chilled and garnish with the additional parsley or mint.

Vinegared Cucumber Salad

Add this tangy salad to your next cold buffet. It is especially good with cold, poached fish of any kind.

Makes about 6 servings

1 large English cucumber, unpeeled, halved
   lengthwise, seeded, and thinly sliced;
   or 2 common cucumbers, peeled, and
   prepared in the same manner
Salt
½ small sweet onion, thinly sliced; or 1 bunch
   (6 to 8) green onions (scallions), white
   and light green parts only, thinly sliced
1 teaspoon sugar
⅓ to ½ cup cider vinegar (or white wine,
   champagne, or rice wine vinegar)
Freshly ground black pepper to taste
2 tablespoons chopped fresh dill

Place the cucumber slices in a colander. Sprinkle well with salt and let drain for 30 to 60 minutes. Rinse well and press to remove as much liquid as possible. Roll up the cucumbers in a dry kitchen towel and twist the ends to remove as liquid as possible.
   Place the cucumbers in a small glass salad bowl. Stir in the onion. Sprinkle with the sugar and pour the vinegar over the mixture. Toss gently to coat the vegetables with the dressing. Season well with pepper. Cover and refrigerate for several hours. Serve the salad cold, garnished with the dill. Pass additional salt and pepper.

Cucumber Sauté

Poach a thick fillet of salmon, drain it, sprinkle on a little extra-virgin olive oil and sea salt, and pass these cucumbers. Easy and delicious.

Makes 6 servings

2 tablespoons butter
1 small onion, halved and thinly sliced
½ green bell pepper, seeded, cut into quarters, and thinly sliced
2 English cucumbers, peeled, halved lengthwise, seeded, and cut on the diagonal into ½-inch slices
2 tablespoons chopped fresh dill, plus additional for garnishing
Salt and freshly ground black pepper to taste
⅓ cup heavy cream

Melt the butter in a medium-size heavy skillet over medium heat. Cook the onion and bell pepper, stirring, until crisply tender, 4 to 5 minutes. Add the cucumbers and cook, stirring or tossing, 5 minutes longer. Season well with dill, salt, and pepper. Cook, stirring, 1 minute. Stir in the cream. Simmer over medium heat until the cream is reduced to a few spoonfuls, about 4 to 5 minutes. Toss to coat the cucumber slices with the sauce. Serve very hot, garnished with additional dill.

Cucumber Slaw with Oil and Vinegar

I think this crisp combination is very good with cold roast meat or chicken.

Makes 6 servings

1 large English cucumber, unpeeled, halved, seeded, and thinly sliced, or cut into 2-inch lengths and then into thin matchstick strips
Salt to taste
½ small onion, very thinly sliced

1 cup thinly shredded Savoy cabbage
½ teaspoon ground cumin
⅓ cup chopped fresh cilantro
2 tablespoons white wine or rice-wine vinegar
⅓ cup extra-virgin olive oil
Freshly ground black pepper to taste

Place the cucumber in a colander or sieve. Sprinkle generously with salt. Let stand for 30 to 60 minutes. Rinse with cold water. Press out as much liquid as possible. Roll up the cucumbers in a dry kitchen towel and twist the ends to remove as much liquid as possible.

Place the cucumbers in a medium-size bowl. Toss with the onion and cabbage. Toss the vegetables with the cumin and cilantro. Sprinkle with the vinegar and drizzle with the olive oil. Toss well. Season well with the pepper. Serve at room temperature.

Cucumber Salsa

This is an extremely versatile condiment. Serve it with corn fritters and cold meats or grilled tuna.

Makes about 2 cups

1 large or 2 medium-size common cucumbers, peeled, halved lengthwise, seeded, and cut into ¼-inch dice
½ medium red bell pepper, seeded and cut into ¼-inch dice
1 bunch (6 to 8) green onions (scallions), white part only, sliced
1 clove garlic, minced
½ jalapeño pepper, seeded and minced, or more to taste
1 medium-size ripe tomato, peeled, halved, seeded, and finely diced
¼ cup chopped fresh cilantro
2 tablespoons fresh lime juice
3 tablespoons olive oil
Salt and freshly ground black pepper to taste

Combine all the ingredients and refrigerate for several hours. Bring to room temperature to serve.

Baked Cucumbers

Cucumber goes very well with grilled fish. Try this dish with thick salmon steaks for a very special treat.

Makes 6 servings

1 cup plain dried bread crumbs
1 bunch (6 to 8) green onions (scallions), white and light green parts only, minced
2 tablespoons chopped fresh parsley
2 cloves garlic, minced
Salt and freshly ground black pepper to taste
2 tablespoons butter, melted
3 large common cucumbers, peeled, halved lengthwise, and seeded (do not use English cucumbers)
Freshly grated Parmesan cheese

Preheat the oven to 350°F.

In a medium-size bowl, combine the bread crumbs, green onions, parsley, garlic, salt, pepper, and butter. Stuff the cucumbers with this mixture.

Place the stuffed cucumbers in a single layer in a shallow baking dish large enough to hold the cucumbers side by side. Pour in enough boiling water to come just halfway up the sides of the cucumbers. Bake, uncovered, until the cucumbers are tender when pierced with the point of a sharp knife and the filling is golden brown, about 30 minutes. Serve very hot, dusted with the cheese.

> Note: *These stuffed cucumbers are also very good when served at room temperature as part of an antipasto platter or cold buffet.*

Cucumbers and Cream

I first ate cucumbers prepared something like this when they were served alongside braised chicken breasts, and I have always thought the combination almost perfect. Roast

chicken or oven-baked chicken breasts are also very good menu companions.

Makes 6 servings

2 tablespoons butter
4 medium-size common cucumbers, peeled, halved lengthwise, seeded, and thickly sliced; or 2 English cucumbers, unpeeled, prepared in the same manner
2 tablespoons dry white wine
2 tablespoons chicken stock
½ cup heavy cream
1 tablespoon chopped fresh thyme
Salt and freshly ground white pepper to taste
Chopped fresh parsley

Melt the butter in a medium-size heavy skillet over medium heat. Cook the cucumbers, tossing or stirring, until crisply tender, 3 to 5 minutes. Stir in the wine, stock, cream, and thyme. Cover and simmer over low heat for 5 minutes. Remove the cover, raise the heat to medium, and boil until the cream thickens into an unctuous sauce, 1 to 2 minutes. Season well with salt and pepper. Serve very hot, garnished with the parsley.

Variation: *Thinly slice half of a small onion and add it to the butter when the cucumbers are being sautéed, then continue with the recipe.*

Eggplant

The eggplant is a member of the nightshade family, a relative of the potato, pepper, and tomato. Perhaps that's why it marries so well with peppers and tomatoes in cooked dishes. The eggplant originated in India or Southeast Asia. Savvy Asian and Arab traders brought it west with them, probably during the fourth century. It spread from the Middle East to all of North Africa and then to Europe. Now some variety or other of eggplant is eaten in many sections of the world. The popularity of eggplant may be in part because it is extremely versatile. The vegetable, which has a delicate flavor on its own, takes on and enhances the flavors of the other ingredients in the dish.

The first eggplants were small and white, shaped like an egg. Until recently it was difficult to find these small eggplants in American markets, but the explosion of vegetable varieties available today has happily included some of the eggplants that have, in the past, been found only in Japan, India, and Italy.

While the Middle Eastern cuisines embraced it, Europeans were extremely wary of the eggplant, just as they had been of the tomato and the potato before it. Whether the "mad apple" was actually thought to drive you mad or simply made you crazy with love for it, the eggplant was approached with caution. Small amounts of it, combined perhaps with tomato and pepper, were eaten as a love potion, and it wasn't until the nineteenth century that full use was made of it—especially in Italy.

Among the types of eggplant you might find in the market is Japanese eggplant, which is 6 to 8 inches long, thin, and white or deep purple. Chinese eggplant is shaped the same, but larger.

Italian eggplant is generally small, more round than oblong shaped, and can be dark purple, light purple, white, or white-and-purple striped. The large familiar globe eggplant is also available in white now. And if you have an extremely well-stocked greengrocer, you may find Thai or Indian eggplant, which are small and egg shaped in green, purple, green and white, and white. Try them all. Most varieties are interchangeable, but the size will depend on the presentation of the dish. The small varieties, which would be useless for stuffing, generally seem to hold together better in baked dishes. And I like the Japanese variety for stir-frying, because I prefer all the pieces to have some skin on them and few or very small seeds.

Large eggplant, left too long on the vine, develop a lot of hard, unappetizing seeds. There was once a theory that there were male and female vegetables, the females being full of seeds. It isn't true, however, and no one needs to examine his or her eggplant for deep indentations in the blossom end, which were thought to indicate a female eggplant. The truth is that overmaturity is the culprit. For that reason it is best to look for small to medium-size vegetables, and avoid any that weigh much more than $1\frac{1}{4}$ pounds. Buy more eggplants rather than a bigger one.

Eggplants are fat free and low in calories, but are very filling, making them good diet fare. They contain small amounts of vitamin C, phosphorus, and calcium.

Selection: Whatever variety you choose, be sure to look for vegetables that are plump, smooth, shiny, and clear colored. Discard any that have lost their sheen, have dents, soft places, brown spots, or shriveled ends. The stem and cap are good indicators. If they are fresh and green, rather than dry and brown, the vegetable should be in good shape. While the texture of eggplant tends to be very slightly spongy, look

for those that are heavy and very firm to the touch.

When choosing globe eggplant, pick out small to medium-size vegetables. Not only are the larger specimens frequently full of seeds, they are often somewhat bitter. Modern varieties are rarely bitter if they are not overmature.

The prime season for fresh eggplant is late July to October, but the globe variety is usually available year round.

You will need about 2 pounds for six people.

Storage and Preparation: Like many other fresh vegetables, eggplant is best when eaten as soon after it is picked as possible. Do not let the outside fool you. Eggplant is perishable and will begin to lose its moisture within a day or two. Long storage will also tend to make the flavor bitter. Keep the eggplant in a perforated plastic bag in the vegetable section of the refrigerator. If the vegetable was very fresh when bought, it will keep up to three days, only a day or two if it was less fresh.

If the recipe calls for peeled eggplant, a vegetable peeler does a good job. Otherwise, wash the eggplant well, dry, trim the stem and blossom end, and leave the skin on. Do not use a carbon-steel knife to prepare eggplant, as it will discolor the flesh. The flesh tends to darken and turn brown once it is cut, so it is best to cook it as quickly as possible after cutting or to toss it with 1 teaspoon or so of lemon juice. Do not soak the cut eggplant in water, because the flesh will absorb quantities of water, releasing it again during the cooking process.

Eggplant also tends to absorb prodigious amounts of oil. Salting the cut-up vegetable, draining, and then drying it can reduce the amount of oil it will soak up. I find broiling the slices, sticks, or cubes, rather than frying or sautéing them, dramatically reduces the amount of oil needed and produces a very acceptable finished dish.

To salt the cut eggplant, sprinkle the cut surfaces liberally with salt, lay on clean kitchen towels or on a rack over towels, and let stand, lightly covered, for at least 30 minutes. Wipe off as much of the salt as you can or rinse very lightly and then dry the eggplant on more towels.

Eggplant Spread

Sometimes called beggar's caviar, this spread is quite good with all kinds of chips or bread. I like to add this to an antipasto plate or any cold buffet. Some recipes call for adding chopped tomato and/or hard-cooked eggs, but I prefer this plain variation.

Makes about 2 cups

1 large eggplant
3 tablespoons olive oil
½ small onion, minced
2 cloves garlic, minced
3 tablespoons chopped fresh parsley, or more to taste, plus additional for garnishing
2 tablespoons fresh lemon juice
Hot pepper sauce to taste
Salt to taste

Heat the oven to 450°F.

Prick the eggplant all over with a fork. Put the whole eggplant in a small shallow baking dish and bake until it is very tender when pierced with a knife, up to 1 hour.

Cool the eggplant. Halve it lengthwise, scoop out the flesh, and place it on a cutting board. Discard the skin. Chop the eggplant, but do not puree. Place the chopped eggplant in a medium-size bowl. Beat in the olive oil, 1 tablespoon at a time, until the mixture is thick. Stir in the onion, garlic, and parsley. Season with lemon juice and hot pepper sauce. Add salt. Chill several hours and garnish with the additional parsley.

Variation: *For a slightly smoky flavor, halve the unpeeled raw eggplant lengthwise and grill over medium coals, turning from time to time, until the eggplant is very tender and almost collapsed. Proceed with the recipe.*

Eggplant Sandwiches

Alone, these make a delightful first course or light lunch. But I like to serve them as a side dish with grilled fish, such as red snapper.

Makes 6 servings

1 medium-size eggplant, peeled and sliced across about ⅜-inch thick
Extra-virgin olive oil
½ pound fresh mozzarella cheese, sliced
1 cup dried bread crumbs, plain or Italian seasoned
¼ cup freshly grated Parmesan cheese
2 tablespoons chopped fresh parsley
1 large egg, beaten in a shallow bowl
Salt to taste

Preheat the broiler.

Brush one side of the eggplant slices with olive oil. Arrange the slices, oiled side up, in one layer on a baking sheet. Broil until just golden brown on top, about 3 minutes. Turn the slices and brush with oil. Broil until just golden on top, another 3 minutes. Remove the baking sheet from the oven.

Cool the eggplant slightly. Make sandwiches using 2 eggplant slices and 1 slice of mozzarella cheese. Combine the bread crumbs, Parmesan cheese, and parsley in a shallow bowl. Dip each sandwich in the beaten egg. Then roll the sandwiches in the crumb mixture, knocking off any excess.

Heat 1 to 2 tablespoons of the olive oil in a large heavy skillet over medium heat. Brown the sandwiches until golden brown on both sides and the cheese begins to melt, 5 to 6 minutes total. Serve very hot, sprinkled with salt.

Variations: *A little fresh tomato sauce can be passed to complement the sandwiches if you like. For a different flavor, pass a dish of Avocado Salsa with these.*

Scalloped Eggplant

Enjoy the real flavor of the eggplant in this dish, unaltered by the more robust taste of tomatoes and peppers. I think it is very good with baked fish or roast poultry.

Makes 6 to 8 servings

3 tablespoons butter, plus additional for buttering
2 small or 1 large eggplants, trimmed, unpeeled, and cut into 1-inch cubes
1 medium-size onion, sliced
2 cloves garlic, minced
2 tablespoons all-purpose flour
Salt and freshly ground black pepper to taste
1 teaspoon dried Italian herbs, such as oregano, marjoram, rosemary, and thyme, or a prepared mix; or 2 tablespoons chopped fresh oregano
2 cups milk, or half-and-half
1/2 cup cracker crumbs (use butter-cracker crumbs for a richer dish)

Preheat the oven to 350°F. Generously butter a medium-size deep baking dish.

Arrange half the eggplant in the bottom of the dish. Sprinkle with half the onion and half the garlic. Sprinkle with 1 tablespoon of the flour and season with salt and pepper and half the herbs. Repeat the layers. Pour the milk over all.

In a small saucepan, melt 3 tablespoons of butter. In a small bowl, combine the melted butter with the cracker crumbs and spread the mixture over the eggplant and onions.

Cover the dish with aluminum foil and bake for 30 to 35 minutes. Uncover and bake until the surface is golden brown, about 15 minutes longer. Serve very hot.

Ratatouille

The combination of these summer vegetables has many variations. This is my version of the classic French

Provençal dish. The specific order of layering the vegetables is important. The vegetables that need the most cooking are on the bottom. This way the more delicate vegetables don't cook into a mush, yet the flavors combine well. The dish can be eaten hot or, better yet, at room temperature. Enjoy it with any kind of entrée, from grilled shrimp to roast pork.

Makes 6 to 8 servings

1/4 cup olive oil
2 medium-size onions, cut into 1/4-inch dice or thinly sliced
2 cloves garlic, minced, or more to taste
2 large green bell peppers, seeded and cut into 1/4-inch dice or thinly sliced
3 to 4 small zucchini, trimmed and thickly sliced
1 medium-size eggplant, trimmed, unpeeled, and cut into 1-inch cubes
4 large ripe tomatoes, seeded and cut into chunks or thick slices
Salt and freshly ground black pepper to taste
1 tablespoon chopped fresh oregano
2 tablespoons chopped fresh basil
1/3 cup dry white wine

Heat the olive oil in a large kettle with a tight-fitting lid over low heat. Add the onions and garlic. Cook, stirring, for 2 minutes. In layers, add the bell peppers, then the zucchini, then the eggplant, then the tomatoes. Season well with salt, pepper, and herbs. Pour in the wine, cover, and simmer over low heat until the vegetables are very tender, but not mushy, 35 to 45 minutes. Stir from time to time after 30 minutes, being careful not to break up the vegetables too much. Uncover, remove from the heat, and let cool. Serve hot or at room temperature.

Variations: *Spoon this mixture between two fish fillets (bluefish or striped bass is nice), drizzle the whole with olive oil, and bake it for 15 to 20 minutes at 375°F. Delicious as a summer entrée.*

Spoon some of the cooled ratatouille onto a pizza or Boboli shell. Spread grated or cubed mozzarella cheese on top and bake at 475°F. until the cheese is melted and golden brown, about 15 minutes. Serve very hot.

Imam Bayildi

There are a lot of translations for the name of this dish. Literally, it means "the imam fainted." But the question might be, did he faint from the ecstasy of eating this delicious dish or did he faint because of the amount of expensive olive oil it contains? In any event, the Middle Eastern origins are clear—even though the basic ingredients are nearly the same as the Italian stuffed eggplant. Serve it with roast lamb—or concoct a large green salad and let it stand on its own at lunch or late supper.

Makes 6 servings

3 small to medium-size eggplants, halved
    lengthwise
Salt
3 tablespoons plus $\frac{1}{3}$ cup olive oil
1 large onion, halved and very thinly sliced
2 small cloves garlic, minced
2 medium-size ripe tomatoes, peeled, seeded,
    and chopped
$\frac{1}{2}$ cup chopped fresh parsley
Salt and freshly ground black pepper to taste
$\frac{1}{3}$ cup water
Juice of 1 lemon

Preheat the oven to 325°F.

Use a sharp knife to make diagonal slashes across the cut surface of the eggplant halves, cutting to within $\frac{1}{4}$ inch of the skin. Make more slashes in the other direction. Salt the cut sides and turn the eggplant cut side down on paper towels to drain for 20 minutes. Rinse the eggplant lightly and then dry on paper towels.

Heat 3 tablespoons of the olive oil in a medium-size heavy skillet over low heat. Add the onion and cook, stirring occasionally, until just softened, 6 to 8 minutes. Stir in the garlic and cook 1 minute longer. Add the tomatoes and parsley. Stir. Remove from the heat and season very well with salt and pepper.

Divide the filling among the eggplant halves. Use a spoon to push the mixture into the cuts in the flesh, mounding more on top. Arrange the stuffed eggplant, filling side up, in one layer, in a large shallow baking dish. In a small bowl, combine the remaining $\frac{1}{3}$ cup of olive oil, the water, and lemon juice. Pour this mixture over and around the eggplant. Cover the dish with aluminum foil.

Bake the eggplant for 1 hour. Remove from the oven. Uncover, baste with pan juices, and cool. Serve at room temperature.

Stacked Eggplant

This combination of eggplant, tomatoes, onion, and cheese goes well with butterflied leg of lamb that has been grilled until pink inside and crusty outside. Lamb chops or kebabs, grilled over medium-hot coals are also good. If you are not fond of lamb, try this with a grilled steak.

Makes about 6 servings

1 medium-size eggplant, trimmed and sliced
    across into rounds about $\frac{1}{4}$ inch thick
Olive oil
2 large ripe tomatoes, sliced about $\frac{1}{4}$-inch thick
1 small sweet onion, thinly sliced
Salt and freshly ground black pepper to taste
1 tablespoon chopped fresh thyme
4 ounces mild goat cheese, such as Montrachet,
    sliced or crumbled

Preheat the broiler.

Brush one side of each eggplant slice with olive oil. Arrange the slices, oiled side up, in one layer on a baking sheet. Broil until golden brown, 2 to 3 minutes. Turn the slices, brush with more oil, and broil 2 to 3 minutes longer. Remove the baking sheet from the oven.

Top each eggplant slice with a slice of tomato and then a slice of onion. Season well with salt and pepper and sprinkle with the thyme. Top each round with cheese and drizzle with a little olive oil.

Broil the stacks just until the cheese begins to melt, 2 to 3 minutes. Serve very hot or cool slightly and serve just warm.

Italian Stuffed Eggplant

The Mediterranean style of cooking has become very popular, not only because it is delicious but because it now appears to be extremely healthful. This Mediterranean dish combines some of the best local ingredients in an attractive accompaniment for baked chicken or almost any roast meat.

Makes 6 servings

2 tablespoons olive oil, plus additional for greasing and drizzling
3 small eggplants, halved lengthwise, flesh scooped out to leave a ¼-inch shell and reserved
4 anchovy fillets, chopped, or more to taste
½ small onion, minced
2 cloves garlic, minced
1 teaspoon capers, drained and minced (if using salted capers, rinse and drain them before mincing)
1 large ripe tomato, peeled, seeded, and cut into ¼-inch dice; or 1 cup drained, canned, diced tomatoes
3 tablespoons chopped fresh parsley
1 tablespoon chopped fresh oregano
Salt and freshly ground black pepper to taste
¼ cup plain dried bread crumbs
¼ cup freshly grated Parmesan cheese

Preheat the oven to 400°F. Grease the bottom of a large shallow baking dish with olive oil.

Heat 2 tablespoons of olive oil in a small skillet over low heat. Chop the eggplant flesh coarsely. Add the chopped eggplant, the anchovies, onion, and garlic to the skillet. Cook, stirring, for 2 to 3 minutes. Cool slightly and turn the mixture into a medium-size bowl. Add the capers, tomato, parsley, and oregano. Season well with salt and pepper. Fill the eggplant shells with the mixture.

In a small bowl, combine the bread crumbs and cheese. Sprinkle the mixture evenly over the filling in the shells.

Arrange the eggplant halves in one layer in the prepared dish. Drizzle with a little more olive oil. Bake until the shells are tender and the filling is bubbling hot, 35 to 40 minutes. Serve hot.

Caponata

This Italian specialty is similar to ratatouille but contains no zucchini and adds olives and celery. Purists believe that each vegetable should be cooked separately and then combined at the last minute. This recipe follows the classic method. Serve this as a part of an antipasto spread or pair it with veal in any form.

Makes 6 to 8 servings

⅓ cup pure olive oil
1 medium-size eggplant, trimmed, unpeeled, and cut into 1-inch chunks
6 to 8 ribs celery, trimmed and cut into 1-inch chunks
2 medium-size onions, thinly sliced
⅓ to ½ cup red wine vinegar
3 large tomatoes, seeded and coarsely chopped
1 tablespoon capers, drained (if using salted capers, rinse and drain them)
Salt and freshly ground black pepper to taste
⅓ cup chopped fresh parsley
2 tablespoons chopped fresh oregano
½ cup oil-cured black olives
Extra-virgin olive oil, optional, according to taste

In a large heavy skillet, heat 2 tablespoons of the pure olive oil over medium heat. Cook the eggplant, celery, and onions separately, one at a time, stirring occasionally, until each is tender and just golden brown, about 15 minutes, and remove each vegetable to a medium-size bowl as it is done. Add olive oil to the skillet as necessary. Add any remaining pure olive oil, the vinegar, tomatoes, capers, salt, pepper, and herbs to the skillet once all the vegetables are cooked and reserved in the bowl. Simmer, stirring, over low heat for 10 minutes. Stir this sauce into the eggplant mixture. Stir in the olives. Add additional salt and pepper if needed. Cool to room temperature. Drizzle with the extra-virgin olive oil if desired.

> Note: *Caponata can also be made by combining all the ingredients (except the olives) in a shallow baking pan and baking it at 325°F. until the vegetables are very tender, 45 to 60 minutes. There is little danger of burning the vegetables that way and overcooking is difficult, but you must stir it from time to time.*

French-fried Eggplant

If there are any dyed-in-the-wool eggplant haters in your household, try serving it prepared this way. It never ceases to amaze me how popular it is. Why not serve these delicious morsels in place of French fries with your next hamburger?

Makes 6 servings

Mild vegetable oil for deep-frying
1 medium-size eggplant, peeled, sliced across into ⅓-inch rounds and then cut into 3-inch sticks
Beer Batter (page 17)
Salt to taste

Heat the oil to 375°F. in a deep-fat fryer or a very deep heavy skillet.

Dry the eggplant sticks with a clean kitchen towel. Dredge the sticks in the batter, drain the excess batter, and fry, a few at a time, in the hot fat until golden brown, 2 to 3 minutes. Remove from the oil with a slotted spoon, drain on paper towels, and keep warm until all the eggplant is fried. Season with salt and serve very hot.

Variation: *Some cooks prefer to fry the eggplant without dipping it in batter. I like the crispy coating the batter*

gives and am convinced it keeps the eggplant from absorbing too much oil. But if you prefer not to use it, shake the sticks in a plastic bag into which you have placed 1 cup all-purpose flour, ½ teaspoon salt, and freshly ground pepper to taste. Knock off any excess flour and fry the eggplant, a few sticks at a time, until golden brown.

Garlicky Stir-fried Eggplant

Serve this alongside grilled fish. I like it with pan-sautéed fish fillets, too.

Makes 6 servings

3 tablespoons mild vegetable oil, preferably peanut; or for a hotter dish, a mixture of 3 tablespoons mild vegetable oil and 1 teaspoon Chinese hot oil
2 cloves garlic, minced
1 medium-size eggplant, trimmed and cut into 1-inch chunks
1 bunch (6 to 8) green onions (scallions), white and light green parts only, sliced on the diagonal into ½-inch pieces
Pinch crushed red pepper
2 tablespoons balsamic vinegar
2 tablespoons sugar
1 tablespoons Chinese black bean paste
¼ cup white wine
3 tablespoons light soy sauce, or teriyaki sauce
2 tablespoons chopped fresh parsley

Heat the oil in a wok over high heat. Add the garlic and stir 1 minute. Stir in the eggplant and cook, stirring constantly, until tender, about 5 minutes. Add the green onions and cook 1 minute longer. Stir in the crushed red pepper.

Combine the vinegar, sugar, black bean paste, wine, and soy sauce in a small bowl. Pour into the eggplant. Cover and steam for 2 minutes. Remove the cover and cook over high heat, stirring, until the sauce is slightly thickened, about 1 minute. Serve very hot, garnished with the parsley.

Eggplant Lasagna

I have often made this for a hoard of hungry teenagers and seen it disappear like snow on a summer's day. They loved it with hamburgers and mounds of fried chicken, but it is also delicious with plain roast chicken.

Makes 6 to 8 servings

3 tablespoons olive oil, plus additional for oiling
3 tablespoons butter, melted
1 large eggplant, trimmed, cut lengthwise into
    1/4-inch-thick slices, sprinkled with salt,
    and drained for 15 minutes
2 small onions, finely chopped
3 cloves garlic, minced
1/2 cup tomato sauce, preferably homemade
    (page 346)
1/2 cup red wine
1/2 cup chopped fresh parsley
Salt and freshly ground black pepper to taste
1 cup skim-milk ricotta cheese
2 medium-size tomatoes, sliced
8 ounces grated mozzarella cheese (2 cups)
1/4 cup freshly grated Parmesan cheese
1/2 teaspoon dried oregano.

Preheat the oven to 350°F. Lightly grease a medium-size lasagna pan.

Combine 3 tablespoons of olive oil and the butter in a small bowl. Brush the eggplant slices with some of the oil mixture. Arrange the slices in one layer on a baking sheet, and bake, turning once, until tender, about 5 minutes per side.

Heat 3 tablespoons of the oil mixture in a medium-size heavy skillet over low heat. Add the onion and garlic and cook, stirring occasionally, until translucent, about 10 minutes. Stir in the tomato sauce, wine, and parsley. Season with salt and pepper, and simmer over low heat for 5 minutes longer.

Layer one-third of the eggplant slices in the prepared pan, then half the ricotta, half the tomato slices, half the tomato sauce mixture, half the mozzarella cheese. Repeat the layers. Top with the remaining one-third of the eggplant. Drizzle with any remaining oil mixture over all and sprinkle with the Parmesan cheese. Season with dried oregano.

Bake until very hot and golden brown on top, 45 to 60 minutes. Serve very hot, or warm.

Parmesan-style Stuffed Eggplant

Who says eggplant Parmesan has to be served in a gratin dish? This variation is very satisfying, and I think it goes quite well with pork; but it's best with veal, especially thick grilled chops.

Makes 6 servings

3 small to medium-size eggplants
Olive oil
1/2 small onion, minced
1 teaspoon chopped fresh oregano
4 ounces mozzarella cheese, cut into small dice
1 cup tomato sauce, preferably homemade
    (page 346)
1/4 cup freshly grated Parmesan cheese

Preheat the oven to 375°F.

Rub the eggplants with olive oil and arrange them in a medium-size shallow baking dish. Bake until just tender when pierced with a fork, but not collapsed, 20 to 25 minutes. Remove the baking dish from the oven and let the eggplants cool slightly.

Increase the oven temperature to 400°F. Lightly oil a baking sheet.

Cut the eggplants in half lengthwise. Cut out the flesh in two or three pieces, leaving a 1/4-inch shell. Cut the eggplant flesh into large dice. In a medium-size bowl, toss the diced eggplant with the onion, oregano, and mozzarella. Pile the mixture into the scooped-out shells. Spoon the tomato sauce over the stuffed eggplants.

Arrange the stuffed eggplants on the prepared baking sheet. Sprinkle them with the Parmesan. Bake until golden and bubbling hot, 30 to 40 minutes. Serve very hot.

Greek-style Eggplant Rounds

The first time I ate eggplant like this was outside Athens. The outdoor café served the best whole grilled fish I have ever eaten. They were simply seasoned with lemon juice, olive oil, and salt. The eggplant went perfectly with the smokiness of the fish.

I still love the combination and like to serve it when I have a whole fish to grill.

Makes 6 servings

1 medium-size eggplant, trimmed and cut across
    into rounds about ⅓ inch thick
3 tablespoons olive oil
2 tablespoons butter
2 small onions, thinly sliced
2 large tomatoes, seeded and chopped
2 cloves garlic, minced
Salt and freshly ground black pepper to taste
½ cup chopped fresh parsley
½ cup crumbled feta cheese

Preheat the broiler.

Brush one side of each slice of eggplant with olive oil. Arrange the slices, oiled side, in one layer on a baking sheet and broil until golden brown on top, 2 to 3 minutes. Turn the slices over, brush with more oil and broil 2 to 3 minutes longer. Remove the baking sheet from the oven and cool the eggplant on a rack.

Preheat the oven to 375°F.

Heat 1 tablespoon of the olive oil and the butter in a medium-size heavy skillet over medium heat. Add the onions and cook, stirring, until soft and golden brown, about 10 minutes. Stir in the tomatoes and simmer over low heat for 10 minutes longer. Stir in the garlic and parsley. Season well with salt and pepper. Cook 10 minutes longer, stirring occasionally.

Arrange the broiled eggplant slices on a baking sheet. Pile the tomato mixture on the rounds and sprinkle each with cheese. Bake until the cheese melts and the mixture bubbles, about 15 minutes. Serve very hot.

Eggplant Cannelloni

Serve these with grilled Italian sausages. I prefer the hot variety because the flavor is enhanced by the delicious pastalike combination of eggplant and ricotta cheese.

Makes 6 to 8 servings

2 medium-size eggplants, trimmed and sliced
    lengthwise into ¼-inch slices
Olive oil
2 cups skim-milk ricotta cheese
¼ cup freshly grated Parmesan cheese, plus
    additional for serving
1 cup chopped fresh parsley, or chopped
    cooked spinach
2 cloves garlic, pressed
1 cup grated mozzarella cheese, or fontina
1 large egg, beaten
Salt and freshly ground black pepper
1 cup tomato sauce, preferably homemade
    (page 346)

Preheat the broiler.

Brush one side of each eggplant slice with olive oil. Arrange the slices, oiled side up, in one layer on a baking sheet. Broil until just golden, 2 to 3 minutes. Turn the slices over, brush with olive oil, and broil another 2 to 3 minutes. Remove the baking sheet from the oven and cool the eggplant.

Preheat the oven temperature to 350°F. Lightly oil a medium-size gratin dish.

In a medium-size bowl, beat together the ricotta, the ¼ cup of Parmesan, the parsley, garlic, mozzarella, egg, salt, and pepper.

Spoon some of the cheese mixture along the short edge of each eggplant slice. Roll up the slices jellyroll fashion and arrange, seam side down, in the prepared dish. Repeat with all the slices, arranging the rolls side by side. Drizzle with a little more olive oil.

Cover the dish with foil and bake 25 minutes. Remove the foil. Spoon the tomato sauce over the rolls and bake until the sauce is bubbling, about 10 minutes longer. Serve very hot. Pass the additional grated Parmesan cheese.

Skillet-steamed Eggplant

The little skinny Japanese eggplants have a delicious flavor. Serve this mixture with grilled shrimp.

Makes 6 servings

3 tablespoons olive oil
2 pounds very small eggplants (Japanese eggplants, if possible), trimmed and cut into large chunks, or if very small, cut in half lengthwise or in quarters
¼ cup water, about
2 cloves garlic, minced
1 teaspoon dried Italian herbs, such as oregano, marjoram, rosemary, and thyme, or a prepared mix; or 1 tablespoon chopped fresh oregano
Salt and freshly ground black pepper to taste
3 tablespoons chopped fresh parsley
Hot pepper sauce to taste (optional)

Heat the oil in a large heavy skillet over high heat and add the eggplant. Cook, tossing or turning with a spatula, until brown, 3 to 5 minutes. Add the water, then the garlic and herbs. Cover and cook over high heat, turning from time to time and covering again, until well browned and soft, about 10 minutes. Add 1 or 2 tablespoons of water as it evaporates in order to keep steam in the skillet so the eggplant continues to cook.

Season well with salt and pepper. Stir in the parsley and add hot pepper sauce, if desired. Serve hot.

Spicy Roasted Eggplant

Here is a very easy way to prepare eggplant. Choose very firm ones, not over 1¼ pounds apiece, so that they will not have too many seeds. Old Bay seasoning is available in the spice department of most supermarkets. Go easy at first, until you know if you like the peppery flavor. Pass these along with any roast meat.

Makes 6 servings

2 medium-size firm eggplants, peeled and cut into 3-inch-long sticks or wedges
2 tablespoons olive oil
1 to 2 tablespoons Old Bay seasoning
Salt to taste (optional)
Blue Cheese Sauce (optional) (recipe follows)

Preheat the oven to 375°F.

In a large bowl, toss the eggplant with the oil. Toss with the Old Bay seasoning. Spread the seasoned eggplant in a single layer in a shallow roasting pan. Roast, turning from time to time with a wide spatula, until golden brown and slightly crisp outside and soft inside, about 20 minutes. Taste, and salt lightly if desired. Serve very hot. Pass blue cheese sauce, if you like.

Blue Cheese Sauce

Makes about 1 cup

2 ounces blue cheese, crumbled (about ½ cup)
⅔ cup mayonnaise, prepared or homemade (page 13)
¼ cup buttermilk, or light sour cream
1 teaspoon white wine vinegar, or lemon juice

Beat together all the ingredients in a medium-size bowl. Refrigerate several hours or overnight. Serve cold, for chipping.

Spicy Eggplant Fritters with Rouille

Try these as nibbles with a glass of white wine or serve them alongside a whole baked fish: shad, striped bass, or grouper.

Makes 6 to 8 servings

1 medium-size eggplant, peeled and cut into ½-inch cubes
3 tablespoons chopped fresh parsley
2 cloves garlic, pressed

Hot pepper sauce to taste
2 large eggs, beaten
Salt to taste
Up to 1½ cups plain dried bread crumbs
Oil for deep-frying
Easy Rouille (recipe follows)

Simmer the eggplant in salted water to cover over low heat until tender, 10 to 15 minutes. Drain. Mash the eggplant with a fork or a potato masher in a medium-size bowl or put through a ricer. Turn the mashed eggplant into a large bowl. Beat in the parsley, garlic, and hot pepper sauce. Beat in the eggs, salt, and enough bread crumbs to make the mixture hold together when pressed. Shape the mixture into balls about 1½ inches in diameter. Let the balls dry for about 30 minutes.

Heat the oil in a deep-fat fryer or heavy kettle to 375°F. Fry the fritters, a few at a time, until golden brown and crisp, turning once, about 3 minutes for each batch. Drain on paper towels. Salt lightly and serve hot with a little easy rouille on the side for dipping.

Easy Rouille

Makes about 1 cup

3 small cloves garlic, pressed
2 small dried red chiles (for example, bird's tongues) ground in a mortar or in a small food processor
1 cup mayonnaise, prepared or homemade with olive oil (page 13)

Beat together all the ingredients in a medium-size bowl. Let stand at least 1 hour to blend the flavors.

Summer Tajine

A tajine is not only a kind of baked dish, it is also the earthenware dish itself. This exceptionally easy to prepare summer vegetable combination with Moroccan origins is also exceptionally popular. Be prepared to have none left over. Serve it with any kind of grilled entrée: lamb, chicken, pork, and even sausages.

Makes 6 servings

1 small eggplant, trimmed and thinly sliced into rounds
2 medium-size zucchini, trimmed and thinly sliced into rounds
1 large onion, thinly sliced
1 large green bell pepper, seeded and thinly sliced
2 tomatoes, thinly sliced
2 cloves garlic, minced
Salt and freshly ground black pepper to taste
Olive oil
3 or 4 large sprigs fresh thyme
1 large sprig fresh oregano

Preheat the oven to 400°F.

In a large gratin dish, arrange the vegetables in rows, overlapping the slices slightly. Do not make more than one layer or the end result will not have the right texture. Sprinkle the garlic over all. Season with salt and pepper. Drizzle generously with the olive oil (but don't drown the vegetables either) and arrange the sprigs of thyme and oregano on top.

Bake until the vegetables are tender and beginning to brown around the edges, 25 to 30 minutes. Serve very hot.

Note: *In the unlikely even you should have any left over, this is delicious cold the next day. I like to bring it to room temperature and make open-faced sandwiches by layering the vegetables on thick slices of toasted Italian bread or sourdough bread. A tiny drizzle of olive oil and a good grinding of fresh black pepper are perfect finishing touches.*

Fennel

While it has somewhat the same anise flavor as the common herb fennel, Florence fennel (bulb fennel or finocchio) is a crisply delicious vegetable. For some, that anise flavor is an acquired taste, for others it is a delicious accompaniment to almost any fish, poultry, veal, or lamb dish.

Florence fennel has a swollen leaf base, somewhat like celery. In fact almost anything that can be done with celery can be done with fennel. The crisp, overlapping ribbed stems are delicious raw in salads and on crudité platters, but they can also be grilled, steamed, braised, or pureed and added to sauces and soups.

Fennel is popular in France and is increasingly available in American supermarkets, but it is truly savored in Italy. Italians love fennel prepared in many ways, including in a very simple dish called Pinzimonio—crisp strips of raw fennel dipped in the finest available extra-virgin olive oil that has been well seasoned with salt and pepper. While it is simplicity itself, I have found that this method of serving fennel is more than just simply delicious.

This is certainly a very versatile vegetable that deserves a larger place in American cooking, especially with the modern emphasis on lightness.

Fennel is low in fat and calories, is relatively high in vitamins A and C, and potassium, and is a moderate source of fiber and calcium.

Selection: The fennel bulbs should be as crisp, plump (rather than desiccated), and white (the greener ones can be bitter) as possible with no tinges of yellow or brown. The stalks should not be limp or spongy. Generally, the bulbs are sold with the upper stalks cut off, leaving only a few wispy, feathery leaves in the center. These leaves can be used like dill as a seasoning in salads and stews. The cut ends of the hollow stalks should look fresh and green, not brown and dry.

162

Fennel is freshest from early October throughout the end of January, but it is often available year round in large markets and at specialty greengrocers.

One medium-size bulb of fennel will be plenty for two people; two large or three medium-size bulbs should serve six.

Storage and Preparation: If you have found fresh fennel bulbs with the stems attached, it is best to cut them off about 2 inches above the bulb itself. If left attached these stems, like carrot leaves, will continue to draw moisture out of the bulb and will tend to make the interior soft and spongy.

Store fennel, unwashed, in a perforated vegetable bag in the vegetable section of the refrigerator. Very fresh bulbs will remain crisp for up to five days or so. Fennel on the edge of freshness should be used as quickly as possible.

To prepare the bulbs for salads or other raw dishes, simply wash the outside well, dry, and cut off the remaining stems. Trim the root end and remove any scarred or blemished ribs. The bulb can be sliced, halved lengthwise, cut into wedges, cut into sticks or matchstick strips, chopped, or diced. If the prepared fennel will be cooked, it can be handled in the same manner or left whole.

Microwaved Fennel

For six servings, trim 3 medium-size fennel bulbs. Halve them lengthwise and arrange in one layer in a microwave dish. Add 3 tablespoons of water or chicken stock, cover with plastic microwave wrap, and vent. Microwave on high for 6 to 7 minutes, depending on the size of the fennel. Let stand for 5 minutes before uncovering.

Boiled Fennel

Plain boiled or braised fennel is delicious if drained, seasoned with salt and pepper, and served with a drizzle of olive oil or melted butter.

For six servings, trim 3 medium-size fennel bulbs. Halve them lengthwise and arrange them cut side down in a large, heavy skillet. Add enough water or chicken stock to just cover the fennel. Cover and simmer until the vegetable is fork tender, 20 to 30 minutes. Drain and season.

Steamed Fennel

Arrange trimmed and halved or quartered fennel bulbs in a steamer basket or colander. Steam, covered, over simmering water until tender when pierced with a sharp fork, 20 to 25 minutes. Serve very hot or marinate in a savory dressing and serve at room temperature.

Braised Fennel with Dill

Once you have prepared fennel this way it will become a permanent part of your vegetable repertoire. I like it best with poached salmon, but it is also wonderful with almost any grilled fish and, of course, with roast veal.

Makes 6 servings

2 tablespoons butter
**3 medium-size fennel bulbs, trimmed and sliced
    lengthwise into ¼-inch slices**
½ cup chicken stock
¼ cup dry vermouth or dry white wine
Salt and freshly ground pepper to taste
3 tablespoons chopped fresh dill

Melt the butter in a large skillet over low heat and arrange the fennel slices in one layer if possible. Pour in the stock and vermouth. Cover and cook until quite tender, up to 40 minutes, depending on the age of the fennel. Uncover the skillet, raise the heat to medium and boil until the liquid is reduced to 2 to 3 tablespoons, about 3 minutes. Season well with salt, pepper, and dill. Serve hot, or at room temperature.

> Note: *If the fennel bulbs have any of their feathery leaves attached, save them, chop, and add them at the end of the recipe along with the salt, pepper, and dill.*

Steamed Fennel Parmesan

The pleasant anise flavor of fennel goes very well with veal, especially thick broiled chops.

Makes 6 servings

**3 to 4 medium-size fennel bulbs, trimmed, any
    tough outer ribs removed, halved lengthwise,
    cut into wedges, and steamed until tender**

2 tablespoons butter, plus additional for buttering
Salt and freshly ground black pepper to taste
⅓ to ½ cup freshly grated Parmesan cheese

Preheat the broiler. Butter a small gratin dish.

Arrange the steamed fennel in the prepared dish. Season well with salt and pepper. Dot with 2 tablespoons of butter. Sprinkle the cheese over the fennel. Broil 3 to 4 minutes until very hot and the cheese is golden brown. Serve at once.

Fennel and Red Pepper Sauté

This is the perfect foil for a crusty grilled whole fish, such as trout, red snapper, or small catfish.

Makes 6 servings

**3 medium-size fennel bulbs, trimmed, any tough
    outer ribs removed, cut into large dice, boiled
    or steamed until just tender, and well drained**
2 tablespoons butter
1 tablespoon pure olive oil
1 small onion, cut into ¼-inch dice
**2 small red bell peppers, seeded and cut into
    large dice**
Salt and freshly ground black pepper to taste
2 tablespoons chopped fresh oregano
Freshly grated Parmesan cheese (optional)
Extra-virgin olive oil (optional)

Melt the butter in a heavy skillet or sauté pan over medium heat. Stir in the pure olive oil. Add the onion and bell peppers and cook, stirring, until the onion is limp and the peppers are crisply tender, 6 to 7 minutes. Stir in the drained fennel, season with salt, pepper, and oregano. Cook, stirring, until the fennel is tender and lightly browned, another 10 minutes or so.

Serve very hot and pass the cheese separately. Or, if you prefer, cool the fennel mixture and serve it at room temperature, without the cheese, and pass the extra-virgin olive oil for drizzling on top.

Roasted Fennel

For the best flavor, parboil the fennel ahead of time and then roast it just before serving. I think this goes very well with broiled or grilled fish—orange roughy, salmon, and even tuna.

Makes 6 servings

3 medium-size fennel bulbs, trimmed, sliced vertically into 4 thick slices per bulb
2 tablespoons olive oil
Salt and freshly ground black pepper to taste

Arrange the fennel slices in a large skillet. Cover with water and simmer over medium heat until the fennel is barely tender when pierced with a sharp knife, about 5 minutes. Drain the fennel and dry it on a cloth kitchen towel.

Preheat the oven to 500°F.

Brush the parboiled fennel on both sides with olive oil. Season with salt and pepper. Arrange the fennel slices in a single layer on a baking sheet and roast in the oven, turning them once or twice, until golden brown on both sides and very tender, 15 to 20 minutes.

Variation: *Cut the fennel bulbs in half vertically, or in large wedges. Parboil them until just tender, up to 15 to 20 minutes, depending on the age and size of the bulbs. Brush the fennel with olive oil and then grill, turning the pieces once or twice, over medium-hot coals until the cut surfaces begin to turn golden brown and the edges become lightly charred.*

Braised Fennel and Red Onion

When it is served at room temperature, I think this is a good addition to any antipasto or appetizer buffet. Or, serve it hot with roast poultry or baked fish.

Makes 6 servings

3 tablespoons butter

2 to 3 medium-size fennel bulbs, trimmed and cut vertically into ¼-inch slices
2 medium-size red onions, thickly sliced
¾ cup well-flavored chicken stock
2 tablespoons anise-flavored liqueur, such as anisette or Pernod
Salt and freshly ground black pepper to taste
2 tablespoons chopped fresh parsley

Melt the butter in a large heavy skillet over medium heat. Add the fennel and onions. Pour in the stock and add the liqueur. Season well with salt and pepper. Cover and simmer over low heat until very tender, 40 to 45 minutes.

Remove the cover and raise heat to medium-high. Boil until the sauce is thick and coats the vegetables, 5 to 10 minutes. Serve very hot, or warm, garnished with the parsley.

Fennel and Parmesan Salad

It is essential that the fennel be absolutely fresh, and the more tender it is, the better. I also suggest splurging on the fruitiest olive oil you can find. This salad is so simple, not unlike pinzimonio (an Italian appetizer of raw vegetables seasoned with extra-virgin olive oil), that the quality of the ingredients will determine the end result. While this is delicious all year long, I think of it as a summer specialty, to accompany cold poached fish.

Makes 6 to 8 servings

1 head leaf lettuce
2 medium-size fennel bulbs, trimmed, thinly sliced lengthwise
Best quality extra-virgin olive oil
Salt and freshly ground black pepper to taste
Aged Parmesan cheese, shaved
Chopped fresh parsley

Arrange the lettuce leaves on chilled salad plates. Divide the fennel among the plates. Drizzle generously with the olive oil and season well with salt and pepper. Top each salad with lots of cheese. Garnish with the parsley.

Stir-fried Fennel

This colorful dish is perfect with lamb and pork. My favorite is to serve it with thick lamb chops that have been cooked until pink inside, crusty on the outside.

Makes 6 servings

2 tablespoons olive oil
2 medium-size fennel bulbs, trimmed, halved
    vertically and thinly sliced across the cut
1 small onion, sliced vertically
1 red or green bell pepper, seeded and cut into
    thin strips
1 clove garlic, minced
2 tablespoons dry white wine, or dry sherry
1 tablespoon chicken stock
1 teaspoon soy sauce
1/4 teaspoon ground ginger
Hot pepper sauce to taste (optional)

Heat the oil to smoking in a wok over high heat. Add the fennel, onion, and bell pepper. Cook, stirring, for 4 to 5 minutes. Stir in the garlic and cook, stirring, 1 minute longer. In a small bowl, mix together the wine, stock, soy sauce, and ginger. Pour this mixture into the wok. Reduce the heat to medium. Cover and cook until the vegetables are crisply tender and are coated with the sauce, about 3 minutes. Add hot pepper sauce if using. Serve very hot.

Fiddlehead Ferns

Fiddleheads must be one of the most difficult vegetables to find in the market, but I included them because I think they are well worth the effort to try if you happen to run across a source. The flavor is fresh, delicate, and slightly bitter, a little like asparagus.

These elusive little gems are in season for only a few short weeks from late April to early May, the mud season, and the best place to find them is in Maine, although they do grow all along the East Coast and in some areas of the Pacific Northwest. The finest fiddleheads are plucked by hand by a few avid hunters, most of whom are extremely jealous of their private caches and will never tell where in the swampy marshes and damp hillocks of Maine or eastern Canada that they find them.

Usually, only the tiny, furled (like the scroll of a fiddle, hence the name), undeveloped shoots of the ostrich fern are eaten, although, in other countries, bracken are also cooked. Most other ferns are not edible, and you must be very careful when buying the fresh variety as the wrong ones can be poisonous. There are canned fiddleheads, usually found in the gourmet section of large supermarkets or in specialty stores. In my estimation these canned fiddleheads are as unappetizing as canned spinach, but they might come in handy if you become addicted and simply must have fiddleheads. The canned variety should be rinsed and well drained before using. They usually have already been overcooked during the canning process, and will need very little additional preparation.

Fresh fiddleheads can be prepared much like asparagus, although I think they are too few and far between not to enjoy in as simple a manner as possible.

While fiddleheads are not readily enough available to seriously affect anyone's diet, they do provide a modicum of both vitamin A and vitamin C.

Selection: Try to find the freshest fiddleheads possible. Look for the brightest green, most succulent (as opposed to old or dried out) ferns available. Fiddleheads less than 3 inches long will be the tenderest. They are often covered with a scaly, papery husk that usually rubs right off. Sometimes this husk will be missing, having fallen off during sorting and packaging. Avoid any fiddleheads that are yellowed, brown, or dry looking. And definitely do not buy any that are not tightly coiled. Once the ferns begin to unroll they become tough, hairy, and unappetizing. The truth of the matter, in my estimation, is that fiddleheads are so expensive that they should be avoided all together if they are not in excellent condition.

The very best fiddleheads are often found at small markets in the Maine countryside, generally sold by the pound in small paper bags. If you find them in a metropolitan specialty greengrocer or market, pick them out individually, selecting only those in prime condition.

Count on ¼ pound per person.

Storage and Preparation: Fiddleheads are best when they are prepared as soon as possible after being picked. If they must be stored, place them, unwashed, in a perforated plastic vegetable bag. Use as soon as possible, within a day or two at the outside.

Wash the fiddleheads in cold water to cover, rubbing off the husks. Drain the tightly curled ferns, trim off the ends, and dry them on cloth kitchen towels.

If the fiddleheads are to be served just lightly sautéed, boil them first in salted water to cover until just tender, 5 to 7 minutes.

> Tip: *Serve fiddlehead ferns any way you might prepare asparagus. Steam or boil them in lightly salted water to cover until crisply tender, generally less than 15 minutes. Drain them well and serve quite warm with Hollandaise or Maltaise sauce spooned over the top. Or drizzle them with a little extra-virgin olive oil and sprinkle with good, freshly grated Parmesan cheese. You can also serve them raw or cooked and cooled to room temperature as part of a spring salad, with a good mustardy vinaigrette. For another tasty preparation, add 1 or 2 tablespoons of toasted sesame oil to mayonnaise, prepared or homemade, and pass it in a sauceboat for adding to barely warm fiddleheads. Sprinkle each serving with freshly toasted sesame seeds for crunch.*

Sautéed Fiddlehead Ferns with Butter and Garlic

If you are lucky enough to find a pound of fresh fiddleheads, try this recipe, either as an appetizer on its own or as a sidekick for a grilled steak.

Makes 4 to 6 servings

3 tablespoons butter
1 pound fiddlehead ferns, husks rubbed off, boiled in salted water to cover for 5 minutes, and drained
Salt and freshly ground black pepper to taste
3 medium-size cloves garlic, minced
¼ cup chopped fresh parsley

Melt the butter in a medium-size heavy skillet over medium heat. Cook the fiddleheads, stirring, until they are tender, 3 to 4 minutes. Season well with salt and pepper. Add the garlic and parsley. Cook, tossing 2 to 3 more minutes. Serve very hot.

Variation: *Pass some freshly grated Parmesan cheese and serve with veal scaloppine.*

Steamed Fiddlehead Ferns with Blender Hollandaise

If you cannot find fresh fiddleheads, skip on to some other vegetable. The canned variety will not be worthwhile in this preparation. Serve this with a perfect spring menu, poached fish or roast chicken would be just right, along with tiny, waxy new potatoes.

Makes 4 to 6 servings

1 pound fiddlehead ferns, husks rubbed off
Blender Hollandaise sauce (page 20)
Fresh bread crumbs, toasted

Steam the fiddleheads in a steamer basket or colander over simmering water, covered, until just tender, 7 to 10 minutes, depending on the size and freshness of the ferns. Or boil the ferns in salted water to cover until tender, 5 or 6 minutes, or 10 minutes or longer if the ferns are large. Drain well and keep warm.

Spoon the blender Hollandaise sauce onto warm, but not hot, serving plates. Arrange the ferns on top of the sauce. Garnish each serving with a sprinkle of bread crumbs. Serve at once.

Garlic

There doesn't seem to be any middle ground when it comes to garlic. Either you love it or you hate it—or, sometimes, it hates you. In cooking, I really don't believe there can be anything like "a little garlic"; either it is definitely present or it should be absent. Sometimes it can be a subtle presence in a delicate dish, i.e., rubbed on toasted bread to make tomato-soaked bruschetta or on the inside of a fondue dish or salad bowl to give just a hint of its character, but generally garlic is incorporated to give both fragrance and flavor.

Garlic is a member of the allium family, which includes lilies, onions of all kinds, leeks, and chives. It will grow nearly anywhere, and has been used in cooking for at least five thousand years. In fact, some cuisines seem almost to be based on it. The Chinese enjoy it in quantity, especially when mixed with blazing hot peppers. In Italy it is less fiery but equally prevalent, India and Mexico indulge without qualm, and America is moving up rapidly in rate of consumption.

While there are actually several hundred types of garlic, we usually find three in quantity in American markets. Spring garlic, which is white, often with small cloves, can have a tendency to sprout quickly. These little green sprouts can add a bitter taste unless they are picked out. The garlic that is harvested in the fall usually has a pink or purple-tinted skin. The cloves are plump and generally somewhat larger than the white variety, and several French chefs I have worked with frequently told me it is less likely to cause heartburn, though I cannot find any evidence to prove this belief. I think those who will be bothered by garlic are affected by all of it. Elephant garlic, a giant head made up of huge cloves that look like the answer to a garlic lover's dream, is more closely related to leeks than common garlic, and the flavor is so mild it adds very little character to cooked dishes. Even though it has its enthusiastic advocates, I just cannot get excited about it.

The odor and flavor of garlic are contained in its natural oils. Garlic actually has several different flavors. Raw, it can be acrid and harsh if eaten in large pieces. Cut up or minced and added to cooked dishes, it contributes both a pleasant aroma and tantalizing taste. Roasted, baked, or simmered until meltingly tender, garlic becomes soft, spreadable, unctuous, and almost sweet—totally unlike its more assertive raw state.

Health claims about garlic have been made practically for as long as it has been eaten. At one time or another it has been touted as a cure for everything from hair loss to heart disease and most ailments in between, including impotence and infertility. Healers in ancient Egypt, Greece, Rome, China, and India prescribed it for almost anything that afflicted their patients. Even today many people are convinced that garlic extract capsules keep them hale and hearty. Actually, garlic does have substantial antibacterial properties, and modern research is beginning to indicate that garlic may reduce cholesterol levels, aid digestion, possibly prevent heart attacks, and act as an anticarcinogenic. While the scientific jury is still out on its true medicinal value, it is abundantly evident that eating garlic in almost anything adds enjoyment to a meal and does little or no harm to the eater.

At one time or another, garlic has also been thought to keep away vampires, witches, and goblins, along with various and sundry other evil influences and troublesome spirits. Whether it is the odor or some other property that keeps them at bay is a matter of conjecture, though.

Garlic is low in fat and cholesterol and contains a substantial amount of vitamin C. Unfortunately, the amounts of garlic eaten at any one time are usually so small that the quantity of vitamin C really isn't significant.

Selection: No matter which type of garlic is in the market, look for plump, heavy, dry heads. Unless it is the only kind available, avoid garlic sold in little cardboard boxes. I find these heads are often dried out—or that the cloves are tiny and difficult to peel. Do not buy garlic that has begun to sprout or that has been stored where moisture can get at it and turn the cloves moldy. Do not buy garlic heads that are light in weight, soft, or dried out.

Storage and Preparation: Most experts store their garlic in a dry, dark, well-ventilated container rather than in the refrigerator. The temperature of the refrigerator doesn't seem to injure the garlic, but the moisture will speed up the tendency to mold, so it will spoil faster than in a dry container at room temperature. If you are not in the habit of using a great deal of garlic, it is probably wisest to buy it in small quantities more frequently, rather than to stock up at one time. True garlic lovers can buy several heads at a time and keep it for several weeks, or longer, in a basket or in one of the commercial clay garlic jars with holes in the sides. I keep mine in a small basket away from drafts and light, and it always seems to be gone before it suffers any adverse effects.

Garlic needs little preparation. The cloves can be separated from the head in any quantity needed. If you must peel a lot of garlic at one time for a recipe, the cloves can be parboiled for 3 to 4 minutes, drained, and cooled slightly. The skins should slip off without much trouble. If a little green sprout has begun to develop in the middle of the clove, halve the clove lengthwise and pop the sprout out with the point of a knife. The sprout can be a little bitter, but some people don't mind the taste, and there is no reason not to include it in the dish if you like. In fact, in China, these sprouts are pried out whole to add to salads or cooked dishes or are allowed to develop into full-fledged shoots. These shoots are often sold in bunches much as we sell green onions, to be cut up and used in stir-fries and other dishes.

> **Tip:** *If the garlic is to be chopped for a given recipe, there is an easy way to peel it. Place the unpeeled cloves on a chopping board and smack them with the flat side of a large chef's knife or a Japanese or Chinese cleaver. The peel will separate from the flesh and can be easily slipped off and discarded.*
>
> *Once the cloves are peeled, sprinkle a little salt on them and chop as finely as you like. The salt helps to hold the chopped garlic together and keeps it from sticking to the knife. Be sure to subtract the amount of salt you used during chopping from the salt called for in the recipe.*

> **Note:** *Some cooks feel that putting garlic through a press results in a strong, somewhat bitter paste, and they advocate mincing garlic as finely as possible, mashing it a little with the flat side of the knife. I agree that pressed garlic can be strong if it is incorporated into uncooked dishes, but if the dish or sauce is going to be cooked for any length of time, pressing is an easy way to process garlic leaving no discernible pieces. The new self-cleaning garlic presses are strong enough to press garlic cloves with the skin still on, although this method sometimes results in garlic spurting all over the presser rather than down into the cup or bowl. You can easily remove the odor of garlic from utensils and hands by rubbing them with the cut side of a lemon.*

Roasted Garlic

Garlic prepared this way loses all of its sharpness and becomes a luscious, creamy puree that enhances any sauce and is delicious on its own, as a spread for crusty bread or served as a natural sauce with slices of roast lamb.

Makes about 6 servings

Melted butter, or olive oil, depending on taste— each gives a different flavor
4 large heads garlic, unpeeled
2 large sprigs fresh thyme (optional)

Preheat the oven to 300°F. Butter or oil a small gratin dish.

Cut a ¼-inch-thick slice from the top of each garlic head. Arrange the whole heads, cut side up, in the prepared dish. Drizzle the heads with a little olive oil or melted butter. Bake the heads, uncovered, about 30 minutes. Remove the dish from the oven and arrange the fresh thyme if using, over the garlic. Cover the dish well with foil and continue to bake until the garlic becomes a creamy paste inside the peel, 1 to 1½ hours longer. Uncover the dish and remove the garlic. Squeeze the soft garlic from the heads into a small dish.

To use, add the garlic to a sauce, beat it into softened butter, spread it on toasted bread, or pass it as an instant sauce for roast meats, especially lamb. Season well with salt and pepper.

Caramelized Garlic Slices

Pass these delicious garlic slices to stir into mashed potatoes, or serve them as an accompaniment to roast pork, grilled steak, or roast lamb.

Makes about 1 cup

3 tablespoons butter
3 large heads garlic, cloves peeled and thickly sliced lengthwise

1 tablespoon sugar
2 tablespoons balsamic vinegar
2 tablespoons dry white wine
¼ cup well-flavored chicken stock
Salt and freshly ground black pepper to taste
2 tablespoons chopped fresh parsley

Melt the butter in a medium-size heavy skillet over very low heat. Add the garlic, cover, and cook, shaking the pan from time to time to keep it from burning, until the garlic is almost tender, 15 to 20 minutes. Sprinkle the sugar over the garlic. Pour in the vinegar, wine, and stock. Increase the heat and boil until the liquid is reduced to a few tablespoons of thick glaze and the garlic is coated and golden brown, 3 to 4 minutes. Season with salt and pepper and toss with the parsley. Serve hot.

> Note: *Garlic chars and burns easily if cooked at too high a heat. Burned garlic has an unpleasant bitter flavor that will spoil the final dish. It is better to add the cut-up cloves to a moderately hot pan and to cook, stirring constantly, for no longer than 1 minute. If you must add garlic to very hot oil or butter, cook it only for a few seconds before adding other ingredients. For a milder flavor, cook a whole peeled clove of garlic in butter or oil over medium heat for 1 minute, being careful not to let it burn. Then remove the clove from the pan with a slotted spoon and discard. The whole clove will impart a mild garlic flavor to the fat and will enhance a delicate dish or sauce.*

Roasted Garlic Custards

The rich flavor of the roasted garlic comes through in these delightful individual custards. I like to serve them along with grilled tuna steaks, but they would make a great addition to any festive meal, including a classic roast turkey Thanksgiving dinner.

Makes six 4-ounce ramekins or 6-ounce custard cups

1 tablespoon butter, plus additional butter, softened, for buttering
1 tablespoon all-purpose flour, plus additional for dusting
1 large head garlic, unpeeled
1 cup chicken stock, hot but not boiling
½ cup heavy cream
5 whole large eggs, beaten until very light
1 teaspoon Dijon-style mustard
Salt and freshly ground black pepper to taste
1 teaspoon *each* chopped fresh thyme, oregano, and basil
Sprigs of fresh parsley

Preheat the oven to 325°F. Generously butter six 4-ounce ramekins. Dust the inside of the ramekins with flour, knocking out any excess.

Cut a ¼-inch-thick slice from the top of the garlic head. Wrap the whole head, cut side up, in a piece of aluminum foil. Bake the head, until soft, about 1½ hours.

Melt 1 tablespoon butter in a small saucepan over medium heat. Stir in 1 tablespoon flour and cook, stirring, for 3 minutes. Do not brown. Whisk in the stock and beat until smooth. Reduce the heat to low and cook, stirring, until just beginning to thicken, about 3 minutes. Set aside.

Squeeze the roasted garlic into a small heatproof bowl. Beat in the cream and the eggs. Beat in the mustard. Finally beat in the hot cream sauce. Season well with salt, pepper, and herbs.

Divide the mixture evenly among the buttered ramekins. Place the filled ramekins in a shallow baking pan. Pour enough boiling water into the baking pan to come halfway up the outside of the ramekins. Cover with foil.

Bake until just set and a sharp knife inserted in the center comes out clean, 25 to 35 minutes. Remove the ramekins from the water bath, uncover, and cool for 5 minutes.

Serve very hot, either in the ramekins or turned out onto heated serving plates. Garnish each custard with a small sprig of parsley.

Garlic Mashed Potatoes

Once you have added this to a menu that features a grilled steak or a crisp-crusted, roast rack of lamb, you will never go back to plain mashed potatoes again—unless, of course, garlic is not high on your list of favorite flavors.

Makes 6 servings

4 tablespoons (½ stick) butter
2 small heads garlic, separated into cloves,
    boiled in water to cover for 5 minutes,
    drained, and peeled
⅓ cup heavy cream
3 large baking potatoes, peeled and cubed
Salt and freshly ground black pepper to taste
3 tablespoons chopped fresh parsley

Melt 2 tablespoons of the butter in a small skillet over very low heat. Add the garlic, cover, and cook, shaking the skillet from time to time to keep the cloves from sticking and burning, until very tender, 25 or 30 minutes. Raise the heat to high and stir in the cream. Cook 1 minute longer.

Pour the garlic and reduced cream into a blender or food processor and process until smooth.

Meanwhile, boil the potatoes in a medium-size saucepan of salted water to cover until tender, up to 20 minutes. Drain the cooked potatoes. Push them through a ricer or mash with a potato masher until fluffy. Stir in the remaining 2 tablespoons of butter. Beat the garlic puree into the potatoes and season well with salt and pepper. Stir in the parsley.

Spoon the mashed potatoes into a medium-size saucepan. Dry over very low heat, stirring from time to time until the potatoes are thick and smooth. Be careful not to scorch them on the bottom. Serve very hot.

Note: *These potatoes can be made ahead of time and reheated, covered, in the microwave for 2 minutes on high.*

Garlic Flan

The secret to this delicious flan is to season it very well with salt and pepper. Serve the hot custard, cut into wedges, with roast beef, lamb, or pork loin, or with grilled pork tenderloin.

Makes 6 to 8 servings

1 large head garlic, separated into cloves,
    boiled in water to cover for 5 minutes,
    drained, and peeled
1½ cups well-flavored chicken stock
Butter
2 cups milk or half-and-half, heated just
    until bubbles appear around the edges
    of the pan, cooled slightly
2 whole large eggs
4 large egg yolks
Salt and freshly ground black pepper to taste
3 tablespoons chopped fresh parsley
Fresh parsley sprigs

In a medium-size saucepan, combine the garlic with the stock. Simmer over low heat, until very soft, 25 to 30 minutes. Drain, reserving the stock for making garlic-flavored sauces. Puree the garlic in a small food processor or herb grinder or in a mortar with a pestle.

Preheat the oven to 350°F. Generously butter a 1-quart flan mold or an 8-inch cake tin.

In a medium-size bowl, beat together the eggs and the egg yolks until they are very light in color. Beat in about ½ cup of the hot milk, then beat this egg mixture into the remaining milk. Simmer over very low heat, stirring, until the mixture just coats the back of a spoon, 1 to 2 minutes. Remove the saucepan from the heat and strain the mixture through a sieve into the same bowl that held the eggs. Beat in the garlic puree and season well with salt and pepper. Stir in the chopped parsley.

Pour the flan mixture into the prepared mold. Set the mold into a larger shallow baking pan. Pour enough boiling water into the baking pan to reach halfway up the outside of the mold. Bake until the flan is set in the middle and a sharp knife inserted in the custard comes out clean, 50 to 55 minutes. Remove from the oven.

Take the mold out of the water bath and let it stand for 5 minutes. Run a knife carefully around the inside edge of the mold and invert the flan onto a heated serving plate. Serve very hot, garnished with the parsley sprigs.

> **Tip:** *Moisten the serving plate very slightly before unmolding the flan. This will allow you to shift the flan if it isn't well centered.*

Aioli

This thick, mayonnaise-like sauce is not for the faint-hearted. It is often served in the south of France as an accompaniment for what is called a grand aioli, *a mammoth meal consisting of soaked and poached salt cod, snails, and boiled eggs and sometimes shrimp, mussels, and other shellfish, along with a vast assortment of steamed vegetables. It is also an essential part of a* bourride, *a terrific fish stew usually made with monkfish or other firm white fish. I think it is also delicious with cold roast meats, while a spoonful or two in a baked potato is truly wonderful. One word of warning: Everyone at the table has to indulge since this sauce is garlic personified and would probably overwhelm any nonparticipant.*

Makes about 2 cups

6 to 8 medium-size to large cloves garlic, mashed to a paste in a mortar with a pestle and a little salt or very finely minced
3 large egg yolks, at room temperature
2 tablespoons boiling water

Salt and freshly ground black pepper to taste
2 tablespoons fresh lemon juice
1½ cups olive oil

Place the garlic and egg yolks in a blender. Blend in short bursts until smooth. Turn the blender on again and add the boiling water in a thin stream. Season with salt and pepper and add the lemon juice. Blend until smooth. Turn the blender on and add the oil in a very thin stream, just a little at the beginning, a little faster as the sauce begins to thicken. The sauce should become thick and fluffy like mayonnaise.

Set the aioli aside for an hour to let the flavor develop. Serve at room temperature.

> **Note:** *The traditional method for making aioli calls for beating the sauce in a mortar, with the water added a little at a time, along with the lemon juice, after about one-third of the oil has been incorporated. Here I have used the blender, which generally keeps the sauce from separating, and I have incorporated hot water, which should raise the temperature of the egg yolks high enough to eliminate the risk of salmonella. Some recipes call for adding a little mashed potato at the end, making a thicker sauce and probably holding it in emulsion, but I prefer it this way.*

> **Tip:** *If the sauce separates, it can usually be reconstituted by beating 1 large egg yolk and 1 teaspoon lemon juice together in a clean bowl and then beating the separated sauce into the egg, a little bit at a time, until it is thick and fluffy again. See page 13 for more information about raw eggs.*

Hominy

While hominy is not a fresh vegetable, it played such a large part, along with fresh corn, in the nurturing of this country's original settlers that I feel compelled to include it here. North and South American natives relied heavily on hominy as a diet staple, and it still plays a substantial role in Mexican cooking. Outside of the Southwest and some parts of the South, however, hominy seems to have gone out of fashion, and I think it really deserves a little attention.

Both white and yellow corn are made into hominy, although some Southerners will only eat the white variety, as dried yellow corn has been traditionally used for animal feed. To make hominy, field-dried corn is removed from the cob, soaked in lime water (originally it was a lye solution made from wood ashes and water) and boiled so that it swells up and the husk or bran comes off the kernels. If the resulting swollen kernels are redried, they can be broken up or ground. Broken into large pieces, the dried hominy is called samp and is made into a nourishing mush; ground, it becomes that wonderful southern staple, hominy grits (although grits are sometimes ground from dried corn that has not

been made into hominy). Ground even more finely into meal, hominy becomes masa harina, the flour traditionally used in Mexico to make tortillas and tamales.

Making your own hominy is certainly not worth the effort today since there is good-quality canned hominy (both yellow and white) widely available. In some areas, frozen hominy may be in the market and can be thawed and substituted for the canned. Occasionally, whole hominy is available dried. It must be rehydrated by soaking overnight and then boiling it until soft again. White hominy has a more delicate flavor than yellow, but they can be used interchangeably.

Hominy is delicious on its own but can be added to your favorite stews and soups at will. I like to stir a cup or so of rinsed hominy into my favorite bean soup for a different flavor and unusual texture.

Preparation: Canned hominy requires little preparation before using. I believe it should be well drained in a sieve and rinsed thoroughly in cold water. I do not like the strong flavor of unrinsed hominy, and occasionally unrinsed hominy will make the milk in a recipe curdle.

Posole

Traditional Mexican posole is a hearty stew, much like this variation but with a generous quantity of cubed pork in it. Served with tortillas, it makes a fun dinner. My adaptation of posole is not a pork-filled main dish but a delicious side dish that can accompany roast pork, grilled pork chops, spareribs, or any kind of grilled fish.

Makes 6 servings

Two 15$\frac{1}{2}$-ounce cans white hominy, drained in a sieve and well rinsed with cold water
1 quart well-flavored chicken stock
$\frac{1}{4}$ pound slab bacon, cut into large dice
2 tablespoons chopped fresh oregano, preferably Mexican, plus additional for garnishing
2 tablespoons good chili powder, or more to taste
1 whole chipotle chile, broken up
1 small onion, finely chopped
2 cloves garlic, minced (optional, but recommended)
3 large ripe tomatoes, seeded and chopped; or one 15$\frac{1}{2}$-ounce can diced tomatoes (chili style if you like), with the juice
Salt to taste
Hot pepper sauce to taste

Combine all the ingredients, except the salt, hot pepper sauce, and the additional oregano for garnishing, in a medium-size heavy covered saucepan or flame-proof casserole. Simmer, covered, over very low heat until the hominy is very tender, but not mushy or falling apart, 2 to 2$\frac{1}{2}$ hours.

If necessary, increase the heat to medium and cook until the posole is thick. Season with salt and hot pepper sauce. Serve hot, garnished with the additional oregano.

Sautéed Hominy and Tomatoes

While this combination is delicious with any kind of grilled whole fish, I think that, at room temperature, it is a great addition to a cold-cut lunch or to any antipasto buffet.

Makes 6 servings

3 tablespoons olive oil
1 tablespoon butter
1 medium-size onion, halved and thinly sliced
$\frac{1}{2}$ small green bell pepper, seeded and coarsely chopped
$\frac{1}{4}$ pound white mushrooms, stems trimmed and sliced
1 clove garlic, minced
Two 15$\frac{1}{2}$ cans yellow or white hominy, drained in a sieve and well rinsed with cold water
2 large ripe tomatoes, seeded and coarsely chopped; or one 15$\frac{1}{2}$ ounce can Italian-style diced tomatoes
Salt and freshly ground black pepper to taste
2 tablespoons chopped fresh oregano

Heat the oil and butter in a large heavy skillet or large saucepan over medium heat. Cook the onion and bell pepper, stirring, for 4 to 5 minutes. Stir in the mushrooms and garlic. Cook, stirring, 1 minute longer. Stir in the hominy and cook 3 to 4 minutes, stirring several times.

Stir in the tomatoes, season with salt and pepper to taste. Stir in the oregano. Cover and simmer gently, over low heat, for 20 minutes. Serve very hot or cool to room temperature.

Buttered Hominy

If you are serving hominy for the first time, I think this easy recipe is the one to cut your teeth on. While the flavor of the hominy is clearly apparent, the milk makes this a delicate dish. Serve it with roast pork or chicken.

Makes 6 servings

Two 15-½ ounce cans white hominy, drained in a
    sieve and well rinsed with cold water
1 cup milk
3 tablespoons butter
Salt and freshly ground black pepper to taste
2 tablespoons chopped fresh parsley

Combine the hominy, milk, and butter in a medium-size saucepan. Simmer over low heat until the milk is almost absorbed, stirring from time to time, 25 to 30 minutes. Season well with salt and pepper. Serve very hot, garnished with the parsley.

Braised Hominy with Garlic and Onion

Serve this with baked ham or smoked pork chops. Add some bitter greens, such as Mustard Greens with Bacon, to complete the menu.

Makes 6 servings

2 tablespoons butter
1 small onion, thinly sliced
2 cloves garlic, minced
Two 15½ ounce cans white or yellow hominy,
    drained in a sieve and well rinsed with
    cold water
Salt and freshly ground black pepper to taste
1 cup strong chicken stock
3 tablespoons finely chopped fresh parsley

Melt the butter in a medium-size heavy skillet over medium heat. Add the onion and cook, stirring occasionally, until tender, 6 to 8 minutes. Add the garlic and cook 1 minute longer. Stir in the hominy. Season well with salt and pepper. Stir in the stock and simmer, uncovered, over low heat for 25 to 30 minutes. Stir in the parsley and serve very hot.

Hominy au Gratin

Corn in almost any form goes very well with grilled steaks or chops, and this is no exception.

Makes 6 to 8 servings

3 tablespoons butter, plus additional for buttering
Two 15½ ounce cans white hominy, drained in a
    sieve and well rinsed with cold water
1 cup milk
1 small onion, minced
Salt and freshly ground black pepper to taste
3 tablespoons chopped fresh parsley
Hot pepper sauce to taste (optional)
¾ cup grated Monterey Jack or Cheddar cheese
¼ cup plain dried bread crumbs

Preheat the oven to 475°F. Generously butter a small deep ovenproof casserole.

In a medium-size saucepan, simmer the hominy in the milk over low heat for 15 minutes. Drain.

Melt 3 tablespoons of butter in a small skillet over medium heat. Add the onion and cook, stirring, until tender, 7 or 8 minutes. Stir in the hominy, salt, pepper, parsley, and hot pepper sauce if using. Spoon the mixture into the prepared casserole.

Mix the cheese and bread crumbs and sprinkle over the hominy. Bake until golden brown and bubbling, 15 to 20 minutes. Serve very hot.

Note: *This dish can be put together and refrigerated, covered, ready to bake, up to 24 hours in advance. To finish, bring to room temperature and bake in a preheated 475°F. oven for 15 minutes.*

Jicama

An unassuming exterior belies the versatility of jicama. This large, round, light brown tuber looks like something you might rather leave in the market than take home and work with. The tan skin is thin, though, and easily removed with a vegetable peeler to reveal a crisp, creamy white flesh underneath. Unlike potato, jicama does not turn brown immediately after it has been peeled but retains its creamy color for a little while. If you like, it can be tossed with lemon or lime juice or covered with acidulated water (2 tablespoons lemon juice to 1 quart of water), but it isn't necessary. Jicama can be cut into any imaginable shape or form to eat raw or cooked.

Jicama is eaten in most tropical countries of the world. It requires a very long growing season and reacts well to hot weather. The tubers store well and can be incorporated into so many different dishes that it can be eaten almost daily without tiring of it. And, best of all, one large tuber provides food for a crowd.

In Mexico they have been using jicama in salads and stews for years. They serve thin slices of it with tequila, to dip in fresh lime juice and sprinkle with salt; and they love to pair it with oranges and onions in a crisp refreshing salad.

New Mexican cooks have found how the delicate, faintly sweet flavor of jicama acts a lot like tofu, absorbing and accentuating other tastes and seasonings without adding too much of its own.

In China, jicama has long been popular as a crisp alternative to water chestnuts, and I recommend using it as a fresh replacement for canned water chestnuts in home-cooked Chinese dishes.

In addition to being versatile, jicama is extremely low in calories and should become a welcome addition to the repertoire of serious dieters. Sticks of it can be served in place of the ever-present celery and carrot; jicama salads can be tossed with lime or lemon juice and just a few drops of olive oil; it can be boiled, baked, stewed, or steamed, and seasoned with fresh herbs, sea salt (my preference over ordinary table salt), and pepper or hot pepper sauce; and it can be combined with almost any other kind of vegetable you choose.

Jicama provides a good source of vitamin C and potassium, and contains a moderate amount of fiber.

Selection: I have seen jicama in the market all year long, but it is at its peak from October to June. That makes it a welcome addition to your winter vegetable selection. Look for plump, heavy tubers. Ranging in weight from 2 to 8 pounds, the larger ones can become a little fibrous but are generally crisp and sweet regardless of the size. Look for vegetables that have a flattened end, with a uniform peel. Occasionally the skin color is blotchy, which should not affect the flesh underneath. The texture of the skin can be nearly smooth or rough to the touch. Avoid any jicama that look bruised or moldy, are marred by spade cuts, or have soft spots.

Count on about $\frac{1}{4}$ pound per person. Once the vegetable is cut, it should be eaten within one or two days, and I suggest selecting a size you can use up before it spoils.

Storage and Preparation: Jicama will keep, unwrapped, in the vegetable drawer of the refrigerator for three weeks or more. Do not wash or peel it until ready to use. Once the tuber has been cut, it should be tightly wrapped in plastic wrap, stored in the refrigerator, and used within a day or two, although I have occasionally kept it up to a week.

Jicama needs little preparation other than peeling and cutting into the desired shape. The peel is thin, and can be removed with a vegetable peeler. Large tubers may have a slightly tough inner layer, which can be pared away if you like. If you are serving jicama in slices for hors d'oeuvres or in salads, add interest by shaping the slices with fancy canapé cutters or cookie cutters. Dry the slices on a kitchen towel before continuing with the recipe.

Boiled Jicama

Jicama cooks relatively quickly and, as it is delightful served raw, it rarely needs parboiling. If the jicama is to be dressed with a sauce of some kind after cooking, it can simply be boiled first. Fresh tomato sauce or a little pesto can be good. Or top simmered jicama with a little fiery hot fresh salsa.

For six servings, place $1\frac{1}{2}$ pounds peeled and cut-up jicama in boiling, salted water to cover. Boil until tender but not falling apart, 8 to 12 minutes. Drain.

Steamed Jicama

Steam peeled and cut-up jicama in a steamer basket or colander over simmering water, covered, until tender, 8 to 12 minutes, depending on the size of the cuts.

Microwaved Jicama

Jicama is easy to cook in the microwave. Arrange 1 pound of cut-up jicama in a microwave dish. Add $\frac{1}{4}$ cup water, cover, and vent. Microwave on high for 4 to 5 minutes. Let stand 3 to 4 minutes before uncovering.

Jicama, Zucchini, and Onion Salad

One of the most rewarding ways to enjoy jicama is to serve it fresh in a crunchy salad. I think this is a super summer salad and a wonderful addition to any cold meal.

Makes 6 servings

1 small head Boston lettuce
1 medium-size sweet onion, such as Vidalia or Walla Walla Sweet, or 1 medium-size red onion, halved and thinly sliced
1 medium-size (about 1 pound) jicama, peeled, sliced, and cut into matchstick strips
2 small zucchini, trimmed and cut into matchstick strips
½ small red bell pepper, seeded and thinly sliced

Vinaigrette

2 tablespoons fresh lemon juice
1 small clove garlic, minced
1 teaspoon capers, drained, rinsed, and chopped
1 tablespoon chopped fresh oregano
Salt and freshly ground black pepper to taste
⅓ to ½ cup extra-virgin olive oil, to taste

Arrange the lettuce in a medium-size salad bowl. Arrange the onion slices on top. In a medium-size bowl, toss the jicama and zucchini together and spoon the mixture over the onion slices. Garnish with the red pepper.

Prepare the vinaigrette. In a small bowl, beat together the lemon juice, garlic, capers, oregano, salt, and pepper. Beat in the olive oil.

Just before serving, pour some of the vinaigrette over the vegetables. Toss. Pass the remaining vinaigrette in a separate sauce boat.

Orange-Jicama Salad

A Mexican accent makes this a perfect salad to refresh diners after a meal of fiery hot chili. Jicama and oranges are often paired in Mexico, and I like the addition of a few drops of hot pepper sauce to the vinaigrette for a spicier finished dish.

Makes 6 servings

1 medium-size (about 1 pound) jicama, peeled, quartered, and sliced
1 medium-size sweet onion or red onion, thinly sliced
½ medium-size red bell pepper, seeded, quartered, and thinly sliced
3 seedless oranges, peeled and sectioned, any juice reserved in a small bowl
1 small cucumber, peeled, halved lengthwise, seeded, and sliced

Dressing

2 tablespoons red wine vinegar
3 tablespoons of the reserved orange juice
1 tablespoon chopped fresh oregano, or ½ teaspoon dried
Hot pepper sauce to taste (optional)
Salt and freshly ground black pepper to taste
⅓ to ½ cup olive oil, to taste
1 small head leaf lettuce
Chili powder

In a medium-size bowl, gently toss together the jicama, onion, red pepper, oranges, and cucumber.

Prepare the dressing. Beat together the vinegar, orange juice, oregano, hot pepper sauce (if desired), salt, and pepper. Beat in the olive oil. Pour the dressing over the salad and toss. Refrigerate, covered, for at least 1 hour.

To serve, arrange the leaf lettuce on chilled salad plates. Toss the salad gently and spoon it onto the lettuce beds. Dust with the chili powder and serve well chilled.

Jicama Rémoulade

Céleri rémoulade is one of my favorite salads. Crisp and refreshing, it is a wonderful addition to any cold buffet. This variation is a delightful change of pace and will be the perfect appetizer for a company meal, but I also like it with barbecued beef ribs or brisket.

Makes 6 servings

1 medium-size (about 1 pound) jicama, peeled, sliced, and cut into thin matchstick strips or shredded
1 bunch (6 to 8) green onions (scallions), white and light green parts only, very thinly sliced
½ small sweet onion, such as Vidalia, Walla Walla, or Texas Super Sweets, very thinly sliced
1 teaspoon fresh lemon juice
1 tablespoon Dijon-style mustard
3 tablespoons chopped fresh parsley, plus additional for garnishing
1 cup mayonnaise, prepared or homemade (page 13)
Salt and freshly ground black pepper to taste

In a medium-size bowl, toss the jicama, green onions, and sweet onion with the lemon juice. In a small bowl, beat together the mustard, parsley, and mayonnaise. Season well with salt and pepper. Toss enough of this dressing with the jicama salad to moisten well. Cover and refrigerate the salad for several hours. Serve at room temperature, garnished with the additional parsley.
Variation: *Use equal amounts of jicama, cut into matchstick strips or shredded, and celery root, cut into matchstick strips or shredded, for a different flavor.*

Jicama Stir-fry

The Chinese have been using jicama for more than a hundred years. It is a nice fresh substitute in recipes calling for water chestnuts and can be exchanged quantity for quantity for them. Do not overcook the jicama; it should remain crisp. Serve this with grilled shrimp and freshly steamed rice.

Makes 6 servings

2 tablespoons mild vegetable oil, preferably peanut
1 teaspoon Chinese hot oil
1 clove garlic, minced
1 tablespoon grated fresh ginger
½ medium-size red bell pepper, seeded and sliced about ⅛ inch thick
1 small to medium-size (about 1 pound) jicama, peeled, cut into 1-inch slices, and then sliced about ⅛ inch thick
1 cup fresh broccoli flowerettes, steamed 3 minutes
1 tablespoon soy sauce
1 tablespoon rice wine, or dry sherry
2 tablespoons chicken stock
1 tablespoon chopped fresh parsley

Heat the vegetable oil and the hot oil in a wok over high heat. Add the garlic and ginger and cook, stirring, for 10 to 15 seconds. Stir in the bell pepper and cook, stirring, for 2 minutes. Add the jicama and broccoli. Cook, stirring, for 2 minutes longer. In a small bowl, stir together the soy sauce, wine, and stock. Pour this mixture over the vegetables, cover, and cook for 2 minutes. Remove the cover, stir, and turn into a heated vegetable dish. Serve very hot, garnished with the parsley.

Jicama Suggestions

1. Replace turnips with jicama for a new take on any old-fashioned stew. Add peeled cubes of jicama to the stew 15 to 20 minutes before it is to be served.

2. Add thick jicama sticks to any crudité basket.

3. Add jicama to a Pinzimonio (page 162) or to a platter of vegetables for Bagna Cauda (page 96).

4. Peel and shred raw jicama and add it to an equal amount of shredded raw potatoes for interesting change-of-pace Potato Pancakes (page 287). Serve them very crisp and hot, with a peppery tomato sauce instead of applesauce or sour cream.

5. Peel jicama, cut it into ¼-inch dice, and steam or parboil 3 minutes, then drain it and add to Russian Salad (page 103).

6. Add ⅓ cup diced raw jicama to potato or shrimp salad for added crunch.

7. Add ½ cup peeled, shredded jicama to any coleslaw recipe.

8. Substitute sticks of peeled jicama for eggplant in French-fried Eggplant (page 157).

9. Substitute jicama in any recipe that calls for potato. It contains more water than potato and will cook down a bit more, but the final texture will be much the same and the flavor is delicate and with a hint of sweetness.

Kale

Curly kale may well be the world's oldest form of cultivated cabbage. Like cabbage, collards, and spinach, kale is important enough in its own right to be considered by itself, rather than being grouped with other hearty greens. While some cooks think of kale as merely a simple country vegetable—and it is true that this meaty, calcium-rich green has helped sustain many throughout slim times—its flavor makes it well worth a place on more sophisticated menus.

Ancient Greeks and then Romans grew and enjoyed kale, but whether it originally grew wild there or further east isn't known. Kale gradually made its way west and north to England and then on to the New World. Available almost everywhere, it is especially popular in the southern states. Kale is not delicate; it has a hearty, almost meaty quality that makes it very satisfactory if it is the mainstay of a meal. Add a little meat, ham hock, salt pork, or bacon along with homemade bread or biscuits, and a kettle of kale becomes a full meal.

Kale is a cold-weather vegetable. It is at its best from September to May, and many cooks think it is definitely better after it has been touched by frost. The plants are hardy enough to withstand even snow, and if you are a gardener, the leaves can be picked all winter long, unless temperatures stay in the teens for prolonged periods of time.

There are often several varieties of kale in the market: the familiar dark, blue-green kind with its very curly leaves; the lighter green, almost flat leaf, only crinkly around the edges; and purple or flowering kale, sometimes called Salad Savoy. Flowering kale ranges in color from purple to creamy white or pale yellow. While it is often planted as an ornamental, it can be used as a decorative plant in the house, added to salads, or cooked and eaten like other kale.

In the past, kale was classed as one of the "bitter greens" and thought to have too strong a taste to eat raw, but I have found that it can be delicious as a salad if only the smallest, most tender leaves are used. Use a well-flavored dressing and enjoy a crisp new taste.

While kale's bulk does diminish to some extent in cooking, it is not like spinach, which practically disappears when it wilts. Also, the heavy leaves are very misleading to the first-time cook. Only the oldest kale is tough. Normally, kale requires only 8 to 10 minutes cooking before it is delightfully tender. This shortened cooking time also helps eliminate the strong odor once associated with cooked kale.

Not only does kale offer vitamins A and C, the same health benefits as its cruciferous cousin cabbage, it contains substantial quantities of iron and absorbable calcium. And kale is also low in calories and fat.

Selection: No matter which kind of kale you choose, pick the brightest, most vibrantly colored leaves available. The leaves should be crisp, with stems that are not the least limp or wilted. Avoid leaves that are brown around the edges, are yellowed (unless you are buying flowering kale), or have rusty-colored stem ends—which would indicate they are less than garden fresh.

Kale is at its best once the weather turns cold and is a good addition to winter menus. Count about 1/3 pound raw kale per person.

Storage and Preparation: Once picked, kale should be eaten as soon as possible. Store it, unwashed, in a perforated plastic vegetable bag in the vegetable bin of the refrigerator for only a day or two.

Just before cooking, wash kale thoroughly, using at least two changes of water to remove any grit. While some old-fashioned cooks just cut off the thick stem end, I prefer to pull off the stems all the way through the leaf, in the same way I prepare spinach. This eliminates any chance that the cooked kale will be stringy. To do this, hold the leaves, folded over, with the stem down and on the right, in your left hand (if you're right-handed). Use your right hand to grasp the stem end and pull up, until it separates from the leaf. Discard the stems.

Kale can be cooked in the water that clings to the leaves after you've washed it, or it can be boiled in a large quantity of water and drained before seasoning. Young kale is so tender that it does not require parboiling.

Wilted Kale

Pile the washed (but not dried) and stemmed kale in a large kettle. Place the kettle over medium heat and cook, tossing once or twice with a fork, until the kale softens and is tender—5 to 8 minutes. Sauce the kale with a little butter or bacon fat and season well with salt and pepper. Pass a small cruet of cider vinegar if you like.

Boiled Kale

Bring a large kettle of water to boil. Add the washed and stemmed kale, and boil until tender, 7 to 8 minutes. Drain. Add butter, salt, pepper, and hot pepper sauce to taste.

For a full-flavored kale, substitute boiling chicken stock for the water. Drain, reserving the cooking liquid to use as a soup stock.

If you would like to cook kale with meat, add a ham bone, ham hock, salt pork, or slab bacon to the boiling water. Simmer for 30 to 45 minutes before adding the kale. Simmer the kale for about 10 minutes. If you are serving old-fashioned diners, simmer the kale for 15 but no longer than 20 minutes. Drain well. Remove the meat, cut up, and toss with the kale before seasoning.

Tangy Wilted Kale

Curly kale is one of the most colorful of fresh greens, dark and almost blue-green. It has a definite personality, but won't overwhelm poached fish or baked chicken. The hot dressing used here is an adaptation of a classic German one, making this a big hit on the same menu as a succulent, spicy sauerbraten.

Makes 6 servings

4 thick slices of bacon, fried until crisp, drained on paper towels, and crumbled, fat reserved (page 42)
1 small red onion, minced
1 tablespoon sugar
¼ to ⅓ cup cider vinegar
Salt and freshly ground black pepper to taste
Hot pepper sauce to taste (optional)
2 pounds darkest green kale, stemmed and coarsely chopped

Heat 3 tablespoons of the bacon fat in a medium-size skillet over low heat. Add the onion and cook, stirring, until translucent, 6 to 8 minutes. Stir in the sugar, vinegar, salt, pepper, and if using, the hot sauce. Simmer over medium heat, stirring, for 1 minute.

Pile the kale in a large heatproof salad bowl. Pour the boiling sauce over the kale and toss well. Serve at once, garnished with the crumbled bacon.

Variations: *Leaf spinach or crisp, fresh beet greens can be substituted for the kale. Try topping the wilted kale with 2 hard-cooked eggs, chopped or sliced. Then sprinkle with the crumbled bacon.*

Sautéed Kale

Kale always goes well with pork and ham. This dish, however, is also delicious with lamb, especially roast leg of lamb. Mashed or boiled potatoes can complete the menu.

Makes 6 servings

2 pounds darkest green kale, stemmed and coarsely chopped
1 tablespoon toasted sesame oil
1 tablespoon olive oil, or a mild vegetable oil
2 small cloves garlic, minced
Salt and freshly ground black pepper to taste
1 tablespoon sesame seeds, toasted (page 70)

Pile the kale in a large kettle. Cover and cook over low heat in the water that clings to the leaves after washing, just until the kale collapses, or wilts, and is tender, 4 to 5 minutes. Drain well in a colander, pressing out any excess water.

Heat the sesame oil with the olive oil in a large heavy skillet over medium heat. Stir in the garlic and cook, stirring, for about 10 seconds. Add the drained kale. Cook the kale, tossing with a fork, until cooked through, 3 to 4 minutes. Season well with salt and pepper. Serve very hot, sprinkled with sesame seeds.

Creamed Kale with Caraway Seeds

The spicy flavor of the caraway seeds makes this a natural with roast duck or goose. It will also go well with such game as venison. If you find a fresh pork shoulder that you can roast with the skin on, this dish will make it a meal to remember.

Makes 6 servings

3 pounds darkest green kale, stemmed and cut into thick slices
2 tablespoons butter
2 medium-size onions, thinly sliced
1 tablespoon caraway seeds
2 tablespoons fresh lemon juice
½ cup heavy cream
Salt and freshly ground black pepper to taste
Hot pepper sauce to taste

Pile the kale into a large kettle of boiling, salted water. Simmer over medium heat for 5 minutes.

Drain the kale well, pressing out as much moisture as possible.

Melt the butter in a large heavy skillet over medium heat. Add the onions and cook, stirring, until just tender, about 10 minutes. Stir in the caraway seeds and cook 2 minutes longer. Add the well-drained kale and the lemon juice. Cook, tossing, until the kale is very tender, about 10 minutes longer. Stir in the cream. Season well with salt and pepper. Simmer, stirring, 2 to 3 minutes, until the kale is coated with the sauce. Serve the kale very hot, with hot pepper sauce on the side.

Kale and Potato Bake

This hearty gratin is perfect for the first cold day of fall. It will go very well alongside baked chicken, shoulder lamb chops, or a wonderful homemade meat loaf.

Makes 6 servings

3 tablespoons butter, plus additional for buttering
1½ pounds darkest green kale, stemmed and very coarsely chopped
4 large new or thin-skinned potatoes, unpeeled, thickly sliced, boiled in salted water to cover until just tender, 8 to 10 minutes, well drained
1 small onion, thinly sliced
Salt and freshly ground black pepper to taste
1 cup chicken stock
¼ cup freshly grated Parmesan cheese

Preheat the oven to 350°F. Generously butter a medium-size deep ovenproof casserole.

Pile the kale in a large kettle. Cover and cook over low heat in the water that clings to the leaves after washing, just until the kale collapses, or wilts, and is tender, 4 to 5 minutes. Drain in a colander, pressing out any excess water.

Melt 2 tablespoons of the butter in a small skillet over medium heat. Add the onion and cook, stirring, until wilted, about 2 minutes. Remove from the heat.

Layer one-third of the boiled potatoes in the bottom of the prepared dish. Top with half of the kale and half of the onion. Season with salt and pepper and dot with butter. Repeat the layers, seasoning again with salt and pepper, and dotting with butter. Arrange the last one-third of the potatoes on top. Pour in the stock. Cover the casserole with aluminum foil.

Bake for 40 minutes. Uncover, sprinkle with the cheese, and bake 10 minutes longer. Serve very hot.

Kale Salad

I like to serve this as a first-course salad, but it is also delicious with a meal that features mouth-blistering Cajun-style blackened fish fillets.

Makes 6 servings

½ pound smallest leaves of darkest green kale, stemmed, dried, and torn into bite-size pieces
2 medium-size seedless oranges, peeled and thinly sliced, any juice reserved
2 bunches (12 to 16) green onions (scallions), white part only, very thinly sliced
2 tablespoons white wine vinegar
1 teaspoon honey mustard
1 tablespoon reserved orange juice
Salt and freshly ground black pepper to taste
1 tablespoon toasted sesame oil
⅓ cup mild vegetable oil
1 tablespoon sesame seeds, toasted (page 70)

Pile the kale into a large salad bowl (glass is pretty). Arrange the orange slices on top of the kale. Spread the sliced green onions over the oranges.

In a jar with a tight-fitting lid, shake together the vinegar, honey mustard, orange juice, salt, and pepper. Add the oils. Shake until well mixed.

Just before serving, pour the dressing over the salad and sprinkle with the toasted sesame seeds. Toss and serve at once.

Braised Kale with Bacon

This easy kale dish is very good with grilled tuna, but it will also enhance a meal based on a good stew, such as beef bourguignon.

Makes 6 servings

2 pounds darkest green kale, stemmed and torn into large pieces
¼ cup chicken stock
¼ cup dry white wine
4 slices bacon, cut into ¼-inch dice, fried until almost crisp, and drained on paper towels (page 42)
Salt and freshly ground black pepper to taste

Pile the kale into a large kettle. Add the stock and wine. Cover and simmer over low heat for 5 minutes. Stir in the bacon. Simmer, tossing the kale with a fork from time to time, until it is tender, 5 to 6 more minutes. Season well with salt and pepper. Toss well with a fork to coat with the sauce remaining in the kettle, and serve very hot.

Colcannon

If you have never tasted this classic pale green combination, you have missed one of life's great pleasures. The Irish have known about it for at least a hundred years. They often used to serve it with a great bowl of hot melted butter; spoonfuls of colcannon were dipped into the golden

liquid. *Given today's attention to the dangers of cholesterol, a little added butter should suffice, but the old-fashioned way was certainly delicious. In some Irish homes, colcannon and great oatmeal griddle cakes made up the whole meal, but I like to serve it with thick grilled lamb chops and lots of mint jelly or Cumberland sauce.*

Makes 6 servings

1 pound darkest green kale, stemmed, chopped, and boiled in salted water to cover until very tender, 15 to 20 minutes, well drained, pressing to remove excess water
3 large Russet potatoes, peeled and cut into chunks, boiled in salted water to cover until very tender, 15 to 20 minutes, well drained and kept hot
¼ to ½ cup milk, half-and-half, or heavy cream, hot
2 tablespoons butter, plus additional optional melted butter
Salt and freshly ground black pepper to taste

Put the potatoes through a ricer, or mash them well with a potato masher. Beat in the milk until the potatoes are light and fluffy. Beat the drained kale into the potatoes (the kale will melt into a puree in the process). Stir in 2 tablespoons of butter and serve very hot.

If you like, pass a small pitcher of melted butter. Each diner can make a small well in his or her serving and pour butter into it.

Variations: *For even more flavor cook the kale in defatted chicken stock. You can substitute Savoy cabbage or New Zealand spinach, also called tetragon, for the kale.*

Kohlrabi

There is some controversy about the origin of kohlrabi. Did it exist in ancient times or was it a purposeful hybrid, developed only about five hundred years ago? If it was not known until the fifteenth century, it would be one of the youngest cultivated vegetables in the world. It certainly has a worldwide following for such a recent addition to the garden. While Americans are not very familiar with this member of the *Brassica* genus (which also includes cabbage), it is relished by Europeans, Middle Easterners, and Asians alike. Its delicate flavor and crisp texture make it a versatile alternative to any of its relatives.

The name is German, meaning cabbage (*kohl*) turnip (*rabi*), and its taste is very much like a cross between the two. It is slightly sweeter than turnip and more delicate than cabbage. Long overlooked here, it is just beginning to appear regularly in supermarkets.

Don't be put off by the otherworldly looks of this interesting vegetable. Kohlrabi is actually the stem of the plant, swollen and round, which grows just above ground. The leaves, which look much like turnip greens, grow out of the bulb at odd angles. Once the bulbs are trimmed of leaves and arranged in the market display, they resemble miniature pale green (or occasionally purple) sputniks with little spikes sticking out all over.

Kohlrabi can be eaten cooked or raw. Raw, it has a flavor somewhat like sweet radishes. Like jicama and fennel, slices or sticks of kohlrabi can be part of a crudité platter, along with any kind of savory dip or sauce. Kohlrabi is a perfect addition to Bagna Cauda or Pinzimonio. Or it can be cubed or cut into matchstick strips to add crunch to salads and dieter's snack trays.

The bulb can be peeled and cubed, sliced, or left whole. It can be boiled, steamed, or roasted. It can be added to soups, stews, and casseroles; served by itself with just a little butter or olive oil and salt and pepper; or mashed and added to potatoes or another root vegetable, such as its cousin rutabaga. It can be cut into matchstick strips and steamed along with sticks of carrots and celery for a delicious low-calorie side dish. If you live near a grower or grow it in your own garden, the leaves are delicious cooked like beet greens. Like garden-fresh beets and turnips, it is two distinct vegetables in one. Unfortunately, you seldom see kohlrabi sold in bunches today with the leaves still on.

And if its versatility were not enough, kohlrabi has many of the same health benefits as its relatives in the cabbage family. It is high in vitamin C, calcium, and potassium and provides some vitamin A. Kohlrabi is a good source of fiber and is low in fat and calories.

Selection: The smaller the better when it comes to kohlrabi. The skin and the layer under it are very fibrous and can be strong tasting when the bulbs are large. Look for palest green (or if you find them, bright purple) bulbs that are plump, crisp, and about the size of a golf ball or slightly larger. Avoid any that have attained baseball size; they will usually be too fibrous. The bulbs should be uniform in color with no brown or soft spots. Do not buy any that are split or cracked. If the stem ends are wilted and yellow, leave them in the display.

If you are lucky enough to find kohlrabi with the leaves on, they should be bright green, not at all limp or yellowed.

Count at least one bulb per serving, more if they are small.

Kohlrabi is available from June to October (and occasionally all year long), but the smallest and best should be sampled in early summer.

Storage and Preparation: If you find the green leaves still attached to the bulbs, they should be trimmed and prepared the day you buy them. The bulbs can be stored in a perforated plastic vegetable bag in a refrigerator drawer for up to a week. Old-time European gardeners left them in the ground until after the first frost or stored them buried in sand for several months. Our modern houses and apartments don't provide space to keep them that way, so they are relegated to the refrigerator.

The outer layer of kohlrabi is very fibrous, and whether eaten raw or cooked, kohlrabi has to be peeled. Once cooked or parboiled, the skin comes off easily and any additional fibers can be pulled off. If you are preparing kohlrabi to eat raw, it will peel much like broccoli stems. Cut a small slice off the top and bottom of the bulb and, with a sharp knife, strip off the outer skin and fibers in a thick layer.

Once peeled, kohlrabi can be cut into any shape or size, or it can be left whole. It can be quartered, diced, sliced, cut into matchstick strips, or cut into large chunks. If you will be adding it to a cold display, it can be sliced and cut into decorative shapes. Any leftover bits and pieces can be used in soups or salads.

Kohlrabi leaves should be well washed and stemmed. They can be left whole or cut into shreds before cooking. Prepare them any way you might prepare beet greens or spinach.

Boiled Kohlrabi

In its simplest form, kohlrabi can be boiled whole, cut up, and served with just a little butter, salt and pepper, and a dusting of chopped fresh parsley or chives.

Place the peeled and cut-up—or unpeeled and whole—kohlrabi in boiling salted water to cover. Simmer on medium heat for about 15 minutes if peeled and cut up, up to 25 minutes for whole bulbs. Drain. Once drained the unpeeled bulbs can easily be peeled, left whole or cut up, and tossed with melted butter.

If the kohlrabi is being used in a gratin, or any other recipe in which it is being parboiled, boil the bulbs whole in their skin for 5 minutes, drain, and peel before continuing with the recipe.

Steamed Kohlrabi

Kohlrabi is also delicious steamed. Place the peeled and cut-up bulbs in the steamer basket or colander over simmering water. Cover and steam until tender but not falling apart, up to 25 minutes.

Microwaved Kohlrabi

Arrange peeled, cut-up kohlrabi in one layer in a microwave dish. Add 2 tablespoons water, cover, and vent. Microwave on high until tender but not falling apart, 4 to 6 minutes. Let stand 5 minutes before uncovering.

Place whole kohlrabi in a microwave dish. Four small kohlrabi can be cooked at one time. Add 2 to 3 tablespoons water, cover, and vent. Microwave on high until tender but not falling apart, 8 to 10 minutes. Let stand 5 minutes, uncover, and peel before continuing with the recipe.

Kohlrabi and Leek Soup

Wholesome and delicious, this soup is enough for a main course when served hot with a salad and lots of good bread. It is also delicious served cold, as a late summer treat, garnished with lots of thinly sliced green onions.

Makes 6 servings

2 tablespoons butter
1 pound leeks, trimmed, white and light green
    parts only, thinly sliced
3 small kohlrabi, trimmed, peeled, and cut into
    1/4-inch dice
1 large Russet potato, peeled and cut into
    1/4-inch dice
1 quart well-flavored chicken stock
1 tablespoon chopped fresh thyme, or
    1 teaspoon dried
1/2 cup heavy cream
Salt and freshly ground black pepper to taste

Melt the butter in a medium-size heavy kettle over medium heat. Add the leeks and cook, stirring, until translucent and tender, 10 to 15 minutes. Stir in the kohlrabi and potato and cook, stirring, 3 to 4 minutes longer. Stir in the stock and thyme. Simmer over low heat until the kohlrabi and potato are very tender, 20 to 25 minutes.

Remove about half of the vegetables and puree them in a food processor or blender, adding a little of the stock if necessary. Return the puree to the kettle and stir in the cream. Season with salt and pepper and simmer over low heat for 10 minutes longer. Serve very hot.

Note: *If the soup will be served cold, be sure to season well with salt and pepper. Low temperatures tend to dull the flavor of salt, making it necessary to season liberally.*

Braised Kohlrabi

Serve this delicate dish like braised celery, alongside roast pheasant or duck, for a wonderful dinner-party menu.

Makes 6 servings

2 tablespoons butter
4 small kohlrabi, trimmed, peeled, and cut into
    ¹/₂-inch cubes
¹/₂ cup well-flavored chicken stock
¹/₄ cup dry vermouth
1 teaspoon sugar
Salt and freshly ground white pepper to taste
¹/₂ teaspoon celery seed
3 tablespoons chopped fresh parsley

Melt the butter in a large heavy skillet over medium heat. Add the kohlrabi and cook, tossing from time to time, for 5 minutes. Stir in the stock and vermouth and season with the sugar, salt, pepper, and celery seed. Cover and cook over low heat until very tender but not falling apart, 15 to 20 minutes. Serve the kohlrabi very hot, garnished with the parsley.

Kohlrabi and Mushroom Sauté

Brighten up a workday dinner of roast chicken with this delicious combination. Add it to a traditional Thanksgiving dinner for a new twist. A mixture of shiitake and white mushrooms is a good combination here.

Makes 6 servings

3 tablespoons butter
¹/₂ small onion, thinly sliced
1 clove garlic, minced
4 small kohlrabi, trimmed, peeled, and sliced
¹/₄ pound fresh mushrooms, wiped and
    thinly sliced
¹/₂ cup well-flavored chicken stock

¹/₄ cup dry white wine
2 tablespoons chopped fresh basil, plus additional
    leaves for garnishing
Salt and freshly ground black pepper to taste

Melt the butter in a large heavy skillet over medium heat. Add the onion and cook, stirring, for 1 minute. Add the garlic and cook 10 seconds longer. Stir in the kohlrabi and cook, stirring, for 3 to 4 minutes.

Stir in the mushrooms and cook for 2 minutes longer. Add the stock, wine, and chopped basil. Simmer over low heat until the kohlrabi is very tender, but not falling apart, 10 to 15 minutes longer. Increase the heat and boil off all but 1 or 2 tablespoons of the liquid. Season well with salt and pepper. Serve very hot, garnished with the basil leaves.
Variation: *Add ¹/₄ cup heavy cream after the excess liquid has been boiled off. Toss to coat the vegetables.*

Kohlrabi Gratin with Onions

The delicate turniplike flavor of kohlrabi makes this dish a perfect foil for a spicy main course such as sauerbraten or baked ham.

Makes 6 servings

1 tablespoon butter, plus additional for buttering
4 medium-size kohlrabi, trimmed, peeled, sliced,
    boiled in salted water to cover until just
    tender, about 15 minutes, and drained
1 large onion, thinly sliced
1 tablespoon all-purpose flour
1 cup milk, heated until bubbles appear around
    the edge and still hot
Salt and freshly ground black pepper to taste
1 teaspoon dried Italian herbs, such as oregano,
    marjoram, rosemary, and thyme, or a
    prepared mix
¹/₃ cup freshly grated Parmesan cheese

Preheat the oven to 375°F. Generously butter a 1¹/₂-quart deep ovenproof casserole or soufflé dish.

Gently toss together the kohlrabi and onion in a medium-size bowl. Pile the vegetables into the prepared dish.

In a small saucepan, melt 1 tablespoon of butter over low heat and stir in the flour. Cook, stirring, for 3 minutes. Stir in the milk all at once. Season with salt, pepper, and herbs. Pour this sauce over the kohlrabi.

Bake the gratin, uncovered, for 20 minutes. Sprinkle with the cheese. Bake until bubbling hot and the top is golden brown, 10 to 15 minutes longer. Serve very hot.

Variation: *For a richer dish, use heavy cream rather than milk.*

Leeks

Leeks have a long and illustrious history as food. Cultivated for thousands of years, they have at times been almost venerated. Egyptians were buried with them (or reproductions of them) to provide food in the hereafter. Very popular with the Romans (Nero is said to have eaten leeks in soup every day to improve the quality of his voice), they carried them to all their outposts and introduced their cultivation to the local inhabitants, who immediately incorporated leeks into their native dishes.

In fact, leeks are so much a part of the diet in England and Wales, former Roman outposts, that they are the national symbol of Wales. Legend has it (and whether you believe it or not is up to you) that the Welsh pulled leeks from the ground and stuck them in their hats on St. David's Day in 640 so they could tell each other from the Saxons they were fighting. It must have worked. Instead of killing their own kin, they beat the Saxons and saved Wales. Every year on St. David's Day the Welsh celebrate the lowly leek by wearing it and enjoying it in all sorts of hot and cold cooked dishes.

And cock-a-leekie, a curious, but delicious, soup made with chicken, vegetables, barley, leeks, and prunes is practically the Scottish national dish—after haggis, that is.

There is nothing like a bowl of humble leek and potato soup to warm a cold and gloomy day, and its chilled counterpart, vichyssoise, is considered an extremely sophisticated treat. Leeks go well with eggs and in stews. They are delicious by themselves either steamed or braised, and served hot or cold. I like to add them to any cooked dish with sliced onions, where they enhance the onion flavor, and I think they make a dynamite first course when steamed and dressed with a mustardy vinaigrette, then chilled.

Although leeks take months to grow and require much labor to mound the rows with earth to keep the stems white, they have virtually no enemies, making them almost a sure crop. For this reason, along with their versatility, they were long known as poor man's food. I cannot for the life of me figure out how anything so delicious should have been relegated in peoples' minds only to rustic soups and farmhouse dishes. Nor can I understand why we eat so few leeks here in America. Today, leeks are considered a basic element in European diets, but here they are often scarce, costly, overgrown, and coarse.

Leeks are part of the lily family and are related to green onions, onions, shallots, and garlic. They have a wonderful flavor and I don't think onions are a good substitution.

Leeks are low in calories and contain relatively large amounts of vitamins A and C.

Selection: Ideally, you should look for long, white, unwrinkled stalks, with bright green tops. Unlike onions and scallions, leeks are pretty much the same diameter from leaf to root, with no obvious bulb. Try to avoid leeks that are too large; a 1-inch diameter is thick enough, especially in the spring when leeks can have a hard fibrous core that must be removed. The green tops should not be limp or yellowed, and if you have a choice, eliminate any leeks that are excessively dirty.

The method of keeping leeks white by mounding soil up the stalk tends to result in dirt seeping down between the leaves, especially during rainy periods. If they are very dirty, it may have rained just before they were dug, which can wash even more dirt into the crevices. If muddy stalks are the only leeks available, don't worry; just take extra care to clean them well.

It may be difficult in any but a specialty market to find leeks thin enough to serve whole. If you have a source, choose all the leeks of the same thickness, about the same as thick asparagus. They are well worth the expense to try them if available.

Leeks are a cold weather crop and are at their best in the fall and early winter. I seem to find them in the market all year long, however, although not in any profusion.

If serving them whole, count four to five slim leeks per person.

Storage and Preparation: Do not wash or trim leeks until you are ready to use them. Store them in a plastic bag in the vegetable drawer of the refrigerator for no longer than seven to ten days, depending on how fresh they were when you bought them.

The one drawback to serving leeks often, other than their cost here in America, is the work it takes to get them clean. It is not a chore you can skimp on, because leeks that are not adequately washed will be very unpleasantly gritty and will ruin any dish they are used in.

To clean the leeks, cut off the root end and most of the green leaves, 2 to 3 inches above the white. If they are very thin, it may be possible to simply separate the leaves a bit and run fresh, cold water into them, from the top down. If the leeks are large, or very dirty, it will be necessary to split them. Take a knife with a sharp point and insert it into the leek where the green begins. Slit the white down almost to the root on at least two sides. If the leeks are very large, you may have to halve them. Wash them thoroughly in copious amounts of water, separating the leaves as much as possible to wash out all the grit. Drain well.

Small leeks can be cut on the diagonal and added to stir-fries. Or they can be boiled whole in salted water to cover for 3 minutes, drained, and then roasted. They can be braised or boiled (whole or cut up), drained, and sauced with everything from vinaigrette to Hollandaise.

Large leeks should be sliced or cut into sticks—thick or thin, depending on the recipe. They can be added directly to soups, stews, or stocks; or they can be sautéed in butter to add to quiches, casseroles, or many other dishes including omelets.

Boiled Leeks

Whole trimmed leeks can be boiled or braised in water to cover for 20 to 30 minutes, depending on the thickness of the leek. Test after 20 minutes with the point of a sharp knife to see if they are tender. The leeks should be easily cut but not falling into a mush. Serve hot or at room temperature, seasoned with salt and pepper and perhaps a drizzle of olive oil or vinaigrette dressing.

Steamed Leeks

Arrange whole trimmed leeks in one layer in a steamer basket or colander. Steam, covered, over simmering water for 20 minutes or longer, depending on the thickness of the leeks. Sliced leeks can be steamed in the same way, but cut the time to 10 minutes or a little longer, depending on the size of the pieces. Test with the point of a sharp knife after about 10 minutes.

Braised Leeks with Garlic and Parsley

I like to serve these with grilled steak or any other entrée you might pair with asparagus.

Makes 6 servings

1 cup well-flavored chicken stock
½ cup dry white wine
3 pounds (about 12) small leeks, trimmed, white and light green parts only

Salt and freshly ground black pepper to taste
2 tablespoons olive oil
1 tablespoon butter
3 cloves garlic, minced
½ cup chopped fresh parsley

Combine the stock and wine in a large skillet. Add the leeks and simmer over low heat until very tender, 30 to 45 minutes, depending on their size. Season well with salt and pepper.

Drain the leeks well, reserving 2 tablespoons of the cooking liquid, and keep warm.

Heat the olive oil and butter together in a small skillet over low heat. Add the garlic and parsley and cook, stirring, for 3 minutes, being careful not to burn the garlic. Stir in the reserved cooking liquid. Cook 30 seconds.

Serve the leeks on a heated plate with the garlic and parsley spooned over them. This dish can be served hot or warm, or as a part of an antipasto plate.

Leeks au Gratin

If you are like me and really love the flavor of leeks, you will want to serve these often, budget permitting. I find this dish goes with many main-course selections, from baked fish to grilled steak.

Makes 6 servings

12 to 18 thin or 6 fat leeks, trimmed, white and light green parts only, fat leeks halved or quartered lengthwise, steamed until tender, about 20 minutes, and drained
3 tablespoons butter
2 tablespoons all-purpose flour
Salt and freshly ground black pepper to taste
1 cup milk, regular or skim, or well-flavored chicken stock, hot
1 tablespoon Dijon-style mustard
1 cup grated Gruyère cheese, or Cheddar, fontina, or Comté
½ cup plain dried bread crumbs

Preheat the oven to 400°F.

Arrange the leeks in a single layer in a shallow oblong baking dish.

In a medium-size heavy saucepan, melt 2 tablespoons of the butter over medium heat. Stir in the flour and season well with salt and pepper. Cook, stirring, being careful not to brown the mixture, for 3 minutes. Whisk in the milk, beating until smooth. Cook, stirring, until the sauce thickens, about 3 minutes. Remove from the heat and beat in the mustard. Add the cheese, stirring until it melts. Pour this mixture over the leeks.

Melt the remaining 1 tablespoon of butter in a small saucepan over low heat. Remove the pan from the heat and stir in the bread crumbs. Sprinkle the buttered crumbs over the leeks. Bake until the sauce is bubbling and the crumbs are dark golden brown, about 20 minutes. Serve very hot.

Leek and Potato Puree

I like this variation of an old Irish dish called Champ (page 279), which is a puree of potatoes and green onions. Here leeks lend additional flavor. Serve with a great homemade meat loaf for a wonderful supper.

Makes 6 servings

2 tablespoons butter
1 tablespoon olive oil
2 large leeks, trimmed, white and light green
    parts only, halved lengthwise and very
    thinly sliced
Salt and freshly ground black pepper to taste
3 large Russet potatoes, peeled and cut into
    chunks, boiled in salted water to cover until
    very tender, 15 to 20 minutes, well drained,
    and kept hot
2 to 3 tablespoons heavy cream
2 tablespoons chopped fresh parsley

Heat 1 tablespoon of the butter with the olive oil in a small skillet over low heat. Add the leeks and cook, stirring from time to time, until very tender but not browned, 20 to 25 minutes. Puree the leeks in a small food processor. Season well with salt and pepper.

Put the drained potatoes through a ricer, or mash with a potato masher. Beat in the cream and the remaining 1 tablespoon butter. Beat in the leek puree.

Serve the puree very hot, garnished with the parsley. Pass more butter if desired.

Leek and Garlic Gratin

While this garlic-redolent dish is perfect with a delicately pink roast leg of lamb, I love to serve it instead of the classic creamed onions at Thanksgiving or Christmas.

Makes 8 to 10 servings

2 tablespoons butter
2 whole heads garlic, separated into cloves,
    boiled in water to cover for 3 minutes,
    drained, and peeled
1 pint boiling onions, boiled in water to cover for
    1 minute, drained, and peeled; or 2 cups
    thawed frozen baby onions
4 medium-size leeks, trimmed, white and light
    green parts only, cut into $1/2$-inch slices
2 bunches (12 to 16) green onions (scallions),
    white and 2 inches of green only, cut into
    1-inch lengths
1 teaspoon ground cumin, or more to taste
$1/2$ cup dry white wine
$1/4$ cup well-flavored chicken stock
$1/4$ cup heavy cream
Salt and freshly ground black pepper to taste
3 tablespoons chopped fresh parsley

Preheat the oven to 350°F.

Melt the butter in a large heavy skillet over low heat. Cook the garlic with the boiling onions and leeks, stirring from time to time, until the garlic is very tender, at least 20 minutes. Stir in the green onions and cook 1 minute. Stir in the cumin. Add the wine, stock, and cream. Season well with salt and pepper. Pour the vegetables into a medium-size gratin dish.

Bake until the vegetables are golden brown on top, about 40 minutes. Serve very hot, garnished with the chopped parsley.

Leek and Onion Tart

Serve a wedge of this delicious quichelike tart on a plate with smoked pork chops or baked ham and a small lettuce and tomato salad. If the leeks are cooked ahead and then warmed 1 minute in the microwave before spreading in the pastry shell, this will be a quick and easy addition to any busy-night dinner.

Makes 6 to 8 servings

Pastry dough for a 1-crust 9-inch pie (page 126)
2 tablespoons butter
2 pounds leeks, trimmed, white and light green parts only, thinly sliced
1 large onion, halved and thinly sliced
1 bunch (6 to 8) green onions (scallions), white and light green parts only, thinly sliced
1 tablespoon chopped fresh thyme, or 1 teaspoon dried
$^1/_3$ pound slab bacon, cut into large dice, fried until almost crisp, and drained on paper towels (page 42)
1 large whole egg
2 large egg yolks
$1^1/_2$ cups half-and-half
Salt and freshly ground black pepper to taste

Preheat the oven to 375°F.

Roll out the pastry dough and line a 9-inch pie plate or tart mold, making a fluted edge. Line the pastry shell with waxed or parchment paper. Fill with dried beans or baking weights. Bake 8 minutes. Remove weights and paper and cool.

Melt the butter in a large heavy skillet over low heat. Add the leeks and onion and cook, stirring, until very tender but not browned, 15 to 20 minutes, or longer. Stir in the green onions and thyme. Cook, stirring, 2 minutes longer. Spread the mixture in the bottom of the pastry shell. Sprinkle the bacon on top of the leek mixture.

Beat together the whole egg, egg yolks, and half-and-half. Season well with salt and pepper. Gently pour this mixture over the leeks. Bake in the middle of the oven until the custard is puffy, the center is set, and a knife inserted near the middle comes out clean, about 30 minutes. Cool 5 minutes (or longer if serving warm). Serve hot or warm.

Variations: *Spread 1 cup grated Gruyère cheese over the leeks in the pastry shell before sprinkling with the bacon. Or, for a more aggressive flavor, beat 2 tablespoons Dijon-style mustard into the egg and cream mixture before pouring it over the cooked leeks.*

Baked Leeks with Barley

Two almost-forgotten ingredients go very well together in a one-dish accompaniment for lamb or game of any kind, especially wild goose. This dish can also be served at room temperature with a meal of cold meats, fish, and cheese.

Makes 6 servings

1 tablespoon butter
1 tablespoon olive oil
3 large leeks, trimmed, white and light green parts only, thinly sliced
2 cloves garlic, minced
1 medium-size green bell pepper, seeded and thinly sliced
$^1/_2$ cup dry white wine
3 cups cooked pearled barley (about $^3/_4$ cup raw)
$^1/_3$ cup chopped fresh parsley
Salt and freshly ground black pepper to taste

Preheat the oven to 350°F. Butter a medium-size shallow baking dish.

Heat 1 tablespoon butter and oil in a medium-size heavy skillet over low heat. Add the leeks and cook, stirring from time to time, until just tender, 15 to 20 minutes. Stir in the garlic and bell pepper. Cook, stirring occasionally, for 5 to 6 minutes longer. Stir in the wine and cook 2 minutes. Stir in the barley and parsley and season well with salt and pepper. Spread the vegetables in the prepared baking dish. Bake until very hot, about 20 minutes. Serve very hot.

Variation: Add ¼ *pound sliced mushrooms, cooked 5 minutes in 1 tablespoon of butter, to the leeks and barley before spreading the mixture into the baking dish. Continue with the recipe.*

Leeks Vinaigrette

In Europe, leeks prepared this way are called poor man's asparagus—in America, things are reversed and asparagus are often less expensive and more readily available than leeks. I think this is the perfect bistro first course, but these leeks go very well with any cold buffet.

Makes 6 servings

18 very thin leeks, trimmed, white and light green parts only
3 tablespoons lemon juice
1 tablespoon Dijon-style mustard
⅓ to ½ cup extra-virgin olive oil
Salt and freshly ground black pepper to taste
3 tablespoons chopped fresh parsley

Steam the leeks, whole, in a steamer basket or a colander, covered, over simmering water until tender, at least 20 minutes. Or boil the leeks in salted water to cover until tender, at least 20 minutes. Drain well. While still hot, halve the leeks lengthwise and arrange them in a flat glass or other nonreactive dish.

In a jar with a tight-fitting lid, combine the lemon juice, mustard, olive oil, salt, pepper, and parsley. Shake until well mixed. Pour this dressing over the warm leeks and let cool. Refrigerate for several hours if not serving within 1 hour. Serve at room temperature.

Lentils

Along with dried beans, lentils provide more protein for more of the world's people than almost any other food. These little dried seeds grow in many parts of the world and, like dried beans, come in various colors, from orange red to brown to green. They can be stewed, pureed, or ground into a sort of flour. Lentils are wonderful in soups and salads, great all year long, though in many countries they are considered hearty winter fare.

In India one variety of lentil (masur or masoor) is soaked to remove the skin, split, and becomes dal, although dried beans and peas—hulled or not and split or not—are also called dal. Stewed and sometimes pureed, dal is served over or with rice or bread. Lentils eaten together with rice or bread provide a source of "complete" protein. In poor families, this combination is virtually the sole source of nourishment; wealthier families will serve it as part of a more widely varied diet.

In some Moslem countries, lentils are considered such an important source of nourishment that a soup of lentils and lamb is often the one dish that breaks the daily fast during Ramadan.

Lentils, like dried beans and peas, are called a pulse. Any edible seed that is taken from the pod and dried is a pulse. Some confusion arises, however, when the mush made in some countries, usually from lentils, is also called pulse.

Unlike dried beans, lentils do not need to be presoaked, although some books and packages will tell you to do so. They do, however, need to be well washed and picked over, especially if you buy them in bulk. Frequently, there are tiny stones that have been scooped up with the seeds and, if not picked out, can break a tooth. Many lentils sold in America are called "quick cooking" and will be ready to eat in 45 minutes or less. Brown and, especially, green lentils keep their shape during long cooking, but red lentils, which turn yellow when cooked—though more colorful—fall into a mush if cooked too long. Otherwise, one variety can pretty much be substituted for another. I usually begin to check lentils of any kind after cooking them about 35 to 40 minutes to be sure they are just tender and not overcooked.

It is unfortunate that lentils share with dried beans the tendency to create uncomfortable gas in people who lack the enzyme that aids in the digestion of the simple sugars in the small intestine. Happily, there is now an over-the-counter product, Beano® (see page 37), that can provide the missing enzyme and relieve this problem for most of us.

Lentils contain no cholesterol and almost no fat. They are high in fiber, carbohydrates, iron, and vitamin B.

Count on 1 cup of dry lentils to provide about 3 cups of cooked.

Storage and Preparation: Like dried beans, lentils should be stored in a cool, dry place, preferably in an airtight container.

While lentils do not need to be presoaked, they must be washed and picked over carefully before using to eliminate any pebbles or dirt. The easiest way to do this is to place the dry lentils in a large bowl and run clear water over them. Any lentils that float to the surface should be discarded, along with other extraneous bits and pieces that appear when the seeds are stirred. Drain the lentils well, look for pebbles or tiny stones, and then continue with the recipe. Most lentils sold in boxes have been prescreened and do not contain stones, pebbles, or other matter, although boxes that have been kept on the shelf for a long period of time may have attracted bugs and should be washed.

Boiled Lentils

Place the lentils in a large pot. Cover with water and bring to a boil over medium heat. Reduce the heat to low and simmer, partially covered, until tender. The cooking time can vary from 45 minutes to 1½ hours, depending on the age and variety you are using. Be sure to check the water level during the cooking process as lentils absorb substantially more water than beans and can quickly boil dry. Burned lentils have a very unpleasant taste.

Boiled lentils should be thoroughly drained. They can be used in other recipes or can be seasoned with salt, pepper, cumin, and fresh parsley—and a little olive oil if you like. Serve with rice as a one-dish vegetarian meal or set them alongside baked ham or hearty, garlicky grilled sausages.

Creamed Lentils

A very homely, yet satisfying dish, this goes very well with lamb, especially charcoal-grilled kebabs.

Makes 6 to 8 servings

1 tablespoon butter
1 bunch (6 to 8) green onions (scallions), white and light green parts only, sliced, plus additional for garnishing
1 tablespoon all-purpose flour
Salt and freshly ground black pepper to taste
1 tablespoon ground cumin, or to taste
1 cup heavy cream, half-and-half, or regular or skim milk, hot
2 cups brown or green lentils, carefully picked over, simmered in water to cover until tender, 45 to 60 minutes, and drained

Melt the butter in a large heavy saucepan over medium heat. Add the green onions and cook, stirring, for 1 minute. Stir in the flour and season with salt, pepper, and cumin. Cook over low heat for 1 minute. Whisk in the hot half-and-half. Stir until thickened, 3 or 4 minutes. Stir in the lentils and heat through. Serve very hot, garnished with the additional green onions.

Variation: *Thinly slice ¼ pound white mushrooms and cook them, stirring, over medium heat in 1 tablespoon of butter until golden, 5 to 8 minutes. Stir them into the lentils before adding to the cream sauce.*

Lentil and Goat Cheese Salad

Here is a nice change of pace for your next picnic. Take the cheese and lettuce along in separate containers and put the salad together at the picnic site. This is perfect with cold cuts; a robust country pâté; lots of cheeses; and good, crusty bread.

Makes 6 to 8 servings

2 cups brown or green lentils, carefully picked over, simmered in beef stock to cover until tender, 45 to 60 minutes, drained, and cooled, stock reserved for another use
¼ cup minced green bell pepper
2 bunches (12 to 16) green onions (scallions), white and light green parts only, thinly sliced
1 clove garlic, minced
2 tablespoons chopped fresh parsley
1 tablespoon chopped fresh thyme
1 tablespoon red wine vinegar
1 teaspoon Dijon-style mustard
Salt and freshly ground black pepper to taste
⅓ cup olive oil
Leaf lettuce
1 cup crumbled goat cheese, or feta

In a medium-size bowl, toss together the lentils, bell pepper, green onions, and garlic.

In a jar with a tight-fitting lid, combine the herbs, vinegar, mustard, salt, pepper, and olive oil. Cover and shake until well combined. Toss this dressing with the lentils. Chill several hours or up to two days.

To serve, bring the lentils to room temperature. Arrange the leaf lettuce in a small salad bowl. Pile the lentils on top. Garnish with the cheese.

Note: *If the salad will be served a day or two after making it, you may want to add a little more dressing to the lentils.*

Mexican Lentil Salad

The robust flavor of this dish makes it a great accompaniment for barbecued beef or pork.

Makes 6 to 8 servings

1 small onion, cut into ¼-inch dice
1 medium-size clove garlic, minced
1 jalapeño pepper, seeded and minced
2 ripe tomatoes, peeled, seeded, and cut into ¼-inch dice

½ green bell pepper, seeded and cut into
    ¼-inch dice
1 teaspoon ground cumin
1 teaspoon well-flavored chili powder,
    or more to taste
3 tablespoons fresh lime juice
⅓ cup olive oil
¼ cup chopped fresh cilantro
1½ cups brown lentils, well picked over,
    simmered in water to cover until tender,
    45 to 60 minutes, well drained, and cooled
Salt and freshly ground black pepper to taste
2 tablespoons thinly sliced green onions
    (scallions)
Leaf lettuce

In a large bowl, toss together all the ingredients except the lentils, green onions, and lettuce. Stir in the drained and cooled lentils. Chill overnight. Bring the salad to room temperature.

Arrange the lettuce on a serving plate. Pile the salad on the lettuce and garnish with the green onions and another grind of pepper.

Lentils with Carrots and Smoked Bacon

This is a favorite way to serve lentils in Europe. It is so popular that there are very acceptable canned versions on sale in almost every supermarket. Today, you can often find lentils prepared like this sealed in plastic in the refrigerated cases of specialty markets. They are almost good enough to make you forego preparing them yourself, and make a fine base for lentil soup. This very hearty cold-weather dish goes well with baked ham, or pork in any form, especially garlicky sausages.

Makes at least 6 servings

2 cups brown lentils, carefully picked over
1 medium-size onion, chopped
¼ pound slab bacon, cut into ¼-inch dice
2 cups well-flavored beef stock
½ cup red wine
Salt and freshly ground black pepper to taste
2 tablespoons chopped fresh thyme, or
    2 teaspoons dried
3 large carrots, peeled and cut into large dice

Combine all the ingredients except the carrots in a large heavy saucepan. Simmer, covered, over low heat until the lentils are tender, 30 to 45 minutes. Stir in the carrots and simmer until most of the liquid is absorbed and the lentils and carrots are very tender but not falling apart, 15 to 20 minutes longer. Season again with salt and pepper if necessary. Serve hot.

Note: *While red lentils are very colorful, they tend to fall apart if cooked too long and should not be used in dishes like this.*

Lettuce and Other Salad Greens

In the continuing quest for health, fitness, and slim figures, Americans have definitely given salads an important place in their diet, even though salad greens have been part of the American scene ever since colonial days. While many cooks rely on only one or two types of lettuce for their entire repertoire, there are many kinds of greens (and reds!) that make wonderful salads, and most can be treated in the same way, although some are heartier than others. The more fragile greens must be treated with respect and a delicate touch or they soon become limp and unattractive. And why stick with just one kind of green? Not only can you make up your own combinations but now many markets and greengrocers sell their own mixes, from mesclun (an eclectic European-type mixture of wild or small early "greens") to more robust mixtures of familiar leaves.

Here are some of the types of lettuce and greens available for your salad creations.

Arugula (rocket or roquette) is a dark green, deeply lobed leaf of Mediterranean extraction that has a delightful almost peppery flavor. Avoid the large leaves, which can be tough and bitter. It is expensive, but combined with other greens, a little goes a long way.

Bibb (limestone or butterhead) is an American development. Its crinkly, soft but not limp leaves are wonderful tossed with oil and vinegar or mixed with more robust greens. I like to use them in sandwiches for an unctuous, buttery taste, but only for sandwiches made just before serving. I think this is wonderful for Vietnamese dishes that combine meat or shrimp, fish sauce, and fresh mint, all wrapped in crisp, freshly washed lettuce leaves.

Boston lettuce has very tender, light green, buttery leaves that wilt quickly once they have been dressed. In France, a similar type (*laitue*) is often served by itself, tossed at the last minute with a mustardy vinaigrette.

Chicory (curly endive, frisée) is a frizzy leaved relative of Belgian endive with a similar bitter edge. The more bitter, dark green outer leaves are delicious if served with a hot vinegar dressing, topped with fried, crumbled bacon and hard-cooked or poached eggs. Toss the more delicate yellow to white inner leaves with a mixture of other salad greens.

Escarole (also called chicory) is less bitter than curly or Belgian endive. The deep green outer leaves can be sliced and tossed with robust dressings or added to soups, beans, or pasta for extra flavor. The lighter inner leaves are delicious in any kind of salad.

Iceberg (crisphead) is the ultra-crisp compact head that is often denigrated by "serious" cooks. I think its mild flavor and decisive crunch make it wonderful for sandwiches; old-fashioned wedge salads; and when shredded, a perfect, sturdy base for composed salads.

Leaf lettuce includes a number of different kinds of greens (and reds), such as green and red leaf, green and red oak leaf, and other more esoteric nonheading lettuces that local producers may have cultivated. Of the commercially available leafs, I am most partial to red oak leaf and red tipped because they have a lovely flavor and make a very attractive salad, even if mixed with other greens.

Mâche (lamb's lettuce, corn salad, *feld salat*) has tiny, delicate oval leaves, and is usually sold in little sprigs of 4 or 5 leaves. It's wonderful all by itself, but when it is expensive or in short supply, it can be combined with other delicate greens. Its nutty, faintly sweet flavor is enhanced by its unctuous texture.

Radicchio is a red-leaf relative of endive. Its leaves have a thick white vein and a robust, pleasantly bitter flavor. This is one "green" that can stand up to highly flavored dressings. It's best when combined raw with other greens, but also can be grilled or quickly stir-fried.

Romaine (cos) is the original Caesar salad green. If legend has it right, it first grew on the Greek island of Kos, where it was supposedly well liked for its crunchy texture. I also like its long, dark and light green leaves shredded and tossed with a hot vinegary dressing.

Watercress grows in flooded fields, and its spriggy little leaves have a wonderful very peppery flavor. It is truly an all-purpose green. Watercress is great on its own for a robustly flavorful salad. It's also good mixed with other greens to add a little spice. Try it as the green in a number of different sandwiches (especially grilled vegetable on sourdough bread), or cook it for wonderful soups, both hot and cold.

Other greens that can be added to salads include tiny crisp beet greens, mustard greens, Swiss chard, and if you can find them, very young dandelion greens.

Many salad greens also have another life that is frequently overlooked. They can be cooked to add interest to everyday and company meals, and I have included several recipes that should pique your interest.

Lettuces and other salad greens are all, for the most part, low in calories, fat free, and high in carbohydrates. Many contain reasonable amounts of vitamins A and C as well as calcium and iron.

Selection: Choose the crispest leaves available. Look for greens, reds, or yellows that have the clearest, most vibrant colors. Avoid any leaves that are limp or browned along the edges. The stems should be crisp, breaking easily when they are bent.

Salad greens are at their best during the summer months, but today many are available all year long. Increasingly, you also can find packaged mixtures of greens, prewashed and ready to use. Be sure to inspect the plastic packages carefully and discard any that show too much moisture on the inside or have leaves that have begun to wilt, turn brown, or show signs of mold.

Storage and Preparation: Greens should be stored, unwashed, in a perforated vegetable bag in the vegetable drawer of the refrigerator, away from any fruit. Tender delicate-leaved greens should be eaten soon after picking or purchasing, two to three days at most. Hardier lettuces will keep up to two weeks. Inspect the greens every day or two, discarding any leaves that have begun to wilt or decay. Changing the bag from time to time will increase the life of the remaining greens.

All greens—except those that are prewashed and packaged—need to be washed and dried before preparing. Some experts suggest washing with lukewarm water rather than cold, claiming that it loosens the dirt and grit more completely than cold, but it does tend to wilt the leaves a bit. However, if the washed greens are dried—preferably spun in a salad dryer—wrapped in paper towels or a kitchen towel, placed in a plastic bag, and refrigerated for an hour or two they will crisp up again beautifully. If the lettuces must be served right after washing, I suggest using the coldest water available, even adding a few ice cubes to the water if you like.

The greens can also be washed, spun dry, and stored in a closed plastic bag for up to two days.

Leaf lettuce can easily be separated from the stem by twisting off the base. The simplest method of coring head lettuces and other heading greens is to hold the head in your hands, stem down, and rap the stem sharply on the counter or other hard surface. This will loosen the core, allowing you to twist it out completely. Iceberg lettuce can be rinsed by holding the cored hole under the faucet, spreading the leaves slightly. Drain by shaking the head well and then turning the cored side down in a colander.

Very large leaves with heavy stems should be stemmed and cut or torn into bite-size pieces. If you like the added crunch, cut the crisp stems into 1-inch lengths and toss with the leaves. Small tender leaves can be left whole or torn into pieces before tossing with dressing.

Some experts say that greens should always be hand torn and never cut with a knife. I have prepared tubs of salad for huge dinners and have used very sharp stainless-steel knives to stem and cut the leaves without any evil effect, so I have some difficulty with this philosophy. However, I suggest you use whichever method you prefer.

Sautéed Lettuce

Cooking lettuce has become a lost art. Old-fashioned menus often included recipes similar to this. Before nouvelle cuisine took over in France, many wonderful restaurants used to serve this dish, especially with delicately flavored poached fish, such as salmon, turbot, or sole.

Makes about 6 servings

3 to 4 tablespoons (up to ½ stick) butter
3 small to medium-size heads Boston lettuce, cut crosswise into thin strips
Salt and freshly ground black pepper to taste
1 generous tablespoon snipped fresh chives

Melt the butter in a heavy skillet over medium heat. Stir in the lettuce and season well with salt and pepper. Cook, stirring gently from time to time, or tossing, just until wilted, less than 3 or 4 minutes. Serve very hot, garnished with the chives.

Lettuce Stir-fry

The secret to this crisp, savory dish lies in quick cooking. All the cutting can be done ahead of time, with the actual cooking accomplished at the last minute. Serve it alongside a spicy meal of blackened fish fillets.

Makes 6 servings

2 tablespoons mild vegetable oil, preferably peanut
1 teaspoon Chinese hot oil
1 clove garlic, minced
1 bunch (6 to 8) green onions (scallions), white and light green parts only, thinly sliced, plus 1 tablespoon for garnishing
1 large head green leaf lettuce, Romaine, or curly endive, sliced crosswise
1 tablespoon light soy sauce
1 tablespoon rice wine, or dry sherry
2 tablespoons chicken stock
1 teaspoon cornstarch
Hot pepper sauce to taste (optional)

Heat the oils in a wok over high heat. Add the garlic and all but 1 tablespoon of the green onions, and cook, stirring, for 10 to 15 seconds, being careful not to burn the vegetables. Add the lettuce and stir-fry until just wilted, about 1 minute.

In a small bowl, stir together the soy sauce, wine, stock, and cornstarch. Stir this mixture into the lettuce and continue to cook, stirring or tossing, constantly, until the sauce is thickened, no longer than 1 minute.

Serve the lettuce at once, very hot, garnished with the remaining 1 tablespoon of green onions. Pass a favorite hot pepper sauce, if desired.

Warm Chicory and Potato Salad

In France, a plate of warm potato slices served alongside slices of savory garlic sausage from Lyon with a mustardy dressing over all is often a bistro appetizer or light lunch with a green salad. I have combined the two into one. Serve it as a first course or pass it along with a golden roast chicken and grilled tomatoes for a lovely impromptu company dinner.

Makes 6 servings

1 medium-size or ½ large head chicory (curly endive), cut into bite-size pieces
6 medium-size waxy potatoes, unpeeled, boiled in salted water to cover until tender but not falling apart, 15 to 20 minutes, drained, sliced, and kept warm
½ medium-size sweet onion or red onion, thinly sliced
8 ounces garlic sausage, such as kielbasa, grilled, thinly sliced, and kept warm
1 small bunch watercress, stemmed
1 tablespoon balsamic vinegar
1 tablespoon Dijon-style mustard
Salt and freshly ground black pepper to taste
⅓ to ½ cup extra-virgin olive oil

Divide the chicory among six salad plates. Arrange 1 warm sliced potato on each plate. Arrange the onion over the potatoes and top with warm sausage slices. Or alternate the potato and sausage slices and arrange the onion on top. Garnish each serving with some of the watercress.

In a small bowl, beat together the vinegar, mustard, salt, pepper, and oil. Spoon some of this dressing over the salads and serve while the potatoes and sausage are still warm. Pass any remaining dressing in a sauce boat.

Chicory Salad

This is a delightful late-summer salad. When everyone needs a break from tomatoes and leaf lettuce, offer the bittersweet goodness of chicory and endive. Perfect for a meal of cold roast meat such as chicken, veal tonnato, or pork, I also think this salad goes well with grilled shrimp. I even like it as the one side dish with mouth-burning Old Bay–seasoned steamed crabs.

Makes 6 servings

½ large head of chicory (curly endive), separated into leaves and cut into bite-size pieces
1 large or 2 medium-size heads Belgian endive, trimmed and cut across into 1-inch rounds
1 small head radicchio, separated into leaves, trimmed, and cut into bite-size pieces
1 large ripe red or green Bartlett pear
Juice of ½ lemon
⅓ cup crumbled blue cheese, such as Maytag, Roquefort, or Gorgonzola
⅓ cup walnut halves, toasted (page 70)
1 tablespoon chopped fresh parsley, plus additional sprigs for garnishing
1 teaspoon balsamic vinegar
Salt and freshly ground black pepper to taste
¼ teaspoon ground ginger
1 tablespoon walnut oil (toasted walnut oil will be more intense if available)
¼ cup mild vegetable oil, such as peanut, corn, or canola

Pile the chicory in a large chilled salad bowl. Arrange the endive and radicchio on top.

In a small bowl, quickly toss the pear slices with the lemon juice and arrange them on the greens like the spokes of a wheel. Sprinkle the blue cheese and walnuts over all.

In a small bowl, beat together the chopped parsley, vinegar, salt, pepper, ginger, and oils. Pour this dressing over the salad and garnish with the parsley.

Just before serving, toss the salad and divide between six chilled salad dishes.

Braised Whole Lettuce

Too often we think lettuce is only for salads. The delicate flavor is also delicious when cooked. These whole braised heads of buttery leaf lettuce make a very sophisticated accompaniment for roast veal, pheasant, or even grilled fish such as red snapper.

Makes 6 servings

6 small heads leaf lettuce, such as Boston or Bibb, trimmed, boiled in salted water to cover for 3 minutes, and well drained
2 tablespoons butter
1 slice smoked ham, cut into ¼-inch dice
1 small onion, halved and thinly sliced
1 large carrot, peeled and cut into ¼-inch dice
1 medium-size rib celery, cut into ¼-inch dice, including the leaves
1 cup well-flavored-chicken stock
¼ cup dry white wine
Salt and freshly ground black pepper to taste
2 tablespoons chopped fresh parsley

Squeeze the drained lettuce to remove as much of the cooking water as possible. Use your hands to shape each head into a firm bundle. Some cooks like to use a little fine string to hold the bundles together, but if the heads are well compressed, it's not necessary.

Over medium heat, melt the butter in a covered flameproof casserole large enough to hold the lettuce bundles in a single layer. Add the ham, onion, carrot, and celery and cook, stirring occasionally, until just translucent, 8 to 10 minutes. Spread the mixture in an even layer in the bottom of the casserole. Arrange the lettuce bundles on top of the vegetables.

Pour in the stock and wine. Season well with salt and pepper. Cover and simmer gently over low heat until the lettuce is very tender, 25 to 30 minutes.

Using a slotted spoon, remove the lettuce to a heated serving plate, cover, and keep warm. Strain the cooking liquid into a small saucepan, pressing on the vegetables to remove as much of the juice as possible. Boil the cooking liquid hard over high heat and until it reduces to ¼ to ⅓ cup of concentrated sauce, about 5 minutes.

Serve the lettuce very hot, with a little of the sauce spooned over each head. Garnish with the parsley.

Variation: *Create a colorful (albeit expensive) version of this dish by substituting small whole heads of radicchio for the lettuce. Radicchio has a more substantial leaf and will not shrink as much as Boston or Bibb lettuce. Add 2 tablespoons vinegar to the boiling water before adding the heads of radicchio to set the color so it will not fade too much or turn brown.*

Note: *Vegetables that are diced, "sweated" (cooked, covered, in a little fat until soft), and used in this manner—as a bed to keep another ingredient from touching the bottom of the cooking dish—are called a* mirepoix.

Cold Lettuce Soufflé with Mustard Sauce

Try this summertime dish with cold roast meats or cold poached fish. It goes very well with poached or home-smoked bluefish.

Makes 6 to 8 servings

1 tablespoon butter
1 bunch (6 to 8) green onions (scallions), white part only, thinly sliced
1 large head leaf lettuce, such as Bibb, Boston, or green leaf, stemmed and chopped; or 2 bunches watercress
½ cup well-flavored chicken stock
3 large eggs, separated, whites beaten until stiff
2 cups skim milk
2 tablespoons (2 envelopes) powdered gelatin
¼ cup water
½ teaspoon ground cumin
Salt and freshly ground black pepper to taste

Hot pepper sauce to taste (optional)
1 cup best-quality plain yogurt, whipped until stiff
Several parsley sprigs
Mustard Sauce (recipe follows)

Melt the butter in a medium-size deep skillet over medium heat. Add the green onions and toss to coat. Stir in the lettuce and cook until just wilted, about 1 minute. Stir in the stock. Simmer over low heat until the lettuce is very tender, 6 to 8 minutes. Drain the vegetables well and puree them in a blender or food processor. Set aside.

In a small bowl, beat the egg yolks until light. Pour them into the top of a double boiler set over simmering, but not boiling, water. Whisk in the milk and cook, whisking, until the mixture coats the back of a spoon, 6 to 10 minutes.

In a small bowl, dissolve the gelatin in the water. Remove the egg mixture from the heat. Beat in the gelatin. Stir in the lettuce puree. Season with cumin, salt, and pepper. Add hot pepper sauce if using. Cool.

When the mixture is cool, fold in the whipped yogurt and then the beaten egg whites. Pile the mixture into a 1-quart soufflé dish. Refrigerate, covered, until set, about 8 hours or overnight. Garnish with the parsley and serve with the Mustard Sauce.

Mustard Sauce

Makes about ¾ cup

½ cup mayonnaise, prepared or homemade (page 13)
3 tablespoons light sour cream
1 teaspoon dry English mustard
2 tablespoons Dijon-style mustard
¼ cup skim milk, or more if a thinner sauce is desired
Salt and freshly ground black pepper to taste
2 tablespoons chopped fresh parsley

In a small bowl, beat together all the ingredients and chill at least 4 hours. Serve chilled.

Roman Escarole

The slightly bitter taste of escarole, like its cousin chicory (curly endive), makes it a good foil for the richness of baked ham or roast spareribs. I have often eaten escarole prepared this way in Italy and in Italian areas of Switzerland. Pass a little freshly grated Parmesan cheese with it if you like. At room temperature, it makes a good addition to an antipasto platter.

Makes 6 servings

2 tablespoons olive oil
2 small cloves garlic, minced
1 to 1½ pounds escarole, trimmed, stemmed if
    necessary, and thickly sliced across
2 tablespoons dry white wine
Salt and freshly ground black pepper to taste
1 tablespoon pine nuts, lightly toasted (page 70)

Heat the olive oil in a large heavy skillet over medium heat. Add the garlic and cook, stirring, for 30 seconds. Add the escarole and cook, tossing, until the escarole begins to wilt, about 1 minute. Stir in the wine, cover, and cook until the leaves are tender but still very green, 2 to 3 minutes. Remove the cover, increase the heat to high, and cook, stirring, to evaporate the liquid, about 1 minute. Season well with salt and pepper. Serve very hot, or at room temperature, garnished with the pine nuts.

Escarole Tarts

These savory little tarts make perfect appetizers, but they are also a delicious side dish with garlicky shrimp scampi or spicy grilled prawns.

Makes six 6-inch tarts

Pastry dough for six 6-inch tarts, for one
    2-crust tart, or two 9-inch tarts, prepared or
    homemade (page 126)

2 tablespoons olive oil
1 large onion, halved and thinly sliced
2 cloves garlic, minced
1 large head escarole, trimmed and chopped
1 large egg, beaten
½ cup freshly grated Parmesan cheese
½ cup heavy cream
½ teaspoon ground nutmeg

Preheat the oven to 350°F.

Roll out the pastry dough, cut it into six 7-inch rounds, and line six 6-inch tart pans.

Heat the olive oil in a large heavy skillet over medium heat. Add the onion and cook, stirring occasionally, until translucent, about 10 minutes. Stir in the garlic and cook 1 minute longer. Stir in the escarole and cook, stirring, until wilted, about 5 minutes. Remove the pan from the heat and cool slightly.

In a medium-size bowl, beat together the egg, cheese, cream, and nutmeg. Stir this into the escarole. Spoon this mixture into the tart shells. Bake until the filling is puffed and the pastry is golden brown, 20 to 25 minutes. Serve very hot.

Mustard Greens with Bacon

While mustard greens can be used in salads, they have a slightly bitter taste. In the past they nourished many a pioneer, and this very old-fashioned dish might have been appetizer, main course, and salad all in one. Serve it with thick grilled pork chops or with an equally old-fashioned roast fresh ham or pork picnic shoulder.

Makes 6 servings

4 thick slices bacon, fried until crisp, crumbled
    and drained on paper towels, fat left in the
    skillet (page 42)
2 pounds mustard greens, stemmed and torn into
    large pieces
Salt and freshly ground black pepper to taste
Cider vinegar or malt vinegar to taste
Hot pepper sauce to taste

Heat the bacon fat in the same skillet the bacon was cooked in over very low heat. Add the greens and cook, stirring from time to time, until the water that clings to the leaves after washing has evaporated and the greens are wilted, tender, and coated with the fat, 3 to 4 minutes. Season well with salt and pepper. Garnish with the bacon.

Pass the vinegar and hot sauce so that diners can add them to suit their taste.

Note: *If a longer-cooked texture is desired, add about* $\frac{1}{3}$ *cup water or chicken stock to the wilted greens, cover, and cook for about 10 minutes.*

Mushrooms

Mushrooms mean only one thing to too many people—the smooth white caps found in most supermarkets, sometimes in bulk, often only in plastic-wrapped baskets. While there is certainly a definite place for this basic white variety, there is a whole world of other choices for the more adventuresome.

Being adventuresome, however, does not extend to collecting mushrooms in the wild by oneself. Even though only a few wild mushrooms are actually deadly, there are many that can cause extreme distress, especially for people with food sensitivities. Too many wild mushrooms mimic each other, deadly or distressing ones appearing to be nearly the same as those that are completely innocuous. In order for you—and me—to be perfectly safe we must rely only on expert pickers—or stick to the cultivated varieties. Knowledgeable restaurateurs who serve mushrooms from the wild say the most important thing about these mushrooms is knowing the expertise of the picker or purveyor.

Even if you have an experienced source for wild mushrooms and you trust their judgment implicitly, never serve them raw. All should be cooked, separately from any other ingredient, for at least 5 minutes. Some European chefs who use wild mushrooms regularly insist they should be cooked at least 15 minutes to ensure they will not cause side effects in susceptible people. The heat of cooking will nullify some of the substances in the mushrooms that cause distress.

Happily for us, there are ever-growing numbers of cultivated mushrooms that are perfectly safe, including heretofore only wild varieties such as chanterelles, cèpes, and even morels.

Mushrooms can add a new dimension to foods. The rich, nutty taste of the more full-flavored varieties greatly enhances soups, stews, and other dishes. They have been so prized in the past for their flavor that some ancient cultures allowed only the wealthy, or sometimes just the priests, to indulge in the "food of the gods."

Fresh Mushrooms

In the beginning, the only mushrooms available were those picked in the wild. Not until almost the beginning of the nineteenth century were the first mushrooms cultivated on a large scale. It was the French who first entered the market with the white mushroom (*champignon de Paris*) we are familiar with today, although the brown or cremini variety was soon grown on a commercial scale as well.

Since those early days, other varieties have become increasingly available. Look for these fresh mushrooms in your market or specialty green grocer.

White mushrooms are the crisp, white fungi most commonly found and are what many people consider to be mushrooms. They have a very delicate flavor and range in size from "button" (about ½ inch in diameter) to large caps more than 2 inches wide. These cultivated mushrooms are available all year long.

The brown mushroom (cremini) is a close relative of the common white mushroom. Light brown in color, with a slightly more robust flavor, they are available in the same sizes as and are virtually interchangeable with white mushrooms. Like white mushrooms, cremini are cultivated and are available all year long.

Portabella mushrooms are cremini mushrooms that have grown into very large fungi. The texture is called steaklike, and the flavor is delicious. Thick slices can be grilled, and whole caps can be basted with olive oil and garlic, roasted over indirect coals, and served in place of meat. Portabella mushrooms are available all year long.

Shiitake (Asian black) mushrooms have flat, brown caps with dark undersides and thin, woody stems that should be discarded as they are usually too tough to eat. The hearty texture and robust flavor that often has a slight garlicky overtone make them wonderful in stir-fries, ragouts, and gratins. Wild until recently, shiitakes are now cultivated and available year round.

Enoki mushrooms are tiny, snowy white, button candy–size caps on long thin stems. These are very delicately flavored morsels with a crisp texture a little like bean sprouts. Do not buy any that are slimy or wet. I think they are best eaten raw, just barely heated or dropped as a garnish into soups. These are also cultivated and are available year round.

Oyster mushrooms (*pleurottes*) have white to beige caps with a very silky texture. The flavor is even more delicate than white mushrooms but is delicious, with slight shellfish overtones, hence the name. They are especially good in combination with other varieties. Oyster mushrooms are now cultivated and can be found year round in some areas.

Wood ear (cloud ear) mushrooms have large, dark brown, sometimes almost black, frilly caps with a curious, crisp but slightly gelatinous texture. These are the mushrooms so often used in Asian dishes.

Hen-of-the-woods, a shelflike mushroom, appears in flat, beige, stemless clusters (usually on tree trunks) and has a rich flavor that is wonderful in ragouts. While these are not universally available, they are common enough from midsummer through the first frost to look for and are well worth trying. These are wild for the most part, though some are now being cultivated.

Cèpes (boletes, porcini, *Steinpiltz*) are pretty, classically shaped fungi with dark brown caps. Until recently these were strictly wild, harvested by independent pickers. A limited supply is now being cultivated. Look for them in specialty stores. Their flavor is rich and delicious. Sliced, or not if small, and sautéed with garlic, parsley, and olive oil, they are food for the gods. If these are being harvested in the wild, they are most available in summer up through October. They are excellent dried.

Chanterelles are another wild mushroom that is finally being cultivated in small amounts. These frilly, horn-shaped, pale orange fungi with thin stems are some of the most sought after for both restaurants and private homes. In season, these are prepared in myriad ways, even added to scrambled eggs. The flavor is rich and full without being overpowering, and the texture is slightly less tender than most cultivated mushrooms. Look for them from midsummer until the end of October or a little later.

Morels are wonderful, almost black, nutty flavored conical mushrooms with a honeycomb surface. Classically served in rich sauces with thick cuts of beef, they are also delicious with game or served in a cream sauce over crisp triangles of toast. These wild, early spring mushrooms are extremely difficult to find fresh. They are available dried all year long. While they are very expensive, dried morels are excellent once they are rehydrated and can be used in any recipe calling for fresh mushrooms.

Mushrooms are a good source of vitamin B and contain fair amounts of protein.

Selection: Mushrooms should be as fresh as possible. They are fragile and spoil quickly. Try to avoid any that are damp or even slightly slimy. Look for bright, even coloring, without any signs of mold or decay.

In mushrooms with gills, the gills should be closed and the caps firm and crisp. Darkened mushrooms with open gills can be added to soups and stews where appearance is not primary, as long as the texture is not leathery, wet, or slippery.

If possible, buy mushrooms from a bulk container so that you can choose each one individually, eliminating any that are not in the best possible condition. If you must buy mushrooms in prepacked containers, choose the crispest looking available, and open them as soon as you get them home.

Mushrooms shrink as much as 50 percent—or more—in volume when cooked, so take this into consideration when buying.

Storage and Preparation: Mushrooms need to be prepared as soon as possible. If they are in prime condition when bought, they can generally be refrigerated two or three days longer. Be sure to pick them over well, opening plastic-wrapped containers and removing any mushrooms that are not in prime condition. If you are going to store mushrooms longer than 24 hours, it is wise to pick them over daily so that any that are spoiling do not infect those remaining in the bag.

Place the mushrooms in a paper or cloth bag and store in the vegetable drawer of the refrigerator. If they appear to be drying out, cover them with a lightly dampened—but not wet—paper or kitchen towel that should be changed daily.

Mushrooms are like sponges. If they are soaked in water for any length of time, they will absorb prodigious quantities, which they will subsequently give off when cooked, which can ruin a recipe. It is best in most cases to just lightly brush the caps or wipe them with a clean kitchen towel, removing any loose dirt; clean them just before cooking. Trim the stem ends—or discard the stems of shiitake mushrooms—and cut out any bad spots. The only mushrooms that should be well washed, in running water, are morels. The little crevices on their surface are favorite hiding places for little creatures that are best not eaten with the fungi.

Leave the mushrooms whole or cut them into halves, slices, or chunks, depending on the recipe. Cook at once.

Dried Mushrooms

Many varieties of wild mushrooms are available fresh for very short periods during the year. In the past, to preserve the delicious flavor and aroma of these succulent morsels, a large portion of the fresh harvest was dried for use during the rest of the year. Mushrooms consist of up to 90 percent water and dehydrate quickly, making them prime candidates for drying. They can be dried whole, sliced, or diced. Some varieties are even dried and then pulverized to a powder for adding to sauces and soups.

Some mushrooms, such as morels, shiitakes, and cèpes rehydrate to a condition very much like that of fresh mushrooms. Other varieties maintain their flavor and aroma but will be somewhat softer in texture when reconstituted than when they were fresh. Almost all dried mushrooms can be substituted for fresh ones in many dishes.

Morels are extremely expensive, but for flavor and aroma, the dried variety is dynamite, especially in areas where fresh morels (which have a brief season) are virtually unavailable. Dried morels need to be carefully rinsed after rehydrating to remove any debris that may have collected in the honeycomb-like surface.

Cèpes are available in some supermarkets and in specialty stores. They are also quite costly, but 1 ounce of dried cèpes can equal 6 or more ounces of rehydrated mushrooms. I think the dried cèpes from Italy have the best flavor.

Chanterelles tend to lose some flavor in the drying process, but they retain their lovely golden color. When fresh are out of the question, dried chanterelles make a very acceptable substitute and go a long way toward satisfying the longing to re-create the delicious dishes you might have sampled in the past.

Wood ear mushrooms are the traditional mushrooms used in Chinese soups and in many vegetable dishes. In China, they are often used exactly like the fresh ones. Once rehydrated, they regain the slightly gelatinous crunch they had when fresh. These mushrooms increase at least three to four times in size once rehydrated.

Shiitakes are the popular Chinese black mushrooms used in many Asian dishes. These, like most other varieties, are dried without the stems. Dried shiitakes are an excellent substitute for fresh ones, and in China are used interchangeably.

Preparation: To rehydrate dried mushrooms, place the desired amount of dried mushrooms (1 ounce dried will yield the equivalent of 6 to 8 ounces of fresh, depending on the variety) in a medium-size heatproof bowl. Pour tepid to warm water over the mushrooms, remembering that they will expand considerably during the rehydrating process. Soak the mushrooms for 15 to 30 minutes, adding more water if necessary.

Drain the mushrooms well. Most rehydrated mushrooms should be rinsed and then drained on paper or kitchen towels. If you would like to use the water left over from soaking the mushrooms for a sauce, soup, or stew, take care to strain it through a very fine mesh strainer or several layers of cheese cloth to remove any grit or debris. This water can be extremely aromatic and will add a delicious flavor to finished dishes.

Ragout of Mushrooms

In Italy, a savory ragout of mushrooms is often spooned over mounds of fresh polenta. Or the polenta can be molded in a loaf pan, sliced, dusted with flour, and fried until crisp in butter or olive oil before being topped with this fragrant "stew." By itself, the ragout goes very well with roast beef, even roast chicken; or, it can top a fluffy baked potato.

Makes 6 servings

3 tablespoons butter
1 clove garlic, minced
1 pound mixed fresh mushrooms, such as
    shiitake (stems discarded), portabella,
    and oyster, stems trimmed, cut into
    bite-size pieces
1 tablespoon all-purpose flour
⅓ cup dry vermouth
⅓ cup well-flavored beef stock
Salt and freshly ground black pepper to taste
1 to 2 teaspoons chopped fresh thyme
2 tablespoons chopped fresh parsley

Melt the butter in a large heavy skillet over medium heat. Add the garlic and cook 30 seconds. Add the mushrooms and cook, stirring, over medium heat until golden, 8 to 10 minutes. Sprinkle the mushrooms with the flour and cook, stirring, for 2 minutes longer. Stir in the vermouth and stock and simmer, stirring, until the sauce is slightly thickened and the mushrooms are coated, 3 or 4 minutes. Season with salt, pepper, and thyme. Serve the ragout very hot, garnished with the parsley.

Variations: *Just before serving, stir 2 to 3 tablespoons of sour cream, regular or light, into the mushrooms. Heat through, but do not boil.*

Or slice 1 small sweet, red, or Spanish onion, and cook it in the butter until translucent, 6 to 8 minutes, before adding the garlic and mushrooms. Spooned over toast, rice, or noodles, this makes a delicious late-night supper with a crisp salad and a glass of red wine. For added zest, stir a few drops of hot pepper sauce into this mushroom ragout.

Mushroom Risotto

A perfectly prepared risotto is such a delightful dish that it often doesn't need any accompaniment. But, in America, we tend to like rice as a side dish rather than a main course. This moistly delicious combination is great with roast or grilled veal or with scaloppine prepared saltimbocca (literally, "jump into the mouth").

Makes 6 to 8 servings

4 tablespoons (½ stick) butter
½ small onion, minced
1 clove garlic, minced
½ pound fresh shiitake mushrooms (stems
    discarded), or other well-flavored
    mushrooms, such as cèpes, chanterelles,
    or morels, stems trimmed, sliced
2 tablespoons chopped fresh parsley
3 tablespoons dry white wine
1½ cups arborio rice, or another very short
    or round-grain rice
4 to 5 cups well-flavored chicken stock,
    simmering
3 tablespoons freshly grated Parmesan cheese,
    plus additional for passing
Salt and freshly ground black pepper to taste

Melt 2 tablespoons of the butter in a small skillet over low heat. Add the onion and garlic and cook, stirring, until translucent, 6 to 8 minutes. Add the mushrooms, raise the heat a little to medium, and cook until golden, 6 to 8 minutes longer. Stir in the parsley and wine and keep the mixture warm over very low heat.

Melt the remaining 2 tablespoons of butter in a large, heavy saucepan over medium heat. Stir in the rice and cook, stirring, until the grains become translucent and are coated with butter, 3 or 4 minutes. Stir in 1 cup of the hot stock and cook, stirring, until most of it is absorbed—but not until the rice is dry. Stir in 1 cup more stock and cook, stirring constantly, until nearly absorbed. Continue stirring in ½ to 1 cup stock at a time, until the rice is cooked, but still very moist, *not* soupy, about 20 minutes.

Stir the mushroom mixture into the rice and heat through, about 3 minutes. Stir in 3 tablespoons of cheese and season well with salt and pepper to taste. Serve at once, very hot. Pass the additional cheese in a separate dish.

Note: *The only drawback to risotto is that a great one is a last-minute dish, and like a soufflé, it should be served the moment it is ready. The total cooking time for the rice is 15 to 20 minutes. To make the final preparation a little easier, cook the mushroom mixture ahead and reheat it for 30 seconds in the microwave on high before stirring it into the rice.*

Shiitake Mushroom Stir-fry

There is a wonderful affinity between roast or grilled beef and mushrooms. This garlicky combination is delicious served next to a succulent grilled steak. For another treat, spoon some on top of a serving of gratinéed potatoes. Or serve it over a mound of freshly cooked polenta, along with a thick slice of herb-roasted pork loin. Use white mushrooms here only if nothing else is available.

Makes 6 servings

2 tablespoons mild vegetable oil,
    preferably peanut
1 teaspoon toasted sesame oil
2 cloves garlic, crushed
1 pound fresh shiitake mushrooms (stems
    discarded), or another full-flavored
    mushroom, or a combination, stems trimmed
1 bunch (6 to 8) green onions (scallions), white
    and light green parts only, cut on the
    diagonal into 1-inch pieces
1 tablespoon Chinese black bean sauce
Pinch sugar
2 tablespoons dry sherry
1 tablespoon sesame seeds, toasted (page 70)

Heat the oils together in a wok over high heat. Add the garlic and fry, stirring, until just golden, but not burned, about 30 seconds. Stir in the mushrooms and cook, stirring, until beginning to brown, 4 to 5 minutes. Add the green onions and cook, stirring, until they are crisply tender, about 2 minutes longer.

In a small bowl, mix together the black bean sauce, sugar, and sherry. Stir this mixture into the mushrooms. Heat through and serve very hot, garnished with the sesame seeds.

Sweet-and-Sour Mushrooms

While these are wonderful with pork, I also think they go very well with a vegetable frittata or with individual Spanish omelets for a special Sunday brunch.

Makes 6 servings

¼ cup mild vegetable oil, preferably peanut
1 small green bell pepper, seeded and sliced
1 pound fresh shiitake mushrooms (stems
    discarded), caps cut into large pieces
1 bunch (6 to 8) green onions (scallions),
    white and light green parts only, cut into
    ¼-inch pieces
3 tablespoons white wine vinegar
2 tablespoons sugar
2 tablespoons well-flavored chicken stock
1 teaspoon cornstarch
Salt and freshly ground black pepper to taste

Heat the oil in a wok over high heat. Add the bell pepper and cook, stirring, for 3 to 4 minutes. Stir in the mushrooms and cook, stirring, until golden, 4 to 5 minutes. Add the green onions and cook, stirring or tossing to keep them from burning, until tender but not dark, about 2 minutes longer.

In a small bowl, mix together the vinegar, sugar, chicken stock, and cornstarch. Stir this mixture into the mushrooms and cook, stirring, until the sauce is thickened and the mushrooms are coated, 1 to 2 minutes. Season with salt and pepper. Serve hot, or at room temperature.

Mushrooms Persillade

This classic mushroom preparation is best when made with wild mushrooms such as cèpes or chanterelles, which have enough flavor to stand up to the garlic. But if wild ones are not available, spring for whatever well-flavored cultivated mushrooms your market has to offer. I cannot think of anything I would rather pair with a thick grilled steak than these delicious morsels.

Makes 6 servings

3 to 4 tablespoons olive oil or butter
1 pound fresh full-flavored mushrooms, such as portabella, shiitake (stems discarded), brown, or any mixture, stems trimmed, halved or, if large, quartered
¼ to ⅓ cup chopped fresh parsley
3 cloves garlic, minced
Salt and freshly ground black pepper to taste

Heat the olive oil in a large heavy skillet over high heat. Add the mushrooms and cook, stirring, until they are golden but not browned, about 5 minutes. Stir the parsley and garlic into the mushrooms. Season well with salt and pepper. Reduce the heat to low and cook, stirring, until the garlic is tender but not burned, 4 to 5 minutes longer. Serve very hot.

Variation: *A few tablespoons of chicken stock, vermouth, or dry white wine can be stirred into the mushrooms for 1 or 2 minutes before serving if a more liquid consistency is desired.*

Mushroom Ratatouille

While this is really at its best when made with the vine-ripened tomatoes of summer, it can be a breath of warm weather in mid-winter if you substitute 6 or 8 ripe plum tomatoes for the garden variety. This is especially good with cold meats, but I think it also goes well with an old-fashioned pot roast.

Makes about 6 servings

3 tablespoons olive oil
1½ pounds large white or brown (cremini) mushrooms, stems trimmed, cut into very thick slices
2 large green bell peppers, seeded and cut into 1-inch or larger pieces
2 small onions, thickly sliced
2 ribs celery, strung and cut into 1-inch pieces
3 large tomatoes, seeded and cut into large dice
1 or 2 cloves garlic, to taste, minced
½ cup dry white wine
1 tablespoon chopped fresh oregano
1 teaspoon crushed fresh rosemary
Salt and freshly ground black pepper to taste

Heat the oil in a large heavy skillet over medium heat. Add the mushrooms and cook, stirring, until just golden, about 5 minutes. Remove the mushrooms with a slotted spoon and set aside.

Add the bell peppers, onions, and celery to the same skillet, and cook, stirring, until just limp, about 10 minutes. Stir in the tomatoes and cook until just softened, about 3 minutes. Stir in the garlic, wine, oregano, and rosemary. Return the mushrooms, and any juice they have given off, to the skillet. Season well with salt and pepper. Cover and cook over low heat for 5 minutes. Remove the vegetables from the heat and allow them to cool. Serve warm, at room temperature, or cold.

Note: *Be careful not to cook the vegetables into a mush. There should be a definable consistency to each individual vegetable. This is also one of those dishes that only gets better with age. It can be made at least 24 hours ahead of time, refrigerated, and then brought to room temperature before serving.*

Variation: *Spread about ⅔ cup of the cooked mixture on a large round of Boboli, sprinkle with 2 tablespoons thinly sliced green onions and ½ to ⅔ cup crumbled feta cheese. Bake at 475°F. for 10 minutes. Serve very hot, cut into wedges, with glasses of hearty red wine. Or cut into small pieces and pass with cocktails.*

Whole Braised Mushrooms

Pair these whole mushrooms with grilled fish, roast pheasant, or roast beef. But I think they are also a delicious addition, along with a mixed green salad, to a cold-cut lunch or Sunday supper.

Makes 6 servings

2 tablespoons butter, plus additional for buttering
1½ pounds large white or brown (cremini)
    mushrooms, stems trimmed
1 bunch (6 to 8) green onions (scallions), white
    and light green parts only, sliced
¼ cup chopped fresh parsley
½ cup heavy cream
¼ cup dry white wine, or dry vermouth
1 teaspoon ground cumin
Salt and seasoned pepper, such as Mrs. Dash,
    to taste

Preheat the oven to 350°F. Generously butter a large shallow covered baking or gratin dish.

Layer the mushrooms, stem side down, in the dish. Spread the green onions and then the parsley over the mushrooms. In a small bowl, beat together the cream and wine. Pour this mixture over the mushrooms. Season well with cumin, salt, and seasoned pepper.

Cover and bake for 15 to 20 minutes. Uncover, baste with the liquid, and bake until the mushrooms are very tender but not totally collapsed, about 10 minutes longer. Serve very hot, with a little of the cooking liquid spooned over them.

Greek-style Marinated Mushrooms

As a snack with wine in the company of friends, these are excellent. They will also complement any antipasto spread. Or make them a part of your next cold buffet with cold roast meats and a variety of cheeses. If button mushrooms are not available, choose uniform-size mushrooms and cut them into quarters.

Makes 6 servings

2 tablespoons olive oil
1½ pounds white or brown button mushrooms,
    stems trimmed
⅓ cup olive oil
⅓ cup fresh lemon juice
½ cup dry white wine
1 cup water
1 bouquet garni made of two 2-inch pieces celery,
    4 parsley sprigs, and 1 bay leaf, tied with
    kitchen string
2 cloves garlic, sliced
Salt and freshly ground black pepper to taste
1 tablespoon tomato paste, regular or Italian style
3 tablespoons chopped fresh parsley

Heat the olive oil in a large heavy saucepan over medium heat. Add the mushrooms and cook, stirring, until browned, about 5 minutes. Add all the remaining ingredients, except for the parsley. Simmer over low heat for 15 minutes. Remove the bouquet garni and cool the mushrooms. Chill, covered, for several hours. To serve, bring to room temperature, and garnish with the parsley.

Note: *I like to increase the heat after 10 or 12 minutes and boil the sauce hard for the remaining 3 to 5 minutes to thicken it. This isn't necessary, but it gives the chilled mushroom dish a good consistency to serve with cold meats.*

Variation: *Add 2 celery ribs, cut into ¼-inch slices, to the mushrooms before adding the liquids, cook 1 minute, then continue with the recipe. This makes a sort of mushroom salad. Sometimes I will replace the celery with ½ large fennel bulb, cut into large dice. The anise flavor of fennel goes very well with the mushrooms.*

Curried Mushrooms

Spoon these savory mushrooms over freshly steamed rice and serve with baked or grilled chicken or fish. Try them sometime with tandoori-style chicken.

Makes 6 to 8 servings

3 tablespoons butter
1 small onion, finely chopped
1 bunch (6 to 8) green onions (scallions), white
    and light green parts only, thinly sliced
1 or 2 cloves garlic, minced
1 pound fresh full-flavored assorted mushrooms,
    stems trimmed, thickly sliced or quartered
¼ cup golden (my preference) or dark raisins,
    plumped in boiling water to cover and
    drained
1 tablespoon hot curry powder, or more to taste
¼ cup dry white wine, beer, or well-flavored
    chicken stock
½ cup heavy cream
Salt and freshly ground black pepper to taste
3 tablespoons chopped fresh parsley
3 tablespoons chopped peanuts (optional)

Melt the butter in a large heavy skillet over medium heat. Add the onion and green onion and cook, stirring, until just translucent, 2 or 3 minutes. Add the garlic and cook, stirring, 1 minute. Add the mushrooms and cook, stirring or tossing from time to time, until golden, 5 or 6 minutes. Stir in the raisins and curry powder. Cook, stirring, about 1 minute, so that the curry powder will release its flavor. Stir in the wine and cream. Season with salt and pepper.

Cook the mixture over medium heat until the liquid thickens into a creamy sauce, 5 or 6 minutes. Stir in the parsley. Serve very hot, garnished with the peanuts if you like.

Variation: *Replace the sliced onions and green onions with 1 cup small boiling onions, boiled in water to cover for 1 minute, drained, and peeled; or 1 cup thawed frozen baby onions.*

Mushroom and Tomato Sauté

Serve these with roast poultry, grilled fish, or veal chops.

Makes about 6 servings

3 tablespoons olive oil
2 cloves garlic, minced
1 pound assorted fresh mushrooms, including
    some shiitake (stems discarded), cloud ear,
    hen-of-the-woods, or portabella, stems
    trimmed, halved or quartered if large
2 large ripe tomatoes, peeled, seeded, and
    coarsely chopped; or one 14½-ounce can
    diced tomatoes, well drained
3 tablespoons chopped fresh parsley
1 teaspoon chopped fresh thyme
Salt and freshly ground black pepper to taste

Heat the oil in a large heavy skillet over low heat. Add the garlic and cook for 1 minute. Stir in the mushrooms and cook, stirring, until beginning to turn golden brown, about 5 minutes. Add the tomatoes and cook, tossing or stirring from time to time just until a thick sauce begins to form, about 5 more minutes. Stir in the parsley and thyme and season very well with salt and pepper. Serve very hot.

Pesto-stuffed Mushrooms

While these make delicious appetizers—count three apiece if served that way—they are dynamite alongside a grilled chicken or steak or a thick, soy-marinated piece of grilled tuna or halibut.

Makes 6 servings

12 large white or brown (cremini) mushrooms,
    stems trimmed and chopped, caps left whole
Olive oil
⅓ cup pesto, prepared or homemade (page 7)
Freshly grated Parmesan cheese

Preheat the oven to 475°F.

Rub the tops of the mushroom caps with the olive oil. In a medium-size bowl, stir together ½ cup of the chopped mushroom stems and the pesto. Spoon this mixture into the mushroom caps, mounding it a bit in the center. Arrange the filled caps in a single layer in a large shallow baking pan. Sprinkle each with a little cheese.

Bake the mushrooms until hot and bubbling, 6 to 8 minutes. Remove the pan from the oven and cool for several minutes before removing the mushrooms. Serve hot, but not scalding.

Note: *These are also good served at room temperature as part of a cold antipasto buffet.*

Okra

I think okra has gotten a bum rap. Of course, I had a Louisiana grandmother, and okra was as much a part of our diet as were collard greens and fried green tomatoes. Her garden yielded small, firm pods, cut just before they were washed and cooked. It was an integral part of summer. But, childhood experiences aside, I think okra can be a delicious addition to any meal. It is, however, important to understand a little about this ancient vegetable.

Okra originally grew wild in Africa. In fact, both the word *okra* and the word *gumbo*, one of the most familiar American okra dishes, are derived from an African language. The vegetable was carried north to Egypt and other countries bordering on the Mediterranean, east to India, and on to Europe, where it was once very fashionable. While some sources suggest it may have been brought to America directly from Africa, it is more likely that it was first imported by Europeans, probably the French.

However okra made its way here, African cooks in the South took the familiar vegetable and combined it with the Creole influence of the Louisiana Territory to create some wonderfully satisfying dishes.

Funny as it may seem, it is the very characteristic that puts most people off that makes okra a wonderful addition to soups and stews. When cut and cooked, it gives off a gelatinous sap that will thicken any liquid it is added to. When okra is in season, gumbos are traditionally thickened with small whole pods or cuts of larger ones. When okra is not available, filé powder (the finely ground dried leaves of sassafras trees) is added as a thickener instead.

It is the slight sliminess of this sap that is so off-putting. There may be as many ways to counteract this as there are cooks. Most will tell you not to pierce the pod before cooking it. Obviously, this will help contain the sap, but the pods will still have some inside, though the smaller and younger the pod, the less sappy it will be. Some chefs will tell you to cook it quickly. Others will tell you to cook it for a long time.

No matter what I have tried, with the possible exception of cutting very small pods into thick slices, dredging them in cornmeal, and deep-frying them in hot oil, there is still some slippery juice. I think it is part of the beast, though, and believe we should take advantage of its tendency to thicken liquid and stop trying to eliminate it.

Older, large okra can become very fibrous, and if this is what you have been exposed to, it can be quite unpleasant. Young, fresh okra is crisp and tender, worth looking for, and once you have sampled it, I think you will want to enjoy it often. The flavor is fresh and delicate, unlike anything else. Okra is wonderful at absorbing or enhancing other flavors, too, and it merges very well with tomatoes and peppers.

Okra is extremely versatile. It can be steamed, boiled, stewed, fried, incorporated in casseroles and soups, pickled, and used in salads or on crudité platters.

Okra is rich in protein and carbohydrates and provides a reasonable amount of vitamin C.

Selection: In my estimation, it is the little pods that are the best. Therefore, I suggest looking for small, bright green, unblemished pods that are firm and crisp to the touch. The stem end should still be green, and the cap should not show any signs of black. Avoid any pods that are spotty or show signs of mold. If you are choosing larger okra for stewing or for gumbos, a little darkening of the tips is okay; the whole okra will darken slightly during long cooking.

There are several varieties of okra on the market. One is totally smooth, one has small ridges running the length of the pod, one has a slight silvery gray fuzz, and one is even deep red, almost purple. All are interchangeable—but the red variety turns dark green when cooked.

Frozen okra, widely available, is fine for use in stews and soups. Canned okra is also available, sometimes combined with other vegetables such as tomatoes, but I think that canning only emphasizes the gelatinous quality. Some commercial okra pickles are quite good, especially those that are hot and spicy.

Okra can be found in the markets all year long, but small tender pods are at their best from late June through August.

Count on 1/4 pound of fresh okra per person.

Storage and Preparation: Okra is much more perishable than it looks. It is at its very best if prepared the day it is picked or at least the day it is bought. If it must be stored, place the pods, unwashed, in a small paper bag or wrap them in paper towels and seal in a perforated plastic vegetable bag for only a day or two.

Wash the okra just before using. Dry on kitchen towels. If the pods are to be used whole, snip off the stem, leaving about 1/8 inch. Do not cut into the pods. For smaller pieces, cut off the stem and cut the larger pods across into thick slices or chunks.

Microwaved Okra

Arrange 1 pound of trimmed okra in a single layer in a microwaveable dish. Add 2 tablespoons water. Cover with plastic microwave wrap and vent. Microwave 4 to 6 minutes, depending on the size of the pods. Remove from the oven and let stand 3 minutes before uncovering.

Boiled Okra

My grandmother loved plain boiled or steamed okra, marinated with a spicy vinaigrette dressing. I like a more elegant dish, with a little Hollandaise sauce over lightly boiled, slightly crisp okra pods. All of the pods should be of nearly equal size to ensure that they are cooked at the same time.

Simmer trimmed okra in salted water to cover for 6 to 10 minutes, depending on the age and size of the pods. They should still be slightly crisp. Drain well and serve plain with a little butter, salt, and pepper; drizzle with a little extra-virgin olive oil; or season with hot pepper sauce.

Steamed Okra

I think steaming results in the freshest-looking, greenest cooked okra, making it perfect for chilling and serving on a crudité platter with a well-flavored dip. Pick pods of equal size to ensure even cooking.

Arrange trimmed okra pods in a steamer basket or colander and steam, covered, over simmering water until crisp tender, 4 to 6 minutes, depending on the age and size of the pods and on the subsequent use of the okra.

Popcorn Okra

These crisp little nuggets are delicious with cocktails, though I think they are also wonderful as a substitute for French fries with anything from hamburgers to crab cakes.

Makes 6 to 8 servings

1 large whole egg, beaten in a shallow bowl
Salt and freshly ground black pepper to taste
1 cup finely ground white or yellow cornmeal
1½ pounds okra, trimmed and cut into
    ½-inch pieces
Mild vegetable oil, preferably peanut, for
    deep-frying
Hot pepper sauce to taste

Season the egg with salt and pepper. Place the cornmeal in a plastic bag. Toss the okra in the egg, then dredge in the cornmeal, shaking off any extra. Arrange the coated okra on a baking sheet to dry for 10 to 15 minutes.

Heat the oil in a deep-fat fryer to 375°F. Fry the coated okra in batches until golden brown, 2 to 3 minutes per batch. Remove from the oil with a slotted spoon and drain on paper towels.

Sprinkle with a little salt and serve very hot. Pass hot pepper sauce on the side.

Variation: *Whole okra can be cooked the same way. Choose the smallest okra available; trim the stem to about ⅛ inch before tossing in the egg and then the cornmeal. Let the coated okra dry for about 10 minutes and then fry for 3 to 5 minutes until crisp and golden.*

Sweet-and-Sour Okra

My Louisiana grandmother always ate her boiled okra hot, with a tangy vinaigrette dressing drizzled over it. This dish gives much the same flavor. She liked to have hers with smothered pork chops (page 88), and that would be a good partner for this, but I also think this preparation goes extremely well with fish, baked, grilled, or breaded and pan fried.

Makes about 6 servings

3 tablespoons mild vegetable oil,
    preferably peanut
1½ pounds smallest okra, stems trimmed
    to about ⅛ inch
½ cup water
3 tablespoons cider vinegar
2 tablespoons sugar

2 tablespoons chopped fresh tarragon
Salt and freshly ground black pepper to taste

Heat the oil in a large heavy skillet or wok over medium heat. Add the okra and cook, stirring, until just tender, 2 to 3 minutes. Add the water and vinegar and simmer, covered, until the okra is quite tender but not soft, 10 to 12 minutes. Stir in the sugar and tarragon and boil the mixture hard until it reduces to about ¼ cup, 1 to 2 minutes. Season well with salt and pepper.

Scalloped Okra

Southerners like to scallop almost anything, and okra is delicious prepared this way. Use commercial cracker crumbs if you like or crush your own saltines. For a richer dish, crush butter crackers such as Ritz instead. Serve this with any kind of roasted poultry.

Makes 6 servings

1 tablespoon butter, plus additional for buttering
1½ pounds small okra, stems trimmed to about
    ⅛ inch, boiled in salted water to cover until
    just tender, about 5 minutes, and drained
1 pint boiling onions, boiled in water to cover for
    1 minute, drained, peeled, simmered in salted
    water until tender, 8 to 10 minutes, and
    drained; or one-half 16-ounce package of
    frozen baby onions, thawed
1 tablespoon all-purpose flour
Salt and freshly ground black pepper to taste
1 cup milk, heated until bubbles appear around
    the edge
¼ cup freshly grated Parmesan cheese
⅓ cup cracker crumbs (commercial, or crushed
    saltines)

Preheat the oven to 350°F. Generously butter a small shallow baking dish.

Combine the okra and onions and spread them in the prepared dish.

Melt 1 tablespoon of butter in a small saucepan over medium heat. Stir in the flour and cook, stirring, until light golden brown, being careful not to burn it, about 3 minutes. Season with salt and pepper. Stir in the milk and whisk until smooth. Cook, stirring, until beginning to thicken, about 2 minutes. Pour this over the okra and onions.

In a small bowl, combine the cheese and cracker crumbs. Spread them over the vegetables. Bake until the sauce is bubbling hot and the crumbs are golden brown, about 20 minutes. Serve very hot.

Okra, Tomatoes, and Green Peppers

I love this variation of a classic okra dish. It can be livened up by adding hot pepper sauce to taste. Serve this with grilled or baked fish, especially blue fish, which has flavor enough to stand up to the vegetables.

Makes 6 servings

3 tablespoons olive oil
2 small cloves garlic, minced
1 small green bell pepper, seeded and cut
    into large dice
1 pound smallest whole okra, stems trimmed
    to about ⅛ inch
¼ cup dry white wine
2 ripe tomatoes, cut into ¼-inch dice
Salt and freshly ground black pepper to taste
3 tablespoons chopped fresh parsley, plus
    additional for garnishing
Hot pepper sauce to taste

Heat the olive oil in a large heavy saucepan over medium heat. Add the garlic and cook, stirring, for 30 seconds. Add the bell pepper and cook it, stirring, until translucent, about 10 minutes. Stir in the okra and wine. Cover and simmer over low heat for about 10 minutes. Stir in the tomatoes and cook over high heat, stirring from time to time, until much of the liquid is reduced, 4 to 5 minutes. Season well with salt and pepper. Stir in the 3 tablespoons of parsley and heat through. Serve the okra very hot, garnished with the additional parsley. Pass the hot pepper sauce separately.

Stewed Okra

I like to serve this old-fashioned, but delicious, combination over rice with baked whole shad. It goes very well with grilled shrimp, too—the larger the better.

Makes 6 servings

3 slices bacon, cut into $1/4$-inch pieces, until just
    crisp, and drained on paper towels (page 42),
    2 tablespoons fat left in the skillet
1 small onion, chopped
1 large clove garlic, minced
$1/2$ medium-size green or red bell pepper,
    seeded and chopped
1 pound smallest okra, stems trimmed to $1/8$ inch
$1/2$ cup well-flavored chicken stock
1 teaspoon dried Italian herbs, such as oregano,
    marjoram, rosemary, and thyme, or a
    prepared mix
Salt and freshly ground black pepper to taste
Freshly steamed rice (optional)
1 tablespoon chopped fresh parsley

Heat the bacon fat left in the skillet over low heat. Add the onion, garlic, and bell pepper and cook, stirring, until the vegetables are wilted, about 3 minutes. Stir in the okra and cook, stirring, for about 2 minutes. Add the chicken stock. Season well with the herbs and salt and pepper. Cover and simmer over very low heat until the okra is very tender but not collapsed, 15 to 20 minutes. Remove the cover, raise the heat to high, and cook until the cooking liquid reduces slightly, about 2 more minutes. Stir in the bacon. Serve very hot, spooned over the rice if you like, and garnished with the parsley.

Vegetable Gumbo

This would be delicious with Louisiana grillades—slices of round steak browned and simmered in tomato gravy until tender. Chicken-fried steak—cubed steak breaded and fried like chicken, often served with cream gravy—
would also be a great partner. Actually, this dish also goes very well with breaded veal cutlets or lamb chops and would be excellent with baked fish. Serve with freshly steamed rice.

Serves 6 to 8 servings

3 tablespoons mild vegetable oil, preferably
    peanut
1 clove garlic, minced
1 large onion, chopped
3 ribs celery, strung and chopped
1 large green bell pepper, seeded and chopped
2 tablespoons all-purpose flour
3 medium-size ripe tomatoes, peeled, seeded,
    and chopped
1 pint (10 ounces) boiling onions, boiled in water
    to cover for 1 minute, drained, and peeled;
    or one-half 16-ounce package frozen baby
    onions, thawed
2 cups water, boiling
Salt and freshly ground black pepper to taste
$1/2$ teaspoon crushed red pepper
2 teaspoons good Hungarian paprika
1 teaspoon dried Italian herbs, such as oregano,
    marjoram, rosemary, and thyme, or a
    prepared mix
$1/4$ pound sugar snap peas
$3/4$ pound smallest okra, stems trimmed,
    halved across
Hot pepper sauce to taste

Heat the oil in a medium-size heavy kettle over medium heat. Add the garlic, chopped onion, celery, and bell pepper and cook, stirring, until the onion is just translucent, 5 to 6 minutes. Stir in the flour and continue to cook, stirring, until browned but not burned, about 5 minutes. Stir in the tomatoes and boiling onions. Pour in the boiling water and season with red pepper, paprika, and herbs. Reduce the heat to low and simmer, stirring once or twice, for 30 minutes.

Stir in the sugar snap peas and the okra. Simmer until tender and thickened, about 15 minutes longer. Verify the seasoning and add pepper sauce to taste. Serve hot.

Baked Okra

This is a make-ahead dish. It can be put together in the morning and then baked just before serving. It's a tasty combination to serve with roasted or baked chicken.

Makes 6 servings

Butter
1½ **pounds large okra, trimmed, and cut into thick slices**
2 **large ripe tomatoes, peeled, seeded, and coarsely chopped**
2 **small onions, very thinly sliced**
½ **jalapeño pepper, seeded and minced**
4 **ounces slab bacon, cut into ¼-inch dice, fried until cooked, but not quite crisp, and drained on paper towels (page 42)**
Salt and freshly ground black pepper to taste
1 **tablespoon chopped fresh sage, or 1 teaspoon dried**
⅓ **cup dry white wine**
½ **cup grated Monterey Jack cheese**

Preheat the oven to 350°F. Generously butter a medium-size deep ovenproof casserole.

Layer half of the okra in the prepared casserole. Top with half the tomatoes and then half the onions. Sprinkle with half the jalapeño. Top with half the bacon. Season the vegetables well with salt, pepper, and half the sage. Repeat the layers. Pour the wine over all.

Cover the casserole with aluminum foil. Bake until the vegetables are tender, 35 to 45 minutes. Remove the foil and spread the cheese over the vegetables. Bake, uncovered, until the cheese is melted and bubbling, about 10 minutes longer.

Onions

Is there anything that smells better than onions cooking in a little butter or oil? I find it never fails to gather a crowd, even if they have to surface from a deep sleep to ask what is on the menu. Apparently this has been true time out of mind, because some form of onion has been cultivated ever since humans came out of the cave and scratched crops into the soil.

Onions have been a flavoring element in almost every part of the world. They are hardy, easily transported, and store well. They can be eaten raw or cooked, cold, warm, or hot, and they make almost any savory food palatable. Monotonous fare, even on the run, will be livened up by adding some variety of onion. In fact, onions held such an important place in parts of the ancient world that the Egyptians even felt them worthy to carry into the next world, and onions are frequently represented in the hieroglyphics on their tombs.

All onions are members of the allium family, along with their cousins garlic and leeks. Onions range from large round bulbs to pencil-thin stalks, from pungent to nearly sugar sweet, from sturdy preservers to more delicate varieties.

Bulb onions—white, yellow, and red—are the most readily available members of this family. These are the "storage" onions that we buy in sacks or in bulk. They tend to be fairly strong-flavored, because of the high concentration of sulfur compounds in their cells. (It is the sulfur that gives onions their "bite.") Large yellow onions, sometimes called Bermuda or Spanish onions, are the mildest of these. Smaller yellow onions are much sharper tasting, although long cooking will make them somewhat sweeter. Red onions are not quite as mild as large yellow ones, but they are still sweet and very attractive to eat raw. They do lose some of their deep maroon coloring when they are cooked, sometimes turning yellow. All of these onions can be used for cooking.

228

For eating raw, I suggest taking advantage of the super sweets, which are becoming more widely available. The best known is the Vidalia, grown in a small corner of Georgia. But there are also Walla Walla, Texas Super Sweets, and Maui, to name a few. All of them are the same basic onion; they are just grown in different localities, in similar low-sulfur soil. These slightly squashed-looking, thin-skinned bulbs contain much more water than ordinary storage onions, and have less of the offending sulfur compounds. They are actually so sweet you can eat them out of hand like an apple and are dynamite in salads and sandwiches. Some cooks feel these super sweets lose much of their flavor when cooked, but I love the taste in some dishes. They tend to be very fragile, though, and spoil very quickly if mishandled or stored too long.

Boiling, or pearl, onions are small bulb onions of various colors that are delicious added to soups, stews, or casseroles or when creamed or pickled. These are almost always used whole. They are available with red, white, or yellow skins and can be very sweet.

Green onions (scallions) are simply bulb onion shoots, young versions of the familiar onion. They are milder than in their larger stages (although some are very sharp if eaten raw). Green onions are delicious in salads, and I love to use them in cooked dishes when only a hint of onion flavor is wanted. I often use them in sauces instead of bulb onions and, sometimes, in place of shallots when I cannot find good ones in the market. Green onions are also delicious added to stir-fries, cooked whole, or combined with other onions in savory dishes.

The shallot, an onion relative, forms a head somewhat like garlic. The individual cloves range in color from grayish white to tan to red skinned. They can be very sweet or slightly sharp and offer a delicate onion flavor. They can be difficult to peel, but the effort is well worthwhile.

The gray variety of shallot has a finer taste—especially when minced raw and mixed with vinegar as a mignonette sauce for raw oysters—but it is hard to find. If shallots are not in the market, are in bad condition, or not at hand when you need them, substitute green onions or a little minced sweet onion.

Selection: All onions should be crisp and fresh smelling. Yellow, white, and red onions should have dry, papery skins, with very dry stem ends. Avoid any that are soft, damp, show bruises, or have begun to sprout. Do not buy onions that have a musty smell (somewhat like rotting leaves). They will contaminate any other onions they are stored near.

Sweet onions, such as Vidalia, Walla Walla, and Texas Super Sweets, are much more fragile than their stronger-tasting brethren. Their season is usually very short, only a few weeks from late May to midsummer at most, and they are shipped as soon as they are pulled. I have noticed in the last year or two, as these onions have become trendy, that markets are selling them into the fall. While some are as crisp and sweet as they are in season, these onions do not store well—even though some growers are experimenting with methods to "harden" them. They contain more water and are much juicier than strong onions and have a tendency to go soft very quickly. I have not had any success trying to cut out the soft areas; the disagreeable taste of spoiled onion seems to penetrate everything. My advice is to enjoy Vidalias, and the other super sweets, to their fullest when they first come into the market, and then return to the longer-lasting varieties until the next year.

Boiling onions are usually sold prepackaged in bags or pint containers. Look for the plumpest, with papery thin skins—regardless of the color. As soon as you get them home, open the container and pick over the onions to remove any that might have begun to sprout or spoil.

Green onions (scallions) are available all year long. They are simply younger versions of the more familiar dry-skinned bulb onions. Scallions are shoots that have not yet developed any bulb and are the same thickness from root to tops. Green onions have a slightly swollen white bulb beneath the dark green tops. Recently, for a week or two just before the mature Vidalias come into the market, I have found small bunches of Vidalia green onions. The bulb is about the size of a shooter marble and the flavor is ultra-sweet. If you find them, indulge. They are wonderful raw. All green onions should be as crisp as possible. They should not have limp or yellowing tops, and the white parts should not be slimy. This is not to say they should not be wet. Many markets these days keep their produce crisp by misting them on a regular schedule. If the green onions are wet from misting, but not slimy, be sure to dry them before placing in a perforated plastic bag to keep them from spoiling too quickly.

Shallots are sold loose or sometimes in small bags. Select plump, heavy cloves with no sign of a green sprout. The skins should be dry, but the cloves should not be. Avoid any that are spongy or light in weight.

Storage and Preparation: All onions except green onions should be stored in a cool, dry, well-ventilated place, preferably in the dark, where they should last at least a month or two, and sometimes up to three. Bulb onions are best when kept in ventilated baskets and away from potatoes. Although storage bins frequently place them side by side, potatoes give off a gas that will cause onions to spoil more quickly than usual.

Vidalia growers, who are well aware of how fragile their onions are, suggest that these onions, and the other super sweets, be stored so that they do not touch or bruise each other. Clean nylon stockings or pantyhose are useful for this. Drop an onion into the toe, tie a knot, and drop in another. Continue until full. The stockings can be hung up in a very cool dark place. Each onion is cut off individually just below the knot, leaving the others untouched. Plan on using them all within three to four weeks.

Boiling onions should be used as quickly as possible because they have a tendency to sprout. It is probably wise to buy them just before using, rather than trying to store them.

Shallots are best kept in a small basket in a cool place. Go over them once a week or so to remove any that may have begun to soften or sprout. They will usually stay fresh for three to four weeks.

Green onions need to be kept refrigerated. Cut off any wilted tops, dry them if they are wet from misting, and store unwrapped in the vegetable drawer of the refrigerator. If you need to keep them for more than a few days, take the bands off the bunches and seal the loose onions in a perforated plastic vegetable bag. Be sure to sort through them every day or two to remove any that may have begun to spoil.

Who has not cried when chopping onions? Once an onion is cut, it gives off a sulfur compound (the same sulfur compound that gives onions their unique strong flavor) that can irritate eyes and cause them to water. To alleviate this unpleasant experience some cooks suggest cutting the onions under running water, but I have not had much success doing this, and I think it can increase the possibility of cutting yourself if the knife slips in a wet hand. Still others have sworn by holding a slice of bread in your mouth while doing the cutting. The bread does absorb some of the sulfur, but I have not been able to get past feeling foolish looking. I think the only convenient way to lessen this effect is to refrigerate the onions you intend to use for several hours before peeling, slicing, or chopping.

Bulb onions need to be peeled before using. If the recipe calls for halving or chopping the onion, halve it lengthwise before peeling. The skin will come off more easily.

To slice whole peeled bulb onions, cut off the stem end. Cut a small round off one side, then set the onion on the flat point and, holding the onion with your fingers, nails pointing under slightly toward your palms, slice the onion to the thickness you want.

To chop peeled bulb onions, cut the onion in half from stem end to root end. Lay the onion down on the cut side with the root end to the left (if you are right-handed). Using a large sharp chef's knife, cut a small wedge from the stem end to remove the tough little point. Then make a series of lengthwise cuts perpendicular to the cutting board. Holding the onion together, make several horizontal cuts from right to left, parallel to the cutting board, almost back to the root end. Then cut across the onion. It should fall into dice. The size of the dice will depend on the thickness of each cut.

I prefer to chop onions by hand. Using the food processor breaks down the cells in such a way that much sulfur is released and the onions become extremely strong and somewhat bitter and watery. For very finely chopped onions, I suggest using either a Japanese or Chinese cleaver to mince onions that have been diced as above, or to invest in an Italian *mezzaluna* (an arc-shaped blade with a vertical handle on each end—the name means "half moon" in Italian), which allows you to use a rocking motion that easily reduces diced onions to a very fine mince.

To peel boiling onions easily, drop them into boiling water to cover for 1 minute, drain, and then slip off the skins. These onions are generally cooked and eaten whole.

Cut the root ends off green onions. Wash them well, peeling off any layers that may be wilted or soft. Slice the onions across thick or thin. Or cut them into 2-inch lengths and then slice lengthwise into thin matchstick strips. They can also be cut into ¼- to 1-inch lengths on the diagonal. Try roll-cutting the green onions the way the Chinese do: Make one cut on the diagonal—slanting across the onion—then roll the onion ¼ turn and cut again on the diagonal. The pieces will have an attractive, irregular shape. Continue to roll and cut, making the pieces as long as you like.

Shallots can be minced using the same system as for chopping whole bulb onions, except that the knife should be smaller and the cuts finer, or sliced before cooking. They can also be easily minced in a small food or herb processor. Shallots, like garlic, burn easily, which makes them bitter. They need long slow cooking—or constant stirring, if cooked over higher heat— to keep them from turning too dark.

Tip: *When there are no super sweet onions in the market, regular bulb onions, especially red ones, can be made less strong for eating raw by soaking them in ice water. Peel and slice the onions or cut them into thin wedges. Place the slices in a deep bowl. Pour in ice water to cover and, if you like, add several ice cubes. Soak for 30 minutes, drain, and then follow the desired recipe. The pieces of onion will be extra crisp and less sharp tasting.*

Fried Onions and Apples

Onions and apples are meant to go with pork. Next time you have a roast pork loin, serve thick juicy slices accompanied by these delicious onions. The sweet-savory combination is a perfect match.

Makes 6 to 8 servings

3 tablespoons butter
3 large yellow or red onions, halved root to stem and cut into thin wedges
2 Golden Delicious apples, peeled, cored, and cut into wedges
Salt and freshly ground black pepper to taste
¼ teaspoon ground allspice
⅓ cup apple cider
⅓ cup chopped fresh parsley

Melt the butter in a large heavy skillet over medium heat. Add the cut up onions and cook, stirring from time to time, until the onions begin to turn translucent, about 10 minutes. Add the apples and cook, covered, stirring occasionally, until the onions are tender and the apples are golden brown, but not falling apart, about 10 minutes longer. Season well with salt, pepper, and the allspice. Pour in the cider and cook over medium heat until the liquid is almost evaporated, leaving only a few spoonfuls of thick sauce, 2 to 3 minutes. Serve the onions and apples hot, garnished with the parsley.

Butter-braised Green Onions

As much as I love fresh asparagus, they are only in their full prolific glory for a short time in the spring. Green onions on the other hand are almost always in the market. Prepared this way, they make a wonderfully delicious alternative to asparagus, and they are generally less expensive. Serve with any grilled whole fish, such as red snapper or striped bass.

Makes 6 servings

3 tablespoons butter
6 bunches (36 to 48) green onions (scallions), outer layer peeled off, tops cut to leave the onions about 6 inches long
¼ cup well-flavored chicken stock, or water
Salt and freshly ground black pepper to taste
Chopped fresh cilantro

Melt the butter in a large heavy covered skillet over medium heat. Add the green onions and toss to coat with the butter. Add the stock. Cover and simmer over low heat until very tender when pierced with a fork, 15 to 20 minutes. Season well with salt and pepper. Serve hot or at room temperature, spooning any sauce over them, garnished with the cilantro.

Creamed Baby Onions

I grew up thinking you could serve these wonderful little onions only at Thanksgiving and Christmas, and then only if you were having the traditional turkey with all the trimmings. Occasionally we had roast beef or goose for Christmas, so that limited us to once a year for creamed onions. Thankfully, once I was out on my own, I learned you can have these any time you want, serving them with everything from roast poultry to a succulent London broil.

Makes 6 servings

2 tablespoons butter
2 tablespoons all-purpose flour
2 pints (1¼ pounds) boiling onions, boiled in water to cover for 1 minute, drained, peeled, simmered in chicken stock to cover until tender, about 15 minutes, and drained, ½ cup stock reserved; or one 16-ounce bag frozen baby onions, thawed, simmered in chicken stock to cover for 5 minutes, and drained, ½ cup stock reserved
¾ cup half-and-half, heavy cream, or milk, hot
Salt and freshly ground black pepper to taste

1 teaspoon ground cumin (optional)
Chopped fresh parsley

Melt the butter in a medium-size saucepan over medium heat. Stir in the flour and cook, stirring, for about 3 minutes. Do not brown. Stir in ½ cup of the reserved stock. Stir in the half-and-half (use cream to produce a very unctuous finished dish).

Simmer the mixture over low heat, stirring to prevent it from sticking, until it is thick and creamy, 5 minutes or longer. Stir in salt, pepper, and if using, cumin. Stir in the onions and heat through. Serve very hot, garnished with the parsley.

Variation: *Replace the cumin with 1 tablespoon hot curry powder.*

Caramelized Baby Onions

Like glazed carrots and turnips (see pages 102 and 356) these little onions are succulent and delicious. Browning the butter a little at the beginning gives the glaze a rich golden caramel color and adds a slightly nutty flavor to the finished onions. I like to serve these with game, such as wild duck or goose, and even with venison steaks.

Makes 6 servings

3 tablespoons butter
2 pints (1¼ pounds) boiling onions, boiled in
    water to cover for 1 minute, drained, and
    peeled; or one 16-ounce package frozen baby
    onions, thawed
3 tablespoons sugar
1 cup well-flavored chicken stock
Salt and freshly ground black pepper to taste
1 tablespoon chopped fresh thyme

Melt the butter in a medium-size deep skillet over medium-high heat. Add the onions and cook, stirring over medium heat, until they just begin to turn golden, and the butter is almost nut brown. This step could take up to 10 minutes. It is very important to watch the butter carefully so it will not burn. Sprinkle the onions with sugar and pour in the stock. Cook over high heat until the onions are tender and the stock is evaporated, 6 to 7 minutes. Continue to cook, tossing or stirring, until the onions are coated with the golden butter glaze. Season very well with salt and pepper. Serve very hot, garnished with the thyme.

Shirred Onions

The most special mornings of my childhood were those when my mother or my grandmother's cook gave us shirred eggs. I have often had them at home for a quiet solitary dinner when comfort food was a must. These onions, cooked in much the same manner even though they don't contain any eggs, are almost as satisfying. A menu including baked chicken breasts, fresh spinach or other hot greens, and these onions will be special enough for unexpected company or for any festive family celebration.

Makes 6 servings

3 tablespoons butter
3 pounds onions, sliced
6 slices bacon, fried until crisp, drained on paper
    towels, and crumbled (page 42)
¾ cup heavy cream
Salt and freshly ground black pepper to taste
¾ cup grated Gruyère, Comté, or Emmenthal
    cheese
3 tablespoons snipped fresh chives

Melt the butter in a large heavy skillet over low heat. Add the onions and cook, stirring occasionally, until soft and pale golden brown, up to 30 minutes.

Preheat the oven to 450°F.

Divide the onions between 6 small shirred egg dishes, or 3-inch ramekins. Sprinkle each serving with some of the bacon. Top each with 2 tablespoons of the cream. Season well with salt and pepper. Spread 2 tablespoons of the cheese over each serving.

Bake until the cheese is melted and golden brown, 5 to 6 minutes. Serve very hot, garnished with the snipped chives.

Variation: *Replace the bacon with 6 anchovy fillets, rinsed, dried, and chopped if you like the flavor.*

Soubise

Soubise can be an onion-based sauce, thickened with just a little cooked rice. Or it can be this delicious, creamy onion and rice dish that is just perfect with roast lamb, especially herb-crusted racks of tiny meltingly tender chops. Some chefs like to puree the mixture before serving it. Some add grated Gruyère cheese. And others spoon the mixture into a gratin dish, top it with a little Parmesan or other salty cheese, and bake it in a hot oven before serving. But I like it this way best.

Makes 6 to 8 servings

3 tablespoons butter
6 large onions (about 3½ pounds), halved and thinly sliced
⅔ cup raw rice, arborio, basmati, or regular converted rice, boiled in salted water to cover for 5 minutes and drained
About ½ cup well-flavored chicken stock
Salt and freshly ground black pepper to taste
2 to 3 tablespoons heavy cream (optional)
⅓ cup chopped fresh parsley

Preheat the oven to 300°F.

Melt the butter in a medium-size heavy covered ovenproof casserole over medium heat. (I like to use Le Creuset or another enameled cast-iron product.) Add the onions and cook, stirring to coat with the butter, for 2 to 3 minutes. Stir in the rice and cook, stirring, until the grains become translucent and are also coated with the butter, 3 to 4 minutes. Stir in the ½ cup stock. Season well with salt and pepper.

Cover and bake, stirring from time to time, until the rice is very tender and the onions seem almost to have dissolved into it. If the onions seem to be taking on any color, reduce the heat to 275°F. The moisture from the onions should provide enough additional liquid to cook the rice, but if the mixture seems too dry or begins to stick, add more stock, 1 tablespoon at a time. Count on cooking the onion mixture 1 to 1¼ hours, or even longer. The texture should be very much like soft oatmeal.

If you are using the cream, stir it into the onions. Check the seasoning. Add more salt and pepper if needed. Stir in the parsley and serve very hot.

Variation: *Substitute 2 large leeks, white and light green parts only, very thinly sliced, for 1 of the onions. Cook the leeks along with the onions, before adding the rice. The finished dish will have a pale green tint.*

Note: *If there is any soubise left over, chill it, form it into thin, 3-inch cakes, and dust with flour. Fry the cakes in 1 tablespoon of butter or mild vegetable oil, preferably peanut, until golden brown and crisp on the outside, about 5 minutes per side. Serve very hot, sprinkled with a little freshly grated Parmesan cheese.*

Easy Fried Onion Rings

The quantity of onion rings may seem excessive, but I find they don't last very long, and more is better. These are a last-minute undertaking, although the rings can be cut and left to soak in ice water in the refrigerator for an hour or so. Pile these on top of thick cuts of grilled or pan-broiled calves' liver, over grilled fish of any kind, or, of course, on top of the best grilled steak you can buy.

Makes 6 servings

Oil for deep-frying
4 large onions, thickly sliced, separated into rings, and soaked in ice water to cover for at least 30 minutes
1 cup all-purpose flour
Salt and freshly ground black pepper to taste

Preheat the oil to 375°F. in a deep-fat fryer.

Drain the onion rings and dry them well.

Combine the flour, salt, and pepper in a paper or plastic bag. Toss the onion rings, a handful at a time, in the seasoned flour.

Fry the rings, in batches, in the hot oil until they are crisp and golden, about 3 minutes or a little longer per batch. Drain on paper towels. Salt to taste. Keep the rings hot until all are fried.

Serve as soon as possible very hot, piled in a heated bowl, or, if you are serving liver, fish, or beef, directly on the meat.

Mini Pissaladières

This very old dish from the Mediterranean coast of France might be called a pizza with a French accent, and it's still much enjoyed locally. Add these to any cold buffet along with a huge tossed salad, or cut them into quarters and pass with drinks.

Makes 6 to 8 servings

3 tablespoons olive oil
1½ pounds onions, thinly sliced
2 cloves garlic, minced
1 tablespoon chopped fresh thyme
1 tablespoon chopped fresh oregano
Salt and freshly ground black pepper to taste
Pizza dough for 2 large pies (about 2 pounds),
    cut into six 6-inch rounds (recipe follows)
Cornmeal
6 anchovy fillets, rinsed, dried, and minced,
    or more to taste
½ cup oil-cured olives, halved, pitted, and,
    if you like, sliced

Preheat the oven to 425°F.

Heat the oil in a medium-size heavy skillet over medium heat. Add the onions and cook, stirring occasionally, until they are very tender and golden brown but not burned, 15 to 20 minutes. Stir in the garlic and cook 3 minutes. Stir in the thyme and oregano and season very well with salt and pepper.

Arrange the rounds of pizza dough on 2 baking sheets that have been sprinkled with cornmeal. Divide the onion mixture among the rounds, spreading it to within ¼ inch of the edges. Sprinkle each with anchovies and olives.

Bake the rounds until the crust is golden brown, 15 to 20 minutes. Cool the pissaladières to room temperature to serve.

Variation: *Roll or pull half the pizza dough into one 12- to 14-inch round. Spread the onion mixture on the dough, leaving a 1-inch rim. Do not mince the anchovies, but arrange them like the spokes of a wagon wheel in the center of the pie. Decorate with the olives.*

Pizza Dough

There is very good commercial pizza dough available nearly everywhere. If you feel inclined to make your own, try this recipe.

Makes two 12-inch pizzas

1 envelope active dry yeast
1 cup warm water (about 110°F.)
3¼ cups unbleached, all-purpose flour, plus
    additional for kneading
½ teaspoon salt
2 tablespoons extra-virgin olive oil, plus
    additional for greasing

In a small bowl, sprinkle the yeast over the warm water, stirring until foamy. Set aside.

In a large bowl, stir together the 3¼ cups flour and the salt. Stir in the yeast mixture and the olive oil, beating until a stiff dough forms. Add a little additional flour if the dough is too sticky to handle.

Turn the dough out onto a lightly floured work surface and knead until it is smooth, shiny, and elastic, 8 to 10 minutes. Add additional flour to the work surface if necessary to keep the dough from sticking.

Place the kneaded dough in a lightly oiled bowl and brush the surface with a little additional olive oil. Cover the dough lightly with a clean towel and let rise in a warm place until double in bulk, up to 1 hour.

Punch down the dough and divide it into 2 rounds. Roll it out or stretch it on a lightly floured work surface into two 12-inch rounds and proceed with the main recipe.

Onion Casserole

The first time I served this as a substitute for the more familiar creamed onions at Thanksgiving, I thought I was going to be lynched. Once the feast had been dispatched, however, several requests for the recipe made me realize this was a winner. I still like it for holiday meals, but find it goes very well anytime with game or beef.

Makes 6 to 8 servings

2 tablespoons butter
2 tablespoons olive oil
2 cloves garlic, very thinly sliced
3 medium-size yellow onions, halved and
    thinly sliced
1 large red onion, halved and thinly sliced
3 large leeks, white and light green parts only,
    halved lengthwise and thinly sliced
3 bunches (18 to 24) green onions (scallions),
    white and light green parts only, thinly sliced
½ cup dry white wine
½ cup well-flavored chicken stock
¼ cup heavy cream
Salt and freshly ground black pepper to taste
¼ cup freshly grated Parmesan cheese
2 tablespoons snipped fresh chives

Preheat the oven to 350°F.

Melt the butter in the olive oil in a large heavy skillet over very low heat. Add the garlic and cook, stirring, for 1 minute. Add the yellow and red onions, leeks, and green onions. Cook, stirring from time to time, until translucent and very tender. This may take 30 minutes or more. Stir in the wine, stock, and cream. Simmer the mixture over medium heat until thickened, about 5 minutes. Season well with salt and pepper.

Spoon the mixture into a medium-size shallow ovenproof casserole. Cover with aluminum foil and bake for 35 minutes. Uncover, sprinkle with the cheese and bake until well browned and bubbling, 10 to 15 minutes longer. Serve very hot, garnished with the chives.

Onion Rings in Beer Batter

The batter on these rings is more substantial than the batter for Easy Fried Onion Rings (page 234) and makes them a bit more filling. These are equally good with liver, grilled fish, or beef.

Makes 6 to 8 servings

1½ cups all-purpose flour
1 teaspoon salt, plus additional for salting
1 teaspoon paprika
One 12-ounce can beer, pale, light,
    or alcohol free
Oil for deep-frying
3 to 4 large sweet onions, Vidalia, Walla Walla,
    or Texas Super Sweets, thickly sliced and
    separated into rings

In a medium-size bowl, stir together the flour, salt, and paprika. Whisk the beer into the mixture.

Heat the oil to 365°F. in a deep-fat fryer or deep heavy skillet.

Dip the onion rings in the batter. Drain off any excess and fry the coated rings in batches until crisp and golden on both sides, 3 to 4 minutes per batch.

Drain on paper towels. Salt lightly and serve the rings at once, very hot.

Rice-stuffed Onions

I love to serve these with grilled fish, but they also go very well with an old-fashioned mixed grill.

Makes 6 servings

6 medium-size sweet onions, such as Vidalia,
    Walla Walla, or Texas Super Sweets,
    peeled, boiled in salted water to cover for
    10 minutes, and drained
2 tablespoons butter
1 large clove garlic, minced

3 tablespoons minced green bell pepper
1 cup cooked (about ⅓ cup raw) rice, hot
½ cup grated fontina cheese
¼ cup chopped fresh parsley
Salt and freshly ground black pepper to taste
¾ cup well-flavored chicken stock
¼ cup dry white wine
Paprika to taste (optional)

Preheat the oven to 375°F.

Cut a small slice off the top of each onion. Using a melon baller or sharp teaspoon, scoop out the inside of the onion, leaving a thick shell about ¼ inch thick. Chop the scooped out onion finely.

Melt the butter in a medium-size heavy saucepan over low heat. Stir in the chopped onions, the garlic, and bell pepper. Cook, stirring occasionally, until the vegetables are tender, about 10 minutes. Remove the pan from the heat, and stir in the rice, cheese, and parsley. Season well with salt and pepper.

Spoon the rice mixture into the hollowed-out onions, mounding the filling slightly. Arrange the filled onions side by side in a shallow baking dish just large enough to hold them in one layer. Pour the stock and wine around the onions. Bake until the onions are very tender and the filling is golden, about 45 minutes.

Remove the baking dish from the oven. Serve the onions very hot, garnished with a little paprika.

Note: These onions are also very good served warm, as part of an outdoor barbecue celebration. The recipe is easily expanded by doubling the quantities in the filling.

Potato and Herb-stuffed Onions

Here is a great way to use leftover mashed potatoes. This is a substantial side dish, needing only a mixed green salad or a light green vegetable to complete the menu. Serve them with barbecued beef ribs or thin slices of barbecued flank steak.

Makes 6 servings

1 tablespoon butter, plus additional for buttering
6 large sweet onions, such as Vidalia, Walla Walla, or Texas Super Sweets, peeled, boiled in salted water to cover for 10 minutes, and drained
1 cup mashed potatoes, warm (½ to ¾ pound Russet potatoes)
3 green onions (scallions), white and light green parts only, thinly sliced
1 large egg, beaten
Salt and freshly ground black pepper to taste
1 teaspoon chopped fresh oregano
1 teaspoon snipped fresh chives, plus 1 additional tablespoon for garnishing
1 tablespoon chopped fresh parsley
1 tablespoon freshly grated Parmesan cheese
½ cup white wine

Preheat the oven to 375°F. Generously butter a shallow baking dish just large enough to hold the onions in one layer.

Using a melon baller or sharp spoon, scoop out the center of the onions, leaving a thick outer shell about ¼ inch thick, and chop the scooped-out onion finely.

Melt the butter in a small skillet over high heat. Add the chopped onions and cook, stirring, until golden, 6 to 8 minutes. Stir these onions into the mashed potatoes. Stir in the green onions. Beat in the egg and season well with salt, pepper, and herbs. Stir in the cheese.

Stuff the onions with the potato mixture, mounding it slightly. Place the filled onions side by side in the prepared baking dish. Pour the wine into the dish around the onions. Bake until the filling is puffy and golden brown, 30 to 40 minutes.

Remove the baking dish from the oven and serve the onions hot, garnishing each with the remaining chives.

Jacket-roasted Onions with Balsamic Vinegar

Just like potatoes, onions can be roasted in their jackets. Sometimes I like to serve whole baked white or sweet potatoes at the same time, with a thick cut of roast beef or fork-tender slices of grilled sirloin steak.

Makes 6 servings

6 medium-size onions, yellow, Vidalia, Walla Walla, or Texas Super Sweets
Pure olive oil
Extra-virgin olive oil
Salt and freshly ground black pepper to taste
Balsamic vinegar to taste

Preheat the oven to 375°F.

Wipe the outside of the onions clean. Rub the skins with a little of the pure olive oil. Place the oiled onions on the rack in the middle of the oven and bake until they are very tender when pierced with a fork, 1 to 1½ hours.

To serve, halve the onions horizontally, remove the peel, drizzle with the extra-virgin olive oil, and season well with salt and pepper. Pass a bottle of good balsamic vinegar for sprinkling.

Pearl Onion and Raisin Ragout

Serve this hot or at room temperature as a condiment with roast poultry or with any cold meat or fish, especially smoked fish. It makes a nice alternative to cranberry sauce on your holiday table.

Makes about 2½ cups

2 tablespoons butter
2 pints (20 ounces) boiling onions, boiled in water to cover for 1 minute, drained, and peeled; or one 16-ounce package frozen baby onions, thawed
1 tablespoon chopped fresh thyme, or 1 teaspoon dried
½ cup well-flavored chicken stock
¼ cup dry white wine
½ cup golden raisins, plumped 10 minutes in boiling water to cover and drained
½ cup dried cranberries, plumped 10 minutes in boiling water to cover and drained (optional)
Salt and freshly ground black pepper to taste
2 tablespoons chopped fresh parsley

Melt the butter in a large heavy saucepan over low heat. Add the onions and toss to coat. Stir in the thyme, stock, and wine. Cover and simmer over low heat until the onions are very tender, 15 to 20 minutes.

Remove the cover and cook over medium heat until all but several tablespoons of the liquid is evaporated, 5 to 6 more minutes. Stir in the raisins and, if using, the cran-berries, and cook, tossing until they are hot and everything is coated with the sauce, 3 to 4 minutes. Season well with salt and pepper, garnished with the parsley.

> Note: *These onions can be served at room temperature, and they keep well in the refrigerator for four or five days.*

Variation: *Replace the cranberries with dried cherries or dried blueberries that have been plumped in boiling water to cover and drained, or use a combination of dried fruit. The resulting ragout will be slightly sweeter.*

Pub-style Pickled Onions

A pub lunch of crusty bread, thick slabs of crumbly Cheddar cheese, and these pickled onions is an age-old and truly satisfying meal. Add thick slices of cold roast beef, pork, or lamb for an extra-simple, impromptu Sunday dinner party.

Makes about 1 quart

1½ cups Madeira, tawny port, or other fortified
   red wine
¾ cup malt vinegar, white wine vinegar,
   or cider vinegar
½ cup packed dark brown sugar
½ teaspoon ground red (cayenne) pepper
2 pounds small (1 to 1½ inches in diameter)
   yellow or white onions, boiled in water to
   cover for 3 minutes, drained, and peeled; or
   2 pints (20 ounces) boiling onions, boiled in
   water to cover for 1 minute, drained, and
   peeled; or two 16-ounce packages frozen
   baby onions, thawed and dried
3 tablespoons mild vegetable oil, preferably
   peanut (not olive oil)
Salt to taste
Hot pepper sauce to taste (optional)

In a medium-size nonreactive saucepan, combine the wine, vinegar, sugar, and red pepper. Bring to a boil over high heat and boil vigorously until the mixture is reduced to about 2 cups of liquid, 5 to 6 minutes.

Arrange the onions in one layer in a large skillet. Pour in the oil and cook the onions over high heat, shaking or tossing, until they are golden but not dark brown. This can take 6 to 8 minutes and requires constant watching to keep them from burning. Once they are browned, add them to the wine mixture.

Simmer the onions in the wine until crisply tender. They must not become mushy but should retain a crunchy texture. If you are using boiling onions or frozen onions, this may take only 1 or 2 minutes. Cool the onions in the liquid.

Add salt and, if you like, season with hot pepper sauce. Refrigerate several days to improve the flavor. Serve at room temperature.

Sweet Onion-Apple Compote

Nothing that I know of goes so well with a crisply roasted duck or goose as this tangy, tart-sweet compote. It is almost a chutney and could certainly be happily paired with any hot spicy curry, especially one featuring poultry of any kind.

Makes about 2 cups

3 tablespoons butter
2 pounds largest onions, thinly sliced
2 large Granny Smith apples, peeled, cored,
   quartered, and thinly sliced
1 medium-size lemon, ends trimmed, halved
   lengthwise, sliced crosswise as thin as
   possible, any seeds removed, simmered in
   water to cover for 5 minutes, and drained
1 cup dry white wine
¼ cup cider vinegar
⅓ cup sugar
⅓ cup currants, raisins, or dried cherries
   plumped 10 minutes in boiling water to
   cover and drained
1 teaspoon ground cumin
⅛ teaspoon mustard seed
3 tablespoon chopped fresh parsley
Salt and freshly ground black pepper to taste

Melt the butter in a large deep heavy skillet over low heat. Add the onions, apples, and lemon, cover, and cook, stirring occasionally, until the onions and lemon slices are translucent and softened, and the apples are tender, 15 to 20 minutes. Stir in the wine, vinegar, and sugar. Add the currants and season with the cumin and mustard seed. Cover and cook until the onions are very soft, but the apples have not fallen apart, about 5 minutes. Stir in the parsley and season well with salt and pepper.

Cool the compote and refrigerate at least overnight. To serve, bring to room temperature and spoon into a 3- to 4-cup glass or other serving bowl.

Note: *It is important that the apples do not fall apart and become applesauce. The slices should retain their shape and have a certain texture.*

Parsnips

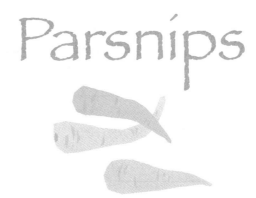

My wonderfully frank grandmother used to say there was nothing she wouldn't eat—except parsnips. Having heard this most of my childhood and never having seen the dreaded vegetable on her table, I avoided it for many years. Finally, in the process of developing recipes for a client, I was more or less forced to make its acquaintance. What a delicious treat I had been missing all that time. Unfortunately, it was long after my grandmother had passed away that I made this amazing discovery, and I was unable to ask her why she spurned the parsnip. I can only guess that she either had eaten only older parsnips that had tough, almost inedible inner cores or had encountered them in blandly spiced and boiled preparations.

The parsnip is an old vegetable that has been cultivated out of the wild for several thousand years. Until potatoes took over the central place as the starch of choice, parsnips were a winter staple. They deserve to be one again.

Parsnips are related to carrots, which they resemble somewhat in shape if not in color. The considerable quantities of starch in the parsnip convert to sugar when the vegetable is touched with the cold of frost. Once this conversion has begun, parsnips are delightfully sweet, with a very agreeable nutty flavor. In fact, parsnips are so sweet that the English used to make a wine with them. On the other hand, the English also make wine with primroses.

In my estimation, home-grown parsnips are best, as they can be pulled before they become overgrown and fibrous. If you do not have a garden, try to find a market that sells young freshly pulled roots rather than those that have been left too long in the ground or kept for months in cold storage.

Once you have added parsnips to soups or stews, you will wonder how you could ever have cooked without them. They can be cut into matchstick strips, sliced, or cut into chunks. The cut-up vegetable can be added to casseroles, mashed, braised, boiled, steamed, or roasted. In fact, they are almost as versatile as the potatoes that replaced them.

Parsnips cook more quickly than carrots and will fall apart if overcooked—which is all right if they are to be mashed but not particularly pleasant if you want them to retain their shape. Do not add them until the last 15 minutes of cooking time in soups and stews.

Parsnips are high in fiber and contain considerable amounts of calcium, potassium, and vitamin C.

Selection: I have never found parsnips with their greens attached. If you can, the greens should be fresh looking and not at all limp. If there are no greens, try to buy clip-top parsnips that are sold in bunches, not in plastic bags. Look for the smallest, firmest cream- or ivory-colored roots. Parsnips are not as regularly formed as carrots. Don't be put off by a knob or two, slightly twisted roots, or clinging garden soil. Do avoid any that are limp and flabby, have black or brown spots, or show any signs of mold.

Parsnips sold in plastic bags like horse carrots are harder to choose. The bags are often difficult to see through, the vegetables inside are frequently older and can have fibrous, woody cores. It may be wise to buy at least one-third more than you need of these, in case you have to discard the core of some of them.

You may see parsnips in the market all year long, but they are at their best from October to January or February. After that they will most likely be from cold storage.

You will need 1½ to 2 pounds of fresh young parsnips with little or no waste for six people. Count on 2½ to 3 pounds of older parsnips that may need coring.

Storage and Preparation: Parsnips are good keepers. If they are young and very fresh, place them in a perforated plastic bag in the vegetable drawer of the refrigerator. They should last at least two weeks. If you need to keep them longer, be sure to go through them every few days, discarding any that may show signs of spoiling. Older parsnips often keep three weeks or longer.

Except for older, very large ones, parsnips don't require a lot of preparation. Small, young roots only need to be well washed, trimmed, and peeled with a vegetable peeler. They can be cooked whole, cut into chunks, slices, matchstick strips, and so on. If you are not going to use cut parsnips immediately, drop the cuts into a bowl of cold water to which you have added 2 tablespoons lemon juice. This acidulated water will keep them from turning dark.

Large, fibrous parsnips should be washed, peeled, quartered lengthwise, and cut into 2- or 3-inch lengths. Use the point of a sharp knife to pop out the woody inner core. I have found these older parsnips are best when used in soups and stews or when mashed.

Steamed Parsnips

Arrange 1½ pounds parsnips, trimmed, peeled, cored if necessary, and cut up, in a steamer basket or a colander. Steam, covered, over simmering water or chicken stock until tender, 6 to 8 minutes.

Boiled Parsnips

Plain boiled parsnips are a little bland, but they can be tossed in some browned butter or with garlic, olive oil, and parsley for added interest. Place 1½ pounds parsnips, trimmed, peeled, cored if necessary, and cut up, in boiling salted water to cover. Simmer over medium heat for 8 to 10 minutes, depending on the age and size of the vegetable. Drain. Toss with a little butter or season well with salt and pepper.

Microwaved Parsnips

Arrange 1 pound parsnips, trimmed, peeled, cored if necessary, and cut up, in one layer in a microwave dish. Add ½ cup liquid. Cover with plastic microwave wrap and vent. Microwave on high for 5 minutes. Remove from the microwave, uncover carefully, and drain.

Parsnips and Pears

There is something wonderful about the nutty flavor of parsnips combined with the fragrant sweetness of pears. I think this is outstanding when served alongside baked or roasted chicken.

Makes 6 servings

1 tablespoon butter, plus additional for buttering
1 firm ripe Bartlett pear, peeled, halved, cored, and thinly sliced across
Juice of ½ lemon
1 pound young parsnips without cores, peeled and thinly sliced

1 small onion, halved and very thinly sliced
Salt and freshly ground black pepper to taste
2 tablespoons chopped fresh tarragon, plus additional for garnishing
½ cup heavy cream

Preheat the oven to 375°F. Generously butter a medium-size gratin or shallow baking dish.

In a small bowl, toss the pear slices with the lemon juice. Layer half the parsnips, then half the onion, and then half of the pear in the prepared dish. Season well with salt, pepper, and 1 tablespoon of the tarragon. Repeat the layers, finishing with the seasonings and another tablespoon of tarragon. Dot with 1 tablespoon of butter. Pour the cream over all. Cover the dish tightly with foil.

Bake until the parsnips and pears are very tender and almost melt together, 30 to 40 minutes. Serve hot, garnished with the remaining tarragon.

Glazed Parsnips

Like their cousin, the carrot, parsnips are delicious and sweet when cooked in a mixture of butter and sugar until it reduces to a shiny glaze. If you have someone at home who dreads the parsnip, like my grandmother did, this is the perfect way to introduce him or her to parsnip reality. I once had these with a piece of delicately poached turbot and have also served them with poached salmon.

Makes 6 to 8 servings

2 to 3 pounds young parsnips without cores, trimmed, cut into 1-inch chunks, simmered in salted water to cover until crisply tender, 4 or 5 minutes, drained, and cooled
2 tablespoons butter
Salt and freshly ground black pepper to taste
2 tablespoons sugar
3 tablespoons chopped fresh parsley

Slip the skins off the cooled parsnips and discard. Cut the parsnips into shapes, such as coins or matchstick strips.

Melt the butter in a medium-size heavy skillet over low heat. Stir in the parsnips. Season with salt and pepper. Sprinkle with sugar. Cook gently, stirring occasionally, until tender and coated with the pale golden glaze, 6 to 8 minutes. Serve very hot, garnished with the parsley.

Variation: *Substitute carrots for half of the parsnips. Season with $1/2$ teaspoon ground ginger. Serve with roast lamb or veal.*

Parsnip-Potato Puree

Parsnips can be boiled and mashed by themselves for a very sweet puree that goes well with pork and smoked ham. This mixture of parsnips and potato is a slightly more balanced puree that complements everything from grilled tuna steaks to a juicy pink rib roast of beef.

Makes 6 servings

1 pound young parsnips, trimmed, peeled, cored
    if necessary, cut into 1-inch lengths, boiled
    in salted water to cover until tender, about
    6 minutes, and drained
1 large Russet potato, peeled, cubed, boiled in
    salted water to cover until very tender, about
    15 minutes, and drained
1 teaspoon grated fresh ginger
2 tablespoons butter
About $1/4$ cup heavy cream
Salt and freshly ground black pepper to taste
Chopped fresh parsley

Mash the parsnips and potato together with a potato masher or put them through a ricer. Beat in the ginger and butter. Beat in enough cream, 1 tablespoon at a time, to make the puree the consistency you prefer—from very stiff to light and fluffy. Season well with salt and pepper. Serve very hot, garnished with the parsley.

Variation: *Just before serving the puree, stir in $1/4$ cup thinly sliced green onions that have been cooked over medium heat in 1 teaspoon butter until tender. The onions should melt into the puree.*

Parsnip Cakes

I like to serve these delicious little cakes alongside grilled tuna or shark. They are also excellent with a hearty pot roast of beef or with thin juicy slices of braised brisket.

Makes 6 servings

3 to 4 tablespoons butter
1 bunch (6 to 8) green onions (scallions), white
    and light green parts only, very thinly sliced
1 tablespoon minced green bell pepper
2 pounds young parsnips without cores, peeled,
    halved lengthwise, and cut into chunks,
    simmered in salted water to cover until
    tender, about 10 minutes, drained, and
    mashed or put through a ricer
$1/4$ cup minced fresh parsley
1 large egg, beaten
$1/3$ cup fine cracker crumbs, such as saltines or,
    for a richer flavor, butter crackers, plus
    additional for coating
Salt and freshly ground black pepper to taste

Melt 1 tablespoon of the butter in a small skillet over low heat. Add the green onions and bell pepper and cook, stirring to keep them from browning, about 5 minutes. In a large bowl, beat these vegetables into the parsnips. Beat in the parsley, egg, and the cracker crumbs. Season well with salt and pepper.

Chill for 2 hours. Make 6 large cakes out of the mixture, patting them with your hands into fairly thin patties (or form them into 12 smaller ones). Coat the cakes with cracker crumbs, knocking off any excess. Let dry for several minutes.

Melt 2 tablespoons of the butter in a skillet large enough to hold all the cakes in a single layer. When the butter is very hot, but not browning, add the cakes. Cook over medium heat until golden brown and crisp on both sides, turning once, about 10 minutes total. Serve very hot.

Fried Parsnips

The slightly sugary flavor of parsnips makes them perfect for a crisp hot chip to serve with roast beef or veal.

Makes 6 to 8 servings

2 pounds young parsnips without cores, trimmed, peeled, and very thinly sliced on the diagonal into oval chips
Oil for deep-frying
Salt to taste
Minced fresh parsley

Soak the parsnips in ice water to cover for 1 hour. Drain and dry well on kitchen towels.

Heat the oil to 375° or 380°F. Fry the parsnip chips in batches, until crisp and golden, 3 to 4 minutes per batch. Drain on paper towels and season with salt. Serve at once, very hot, sprinkling each serving with the parsley.

Note: *These can be twice fried like potato chips if you like. Fry them the first time for 2 to 3 minutes, but do not let them brown. Drain them on paper towels, separating the slices. Just before serving, drop the slices back into the hot oil until crisp and golden brown, about 1 minute.*

Roast Parsnips

Serve these sweet sticks with a rare charcoal-grilled steak for a real treat. Or for a more everyday meal, accompany them with quickly pan-fried cubed steaks or thick braised pork chops. I also like to combine these with roasted carrots, leeks, potatoes, and zucchini for a colorful vegetable platter.

Makes 6 to 8 servings

3 pounds young parsnips without cores, peeled and cut into 3-inch wedges
1 to 2 tablespoons butter, melted, or olive oil
Salt and freshly ground black pepper to taste
2 tablespoons chopped fresh parsley

Preheat the oven to 400°F.

In a large bowl, toss the parsnips in the butter or olive oil and spread them in one layer on a baking sheet. Roast, turning from time to time, until golden brown and very tender when pierced with a sharp fork, 45 minutes or longer. Season with salt and pepper. Toss with the parsley and serve very hot.

Variation: *These Roast Parsnips are delicious if served with a dipping sauce made by combining 3 tablespoons hot honey mustard with ¹/₂ cup mayonnaise.*

Peanuts

W hile most people think of peanuts in terms of cocktail snacks or the ubiquitous commercial spread, they really are a valuable food source. Even spread on bread in the form of a peanut butter sandwich these legumes offer a considerable amount of protein, as well as some oil, and fiber. For this reason, a peanut butter sandwich (no jelly) on crunchy whole-grain bread, along with a glass of skim milk and some fruit is a nearly perfect meal.

Peanuts are not true nuts; they are legumes. They do not, however, grow by hanging on the plant, as do beans. When the flowers wither, they droop down to the ground, pushing a sort of spike into the soil where the pod develops. Peanuts must be carefully lifted out of the soil somewhat like potatoes. Raw or dried, but unroasted, peanuts can be cooked in any way that beans can be prepared. Roasted, unsalted peanuts can also be cooked like dried beans and give a delicious smoky flavor to dishes. They do not need to be presoaked before cooking.

Also called ground nuts, peanuts may be a New World vegetable, most likely originating in Brazil. It is possible that Native Americans knew of the peanut's value as a food long before the first Europeans arrived on the scene. Since the fifteenth century, however, peanuts have spread to many other parts of the world, primarily wherever it is hot and humid. Peanuts like a lot of heat and sun to mature. In Africa, India, and China, substantial amounts of peanuts are grown and eaten, but the United States grows more than any other country.

The peanut is a versatile plant. The nuts are not only eaten, they are also pressed to extract cooking oil. The nuts and shells have been used in thousands of processes from animal fodder to paper products.

While peanuts are relatively high in fat, they contain no cholesterol. They are high in fiber, protein, vitamin E, iron, and potassium.

Selection: Peanuts in the shell, roasted or unroasted, keep better than loose shelled peanuts. Look for dry, plump nuts, avoiding any that are shriveled or show signs of mold. Processed peanuts—for example, roasted and/or salted—are fine as long as the seal of the container has not been broken.

Fresh peanuts are in some local markets in late August and early September.

Storage: Peanuts should be stored in a cool dry atmosphere. Excess moisture tends to encourage the formation of a mold that can be toxic. Roasted peanuts can become stale and rancid if stored over long periods of time, especially at high temperatures.

Peanuts keep well in the refrigerator if they are sealed in airtight plastic bags. But I prefer to freeze them if they will be on hand longer than two or three weeks. Sealed in airtight jars or plastic freezer bags, they will maintain their freshness up to three months or more in the freezer. They thaw quickly for use as snacks or in recipes.

Peanut and Cabbage Sauté

Try this if you ever come across raw, unroasted peanuts. Adapted from a West African recipe, it is a delicious change of pace. In the South, there are several brands of canned raw peanuts. They can be substituted if you like, but be sure to rinse them thoroughly and do not boil them as they are already cooked. This is a natural with baked, smoked ham.

Makes 6 servings

1 cup whole raw shelled peanuts, soaked
    overnight and drained
2 tablespoons butter
1 tablespoon mild vegetable oil, preferably peanut
1 small onion, halved and thinly sliced
½ small head Savoy cabbage, shredded
1 teaspoon ground cumin
¼ cup chicken stock

Salt and freshly ground black pepper to taste
Hot pepper sauce to taste

Simmer the peanuts in salted water to cover over low heat until tender, about 1 hour, depending on the age of the peanuts. Drain.

Melt the butter in the oil in a large heavy skillet over medium heat. Add the onion and cook, stirring from time to time, until translucent, about 10 minutes. Stir in the drained peanuts and cook, tossing, until they are golden brown, about 10 minutes.

Stir in the cabbage and cook, stirring, until coated with the butter mixture, about 1 minute. Stir in the cumin and stock. Season well with salt and pepper. Cover and cook, stirring once or twice, until the cabbage is just tender, about 10 minutes. Serve very hot, passing hot pepper sauce on the side.

Note: *If raw peanuts are not available, use unsalted, roasted peanuts, but do not presoak them before boiling.*

Collards and Peanuts

This is delicious with barbecued spareribs. Serve with freshly steamed rice on the side.

Makes 6 servings

2 tablespoons butter
1 small onion, halved and thinly sliced
½ cup unsalted roasted peanuts,
    coarsely chopped
2 medium-size ripe tomatoes, chopped
2 pounds young collard greens, stemmed,
    chopped, and steamed in the water that clings
    to their leaves until wilted, about 6 minutes
Salt and freshly ground black pepper to taste

Melt the butter in a large heavy skillet over medium heat. Add the onion. Cook, stirring, until translucent, 6 to 8 minutes. Stir in the nuts. Cook

2 minutes. Add tomatoes and cook, stirring, 3 minutes longer. Stir in the cooked collards. Cook 3 minutes longer. Season well with salt and pepper. Serve very hot.

Cold Marinated Eggplant and Peanuts

Add this to your next cold antipasto buffet. Or serve it with cold roast chicken.

Makes about 6 servings

**1 medium-size eggplant, trimmed, cut across into
    ¼-inch rounds**
Pure olive oil
¼ cup extra-virgin olive oil
Juice of 1 lemon
1 clove garlic, minced
⅓ cup roasted peanuts, very coarsely chopped
½ jalapeño pepper, seeded and minced
Salt to taste
**3 green onions (scallions), white and light green
    parts only, very thinly sliced**

Preheat the broiler.

Arrange the eggplant in one layer on a baking sheet. Brush the tops with the pure olive oil. Broil about 2 inches from the heat until golden brown on top, about 2 minutes. With a spatula, turn the eggplant rounds and brush again with pure olive oil. Broil until golden on the second side, 1 to 2 minutes longer. Cool to room temperature.

Layer the eggplant rounds in a shallow dish (glass is pretty). In a small bowl, combine the extra-virgin olive oil, lemon juice, garlic, peanuts, jalapeño pepper, and salt. (Add salt sparingly if salted peanuts are used.) Pour this marinade over the eggplant. Cover and refrigerate for several hours or overnight, basting the eggplant with the marinade once or twice. Serve at room temperature, garnished with the green onions.

Peas

Tender fresh green peas in the pod may soon be a vegetable available only to home gardeners. You can find unshelled peas in many markets during spring and early summer, but they are usually old. The pods are fibrous, and the peas are sometimes so tough that no amount of cooking will render them tender enough to eat.

If you have ever eaten garden-fresh peas, you surely became an instant addict who takes advantage of every opportunity to try to re-create that initial sublime experience. It will not be often repeated, and the experience will have spoiled you for shelled peas in any other form. There is almost nothing as tender and sweet as tiny, freshly picked peas, quickly cooked and tossed with a little butter and fresh mint. Very fresh shelled peas can be sprinkled raw over salads, too.

Green peas, or English peas, are legumes meant to be shelled just before they are eaten. Their season is very short, usually late May to very early July at most. Shelling peas are like corn. As soon as they are picked, the sugars begin to turn to starch, and only a few hours from vine to pot can cause the loss of much of their sweetness. Older peas become tough and unappetizing. For this reason, most of the crop in the United States is preserved, either by canning or freezing. While canned baby peas do have a certain following, I think they bear no resemblance to the fresh vegetable. Frozen peas, on the other hand, are flash frozen only hours out of the field and, if handled properly, can be a fairly good substitute for fresh—especially the tiny baby peas that are increasingly available in the freezer.

The pod of green, or English, peas is not edible. While it isn't harmful, the lining of the pod is fibrous and unappealing. Occasionally, one or two empty pods can be added to the pot during cooking for added flavor, but they should be removed before serving the finished dish. There are, however, two varieties of fresh peas now on the market that are meant to be eaten whole, pod and all.

Snow peas, also known as sugar peas—or *mangetouts* in France; literally, "eat everything"—have been around for quite a while. Most of us are familiar with them because they are a staple ingredient in Chinese stir-fries.

Lately, they have been increasingly available fresh in greengrocers, and now also appear in many supermarkets. These long, thin, and almost flat pods are crisp and full of flavor. Picked while the little peas are still immature, they are meant to be cooked quickly, for only 1 or 2 minutes. Once they have been topped, tailed, and strung, snow peas can also be sliced or left whole, and added raw to salads and crudité platters.

Sugar snap peas, the darlings of the restaurant scene right now, are a wonderful cross between English and snow peas. Although they seem to have been around for quite a while, it was only in the 1970s that they were bred to perfection. Unlike snow peas, the peas themselves are well developed inside the thin, crisp pod. These are plump little green pods, full of flavor and, when not overcooked, snap. Like snow peas, they should be cooked quickly and served while they are still quite crisp. They can be strung and tossed raw into salads or added to cold vegetable platters.

Snow peas are available nearly all year long fresh, and they are also found frozen. The frozen variety are limp and frequently dark colored and are really only a last resort for adding at the final moment to a stir-fry or vegetable medley.

Sugar snap peas have about the same fresh season as English peas, but they seem to stay fresh longer, since they are also enjoyed for the flavor and texture of the pod as well as the interior pea. Some companies are now selling frozen sugar snaps, which are infinitely better than frozen snow peas, but cannot be substituted for raw sugar snaps. Blanched (boiled briefly, rinsed in cold water, and drained) before freezing, they become slightly limp when thawed. I frequently use them in the winter, but once they are thawed, I only reheat them quickly and do not let them cook further.

The Chinese have long known about pea shoots. These fragile but delectable tendrils and first leaves of the pea runners, with or without the blossoms, are beginning to appear on the menus of chic restaurants. And specialty markets will sometimes have them for sale in bulk. They can be extremely expensive, but if you are serving them raw, a little goes a long way. If you are going to be cooking them, consider adding them to stir-fries or light sautés, perhaps along with snow peas or sugar snap peas to reinforce the pea theme.

If you do not find the shoots locally, try to persuade a gardener friend to let you graze through his or her pea patch in the early spring. Any kind of edible pea will do. Snip off the tendrils and first few leaves, along with a blossom or two if you like. Don't worry, the plant will produce more. Take the shoots home and wash and dry them very gently. Add them to any mixed green salad for a very fresh pea flavor—delicious when combined with a little peppery watercress along with some tiny garden fresh lettuce leaves. Do not add dressing until the last minute as the shoots wilt almost immediately.

When adding pea shoots to stir-fries or sautés, add only 30 seconds or so before serving. A very short cooking time is enough to wilt them slightly while preserving the lovely bright green color and fresh pea flavor.

Fresh peas are an excellent source of protein, carbohydrate, and fiber. They are low in fat and high in vitamin A.

Selection: If you are fortunate enough to find a source of truly fresh green peas, select the plumpest, most vibrantly green pods available. Avoid any that appear in the least shriveled or yellowed, have spotted pods, or show any signs of mold. *Never* buy shelled fresh peas. No matter how appealing they look, they will be less than sweet and are often tough little balls that will never tenderize satisfactorily. If garden-fresh English peas are not available, it is best to substitute frozen peas instead. These should simply be reheated after thawing, cooked only 1 or 2 minutes, or they will lose their fresh color, flavor, and crisp texture.

From 1 pound of peas in the pod you will get approximately 1 cup shelled peas. You will need 3 or more pounds for six servings. Snow peas and sugar snap peas should be as firm and crisp as possible. Look for the brightest green color with no splits, brown spots, or signs of mold. Avoid any pods that are limp and tired looking. You can count on $\frac{1}{4}$ pound snow or sugar snap peas per serving.

Storage and Preparation: Like corn, all varieties of fresh peas should be eaten as soon after picking as possible, certainly the same day they are purchased. If something unexpected happens and you must keep them longer than a few hours, seal them, unwashed, in a perforated plastic vegetable bag and use as soon as possible, preferably within a day or two.

Shell peas just before they are going to be cooked. To shell peas, each pod must be opened individually. I find it easiest to string the pods first. Grasp the blossom end and pull along the "seam." The string should come away in one long fiber. Then use the pressure of your thumb and forefinger to press the pods along the same seam. If they do not pop open with this pressure, run your thumbnail along the seam until the pod opens. Then run your thumb down the inside of the pod to release the peas. The shelled peas should be washed lightly in running water and cooked immediately. In our house, shelling was often a job relegated to children, and I remember many wonderful early summer evenings sitting on the back (or front) steps with my mother, shelling peas for dinner and talking.

Sugar snap peas and snow peas need to be strung before eating. Grasp the blossom end and pull gently along the seam. The string should come away in one long fiber. Sugar snaps will have to be strung along both seams. Wash the strung pods well and drain. Once washed, the pods are ready to arrange raw in salads or to be cooked immediately. If you are adding sugar snaps to a stir-fry or cooking them in hot oil, it is best to dry the pods so that they do not spit fat on the cook.

Boiled Peas

Place shelled peas in boiling (unsalted) water just to cover. Simmer 8 to 10 minutes if very fresh, depending on the size of the peas, and drain. Truly fresh peas need very little cooking time. If they will be chilled and used in salads, they can be cooked 1 or 2 minutes less. Older peas may require up to 15 minutes cooking time. Very old peas may never become tender.

Fourth of July Peas

Down East, in New England, it used to be a matter of pride to have enough fresh green peas from the garden ready to serve on the Fourth of July, along with poached fresh salmon. Peas go very well with fish, and with almost everything else as well.

Makes 6 to 8 servings

3 pounds young peas in the pod, shelled
1 bunch (6 to 8) green onions (scallions), white and as much dark green as is crisp, thinly sliced
1 tablespoon butter
4 large lettuce leaves, halved or shredded
Salt and freshly ground black pepper to taste
$\frac{1}{4}$ cup heavy cream
1 tablespoon chopped fresh mint, or more to taste

In a large saucepan, combine the peas, green onions, butter, and lettuce. Add enough water to just begin to show through the top layer of peas. Season well with salt and pepper. Cover and simmer over low heat until tender but not mushy, 10 to 12 minutes. Uncover. Stir in the cream, increase the heat to medium, and boil until the liquid reduces to a few tablespoons, about 2 minutes. Serve very hot garnished with the mint.

Note: *Old-fashioned cooks used to toss several well-washed empty pea pods into the saucepan with the peas. They were removed before serving the dish. I have tried this and find it does emphasize the pea flavor slightly, and they are very pretty in the pot.*

Spring Peas with Carrots and Green Onions

This colorful dish will be right at home on an Easter menu with baked ham and sherried acorn squash.

Makes 6 servings

2 to 3 tablespoons butter
2 pounds fresh young peas in the pod, shelled, simmered in water to cover until just tender, about 10 minutes, and drained; or 2 cups thawed smallest frozen peas, prepared in the same manner
2 bunches (12 to 16) green onions (scallions), white and as much green as is crisp (up to 3 inches), sliced 1/4 inch thick and steamed until tender, 4 to 5 minutes
4 small carrots, peeled, sliced 1/4 inch thick, and steamed until tender, 8 to 10 minutes
Salt and freshly ground black pepper to taste
1 cup shredded lettuce
Chopped fresh parsley

Melt the butter in a medium-size saucepan over medium heat. Stir in the peas, green onions, and carrots. Season well with salt and pepper, and add the lettuce. Toss just until well mixed and very hot, with the lettuce still barely wilted, about 2 minutes. Serve very hot, garnished with the parsley.

Spring Pea and Baby Onion Sauté

Enjoy this dish often during the short period when fresh peas are in the market. If boiling onions are not available, frozen baby onions are an acceptable substitute. Frozen peas are fine, too, but are practically a different vegetable from the just-picked fresh green peas. Serve with roast chicken or turkey.

Makes 6 to 8 servings

2 tablespoons butter
1 pint (10 ounces) boiling onions, boiled in water to cover for 1 minute, drained, and peeled and then simmered in salted water for 5 minutes, and drained; or 2 cups thawed frozen baby onions, simmered in salted water for 5 minutes, and drained
2 pounds fresh young peas in the pod, shelled, simmered in water for 5 minutes, and drained
1 tablespoon fresh lemon juice
Salt and freshly ground black pepper to taste
2 tablespoons snipped fresh dill, plus additional for garnishing

Melt the butter in a medium-size skillet over medium heat. Add the onions and cook, stirring, until just beginning to turn golden, 6 to 8 minutes.

Stir in the peas. Toss to coat and cook for 1 to 2 minutes. Stir in the lemon juice. Season well with salt, pepper, and 2 tablespoons of dill. Cook over low heat until the peas are tender, about 5 minutes. Serve very hot, garnished with the additional dill.

Tarragon Peas and Limas

The tarragon in this dish makes it a good companion for baked chicken breasts or for a whole baked fish, such as shad or striped bass.

Makes 6 servings

1 pound fresh baby limas in the pod, shelled, simmered in water for 10 minutes, and drained; or 1½ cups thawed frozen baby limas

1½ pounds fresh young peas, shelled, boiled in water for 4 or 5 minutes, and drained; or 1½ cups thawed small frozen peas, prepared in the same manner

½ cup chicken stock

1 tablespoon butter

1 tablespoon heavy cream, or more to taste (optional)

3 tablespoons chopped fresh tarragon, plus additional for garnishing

Salt and freshly ground black pepper to taste

Combine the limas and peas in a large saucepan. Add the stock and cook, covered, over low heat until both are tender, for 5 to 10 minutes. Drain.

Stir in the butter, cream, and tarragon. Season well with salt and pepper. Heat through. Serve very hot, garnished with a little more tarragon.

Peas and Pasta

This delicious hot dish goes well with veal, with a small grilled steak, or with grilled fish.

Makes 6 servings

3 tablespoons butter

1 bunch (6 to 8) green onions (scallions) white part and all the green that is crisp, sliced about ¼ inch thick

3 tablespoons chopped fresh parsley, plus additional for garnishing

½ teaspoon ground cumin, or more to taste

Salt and freshly ground black pepper to taste

½ cup heavy cream

1½ pounds fresh young peas in the pod, shelled, simmered in water to cover until tender, about 10 minutes, and drained; or 2 cups thawed frozen peas, prepared in the same manner

1 cup small pasta shapes, such as bow ties or elbows, cooked in salted water until al dente, drained, and kept hot

Melt the butter in a large heavy saucepan over medium heat. Add the green onions and cook, stirring, for 1 minute. Stir in 3 tablespoons of parsley. Season with the cumin, salt, and pepper. Stir in the cream. Add the peas and heat through. Stir in the pasta and toss well. Serve very hot, garnished with the additional parsley.

Peas and Barley

I do not understand why barley has gone out of style as a grain to be served with meals. Here the combination of peas and mushrooms enhances the nutty flavor of the barley. I don't know anything better to serve with a grilled veal chop. Pass freshly grated Parmesan cheese in a small dish if you like.

Makes 6 to 8 servings

Butter

1 pound fresh young peas in the pod, shelled, simmered in water to cover until tender, 8 to 10 minutes, and drained; or 1 cup thawed small frozen peas, prepared in the same manner

¼ pound fresh shiitake (stems discarded), or portabella mushrooms, stems trimmed, sliced, and browned in 1 tablespoon butter

1 bunch (6 to 8) green onions (scallions), white part only, thinly sliced

2 cups cooked pearled barley (see Note)

Salt and freshly ground black pepper to taste

½ cup sour cream, regular or light

3 tablespoons chopped fresh oregano,
    plus additional for garnishing

Preheat the oven to 375°F. Generously butter a
1-quart ovenproof casserole.

Combine the peas, mushrooms, green onions, and
barley in the prepared casserole. Season well with
salt and pepper. Stir in the sour cream and 3 tablespoons of oregano. Bake until just heated through,
about 15 minutes. Serve very hot, garnished with the
additional oregano.

Note: Simmer ½ cup pearled barley, covered,
in 2 cups salted water until tender and most of
the water is absorbed, 45 to 50 minutes. Stir
with a fork before adding the barley to the peas
and mushrooms. The barley can be cooked in
advance and refrigerated until ready to use.

Sesame Snow Pea Salad

I like to see the bright colors of this crunchy salad on the
same plate as thick charcoal-grilled chicken burgers.

Makes 6 to 8 servings

½ pound snow peas, topped, tailed, and strung
    if necessary
¼ pound thinnest fresh green beans, topped,
    tailed, steamed until crisply tender, 4 to
    5 minutes, and chilled; or 1 cup thawed
    thinnest frozen green beans
¼ pound white mushrooms, stems
    trimmed, sliced
2 tablespoons teriyaki sauce
Pinch sugar
½ teaspoon grated fresh ginger
2 teaspoons toasted sesame oil
3 tablespoons olive oil
Freshly ground black pepper to taste
1 head leaf lettuce, chilled
1 tablespoon sesame seeds, toasted (page 70)

In a medium-size bowl, toss together the snow peas,
green beans, and mushrooms. Chill.

Prepare the dressing. In a small bowl, beat together
all the remaining ingredients, except the lettuce and
sesame seeds. Chill.

Just before serving, toss the vegetables with the
dressing. Arrange the lettuce on a serving plate. Pile
the salad on the lettuce bed. Sprinkle the salad with
the sesame seeds and serve.

Sugar Snap Peas and Onions

Put these on the same menu as a thick slice of roast beef,
a grilled steak, or any kind of cooked poultry.

Makes 6 to 8 servings

2 tablespoons butter or olive oil
2 pints (1¼ pounds) boiling onions, boiled in
    water to cover for 1 minute, drained, and
    peeled; or one 16-ounce package frozen baby
    onions, thawed
½ cup well-flavored chicken stock
1 pound sugar snap peas, topped and strung
Salt and freshly ground black pepper to taste
2 tablespoons chopped fresh basil
⅓ cup sliced almonds or pecan pieces, toasted
    (page 70)

Heat the butter or oil in a large heavy skillet over
low heat. Add the onions and cook, stirring, until
golden, 6 to 8 minutes. Stir in the stock. Simmer
5 minutes. Stir in the peas. Cover and simmer over
low heat for 5 more minutes. Season well with salt,
pepper, and the basil. Simmer over low heat until
the peas are crisply tender, about 5 minutes longer.
Stir in the nuts, heat through, toss well, and serve
very hot.

Note: If fresh sugar snaps are not in the market, use frozen pods, but check often so they do
not overcook.

Dilly Sugar Snaps and Carrots

I think the colors of this dish will enliven any dinner plate. The mustardy dill flavor makes it delicious with fish. Why not put it beside some freshly made salmon cakes?

Makes 6 servings

½ cup well-flavored chicken stock
½ pint boiling onions, boiled in water to cover for 1 minute, drained, and peeled
½ pound tiny carrots, peeled
½ pound sugar snap peas, topped, tailed, and strung if necessary; or ½ pound snow peas if sugar snaps are not available
2 tablespoons heavy cream
2 tablespoons dry white wine
1 teaspoon Dijon-style mustard
3 tablespoons chopped fresh dill, plus additional for garnishing
Salt and freshly ground black pepper to taste

In a large saucepan, combine the stock, onions, and carrots, and simmer over medium heat until just tender, 10 to 15 minutes. Add the peas and simmer until they are crisply tender, 3 to 4 minutes longer.

Combine the cream, wine, and mustard with 3 tablespoons of dill in a small saucepan. Simmer over medium heat, stirring, until thickened slightly, 3 to 5 minutes. Stir this sauce into the vegetables and simmer, tossing, until hot and the vegetables are well coated, 2 to 3 minutes longer. Season well with salt and pepper. Serve very hot, garnished with the additional dill.

Two-Pea Salad

Nothing complements cold-poached salmon or other cold fish as well as this colorfully delicious salad.

Makes 6 to 8 servings

¼ cup chopped fresh mint, plus whole leaves for garnishing
⅓ cup mayonnaise, or more if the salad appears a little dry, prepared or homemade (page 13)
¼ cup sour cream, regular or light, or plain yogurt
Salt and freshly ground black pepper to taste
3 pounds fresh young peas in the pod, shelled, steamed until just tender, about 10 minutes, and chilled; or 3 cups thawed small frozen peas, prepared in the same manner
1 bunch (6 to 8) green onions (scallions); or ½ small Vidalia or other super sweet onion, very thinly sliced
Fresh lettuce leaves, chilled
½ cup whole sugar snap peas, simmered in water to cover for 6 to 8 minutes, drained, and chilled

In a small bowl, combine ¼ cup of chopped mint, the mayonnaise, and sour cream. Season well with salt and pepper. In a medium-size bowl, toss this dressing with the peas and green onions. Chill 3 hours.

Arrange the lettuce leaves in a medium-size salad bowl (glass is nice). Mound the salad on top. Garnish with the sugar snap peas and the mint leaves.
Variation: *Substitute chopped fresh parsley for the mint. Beat 1 tablespoon medium-hot curry powder into the dressing. Combine with the peas and chill several hours.*

Sugar Snap Pea, Turnip, and Carrot Stir-Fry

I like to serve this along with the largest shrimp I can find. I brush the shrimp with olive oil and garlic, and grill them, in the shell, over hot coals until just cooked through.

Makes 6 servings

2 tablespoons mild vegetable oil, preferably peanut
3 small white turnips, peeled and cut into ¼-inch matchstick strips

2 medium-size carrots, peeled and cut into
  ¼-inch matchstick strips
1 cup sugar snap peas, topped, tailed, and strung
1 large clove garlic, minced
1 teaspoon soy sauce
2 tablespoons chicken stock
1 teaspoon dry sherry
2 green onions, white and light green parts
  only, sliced
2 tablespoons chopped fresh tarragon

Heat the oil in a wok or large deep heavy skillet over high heat until almost smoking. Add the turnips and carrots and cook, stirring, until crisply tender, 3 to 4 minutes. Remove from the wok with a slotted spoon. Add the snow peas and cook, stirring, for 1 minute. Remove from the wok with a slotted spoon. Return the turnips and carrots to the wok.

Add all the remaining ingredients, except the green onions, tarragon, and the reserved snow peas, to the wok. Cover and cook over low heat until the carrots and turnips are just tender, 3 to 5 minutes. Return the snow peas to the wok. Cover and simmer 1 minute longer. Uncover, toss to coat the vegetables. Serve the vegetables very hot, garnished with the scallions and tarragon.

Sugar Snap Peas and Tiny New Potatoes

If early summer has a taste, the combination of fresh green peas and tiny new potatoes may epitomize it. Serve this with any delicate-flavored poached fish fillet.

Makes 6 servings

1 pound smallest white or red truly new potatoes,
  unpeeled, left whole if small, quartered
  if large
1 cup water or well-flavored chicken stock
3 tablespoons butter
¼ cup dry white wine
1 teaspoon fresh lemon juice

2 tablespoons snipped fresh chives, plus
  additional for garnishing
¾ pound fresh sugar snap peas, topped, tailed,
  and strung if necessary, simmered in water
  to cover until crisply tender 5 to 7 minutes,
  drained, and kept warm; or 2 cups frozen
  sugar snaps, thawed, prepared in the
  same manner
Salt and seasoned pepper, such as Mrs. Dash,
  to taste

In a medium-size saucepan, simmer the potatoes over medium heat in the water until tender when pierced with a fork but not falling apart, about 10 minutes. Drain, reserving the liquid for use in sauces or as a soup base. Keep the potatoes warm.

In a small saucepan, melt the butter. Add the wine, lemon juice, and 2 tablespoons of chives, stirring, over medium heat until reduced to a thick sauce, 4 to 5 minutes. Take care not to let all the liquid evaporate.

In a large bowl, toss together the hot, drained potatoes with the sugar snaps. Pour the hot butter sauce over all and toss gently to heat through. Season well with salt and pepper. Serve very hot, garnished with the additional chives.

Risi Bisi

This Italian combination is best when made with the wonderfully tender first peas of spring, but in a pinch, you can use very small frozen peas. In the region around Venice risi bisi is often served alone, as a separate course, but I like to serve it on the same plate as a beautifully poached salmon fillet, or with grilled fish of any kind.

Makes 6 to 8 servings

3 tablespoons olive oil
$^1/_2$ medium-size onion, minced
1 bunch (6 to 8) green onions (scallions), white
    and light green parts only, very thinly sliced
1 cup raw arborio rice
2 cups well-flavored chicken stock
1 pound fresh peas in the pod, shelled, simmered
    until just tender in water to cover, no more
    than 8 to 10 minutes, and drained; or 1 cup
    thawed smallest frozen peas, prepared in the
    same manner
$^1/_4$ cup freshly grated Parmesan cheese
Salt and freshly ground black pepper to taste
Hot pepper sauce to taste (optional)

Heat the oil in a medium-size heavy saucepan over medium heat. Add the minced onion and cook, stirring, until tender and golden brown, about 5 minutes. Stir in the green onions and cook 1 minute. Stir in the rice and cook, stirring, until translucent and all the grains are coated with oil, 2 to 3 minutes. Stir in the stock. Simmer the rice, uncovered, over low heat until the stock is absorbed and the rice is tender, about 20 minutes. The consistency should be moist, but not soupy.

Gently stir in the peas and cheese. Season well with salt and pepper. Heat through but do not cook further. Serve very hot, garnished with the parsley. Pass the hot pepper sauce, if desired, separately.

Puree of Peas

There are a lot of people who think mashed potatoes are the only pureed vegetable they will accept. Once they have tried this simple but delicious dish, however, I think they will change their minds. Serve with Two-Celery Puree (page 114), along with broiled salmon.

Makes 6 servings

3 pounds fresh young peas in the pod, shelled,
    simmered in boiling water until very tender,
    10 to 15 minutes depending on age, and
    drained; or 3 cups thawed frozen peas,
    prepared in the same manner
2 tablespoons butter, softened
2 tablespoons heavy cream
Salt and freshly ground black pepper to taste
1 tablespoon chopped fresh chervil, plus
    additional for garnishing

Puree the partially cooked peas in a food processor until very smooth. Push the puree through a coarse sieve to remove the skins. Place the puree in a medium-size saucepan and stir in the butter and cream. Season well with salt, pepper, and the chervil. Cook over very low heat, stirring, until the puree is thick and unctuous, being careful that it does not burn, about 5 to 6 minutes. The puree should be thick enough to hold its shape when spooned onto a plate and it should not weep any liquid. Serve very hot, garnished with the additional chervil.

Variation: *Substitute fresh mint for the chervil.*

Note: *This puree can be made ahead, cooled, and refrigerated for several hours. Reheat it in the microwave for 1 to 2 minutes (in 30-second increments) on high. Serve very hot.*

Peppers

Peppers are not really pepper (in the peppercorn sense) at all. They were misnamed by the Spaniards who went with Columbus on his second attempt to find the passage west to India. The vegetables (which are really fruits) encountered in the New World were hot, rather than sweet, and it is probably logical that they were called by the same name as the familiar spice that added heat and character to food. The Spaniards carried them home from their voyages, and from there the vegetable migrated with travelers throughout the world. It wasn't long before "peppers" were almost universally popular.

Sweet Peppers

Hot and sweet peppers are all related, but it wasn't until about one hundred years ago that the sweet peppers we know today were bred from the hotter varieties that first made the transatlantic voyage. Sweet peppers are relatively new on the culinary scene. They play such a large part in modern cooking, though, it is hard to believe they haven't always been as important a flavoring element as onions, or garlic.

The common red bell pepper is the same as the green; it has simply been left on the plant until fully ripe. (In fact, almost all peppers, sweet and hot, will turn from their initial green to red if they are left to mature on the plant.) We are no longer limited to these two familiar peppers. A whole spectrum of very colorful, super sweet, thick-skinned peppers are appearing in the markets. These ultra-fancy hybrids are still quite expensive since the majority of them are grown in Europe and shipped here by air, but the seeds are becoming more readily available, and specialty growers are beginning to cultivate them. If you are creating an eye-appealing platter of raw vegetables, or want a colorful sauce or stir-fry, they may well be worth the high price.

Look for deep vibrant yellow, an intense, almost maroon red, rich shining orange, creamy white, brilliant eggplant purple, even a deep chocolate brown. All begin their lives as green peppers and mature into these luscious hybrid colors. All maintain their color when they are used raw, but the purple and brown varieties turn a dark olive green if cooked for more than a minute or two. All can be substituted in recipes for the more familiar bells.

Peppers are an excellent source of vitamins C and A; the red ones provide large amounts of beta-carotene.

Selection: Look for the plumpest, juiciest, most brightly colored peppers available. Regardless of the color it should be clear and shiny. Avoid peppers that are shriveled or wrinkled, have soft spots or cracks, are dull looking, or show signs of mold. In general, the redder the pepper, the sweeter it will be.

Most sweet peppers are available in the market year round, though you may find locally grown, very freshly picked peppers at farm stands during the summer and into the early fall.

Storage and Preparation: Fresh sweet peppers will keep a week or longer. Seal them, unwashed, in a plastic bag, or in a perforated plastic vegetable bag.

Peppers should be washed just before using. To prepare peppers without cutting them up, cut out the stem and remove the seeds and ribs by pulling them out with your hands. The stem, seeds, and ribs should come out in one piece. Turn the pepper upside down and knock out any remaining seeds. For cut peppers, it is easier to core them by slicing the whole pepper in half lengthwise and pulling out the seeds and ribs.

Roasted Peppers: In my estimation there is almost nothing like freshly roasted peppers in olive oil with just a touch of garlic and salt and pepper. For a long time I resisted roasting the peppers for my favorite antipasto dish, thinking it was just too much trouble. Then, after too tentative beginnings, I finally learned to roast them to perfection. It would have been much easier if I had just been able to watch it being done, but I was working from written directions and knew only how the peppers looked before roasting and after they were peeled.

It really doesn't matter if you want to roast the peppers whole, in halves, or in pieces. One of my favorite cooks prefers to cut the raw peppers into the finished size before starting to roast them. The end result is the same, but it may require more attention to roast whole peppers.

Whether you are going to roast the peppers whole or cut up, the process is pretty much the same. In fact, while they are usually called roasted peppers, they aren't actually baked in the oven like, say, roast beef. Rather, they are broiled, grilled, or singed over an open flame. The key is to have very hot coals, a preheated broiler, or a gas burner set on high, and to have the courage to char the skin until it is completely black. Not only will that make the peppers a cinch to peel, it gives them that wonderful smoky flavor that makes them so special.

My gas grill has lava rocks, and I put the peppers directly on the rocks. If you are grilling over charcoal, bring the rack as close to the coals as you can, or lay the whole peppers directly on the coals. If you are using the broiler in your electric stove, it may be best to at least cut the peppers in half lengthwise and to move the rack as close to the broiler burner as possible. If you have a gas salamander or your broiler is open-flame gas, move the rack up until the peppers are almost in touch with the flame. An open-flame gas burner is fine, too. Simply spear the whole peppers on a long-handled fork and turn them in the flame until well charred. And, in a pinch, I have put the peppers—or at least pieces—directly on an electric burner.

Roast the peppers, turning from time to time so that all the skin becomes black and blistered. The ends will be the most difficult and you may have to hold them down onto the grill. If you are roasting cut-up peppers, they do not need to be turned, as only the skin side should be charred.

Once the skin is crisp and black, place all the peppers in a paper or plastic bag. Seal and let stand 10 to 15 minutes. The charred skin should then peel off easily if you scrape them gently with a knife.

Once peeled, the peppers are ready to be used in salads, sandwiches, terrines, or anywhere else you want the smoky flavor.

Chiles (Hot Peppers)

In the past few years, hot chiles have burst on the culinary scene in a big way. They have created a whole new range of flavors and sensations in American cooking. Other countries, however, have long known the delicious qualities of these fiery morsels. Like many other American "discoveries," hot peppers have now developed almost a cult following. There are magazines and books devoted to them and cook-offs centering around the most volcanic productions possible. There are also commercial condiments, sources of dried and fresh peppers, even sweet confections with the bite of chile. Some chile lovers even sport jewelry and clothing giving homage to the fiery qualities of these vegetables.

But chiles are nothing new. It is believed they existed in South and Central America as long ago as 2500 B.C., where their qualities were extolled, almost worshiped, by the local inhabitants. Well before the arrival of Columbus to the shores of the New World, the Aztecs and Incas knew of the benefits of hot chiles. The Spanish fell under the fiery spell of the chiles and brought them back to Europe (calling them peppers, mistakenly believing they were related to the peppercorn plant). Once in Europe, it wasn't long before the hot little numbers began their worldwide migration. Today, they are enjoyed nearly everywhere: Spain, the Middle East, India, Thailand, China, the Caribbean, Mexico—especially anywhere the climate leans toward the hot and sultry.

While all hot peppers are not the same, and each one adds its own special character and taste to various dishes, there are some general rules to follow.

Fresh chiles are generally hotter than canned ones, and I would only recommend the canned varieties if you cannot find fresh. Hot peppers are very individual. The heat can differ from one pepper of the same variety to another—even on the same bush—and though each variety has a certain range of heat, it should be used only as a rule of thumb. The fire may be all that the uninitiated can detect when they first encounter hot chiles, but each species has its own distinct flavor, some very pronounced, some overshadowed by the raw heat.

The heat in these peppers is caused by a compound called capsaicin, located in the stem and inner ribs. The seeds are hot because they are in close contact with the ribs. Capsaicin can be extremely irritating and must be treated with respect. If mishandled it can cause blisters on hands and skin—it is so concentrated in some varieties that it can even cause severe burns. Capsaicin is especially painful if it gets into your eyes. When preparing hot peppers it is important to use plastic or latex gloves while removing the ribs, membranes, and seeds and cutting up the cleaned chiles. Capsaicin is not water soluble—which is why no amount of water will quench the fire that erupts in your mouth and throat after biting into one.

Remember that anything used to prepare the peppers may absorb some of the capsaicin and thus will transfer the heat to anything else that the utensil or surface touches. A mild solution of chlorine bleach will remove capsaicin from hands, knives, and cutting surfaces; and anything fatty and/or sweet, such as milk, yogurt, sour cream, and ice cream will help calm the heat in your mouth. Sugar, salt, potatoes, bread, and tortillas might aid the distress as well—but not water or beer, which sometimes makes it worse.

Chiles vary widely as far as heat is concerned. In 1912, Wilbur Scoville, an early chilehead, devised a standard for measuring the amount of capsaicin in various species. While the number of Scoville units can vary from zero for bell peppers to more than two hundred thousand for the habañero—reputed to be the hottest of the chiles—most rankings are given as one to ten, with the habañero being about ten.

Some of the more readily available chiles, with their approximate heat ranking listed in parenthesis, are discussed below.

Ancho chiles (5) are dried poblanos. They are deep reddish brown in color. They should be heated in a hot skillet or on a grill for a few minutes before using to bring out the smoky flavor. They can be soaked to rehydrate them and then stuffed or added to sauces such as the classic mole, often served with poultry.

Cayenne (10) are small bright red peppers with almost no taste of their own, but they do pack a wallop as far as heat is concerned. Most often cayennes are dried and sometimes mixed with other dried peppers to be sold as crushed red pepper or ground red (cayenne) pepper. Ground red (cayenne) pepper is usually added to a dish when only heat is wanted.

Chipotle (10) chiles are smoked and dried jalapeños. The flavor is unusual and delicious.

For the most part, these are used in salsas and egg dishes and are generally not seeded.

Habañeros (10+), also known in Jamaica as Scotch Bonnets, are generally thought to be the hottest chiles. They are beautiful lantern-shaped little peppers that range in color from green to orange to deep red. Approach with caution. While they have a lovely aroma and a definite pepper flavor, even a little can blow your head off, if you are not accustomed to their heat.

Jalapeños (8) are pretty little blunt chiles 2 to 2½ inches long. They can range in color from a deep hunter green to bright red and are one of the most readily available hot chiles. Jalapeños are generally quite hot, though you will sometimes come across one that is barely warm, and they can be used in salsas, casseroles, egg dishes, and salads. They are often cut into strips or rounds and fried or pickled.

New Mexican chiles (3 to 4)—formerly known as Anaheim chiles—are 5 to 8 inches long and are bright green or red. They can be used raw and are also good roasted and peeled. They are mild enough to be stuffed.

Pasilla chiles (5) are often mistaken for anchos. They are long dark green chiles when fresh but are usually sold dried. Their wonderful flavor is delicious in rustic sauces.

Piquin chiles (9) are tiny, fiery hot red chiles that are sold both fresh and dried. They are also called chiltecpin or, in North Africa, India, and Mauritius, bird peppers.

Poblano (3 to 6) are long, almost black green chiles that range from almost mild to fairly hot. They can be stuffed, used in Chiles con Queso, incorporated into casseroles, or cut into strips and fried with onions.

Serrano (8) are small thin chiles, littler than jalapeños. The color can range from bright green to orange red. Generally, they become slightly milder as they redden. They have a lovely flavor and are probably the most popular chile in

Mexican cooking, where they are used in everything from salsas to fiery main courses.

Various cultures have attributed many benefits to hot chiles. While they do contain massive amounts of vitamins C and A, and they do no harm to healthy digestive tracts, the capsaicin in them may tend to irritate existing ulcers, and thus they should be avoided or at least indulged in sparingly by ulcer sufferers. One recent study indicates that using hot pepper sauce on raw oysters may help destroy harmful bacteria the oysters may have ingested. The jury is still out on how much pepper sauce you might have to add to accomplish the task, though.

Selection: While you may always grow your own hot peppers, they are becoming much more readily available commercially. If your local supermarket does not carry at least two or three different varieties, they can easily be ordered from mail-order supply houses. However, no matter what variety of fresh hot chiles you may be selecting, choose only those that are fresh looking, smooth skinned, firm, and generally untwisted. Look for those that are bright colored and shiny. Avoid any peppers that are cracked, limp, or shriveled or that show black spots or signs of mold.

Storage and Preparation: Once dried, many chiles can be kept for months, even years. The fresh ones are much more fragile. Store them wrapped in paper towels or place them in a small brown paper bag in the vegetable drawer of the refrigerator and use within a few days or a week at most. Do not seal them in plastic bags. The condensation that collects on the peppers in a sealed bag speeds up spoilage and often causes mold. Check them every day or two to remove any that have begun to spoil.

Unless you, and everyone you are feeding, are used to the heat of fresh (or dried) chiles, it is best to remove the stem, ribs, and seeds, which contain most of the heat. Remember, the cap-

saicin in chiles can cause painful blisters and/or burns, so treat chiles with respect. I recommend using latex or plastic gloves when handling chiles, splitting them lengthwise, cutting out the stems, ribs, and seeds—even when washing them. Avoid putting your fingers anywhere near your mouth, eyes, or skin. Everything used in their preparation should be washed in a solution of water and chlorine bleach to remove most of the capsaicin from their surfaces.

Hot chiles can also be roasted like sweet peppers (page 258), but remember, cooking does not take away the fiery effects. Use gloves while peeling, seeding, and preparing roasted chiles, just as you would for raw ones.

Three-Pepper Sauté

Serve this very colorful vegetable hot, with grilled swordfish or chicken breast. I also like it at room temperature as part of an antipasto buffet or with cold roast veal.

Makes 6 to 8 servings

3 tablespoons pure olive oil
1 large onion, peeled, halved and thinly sliced
1 large red bell pepper, seeded and cut lengthwise into strips
1 large green bell pepper, seeded and cut lengthwise into strips
1 large yellow or orange bell pepper, seeded and cut lengthwise into strips
2 cloves garlic, minced
½ teaspoon dried thyme
½ teaspoon dried oregano
Salt and freshly ground black pepper to taste

Heat the olive oil in a large heavy skillet over low heat. Add the onion and cook, stirring, until translucent, 10 to 15 minutes. Stir in the peppers and garlic. Cook, stirring, until the peppers are tender, but the colors are still very vibrant, 10 or 15 minutes longer. Season well with the thyme, oregano, salt, and pepper. Serve very hot or at room temperature.

Grilled Pepper and Bean Salad

A crusty grilled butterflied leg of lamb is the perfect foil for this delicious easy-to-make salad, but it goes well with any cold roast meat, too.

Makes 6 servings

Pure olive oil
2 large bell peppers, halved and seeded
2 large onions, halved lengthwise
1 clove garlic, minced
1½ cups cooked white beans, such as cannellini, navy, or Great Northern, chilled
2 to 3 tablespoons chopped fresh oregano
⅓ to ½ cup extra-virgin olive oil
2 tablespoons balsamic vinegar
Salt and freshly ground black pepper to taste
½ cup ripe cherry tomatoes, halved
⅔ cup crumbled feta cheese

Prepare a fire in a barbecue grill or preheat the broiler.

Brush the pepper halves and onion halves with the pure olive oil. Place them on the grill or broiler rack 3 to 4 inches from the heat and grill until lightly charred (the peppers will not be peeled, so they do not need to be blackened) and tender when pierced with a fork, 15 to 20 minutes. Turn the vegetables several times. Cool.

Cut the peppers and onions into strips. Toss with the garlic, beans, and oregano. Beat together the oil and vinegar, pour over the salad, and toss. Season well with salt and pepper.

Serve at room temperature, tossing with the cherry tomatoes and cheese at the last minute. Pass a pepper mill with the salad.

Roasted Peppers in Olive Oil

Serve these for lunch or late supper, with lots of cheese, cold roast chicken, and plenty of crusty bread. I like to combine them with thick slices of vine-ripened tomatoes and fresh mozzarella cheese. A dusting of freshly ground pepper and a little salt, especially sea salt, make it a wonderful first-course salad—or a light lunch with lots of good bread for soaking up the olive oil.

Makes 6 to 8 servings

6 to 8 bell peppers, red, green, or both
1 clove garlic, halved lengthwise and very thinly sliced crosswise
Extra-virgin olive oil
Fresh oregano sprigs
Salt and freshly ground black pepper to taste

Prepare a fire in a barbecue grill or preheat the broiler.

Place the peppers on the grill/broiler rack about 2 inches from the heat and cook, turning, until well charred, virtually black, on all sides, about 15 minutes or more. Place the charred peppers in a plastic or paper bag. Close tightly and let stand for 10 minutes. Peel the peppers, seed them, then cut into thick slices or quarters.

Arrange the peppers in a pretty serving dish. Sprinkle with the garlic. Drizzle with the extra-virgin olive oil and garnish with the oregano. Chill several hours.

Warm to room temperature to serve. Pass lots of crusty bread, salt, and a pepper mill.

Note: *If you want to preserve these peppers longer than a day or two, pour in enough olive oil to cover them completely. They will be fresh for several days. Drain well before serving, saving the olive oil to use for salad dressings.*

Oven-roasted Peppers and Pasta

Make this in midsummer with the freshest sweet peppers you can find. I like to serve it with grilled chicken or fish, such as tuna or mako shark. Besides red and green bell peppers, you can use any mix of colors for this dish except brown and purple.

Makes 6 servings

4 large bell peppers, 2 red and 2 green, halved, seeded, and thickly sliced
2 large onions, cut into thick slices
2 to 3 tablespoons olive oil
1/3 cup chopped fresh parsley
3 tablespoons chopped fresh oregano
3 cloves garlic, minced
2 cups cherry tomatoes, halved
Salt and freshly ground black pepper to taste
1 pound small pasta shapes, such as shells, bow ties, rigatoni, or radiatore, cooked and kept hot
Freshly grated Parmesan cheese

Preheat the oven to 400°F.

In a large bowl, toss the peppers and onions in the olive oil. Spread them in a shallow roasting pan. Roast in the oven, turning the vegetables from time to time with a spatula, until they are tender and beginning to brown, 30 to 45 minutes. Sprinkle with the parsley, oregano, garlic, and cherry tomatoes. Season well with salt and pepper. Roast 5 minutes more. Remove the roasting pan from the oven.

Toss the pasta with the roasted vegetables and pile in a heated serving bowl. Sprinkle with the cheese and serve very hot.

> Note: These vegetables are also delicious if tossed with cooked cheese-stuffed tortellini or mini cheese ravioli.

Peppers Stuffed with Rice and Corn

These are so delicious you will want them often. Serve them alongside roast chicken or baked chicken breasts.

Makes 6 servings

2 tablespoons pure olive oil, plus additional for greasing
1 small onion, minced
1 small (or 1/2 large) red bell pepper, seeded and minced
1 clove garlic, minced, or more to taste
1 teaspoon ground cumin
1/4 teaspoon crushed red pepper (optional)
1/2 cup fresh corn kernels cut from the cob (about 1 ear), or 1/2 cup thawed frozen corn kernels
2 cups cooked (about 2/3 cup raw) long-grain rice
3 tablespoons chopped fresh cilantro
Salt and freshly ground black pepper to taste
6 medium-size green bell peppers, seeded and steamed 5 to 6 minutes, or microwaved on high for 4 minutes
1/2 cup grated Monterey Jack cheese
Extra-virgin olive oil (optional)

Preheat the oven to 350°F. Using some pure olive oil, lightly grease a shallow baking dish large enough to hold the stuffed peppers in one layer.

Heat 2 tablespoons of pure olive oil in a medium-size heavy skillet over medium heat. Add the onion and red bell pepper and cook, stirring, until just translucent, about 10 minutes. Stir in the garlic and cook 1 minute longer. Season with cumin and crushed red pepper. Stir in the corn, rice, and cilantro. Season well with salt and pepper to taste.

Stuff the green bell peppers with the mixture, mounding it slightly, and sprinkle each filled pepper with cheese. Arrange the peppers upright in one layer in the prepared baking dish.

Bake until very hot, the cheese is melted, and the peppers are crisply tender but not collapsed, 25 to 30 minutes. Serve very hot, or cool to room temperature. If served at room temperature, pass a little extra-virgin olive oil separately for drizzling over the top of each.

Fried Peppers and Onions

Grilled veal chops are a perfect companion to these luscious peppers, but they also go well with a well-flavored meat loaf. Use them as part of an antipasto buffet or pile them onto grilled Italian sausages in crusty rolls.

Makes 6 servings

2 tablespoons olive oil
8 large Italian banana or frying peppers, seeded and cut into strips
2 large onions, halved lengthwise and cut lengthwise into strips
1 teaspoon dried Italian herbs, such as oregano, marjoram, rosemary, and thyme, or a prepared mix
Salt and freshly ground black pepper to taste

Heat the oil in a medium-size heavy skillet over medium heat. Stir in the peppers and fry, stirring, until translucent, 18 to 20 minutes. Stir in the onions and herbs, and fry, stirring, until the peppers and onions are golden, about 15 minutes longer. Season with salt and pepper. Serve hot.

Note: *I also like this at room temperature on a cold buffet along with ham, salami, sausages, and plenty of cheeses.*

Three-Cheese Stuffed Banana Peppers

Nothing goes better with spicy slices of barbecued beef and beans than one or two of these delicious peppers. Of course, if there are some hot Italian sausages around, you might want to grill them to serve alongside. The peppers can be stuffed in advance and baked when ready to serve. If they are still cold from the refrigerator, add 5 to 10 minutes to the cooking time.

Makes 6 servings

6 ounces Monterey Jack cheese, grated (1½ cups)
6 ounces Cheddar cheese, grated (1½ cups)
½ cup ricotta cheese
3 tablespoons chopped fresh cilantro, or parsley
12 golden or pale green banana peppers, slit tip to stem and seeded, steamed until soft enough to stuff without tearing, 3 to 4 minutes, or microwaved on high for 1 minute
1 cup prepared enchilada sauce, hot (my preference) or mild

Preheat the oven to 375°F.

In a large bowl, combine the cheeses. Stir in the cilantro. Stuff the mixture into the peppers, mounding it a little.

Spoon half of the enchilada sauce into the bottom of a large shallow baking dish. (Glass or pottery is nice to serve from.) Arrange the peppers in one layer, the open side up.

Pour the remaining sauce over the filled peppers. Bake until the cheese is melted and the sauce is bubbling, 30 to 35 minutes. Serve very hot with the sauce spooned over the peppers.

Variation: *For a delicious easy supper dish, add 2 chorizo sausages, chopped, to the cheeses. Bake and serve hot with a green salad and warm tortillas or crusty sourdough French bread.*

Peperonata

Serve these versatile vegetables with an omelet, fried or scrambled eggs, cold roast meats, or grilled tuna.

Makes 6 servings

¼ cup olive oil
1 large onion, chopped
2 ribs celery, trimmed, strung if necessary, and chopped
4 large bell peppers (all green or a combination of red, green, and yellow), seeded and cut into ¼-inch slices

1 serrano chile, seeded and minced
4 large ripe tomatoes, peeled, seeded,
    and chopped
2 cloves garlic, very thinly sliced, or more
    to taste
Salt and freshly ground black pepper to taste
2 tablespoons chopped fresh oregano

Heat the olive oil in a large heavy saucepan or skillet over medium heat. Add the onion, celery, and peppers and cook until the vegetables just begin to turn golden along the edges, about 10 minutes. Stir in the chile, tomatoes, and garlic. Season well with salt, pepper, and oregano.

Reduce the heat to low and cook until the vegetables are very tender, about 20 minutes. Remove from the heat, stir, and cool to room temperature. Refrigerate for a day or two if you wish, but warm to room temperature to serve.

Zucchini, Cheese, and Chiles

This colorful dish might be a good way to ease into cooking with hot chiles. The zucchini benefits from the wonderful flavor of New Mexican chiles without being overshadowed by the heat.

Makes 6 servings

1 tablespoon pure olive oil
1 bunch (6 to 8) green onions (scallions), white
    and light green parts only, thinly sliced
2 New Mexican chiles, roasted, peeled, seeded,
    and finely chopped
2 medium-size ripe tomatoes, peeled, seeded, and
    coarsely chopped
1/4 cup chicken stock
4 small zucchini, trimmed and cut into
    1/4-inch slices
Salt to taste
1 cup grated Monterey Jack cheese

Heat the oil in a large heavy skillet over medium heat. Add the green onions and chiles and cook

until softened, 2 to 3 minutes. Stir in the tomatoes and cook, stirring, for 2 minutes longer. Stir in the stock and the zucchini. Season with salt. Simmer the zucchini over low heat until crisply tender, about 10 minutes.

Stir in the cheese and cook 1 minute, or until the cheese is just melted. Serve hot.

Chiles con Queso

Make your own tortilla chips to serve with this delicious cheese and chile dish. It is also wonderful as a hot dip for crisp raw vegetables, such as broccoli, celery, fennel sticks, and so on. I like to serve it spooned over new potatoes boiled in their jackets and cut up on the plate—unorthodox, but a perfect companion to grilled pork chops.

Makes 6 to 8 servings if spooned over potatoes

2 tablespoons pure olive oil
1 large onion, finely chopped
2 small cloves garlic, minced, or more to taste
2 large ripe tomatoes, peeled, seeded,
    and chopped
6 fresh poblano chiles, roasted, peeled, seeded,
    and chopped
Salt to taste
8 ounces Monterey Jack cheese, grated (2 cups)

Preheat the oven to 375°F.

Heat the oil in a medium-size heavy skillet over medium heat. Add the onion and garlic and cook, stirring, until translucent, about 5 minutes. Stir in the tomatoes and chiles and cook just until the chiles are wilted, about 3 minutes longer. Remove the pan from the heat, and season the mixture with salt. Turn the mixture into a 1 1/2-quart deep ovenproof casserole. Stir in one-third of the cheese. Spread the remaining cheese on top.

Bake until the cheese is bubbling and golden brown, 15 to 20 minutes. If using as a dip, put the casserole as is on a serving platter, surrounded by crisp tortilla pieces or vegetables. If you will be spooning it over potatoes, stir to combine before serving. Serve very hot.

New Potatoes, Onions, and Chiles

I like to use the tiniest new potatoes that I can come by for this dish: brown skinned, red, or yellow, or a mixture of colors. Serve it with grilled fish.

Makes 6 servings

3 tablespoons olive oil
1 tablespoon soy sauce
1 pint (10 ounces) boiling onions, boiled in water to cover for 1 minute, drained, and peeled; or one-half 16-ounce package frozen baby onions, thawed
2 pounds smallest (about 1 inch in diameter if available) new potatoes, simmered in salted water to cover until just tender, 8 to 10 minutes, and drained
1 small jalapeño chile, seeded and minced
¼ cup dry white wine
¼ cup chicken stock
3 tablespoons chopped fresh cilantro

Heat the olive oil in a medium-size sauté pan with sloped sides over medium heat. Stir in the soy sauce and onions. Cook, tossing, until the onions are tender and begin to turn golden brown, about 10 minutes. Add the potatoes, chile, wine, and stock. Simmer until the sauce thickens, tossing to coat the vegetables, 3 to 4 minutes. Serve very hot, garnished with the cilantro.

Pepper, Onion, and Chile Salad

This fresh-tasting salad is all you need to accompany thin slices of grilled skirt steak and crusty baked potatoes.

Makes 6 servings

2 medium-size green bell peppers, seeded and thinly sliced
2 medium-size red bell peppers, seeded and thinly sliced
1 large sweet onion, halved from stem to root, and very thinly sliced
1 large poblano chile, seeded and thinly sliced
2 cloves garlic, minced
⅓ cup olive oil
1 tablespoon red wine vinegar
3 tablespoons chopped fresh cilantro, plus additional for garnishing
Salt and freshly ground black pepper to taste
Leaf lettuce, chilled

Combine the bell peppers, onion, chile, and garlic in a medium-size nonreactive bowl. In a smaller bowl, beat together the olive oil, vinegar, 3 tablespoons of cilantro, salt, and pepper. Toss this dressing with the vegetables. Refrigerate several hours.

To serve, line a medium-size salad bowl (glass or colorful pottery is nice) with the lettuce and mound the chilled pepper mixture in the middle. Garnish with the additional cilantro.

Plantains

Oddly enough, plantains, like bananas, are not natives of the Caribbean or South America. They were first cultivated in Asia thousands of years ago and then made their tortuous way west to the islands, traveling in the company of traders and explorers.

A cousin of the sweet bananas that are eaten by the truckload in this country, plantains are, in reality, a fruit. Like bananas, the riper they become, the sweeter the flesh. Unlike bananas, they must be cooked before eating.

The flavor of unripe plantains is mild and very starchy, a little bit like potatoes, and they make a nice occasional substitute. In some countries, especially in the Caribbean and South America, they are not only the principal starch but are a principal food, served at virtually every meal.

Riper plantains, those with a dark, blackened skin, begin to taste somewhat like a slightly sweet squash and can be prepared much like sweet potatoes: You can bake them, boil them, mash them, and so forth.

Plantains are low in fiber, high in carbohydrates, and provide a good source of vitamin A.

Selection: Except in ethnic markets, plantains are often piled individually in the produce bin, unlike bananas, which are sold in "hands" or small bunches. Look for smooth, firm, unbruised fruit. Do not buy any that have soft spots, cut ends or show any signs of mold. If there is time, you will have a better quality if you ripen plantains at home. Plantains are available all year.

Unless they are very large, you should count one plantain per person.

Storage and Preparation: Green, yellow, and black spotted plantains should be stored at room temperature. Once the plantains are fully ripe and turn completely black, they should be placed in the vegetable drawer of the refrigerator. They will keep a day or two longer, but should be cooked as soon as possible.

Green plantains will ripen at room temperature at home. Simply place them in a cool dry spot. Depending on the original age of the plantains, it could take up to two weeks for them to turn from green to almost completely black. The blacker the skin, the sweeter the flesh.

All plantains, even fully ripe ones, should be cooked before eating. For most recipes they will need to be peeled, but not until they are ready to cook. Fully ripe plantains peel almost as easily as their banana cousins, but green and slightly yellow plantains can be somewhat difficult. The skins seem to stick to the flesh.

To peel green plantains, cut a small slice off each end. Cut the plantain in half across. Use the point of a very sharp knife to make four cuts through the skin lengthwise down the whole length of the vegetable. Take the point of the knife and pry up one corner of one of the strips of peel. Pull off the strip. It may be easier to pull the strip sideways rather than down the length of the plantain. Repeat with the other strips of peel. If you want to use the peeled plantains whole, simply cut off the ends and make the four cuts down the whole length of the vegetable. It may be a little difficult at first, but persevere and it will become easier. The peeled plantains are ready to be sliced.

Baked or Roasted Plantains

This very simple method of cooking plantains makes them a delicious substitute for the ever-popular baked potato. Use green plantains or ones that have only have a slight tinge of yellow. Preheat the oven to 350°F. Place the whole, unpeeled plantains, one per person, directly on the rack in the preheated oven. Bake until very tender when pierced with a sharp fork, 30 to 40 minutes. To serve, remove one strip of peel from the top of each plantain. Mash them slightly with a fork, inside the skin. Season with a little butter, salt, and pepper, just as if it were a baked sweet potato.

Plantain Chips

This is a classic Caribbean recipe, which has a dozen different names. These are twice fried, which makes them a lot of work, but the end result is worth the effort. Not only are these crisp chips delicious with drinks before dinner but they are a perfect accompaniment for steamed fish of any kind, but most especially grouper that has been dressed with a little lime juice and hot pepper sauce.

Makes 6 to 8 servings

3 large green plantains, peeled and sliced thickly on the diagonal
Salt to taste (sea salt is especially good)
Mild vegetable oil, preferably peanut for deep-frying
Hot pepper vinegar to taste

Soak the plantain slices in salted ice water to cover for 30 minutes. Drain and dry well on cloth kitchen towels.

Heat the oil in a deep-fat fryer or very heavy deep skillet to 375°F.

Add the slices of plantain in batches and fry until just beginning to brown, 3 or 4 minutes per batch. Remove from the hot fat with a slotted spoon and spread out on paper towels. Use the flat side of a wide spatula to press the slices hard while they are still hot so they become as thin as possible. Repeat with remaining slices.

Cool the chips and return them to the bowl of salted ice water. Drain well after just 1 or 2 minutes; dry thoroughly on kitchen towels. Just before serving, fry the chips again, in batches, in oil heated to 375°F., until deep golden brown and very crisp, 2 to 3 minutes per batch.

Remove the chips with a slotted spoon, drain well, salt, and serve while still hot. Pass hot pepper vinegar to shake over the chips if you like.

Note: *The peeled plantain can be thinly sliced and fried only once until crisp and golden, 2 to 3 minutes per batch. Serve them hot, salted.*

Candied Baked Plantains

Try these instead of sweet potatoes with roast pork or baked ham.

Makes 6 servings

4 tablespoons ($\frac{1}{2}$ stick) butter, plus additional
    for buttering
$\frac{1}{3}$ cup firmly packed dark brown sugar
$\frac{1}{4}$ cup granulated sugar
$\frac{1}{2}$ teaspoon ground cinnamon
$\frac{1}{2}$ cup apple cider, or unsweetened apple juice
3 very ripe (blackened outside) plantains, peeled
    and halved lengthwise
$\frac{1}{3}$ cup unsalted roasted peanuts, very
    coarsely chopped
Chopped fresh parsley

Preheat the oven to 325°F. Generously butter a shallow baking dish that will just hold the plantains in one layer, cut side up.

Melt 4 tablespoons of butter in a small saucepan over medium heat and stir in the sugars. Add the cinnamon and apple juice. Cook, stirring, until thick and syrupy, 2 to 3 minutes.

Pour the syrup over the plantains, sprinkle the peanuts over the top, and bake until the plantains are very tender, 45 minutes or longer. Baste with the syrup from time to time. Serve very hot, with the syrup spooned over the plantains, garnished with the parsley.

Potatoes

For a tuber that originally developed on this side of the Atlantic, the potato had to follow a circuitous route before it reached North America and finally became our most popular vegetable.

This is a food source that was known to the native inhabitants of South America long (perhaps twelve thousand years) before the Spanish arrived on the scene. Oddly enough, the conquistadors took the vegetable back home to Europe but did not seem to carry it north when they began their explorations of the Pacific coast.

Not that the potato was greeted with open arms in Europe. Even though it had been a major food source among the Incas, the potato was associated with its cousin the deadly nightshade by Europeans, who developed a severe mistrust for the vegetable. The first to readily accept the potato seem to have been the Irish. By the middle of the seventeenth century, it constituted a large part of the diet of the poor. Combined with buttermilk, another Irish staple, the potato provided a complete protein source as well as a substantial amount of vitamin C in an easy to grow, easy to store crop.

In Germany it was not so readily accepted, and it wasn't until a government decree forced farmers to grow the potato that it became widely used. In France, agriculturist Antoine-Auguste Parmentier, who had survived on potatoes in a Prussian prisoner-of-war camp during the Seven Years' War, resorted to reverse psychology to convince his compatriots that potatoes were safe to eat. He grew them in a "secret" field that was guarded by soldiers during the day but not at night. Under cover of darkness curious local farmers "stole" the plants and put them in their own gardens to find out what the secret was all about. Even today in France the word *parmentier* in a recipe title or on a menu usually indicates that the dish contains potatoes.

The potato played a considerable part in the development and industrialization of Europe. Not only was it easy to grow but it provided more nourishment per acre than any grain crop previously cultivated. Better nutrition increased the overall health of the population, leading to lower infant mortality and longer, more productive lives for most people.

Unfortunately, the growing dependency on potatoes as a life-sustaining crop led to one of the greatest tragedies and major population shifts in modern times. By the 1840s, Ireland was virtually a one-crop country, certainly among the poorest of its citizens. In the unusually warm, wet summer of 1845, the potato blight hit for the first time, virtually destroying the entire Irish crop. Before it was over, millions had died of starvation and another million or more had emigrated—mainly to the United States. While the same fungus struck in other countries at the same time, those populations did not depend on the potato as the sole source of nourishment and were able to survive until the blight had been temporarily overcome.

Potatoes are more than a food crop. They have been used in wartime to make a fuel for machinery. The starch is used in cosmetics, glues, paper, medicine, and absorbent materials as well as for machine lubricant and animal fodder. The potato is also the main ingredient in vodka. Like the peanut, the potato seems to have nearly unlimited uses.

There is almost nothing you cannot do to a potato. It can be boiled, steamed, braised, baked, roasted, or fried. It can be sliced, diced, mashed, grated, or pureed; it can be cut into matchstick strips, thick sticks, balls, egg shapes, curlicues, or ruffles. Put potatoes into soups, stews, and casseroles; cook them around roasts; or serve them on their own, sauced or not, depending on your whim.

But not all potatoes do all things well. There are two fundamentally different types of potato—floury (or starchy) and waxy. Starchy potatoes are good for baking and frying and make light, fluffy mashed potatoes. The most readily available starchy potatoes in the United States are the Russet Burbank, usually marketed as Russets or Idahos. These were developed in California by Luther Burbank at the end of the nineteenth century and have become the most widely available Idaho-grown potato.

Waxy potatoes are excellent for boiling as well as for frying and cooking in soups, stews, gratins, and casseroles. But they become gluey when mashed and do not bake up well. There are dozens of varieties of waxy potatoes. The most commonly found are round whites, which have either brown or red skins. Specialty markets and some supermarkets are beginning to carry others. You may find the yellow-skinned and -fleshed Yellow Finn potato, sometimes called the butterless potato because it looks and tastes somewhat richer than its white cousins. Also increasingly available are the Yukon Gold and two popular European varieties, Bintje and Ratte, all yellow-fleshed, rich-tasting varieties. There are also Peruvian Purple and All Blue, with deep indigo blue skins and blue flesh, which are sort of all-purpose potatoes that can be both baked and boiled. I think they are fun to serve but are expensive and frequently in short supply. You might also occasionally come on Cherries Jubilee and Ruby Crescents, which are pink skinned and have a sort of attractive rosy tint to the flesh.

If you cannot find these (and the hundreds of other "boutique" potatoes) in your area, they are readily available by mail—even as "potato-of-the-month"!

All-purpose, or long white, potatoes claim to be just that, all-purpose. Like anything that claims to do everything, they don't do anything extremely well. They do not contain enough starch to fluff up well as a baking or mashing potato, nor are they as waxy as you would really want in a boiling or salad potato. They are at least adequate in all these preparations, though, and in some markets they might be all that is available at some times of the year.

True new potatoes are not a separate type of potato, although some farmers do grow certain varieties specifically to lift early. Generally, they are simply any potato that has been dug up before the normal harvest time. Sometimes they are tiny, like marbles, sometimes almost as large as the full-grown size. The key is the skin. New potatoes have a very thin papery skin that peels off in rolls, especially when rubbed, a little like the bark on a birch tree. Once the potato is fully developed, the skin thickens slightly and clings tightly to the flesh.

New potatoes are often dirty, with dried earth clinging to them, indicating that they have not been prewashed and have been shipped without passing through a storage facility. Real new potatoes are delicious, especially for boiling or making into salads. They are generally only available for a short time at the beginning of each crop, starting in late June and recurring several times until the fall. Occasionally, you can find them in the winter, shipped in from other growing areas.

The skin will also help you tell the difference between long white, all-purpose potatoes and Russet or other starchy baking potatoes. Long whites have a thin, pale brown skin that is smooth to the touch. Baking potatoes have thicker, darker brown skins that are slightly rough to the touch, some with a meshlike pattern on the surface. In my experience, the rougher the skin the better the baker.

Potatoes have taken a beating in this time of diet-conscious living. Although Americans still eat more than 120 pounds of potatoes each every year, it seems that most of them are consumed with a guilty conscience. Potatoes on their own, however, are not fattening. What we put in them or on them certainly is. A medium-size baked or boiled potato, served with just salt and pepper, has less than 120 calories. The rich tasting, buttery-looking Yellow Finns contain the same low number of calories but *taste* as if they have been seasoned with butter. Don't eliminate potatoes from your menu, even if you are on a diet. Instead, eat them baked, mashed, boiled,

roasted, almost any way you like, just minimize the amount of fat calories you add to them in the form of oil, butter, cream, and cheese.

Potatoes can be the perfect food. Combined with dairy products, they provide almost every nutrient needed to survive. They are high in carbohydrates, low in calories, and are fat and cholesterol free. In addition they contain large amounts of vitamins C and B and are a good source of potassium.

Selection: Regardless of whether you are buying starchy baking potatoes or waxy boiling potatoes, look for firm, plump specimens with shallow eyes and no sprouts. Do not buy any that are soft to the touch, wrinkled, or have spade cuts in the surface. Avoid any with black spots or that show signs of mold.

Stay away from potatoes of any kind that have even a slight green tinge to the skin color. This can sometimes be difficult to see in red skinned or the currently popular purple skinned potatoes, but look out for it. Lately, I have been seeing it more often. The green is a chemical called solanine, and it is the result of improper storage and overexposure to light. In large quantities it is poisonous and, at the very least, can cause nausea, cramps, and other stomach distress if one is sensitive to it. If you find green-tinged potatoes at home, I suggest you discard them altogether. In the past, I thought that simply cutting out the green, along with a good margin of the surrounding potato, was good enough. There are indications now, however, that the entire potato will have a high concentration of solanine.

Unless you serve large quantities of potatoes daily, it is probably no more expensive to choose them one at a time than it is to buy them in bulk. I like to pick out my potatoes individually, depending on how I am going to serve them, and I frequently have several different kinds at home at the same time. Buying in sacks or bags often results in finding several that have begun to spoil and must be thrown out, or the sizes may be so varied it is difficult to control portions. The one exception to this observation is when you go to the source and can see what is being bagged. Even so, 50 pounds for five or ten dollars is not a bargain unless you can eat them all before they begin to lose their moisture and spoil.

Choose uniformly sized potatoes for baking so they will all be cooked at the same time. Tiny little waxy ones are fine for boiling and for making into a fancy salad, in which they are only halved or quartered. Large, round white potatoes, whether brown or red skinned, are good for stew, soup, salad, and gratins. The odd-shaped yellow potatoes are excellent for boiling and layering in gratins.

Storage potatoes are available all year long. True new potatoes have several short seasons as each type of potato begins to mature.

Count on 2½ to 3 pounds of potatoes for six people, unless they are being combined with other ingredients, then ¼ pound per person is usually enough.

Storage and Preparation: Under the right conditions, potatoes are long-lasting vegetables. If you have a room that is cool and dry, where the temperature remains around 55°F., unwashed potatoes will store well for up to three months. Be sure to cull them occasionally, removing any that have begun to sprout or spoil. If you must keep them in the kitchen, or some other part of a heated house, the optimum storage time is about three weeks. The longer you store potatoes, the more flavor and vitamin C they will lose. That is why they seem to taste so good in September right after they have been harvested and then appear to become blander as the winter wears on. A good rule is to use potatoes as quickly as you can after buying them.

Do not store potatoes in an unheated garage or shed where the temperature falls below about 50°F. Never put potatoes in the refrigerator. The moisture speeds up the spoiling process, and the cold turns their starch to sugar, giving them an unpleasant sweet taste. Try not to keep apples and potatoes in the same area; the ethylene gas given off by the apples speeds up the spoiling process in the potatoes. Do not store potatoes and onions in the same bin, either; although many ready-made bins seem to indicate they are companionable. The proximity tends to make them both spoil quickly.

Do not wash potatoes until you are ready to prepare them. Then scrub the skins with a brush and cold water. Remove any deep-set eyes and cut out any portions that seem black or appear discolored.

For the most part, don't peel potatoes before cooking, unless the dish calls for raw potatoes that have been sliced or cut up. Cooking with the skin on retains more of the vitamins and minerals—and starch. These tend to leach out into the cooking water if the potatoes have been peeled. Cooked potatoes can be peeled very easily, in fact the skins will almost slip right off.

Once they are cut, potatoes immediately begin to oxidize and turn dark. If they are not going to be cooked right away, this process can be slowed down by soaking the cut potatoes in water. However, soaking also tends to leach out some of the starch. This effect is good when you are making chips or fried potatoes because it will lessen their tendency to stick together in the deep-fat fryer, but it can be a problem when you are making potato pancakes or rosti, for which you want the potatoes to retain a compact shape. The best solution is to prepare the potatoes just before cooking.

Cutting with a carbon-steel knife or cooking cut potatoes in an aluminum saucepan can also turn them an unappetizing shade of brown or gray. Use stainless-steel knives and nonstick or enameled cookware to eliminate the problem.

Boiled Potatoes

While other vegetables may be bland and insipid when boiled, not so potatoes. Simple boiling brings out the true flavor and texture of these appealing tubers, especially those that are bred expressly for a rich nutty taste.

Some old-fashioned cooks felt there was nothing that went so well with poached or baked fish as plain boiled potatoes, skinned, seasoned with salt and pepper, and drizzled with just a little melted butter. I still agree.

I prefer to boil potatoes in their skins. They retain more of their vitamins and minerals and do not become waterlogged. They can easily be peeled afterward if you do not want the skins. For small, true new potatoes, a thin strip of peel can be removed from around the equator of each to keep them from splitting while they cook. It also helps them absorb some of the melted butter you might want to toss them in just before serving.

Unpeeled potatoes don't absorb the salt in boiling, salted water, but the skin does. If you are not going to peel them before serving and plan to eat skin and all, I find adding salt to the water gives a delicious, slightly salty flavor to the potato.

Scrub the number of potatoes you want—try the yellow-fleshed Yellow Finn or Ratte if you find them. Place them in a pan of cold, salted water that covers the potatoes completely. Bring the water to a boil, and then reduce the heat until the water simmers constantly but does not boil vigorously. Cover the pan and simmer over medium-low heat until the potatoes are very tender when pierced with a sharp fork, but do not fall apart. The length of time will vary according to the size and age of the potatoes. Small, really new potatoes will take only about 10 minutes. They should be drained, tossed gently in the pan over the heat until they appear dry, then sauced with butter, salt, pepper, and lots of chopped fresh parsley.

Medium-size, or cut-up potatoes will need 15 to 20 minutes cooking time. They should also be drained and dried. Do not leave cooked potatoes in water as they tend to soak it up and become bland and watery tasting. Whole large potatoes can simmer up to 45 minutes before they are ready to eat. They should be drained, peeled (the skins will almost fall off), and cut up according to the recipe instructions.

Fried Potatoes

One of life's great temptations is fried potatoes. Whether you like them plain, lightly salted, sprinkled with malt vinegar, slathered in catsup, or dipped in mayonnaise, they seem to be everyone's favorite. Some like them string-thin and golden; others love them cut into thick sticks with a little of the peel on each one and fried to a rich dark brown; still others want them somewhere in between. I am not finicky; I like them every way I can get them.

In my estimation, the best fried potatoes are plunged into deep fat twice. While this may seem like a lot of work, it actually makes serving them easier because you can cut, peel, and fry them up to several hours ahead of time and then fry them again just before serving. The potatoes—which will darken if cut too long ahead—retain their color and texture and become crisp on the outside with the creamy interior that is so irresistible.

Scrub the potatoes. Large Russet potatoes make wonderful fries. Peel or not, according to your taste. Cut the potatoes into spears, wedges, shoestrings, or whatever shape you like. Soak the cut potatoes in ice water to cover for at least 30 minutes to remove as much of the surface starch as possible. Dry well on paper or cloth towels. (They must be completely dry before sliding into the hot oil, or the oil will spatter dangerously and boil up excessively.)

Heat the oil in a deep-fat fryer to 375°F. Fry the potatoes in batches, until just beginning to turn light golden brown, 3 to 5 minutes per batch, depending on the size of the cut. Drain on paper towels. Do not crowd the potatoes in the fryer. They should have room enough to float without sticking together.

Just before serving, heat the oil to 400°F. Fry the potatoes again until very hot, well browned, and crisp, 1 to 2 minutes. Drain and serve at once, sprinkled with a little salt. These cannot wait once they have been fried the second time.

Note: *Be sure to allow plenty of headroom in the deep-fat fryer. The oil will boil up when you add the potatoes. You do not want the extremely hot oil to spill over onto the element or floor. A good rule of thumb is to have the container no more than one-third to one-half full of oil.*

Steamed Potatoes

Except for tiny new potatoes, I do not think potatoes steam well, although it is a good way to preserve as many nutrients as possible. But once they are boiled they can be arranged in a colander or the basket of a steamer and kept warm over simmering water.

Arrange potatoes, peeled or not, according to taste, in a steamer basket or a colander. Cover and steam over simmering water until tender, 15 to 20 minutes for small new potatoes and up to 45 to 55 minutes for whole unpeeled potatoes. Check the water level from time to time to keep it from boiling dry.

Microwaved Potatoes

I have not always been a proponent of baking potatoes in the microwave. For a long while, no matter what I did, I produced something resembling a steamed potato with an unpleasant, inedible hard place on the bottom. Then a few years ago I was taken in hand by a representative of the Idaho Potato Commission and was taught how to make an acceptable "baked" potato in a lot less than half the time it takes to bake them conventionally. I still use my conventional oven most of the time, but when the urge strikes at the last minute or I don't want to turn on the oven for a potato or two, I use the Idaho method.

Start with one large Russet potato per person. Wash them, but do not dry. Using a sharp fork, prick the potatoes once or twice.

Wrap each potato separately in a microwave-safe paper towel, using the butcher style of wrap: Lay the potato across one corner of the paper towel. Roll up, folding in the edges as you go to form a compact bundle. Lay the bundles on the turntable of the microwave. If microwaving three or more, arrange them in a circle, end to end. Microwave on high: one to two potatoes will take 6 to 10 minutes; three potatoes need 12 to 14 or 15 minutes; four potatoes require up to 25 minutes or a little longer.

It probably is no time saver to try to microwave more than four potatoes at a time. Remove the cooked potatoes from the microwave and let stand 5 minutes before unwrapping. Serve very hot.

Note: *If your microwave does not have a turntable, turn the potatoes over after half the cooking time has elapsed.*

Tarragon Potatoes

Children like to call these "smashed" potatoes and somehow the rustic texture seems to make them a lot of fun to eat. I like to serve them with roast chicken or duck or with a homely meal of oven-braised beef.

Makes 6 servings

1½ pounds small waxy potatoes, brown, red,
    or yellow skinned, unpeeled, simmered in
    salted water to cover until tender, up to
    20 minutes, depending on size, and drained
3 tablespoons butter
1 tablespoon fresh lemon juice
2 to 3 tablespoons chopped fresh tarragon, plus
    additional for garnishing
Salt and freshly ground black pepper (sea salt is
    especially good)

With a fork, lightly squash the potatoes in the pan, just enough to split the skins and break the flesh slightly. Add the butter, lemon juice, and tarragon to the pan and toss all together to mix. Season well with salt and pepper. Serve the potatoes very hot, garnished with the additional tarragon.

Curried Potatoes

These well-flavored potatoes are delicious, especially with pink slices of roast leg of lamb, or hearty servings of braised beef or veal.

Makes 6 servings

¼ cup mild vegetable oil, preferably peanut
2 small onions, halved and thinly sliced
2 tablespoons hot curry powder
3 to 4 large waxy white potatoes, peeled
    (optional) and cut into large dice
2 cloves garlic, minced
Salt and freshly ground black pepper to taste

½ teaspoon crushed red pepper
1 cup water, or well-flavored chicken stock
⅓ cup heavy cream (optional)

Heat the oil in a large heavy skillet over medium heat. Add the onions and cook, stirring occasionally, until golden brown, about 10 minutes. Stir in the curry powder and cook, stirring, 1 minute to bring out the flavor. Stir in the potatoes and garlic, and cook, stirring, until the potatoes begin to brown, 10 to 15 minutes. Add the water and stir in the red pepper. Simmer, uncovered, until the potatoes are very tender but not falling apart, and the liquid is nearly evaporated, 10 to 15 minutes. If using, stir in the cream and heat thoroughly. Serve very hot.

Gratin Dauphinoise

This is the granddaddy of all potato gratin dishes. Some chefs simmer the potato slices in milk or chicken stock before putting them into the gratin dish, but I think this classic version is much more unctuous. When my children were young, they could practically eat their own weight in these potatoes and loved it when they were on the menu. These are good enough for any dinner party and go very well with roast beef, lamb, or veal.

Makes 6 to 8 servings

3 tablespoons butter, softened, plus additional
    for buttering
6 large waxy white potatoes, peeled, sliced,
    soaked in cold water to cover, well drained,
    and dried on a kitchen towel
Salt and freshly ground black pepper to taste
1 cup heavy cream

Preheat the oven to 300°F. Generously butter a medium-size gratin dish.

Arrange a layer of potato slices, slightly overlapping, in the bottom of the prepared dish. Season with salt and pepper. Repeat until all the potatoes are used, seasoning each layer. Dot the surface with

3 tablespoons of butter. Pour in the cream. Bake until the potatoes are very tender but not mushy, and golden brown on top, 1 to 1¼ hours. Serve very hot.

Variations: *Some classic cooks like to shred the potatoes, soak them in cold water to cover, and then dry them well on a kitchen towel. Then they pile the shredded potato into the prepared gratin dish, season well with salt and pepper, and dot the top with butter. Pour in the cream and bake as above.*

While not classic, 1 cup grated Gruyère cheese can be spread over the top of the potatoes 15 to 20 minutes before the potatoes finish cooking.

Old-fashioned·Creamed Potatoes

This tasty dish from out of the past is still a valid accompaniment to a succulent roast beef. The addition of a little onion gives it just the right shot in the arm to elevate the potatoes out of the remembered state of blandness.

Makes 6 servings

2 tablespoons butter
½ small onion, minced
2 tablespoons all-purpose flour
Salt and freshly ground black pepper to taste
2 cups milk, heated until bubbles appear around the edge and hot
4 large waxy white- or yellow-fleshed potatoes, red, white, or yellow skinned, peeled, cut into cubes, simmered in salted water to cover until just tender, 10 to 15 minutes, and drained
3 tablespoons chopped fresh parsley

Melt the butter in a large heavy saucepan over low heat. Add the onion and cook, stirring, until tender, 5 to 7 minutes. Stir in the flour. Season with salt and pepper. Cook, stirring, without browning for 3 minutes. Pour in the milk, all at once, whisking constantly until smooth. Simmer gently over low heat until thick, 3 to 5 minutes. Stir in the potatoes and cook over low heat until the potatoes are very hot, about 5 minutes.

Check the seasoning and add more salt and pepper if needed. Serve the potatoes very hot, garnished with the parsley.

Pesto Mashed Potatoes

I love the flavor of fresh basil, and I think the character of pesto makes these potatoes something special indeed. They are excellent when served with crusty grilled tuna steaks.

Makes 6 to 8 servings

5 or 6 large Russet potatoes, peeled, cut into large chunks, boiled in salted water to cover until very tender, about 20 minutes, and drained
⅓ cup pesto, prepared or homemade (page 7)
Freshly ground pepper to taste
Heavy cream, heated until bubbles appear around the edge and still hot
Chopped fresh basil

Put the potatoes through a ricer into a large bowl, or mash them with a flat potato masher, adding a little of the potato water if the puree is too thick. Beat in the pesto and season well with freshly ground pepper. Stir in the hot cream, 1 tablespoon at a time, as needed to make the potatoes light and fluffy. Serve the potatoes very hot, garnished with the basil.

Note: *Mashed potatoes are one of those vegetables that reheat beautifully in the microwave. If you are pressed for time or have mashed potatoes left over in the refrigerator, simply spoon them into a microwave dish, cover, vent, and microwave on high for 1 minute. Check and continue microwaving, in 20-second increments, until the potatoes are steaming. Beat with a fork and serve in a heated serving dish.*

Potato Croquettes

Children love these and will eat enormous quantities, dipping them into puddles of ketchup and having contests over who can eat the most.

I haven't found too many grownups who do not like them, either, especially if you serve them alongside juicy home-grilled hamburgers or steak.

Makes 6 servings

3 large Russet potatoes, unpeeled, boiled in
    salted water to cover until just tender, about
    20 minutes, drained, peeled, and grated
    or shredded
1/4 small onion, minced
2 large eggs, beaten
2 tablespoons heavy cream or milk
2 tablespoons finely chopped fresh parsley
Salt and freshly ground black pepper to taste
1 cup plain dried bread crumbs
Mild vegetable oil for deep-frying

In a large bowl, stir together the potatoes, onion, eggs, cream, parsley, salt, pepper, and 1/2 cup of the bread crumbs.

Form by tablespoonfuls into balls or small logs (like Tatertots). Roll the prepared shapes in the remaining crumbs to coat thoroughly. Gently knock off any excess. Lay the coated croquettes on waxed paper to dry slightly, about 10 minutes or longer.

Heat the oil in a deep-fat fryer to 375°F. Fry the croquettes in batches until golden brown, 2 to 3 minutes per batch. Remove from the hot fat, drain on paper towels, and salt. Spread the croquettes on a flat baking sheet and keep hot in a 400°F. oven. Continue until all the croquettes are fried. Serve very hot, sprinkled with salt.

Note: *If you like a smoother croquette, the boiled potatoes may be put through a ricer or mashed instead of being grated.*

Classic Mashed Potatoes

I do not think anything is more satisfying or comforting than a large serving of hot fluffy mashed potatoes. As far as I am concerned there is no entrée that isn't enhanced by them. We all know that Russets make great mashed potatoes. But if you are careful and rice them rather than whip them, yellow-skinned potatoes also make rich-looking and tasting mashed potatoes.

Makes 6 to 8 servings

5 or 6 large Russet or yellow-skinned potatoes
    (about 3 pounds), peeled, cut into large
    chunks, boiled in salted water to cover until
    very tender, 15 to 20 minutes, and drained
3 tablespoons butter, about, to taste
About 1/2 cup cream, milk, or potato water,
    to taste
Salt and freshly ground black pepper to taste

Push the potatoes through a potato ricer into a large bowl. Or mash them with an old-fashioned flat potato masher. Stir in the butter and then add the cream until the potatoes are thick and fluffy. Season well with salt and pepper. Serve very hot, garnished with more butter if you like.

Note: *Often potatoes, especially long whites and other thin-skinned ones, become gluey if they are pureed with an electric mixer or food processor. A ricer eliminates lumps and prevents the glueyness. If you have never used this gadget, once you become accustomed to it, I think you will agree ricing produces deliciously light fluffy potatoes, even with yellow-skinned or other waxy potatoes. A flat potato masher with openings in the flat surface also does a good job, but I think the ricer is quicker and easier.*

Variations: *Once the potatoes are mashed, you might beat in 1/4 cup of snipped fresh chives, freshly grated*

Parmesan cheese, or chopped fresh parsley. Serve very hot. For a slightly different flavor and texture, bake the potatoes in a 375°F. oven until very tender when pierced with a sharp fork, 45 to 60 minutes. Split the skins and scoop the insides into the ricer. Continue with the recipe.

Champ

The Irish knew a good thing when they came on it. Potatoes were a large part of their diet—in the early nineteenth century, potatoes were practically their entire diet—but cooks learned to combine them with various other vegetables to produce wonderfully different flavors. The green onions in this dish give it just the right hint of onion. Serve it with thick grilled lamb chops.

Makes 6 to 8 servings

2 tablespoons butter, plus additional butter for
    serving (optional)
3 bunches (18 to 24) green onions (scallions),
    white and light green parts only, thinly
    sliced
5 to 6 large Russet potatoes, peeled, cut into
    large chunks, boiled in salted water to cover
    until tender, about 20 minutes, and drained
2 tablespoons heavy cream
Salt and freshly ground black pepper to taste

Melt 2 tablespoons of butter in a very small skillet over low heat. Add the green onions and cook, stirring, until tender, about 5 minutes.

Put the potatoes through a ricer into a large heated bowl. Beat in the cooked green onions and any butter that remains in the skillet. Beat in the cream, if needed, a little at a time, until the potatoes are fluffy. Season well with salt and freshly ground pepper. Serve very hot with, if you like, the additional butter.

Variations: For a different flavor, use Yellow Finns or any other yellow fleshed potatoes you find in the market. The result will be rich and buttery looking. You may also substitute buttermilk for the heavy cream. The flavor is just as rich, but the calories are less.

Note: *When this was considered a nursery dish, it was often served like colcannon with vats of melted butter. Each child made a deep well in his or her serving and poured in butter until it threatened to overflow the well. It was traditional to eat from the outside of the serving in, dipping each fork or spoonful into the butter in the center before swallowing it. Heaven.*

Summer Potato Bake with Thyme and Rosemary

I hope you are a gardener or have a gardening neighbor or an excellent farm stand or greengrocer nearby because it is essential that everything be as fresh as possible. Put it alongside a fillet of bluefish or striped bass.

Makes 6 to 8 servings

2 pounds tiny truly new potatoes, unpeeled,
    boiled in salted water to cover until tender,
    10 to 15 minutes, drained, and halved
1 medium-size onion, halved and thinly sliced
2 small (about 8-inch long) zucchini, trimmed
    and cut into $\frac{1}{4}$-inch dice
2 large, ripe tomatoes, peeled, seeded,
    and coarsely chopped
Salt and freshly ground black pepper to taste
3 to 4 tablespoons olive oil
2 teaspoons chopped fresh thyme
1 teaspoon chopped fresh rosemary
2 tablespoons chopped fresh parsley

Preheat the oven to 350°F.

In a large bowl, toss together the potatoes, onion, zucchini, and tomatoes. Season well with salt and pepper. Pile the vegetables into a medium-size gratin dish or shallow baking dish. Drizzle with olive oil and sprinkle with the herbs. Bake until all the vegetables are tender, 25 to 30 minutes. Serve very hot, or at room temperature.

Home-fried Potatoes

I love to add these to a brunch menu that features a light and fluffy omelet that is oozing melted Appenzeller, Comté, or another nutty-tasting Swiss-type cheese.

Makes 6 to 8 servings

2 tablespoons mild vegetable oil, such as peanut, or olive oil
1 tablespoon butter
2 large onions, halved and thinly sliced or chopped
½ large green or red bell pepper, seeded, quartered, and sliced crosswise
2 pounds waxy white potatoes, brown or red skinned, unpeeled, boiled in salted water to cover until tender, 15 to 20 minutes, drained, halved lengthwise, and sliced crosswise
Salt and freshly ground pepper to taste

Heat the oil and butter in a large heavy skillet over medium heat. Add the onions and bell pepper and cook, stirring occasionally, until wilted, about 5 minutes. Add the potatoes and cook, turning often with a spatula to keep the mixture from burning, until golden brown and crusty around the edges, up to 20 minutes. Season with salt and freshly ground pepper to taste. Serve hot.

Variations: *For a little extra character, add 1 small fresh jalapeño pepper, seeded and minced, to the onion and bell pepper. An entirely different, unique flavor can be had by substituting an equal amount of peeled, parboiled sweet potatoes for the waxy potatoes.*

Roasted Potato Skins

Fill these with all manner of good things from homemade chili to creamed spinach to curried vegetables or try any combination of stir-fried vegetables. Serve with baked chicken, homemade Salisbury steak, or miniature meat loaves.

Makes 6 servings

3 large Russet potatoes, unpeeled, baked at 375°F. until tender, abut 45 minutes, and halved lengthwise
1 tablespoon mild vegetable oil, preferably peanut
1 tablespoon butter, melted
1 tablespoon freshly grated Parmesan cheese

Preheat the oven to 475°F.

Scoop out the potato insides, leaving a shell at least ¼ inch thick. Reserve the potato insides for another use.

In a small bowl, stir together the oil, butter, and cheese. Brush the mixture inside the potato shells. Arrange the shells, cut side up, on a baking sheet. Bake until the shells are well browned and crisp, about 10 minutes. Serve these shells very hot, filled with other vegetables.

Potatoes Anna

This is a very rich, but wonderful potato dish. Just contemplating the amount of butter might cause some people cardiac distress, but once in a great while this is the perfect very special dinner vegetable. Serve it with a whole grilled fish, such as red snapper, or with roast poultry of any kind.

Makes 6 large or 8 to 10 small servings

5 tablespoons (⅓ cup) butter, melted and clarified (see Note)
2 pounds large Russet potatoes, peeled, very thinly sliced, and well dried on kitchen towels
Salt and freshly ground black pepper to taste

Preheat the oven to 450°F.

Pour 2 tablespoons of the butter into the bottom of a *pommes de terre Anna* pan or a heavy 9-inch skillet. Arrange one layer of potato slices in an overlapping circular pattern over the entire bottom of the skillet. Season well with salt and pepper. Spoon a little melted butter over the potatoes. Arrange another layer of potatoes on top of the first. Spoon a little more butter over the finished layer. Continue making thin layers of potato, spooning a little butter over each and seasoning with salt and pepper, until all the potatoes are used up. Season the whole with salt and pepper. Using a wide spatula or wooden spoon, press the layers down hard to compress them into a thick cake, taking care not to break up the slices.

Cover the skillet tightly with a close-fitting lid or aluminum foil. Place it in the oven and bake 20 minutes. Remove the foil and bake until the surface is golden brown and crisp, about 20 minutes longer. (If using a *pommes de terre Anna* pan, simply turn the pan over and return it to the oven with the cover on.) Invert the potato cake onto a heated serving plate. Serve the potatoes very hot, cut into wedges.

> Note: *To clarify butter, melt it over low heat until the clear yellow fat rises to the top and the white milk solids along with any water fall to the bottom. Pour off the golden butter and throw away the rest.*

> Tip: *In France there are beautiful, special heavy tin- or stainless steel-lined copper pans with deep covers and two stubby handles for making pommes Anna. But any heavy, round covered skillet will do. The secret is to slice the potatoes as thinly as possible. The end result should be creamily tender inside, crisp and golden on the outside.*

Potato and Mushroom Gratin

This rich, cold-weather dish may be just the thing for dinner after a hard day on skis. I think it is very good with thick grilled veal chops, but it is equally delicious with roast beef or poultry.

Makes 6 servings

3 tablespoons butter, softened, plus additional for buttering
½ pound shiitake (stems discarded), portabella, or other full-flavored mushrooms, stems trimmed and cut into thick slices
2 cloves garlic, minced
¼ cup chopped fresh parsley
5 large waxy white potatoes, brown or red skinned, unpeeled, boiled in salted water to cover until just tender, 15 to 20 minutes, drained, and thinly sliced
Salt and freshly ground black pepper to taste
1 cup well-flavored chicken stock
⅓ cup freshly grated Parmesan cheese

Preheat the oven to 350°F. Generously butter a medium-size gratin dish.

Melt 2 tablespoons of the butter in a medium-size heavy skillet over medium heat. Add the mushrooms and cook, stirring occasionally, until just beginning to turn golden brown, about 5 minutes. Stir in the garlic and parsley and cook 2 minutes longer. Remove from the heat and set aside.

Arrange half the potatoes in one layer in the prepared dish. Spread the mushrooms on top. Season well with salt and pepper. Arrange the remaining potatoes on top. Dot with the remaining 1 tablespoon butter and pour in the stock. Sprinkle with the cheese.

Bake until the dish is bubbling hot and golden brown on top, 30 to 45 minutes. Serve very hot.

> Note: *If you are serving this as part of a meal after watching the game, skiing, or sailing or at the end of a long day of trying to catch up on those chores that never get done, prepare everything and put the dish together in the morning.*
>
> *Do not pour the chicken stock into the dish or top with the cheese until just before baking. Bake an extra 5 to 10 minutes if the dish is still cold when you put it in the oven.*

Three-Cheese Potatoes with Sautéed Tomatoes

These are very hearty potatoes. I recommend them for teenage boys or as a filling snack for Super Bowl watchers. They are also delicious as a luncheon dish, with a small green salad on the side and some good hot bread. If you have a group with big appetites, put these on the same plate as a thick slice of roast beef. This recipe is also very good without the tomatoes.

Makes 6 servings

6 medium-size Russet potatoes, unpeeled, baked at 375°F. until very tender, about 1 hour
Freshly ground black pepper to taste
²/₃ cup grated extra-sharp Cheddar cheese
²/₃ cup grated Monterey Jack cheese
²/₃ cup grated fontina cheese
Sautéed Tomatoes (recipe follows)
1 teaspoon dried Italian herbs, such as oregano, marjoram, rosemary, and thyme, or a prepared mix

Preheat the broiler.

Make a cut lengthwise through the top of each potato, splitting the potatoes almost in half. Spread them open. Season with pepper. In a medium-size bowl, toss together the cheeses. Fill the opening in each potato with the sautéed tomatoes and top generously with the cheese mixture. Sprinkle each with the Italian herbs.

Place the filled potatoes on a baking sheet. Broil about 6 inches from the element until the cheese melts and bubbles, 3 to 5 minutes. Serve at once, very hot.

Sautéed Tomatoes

Makes about 1 cup

1 tablespoon olive oil
1 bunch (6 to 8) green onions (scallions), white and light green parts only, thinly sliced
1 small clove garlic, minced
2 medium-size tomatoes, peeled, seeded, and chopped
3 tablespoons tomato sauce, homemade or prepared
Salt and freshly ground black pepper to taste
½ teaspoon dried Italian herbs, such as oregano, marjoram, rosemary, and thyme, or a prepared mix

Heat the olive oil in a small skillet over low heat. Add the onions and garlic and cook, stirring occasionally, until just translucent, about 5 minutes. Add the tomatoes and cook 5 minutes longer. Stir in the tomato sauce, season well with salt, pepper, and herbs. Simmer for 10 minutes. Serve hot.

Potatoes and Tomatoes au Gratin

I like to serve this easy dish with pot roast or meat loaf, but it is delicious enough to accompany a wonderful grilled steak or fish.

Makes 6 servings

3 tablespoons butter
4 large Russet potatoes, unpeeled, baked at 375°F. until just tender, about 45 minutes, peeled, and very thickly sliced
Salt and freshly ground black pepper to taste
1 large onion, thinly sliced
3 cloves garlic, minced
3 large ripe tomatoes, seeded and cut into ¼-inch dice; or one 16-ounce can diced tomatoes, well drained
1 tablespoon Dijon-style mustard
⅓ cup plain dried bread crumbs
2 tablespoons chopped fresh parsley

Preheat the oven to 450°F.

Melt 2 tablespoons of the butter in a small saucepan over medium heat and then, in a large bowl toss it gently with the potatoes. Arrange the buttered potato slices in the bottom of a medium-size gratin dish or shallow ovenproof casserole. Season well with salt and pepper.

Melt the remaining butter in a heavy skillet over medium heat. Add the onions and garlic and cook, stirring, until just wilted, 6 to 8 minutes. Stir in the tomatoes and cook until just tender, about 5 minutes. Season with salt and pepper and stir in the mustard. Spread the tomato mixture evenly over the potatoes.

Mix the bread crumbs and parsley in a small bowl and spread over the tomatoes. Bake until very hot, bubbling, and golden brown on top, about 20 minutes or a little longer.

Note: The gratin can be put together, except for the bread crumbs, ahead of time and refrigerated for several hours. Bring to room temperature, spread with the crumbs, and bake—but increase the cooking time to 25 or 30 minutes.

Oven-fried Potato Chips

If you do not like deep-fat frying, these crisp chips may be just what you are looking for. Pile them on a plate alongside grilled fish fillets or pair with juicy grilled bratwurst on long rolls. Make a big bowl to serve, hot, the next time the crowd convenes for a TV ball game.

Makes 6 servings

Mild vegetable oil or cooking oil spray
3 large Russet or all-purpose long white potatoes, peeled, thinly sliced, and soaked in ice water to cover
2 tablespoons olive oil
Salt to taste
Malt vinegar (optional)

Preheat the oven to 400°F. Lightly grease or spray one or two large baking sheets.

Drain and dry the potato slices on kitchen towels. In a large bowl, toss them with the olive oil. Spread the chips in one layer on the baking sheets. Bake in the hot oven until the chips are beginning to brown, up to 20 minutes. Remove the pans from the oven and turn the chips over. Bake until crisp and golden, 15 to 20 minutes longer. Dust with salt and serve very hot. Pass a shaker of malt vinegar if you like.

Oven-roasted Potatoes

The small quantity of oil used here is enough to keep these crisp potato wedges from sticking to the baking sheet and helps them turn a delightful golden brown. These are delicious if served with a savory dip—such as blue cheese or Ranch. I like them alongside thick, juicy, homemade hamburgers on sourdough rolls.

Makes 6 to 8 servings

5 large Russet potatoes, or large waxy round potatoes with brown or red skins, unpeeled, halved horizontally and cut into thick wedges
1 to 2 cloves garlic, minced (optional)
1 tablespoon olive oil
Salt and seasoned pepper, such as Mrs. Dash, to taste

Preheat the oven to 375°F.

In a large bowl, toss the potatoes, garlic (if using), and olive oil together. Season with salt and pepper. Spread the potatoes in one layer on a baking sheet with sides.

Roast, turning the potatoes several times with a wide spatula, until golden brown and crisp. This will take 45 to 60 minutes. Serve very hot.

Variation: Combine 2 tablespoons Old Bay crab seasoning and 2 tablespoons grated Parmesan cheese in a plastic bag. Toss the oiled potato wedges in the seasoning. Do not season with salt and pepper. Spread the seasoned potatoes in one layer on a baking sheet with sides. Continue with the recipe. These potatoes are spicy. If you like them even more peppery, increase the amount of the Old Bay seasoning. If Old Bay is not available, chili powder can be substituted.

Half-baked Potatoes

These are quite good when you want the goodness of potatoes, but are looking for less on the plate than a whole baked potato. I like them for brunch along with an omelet, maybe one with a sour cream, green onion, and smoked salmon filling.

Makes 6 servings

**3 large Russet potatoes, unpeeled, halved
    lengthwise
3 tablespoons butter, melted
1 tablespoon freshly grated Parmesan cheese
Snipped fresh chives**

Preheat the oven to 350°F.

Score the cut surface of the potatoes in a cross-hatched pattern with a sharp knife. Combine the butter and cheese in a small bowl. Spread this mixture on the scored halves of the potatoes. Let it soak in for 5 minutes.

Place the potato halves cut-side down on a baking sheet. Bake until very tender, 35 to 45 minutes. Turn the potatoes over. Serve very hot, garnished with the chives.

Potato Lasagna

Next time you want to grill some spicy hot Italian sausages, serve them with generous squares of this delicious potato dish. I also think this goes well with baked fish fillets.

Makes 6 to 8 servings

**2 tablespoons olive oil, plus additional
    for greasing
1 small onion, minced
2 cloves garlic, minced
1 tablespoon chopped fresh thyme
1 cup homemade tomato sauce, or good-quality
    prepared marinara sauce**

**4 large Russet potatoes, peeled, thinly sliced
    lengthwise, boiled in salted water to cover for
    3 minutes, drained, well dried, and separated
    into individual slices
1 cup skim-milk ricotta cheese
1 cup grated mozzarella cheese
Salt and freshly ground black pepper to taste
1/4 cup freshly grated Parmesan cheese, plus
    additional for serving**

Preheat the oven to 375°F. Generously oil a shallow 9-inch square glass or other baking dish.

Heat 2 tablespoons of oil in a medium-size heavy skillet over medium heat. Add the onion and garlic and cook, stirring from time to time, until translucent, about 10 minutes. Stir in the thyme and tomato sauce and simmer over low heat for 5 minutes longer. Set aside.

Layer one-third potatoes in the bottom of the prepared dish. Spoon half the tomato mixture over the potatoes. Top with half the ricotta and then half the mozzarella. Repeat the layers. Finish with the final one-third of the potatoes. Season well with salt and pepper. Sprinkle with the Parmesan cheese.

Cover and bake for 25 minutes. Uncover and bake until the potatoes are very tender and the top is golden brown, 10 to 15 minutes longer. Serve this very hot and pass the additional Parmesan cheese.

Souffléed Potatoes with Green Onions and Chives

If you can find thick slices of calves' liver to grill to tender pinkness, these potatoes will be just the thing to round out the menu.

Makes 6 servings

**3 large Russet potatoes, unpeeled, baked at
    375°F. until tender, about 1 hour, each
    halved lengthwise, insides scooped into a
    large bowl, leaving a 1/4-inch shell
2 tablespoons butter, plus 1 tablespoon
    melted butter**

3 tablespoons heavy cream or buttermilk
1 bunch (6 to 8) green onions (scallions), white
    and light green parts only, chopped
2 large eggs, separated, whites beaten until stiff
Salt and freshly ground black pepper to taste
3 tablespoons snipped fresh chives

Preheat the oven to 375°F.

Put the potato through a ricer or mash with a potato masher. Beat in 2 tablespoons of butter and the cream. Stir in the green onions. Beat in the egg yolks. Season well with salt and pepper and stir in half of the chives. Carefully fold in the beaten egg whites. Spoon this mixture into the potato shells, mounding slightly. Brush the surface of each lightly with a little melted butter.

Bake the filled potatoes for 30 minutes, or until puffed and golden brown. Serve very hot, garnished with the remaining chives.

Variation: *Beat ¼ cup freshly grated Parmesan cheese into the potato mixture just before folding in the egg whites.*

Twice-baked Spinach Potatoes

I love to serve these with crisply roasted Cornish hens, counting one hen for every two diners. They are also delicious with grilled flank steak. These potatoes will be light and fluffy, but will not be as puffy as souffléed potatoes.

Makes 6 servings

3 large Russet potatoes, unpeeled, baked at
    375°F. until tender, about 1 hour, halved
    lengthwise, insides scooped into a large bowl,
    leaving a ¼-inch shell
3 tablespoons butter
2 to 3 tablespoons heavy cream
1 large egg, beaten
½ cup finely chopped, cooked fresh spinach, well
    pressed to squeeze out as much liquid as
    possible; or one 10-ounce package frozen
    chopped spinach, thawed, rechopped as finely
    as possible, and squeezed until dry

1 bunch (6 to 8) green onions (scallions), white
    part only, minced
Salt and freshly ground black pepper to taste
1 cup grated Cheddar cheese

Preheat the oven to 350°F.

Put the potato through a ricer or mash with a potato masher. Beat in the butter and cream. Beat in the egg. Stir in the spinach and green onions. Season well with salt and pepper. Stir in the cheese.

Spoon the mixture into the potato shells, mounding it. Bake in the oven until well browned, about 30 minutes. Serve very hot.

Rissole Potatoes

Potatoes prepared like this are a classic French accompaniment for poached fish of any kind. Just because it is old-fashioned does not mean it has no place on modern menus. These meltingly tender little morsels with a slightly crisp exterior are almost habit forming, and I generally make half again as many as I think I will need. Since they require some work, make the menu worthwhile, maybe veal scaloppine and fresh spinach.

Makes 6 servings

2 tablespoons butter, or more, up to
    4 tablespoons (½ stick), to taste
2 pounds large waxy white potatoes, red or
    brown skinned, peeled, cut into balls with a
    large melon baller or sharp paring knife,
    boiled in salted water to cover until just
    tender, about 10 minutes, and drained,
    leftover potato reserved for another use
Salt and freshly ground black pepper to taste

Melt the butter in a medium-size skillet over medium heat. Add the drained potatoes and cook, tossing from time to time, until the balls are crisp and golden brown, up to 15 minutes. Season well with salt and pepper and serve very hot.

Variation: *Just before serving, dust the potatoes lightly with a little ground cumin and minced parsley.*

Duchess Potatoes

These potatoes, called pommes de terre à la duchesse *in French, are not only delicious but are spectacular looking when served as a border around an ovenproof serving platter or cutting board that also displays succulent slices of a thick grilled sirloin steak or butterflied leg of lamb.*

Makes 6 servings

2 pounds Russet potatoes, peeled, cut into large chunks, boiled in salted water to cover until tender, 15 to 25 minutes, and drained
2 tablespoons butter, plus 2 additional tablespoons melted butter
3 tablespoons cream
1 large whole egg
2 large egg yolks
Salt and freshly ground white pepper to taste
Pinch grated nutmeg (optional)
Mild vegetable oil or cooking oil spray

Preheat the oven to 425°F. Lightly oil or spray a heavy baking sheet, ovenproof serving platter, or ovenproof cutting board.

Toss the potatoes in a large saucepan over medium heat until all the water is evaporated. Press them through a ricer or mash with a potato masher. Beat in 2 tablespoons of the butter and the cream. Beat in the whole egg and the extra yolks. Season well with salt and pepper. Add the nutmeg if using. (I find Americans do not like the flavor very much.)

Fit a large pastry bag with a large star tip. Fill the bag with the potato mixture and pipe into 2-inch rosettes on the prepared baking sheet. Or pipe a border around the edge of a serving platter or cutting board.

Very gently brush the surface of the potato with the melted butter, taking care not to squash the design. Bake until the edges of the design are golden brown and the potatoes are slightly puffed, 8 to 10 minutes.

Remove the rosettes from the baking sheet with a wide spatula, and serve very hot on heated dinner plates. Or serve from the platter or cutting board directly.

Note: *If you do not have a pastry bag or lack the skill to pipe plump rosettes or garlands, drop the mixture by large spoonfuls onto the prepared baking sheet, platter, or cutting board. Use the tip of a teaspoon to swirl the mounds into a simple design. Brush with melted butter and bake until touched with glints of golden brown.*

Scalloped Potatoes and Peas

At one time it seemed as if Americans would scallop everything, from oysters to tomatoes. Then, like so many cooking trends, scalloping fell out of fashion. With the recent return to heartier foods, I think this delicious combination deserves a tasting. If you like, use a full-flavored, well-skimmed chicken stock instead of the milk for a slightly less rich dish. Serve with barbecued chicken.

Makes 6 servings

3 tablespoons butter, plus additional for buttering
6 large waxy round red- or white-skinned potatoes, unpeeled, sliced
1 large onion, thinly sliced
1 cup freshly shelled green peas, simmered in boiling water to cover for 10 minutes and drained
Salt and freshly ground black pepper to taste
2 tablespoons all-purpose flour
1 cup milk, heated until bubbles appear around the edge and still hot
½ cup cracker crumbs

Preheat the oven to 325°F. Generously butter a 2-quart ovenproof casserole.

Arrange half of the potatoes in a layer in the bottom of the casserole. Top with half of the onion.

Spread two-thirds of the peas over the onions. Season well with salt and pepper. Finish with the remaining potatoes, onions, and peas.

Melt 2 tablespoons of the butter in a medium-size heavy saucepan over medium heat. Stir in the flour and cook, stirring, for 2 minutes. Stir in the milk and beat with a whisk until smooth. Season lightly with salt and pepper. Cook over low heat, stirring from time to time, until thickened, 3 to 4 minutes. Pour this sauce over the potatoes and peas.

Spread the cracker crumbs over the surface. Dot with the remaining butter. Bake until the potatoes are very tender and the casserole is bubbling and golden brown on top, about 1 hour. Serve very hot.

Potato Pancakes

There are two schools of thought when it comes to potato pancakes. While there is little discussion about their overall merit, there are those who like them very thin, crispy all the way through, and those who like only the exterior crisp, with the inside deliciously creamy. You decide which you like—the same recipe will make both, depending on how thick you make the cakes. (The thicker the pancake, the creamier it is inside.) Serve these with applesauce, whole-berry cranberry sauce, sour cream, or horseradish sauce alongside thick slices of roasted pork loin. Be aware that these pancakes are usually consumed with incredible speed and in vast quantities.

Makes 6 servings

1 medium-size onion, minced
2 cloves garlic, grated or pressed
2 large eggs, beaten
3 tablespoons all-purpose flour
1 teaspoon salt
Pepper to taste
3 large Russet potatoes, peeled, grated, or
    shredded, and dried in a kitchen towel
2 tablespoons chopped fresh parsley
Mild vegetable oil, preferably peanut or melted
    clarified butter

In a small bowl, combine the onion, garlic, and eggs. In a medium-size bowl, stir together the flour, salt, and pepper. Beat this mixture into the eggs. Stir the potatoes into the egg mixture. Stir in the parsley.

Heat 1 tablespoon of the oil in a large, heavy skillet over medium-high heat. Using a large spoon, drop spoonfuls of the potatoes onto the hot skillet, flattening them with a wide spatula into very thin or about 1/4-inch-thick pancakes, depending on taste. Fry the pancakes on both sides, turning once, until well-browned and crisp, 5 to 6 minutes per side. Remove to a heated platter. Repeat until all the potatoes are used, adding oil or butter as needed. Serve very hot.

Note: *If you are making these ahead, preheat the oven to 425°F. Arrange the finished pancakes in one layer on a large baking sheet. Bake the pancakes, watching carefully so you not to burn them, until they are hot and crisp again, 7 to 8 minutes.*

Variation: *I have a dear friend who prefers to use mashed potatoes instead of freshly grated ones as the base for his potato pancakes. He starts with 2 cups mashed potatoes—he especially likes to use them leftover from dinner the night before—adds 1/2 small onion, minced; 1 clove garlic, minced; 1 large egg; 2 tablespoons all-purpose flour; 2 tablespoons chopped fresh parsley; and salt and pepper to taste. He refrigerates the mixture for 2 hours. Then he drops it by large spoonfuls onto a preheated griddle or lightly oiled skillet. He fries them until they are golden and crisp on the bottom, turns them, pressing down gently with a wide spatula and fries until browned on the second side. He often adds a little more butter or oil if they begin to stick.*

These pancakes are more fragile than the ones made with grated potatoes. Do not give up if the first two or three fall apart. You will begin to get the hang of it soon enough. One of the secrets is not to turn them more than once. Use the spatula to pick up an edge so you can peek underneath to see if the bottom is browning. Serve very hot. These are best if made and eaten right away.

Jansson's Temptation

This could well be Sweden's national dish. Erik Jansson (or Janson) evidently led such an exemplary life that he only ever gave in to one temptation, this one. Being an anchovy lover, I can certainly see how he fell victim. This is not for the fainthearted. The calorie content is high, and we won't even talk about the cholesterol. But once in a while you might indulge. Frequently in Sweden it is eaten by itself, with a refreshing green salad on the side, but I like to pair it with a tomatoey Swiss steck and a tasty green such as curly kale or collards.

Makes 6 to 8 servings

3 tablespoons butter, plus additional for buttering
2 large onions, thinly sliced
5 large waxy white or yellow-fleshed potatoes, peeled, cut into $1/4$-inch-thick slices and then into matchstick strips, soaked in cold water to cover for 5 minutes, drained, and dried on a kitchen towel
One 2-ounce can flat anchovy fillets, or more to taste, drained and rinsed if you like
Freshly ground black pepper to taste
1 cup heavy cream
Chopped fresh parsley (not traditional, optional)

Preheat the oven to 375°F. Generously butter a $1\frac{1}{2}$-quart deep ovenproof casserole or baking dish.

Melt 2 tablespoons of the butter in a medium-size heavy skillet over medium heat. Add the onions and cook, stirring occasionally, until tender, 10 to 15 minutes.

Arrange one-third of the potatoes in the bottom of the prepared dish. Top with half the onions and then half the anchovies. Season with pepper. Repeat the layers. Finish with the remaining one-third of the potatoes.

Pour in the cream and dot with the remaining 1 tablespoon of butter. Bake, uncovered, until the potatoes are well cooked, very tender, and have absorbed all the cream, 45 to 60 minutes. Serve on heated dinner plates, dusted with the parsley if you like.

Note: *I have also eaten this with the anchovy oil from the can drizzled over the potatoes before they were cooked, but I think it is a bit strong that way, and I love anchovies.*

Butterfly Bakes

These take a little effort, but everyone seems to enjoy them very much. Children like these when they are made with smaller potatoes such as Yellow Finn or Rattes. They will often eat two.

While they are cooking, they open up, a little like butterfly rolls. If you do not have chopsticks, the handles of 2 wooden spoons will do quite well. Serve with barbecued ribs or chicken.

Makes 6 servings

6 small to medium-size Russet potatoes, unpeeled
2 tablespoons olive oil
1 tablespoon butter, melted
2 cloves garlic, pressed
2 tablespoons minced fresh parsley
Salt and freshly ground black pepper to taste

Preheat the oven to 400°F.

Place one chopstick lengthwise on one side of one potato. Place a second chopstick parallel to the first on the other side of the potato. Using a sharp knife, slice the potato across into $1/4$-inch slices, cutting down only to the level of the chopsticks. Do not cut the slices completely through the potato or it will fall apart. Repeat with the other potatoes.

In a small bowl, combine the olive oil, butter, garlic, and parsley. Place the potatoes, cut sides up, on a baking sheet. Brush the oil mixture generously over the potatoes, letting it drip a little into the cuts. Season with salt and pepper.

Bake about 30 minutes. Remove from the oven, brush again with the oil mixture. Return the potatoes to the oven and bake until tender and golden brown, another 20 to 30 minutes. Serve very hot.

Note: *I have tried these with long white all-purpose potatoes, and while it works, I think they are substantially better when made with Russets.*

Potatoes Polonaise

Polonaise is a nearly forgotten way to garnish vegetables. You can use the same combination for green beans, sugar snap peas, zucchini, spinach—almost any vegetable you can think of. Serve these alongside generous portions of poached salmon.

Makes 6 servings

1½ pounds tiniest new potatoes, or small Yellow
    Finn potatoes
3 tablespoons butter
2 large hard-cooked eggs, peeled and very
    coarsely mashed with a fork
3 tablespoons chopped fresh parsley
3 tablespoons plain dried bread crumbs

In a medium-size saucepan, simmer the potatoes over medium heat in salted water to cover until just tender, 10 to 15 minutes. Drain. Add 2 tablespoons of the butter. Cover and cook over very low heat, tossing from time to time, until very tender.

Place the potatoes in a heated serving bowl. Combine the eggs and parsley in a small bowl and sprinkle over the potatoes. In a very small skillet, melt the remaining 1 tablespoon of butter over medium heat. Add the bread crumbs and cook, stirring, until browned, about 5 minutes. Serve the potatoes very hot, garnished with the browned crumbs.

Rösti (Rusty Potatoes)

No matter where you go in Switzerland, especially in the mountains, you will come across some form of this potato cake. *It is truly a national dish, and deservedly so. Often it is served with veal roast or grilled chops or nothing else but a salad. But one restaurant in the mountains used to send out golden rounds of rösti to devour along with monstrous Porterhouse-like steaks, grilled to crusty rare perfection. Whenever I have the chance, I re-create this menu at home.*

Makes 6 servings

4 large Russet potatoes, unpeeled, boiled in salted
    water to cover until just barely tender, 10 to
    15 minutes, peeled, and shredded or grated
Salt and freshly ground black pepper to taste
4 tablespoons (½ stick) butter

Season the potatoes with salt and pepper, tossing them well. Melt 2 tablespoons of the butter in a heavy 10-inch skillet over medium heat. Add the potatoes, pressing down with your hands or the flat side of a wide spatula, to form a large compact cake. Cover with a tight-fitting lid or aluminum foil, and cook until the cake is dark golden brown on the bottom, 10 to 12 minutes or more.

Invert the pancake onto a large flat plate or baking sheet with no rim. Melt the remaining butter in the same skillet. Slide the cake back into the skillet, browned side up. Cook, uncovered, until the second side is browned and crisp on the bottom. Invert the cake onto a heated serving plate. Serve very hot, cut into wedges.

Variations: *Toss with the grated potatoes before turning them into the skillet:* ½ *small sweet onion, minced;* ½ *cup grated Gruyère cheese; or 4 thick slices bacon, fried until crisp, drained on paper towels, and crumbled, (page 42); or any combination (or all) of these.*

Note: *The potatoes can be boiled the day before if you need the time, and then peeled and grated just before frying the cake. Some cooks do not boil the potatoes before grating or shredding them, but I think precooking makes the contrast greater between the crisp outside and tender creamy inside.*

Potato-skin Nachos

I like these better than nachos made with tortilla chips. Serve them alongside steaming bowls of black bean and turkey chili.

Makes 6 servings

6 large Russet potatoes, unpeeled, baked at
    375°F. until tender, about 1 hour
Salt to taste
2 cups grated Cheddar cheese
1 bunch (6 to 8) green onions (scallions), white
    and light green parts only, very thinly sliced
½ cup sliced stuffed olives
1 cup salsa, prepared or homemade
Sour cream, regular or light

Preheat the oven to 500°F.

Halve the potatoes lengthwise, scoop out the insides, leaving only the skins. Reserve the potato insides for another use. Spread the skins open on a lightly greased baking sheet. Salt lightly. Bake in the upper third of the oven, checking from time to time so they do not burn, until very crisp, 10 to 15 minutes.

Remove the skins from the oven, cool, and break them into large chips. Arrange the skins in a large gratin dish. Sprinkle the cheese generously over the chips. Scatter the green onions and olives on top.

Preheat the broiler. Broil just until the cheese melts and begins to bubble, 2 to 3 minutes.

Divide the chips among serving plates. Top each piece with a little salsa and pass the sour cream on the side.

Potato and Apple Pie

This is my version of an old Cornish dinner pie. It is very good for a busy-night dinner, especially when wedges of it are served with lengths of grilled smoked sausage and a crisp green salad.

Makes 6 to 8 servings

Pastry dough for a 2-crust 9-inch pie, prepared or
    homemade (page 126)
3 large waxy white potatoes, brown or red
    skinned, peeled and thinly sliced
2 large onions, very thinly sliced
2 Granny Smith apples, peeled, halved, cored,
    and very thinly sliced
3 large hard-cooked eggs, peeled and sliced
2 tablespoons chopped fresh parsley
1 tablespoon butter
⅓ cup heavy cream
Salt and freshly ground black pepper to taste
Light sour cream (optional)

Preheat the oven to 375°F.

Roll out half the pastry dough and line a deep 9-inch pie plate. Layer the potatoes, onions, apples, and eggs, in that order, in the pastry shell. Sprinkle with parsley. Dot with the butter, and season well with salt and pepper. Pour the cream over all.

Roll out the remaining pastry dough and cover the filling. Seal the top layer of dough to the bottom, flute the edge, and cut steam vents.

Bake until the crust is a dark golden brown, about 1 hour. Remove the pie from the oven and allow it to cool for 15 to 20 minutes. Serve it very warm, or cool to room temperature. Pass a bowl of light sour cream if you wish.

Picnic Potato Salad

No matter what quantity I make of this I have never had much left over. It goes well with almost any picnic fare but especially with hamburgers or hot dogs.

Makes 6 to 8 servings

3 tablespoons chopped dill pickle, or dill
    pickle relish
⅔ cup mayonnaise, prepared or homemade
    (page 13)
⅓ cup light sour cream
1 heaping tablespoon Dijon-style mustard
1 teaspoon celery seed
3 tablespoons finely chopped fresh parsley

2 pounds waxy white potatoes, red or brown
    skinned, unpeeled, boiled in salted water to
    cover until tender, about 15 minutes,
    drained, cooled, and cut into ½-inch cubes
3 large hard-cooked eggs, peeled and chopped
1 rib celery, trimmed, strung if necessary,
    and minced
1 medium-size onion, finely chopped
Salt and freshly ground black pepper to taste

In a small bowl, beat together the dill pickle, mayonnaise, sour cream, mustard, celery seed, and parsley.

In a large bowl, gently toss together the potatoes, eggs, celery, and onion. Season well with salt and pepper. Toss the dressing with the potatoes. There may appear to be too much dressing, but it will be absorbed as the potatoes cool. Refrigerate several hours or overnight.

Potato Salad with Avocado

The unctuous flavor and texture of avocado sets off the tomato and green onions. Serve this with Cajun grilled fish or fiery hot slices of Texas-style beef barbecue.

Makes 6 servings

1½ pounds small waxy white potatoes,
    red or brown skinned, unpeeled, boiled in
    salted water to cover until tender, about
    15 minutes, drained, cooled, and cut into
    1-inch cubes
1 bunch (6 to 8) green onions (scallions), white
    and 2 inches of green only, thickly sliced
1 large ripe tomato, seeded and cut into
    ¼-inch dice
½ cup sour cream, regular or light
2 tablespoons mayonnaise
1 tablespoon fresh lime juice
Salt and freshly ground black pepper to taste
⅓ cup chopped fresh cilantro
Hot pepper sauce to taste
1 large ripe Haas avocado, halved, seed removed,
    peeled and cut into ½-inch cubes
Fresh cilantro sprigs

Toss the potatoes with the green onions and tomato in a large bowl. In a small bowl, stir together the sour cream, mayonnaise, lime juice, salt, pepper, and chopped cilantro. Season with hot pepper sauce.

Toss the vegetables lightly with the dressing. Gently toss in the avocado. Chill 1 hour. Serve the salad garnished with the fresh cilantro sprigs.

Warm Potato Salad

In France and Spain warm seasoned potato slices are often served as an appetizer, with a little olive oil and vinegar drizzled over the top. I think these warm little pyramids go very well with sausages, barbecued chicken, or slabs of barbecued ribs—garlicky if you like.

Makes 6 servings

¼ cup extra-virgin olive oil
1 tablespoon red wine vinegar
¼ teaspoon caraway seeds, crushed
Salt and freshly ground black pepper to taste
1 medium-size head leaf lettuce, torn into
    bite-size pieces
6 medium-size waxy white potatoes, red or brown
    skinned, unpeeled, boiled in salted water to
    cover until tender, drained, and sliced
4 ounces muenster, fontina, or other melting
    cheese, thinly sliced
Pub-style Pickled Onions (page 238)

Preheat the broiler.

In a small bowl, beat together the oil, vinegar, caraway seeds, salt, and pepper. In a large bowl, toss this dressing with the lettuce and arrange on six chilled plates.

Arrange the warm potato slices, overlapping, in six small mounds on a lightly oiled baking sheet. Place several thin slices of cheese on each mound. Broil about 3 inches from the burner until the cheese is melted and bubbling, 2 to 3 minutes.

Using a thin-bladed spatula, transfer one mound to each salad plate. Season well with freshly ground pepper. Serve at once, garnished with the Pub-style Pickled Onions.

German Potato Salad

The hot, astringent dressing makes this salad a refreshing addition to any informal meal. I think it goes very well with roast pork—especially a fresh pork shoulder that has been roasted with the skin on so it becomes crisp and crackling.

Makes 6 servings

¼ pound bacon, fried until crisp, drained on paper towels, and crumbled (page 42), fat left in the skillet

1 medium-size sweet onion, such as Vidalia, Walla Walla, or Texas Super Sweets, cut into ¼-inch dice

2 ribs celery, trimmed, strung if necessary, cut into ¼-inch dice

3 tablespoons white wine vinegar or cider vinegar

½ cup hot water or well-flavored chicken stock

1 teaspoon sugar

Salt and freshly ground black pepper to taste

3 tablespoons chopped fresh parsley

2 pounds small white potatoes, truly new if available, unpeeled, boiled in salted water to cover until just tender, about 15 minutes, drained, and sliced or quartered into a heated salad bowl

3 green onions (scallions), white and light green parts only, very thinly sliced

Pour off all but 3 tablespoons of the bacon fat. Add the onion and celery and cook over medium heat, stirring from time to time, until translucent but crisply tender, about 10 minutes. Stir in the vinegar, hot water, sugar, salt, and pepper. Simmer until well mixed and very hot, 2 to 3 minutes. Stir in the parsley.

Pour this hot dressing over the potatoes. Toss gently to coat the potatoes. Garnish with the bacon and green onions and serve while it is still warm. The potatoes will soak up the dressing.

Pumpkin

Most Americans think of pumpkins in only two ways, as jack-o'-lanterns and as the ever-popular pumpkin pie. Pumpkins are, however, a very versatile vegetable. In the past few years pumpkin muffins, pumpkin soup, and pumpkin-filled ravioli have made an appearance. Still, the offerings have mostly been the traditional sweet variety.

Even though they have the outward appearance of winter squash, pumpkins are in the same family as cucumbers and summer squash. Native North and South Americans grew them long before the first settlers arrived from Europe and may well have interspersed them with corn, just the way some small farmers do today.

In any event, they were a popular harvest-time vegetable, which, with a little care, could be stored to last much of the winter. It was just this quality that may have kept the Pilgrims from dying of hunger that first winter. The diet may have been monotonous, but it sustained life. American Indians taught the Europeans to use pumpkins not only as food but also as utensils. The dried shells were used as bowls and storage containers. And whatever seeds were not needed for the next year's crop were roasted and occasionally doled out as a rare treat.

Today, we see pumpkins displayed from mid-September up through Halloween, a few at a time in the supermarkets, and by the hundreds in farm stands all across America.

Eating, or sugar pumpkins, are not the same as the thick-skinned, sturdy fibrous varieties that are best for carving and lighting up, although these are certainly edible in a pinch. Sugar pumpkins are fine textured, quick cooking, sweet squash that lend themselves to all sorts of preparations, both sweet and savory. Today they range in size from the tiny little individual-serving Munchkins and Jack-Be-Littles to larger 5- to 10-pound Cinderellas and New England Sugar Pies. Sugar pumpkins can be prepared in almost any way that winter (hard-skinned) squash can, but may contain more water than some of the more dense squash varieties, which should be taken into consideration when adding additional liquid to some recipes.

I think most canned vegetables are useful only when fresh or frozen are not available, but canned pumpkin puree is a very acceptable substitute for the fresh preparation. If you cannot find sweet sugar pumpkins in your market, or are pressed for time, canned pumpkin can be used in any recipe calling for puree. (A 2-pound wedge of pumpkin makes about 2 cups of pumpkin puree.)

Pumpkin is low in fat and calories and provides large amounts of beta-carotene, vitamin B, and potassium. It is a perfect diet food that may also have cancer-inhibiting properties.

Selection: Shape should not be the prime criterion when choosing sugar pumpkins, except when using one as a container for soup, stew, or salad or when presenting the tiny ones as individual servings. Instead, look for a bright clear orange color with unblemished skin. Avoid any that have soft spots, brown spots, or cracks, or show signs of mold. Choose pumpkins that have been harvested with at least 2 to 3 inches of stem left on, which will keep them from drying out through the stem scar.

Pumpkins are in the markets from mid-September through early winter.

Because there is a lot of waste, you will need at least ¾ pound raw pumpkin per person.

Storage and Preparation: Pumpkins keep very well in cool, dry places. If you have a basement or storage area that remains around 50°F., they will last whole up to 3 months. Never refrigerate pumpkins or leave them in a damp or humid place. The moisture and cold will hasten spoiling. Sugar pumpkins will last in the kitchen at room temperature about two weeks. They make pretty table decorations that can be enjoyed with the eyes once, then cooked and eaten, and enjoyed again.

Pumpkin needs to be peeled and seeded before eating. The best way to do this is to cut out the stem, and then cut the pumpkin into wedges. Remove the seeds and any stringy fibers, and then peel the wedges with a sharp knife. Or if you are ultimately going to puree the pumpkin, bake the wedges for about 30 minutes at 350°F. Cool slightly and the peel will come off easily with a little encouragement from a knife. Pumpkin can also be boiled, steamed, and microwaved in the peel. If you will be stewing, frying, or using the pumpkin in slices, it is better to remove the peel while it is still raw. Once peeled, the pumpkin is ready to cut into pieces of the desired shape and size.

Boiled Pumpkin

Pumpkin can be boiled, then seasoned with a little butter and salt and pepper, but it isn't a very interesting dish. To prepare boiled pumpkin for other uses, place the cut-up, unpeeled or peeled, and seeded pumpkin in boiling, salted water to cover. Simmer over medium heat until very tender when pierced with a fork but not falling apart, 20 to 30 minutes, depending on the size of the cuts and the variety of pumpkin. Drain well. Peel if necessary.

Steamed Pumpkin

Place the cut-up, peeled or unpeeled, and seeded, pumpkin in a steamer basket or a large colander. Steam, covered, over simmering water until very tender, 30 to 45 minutes, depending on the size of the cuts and the variety of the pumpkin. Peel if necessary.

Microwaved Pumpkin

Place 1 pound cut-up, peeled or unpeeled, and seeded pumpkin in a microwaveable dish. Add 2 tablespoons water, cover, and vent. Microwave on high for 8 to 10 minutes. Let stand 5 minutes before uncovering. Peel if necessary.

If you are going to use a small 4- or 5-pound sugar pumpkin as a serving container for soup or stew, cut out a lid, leaving the stem on. Scoop out all the seeds and fibrous material. Brush the inside of the pumpkin with olive oil or melted butter. Microwave on high for 6 to 8 minutes, then let stand for 2 to 3 minutes. The flesh will be tender, but the shell will not be too soft. Fill the hot shell with the soup or hot stew and serve at once, cocking the lid on top.

I have tried cooking pumpkin soup in the pumpkin shell in the oven many times. So much depends on the pumpkin itself, and more times than I care to think about I have opened the oven door to find my soup leaking out all over the oven floor; and once the whole pumpkin had collapsed in on itself, long before the allotted baking time had passed. I don't know if you have ever tried to clean up 2 quarts of boiling hot soup that is running out of the oven, but I have no desire to repeat the experience. Since that time I have put cooked soup or stew together with cooked pumpkin at the last minute and have been very satisfied with the result. The presentation is the same, and only those who have been in the kitchen will know the difference!

Munchkins and Jack-Be-Littles are delicious individual serving pumpkins. Cut off the tops with the stems, like little lids. Scoop out the seeds and any fibers. Brush the insides with melted butter. Season inside well with salt and pepper. Microwave on high for 5 minutes for one pumpkin, 7 to 8 minutes for two pumpkins, and about 10 minutes for three or four pumpkins. Let stand for 5 minutes before eating. Replace the lids, serve as is with more butter, or fill with vegetable gumbo, green rice, or anything else you like.

Spicy Fried Pumpkin

I love to serve these spicy sticks with grilled whole fish, such as bluefish, trout, or red snapper. But they also go very well with fat, juicy turkey burgers.

Makes 6 servings

1 cup all-purpose flour
2 tablespoons Old Bay or Cajun seasoning;
      or 2 teaspoons ground red (cayenne) pepper
3 pounds pumpkin, peeled, seeded, and cut into
      thick sticks, as for French fries
Mild vegetable oil, preferably peanut for
      deep-frying
Salt to taste

Combine the flour with the Old Bay or Cajun seasoning in a plastic bag. Toss the pumpkin sticks in the seasoned flour, tapping off the excess.

Heat the oil to 375°F. in a deep-fat fryer. Fry the pumpkin sticks, in batches, until crisp and golden brown, 3 to 4 minutes per batch. Remove the fried pumpkin from the oil with a slotted spoon and drain on paper towels. Keep the fries warm in a 375°F. oven while frying the remaining pumpkin. Sprinkle with salt and serve hot.

Mashed Pumpkin and Potato

The fresh winter flavor of pumpkin works very well with potatoes, and this combination provides an alternative to plain mashed potatoes. Pair it with roast pork or even oven-braised pork chops.

Makes 6 servings

2 pounds pumpkin, peeled, seeded, cut into chunks, steamed or boiled in salted water to cover until very tender, up to 20 minutes, and drained

3 large Russet potatoes, peeled, cut into chunks, boiled in salted water to cover until just tender, 15 to 20 minutes, and drained

2 tablespoons butter, plus additional butter (optional) for serving

About 2 tablespoons buttermilk

Salt and freshly ground black pepper to taste

1/4 teaspoon ground nutmeg (optional)

2 green onions (scallions), white part and light green parts only, minced

Puree the pumpkin in a blender or food processor. Pour the puree into a fine-meshed sieve and drain for 10 to 15 minutes. Put the potatoes through a ricer. In a medium-size saucepan, beat the pumpkin and potatoes together with the butter and buttermilk, until smooth. Season well with salt and pepper and stir in the nutmeg if using. Place the puree in a medium saucepan and dry it over low heat until the puree is light and fluffy. Serve very hot, garnished with the green onions. Pass the additional butter on the side.

Gingered Pumpkin Puree

Weary winter menus get a perking up when you include this delicious puree. Serve it with smoked pork chops or baked ham.

Makes 6 servings

3 1/2 to 4 pounds pumpkin, peeled, seeded, cut into chunks, and steamed until very tender, up to 20 minutes

1 tablespoon butter

1 teaspoon grated fresh ginger

1/2 teaspoon ground ginger

2 tablespoons heavy cream

Salt and freshly ground black pepper to taste

Chopped fresh parsley

Puree the pumpkin in a food processor. Pour the puree into a fine-meshed colander and drain for 10 to 15 minutes. Place the puree in a medium-size saucepan and set over very low heat. Stir in the butter, both kinds of ginger, and the cream, and season with salt and pepper. Dry out the puree, stirring from time to time, until it is thick and will retain its shape when mounded in a spoon. Serve very hot, garnished with the parsley.

Stewed Pumpkin

This Thanksgiving invest in a fresh-killed turkey, stuff it with a savory sage-and-onion dressing, and roast it until the skin is golden brown and crackling. Carve thick juicy slices and spoon up big servings of this delicious pumpkin stew. Make mounds of fluffy mashed potatoes and finish with another holiday favorite—spicy pumpkin pie.

Makes 6 to 8 servings

2 tablespoons olive oil

1 small onion, cut into 1/4-inch dice; or 1 pint (10 ounces) boiling onions, boiled in water to cover for 1 minute, drained, and peeled; or one-half 16-ounce package frozen baby onions, thawed

1/2 large green bell pepper, seeded, and cut into 1/4-inch dice

1 small zucchini, trimmed, halved lengthwise, and cut across into 1-inch chunks

3 pounds pumpkin, peeled, seeded, and cut into 1-inch chunks

2 large ripe tomatoes, cut into ¼-inch dice; or
    1 cup well-drained, canned diced tomatoes
½ cup well-flavored chicken stock
Salt and freshly ground black pepper to taste
2 tablespoons chopped fresh oregano, plus
    additional for garnishing
Freshly grated Parmesan cheese

Heat the oil in a large heavy skillet over medium heat. Add the onion and bell pepper, and cook, stirring from time to time, until translucent—6 to 8 minutes. Add the zucchini and pumpkin, and toss until the chunks are well coated with the oil. Stir in the tomatoes. Stir in the stock. Season well with salt, pepper, and oregano. Cover, reduce the heat to low, and simmer gently until the pumpkin is tender but not falling apart, 15 to 20 minutes. Serve the stew very hot, garnished with the additional oregano, along with a bowl of Parmesan cheese on the side.

Notes: *This is very pretty on a holiday table when presented in a pumpkin shell. See the Microwaved Pumpkin for information on how to prepare the shell. This recipe can easily be doubled to serve a crowd.*

Savory Pumpkin Soufflé

Like most other soufflés, this one cannot wait for latecomers. Make it up to 1 hour ahead, cover tightly with plastic wrap, and let it stand at room temperature. Pop it into the oven once everyone is on hand. By the time the first course is finished, this will be ready to serve alongside the pièce de resistance of herb-grilled tenderloins of pork and steamed spinach with garlic and olive oil.

Makes 6 to 8 servings.

2 tablespoons butter, plus additional for buttering
Freshly grated Parmesan cheese
2 tablespoons all-purpose flour

1 cup chicken stock
½ cup heavy cream
Salt and freshly ground black pepper to taste
½ teaspoon ground ginger
3 pounds pumpkin, peeled, seeded, cut into
    chunks, and boiled in salted water to cover
    until tender, about 20 minutes or a little
    longer, well drained, pureed, and drained
    again, 2 cups measured out, remaining puree,
    if any, reserved for another use
3 whole large eggs, separated, whites beaten until
    very stiff

Preheat the oven to 350°F. Generously butter a 1½-quart soufflé dish. Dust the inside well with the cheese. Turn the dish upside down and gently knock out any excess.

Melt 2 tablespoons of butter in a medium-size saucepan over medium heat. Stir in the flour and cook, stirring to prevent it from burning, for 3 minutes. Whisk in the stock and cream all at once. Season well with salt, pepper, and ginger. Whisk over medium heat until smooth and thickened, about 10 minutes. Remove the mixture from the heat and beat in the pumpkin puree. Cool slightly.

Beat in the egg yolks, one at a time, beating very well after adding each one. Stir one-third of the egg whites into the pumpkin mixture to lighten it. Gently fold in remaining egg whites.

Spoon the mixture gently into the prepared dish. Sprinkle lightly with cheese. Bake until puffed and well browned on top, 40 to 45 minutes. Serve immediately, very hot.

Pumpkin Gratin

A tender pot roast, made with lots of sliced onions, would be the perfect accompaniment for this delicious cheesy pumpkin dish.

Makes 6 to 8 servings

2 tablespoons butter, plus additional for buttering
3½ to 4 pounds pumpkin, peeled, seeded, cut
    into ¼-inch slices, boiled in salted water to
    cover for 4 to 5 minutes, and drained
2 large Russet potatoes, peeled, sliced, boiled in
    salted water to cover for 5 minutes, drained,
    dried, and separated into slices
1 small onion, thinly sliced
Salt and freshly ground black pepper to taste
Pinch nutmeg

1 cup well-flavored chicken stock, hot
1 cup grated Monterey Jack cheese

Preheat the oven to 350°F. Generously butter a medium-size gratin dish.

Arrange half the pumpkin slices in the bottom of the prepared dish. Arrange the potato slices in an overlapping pattern on top of the pumpkin. Top with half the onion. Repeat the pumpkin and onion layers. Season well with salt, pepper, and nutmeg. Dot with the remaining 2 tablespoons of butter. Pour in the stock.

Cover tightly with aluminum foil. Bake 30 minutes. Remove the gratin dish from the oven and spread the cheese on top. Return the gratin to the oven, uncover, and bake until most of the liquid is absorbed and the cheese is melted and bubbling, about 15 minutes. Serve very hot.

Radishes

Radishes are not just for serving raw. Many cooks think they are not interesting once cooked, but I find the distinctive sweet/peppery flavor, somewhat like a turnip, is delicious with certain foods. I also think tiny cooked radishes add a little extra interest to the plate. The recent craze for tiny vegetables has led many creative chefs to add butter-braised or steamed radishes to their vegetable medleys that also often include baby carrots, zucchini, tiny pattypan squash, and miniature turnips. Not only are the radishes crisp and flavorful, they add another color to the rainbow on the plate. Radishes vary in color from black to dark red, with shades of purple, pink, and white in between. In fact, if you are a gardener, you can even buy seeds in a combination called Easter Egg that produces radishes in several different colors, including violet. Washed and arranged together on a plate or in a small bowl, they add an edible decorative touch to any table.

Radishes are a very old vegetable. Known for several thousand years, they have been eaten, relished, and literally revered since the ancient Greeks and Egyptians. Originally cultivated by the Chinese, radishes are still very popular in Asia, including the thick white daikon variety that is used in salads, stir-fries, soups, and stews.

There is no commercially available radish that can compare with one that has just been pulled from the garden, washed, and downed with only a sprinkling of salt. Even the very peppery ones that develop when the weather is baking hot are better just pulled than they are at any other time. If you do not grow them yourself, try to find someone who does. Be sure the radishes are pulled young, before they have time to turn woody or become hollow and spongy in the middle. You have a real treat in store.

In France I was introduced to radish sandwiches that are so good they can be habit forming. As with most French sandwiches they are made with a length of baguette, *ficelle* (a smaller, narrower version of baguette), or even a *petit pain*, or roll. Sliced lengthwise, slathered with sweet butter, and filled with thick slices of round red, or the longer radish they call breakfast radish, the only embellishment is a sprinkle of salt and a grind or two of pepper. The combination of the crisp bread, creamy butter, and peppery radish is absolutely delicious. During Oktoberfest in Munich, a variation of the same dish substitutes slices of blackest pumpernickel bread for the baguette, and sometimes the radishes are left whole. Of course huge steins of beer are necessary to wash it all down.

Here are some of the radishes most commonly found in the market. Red globes are the very familiar bright red radishes shaped like little beets. Some varieties can be very hot indeed.

Breakfast radishes are an elongated radish with a red top and a white bottom. They are colorful and usually very crisp and fairly mild.

White icicles, even more elongated—as much as several inches longer than breakfast—are crisp, all-white radishes with a pleasantly mild flavor.

Daikon are thick, very long—often up to 1 foot—carrot-shaped radishes from Asia that have a crisp texture and peppery flavor. This radish is used extensively, literally daily, in Japan.

Black radishes are somewhat difficult to find and can be either beet shaped or elongated. They are much larger than red radishes, nearly the size of small turnips, with a very black skin but white interior. Black radishes have a crisp texture and very peppery flavor.

Radishes have few calories and offer little nutritional value, but they are one of the cruciferous vegetables, like broccoli and cauliflower, and so may aid in preventing cancer. They are an excellent addition to any diet menu. They are also a good source of vitamin C.

Selection: Most globe and icicle radishes are sold either prepackaged in plastic bags or in bunches with the tops still attached. Black radishes and daikons are generally sold loose, without their tops. As a general rule, I suggest avoiding any radishes sold in a bag. Frequently, they are old, pithy, and have been subjected to condensation so that they are musty smelling and unpleasant tasting.

Look for radishes that are crisp and firm and not in the least limp; usually, the smaller the radish, the better. Do not buy any that are spongy to the touch, are cracked, or have brown spots. If the radishes are sold in bunches, choose only those with crisp green leaves. Do not buy them if the leaves are wilted, yellowed, or at all slimy to the touch. If the radishes are clipped and have no leaves, the green stems should be fresh looking, not brown, wilted, or dried out.

If you have no choice and have to buy prepackaged radishes, inspect them very carefully before buying for signs of spoilage or mold and open them as soon as you get them home, removing any that are less than fresh.

Daikons should be a shiny creamy color, firm, heavy, and up to 10 or so inches in length. Avoid any that have brown spots, bruises, cracks, or soft places.

Radishes are generally in the market all year long. They are quick growers—some varieties take only four or five weeks from planting to pulling—but do not tolerate extremely hot weather well. For that reason, local radishes are frequently only available in the spring and early summer and then again sometimes in early fall.

Storage and Preparation: Like many other vegetables, radishes do not store well. They should be prepared and eaten as quickly as possible after they are bought, preferably the same day. If you have to keep them, cut off the leaves. Like carrots, radish leaves tend to extract moisture quickly from the root, which results in a limp, unappetizing vegetable. Do not wash the clipped radishes before storing. Dry them well if they have been misted in the market, and seal in a perforated plastic vegetable bag in the vegetable drawer of the refrigerator. Use them within a few days, certainly within a week.

Daikons will keep up to two weeks, and black radishes even longer, though they will never be as good as when they are first pulled. Be sure to check them from time to time to remove any that have begun to spoil.

All radishes must be washed before eating. Scrub gently to remove any dirt that clings to them. Trim the root end. If the leaves are still very fresh and you are serving the radishes raw, they can be left on, washed, dried, and the whole radishes arranged on a serving platter for an attractive raw salad.

Most radishes can be served with their skin on. Black radishes, if you can find them, and daikon can be peeled with a vegetable peeler if the skin is thick or rough.

> **Tip:** *If, in spite of your best efforts, the radishes have gone a little limp, soak the washed and clipped vegetables in ice water for 30 to 60 minutes. They should crisp up again, though, in my estimation, they will have lost some of their fresh flavor.*

Radishes can be carved or cut into many decorative patterns and shapes. The simplest is to make parallel cuts close together straight down, from root end toward the stem, but not clear through. Toss these into ice water and they not only will become crisp again but will spread open into attractive fan shapes.

Radish and Lettuce Stir-fry

Radishes can taste a little like turnips, only a bit more peppery. I like them to be crisp, even when cooked. Try these the next time you want a little bit of color on the plate. The pink and green is especially pretty if the entrée is a baked fillet of striped bass or bluefish.

Makes 6 servings

1 tablespoon mild vegetable oil, preferably peanut
1½ pounds (about 3 bunches) crisp red radishes, trimmed, cut into thick slices
½ small onion, halved lengthwise (stem to root) and cut into thin wedges
1 tablespoon dry sherry
1 tablespoon well-flavored chicken stock
1 teaspoon soy sauce
1 teaspoon grated fresh ginger
2 cups thickly shredded Romaine, curly chicory, or escarole
Freshly ground black pepper to taste

Over high heat, heat the oil in a wok or a large heavy slope-sided sauté pan until almost smoking. Add the radishes and onion, and cook, stirring, for 1 minute.

In a small bowl, stir together the sherry, stock, soy sauce, and ginger. Pour into the wok, stirring. Cover and cook 2 to 3 minutes. Uncover and add the greens. Cook, tossing, until the lettuce is just beginning to wilt, and all the vegetables are coated with the sauce, about 1 minute. Do not overcook; the lettuce should still be quite crunchy. Season well with the pepper.

> **Note:** *Daikon can be peeled, sliced, and substituted for the radishes in this recipe, but the dish will not be as pretty.*

Butter-braised Radishes

Their fresh, slightly spicy flavor makes cooked radishes a good partner for baked and grilled chicken.

Makes 6 servings

2 to 3 tablespoons butter
1½ pounds small crisp red globe radishes (about 3 bunches) trimmed and quartered, or if very small, left whole
3 tablespoons dry white wine
Salt and freshly ground black pepper to taste
Minced fresh parsley (optional)

Melt the butter in a large heavy skillet over medium heat. Stir in the radishes and toss to coat with the butter. Stir in the wine. Cover and simmer over very low heat until the radishes are crisply tender but still colorfully pink, 4 to 5 minutes. Uncover and season well with salt and pepper. Serve very hot, garnished with the parsley if you like.

Variation: *Stir about ¼ cup heavy cream into the radishes just before seasoning with salt and pepper. Increase the heat and cook until the sauce begins to thicken slightly, 1 to 2 minutes longer. Toss to coat the pieces with the sauce. Serve hot.*

I usually use less butter if I am going to add the cream, only about 1½ tablespoons.

Note: *The radishes will lose some of their color during cooking, but should still retain a deep pink tint.*

Sesame-Radish Salad

When the first very plump radishes come into season, make this salad and serve it with cold grilled chicken or cold roast meats.

Makes 6 servings

1 tablespoon toasted sesame oil
2 tablespoons mild vegetable oil, preferably peanut
2 tablespoons sesame seeds
1 teaspoon grated fresh ginger
1 teaspoon sugar
1 tablespoon teriyaki sauce
2 tablespoons rice wine vinegar
1 bunch (6 to 8) green onions (scallions), white and light green parts only, very thinly sliced
1 pound crisp radishes (about 2 bunches), trimmed, and very thinly sliced
1 rib celery, trimmed, strung, and very thinly sliced slightly on the diagonal
3 tablespoons chopped fresh cilantro, plus additional for garnishing
Leaf lettuce
Freshly ground black pepper to taste

Heat the oils in a very small skillet over medium heat. Add the sesame seeds and cook, stirring, until they are well browned, being very careful not to let them burn, about 2 minutes. Remove from the heat. Stir in the ginger. Cool.

In a small bowl combine the cooled sesame seeds, their oil, and the ginger with the sugar, teriyaki sauce, and vinegar. Beat until well mixed.

In a glass, pottery, or china bowl toss together the green onions, radishes, and celery with the cilantro. Pour the dressing over all and toss to coat.

To serve, line a medium-size glass or other salad bowl with the lettuce. Mound the radish salad on the lettuce. Season well with the pepper, and garnish with the additional cilantro.

Pickled Radishes

Choose the crispest little radishes you can find for these crunchy, sweet/sour pickles. Do not worry if some of the bright color fades. Serve them as a nice change-of-pace condiment on a cold meat platter.

Makes about 2 cups

2 to 3 bunches (1 pound) small crisp,
    bright red, pink, or white globe radishes
    (or a combination of all three), trimmed,
    steamed for 3 minutes, refreshed with ice
    water, and drained
1 cup sugar
3 tablespoons salt
1 cup water
½ cup white wine or rice wine vinegar
½ teaspoon mustard seed, crushed
¼ teaspoon dill seed
2 large sprigs fresh dill

Place the radishes in a medium-size glass or other
nonreactive bowl.

In a small nonreactive saucepan, combine the
remaining ingredients. Bring to a boil and simmer
1 minute. Remove from the heat and cool until just
warm. Pour the warm pickling liquid over the radishes. Cover and refrigerate at least three days. Drain
to serve.

Note: *The pickles will not be as colorful, but
daikon can be substituted for the globe radishes
in this recipe. Peel 1 pound daikon, grate it (as
they do in Japan) or thinly slice it, but do not
steam before pouring the pickling liquid over it.
Continue with the recipe.*

Rutabagas

This member of the cruciferous family is in reality a combination of turnip and cabbage. Whether it's a wild, accidental cross or intentionally bred isn't known. A recent addition to the vegetable realm, rutabagas were chiefly grown as animal food during the early part of the seventeenth century. Like other members of the turnip family, rutabagas grow best where the summers are cool; therefore, their centers of popularity are in northern Europe, Canada, and wherever Scandinavians have tended to migrate. In fact, the large, yellow-fleshed vegetable is often called the Swedish turnip, or Swede, though the Scots call them neeps.

Rutabagas are larger than their turnip cousins. Generally about the size of a softball, they can grow much larger. Very large ones can be pithy and unappetizing; smaller ones can be especially sweet and crisp. All rutabagas come to market without their tops—which resemble cabbage leaves rather than turnip greens. They have a woody looking scar where the greens were cut off and dark brownish purple shoulders. To prolong storage life, nearly all rutabagas come with a thick wax coating. This comes off easily with the peel.

Rutabagas are extremely versatile. They can be baked, boiled, steamed, and mashed. They can be added to soups and stews or served raw in salads. Sticks or raw slices of rutabaga are delicious alongside carrots and celery as low-calorie snacks. They have a sweet, almost nutty flavor that is not as strong as that of large turnips. While their scruffy appearance is frequently off-putting, once you get beyond the ugly waxed exterior they can be a welcome addition to winter menus.

Rutabagas contain no fat or cholesterol and are low in calories. If butter and other fats are kept at a minimum, they are excellent fare for anyone on a diet. Like other cruciferous vegetables, rutabagas may help prevent some forms of cancer. They provide moderate amounts of vitamin C and potassium.

Selection: Look for medium-size, plump, heavy roots. It can be hard to tell through the wax if the outside is blemished, but you should avoid any rutabagas that have obvious cuts, bruises, cracks, or soft spots. The outside should be firm to the touch, with an even coating of shiny wax. Do not buy any that feel spongy.

Rutabagas are in the markets all year, but newly harvested ones begin to appear in the fall and early winter and are at their prime then. Like most other vegetables, the flavor and texture suffers with long storage.

Count on at least $1/4$ pound per person. One medium-size rutabaga should serve four.

Storage and Preparation: Rutabagas will keep well. Do not wash or peel them before storing. If you have a cool, dry storage area with temperatures around 50°F., they will keep two to three weeks. At room temperature they last about one week, and unwrapped in the vegetable drawer of the refrigerator they will keep up to two weeks. If you will not be using the whole rutabaga, cut off the amount needed and refrigerate the rest tightly wrapped in plastic wrap. Use the remainder within a day or two.

Rutabagas need only to be peeled before being cut into the desired shape for cooking. There is usually no waste except for the peel.

The thick coating of wax can make peeling a little difficult. One method I use with considerable success is to cut a slice off the stem and root ends. Rest the rutabaga on the cut side, and slice off sections of the peel from top to bottom, around the root, much the same way as you would peel a grapefruit. Or cut the root into quarters and then remove the peel.

Boiled Rutabaga

Plain boiled rutabaga, with just a little butter and minced parsley, is surprisingly delicious, especially if you use small roots early in the fall when they are sweetest.

To serve six people, plan on about 2 pounds of the smallest roots available. Peel and cut into cubes or slices. Place the cut-up rutabaga in a medium-size saucepan and cover with cold water. Add about $1/2$ teaspoon salt. Bring to a boil and simmer over medium heat until very tender when pierced with a fork but not falling apart, about 15 minutes. Toss with butter, salt, pepper, and a little minced fresh parsley. Serve very hot.

Steamed Rutabaga

Prepare the rutabagas as for boiling. Arrange the cut pieces in the basket of the steamer or in a colander. Steam, covered, over simmering water until tender, 20 to 25 minutes. Drain well, season with salt and pepper. If you like, toss with a little olive oil and minced garlic.

Microwaved Rutabaga

Peel and cut up 1 pound of small rutabagas. Arrange the pieces in a microwave dish. Add 2 tablespoons water. Cover with microwave plastic wrap and vent. Microwave on high 10 to 14 minutes, checking from time to time so the vegetable does not overcook. Let it stand 2 minutes before uncovering.

Rutabaga and Potato Bake

Rutabagas and potatoes are a great combination. If there is a hunter in your family, serve this the next time you make a venison roast or chops. If there is no game in the offing, a crisply roasted duck or goose will do very well as an alternative.

Makes 6 to 8 servings

1 1/2 tablespoons butter, plus additional
    for buttering
1 medium-size rutabaga, peeled, halved, and
    thinly sliced
2 medium-size Russet potatoes, unpeeled,
    thinly sliced
1 small onion, thinly sliced
1 1/2 tablespoons all-purpose flour
1 1/2 cups well-flavored chicken stock, hot
Salt and freshly ground black pepper to taste
1/4 cup plain dried bread crumbs, or butter-
    cracker crumbs
2 tablespoons freshly grated Parmesan cheese

Preheat the oven to 400°F. Generously butter a medium-size gratin dish or 2-quart shallow ovenproof casserole.

In a large bowl, toss together the rutabaga and potato slices. Spread half of the vegetables in the bottom of the prepared dish. Top with the onion. Add the remaining vegetable slices.

In a medium-size saucepan melt 1 1/2 tablespoons of butter over medium heat. Stir in the flour and cook, stirring to keep it from burning, for 3 minutes. Whisk in the stock all at once, whisking continuously until it is smooth. Cook over low heat until the mixture is thickened, about 3 minutes. Season well with salt and pepper. Pour the sauce over the vegetables in the dish. Cover tightly with foil.

Bake for 40 minutes. Remove the casserole from the oven. Uncover. Spread the bread or cracker crumbs over the top. Sprinkle with cheese. Return the dish to the oven and bake until the top is well browned and crusty, about 20 minutes longer. Serve very hot.

Glazed Rutabaga

The sweet flavor of honey-glazed rutabaga goes very well with grilled tuna. It will also be delicious with baked ham or smoked pork chops.

Makes 6 servings

2 tablespoons butter
1 teaspoon sugar
1 teaspoon honey
2 tablespoons dry white wine
1 large or 2 medium-size rutabagas, peeled,
    cut into 1/2-inch cubes, boiled in salted water
    to cover until tender, 15 to 20 minutes,
    and drained
Salt and freshly ground black pepper to taste
Chopped fresh parsley

Melt the butter in a large heavy skillet over medium heat. Stir in the sugar, honey, and wine. Add the rutabagas and toss to coat with the butter mixture. Season well with salt and pepper.

Cover the skillet and cook over medium heat for 2 minutes. Remove the cover and cook, tossing, until the sauce is reduced to a few teaspoons, and the rutabaga cubes are glazed and shiny, no more than 5 minutes. Do not overcook. Serve very hot, garnished with the parsley.

Rutabaga in Cream

If you have not yet acquainted yourself with the distinctive flavor of rutabaga, this is the perfect dish for remedying the situation. I like to serve it with baked chicken or grilled fish.

Makes 6 to 8 servings

2 medium-size rutabagas, peeled and cut into
    1-inch cubes
Salt and freshly ground black pepper to taste
1/2 cup heavy cream, or half-and-half
2 tablespoons snipped fresh chives

In a medium-size saucepan, simmer the rutabaga cubes in salted water to cover over medium heat until crisply tender, 15 to 20 minutes or longer, depending on age. Drain well. Season well with salt and pepper, and pour in the cream. Simmer over medium-low heat until the cream thickens and coats the rutabaga, about 10 minutes. Stir in the chives and serve very hot.

Rutabaga Salad

Although this unusual winter salad is delicious as a simple appetizer or as part of an antipasto buffet, I like to serve it on nights when hamburgers or foot-long hot dogs are on the menu.

Makes 6 to 8 servings

1 small rutabaga, peeled, thinly sliced, and cut into thin matchstick strips
1 cup peeled matchstick strips of broccoli stem
1 medium-size carrot, peeled, cut into 2-inch lengths, sliced lengthwise, and cut into thin matchstick strips, or grated
½ small celeriac, peeled, thinly sliced, and cut into thin matchstick strips, or grated
1 cup mayonnaise, prepared or homemade (page 13)
3 tablespoons light sour cream
2 tablespoons Dijon-style mustard, or more to taste
3 tablespoons minced green onions (scallions), white part only
½ teaspoon celery seed
1 large hard-cooked egg, peeled and finely chopped
3 tablespoons chopped fresh parsley, plus additional for garnishing
Coarsely ground black pepper to taste

In a large salad bowl, toss together the rutabaga, broccoli, carrot, and celeriac.

In a small bowl, beat together the mayonnaise, sour cream, mustard, green onions, celery seed, egg, and 3 tablespoons of parsley. Season well with the pepper. Combine enough of the dressing with the vegetables to create a moist salad, like coleslaw. Cover and refrigerate.

Serve the salad mounded in a large glass or other bowl, garnished with the additional parsley. Pass the remaining dressing in a separate dish, along with a pepper mill.

Clapshot

This simple but delicious dish from the Orkney Islands of Scotland has been traditionally served with haggis (sheep lights cooked with onions and oatmeal, which is then boiled in a sheep's stomach). We don't have much haggis in this country, so I like to serve clapshot with lots of grilled bratwurst or another sausage, instead. This makes a wonderful blustery winter evening supper.

Makes 6 servings

3 large Russet potatoes, peeled, cut into chunks, and boiled in salted water to cover until tender, about 15 minutes, and drained
1 large rutabaga, peeled, cut into chunks, and boiled in salted water to cover until tender, 20 minutes or longer, and drained
2 to 3 tablespoons butter
Salt and freshly ground black pepper to taste
¼ cup snipped fresh chives

Drain the potatoes and rutabaga. Mash them together, beating in the butter. Season well with salt and pepper. Stir in the chives and serve very hot.

Salsify

This is a vegetable you may have to grow yourself to enjoy to its fullest extent. Salsify, also known as oyster plant, is a root vegetable that looks very much like a thin brownish carrot or parsnip, with a grayish white flesh. It is sometimes available in specialty markets or large supermarkets.

Salsify has been around for a long time, certainly since the Middle Ages in Europe, where it is still a fairly common cold-weather vegetable. For some reason salsify has never become as popular in the United States as it has always been in Europe, and even there it has gone in and out of fashion over the years.

Like the parsnip, salsify is best once it has been touched by frost—when its starches begin to turn to sugar—and it can be left in the ground to be harvested as needed, until the first hard freeze.

Black salsify, or scorzonera, may be more readily available, especially in areas where there are markets catering to Spanish and Italian customers. The flavor is similar, though I think salsify is a little tastier. Scorzonera can be substituted in any of the recipes in this section. It does, however, have a tendency to bleed liquid if it is cut while raw, and it will turn hands and cutting surfaces black. For this reason it is advisable simply to wash scorzonera first, simmer it whole until tender, and then peel it before cutting into serving-size pieces.

Salsify does not bleed as much as scorzonera, although if you have pounds and pounds to peel, it will stain fingers and nails. Salsify will begin to turn dark as soon as it has been peeled or cut, and I think it is a good idea to prepare a large bowl of acidulated water—1 quart water mixed with 2 tablespoons lemon juice or white vinegar—before beginning to peel the salsify. Drop the prepared vegetable directly into the acidulated water. Cook the salsify in the same water.

Although the name oyster plant seems to indicate an affinity for oysters, and many people think the flavor of salsify is similar to the bivalve, I think it has a taste much more like artichoke bottoms than oysters. For that reason it makes a nice substitution for baby artichokes in Artichokes à la Barigoule.

One word of caution: Salsify, like the Jerusalem artichoke, contains a starch called inulin, which some sensitive people find difficult to digest. It can cause them gastric distress. The best way to try salsify for the first time is in moderation. If you are one of the sensitive few, don't repeat the experience, otherwise enjoy them whenever you find them.

Salsify and scorzonera are both fairly low in calories and fiber. They contain some vitamin C and potassium.

Selection: Frequently, you will find salsify in the market with dirt still clinging to the root. That is fine. Salsify will be brownish in color, longer and thinner than a carrot or parsnip, sometimes with lots of little rootlets protruding all along the length (which probably led to its Italian nickname of priest's beard). Scorzonera is almost black. While the roots look slightly dry, they should not be dried out, wrinkled, shriveled, or limp. Look for the firmest, straightest roots. Avoid any that are not in prime condition, show any signs of mold, or have slight cuts that may have made them begin to weep.

I have bought peeled, cut-up, parboiled salsify in a small cryovac plastic package. If these packages have been handled well, the salsify may be used in soups and stews, but I don't think it is very satisfactory in dishes where the vegetable is meant to stand on its own.

Salsify is available fresh from late summer through the first hard freeze. Once in a while, if you live in a fairly temperate area, you will find them again fresh in the early spring, but those will be the roots that have been left in the ground all winter. I usually avoid these as they are sometimes dried out.

You will need about 1/4 pound of the plumpest salsify for each serving.

Storage and Preparation: Salsify is very fragile. It loses its moisture quickly and becomes limp and unappetizing. I suggest cooking it the day it is purchased, or within one to two days at most. If you will be keeping it for a day or two, wrap the roots tightly in plastic wrap and store in the vegetable drawer of the refrigerator.

Salsify and scorzonera are best when cooked. They should both be peeled, and this is where the one drawback arises. Once the peel is removed, or the flesh is cut, salsify immediately begins to turn dark—an unappealing gray green color. And it weeps, discoloring hands and cutting surfaces.

To prevent the darkening of the vegetable, it should be immediately immersed in acidulated water (1 quart of water mixed with 2 tablespoons lemon juice) and cooked in the same water. Or it should be cooked *à blanc*. Cooking *à blanc* is an old-fashioned French method of keeping vegetables from discoloring.

Boiled Salsify

Because of its tendency to turn an unappetizing color of gray when mishandled, it is best to cook salsify in acidulated water, or *à blanc* as the French do.

To make an *à blanc* solution, mix ¼ cup unbleached flour with ¼ cup water and 2 tablespoons lemon juice in a small bowl to form a paste. Stir the paste into 2 quarts of water, stirring until the paste is totally dissolved. Add the salsify to the cold solution and bring to a boil. Simmer, uncovered, until just fork tender, from 5 to 12 minutes, depending on the age of the salsify and the size of the pieces.

If you have put the cut salsify directly into acidulated water as suggested in the recipes that follow, make an *à blanc* solution with that as the base. Make a paste of ¼ cup unbleached flour and ¼ cup water. Stir the paste into 1 quart plain water. Add this mixture to the acidulated water that contains the salsify. Bring to a boil and simmer until the vegetable is tender, 5 to 12 minutes.

Note: *If you are going to substitute scorzonera, or black salsify, for the white variety, it is better to wash it and leave it unpeeled and uncut until it is cooked. Raw scorzonera bleeds and will stain hands and cutting surfaces. Once it is cooked, it is easy to peel and cut up. Count on 30 to 40 minutes in simmering water to cover for whole scorzonera to become tender.*

Scalloped Salsify and Carrots

This creamy, delicate combination of flavors goes very well with poached or grilled salmon fillets.

Makes 6 servings

1 tablespoon butter, plus additional for buttering
1 pound salsify, trimmed, peeled, sliced thinly on the diagonal, boiled in acidulated water (1 quart water and 2 tablespoons lemon juice or white vinegar), or *à blanc*, until just tender, 15 to 20 minutes, and drained
1 pound carrots, peeled, thinly sliced on the diagonal, simmered in salted water to cover until crisply tender, about 10 minutes, and drained
1 small onion, very thinly sliced
2 cups heavy cream, simmered over medium heat until reduced to 1 cup, 25 to 30 minutes
Salt and freshly ground black pepper to taste
2 tablespoons chopped fresh dill
⅓ cup plain dried bread crumbs

Generously butter a small glass, pottery, or other deep nonreactive baking dish. Alternate layers of the salsify, carrots, and onion in the dish. Pour in the cream. Season well with salt, pepper, and dill.

In a small saucepan, melt 1 tablespoon of butter over medium heat. Remove the pan from the heat and stir the bread crumbs into the melted butter. Spread this mixture on top of the vegetables. Bake until bubbling and golden brown, about 30 minutes. Serve hot.

Salsify Persillade

The delicious flavor of salsify cooked with garlic makes this a great partner for a crisply roasted duck. If there is no duck on hand, serve this dish with crisply grilled chicken that has been brushed with a soy sauce marinade.

Makes 6 to 8 servings

2 tablespoons olive oil
2 tablespoons butter
2 pounds salsify, trimmed, peeled, cut into
    ½-inch slices, boiled in acidulated water
    (1 quart water and 2 tablespoons lemon juice
    or white vinegar), or *à blanc*, until tender,
    20 to 30 minutes, depending on the age of
    the roots, drained, and dried in a kitchen
    towel
2 cloves garlic, minced
¼ cup chopped fresh parsley
Salt and freshly ground black pepper to taste

In a medium-size heavy skillet, heat the olive oil and butter together over low heat. Add the salsify and cook until golden brown and very tender, but not falling apart, about 10 minutes. Toss from time to time to coat with the butter mixture. Stir in the garlic and parsley. Raise the heat to medium and cook, tossing to keep the garlic from burning, about 3 minutes longer. Season with salt and pepper. Serve hot.

Butter-braised Salsify

The delicate, almost artichoke-like, flavor of salsify should not be overwhelmed by the main course. I generally serve it with roast or baked poultry, or fish.

Makes 6 servings

3 tablespoons butter
2 pounds salsify, trimmed, peeled, cut into
    2-inch lengths, boiled in acidulated water
    (1 quart water and 2 tablespoons lemon juice
    or white vinegar), or *à blanc* for 5 minutes,
    and drained
½ cup well-flavored chicken stock
Salt and freshly ground black pepper to taste
2 tablespoons chopped fresh chervil, or snipped
    fresh chives

Melt the butter in a medium-size heavy saucepan over medium heat. Stir in the salsify and toss to coat with the butter. Stir in the stock and season with salt and pepper. Cover and simmer over low heat, tossing from time to time, until tender when pierced with a fork but not falling apart, 20 to 30 minutes, depending on the thickness and age of the roots. Remove the cover, raise the heat to high, and evaporate most of the liquid, tossing occasionally to keep the salsify from sticking or turning dark brown, about 2 minutes. Serve very hot, garnished with the chervil or chives.

Spinach

The most compelling reason for going to all the trouble of preparing fresh spinach is, basically, flavor. The difference between garden-fresh spinach, cooked only hours after picking, and the quick-to-fix, frozen variety is enormous. Frozen spinach is fine in cooked dishes, especially if there is no fresh spinach in the market, but if you plan to eat it plain, or simply creamed, there is no substitute for fresh. Fresh spinach is truly a sublime vegetable, well worth the effort it takes.

While spinach has been grown in Europe for several hundred years, it was known in the Middle East long before it was brought west by Arab traders. It is still a favorite vegetable in Iran, Turkey, and Greece, where it is baked into pastries, made into stews with lamb or beef, combined with oranges, and eaten on its own, simply cooked with onions and maybe a little chopped tomato.

There are two major drawbacks to preparing fresh spinach: the prodigious quantities needed for feeding more than two people, and its maddening quality of carrying large amounts of dirt with it from the garden to the kitchen. There is no shortcut for dealing with either of these problems. Spinach wilts substantially when heated, and a large kettle full of fresh leaves will produce hardly a cup of cooked vegetable. It is a time-consuming task to pull the stems from all the leaves you will need, but I think spinach cooked with the stems ends up being almost too stringy to eat. And, if you have ever eaten inadequately washed spinach and gotten a mouthful of grit, you know why it is essential to clean it extremely carefully.

The leaves must be washed in quantities of water, changed several times. After each washing, the leaves must be taken out of the water and set aside. Do not let the water drain through the leaves, or the dirt and grit will simply settle back on them and you will be right back where you started. Home-grown spinach may need as many as three or four water changes, especially if it rained just before it was picked. Commercially packaged spinach has been prewashed, but still should be thoroughly rinsed before using.

You will find several kinds of spinach in the market. Savoy is the very dark green, curly leaf variety that is often sold in prepackaged plastic bags. There is a slightly paler green, flat-leaf variety, which is increasingly more available and is a little easier to clean. New Zealand spinach, or tetragonia, has light green, triangular leaves and is not really spinach at all. It collects less grit, however, has smaller stems, is easier to clean, and has a deliciously delicate flavor that I, personally, enjoy very much.

While frozen spinach can have a good taste and is certainly easier to use than fresh, especially if you are going to chop it finely, there is absolutely nothing to recommend the canned version. It is overcooked, salty, and has a decidedly metallic flavor that no amount of doctoring can overcome.

And, regardless of what Popeye says, spinach is not the muscle-building paragon of a food that it might seem. Spinach contains large quantities of oxalic acid that combine with the considerable amounts of calcium and iron in the leaves. The combination cannot be absorbed by the body and passes through almost virtually untouched. While spinach is also a good source of protein, it should be eaten along with rice or other grains, meat, or dairy products in order to derive its maximum benefit.

All is not lost, however. Spinach is very low in calories, has no cholesterol, and contains large quantities of beta-carotene as well as vitamin C. The antioxidant qualities of the beta-carotene could help in preventing some kinds of cancer.

Selection: No matter where you buy it, fresh spinach will contain a certain amount of dirt and grit. Prepackaged spinach usually has the least. Pick out the deepest-colored, freshest-looking, crispest leaves. Medium-size leaves tend to be younger and more tender than the giant ones, and the stems are smaller, giving less waste per pound. Avoid any leaves that are thick and tough looking, are broken or torn, have yellow or brown spots, or are limp and wilted. The leaves should be dry and firm. Do not buy any spinach that has a musty odor, or smells like wet leaves.

I like to pick out my spinach leaf by leaf from a bulk display, but if your market carries only prepackaged spinach, you will have to choose carefully. Some prepacked spinach is of very high quality, especially if it has been well handled all down the line. Sometimes the bagged spinach will be poor quality, wilted, even spoiled. It is important to inspect the packages closely. The leaves should be very green and appear dry. None should be wet or slimy, and none should be yellowed or limp looking. Squeeze the package very gently; it should almost feel like it is pushing back slightly. Reject any bags that feel soft and squishy.

Fresh spinach is generally available all year long, especially the prepackaged variety, because it will be shipped in from other growing areas. Local spinach will be at its best in the spring.

Because of the waste in preparing fresh spinach, you will need to count on at least ½ pound of raw spinach per person for cooked dishes, about half that for salads.

Storage and Preparation: Spinach is one of those vegetables that is at its best if eaten as soon after it is picked as possible. I suggest preparing it the same day it is bought. If it appears very fresh, it will keep two to three days in the refrigerator. Loose spinach should be sealed, unwashed, in a plastic vegetable bag and placed in the vegetable drawer of the refrigerator. Plan to use as soon as possible. Some cooks suggest leaving prepackaged spinach in the bag until you are ready to prepare it. I prefer to open the bags, pick over the leaves, and discard any that have blackened edges, are yellowed or wilted, or are too coarse to use. The remaining leaves should be sealed in a plastic vegetable bag and stored in the refrigerator. Not only does this method remove any spoiled leaves, it gives you an accurate idea of how much spinach you actually have, allowing you to buy more if the quantity is less than you thought.

All spinach must be washed and should be stemmed before cooking. I like to wash before I stem because if the spinach is very muddy or gritty, stemming becomes unpleasant work. I choose lukewarm water to wash the leaves, especially if they are the very curly variety. The warm water seems to wilt the leaves slightly, loosening some of the more embedded grit. Spinach that will be served raw can be dried in a salad spinner, wrapped in a towel, and refrigerated for 1 or 2 hours to recrisp before using.

The best way to wash spinach is in a double sink. If you do not have a double sink, place a large pot or plastic basin on the counter next to the sink. Place the spinach to be washed in one side of the sink and run the water over it until the sink is full. Swish the spinach up and down, agitating it well to loosen as much of the dirt as possible. Remove the spinach from the water and place it in the other sink. Drain the water and wash the grit out of the first sink. Repeat the process until no grit or dirt remains in the bottom of the sink. If you are using one sink and a basin, remove the spinach to the basin, flush out the sink, and return the spinach to it for the next rinse.

Once the leaves are clean, each one must be stemmed individually, or the finished dish could be unpleasantly fibrous or stringy. It is a tedious job, and company makes it a much more enjoyable task. I suggest enlisting a child, spouse, or friend to help; turning on the TV; or listening to your favorite tape or CD.

Spinach is stemmed like any other green, such as collards or Swiss chard. The easiest method is to fold the leaf in half with the back side out. Hold the leaf in the left hand (if you are right-handed) with the stem to the right side. Grasp the bottom of the stem with the right hand and pull up (or down if that seems easier). The stem should come away in one piece. The leaves are ready to cook or use raw, whole or cut up.

Unless the spinach is going to be served raw, do not dry the leaves. Place the washed and stemmed spinach directly into the cooking pot. It will look like a lot, but remember it cooks down considerably.

Spinach can be left whole, torn into bite-size pieces, cut into shreds, or chopped. The quickest way to shred or chop is to pile several leaves together and slice across with a sharp knife for shreds. Turn and cut in the other direction for chopped. This does not have to be done with painstaking care, because the size and shape of the pieces will not be evident in the cooked dish.

Wilted Spinach

Old-fashioned cooks boiled spinach in a large quantity of salted water. This did set the color, but it also removed many of the vitamins. Steaming spinach in the water that clings to the leaves after washing is simple and provides the most nutritious finished vegetable.

Pile the washed spinach (whole leaves, shredded, or chopped) in a large kettle. Packing the leaves in won't hurt anything. Cover the kettle and cook over high heat for several minutes—the time will depend on the amount of spinach, but 3 minutes for 2 or 3 pounds is about right. Remove the cover after 1 minute and use a long-handled fork to toss the spinach, moving the less wilted leaves into contact with the bottom of the kettle. Once the spinach is wilted and still very green, drain off any remaining water, pressing slightly to remove excess liquid. Add a little butter, season with salt and pepper, and serve at once. Do not overcook or the spinach will lose its bright green color and fresh flavor.

For a slightly fancier dish, top the cooked spinach with chopped hard-cooked egg. This will give you a dish called spinach mimosa. Or arrange sliced hard-cooked eggs on top.

Freezing Your Own Spinach

If you love spinach and want the convenience of frozen, make your own. Set aside a day in the spring when your local greengrocer has an abundant supply of fresh-picked spinach and enlist the children or a friend or two to help with the washing and stemming. Cook the cleaned spinach in the water that clings to the leaves after washing until barely wilted, about 2 minutes, cool slightly and seal it by cupsful in airtight plastic freezer bags. Freeze. Thaw in the refrigerator or in the microwave, before using.

Steamed Spinach

Steaming is an excellent method for preparing spinach that will be sautéed or cooked further by some other method. It can be wilted quickly without being overcooked.

Pile the washed and stemmed spinach in a steamer basket or a large colander and cook, covered, over simmering water until barely wilted, 3 to 4 minutes. Drain well, pressing on the spinach to remove any excess moisture.

Microwaved Spinach

Microwaving is a good way to prepare a small quantity of spinach, but it is easier and quicker to cook large amounts by wilting or steaming.

Place about $\frac{1}{2}$ pound washed, but not dried, stemmed, and cut-up spinach in a microwaveable dish. Cover with microwave plastic wrap and vent. Microwave on high 2 to 3 minutes. Let stand 2 more minutes, uncover, drain, and press out any excess moisture.

Stir-fried Spinach

For a slightly different flavor and texture, dry 1 pound of spinach in a salad spinner, then shred it. Heat 1 tablespoon olive oil in a large skillet. Add the dried spinach. Cook, tossing all the time, until it collapses, 2 to 3 minutes. Season with 1 teaspoon soy sauce, toss, and serve very hot.

Best Ever Creamed Spinach

Not exactly classic, this recipe contains green onions and does not contain flour, but I think it is a definite improvement on the original. I like to serve this with almost anything, from poached and grilled fish to grilled steak, steamed lobster, or thick grilled veal chops.

Makes 6 servings

3 pounds spinach, stemmed and chopped
2 tablespoons butter
1 bunch (6 to 8) green onions (scallions), white and light green parts only, very thinly sliced
Salt and freshly ground black pepper to taste
Pinch nutmeg (optional)
½ cup heavy cream, simmered over medium heat until reduced to about ⅓ cup, about 15 minutes

In a large kettle over medium heat, cook the spinach in the water that clings to the leaves after washing until wilted, 2 to 3 minutes. Raise the heat to high and evaporate the moisture in the bottom of the pan, tossing the spinach to keep it from burning.

Melt the butter in a medium-size heavy saucepan over medium heat. Add the green onions and sauté for 1 minute. Stir in the spinach. Season well with salt, pepper, and nutmeg, if using. Stir in the cream. Heat through, simmering until the vegetable is thick and creamy, 2 to 3 minutes longer. Serve very hot.

Parmesan Creamed Spinach

This spinach dish is exactly the right accompaniment for roast lamb or standing ribs of beef.

Makes 6 servings

1 tablespoon butter
1 clove garlic, minced

3 pounds spinach, stemmed and torn up
½ cup heavy cream
¼ cup freshly grated Parmesan cheese
Freshly ground pepper to taste

Melt the butter in a large kettle over medium heat. Add the garlic and cook, stirring, for 30 seconds. Add the spinach and cook it in the water that clings to the leaves after washing until it is wilted and tender, about 3 minutes. Drain well.

In a small bowl, beat together the cream and cheese. Stir this mixture into the spinach. Toss well and cook until very hot and the cheese is melted, 3 or 4 minutes longer. Season well with the ground pepper. Serve hot.

Creamed Spinach and Sorrel

Do not be concerned if the color of this finished dish is not as bright green as creamed spinach. Sorrel tends to turn slightly yellow when cooked, but the color change does not affect the flavor. An old friend of mine, a very talented French chef, believed sorrel was the most wonderful accompaniment for veal. I love this with veal scaloppine, but have also enjoyed it with sautéed skinless chicken breasts as well.

Makes 6 to 8 servings

1 tablespoon butter
3 pounds spinach, stemmed and chopped
1 pound sorrel, stemmed, and chopped
One-half 3-ounce package cream cheese
½ cup heavy cream
Salt and freshly ground black pepper to taste
½ teaspoon ground cumin

Melt the butter in a large kettle over low heat. Pile in the spinach. Cover and cook, stirring occasionally, in the water that clings to the leaves after washing until the spinach is just wilted, about 3 minutes. Add the sorrel and cook 2 or 3 minutes longer. The sorrel will wilt into a puree and turn a yellower green than the spinach. Stir together and cook until tender, about 2 minutes longer. Drain, pressing out some of the moisture.

In a medium-size saucepan, combine the cream cheese and the cream. Simmer over low heat until the mixture is thick and creamy. Season with salt, pepper, and cumin. Stir in the spinach/sorrel combination. Heat, stirring, until the greens are hot and well coated, about 2 minutes. Serve at once.

Spinach Soufflé with Onion Sauce

Soufflés have a reputation of being elegant but difficult. Nonsense. If you can make a cream (white) sauce and beat an egg white, you can make a perfect soufflé. This delightfully colored, delicious spinach soufflé is elegant enough to serve with pheasant, simple enough to pair with pan-fried fillets of sole.

Makes 6 to 8 servings

2 tablespoons butter, plus additional for buttering
2 tablespoons freshly grated Parmesan cheese
1½ pounds fresh spinach, stemmed, finely chopped, cooked in the water that clings to the leaves after washing until wilted, about 3 minutes, and well drained; or one 10-ounce package frozen chopped spinach, thawed, squeezed very dry, and rechopped very finely
2 tablespoons fresh lemon juice
1 tablespoon grated onion
Salt and freshly ground black pepper to taste
2 tablespoons all-purpose flour
1 cup milk, heated but not boiling
4 large eggs, separated, whites beaten until stiff
Onion Sauce (recipe follows)

Preheat the oven to 350°F. Generously butter a 1½-quart soufflé dish and dust the inside with the cheese. Turn the dish upside down and gently knock out any excess.

In a medium-size bowl, stir together the spinach, lemon juice, and onion. Add salt and pepper.

In a medium-size saucepan, melt 2 tablespoons of butter over medium heat. Stir in the flour and cook, stirring, for 3 minutes. Whisk in the warm milk all at once. Cook gently, stirring, until smooth and thickened, at least 3 minutes. Remove the pan from the heat and cool. Beat in the egg yolks, one at a time. Beat in the spinach. Turn the mixture into a medium-size bowl.

Stir one-third of the egg whites into the spinach mixture to lighten it. Gently fold in the remaining egg whites, being careful not to break them down too much.

Spoon the mixture into the prepared dish. Bake until well risen and golden brown on top, 35 to 40 minutes. Serve very hot, with a little of the onion sauce spooned over the top of each portion.

Onion Sauce

Makes about 1¼ cups

3 tablespoons butter
3 medium-size sweet onions, such as Vidalia, Walla Walla, or Texas Super Sweets, chopped, simmered in salted water for 6 to 7 minutes, and drained
¼ cup hot cooked rice
Salt and freshly ground black pepper to taste
½ cup heavy cream
2 tablespoons minced fresh parsley

Melt the butter in a medium-size saucepan over low heat. Add the onions and cook, stirring, until just beginning to take on a golden brown color, 6 to 8 minutes. Stir in the rice and season with salt and pepper. Cover and cook over low heat for 5 minutes. Puree the mixture in a food processor.

Return the puree to the saucepan and stir in the cream. Heat through. Season again with salt and pepper if necessary. Stir in the parsley. Serve very hot over the soufflé.

Spinach with Garlic and Olive Oil

Roman spinach, redolent with garlic and olive oil, is to me the perfect side dish for veal marsala, saltimbocca, or even delicate little veal (or chicken) sausages.

Makes 6 servings

2 tablespoons olive oil, plus additional for serving
3 cloves garlic, minced
3 pounds fresh spinach, stemmed and shredded, cooked in the water that clings to the leaves after washing until wilted, 3 or 4 minutes, drained, and pressed to remove as much liquid as possible; or three 10-ounce packages frozen chopped spinach, thawed and squeezed dry
Salt and freshly ground black pepper to taste

Heat the oil in a medium-size heavy skillet over medium heat. Cook the garlic, stirring, until just golden, but not browned or burned, no more than 1 minute. Stir in the spinach and toss until coated with the oil and garlic. Season well with salt and pepper. Serve very hot, drizzled with a little more olive oil.

Greek Spinach

Ask your fishmonger for a very fresh, whole red snapper, well cleaned. Grill it to perfection, brushing it with olive oil. Serve it with this wonderful spinach dish.

Makes 6 servings

3 tablespoons olive oil
3 pounds fresh spinach, stemmed, dried, and chopped
1 bunch (6 to 8) green onions (scallions), white and light green parts only, sliced
2 cloves garlic, minced
1 tablespoon chopped fresh oregano; or 1 teaspoon dried

2 tablespoons fresh lemon juice
Salt and freshly ground black pepper to taste
1/3 cup crumbled feta cheese

Heat the oil in a large heavy skillet over medium heat. Stir in the spinach and cook, stirring, for 1 minute. Stir in the green onions, garlic, and oregano. Cook, uncovered, stirring from time to time, until very tender but still very green, 5 or 6 minutes. Stir in the lemon juice. Season well with salt and pepper. Serve the spinach very hot, topped with the crumbled feta cheese.

Baked Spinach

This can be assembled ahead of time and baked just before serving. Roast poultry of any kind will be enhanced by sharing a plate with this dish, but I also love to serve it for brunch or late supper with carefully scrambled eggs and paper-thin slices of smoked salmon.

Makes 6 servings

1 tablespoon butter, plus additional for buttering
1 tablespoon olive oil
1/2 small onion, minced
3 pounds fresh spinach, stemmed, chopped, cooked in the water that clings to the leaves until just wilted, about 2 minutes, drained, and pressed to remove as much liquid as possible; or three 10-ounce packages frozen chopped spinach, thawed, and squeezed dry
Salt and freshly ground black pepper to taste
1/4 teaspoon nutmeg
1/2 cup heavy cream
1/4 cup plain dried bread crumbs
1/4 cup freshly grated Parmesan cheese

Preheat the oven to 325°F. Butter a 1-quart shallow baking or gratin dish.

Heat the olive oil in a small skillet over low heat. Add the onion and cook over low heat until translucent, about 10 minutes. Stir in the spinach. Season well with salt, pepper, and nutmeg. Stir in the cream.

Spoon the mixture into the prepared dish. Dot with 1 tablespoon of butter. Mix the bread crumbs and cheese. Sprinkle on top of the spinach. Bake until hot and bubbling, 15 to 20 minutes. Serve very hot. **Variation:** *Substitute kale or Swiss chard for all or some of the spinach for a somewhat different flavor.*

Spinach and Potato Gratin

A square of this hearty gratin is wonderful served with chops of any kind, but I especially like it alongside crusty pink loin lamb chops cooked over the grill. If loin chops are too expensive, try thick shoulder chops instead.

Makes 6 to 8 servings

Butter, softened
1 tablespoon olive oil, plus additional for drizzling
½ pound brown (cremini) or white mushrooms, stems trimmed, thinly sliced
3 large Russet potatoes, peeled, simmered in well-flavored chicken stock until just tender, about 20 minutes, drained, and thinly sliced
1 small onion, very thinly sliced
2 pounds spinach, stemmed, chopped, cooked in the water that clings to the leaves after washing until wilted, about 3 minutes, and well drained
3 tablespoons pine nuts
2 cloves garlic, minced
1 cup ricotta cheese, whole milk or skim
6 ounces mozzarella cheese, grated (1½ cups)
Salt and freshly ground black pepper to taste
¼ cup freshly grated Parmesan cheese

Preheat the oven to 400°F. Generously butter a 2-quart deep baking dish.

Heat 1 tablespoon of olive oil in a small heavy skillet over medium heat. Add the mushrooms and cook over medium heat, tossing from time to time, just until they begin to brown, 6 to 7 minutes.

Layer half of the potato slices in the prepared dish. Spread the onion on top of the potatoes. Spread the spinach on top of the onion. Layer the cooked mushrooms on top of the spinach. Sprinkle with the pine nuts.

In a medium-size bowl beat together the garlic, ricotta, and mozzarella cheese. Season well with salt and pepper. Spread half of the mixture over the spinach. Top with remaining potatoes. Season with salt and pepper and drizzle with a little olive oil. Spread remaining cheese mixture over the potatoes.

Cover with aluminum foil. Bake 30 minutes. Remove the foil, sprinkle with the Parmesan cheese. Bake until the whole is golden brown and bubbling, about 15 minutes. Serve very hot, cut into squares.

Green Rice

This is a delicious alternative to plain rice, especially when grilled lamb kebabs are on the menu. Chicken or beef kebabs are also good partners.

Makes 6 servings

2 tablespoons butter
1 large or 2 small cloves garlic, minced
2 pounds fresh spinach, stemmed, chopped, cooked in the water that clings to the leaves after washing until wilted, about 3 minutes, drained, and pressed to remove as much liquid as possible; or two 10-ounce packages frozen chopped spinach, thawed and squeezed dry
Salt and freshly ground black pepper to taste
½ teaspoon ground ginger
2 tablespoons heavy cream
2 cups cooked (⅔ cup raw) rice, hot
3 tablespoons slivered almonds, toasted (page 70)

Melt the butter in a large heavy saucepan over low heat. Add the garlic and cook, stirring, until just tender, about 1 minute. Stir in the spinach. Season with salt, pepper, and ginger. Stir in the cream and rice. Cover, cook over low heat, stirring once or twice, until very hot, 4 to 5 minutes. Serve very hot, garnished with the almonds.

Spinach and Citrus Salad

Sometimes a refreshing citrus flavor is just what the menu needs. The slightly sweet nature of the dressing keeps it from being too acidic. Why not put this on the table the next time you dish up fiery hot bowls of red beans and rice or chili?

Makes 6 servings

1 pound spinach, stemmed and dried
1 large seedless pink grapefruit, peeled
    and sectioned
2 large seedless oranges, peeled and sectioned
3 ounces feta cheese, crumbled (about ¾ cup)
1 small sweet onion, thinly sliced and separated
    into rings
⅓ cup small oil-cured olives
2 tablespoons white wine vinegar
2 tablespoons fresh orange juice
1 teaspoon honey
½ teaspoon Dijon-style mustard
½ teaspoon ground cumin
Salt and freshly ground black pepper to taste
1 teaspoon poppy seeds
⅓ cup mild vegetable oil, preferably peanut
Snipped fresh chives

Pile the spinach in a large glass or other salad bowl. Arrange the grapefruit and orange sections in an attractive pattern on the spinach. Sprinkle the cheese over the fruit. Garnish with the onion rings and olives. Chill, covered for 30 minutes.

In a small bowl, beat together all the remaining ingredients, except the chives. Just before serving, pour the dressing over the salad. Serve with the chives sprinkled over the top.

Classic Spinach Salad

Somehow I can never get enough of this old favorite. I love spinach in salads and frequently combine small tender leaves with other greens, both for color and flavor. But this classic combination is still the one I prepare whenever I grill a thick sirloin steak. I might also include a souffléed baked potato on the plate.

Makes 6 servings

2 pounds spinach, stemmed and dried
6 large white mushrooms, stems trimmed,
    thinly sliced
3 hard-cooked large eggs, peeled and quartered
¼ pound thick sliced bacon, fried until crisp,
    drained on paper towels, and crumbled
    (page 42)
½ cup crumbled Roquefort cheese (optional, but
    recommended)
3 tablespoons red wine vinegar
1 tablespoon Dijon-style mustard
Salt and freshly ground black pepper to taste
½ cup extra-virgin olive oil

Pile the spinach in a large chilled salad bowl. Top with the mushroom slices. Arrange the egg wedges on top. Sprinkle with the crumbled bacon and the cheese if using.

In a small bowl, beat together the vinegar and mustard. Season well with salt and pepper. Beat in the olive oil. Just before serving, pour some of the dressing over the salad and toss. Serve with the remaining dressing on the side.

Variation: *Toss half a medium-size bunch watercress, trimmed, along with a little thinly sliced sweet onion into the salad before adding the dressing.*

Squash

As the name might indicate, squash is native to America, not necessarily North American but certainly from this side of the Atlantic. *Squash*, the word we use to cover a multitude of varieties of the Cucurbitaceae family, seems to come from a Native American word—*askooot-asquash*. This ancient vegetable helped sustain life, and the hard-skinned varieties and their cousins the gourds provided our ancestors with handy containers for water and other foods, as well as eating utensils and dishes—the original disposable kitchenware.

There are dozens of varieties of squash, which can generally be divided into two main categories. The older classification divided squash into summer and winter types. But these vegetables are no longer seasonal and are now in the market all year long. A more exact distinction is between thin-skinned and hard- or thick-skinned varieties.

Thin-skinned squash includes yellow summer squash, zucchini (page 357), pattypan or cymling (both celadon green and sunburst yellow), chayote (page 128), cucumber (page 146), and pumpkin (page 293). Thin-skinned varieties are best when picked very young and small, long before they reach their maximum size, while the seeds are still very immature and the flavor is delicate and fresh. The skins should be thin enough to be easily pierced with your fingernail. These squash are fragile, spoil easily, and require refrigeration.

Hard- or thick-skinned squash takes in all of the long-keeping varieties, including buttercup, butternut, delicata, Hubbard, Kabocha, spaghetti, sweet dumpling, turban, and the most popular acorn. There are many other hard-skinned varieties, but most are unavailable commercially or are found only in very small quantities in specialty greengrocers. The thick-skinned squash are left on the vine until they are fully mature and the shells are too hard to pierce easily. The seeds are fully developed and, for the most part, are inedible. The size of these squash is not the indication of quality that it is in the thin-skinned varieties. Some very large specimens can be even sweeter, more flavorful, and less fibrous than smaller ones. These squash are best when picked and allowed to age, or cure, slightly before storing. If stored in a dry place at an optimum temperature of about 50°F., they will keep through the winter—a real blessing before the advent of interstate trucking and refrigeration.

Squash are multipurpose vegetables. They can be boiled, baked, steamed, stewed, roasted, mashed, fried, and combined with meats, fruits, and other vegetables to create hundreds of different dishes, both savory and sweet. In fact you could serve some kind of squash 365 days in a row and never repeat a recipe.

The following are the types of squash most readily available in supermarkets and greengrocers.

Summer squash is also called yellow squash and can be both straight, like yellow zucchini, and crooked neck. Thin-skinned and fully edible, summer squash is delicious raw in salads or on crudité platters.

Pattypan (cymling, scallop, custard squash) squash is a tiny-to-small, saucer-shaped, thin-skinned squash with scalloped edges. It ranges in color from a beautiful pale celadon green to cream and to the vibrant yellow of the Sunburst variety. It's a frequently neglected squash that can be stuffed, eaten raw, or substituted in any recipe calling for summer squash or zucchini.

Acorn squash, as its name suggests, is shaped like a large acorn. This very thick-skinned variety may be golden yellow, orange, deep green tinged with orange, or white (a new variety). This can be a sweet delicious squash, or it can

be watery tasting and stringy. Look for smaller sizes that can be split in half, yielding two servings. Larger ones can be cut into wedges or sliced across into rings.

Buttercup squash, shaped somewhat like a small flattened green turban squash, is small at the blossom end and bulbous at the stem end. The flesh is deep orange, solid, sweet tasting, and full of beta-carotene. Buy it when you see it for a real treat.

Butternut is an elongated, beige-yellow, bell-shaped squash that can grow to be quite large. It is usually available all year long. The orange flesh is sweet and creamy tasting. The smaller ones are good for stuffing; larger ones can be cut up and used in soups, casseroles, and gratins.

Delicata is a relatively small, elongated green-and-yellow-striped squash. The pale yellow flesh is sweet with a flavor sort of like fresh corn. The skin is thinner than other hard-skinned varieties, and it does not store well. Plan to eat it within a week or two of buying it.

Hubbard is an often extremely large, warty skinned squash, shaped somewhat like an old-fashioned top. Colors can range from dark pine green and deep pumpkin orange to gray. Sometimes it is sold already cut into pieces. If cut, look for the deepest orange flesh, regardless of the skin color. It's very good for stewing or combining with other vegetables and meats.

Kabocha looks like a small green pumpkin. The skin can be mottled and bumpy. This Asian favorite has a dense, sweet flesh that is less watery than some of its cousins.

Spaghetti squash is an oval-shaped, golden yellow squash with a relatively thin skin (thus it is sometimes categorized with thin-skinned varieties). When this squash is cooked, the flesh falls into long, pale golden strands, which can be sauced and served much the same as pasta. The crisp texture and delicate flavor make it a natural to combine with all sorts of sauces, but it can also be very good tossed with just butter, salt, and pepper.

Sweet dumpling squash is small (one yields one or two servings at the most) with a flattened pumpkin shape and mottled dark green to beige or orange stripes. The yellow-orange flesh is sweet and very tasty. This squash can often be substituted for acorn squash, though the flavor is different.

Turban is a large flat-based squash with a three-knobbed topknot. It looks a great deal like an old-fashioned Turkish turban, hence the name. The color can range from golden to pumpkin orange with green stripes, all on the same squash. Choose a dense, heavy specimen. This is a wonderful keeper that can be part of a harvest display on the table, then popped into the pot to enjoy as part of a meal. It combines well with other flavors and is especially good in gratins and other baked dishes.

While squash is available in myriad shapes, sizes, colors, and tastes, all provide much the same nutritional elements. They contain large quantities of beta-carotene; and the more orange the flesh, the more it contains. All are low fat, have no cholesterol, and supply moderate amounts of fiber as well as vitamins B and C.

Selection: Thin-skinned squash should be small, firm, crisp, and brightly colored. There should be no brown spots, dents, soft spots, or signs of mold.

Hard-skinned squash can be more difficult to select. Look for squash that feel heavy in the hands, with skins that cannot be pierced with a fingernail. They should be dry looking, with no soft spots, blemishes, or signs of mold. The one exception to the rule might be the butternut squash, which sometimes has cracks in the shell. Check the stem, which should still be attached with no indications of mildew or mold. Do not buy a squash that has no stem attached; it can be dried out and fibrous.

Thin-skinned squash is almost totally edible, so ¼ to ⅓ pound per person is adequate. Thick-skinned squash has a lot of waste. The seeds, fibers, and skin are generally discarded; therefore, it is best to count on at least ½ pound per person, unless the squash is being combined with other vegetables or meat.

Most squash is now available all year around.

Storage and Preparation: Thin-skinned varieties are fragile and relatively perishable. They quickly lose their moisture and become flabby and uninteresting. It is best to buy what you need and to prepare it as soon as possible. If you have to keep it, store unwashed squash in a perforated plastic vegetable bag in the vegetable compartment of the refrigerator for no longer than two to three days.

Thick-skinned squash keeps best at temperatures of 50° to 55°F. Most will last three to four months. If they must be stored at room temperature, plan to eat them within three to four weeks. They will last another week or so in the refrigerator, but do not do well for long periods at temperatures below 50°F. Cut squash can be tightly wrapped in plastic wrap and kept in the refrigerator for up to a week, but plan to use it as soon as possible after cutting. The same goes for any squash you buy already cut and wrapped. It is best to cook precut squash within a day or two of buying it.

Thin-skinned squash needs to be washed, and the stem ends should be trimmed. Otherwise it is ready to eat or cut up for cooking. Tiny baby yellow squash and pattypans are ready to steam or braise whole. These squash do not need to be peeled.

Thick-skinned squash should be peeled (although the skin is technically edible) and is generally cooked before eating. Actually, the most difficult part of preparing these squash is cutting them open. A heavy knife or sharp Japanese or Chinese cleaver will do a good job on acorn, butternut, delicata, and spaghetti squash, but some of the other very thick-skinned varieties almost need to be attacked with an ax. Try this method: Once the stem has been removed and a very heavy knife can be inserted in the hole, use a rocking motion to pry an opening. Once the skin has begun to split, tap the blunt edge of the knife with a wooden mallet to break it open. Once opened, scoop out the seeds and all the fibers that cling to them. Cut the remaining squash into chunks, wedges, slices, and so on.

Small whole hard-skinned squash, like some acorn and sweet dumpling, can be microwaved whole on high for about 2 minutes. Once removed from the microwave oven they will be easier to cut. Large squash can be softened slightly in the same way—providing you can get them in and out of the microwave. Increase the time to 3 or 4 minutes.

Hard-skinned squash is much easier to peel after it has been parboiled or cooked. If you want to peel it raw for a particular recipe, hack, chop, or cut it into manageable pieces and use a very sharp paring knife or vegetable peeler to remove the skin.

Baked Squash

Small squash can be baked whole. They can be wiped clean, placed on a baking sheet or in a roasting pan, and baked at 350° to 375°F. for 35 to 40 minutes per pound. I prefer to cut out a lid, remove the seeds and fibers, and brush the inside with butter or oil before baking. Check the squash about 15 minutes before you think it will be done so that it does not collapse. This is particularly important if you want to fill it with soup or stew.

Squash can also be baked in pieces. Brush the flesh very lightly with oil and bake, uncovered, for about 30 minutes. Test with a fork or sharp knife. Baked squash can be eaten as is, with butter and herbs or salt and pepper, or it can be treated like parboiled squash and cooled slightly, peeled, and used in another recipe. Squash prepared this way retains more of its vitamins and minerals than when it is boiled.

Microwaved Squash

The quickest way to prepare squash is to cook it in the microwave. This method also retains the maximum amount of nutrients.

Small, whole squash can be microwaved on high for 6 to 10 minutes. Be sure to pierce them several times with a sharp fork to prevent them from exploding. I prefer to cut out a lid, remove the seeds and fibers, and brush the inside with a little oil or butter. They do not need to be pierced if the lid is left slightly ajar. Let the squash stand several minutes before stuffing or serving.

Larger squash can be cut up, placed in a microwaveable dish, covered with plastic microwave wrap, vented, and microwaved on high for 4 to 5 minutes. Let stand 3 or 4 minutes before uncovering.

Boiled Squash

Plain boiled squash is basically uninteresting. Some recipes call for parboiling, though, and very thick-skinned squash is much easier to peel after being parboiled.

Place the cut up unpeeled squash in a saucepan of boiling salted water to cover. Simmer, uncovered, over medium heat, until the skin is easily pierced with a sharp knife. The time will depend on the type of squash, but begin checking after about 10 minutes. Drain well, cool, and peel. Cut the squash into whatever size or shape the recipe calls for.

Steamed Squash

Squash can be oven steamed or steamed over simmering water. To oven steam, preheat the oven to 375°F. Place the squash halves—acorn, butternut, delicata, spaghetti, and so on—cut side down in a baking pan. Add about ¼ inch water. Bake, uncovered, until tender, 30 to 40 minutes. Remove from the oven and drain. Continue with the recipe.

To steam over simmering water, place the squash, cut side down, in a steamer basket or a colander. Steam, covered, for 20 to 25 minutes. Remove from the steamer and continue with the recipe. Pieces of larger squash can be steamed in the same way.

Stuffed Pattypan Squash

Pattypans and their near cousins, the brilliant yellow Sunburst squash, are often neglected, probably because of the incredible onslaught of zucchini and yellow squash from the garden. Pattypans are a perfect size for stuffing, and this green bean puree is both different and delicious. This is a perfect "company" dish, and I would pair it with a thick, juicy grilled steak and steaming hot crisp-skinned baked potatoes.

Makes 6 servings

1 tablespoon butter, softened, plus additional for buttering
6 pattypan (cymling) or Sunburst squash, all the same size, about 3½ inches in diameter, steamed whole until just tender, 15 to 20 minutes
¼ pound green beans, topped and tailed, chopped, simmered in salted water to cover until very tender but still very green, 6 to 8 minutes, and drained
3 tablespoons minced onion
Salt and freshly ground black pepper to taste
½ cup grated fontina cheese
½ cup water
1 tablespoon chopped fresh parsley

Preheat the oven to 375°F. Generously butter a glass or other shallow baking dish just large enough to hold the squash in one layer.

Cut the stems out of the pattypans. With a sharp spoon, scoop out the flesh, leaving a shell at least ¼ inch thick. Chop the removed squash.

Puree the green beans with the onion. Stir into the chopped squash. Season the mixture with salt and pepper. Stir in half of the cheese and the parsley. Spoon the mixture into the prepared shells.

Arrange the stuffed squash side by side in the prepared dish. Dot each squash with a little of the 1 tablespoon butter and sprinkle with more cheese. Pour the water around the squash, being careful not to pour any on them.

Bake until the cheese is bubbling and golden brown, 20 to 25 minutes. Remove the squash from the baking dish and drain it on a paper towel. Serve very hot.

Spaghetti Squash Cakes

Prepare the batter for these crisp, little pancakes ahead of time and then fry just before serving. If you are grilling outdoors, put the skillet directly on the grill or on a portable gas burner alongside, and you will not have to be confined to the kitchen while everyone else is enjoying the fresh air. Serve with grilled fish or chicken.

Makes 6 to 8 servings

1 medium-size spaghetti squash, skin well
    pierced, baked at 375°F. until tender,
    1 to 1½ hours
¼ cup minced onion
¼ cup unbleached all-purpose flour
1 whole large egg, beaten
½ teaspoon dried Italian herbs, such as oregano,
    marjoram, rosemary, and thyme, or a
    prepared mix
Salt and freshly ground black pepper to taste
Butter
Freshly grated Parmesan cheese

Halve the squash lengthwise and use a fork to scrape the insides into a medium-size bowl. Toss with the onion and flour. Stir in the egg. Season well with the herbs, salt, and pepper.

Melt 1 tablespoon butter in a large heavy skillet over medium heat. When the butter bubbles, drop the squash by large spoonfuls into the skillet. Press down with the back of a spoon into large, flat, irregularly shaped cakes. Fry until just golden brown on the bottom, 2 to 3 minutes. Turn the pancakes over with a spatula and brown the other side. Repeat with the remaining squash, adding more butter if necessary. Serve very hot, garnished with a sprinkling of the cheese.

Spaghetti Squash Gratin

Often this delicately flavored squash is sauced just like pasta. (Try it with Fresh Tomato Pasta Sauce Pronto.)

There are many other ways to serve it, though, and this gratin is just one. Serve it with grilled fish, such as halibut, tuna, or swordfish, or a whole red snapper.

Makes 6 servings

3 tablespoons pure olive oil, plus additional
    for oiling
Freshly grated Parmesan cheese
1 large spaghetti squash, skin well pierced
    with a fork, baked at 325°F. until tender,
    about 1½ hours
½ small sweet onion, minced
¼ cup green bell pepper, minced
2 tablespoons chopped fresh oregano;
    or 1½ teaspoons dried
Salt and freshly ground black pepper to taste
1 cup grated Gruyère cheese

Preheat the oven to 400°F. Generously oil a 1½-quart soufflé dish. Dust with the Parmesan cheese. Set aside.

Halve the squash lengthwise and use a fork to scrape the insides into a large bowl. Toss with the onion, pepper, oregano, and 3 tablespoons of oil. Season well with salt and pepper. Pile the squash into the prepared dish. Spread the cheese on the squash. Bake until the cheese is melted and golden brown, 15 to 20 minutes. Serve very hot.

Note: *This dish can be assembled ahead of time, covered, and refrigerated, to be cooked just before serving. Bring the dish to room temperature before baking and increase the cooking time by 5 to 10 minutes.*

Pasta and Two-color Squash

Here is a colorful summer dish that will go well with almost anything you might want to grill. For a lighter meal, serve this pasta with a green salad and lots of good bread.

Makes 6 to 8 servings

2 tablespoons olive oil
1 bunch (6 to 8) green onions (scallions), white
    and light green parts only, sliced
1 large clove garlic, minced
1 teaspoon chopped fresh thyme
2 small yellow squash, trimmed and grated
2 small zucchini, trimmed and grated
Salt and freshly ground black pepper to taste
1 pound thin spaghetti, cooked, drained,
    and kept hot
Freshly grated Parmesan cheese

Heat the oil in a large skillet over medium heat. Add the green onions and cook, stirring, for 2 minutes. Stir in the garlic and thyme. Add the yellow squash and zucchini. Cook over high heat, tossing with a fork, 2 minutes. Season well with salt and pepper.

Add the hot spaghetti to the vegetables in the skillet. Toss well to combine. Remove from the heat. Serve immediately, very hot, with the cheese passed separately.

Creole Summer Squash

I really enjoy this colorful dish alongside Cajun grilled pork chops, or with blackened fish fillets.

Makes 6 servings

2 tablespoons olive oil
1 large onion, sliced
1 large green bell pepper, seeded, and chopped
2 large tomatoes, peeled, seeded, and chopped
3 medium-size yellow squash, trimmed, and
    thinly sliced
3 small zucchini, trimmed and thinly sliced
1 tablespoon chopped fresh thyme;
    or 1 teaspoon dried
1/2 cup dry white wine
Salt and freshly ground black pepper to taste
Hot pepper sauce to taste

Heat the olive oil in a very large heavy skillet over medium heat. Add the onion and bell pepper, and cook, stirring, until just translucent, about 10 minutes. Stir in the tomatoes and cook, stirring, about 3 minutes. Stir in the squash. Toss for about 2 minutes.

Stir in the thyme and white wine. Season well with salt and pepper. Cook, tossing from time to time, until the squash is tender, 5 to 6 minutes. All the vegetables should retain their shape and not dissolve into a mush. Serve very hot. Pass the hot pepper sauce on the side.

Texas Summer Squash Casserole

I first had a variation of this at a barbecue beside a placid Texas lake. It was the perfect summer accompaniment for the fiery barbecued brisket and ribs that were on the menu. If you have squash haters in the house, this could be a great way to change their minds.

Makes 6 to 8 servings

2 tablespoons butter, plus additional for buttering
1 small onion, finely chopped
4 medium-size yellow squash, trimmed, cut into
    1/2-inch cubes, boiled or steamed until crisply
    tender, about 5 minutes
1 small jalapeño pepper, or more to taste, seeded
    and minced
1/2 teaspoon dried oregano
1 cup grated Cheddar cheese
Salt and freshly ground black pepper to taste
3/4 cup plain dried bread crumbs,
    or cracker crumbs

Preheat the oven to 350°F. Generously butter a 1-quart deep baking dish.

Melt 2 tablespoons of butter in a medium-size skillet over medium heat. Add the onion and cook until just translucent, 6 to 8 minutes. Remove from the heat. Stir in the squash, jalapeño pepper, oregano, and cheese. Season well with salt and pepper. Transfer the mixture to the prepared baking dish. Spread the crumbs on top. Bake until hot and bubbling, about 30 minutes. Serve very hot.

Summer Squash Tart

Actually this is a sort of quiche. It is especially fine as the one hot dish on a cold summer menu. Serve with lots of cold meats or fish, and a crisp green salad.

Makes 6 to 8 servings

Pastry dough for a 1-crust 9-inch pie (page 126)
2 tablespoons butter
1 medium-size onion, thinly sliced
3 medium-size yellow summer squash, trimmed, thinly sliced, and steamed until barely tender, 4 to 5 minutes
2 medium-size zucchini, trimmed, thinly sliced, and steamed until barely tender, 4 to 5 minutes
Salt and freshly ground black pepper to taste
1 teaspoon dried Italian herbs, such as oregano, marjoram, rosemary, and thyme, or a prepared mix
$\frac{1}{2}$ cup grated Monterey Jack cheese
2 large eggs, well beaten
$\frac{2}{3}$ cup heavy cream

Preheat the oven to 375°F.

Roll out the pastry dough and line a 9-inch pie pan, making a high fluted edge. Line the pastry shell with wax or parchment paper, and fill with dried beans or baking weights. Bake the pastry shell for 10 minutes. Remove from the oven, remove the weights or beans and paper, and cool the shell.

Melt the butter in a small skillet over medium heat and cook the onion, stirring, until translucent, about 10 minutes.

In a large bowl, toss the squash with the onions. Season well with salt, pepper, and herbs. Spread in the partially baked pastry shell. Spread the cheese over the vegetables.

In a small bowl, beat together the eggs and cream. Pour the mixture over the squash and cheese. Bake the tart until the custard is set and a knife inserted in the middle comes out clean, about 30 minutes. Serve the tart hot, or cool until warm, cut into wedges.

Variation: *Serve the tart warm or at room temperature, with Cooked Tomatillo Salsa spooned over each wedge.*

Stuffed Butternut Squash

The filled squash is very pretty on a serving plate. Cut it across into thick slices to serve. The flavor goes well with a roast loin of pork.

Makes 8 servings

1 medium-size butternut squash (4 to 5 pounds), halved lengthwise, seeds and fibers removed
$\frac{1}{2}$ cup water
5 thick slices bacon, cut into $\frac{1}{4}$-inch dice
$\frac{1}{2}$ small onion, minced
$\frac{1}{2}$ small green bell pepper, minced
$\frac{1}{2}$ cup plain dried bread crumbs
Salt and freshly ground black pepper to taste
1 tablespoon chopped fresh oregano; or 1 teaspoon dried
Hot pepper sauce to taste
Butter
Chopped fresh parsley

Preheat the oven to 400°F.

Place the squash, cut side down, in a shallow baking dish large enough to hold the squash in a single layer. Pour in the water. Bake, uncovered, for 30 minutes. Remove the dish from the oven, turn the squash over, and cool.

Use a sharp spoon to remove the insides, leaving a shell about $\frac{1}{2}$ inch thick. Chop the removed insides.

Fry the bacon in a small heavy skillet over medium heat until crisp, 6 to 8 minutes. Remove the bacon from the skillet with a slotted spoon and drain on paper towels. Add the onion and bell pepper to the bacon fat in the skillet and cook, stirring, until the vegetables are just translucent, 5 to 6 minutes.

In a bowl, toss together the chopped squash, the onion and pepper, the bread crumbs, salt, pepper, and oregano. Season with the hot pepper sauce.

Spoon the mixture back into the prepared shells. Arrange them side by side in the baking dish. Dot the surface with a little butter. Bake until the squash is tender and the filling is very hot, about 25 minutes. Serve hot, cut across into thick slices, garnished with the parsley.

Delicata Squash with Potatoes, Pearl Onions, and Mushrooms

The fresh, almost cornlike flavor of delicata makes this a delicious side dish for a dinner featuring grilled lamb or beef, or even fried chicken.

Makes 6 to 8 servings

2 to 3 tablespoons olive oil or butter
1 pint (10 ounces) boiling (pearl) onions, boiled in water to cover for 1 minute, drained, and peeled; or one-half 16-ounce package frozen baby onions, thawed
2 pounds delicata, or other hard-skinned squash, peeled, seeded, cut into 1-inch chunks, and steamed until just tender, 15 to 20 minutes
2 large waxy round white potatoes (brown or red skinned), unpeeled, cut into 1-inch chunks, boiled in salted water to cover until tender, about 15 minutes, and drained
¼ pound white button mushrooms, stems trimmed, halved if large
Salt and freshly ground black pepper to taste
¾ teaspoon dried thyme, crushed; or 1 tablespoon chopped fresh

Heat the oil in a large heavy skillet over medium heat. Add the onions and cook over medium heat for 5 minutes. Add the squash and potatoes and cook, tossing, until the vegetables begin to turn golden brown, 6 to 8 minutes. Stir in the mushrooms and cook 5 to 6 minutes. Season well with salt, pepper, and thyme. Serve very hot.

Gratin of Butternut Squash with Onions and Tomatoes

Butternut squash has a naturally sweet flavor that goes very well with roast meats. This gratin would be fine with a roast chicken or turkey, beef ribs, or even thick slices of homemade meat loaf.

Makes 6 servings

2 tablespoons olive oil, plus additional for greasing
2 large onions, thinly sliced
2 cloves garlic, minced
3 pounds butternut squash, or another hard-skinned squash, seeded, peeled, sliced, boiled in salted water to cover for 5 minutes, drained, and dried on kitchen towels
2 large ripe tomatoes, thinly sliced
Salt and freshly ground black pepper to taste
1 cup milk
¼ cup freshly grated Parmesan cheese

Preheat the oven to 350°F. Lightly grease a 1½-quart ovenproof casserole.

Heat 2 tablespoons of oil in a medium-size heavy skillet over medium heat. Add the onions and cook, stirring, until just wilted, about 5 minutes. Stir in the garlic. Cook 1 minute.

Arrange one-third of the squash slices in the bottom of the prepared dish. Spread half of the onion and garlic mixture over the squash and then with half of the tomato slices. Season well with salt and pepper. Repeat the layers, ending with squash. Season well with salt and pepper. Pour in the milk and sprinkle the cheese over the top.

Bake until very tender and most of the milk has been absorbed, about 1 hour. Serve very hot.

Winter Squash and Apples

The sweetness of this very tasty winter dish means it is a perfect companion for baked ham, pork roast, or grilled smoked sausages.

Makes 6 servings

2 tablespoons butter
1 rib celery, trimmed, strung, and thinly sliced on
     the diagonal
1 large onion, halved and thinly sliced
1 Granny Smith apple, peeled, cored, quartered,
     and sliced
2 pounds turban, Hubbard, or buttercup squash,
     peeled, seeded, cut into 2-inch square sticks,
     then sliced
1 teaspoon grated fresh ginger
½ cup apple cider
½ cup dry white wine
Salt and freshly ground black pepper to taste
½ teaspoon dried marjoram, crushed

Melt the butter in a large heavy skillet over medium heat. Add the celery and onion and cook, stirring, until translucent, about 8 minutes. Stir in the apple, squash slices, and ginger. Cook, tossing from time to time, until the apples and squash are coated with butter. Stir in the cider and wine. Season with salt, pepper, and marjoram. Cover and simmer over low heat until the squash is very tender but not falling apart, 15 to 20 minutes. Remove the cover, increase the heat to medium-high, and cook until the sauce thickens, 2 or 3 minutes. Toss the vegetables gently and serve very hot.

Wonderfully Rummy Acorn Squash

These slices are easy to eat and seem to appeal to young and old alike. Roast duck and goose are good accompaniments, but a gloriously golden roast turkey or oven-roaster chicken will do just as well.

Makes 6 servings

3 tablespoons butter
½ cup dry white wine
2 large acorn squash, halved lengthwise,
     seeds and fibers removed, cut across into
     ¾-inch slices
Salt and freshly ground black pepper to taste
¼ cup packed brown sugar
3 tablespoons dark rum

Combine the butter and wine in a large covered skillet over low heat. Arrange the squash slices in one layer. Season with salt and pepper. Cover. Simmer over low heat for 15 minutes. Turn the squash slices and simmer until tender, 15 to 20 minutes longer.

Remove the squash and keep warm. Stir the sugar and rum into the juices left in the skillet. Increase the heat to high and boil hard, stirring, until reduced to a buttery glaze, about 5 minutes. Return the squash to the skillet. Cook over low heat, turning the slices to coat well with the glaze. Serve very hot.

Turban Squash with Onions

Braised beef goes very well with this simple combination, and a large bowl of fluffy buttered rice will round out the bill of fare very nicely.

Makes 6 servings

2 tablespoons butter
2 onions, thickly sliced
3 pounds turban or butternut squash, peeled,
     seeded, and cut into 2-inch pieces

¾ cup well-flavored chicken stock
¼ cup dry white wine
½ teaspoon dried thyme, crushed
Salt and freshly ground black pepper to taste
Chopped fresh parsley

Melt the butter in a large deep skillet over medium heat. Add the onions and cook, stirring from time to time, until wilted and translucent, 6 to 8 minutes. Stir in the squash and toss for 2 to 3 minutes, until the squash is coated with butter. Stir in the stock, wine, and thyme. Season well with salt and pepper. Cover and simmer over low heat until the squash is tender, 20 to 25 minutes.

Remove the cover, raise the heat to medium-high, and evaporate most of the liquid, 2 to 3 minutes. Serve very hot, garnished with the parsley.

Ginger-Garlic Acorn Squash

Grilled or baked salmon fillets or, if you are very fortunate, grilled mahimahi will be even better with these delicious little squash on the same plate. The bite of the black bean paste is a pleasant surprise.

Makes 6 servings

3 small acorn squash, or sweet dumplings if you can find them, split lengthwise, seeds and fibers removed, a small slice cut off each bottom so the squash will sit firmly
¼ cup teriyaki sauce, or light soy sauce
1 teaspoon Chinese black bean paste
2 teaspoons grated fresh ginger
3 tablespoons butter
¼ cup dry sherry or rice wine
¼ cup well-flavored chicken stock

Preheat the oven to 375°F.

Arrange the squash, cut side down, in a deep roasting pan large enough to hold them in a single layer. Pour in about ¼ inch water. Bake until the squash is barely tender, 25 to 30 minutes. Remove the pan from the oven, drain, and turn the squash right side up in the pan.

While the squash are baking, combine the teriyaki sauce, black bean paste, ginger, butter, sherry, and stock in a small saucepan. Simmer over low heat, stirring, until well mixed and slightly reduced, 3 to 4 minutes. Divide the mixture evenly among the centers of the squash halves. Cover the pan tightly with aluminum foil.

Bake until the squash are tender, 35 minutes. Remove the aluminum foil. Bake until most of the liquid has been absorbed, about 10 minutes longer. Serve very hot.

Wine-braised Squash

Boiled potatoes, steamed cabbage, and succulent slices of corned beef will go very well with this dish of tender squash.

Makes 6 to 8 servings

1½ tablespoons butter, plus additional
    for buttering
2 small onions, thinly sliced
Salt and freshly ground black pepper to taste
3 pounds hard-skinned squash, such as butternut, Hubbard, turban, or Kabocha, peeled, seeded, and thinly sliced
⅓ cup well-flavored chicken stock
⅓ cup dry white wine
2 tablespoons plain dried bread crumbs
2 tablespoons chopped fresh parsley

Preheat the oven to 350°F. Generously butter a large shallow baking or gratin dish.

Spread the onions in the bottom of the prepared dish. Dot with some of the 1½ tablespoons of butter and season with salt and pepper. Arrange the squash slices over the onions. Dot with more butter and season with salt and pepper. Pour in the stock and wine. Cover tightly with aluminum foil.

Bake 35 to 40 minutes. Uncover. Raise the heat to 450°F. In a small bowl, combine the bread crumbs and parsley. Sprinkle this mixture over the squash. Bake until the crumbs are golden, 5 to 6 minutes. Serve hot, or warm.

Fruit-stuffed Acorn Squash

*I have always loved acorn squash, even with just a spoon-
ful of brown sugar, a little rum, and some butter baked in
the middle until it soaks into the flesh. The slightly sweet
flavor of this delicious squash lends itself to combining
with fruit, too. Serve with medallions of braised pork
tenderloin, or thick braised pork chops.*

Makes 6 servings

3 small acorn squash, or sweet dumplings if you
    can find them, halved lengthwise, seeds and
    fibers removed, a small slice cut off the
    bottom of each so it will sit firmly without
    rocking
2 tablespoons butter
½ small onion, thinly sliced
2 Golden Delicious apples, peeled, cored,
    and chopped
¼ cup golden raisins, plumped in boiling water to
    cover, and drained
¼ cup dried cherries or cranberries, plumped in
    boiling water to cover, and drained
1 teaspoon finely minced candied ginger
⅓ cup dry white wine
⅓ cup firmly packed dark brown sugar
⅓ cup chopped pecans, toasted (page 70)

Preheat the oven to 375°F.

Arrange the squash, cut side down, in a large roasting pan. Pour in about ¼ inch of water. Bake until
barely tender when pierced with a sharp fork, 25 to
30 minutes.

While the squash are baking, melt the butter in a
small skillet over low heat. Add the onions and cook,
stirring, until translucent, 6 to 8 minutes. Add the
apples, raisins, cherries or cranberries, ginger, and
wine. Cover and cook over low heat until the apple
is very tender but not falling apart, about 15 minutes. Remove from the heat and cool. When cool,
stir in the brown sugar and pecans.

When the squash is tender, remove the roasting
pan from the oven. Drain. Turn the squash right side

up in the baking pan. Mound the apple mixture in
the center of each half, and bake until the squash is
very tender, 20 to 25 minutes longer. Serve very hot,
or warm.

Summer Squash Salad

*Add this to your next cold buffet. With yellow squash
and zucchini available all year long now, you might want
to include this in a festive winter celebration, like Super
Bowl Sunday*

Makes 6 servings

⅓ cup extra-virgin olive oil
1 tablespoon white wine vinegar
1 teaspoon Dijon-style mustard
Sald and freshly ground black pepper to taste
2 tablespoons freshly snipped chives, plus
    additional for garnishing
2 small yellow squash, trimmed and grated or cut
    into thin matchstick strips
2 small zucchini, trimmed and grated or cut into
    thin matchstick strips
2 pattypan squash (about 2 inches in diameter),
    stem removed and grated or cut into thin
    matchstick strips
1 small red bell pepper, roasted, peeled, seeded,
    and very thinly sliced
1 small sweet onion, very thinly sliced and
    separated into rings

In a small bowl, beat together the oil, vinegar,
mustard, sald, pepper, and chives.

In a medium-size bowl, toss together all the squash
and the bell pepper. Pour the dressing over the vegetables and toss well. Let stand 30 minutes at room
temperature.

Arrange the salad on a serving plate, top with the
onion rings, and garnish with the additional chives.

Sweet Potatoes

Sweet potatoes are not really potatoes, nor are they yams. This tuber, like its relative the morning glory, is a native American vegetable. Grown in Central and tropical America long before the arrival of Columbus and the other European explorers, it was a diet staple, along with corn and pumpkin. The explorers evidently liked the sweet taste and carried it home with them at the end of their travels, where it was planted with some success. In America, it was quickly adopted by colonial gardeners and, like pumpkin, was one of the foods that helped sustain life during the first long, cold winters when other crops had failed or performed badly in the unfamiliar soil.

Yams, on the other hand, are an African vegetable, transplanted to South America and the Caribbean, but rarely available in the United States, outside of certain ethnic markets. The confusion comes from transplanted Africans referring to the sweet potato by the same name as the more familiar starchy root vegetable from their homeland, although they have nothing in common as far as taste is concerned.

Sweet potatoes are widely eaten in the southern part of the United States and are usually included in holiday menus everywhere else—often buried beneath a thick layer of marshmallow. They deserve better.

There are several varieties of sweet potato. The very familiar moist potato with a deep russet-colored skin and dark orange flesh is the variety most frequently eaten in the South and the one often mistakenly called a yam. There is also a sweet potato with a drier, yellower flesh. These are delicious baked and used in gratins and casseroles, while the more orange variety takes well to sweeter preparations, including certain desserts and pies, although the two kinds are basically interchangeable. In addition to these two most commonly available, there are other varieties, including one with a purplish skin and a pale grayish blue flesh. Most of these are drier fleshed than the deep orange variety.

The starch in sweet potatoes is converted to sugar as it matures, which accounts for the sweet flavor. In fact, some growers cure sweet potatoes by heating them to 85°F. for several days before shipping them. This may stabilize the sugar and seems to increase the storage time.

Because most people associate sweet potatoes with ultra-sugary preparations, they are often neglected in everyday cooking. If you have never had a sweet potato plainly baked, opened, fluffed, and served with nothing more than a little butter, salt, and pepper, you have missed a major treat. Sweet potatoes can be prepared in many of the ways white potatoes are served. They can be boiled, baked, fried, roasted, mashed, and gratinéed and made into casseroles, salads, and soups as well as sweetened dishes.

Not only are sweet potatoes versatile, they are extremely nutritious. They are low calorie, less than an equal-sized white potato, low fat, cholesterol free, relatively high in carbohydrates, and exploding with beta-carotene. The deeper orange the flesh, the more beta-carotene it contains. Given the most recent research into the benefits of foods rich in beta-carotene, sweet potatoes could be very helpful in preventing certain types of cancer. They also provide moderate amounts of fiber, vitamin C, and potassium.

Selection: No matter which variety you select, look for plump, smooth, hard tubers that are heavy in the hand. They should be somewhat elongated, thick in the middle, and tapering on both ends. The skins can be of various colors, from light brown to a deep russet, even purple, but should not have off-colored spots, spade cuts, or bruises. The tubers should not be limp or spongy feeling. Do not buy any that show signs of mold, especially at the tips.

Sweet potatoes are in the market year round but are at their freshest between late September and January and are most abundant during the winter holidays.

You will need from $\frac{1}{3}$ to $\frac{1}{2}$ pound of sweet potatoes per person, unless they are being combined with other vegetables.

Storage and Preparation: Sweet potatoes are not as hardy as white potatoes. The thin skins are readily broken, and the flesh can be easily bruised, which causes them to spoil quickly. Store them, unwashed, in a cool dry place, for up to two weeks. Check them from time to time to be sure they have not begun to spoil. Look at the ends of the potatoes, where decay often begins. If they must be stored at kitchen temperature, plan to use them within a few days or a week at most. Do not refrigerate uncooked sweet potatoes.

For the most part, sweet potatoes require little preparation. They should be scrubbed before peeling or cooking, although the skin is edible, so peeling is not a necessity. Sweet potatoes are easily peeled after being parboiled or baked, but for recipes calling for raw peeled potatoes, it is best done with a sharp paring knife. The peeled potato can be sliced, diced, or cut into any desired shape. If you are preparing the sweet potatoes a long time before they will be cooked, toss them with a little lemon juice. They do not discolor rapidly, but will darken after a while.

Boiled Sweet Potatoes

Sweet potatoes can be boiled, whole, in the skins or can be peeled and cut up before boiling, although they will be much easier to peel once cooked. Place the potatoes in a large saucepan of boiling water deep enough to cover them completely. Simmer over medium heat until tender, 10 to 20 minutes for cut up potatoes, 20 to 40 minutes for whole, unpeeled potatoes, depending upon the size and variety of potato. The moist, deep orange–fleshed potato frequently takes longer to cook than the drier varieties. Drain the potatoes well, cool slightly, then peel if desired.

Baked Sweet Potatoes

Plain, baked sweet potatoes are delicious with just a little butter, salt, and pepper. Potatoes to be used in recipes calling for precooking can also be baked rather than boiled. Baking makes candied sweet potatoes especially good as none of the flavor has been leached out during the boiling process.

Prick the washed, dried sweet potatoes several times with a fork. Place them directly on the rack in a preheated 375°F. oven. Bake for 45 to 60 minutes, depending on the type and size of the potato. They are done when a sharp knife or fork can be easily inserted to the middle. Remove from the oven and let stand about 5 minutes. Serve while still very hot.

Peeled sweet potatoes can be baked or roasted whole around a loin of pork, or other thick cut of meat. Peel the potatoes, brush them with butter or a mild vegetable oil, preferably peanut, and place in the pan with the roast when there is about 1 hour of cooking time left. Turn the potatoes from time to time until they are tender when pierced with a fork and nicely browned all over. Serve alongside the meat.

Microwaved Sweet Potatoes

While sweet potatoes can be cooked in the microwave, I find it is not really a time saver unless you decide at the last minute that you want one baked tuber. And I prefer the texture and taste of conventionally baked potatoes.

Wash and prick the potatoes but do not dry them. Wrap them individually in paper towels, using the butcher wrap: Lay the potato across one corner of the towel. Fold the edges over and roll up into a neat bundle. Lay the bundles on the turntable of the microwave. If you are cooking 3 or more, lay them in a circle, end to end. Microwave on high, 5 to 7 minutes for one, 10 to 12 minutes for two, up to 15 to 20 minutes for four. If the microwave does not have a turntable, turn the potatoes over about halfway through the cooking time. Remove the potatoes from the oven and let stand 5 minutes before unwrapping and serving.

Fanny's Candied Sweet Potatoes

I was practically a teenager before I realized anyone ever made candied sweet potatoes with marshmallows on top. This crusty, marshmallowless dish was what my grandmother's cook taught us all to make instead. We loved it so much that it was a winter staple, especially at Sunday lunch. It is still my favorite holiday accompaniment for roast turkey.

Makes 6 to 8 servings

**3 pounds sweet potatoes, unpeeled, simmered
    in water to cover until tender, about
    20 minutes, drained, peeled, and thickly
    sliced**
1 cup sugar
3 tablespoons butter, softened
Ground cinnamon
½ cup water, or apple cider, boiling

Preheat the oven to 375°F.

Butter a glass or other medium-size deep baking dish. Make a layer of potato slices in the bottom of the dish. Sprinkle with some of the sugar. Dot with some of the butter, and sprinkle with some cinnamon. Continue to layer the potatoes, topping each layer with sugar, butter, and cinnamon. Pour the water into the baking dish, around the potatoes. Sprinkle with the remaining sugar.

Bake until the syrup is thick and sticky and the top is crusted with sugar. Serve very hot, spooning the syrup over each portion.

Baked Sweet Potatoes with Candied Butter

The candied butter should be spooned into the fluffy baked potato, with abandon if you like. It can also be the filling for tender baked apples. Serve these with roast poultry or smoked ham.

Makes 6 servings

8 tablespoons (1 stick) butter, softened
¼ cup packed dark brown sugar
2 tablespoons bourbon
1 teaspoon minced candied ginger
¼ cup chopped pecans, toasted (page 70)
6 medium-size sweet potatoes

In a small bowl, beat together the butter and brown sugar until light and fluffy. Beat in the bourbon. Stir in the ginger and pecans. Spoon into a small serving dish. Cover, refrigerate until firm, or overnight.

Preheat the oven to 375°F.

Bake the potatoes directly on the oven rack until tender, about 1 hour. Remove the potatoes from the oven. Cut an X in the top of each and push both ends inward to "blossom," or open the potato. Serve very hot, with the candied butter on the side.

Sweet Potatoes and Apples

Smoky garlic sausages, grilled over a hardwood fire, along with a big bowl of Summer Slaw, and thick slices of pumpernickel bread will combine very well with this dish.

Makes 6 servings

1 tablespoon butter, plus additional for buttering
4 large sweet potatoes, peeled and sliced
**2 medium-size Golden Delicious apples, peeled,
    halved, cored, and sliced**
1 cup apple cider
**2 tablespoons applejack or apple brandy
    (optional)**
½ teaspoon ground cinnamon
¼ cup packed dark brown sugar

Preheat the oven to 375°F. Generously butter a 1-quart ovenproof casserole.

In a large bowl, toss together the potato and apple slices, and spread them in the prepared casserole. Dot with 1 tablespoon of butter. Pour in the cider and, if using, the applejack. Sprinkle the cinnamon on top. Bake for 40 minutes. Spread the brown sugar on top and bake until melted and bubbling, about 10 minutes longer.

Oven-fried Sweet Potatoes

Root vegetables all seem to do very well when roasted or oven fried. We like these alongside hamburgers, especially ones that have a slice of blue cheese melted on top.

Makes 6 servings

6 medium-size sweet potatoes, peeled and cut into sticks like French fries
2 tablespoons olive oil
1 teaspoon ground allspice
Salt to taste

Preheat the oven to 400°F.

In a large bowl, toss the potato sticks with the oil. Spread on a large baking sheet with sides. Sprinkle with the allspice. Bake 15 minutes. Turn with a spatula and bake 15 minutes longer. Turn the potatoes again. Bake until crisp outside and tender inside, 15 to 20 minutes longer. Season with salt and serve very hot.

Cumin Roast Sweet Potatoes

Try these with blackened fish of any kind, redfish if you can get it, otherwise river catfish will be delicious. I also like to spit-roast a boneless pork loin that has been rolled in dried herbs, to serve alongside these fragrant chunks.

Makes 6 servings

3 tablespoons butter, melted
1 large clove garlic, minced
2 tablespoons minced fresh parsley
4 large sweet potatoes, peeled, and cut into 1-inch chunks

½ teaspoon ground cumin
Salt and freshly ground black pepper to taste

Preheat the oven to 350°F.

In a small bowl combine the butter, garlic, and parsley. In a large bowl, toss the potato chunks with the butter mixture. Sprinkle with the cumin. Spread the potatoes in a large shallow baking dish. Roast, turning from time to time with a spatula, until golden brown and tender, about 45 minutes. Serve very hot, seasoned with salt and pepper.

Twice-baked Sweet Potatoes

For a more elegant presentation, fill a pastry bag fitted with a large star tip with the potato mixture. Pipe the potato into the skins, making a peaked star at the top. Serve at a very special holiday dinner, with roast turkey or baked ham.

Makes 6 servings

3 large sweet potatoes, unpeeled, rubbed with oil, and baked at 350°F. until just tender, about 45 minutes
1 tablespoon butter
3 tablespoons packed dark brown sugar
1 large egg, beaten
1 tablespoon dark rum
Salt and freshly ground black pepper to taste

Preheat the oven to 375°F.

Halve the potatoes lengthwise. Scoop out the insides into a medium-size bowl, leaving a shell about ¼ inch thick. Put the insides through a ricer or mash with a potato masher. Beat in the butter until smooth. Stir in the sugar, egg, and rum. Season well with salt and pepper.

Spoon the mixture into the empty shells. Arrange the filled shells in one layer in a medium-size shallow baking or gratin dish. Bake until the filling is slightly puffy and golden brown, 20 to 30 minutes. Serve very hot.

Roast Sweet Potato Salad

Why not try the blue-fleshed sweet potatoes that some markets carry in late summer and early fall for this wonderful salad? I like to pair it with cold, poached fish, but if there is cold roast lamb left over, that will be great.

Makes 6 to 8 servings

4 medium-size sweet potatoes, peeled, halved
    across, and cut into wedges
2 tablespoons mild vegetable oil
Salt and freshly ground pepper to taste
1 large sweet onion, halved, and thinly sliced
2 ribs celery, trimmed, strung, and thinly sliced
1/2 large green bell pepper, seeded, and cut into
    1/4-inch dice
1/2 pound sugar snap peas, ends trimmed,
    strung, and steamed until just tender, about
    5 minutes; or 2 cups thawed frozen sugar
    snap peas, not cooked
1/2 cup mayonnaise, prepared or homemade
    (page 13)
1/4 cup plain yogurt
1 tablespoon honey
1 teaspoon celery seed
1/2 cup cherry tomatoes, halved
2 tablespoons chopped fresh cilantro

Preheat the oven to 375°F.

In a large bowl, toss the potatoes in the oil and spread on a shallow baking sheet. Roast, turning from time to time, until the wedges are browned and tender, 45 to 60 minutes. Remove the potatoes from the oven and cool.

In a large bowl, toss the cooled potatoes with the onion, celery, bell pepper, and peas.

In a small bowl, combine the mayonnaise, yogurt, honey, and celery seed. Spoon over the vegetables and toss to coat well.

To serve, pile the salad in a large glass or other salad bowl. Add the cherry tomato halves, and garnish with cilantro.

Gingered-mashed Sweet Potatoes

This savory, rather than sweet, puree can be paired with barbecued pork, ribs, crisply grilled duck halves, or grilled tuna or salmon steaks.

Makes 6 to 8 servings

2 to 3 tablespoons butter
3 green onions (scallions), white and light green
    parts only, thinly sliced
2 pounds sweet potatoes, peeled, cut into chunks,
    boiled in salted water to cover until tender,
    about 20 minutes, drained, and mashed, or
    put through a ricer
Salt and freshly ground black pepper to taste
1 tablespoon grated fresh ginger
1 teaspoon ground ginger
3 tablespoons sour cream, regular or light
Freshly snipped chives

Melt the butter in a very small skillet over medium heat. Add the green onions and cook, stirring, 2 minutes. Beat the green onions and butter into the potatoes. Season with salt and pepper to taste. Stir in the grated ginger and the ground ginger. Beat in the sour cream.

Turn the puree into a medium-size saucepan. Cook over low heat, stirring to keep it from burning until thick and fluffy, 5 to 8 minutes. Serve very hot, garnished with the chives.

Curried Sweet Potatoes and Rutabaga

If you should have any goat to roast, this would be a marvelous accompaniment. Lacking goat, a roast leg of lamb or lamb shoulder will go along very well, too.

Makes 6 to 8 servings

3 tablespoons mild vegetable oil, preferably
    peanut
1 medium-size onion, cut into $^1/_4$-inch dice
2 large sweet potatoes, peeled and cut into
    1-inch cubes
1 medium-size rutabaga, peeled, cut into
    1-inch cubes
1 medium-size clove garlic, minced
1 tablespoon hot curry powder, or more to taste
1 cup well-flavored chicken stock
Salt and freshly ground black pepper to taste
$^1/_2$ cup plain yogurt
2 tablespoons chopped fresh cilantro

Heat the oil over high heat in a large wok or slope-sided sauté pan. Add the onion and cook, tossing, 2 minutes. Add the sweet potato and rutabaga. Cook, tossing, until the vegetables begin to brown, 3 to 4 minutes. Add the garlic and sprinkle in the curry powder. Cook, tossing, to release the aroma of the curry powder, about 30 seconds. Stir in the stock. Reduce the heat and simmer over low heat until the vegetables are tender and the liquid is almost evaporated, about 15 minutes.

Season well with salt and pepper. Remove the pan from the heat. Stir in the yogurt and cilantro. Serve immediately, very hot.

Variation: Add 1 large Russet potato, peeled and cut into 1-inch cubes, to the sweet potato and rutabaga in the wok or pan.

Gratin of Sweet Potatoes

This savory sweet potato bake will go well with pot roast or braised brisket. But, if you can find quail, partridge, or even Cornish hens, this will be a perfect accompaniment.

Makes 6 to 8 servings

2 tablespoons butter, softened, plus additional
    for buttering
5 large sweet potatoes, peeled and sliced

1 small onion, thinly sliced
$^1/_2$ teaspoon dried thyme, crushed
Salt and freshly ground black pepper to taste
1 cup well-flavored chicken stock
$^1/_3$ cup heavy cream
$^1/_2$ cup grated Monterey Jack cheese

Preheat the oven to 375°F. Generously butter a medium-size gratin dish.

Layer one-third of the potatoes in the bottom of the prepared dish. Spread half of the onions on top. Dot with some of the 2 tablespoons of butter and season with thyme, salt, and pepper. Repeat the layers, ending with the last third of potatoes. Dot with more butter and pour in the stock. Cover tightly with foil.

Bake for 45 minutes. Raise the heat to 425°F. Remove the foil. Pour the cream over the potatoes and sprinkle with the cheese. Bake until the liquid is reduced and bubbling, and the cheese is melted and browned, about 15 minutes longer. Serve very hot.

Tomatillos

Even though tomatillos look like shiny green cherry tomatoes, they are actually a berry relative inside a thin, papery outer husk. Related to the cape gooseberry and ground cherry, they have a lovely almost acid lemony flavor when raw, that becomes more subtle and fruity when it is cooked.

These Mexican natives were an Aztec favorite. For some reason they never migrated east with the rest of the native American vegetables and fruits, and have remained primarily in Mexico and the southwestern United States. Until now. I have begun to see them increasingly in many supermarkets, especially those with a section for fancy fresh produce. While they are not an important food, they are interesting enough to include here. They are also high in vitamin C.

Tomatillos can be eaten both raw and cooked. They are especially good when roasted—over charcoal or a mesquite fire—until the bright green skin takes on a golden yellow cast. Incorporated into salsas, soups, and stews, roasted tomatillos add a very special smoky flavor. They can be husked, stemmed, and very thinly sliced to add to salads. Try a few thin slices in the Jicama, Onion, and Orange Salad for a deliciously different taste.

Selection: Tomatillos should be bright, shiny pale green, like unripe tomatoes. They should be enclosed in a papery thin, pale green husk, with the stem attached. Avoid any that have begun to ripen to yellow. Do not buy them if they have bruises, cuts, or soft places. They should be very firm, almost hard, to the touch. Size is not particularly important, as long as they are in good condition.

Storage and Preparation: Store tomatillos, unwashed, in a small paper bag in the vegetable drawer of the refrigerator for up to three weeks. Do not put them in a plastic bag, or they will suffer from the effects of condensation and begin to spoil.

Tomatillos need little preparation. Remove the husk, wash well, cut out the stem, and they are ready to slice, dice, or mince, depending on the recipe.

Cooked Tomatillo Salsa

The fresh, almost lemony taste of tomatillo makes this lovely green salsa (salsa verde) the perfect condiment for grilled fish or poultry. For a slightly different flavor, roast the tomatillos on a fish grid over a hot grill until they are slightly charred and begin to show a yellowish color. Husk the cooled tomatillos and continue with the recipe.

Makes about 1½ cups

2 tablespoons olive oil
1 small onion, chopped
1 bunch (6 to 8) green onions (scallions), white and light green parts only, thinly sliced
2 small cloves garlic, minced
1 pound tomatillos, husk removed, stemmed, and finely chopped
1 medium-size or 2 small jalapeño chiles, stemmed, seeded, and minced
1 cup well-flavored chicken stock
Salt and freshly ground black pepper to taste
¼ cup chopped fresh cilantro

Heat the olive oil in a medium-size heavy saucepan over low heat. Add the onion and cook, stirring, until translucent, about 5 minutes. Stir in the green onions and garlic. Cook 1 minute. Stir in the tomatillos and jalapeño. Add the stock and season well with salt and pepper. Simmer 15 minutes. Remove from the heat, cool to room temperature.

Stir in the cilantro and refrigerate several hours. Bring to room temperature before serving.

Tomatoes

It is very difficult to believe that only a little over one hundred years ago Americans considered the tomato to be poisonous. In that short time it has become the second most important commercial crop grown in the United States. Only the potato outstrips the tomato in per capita consumption. Can you imagine what our culinary world would be like without tomato juice; ketchup; chili sauce; tomato paste; pizza sauce; pasta sauce; bacon, lettuce, and tomato sandwiches; or hamburgers with the works? We eat tomatoes in almost every form imaginable, from raw to cooked to pickled to sun dried.

The Aztecs knew all about tomatoes, at least all about some tiny little ancestors of our delicious cherry tomatoes. Columbus and his fellow explorers took them back to Europe, where only the Italians had courage enough to eat them. Because they are a member of the deadly nightshade family, most other Europeans considered them to be poisonous. Thomas Jefferson recognized their value as food, but he had little success trying to convince many other Americans they were good to eat.

Modern tomatoes—some bigger than 6 inches across; some in varying shades of orange, yellow, and red—are a far cry from their tiny Mexican forebears. Flavors range from sweet and intense, to fruity and slightly acidic. And when they are good, they are an incomparable treat.

The problem today is finding good tomatoes to begin with. All of us have some sort of memory of the perfect home-grown tomato—except, perhaps, some of our children who have never even seen a tomato growing—that causes us to lament the quality of most store-bought ones. This lament is usually silenced during the months of July and August when home gardens and local growers provide us with tomatoes that have been allowed to fully ripen on the vine. The flavor is incomparable. Who can turn down a sandwich made of flabby white bread, slathered with mayonnaise, stuffed with thick slices of tomato adorned only with salt and pepper? I cannot. I eat them every day if the tomatoes are really good.

When local tomatoes are not available, rather than use the hard-ripe commercial ones, I often turn to canned ones, especially for sauces and tomato-based casseroles. These are tomatoes that were allowed to ripen on the vine, and were picked only after turning red. The flavor is much more like a garden-grown tomato.

Fresh, commercially grown tomatoes are not fully ripened on the vine. They would never make it to market if they were. When you have once seen a gondola truck full of tomatoes racing from field to packing plant you can easily realize that the tomatoes 6 feet down in the load would be tomato paste if they were vine ripened. So these commercial vegetables are "fully matured," meaning they will not get any bigger or have less jelly in the middle—they will only redden and hopefully develop flavor.

Unfortunately, immature tomatoes are often picked by accident, and these are the ones that give production tomatoes their bad rep, along with poor handling, refrigeration, and several other factors, including the variety that was grown in the first place. Cross-breeding that has created tomatoes with skins so thick they can be dropped from a height of 6 feet and still not split has not centered on developing taste. New varieties are being tested, however; and in the future there may well be a winter tomato that will taste nearly as good as the home-grown summer treat.

Sun-dried tomatoes can be a winter alternative. They cannot be substituted for fresh, but the intense tomato flavor can be used to enhance salads, pastas, and other dishes.

Tomatoes are a dieter's delight. They are low in calories and fat, and contain no cholesterol. High in vitamin C, they also contain substantial amounts of beta-carotene.

Selection: No matter what kind or color of tomato you buy, it is important to pick out ones that have bright, clear color and smooth, unblemished skins—that is not to say they cannot be irregularly shaped—with no bruises, cuts, or soft spots. In the wintertime, choose heavy, unblemished tomatoes that have an even light red color. They can be ripened further at home.

In the summer, during the peak of locally fresh tomato season, look for tomatoes that are heavy, that give a little when slightly pressed, but do not have any obvious soft spots or bruises. These fully ripened tomatoes should give off a heady tomato fragrance, much like that of the vines. When buying orange or yellow tomatoes, the criteria are the same, but the color should be bright and uniform.

Plum, or roma, tomatoes have fewer seeds than round tomatoes, and even vine-ripened ones will be slightly harder to the touch. Sometimes these are the best bet in the wintertime, even for salads. Their normally thicker skin, and smaller commercial production for market allows growers to let them ripen longer on the vine, and they will have a more "real" tomato flavor. Choose only those that are totally red and have no blemishes or bruises.

The increasing number of small tomatoes, from the tiny little cherries to the colorful red and yellow pear-shaped tomatoes should be carefully selected. Do not buy any that have any green on them because they will never mature and will be sour and green inside.

Some farm stands will sell very ripe tomatoes by the quart or peck. I often buy these if I am making pasta sauce. The soft parts can be removed before cooking. Just be careful that they have not begun to rot.

Storage and Preparation: Aside from all the problems inherent in providing an acceptable tomato on a commercial scale, the main enemy tomatoes face is cold. If there is one rule of thumb for keeping tomatoes, it is, do not refrigerate. At least not until the tomato is cut, or until it is so ripe it is in danger of spoiling. Temperatures below 55°F. will not just retard, they will halt ripening and flavor development.

Commercially grown tomatoes can easily be ripened at home. If they were picked when fully mature—even though they might be totally green—and were exposed to ethylene gas, which begins the ripening process, they will reach the market still quite hard. Pile these hard, pink, or pale red tomatoes in a bowl or place them in a closed, but perforated, paper bag. They will give off more natural ethylene gas and continue to ripen, soften, and develop flavor. Check them from time to time to be sure they do not begin to spoil. If the tomatoes were accidentally picked before they were fully mature, they will continue to turn red, but will not develop flavor and will become one of those cardboardy, tasteless tomatoes we all hate. Unfortunately, it is sometimes difficult for pickers to tell which tomatoes are fully mature, and no matter how hard they try, commercial growers will sometimes ship some tomatoes that were accidentally picked too early. If you come across one of these in your baskets, you might as well discard it. If your market consistently sells them, complain. Their purveyor should be able to change suppliers.

Genetically altered tomatoes are beginning to come into the commercial market. In these tomatoes, the gene that signals them to soften during the ripening process has been "turned off." Such tomatoes, technically, can be left on the vine until they turn pink or light red, so that they develop a more real tomato flavor. The tomato, because it does not begin to soften, is still hard enough to withstand the rigors of grading,

packing, and shipping. Once at home, they can be further ripened in a paper bag, which should then soften them. The flavor should be consistently higher than tomatoes picked green. Your local market will be required to identify these tomatoes, and you can try them if and when you see them.

Fully vine-ripened tomatoes, of any color or shape, should be kept at room temperature and either eaten or prepared as soon as possible. Fully ripe tomatoes are somewhat fragile. They should not be piled up, but spread out in one layer, stem up. Oddly enough, the shoulders of the tomato are the tenderest part, and will bruise or break down easily. I found this out the hard way one summer when I had a bumper crop of tomatoes, all ripening at the same time, or so it seemed. I spread them out in one layer, but stem down. They quickly split, leaking the precious juices all over the counter.

If the tomatoes have reached ultimate ripeness and softness, and there is no time to prepare or eat them, place them in the refrigerator for up to two days. Bring them to room temperature to serve. If you cannot eat them all within two days, stem, chop, and simmer them with a little lemon juice in a heavy skillet over low heat for 15 to 20 minutes. Pack them in freezer containers and freeze immediately. They will be fine for soups, sauces, or cooked dishes calling for cut-up tomatoes.

Tomatoes need little preparation. Wash and dry them just before eating or cooking. Remove the stem. The skins are edible and do not have to be removed, especially if they will be eaten raw, although they tend to roll up into hard little tubes in some cooked dishes. Tomatoes do not need to be seeded, either, although some dishes are prettier without all the seeds in them. Once the core is removed, tomatoes are ready to be sliced, wedged, cut up, or diced. They can be peeled and seeded if desired.

Sun-dried tomatoes are available either in hard dried form, or soft, packed in olive oil. The dried ones can be crumbled and used as is on top of salads, for crunch and flavor, or they can be rehydrated by pouring boiling water to cover over them and soaking for 10 to 15 minutes. The soaking water can then be added to the sauce, stock, or soup. Oil-packed sun-dried tomatoes need only to be drained.

> **Tip:** *Seeding tomatoes is quick and easy if you follow these suggestions. Remove the core with a sharp knife. Cut the tomato in half horizontally. Turn the tomato, cut side down, over a bowl or sink, and squeeze gently. The jelly and seeds should drop out. A small spoon can be used to pry out any reluctant seeds that remain in the crevices. The tomato is ready to chop, dice, or slice.*
>
> *If the tomatoes are to be peeled before seeding, cut an X in the skin at the blossom end and drop them into boiling water to cover until the skin at the X begins to curl, about 1 minute. Remove with a slotted spoon, drain, cool sightly, and peel. Remove the core and cut the tomatoes in half horizontally. Follow the same procedure as above.*

Tomato Soufflé

Make this the next time you have summer-ripe tomatoes on hand and a dinner party to give. Serve it along with charcoal-grilled chicken breasts, tuna steaks, or T-bone steaks. For a light luncheon party, serve this soufflé with a mixed green salad dressed with a simple vinaigrette, and add some crusty bread or homemade muffins.

Makes 6 servings

2 tablespoons butter, plus additional for buttering
1 tablespoon finely ground dried bread crumbs

2 tablespoons olive oil
½ small onion, minced
2 small cloves garlic, minced
2 large ripe tomatoes, peeled, seeded, and chopped
2 teaspoons finely chopped fresh oregano
Salt and freshly ground black pepper to taste
2 tablespoons all-purpose flour
1 cup milk, hot but not boiling
4 whole large eggs, separated, whites beaten until stiff
¼ cup freshly grated Parmesan cheese, plus additional for serving

Preheat the oven to 350°F. Generously butter the bottom and sides of a 1½-quart soufflé dish. Dust with the bread crumbs, gently knocking out any excess.

Heat the oil in a medium-size skillet over medium heat. Cook the onion until translucent, about 10 minutes. Add the garlic and cook 1 minute longer. Stir in the tomatoes, oregano, salt, and pepper. Simmer over low heat for 10 minutes.

Remove the skillet from the heat and pour the tomato mixture into the bowl of a food processor. Pulse to chop the tomatoes coarsely, but do not puree them until smooth. Pour the mixture into the prepared soufflé dish.

Melt 2 tablespoons of butter in a small saucepan over low heat. Stir in the flour and cook, stirring, until smooth. Whisk in the milk all at once, and cook, whisking until smooth and thickened, about 3 to 4 minutes. Remove the pan from the heat.

Beat in the egg yolks, one at a time. Season well with salt and pepper. Stir in the cheese. Turn the mixture into a medium-size bowl. Stir one-third of the egg whites into the sauce to lighten it, then gently fold in the remaining egg whites. Spoon the mixture over the tomatoes.

Bake until well puffed and golden brown, 30 to 35 minutes. Serve the soufflé at once, very hot, spooning the tomatoes from the bottom of the dish over each serving of soufflé like a sauce. Pass a small bowl of additional cheese separately if you like, to sprinkle over the soufflé.

Fresh Tomato Sauce Pronto

When the abundance of summer makes you wonder what to do with all the tomatoes on hand, this very plain combination is delicious on all manner of dishes. Serve it with pasta of any kind or shape. Spoon it over grilled fish. Garnish a wedge of quiche with it, or use it to top some grilled eggplant slices. It freezes very well, to provide a little taste of warm weather on a gray, sleety winter day.

Makes about 3 cups

3 tablespoons olive oil
3 cloves garlic, minced
2 pounds ripe plum or large round tomatoes, seeded and chopped
1/3 cup finely chopped fresh basil
Salt and freshly ground black pepper to taste

Heat the oil in a large skillet over medium heat. Add the garlic and cook, stirring for 1 minute. Stir in the tomatoes. Simmer 4 to 5 minutes. Stir in the basil. Simmer until the tomatoes are just tender but not falling apart, 5 to 8 minutes. Season well with salt and freshly ground pepper. Cook over high heat to evaporate the excess liquid, 2 to 3 minutes longer.

Tip: *To counteract the acidity of some tomatoes, add a pinch of sugar to the tomato mixture before cooking. This can make all the difference in some tomato-based pasta sauces. Some old timers sprinkle sugar, rather than salt, on sliced tomatoes in a salad, claiming the sugar enhances the fresh flavor. Experiment, starting with very little sugar, adding more if you like.*

Marinated Tomatoes

This simple but excellent dish is perfect with cold meats and cheeses for an ultra-easy sultry-day supper. Be sure to offer plenty of crusty bread to sop up the juices.

Makes 6 servings

1/2 cup olive oil
3 tablespoons red wine vinegar
1/2 small onion, minced
3 tablespoons chopped fresh parsley
1 teaspoon chopped fresh oregano
1 tablespoon chopped fresh chives
Salt and freshly ground black pepper to taste
4 ripe tomatoes, peeled and cut into wedges
2 green onions (scallions), white and light green parts only, thinly sliced

In a small bowl, beat together the oil, vinegar, onion, herbs, salt, and pepper. Arrange the tomatoes in a medium-size glass or other nonreactive bowl. Pour the dressing over the tomatoes. Cover and refrigerate for several hours. Serve at room temperature, garnished with the green onion.

Old-fashioned Stewed Tomatoes

My mother makes the best stewed tomatoes you will ever eat. Even at age eighty-one, she still uses much of the summer crop for this delicious treat, freezing containers of it to break out when she cannot wait another minute for the flavor of "real tomatoes." In midsummer, she may serve them with grilled steak or, more often, with braised lamb shanks; in winter, she pairs them with meat loaf or pot roast.

Makes 6 to 8 servings

3 tablespoons butter
1/2 small green bell pepper, seeded, and chopped
1 small onion, chopped
1 to 2 cloves garlic, minced (optional, but recommended)
5 large ripe tomatoes, peeled, seeded, and chopped
1/4 cup sugar, or more to taste (my mother likes them sweeter than I do)
1/2 cup water, white wine, or chicken stock

Salt and freshly ground black pepper to taste
2 slices stale white bread, torn into 1-inch pieces
Chopped fresh parsley, basil, thyme, or oregano;
   or a combination of these

Melt the butter in a large heavy skillet over medium heat. Add the bell pepper and onion. Cook, stirring, until almost translucent, about 5 minutes. Stir in the garlic and cook 1 minute. Stir in the tomatoes, sugar, and water, and season well with salt and pepper.

Simmer over low heat until the tomatoes are beginning to fall apart, about 20 minutes. Stir in the bread and cook until the bread is very soft but still holds its shape slightly, about 5 to 6 minutes longer.

Serve the tomatoes hot, garnished with the parsley or other herbs.

Scalloped Tomatoes

This is one of my favorite tomato dishes. I can eat them all by themselves with a salad on the side, but they are delicious with grilled fish.

Makes 6 to 8 servings

1 tablespoon butter
1 small onion, thinly sliced
1 small green bell pepper, seeded and thinly sliced
4 large ripe tomatoes, seeded and cut into
   large pieces
1 tablespoon sugar
1/2 cup heavy cream
Salt and freshly ground black pepper to taste
1 tablespoon Dijon-style mustard
1 teaspoon dried Italian herbs, such as oregano,
   marjoram, rosemary, and thyme, or a
   prepared mix; or 1 tablespoon mixed
   chopped fresh oregano, marjoram, rosemary,
   and thyme
1/2 cup cracker crumbs, or plain dried
   bread crumbs

Preheat the oven to 350°F. Generously butter a 1-quart deep baking dish.

Melt 1 tablespoon of butter in a medium-size skillet over medium heat. Add the onion and bell pepper and cook, stirring, until translucent, about 10 minutes. Stir in the tomatoes and toss to mix well. Spoon the mixture into the prepared dish.

In a small bowl, mix together the cream, sugar, salt, pepper, mustard, and herbs. Pour this mixture over the vegetables. Sprinkle the cracker crumbs over the top.

Bake until the tomatoes are bubbling and the top is golden brown, about 45 minutes. Serve very hot.

Tomato-Barley Pilaf

The rich flavor of barley makes this an excellent dish to serve with a whole baked or grilled fish.

Makes 6 to 8 servings

4 tablespoons (1/2 stick) butter
1 small onion, minced
3 medium-size tomatoes, peeled, seeded,
   and chopped
1 clove garlic, minced
1/3 cup chopped fresh parsley, plus additional
   for garnishing
1/2 cup pearled barley
3 cups well-flavored chicken stock, boiling
Salt and freshly ground black pepper to taste

Preheat the oven to 350°F.

Heat the butter in a large, heavy, covered flameproof casserole over medium heat. Add the onion and cook, stirring occasionally, until translucent, about 10 minutes. Stir in the tomato and cook 5 minutes longer. Add the garlic, parsley, and barley. Cook, stirring, for 3 minutes. Stir in half the stock; season well with salt and pepper. Cover tightly and bake for 30 minutes. Stir in the remaining stock and cook until all the liquid is absorbed, 30 to 40 minutes longer.

Remove the casserole from the oven. Toss gently with a fork to fluff and serve hot, garnished with the additional parsley.

Fried Ripe Tomatoes

The flavor of these tomatoes is entirely different from that of fried green tomatoes. We used to have these with fried chicken or chicken fried steak, but now I prefer them with grilled or roast chicken.

Makes 6 to 8 servings

1 cup all-purpose flour
Salt and freshly ground black pepper to taste
1/4 cup chopped fresh cilantro, or parsley
6 large ripe tomatoes, thickly sliced
1 tablespoon olive oil
2 tablespoons butter
Freshly grated Parmesan cheese (optional)

Mix together the flour, salt, pepper, and cilantro in a shallow bowl. Dredge the tomato slices in the flour mixture, coating them well on both sides.

Heat the oil and butter in a large nonstick skillet until almost smoking. Fry the tomato slices quickly in one layer, turning them once, until crisp and golden brown on the outside, about 2 minutes per side. Drain the tomatoes on unprinted brown paper. Serve very hot, sprinkled with salt and the cheese if desired.

Southern Fried Green Tomatoes

We ate these for Saturday breakfast when I was a child, with cream gravy, eggs, bacon, and grits, and we ate them until we couldn't move. They are also very good with grilled sausages. Try some of the more exotic varieties, like duck with port, or pork with fennel, or venison.

Makes 6 servings

1 cup yellow or white cornmeal
1/2 cup all-purpose flour
Salt and freshly ground black pepper to taste
Pinch ground red (cayenne) pepper
2 tablespoons chopped fresh parsley

1 tablespoon freshly grated Parmesan cheese
4 large or 6 medium-size green tomatoes, thickly sliced
Fat for frying, such as olive oil, mild vegetable oil, preferably peanut, bacon fat, or as in the Old South, lard
Cream Gravy (optional, recipe follows)
Raw Salsa (optional, page 349)
Hot pepper sauce to taste (optional)

In a shallow bowl, toss the cornmeal, flour, salt, black pepper, red pepper, parsley, and cheese. Dredge the tomato slices in this mixture and set them out on a baking sheet to dry for 10 minutes.

Heat 2 tablespoons of the fat in a large heavy skillet over medium heat. Fry the dredged tomato slices in the hot fat, turning once, until crisp and golden, 4 to 5 minutes per side. Continue with the remaining tomato slices, adding more fat when necessary.

Drain a moment or two on unprinted brown paper. Serve immediately, seasoned with salt and pepper. Spoon a little of the Cream Gravy over each serving if you like. Or if you would rather, serve with Raw Salsa, or with hot pepper sauce.

Cream Gravy

Makes about 1 1/2 cups

2 tablespoons butter, bacon fat, or lard
2 tablespoons seasoned cornmeal and flour mixture used for breading the tomatoes (above)
1 1/2 cups milk, hot
Salt and freshly ground black pepper to taste

Melt the butter in a small skillet over medium-high heat. Stir in the breading mixture. Cook, stirring constantly, until the roux is dark golden brown; this could take 10 to 15 minutes. Be very careful not to burn the mixture. Whisk in the hot milk all at once. Cook over medium heat, whisking until smooth and thick, about 5 minutes. Season with salt and pepper if needed. Serve the gravy very hot, spooning it over the tomatoes.

Salade Caprese

A summer classic in Italy, this salad can be served by itself for lunch, with bread and a glass of wine; as an appetizer at dinner; or as an accompaniment for a grilled steak or veal chop.

Makes 6 servings

3 large or 4 medium-size vine-ripened tomatoes, thickly sliced

1 pound fresh mozzarella cheese, sliced (buffalo mozzarella has the most flavor)

$\frac{1}{3}$ cup chopped fresh basil, plus whole leaves for garnishing

2 tablespoons balsamic vinegar (optional)

$\frac{1}{3}$ cup finest extra-virgin olive oil, or more to taste

Salt and freshly ground black pepper to taste

Alternate slices of tomato and mozzarella cheese on a serving platter. Sprinkle with the chopped basil. Sprinkle with vinegar, and drizzle generously with olive oil. Season well with salt and freshly ground pepper. Just before serving, garnish with plenty of whole basil leaves.

Variation: *Add slices of sweet onion, and/or roasted red or green bell peppers to the platter.*

Tomato Salad with Chèvre and Sprouts

This colorful salad can be an appetizer all on its own, or it will be the perfect foil for a light dinner along with a classic herb omelet.

Makes 6 to 8 servings

3 large ripe tomatoes, peeled and sliced

1 medium-size super-sweet onion, very thinly sliced

1 ripe avocado, peeled, seed removed, and thinly sliced

1 tablespoon fresh lime juice

1 cup alfalfa or radish sprouts

Extra-virgin olive oil

Six $\frac{1}{4}$-inch-thick slices Montrachet or other fresh chèvre cheese; or 3 crottins de Chavignol, halved horizontally

$\frac{1}{2}$ teaspoon ground cumin

Red wine vinegar

Salt and freshly ground black pepper to taste

Arrange the tomato slices on a chilled serving plate. Top with the onion slices. Fan the avocado slices on top of the onion. Sprinkle the avocado with the lime juice. Spread the sprouts over the avocado.

Lightly drizzle the olive oil over the salad. Arrange the cheese rounds on top. Sprinkle with the ground cumin.

Serve the salad, passing cruets of olive oil and vinegar on the side, along with salt and a pepper mill.

Raw Salsa

This is really a condiment, rather than a side dish, but it enhances so many other foods that I feel it should be included here.

Makes about $1\frac{1}{2}$ cups

3 small or 2 medium-size ripe tomatoes, seeded and chopped

2 jalapeño peppers, seeded and minced, or more to taste

$\frac{1}{2}$ medium-size red onion, minced

2 bunches (12 to 16) green onions (scallions), white and light green parts only, minced

1 clove garlic, minced

$\frac{1}{3}$ cup chopped fresh cilantro

$\frac{1}{4}$ cup fresh lime juice

$\frac{1}{4}$ cup olive oil

Salt and freshly ground black pepper to taste

Combine all the ingredients in a small bowl. Cover and refrigerate several hours or overnight. Serve at room temperature.

Grilled Tomatoes

These are good the English way, for breakfast with scrambled eggs and thick, crisp slices of bacon. They will also be perfect alongside grilled lamb chops, or with a savory dish of kidneys in mustard sauce, and a mound of fluffy steamed rice.

Makes 6 servings

Oil
3 large tomatoes, thickly sliced, or halved
    horizontally
2 teaspoons minced onion
1 tablespoon butter, softened
2 tablespoons chopped fresh parsley
Salt and freshly ground black pepper to taste

Preheat the broiler. Lightly oil a shallow roasting pan.

Arrange the tomatoes in one layer in the prepared pan. In a small bowl, mix together the onion, butter, and parsley. Spread a little on each tomato slice. Season well with salt and pepper.

Broil until hot and bubbling and the tomatoes are softening but not collapsed, about 5 minutes. Serve very hot, while the topping is still bubbling.

Panzanella

The ingredients in this Tuscan bread salad are much the same as for bruschetta, but the flavor and effect are quite different. There are as many variations for this as there are cooks making it. I love to serve this one on a hot August evening alongside thick steaks of marinated grilled tuna, for a nearly painless dinner.

Makes 6 servings

Four 1-inch thick slices stale Italian sourdough
    bread, soaked in ice water to cover for
    1 minute, squeezed dry, and torn into
    bite-size pieces

3 large ripe tomatoes, peeled, seeded, and
    coarsely chopped
1 large cucumber, peeled, halved lengthwise,
    seeded, and very coarsely chopped
1 bunch (6 to 8) green onions (scallions), white
    and light green parts only, thinly sliced
2 cloves garlic, very finely minced
2 tablespoons red wine vinegar
$\frac{1}{3}$ cup extra-virgin olive oil, plus additional
    for serving
Salt and freshly ground black pepper to taste
3 tablespoons chopped fresh basil, or oregano
    (optional)

In a large salad bowl, toss together the bread, tomatoes, cucumber, green onions, and garlic. Sprinkle the salad with the vinegar. Pour the olive oil over all and toss. Season well with salt and pepper. Sprinkle with basil, if using. Let the salad stand at least 1 hour and up to 4 hours. The bread should soak up the juices from the tomatoes, along with the oil. Toss again just before serving. Pass the additional olive oil and a pepper mill with the salad.

Turnips

Turnips are actually two vegetables in one. The leaves are a delicious, slightly bitter alternative to spinach, collards, Swiss chard, or other greens. If you have a good farm market nearby and can buy turnips in bunches with the crisp fresh greens still attached, rush them home and cook the greens for dinner. The turnips themselves can wait a day or two before they are served.

Turnips are not a favorite American vegetable. Long thought of as animal fodder or poor people's food and often overgrown and stored too long to be at their peak, turnips were pretty much abandoned after more fashionable vegetables came on the scene. European and Asian cuisines make much more use of these delicious root vegetables, however, and they deserve a wider following in this country. This very old vegetable, eaten and enjoyed by the ancient Romans, was a part of the peasant's basic diet throughout Europe for centuries. The French still enjoy turnips, especially with game and duck.

I think one of the major reasons that Americans stay away from turnips in droves is that they have never eaten a good one. Frequently they find storage turnips in the market that have become pithy and strong tasting. Or they have fallen victim to the idea that bigger is better, which usually results in unappetizingly woody vegetables. Small, freshly pulled turnips are crisp and sweet, good enough to eat out of hand, like an apple.

White turnips are shaped like old-fashioned spinning tops, with purple or green shoulders, although there is now a small all-white turnip as well.

Like their cousins rutabagas, turnips are one of the cruciferous vegetables, along with broccoli, cauliflower, and cabbage. While they do not contain beta-carotene, they could be helpful in preventing some kinds of cancer. Turnips are low in calories and fat, and provide moderate amounts of vitamin C, calcium, and potassium.

Selection: Smaller is better when it comes to turnips. If you can find them in bunches with the leaves attached, they will be the freshest available. Choose small turnips, about 2 inches in diameter, with crisp, dark green leaves. Do not buy them if the leaves are yellowed, wet, or the least slimy. If the tops have been clipped, there should still be 2 or 3 inches of stem attached. Look for creamy white roots with purple or green shoulders. They should be plump and not the least shriveled, cut, or bruised. Avoid any that are soft or spongy when squeezed, have brown spots, or show signs of mold or decay around the stem.

Turnips are available all year round, but I do not like storage roots. I think they are wonderful in the early spring and again in the fall when they are just pulled, juicy, and sweet. Turnips stored over a long period of time lose their crisp freshness and, in my estimation, become unpleasantly strong flavored—or lose their taste altogether.

About ¼ pound of turnips per person should be enough.

Storage and Preparation: I am a firm believer that turnips are best when eaten as soon after they are pulled as possible. I enjoy them in season and tend not to serve them in the middle of winter or in the hot weather of summer when they are sure to be from long storage. If you have been lucky enough to buy turnips with the leaves attached, cut them off as soon as you arrive home, leaving 2 to 3 inches of stem. Store the tops and roots separately. Do not wash either the tops or the roots until just before they will be prepared. Prepare the greens the same day they are purchased. If you are not going to eat the turnips the day they are purchased, place the unwashed roots in a perforated plastic vegetable bag and keep them in the vegetable bin of the refrigerator for four or five days. Do not plan to keep them for more than a week.

Turnips are easy to prepare. They should be thoroughly washed. The stem and root ends need to be trimmed. If the turnips are small, and are to be cooked whole or left in wedges or large pieces, I suggest leaving the skin on. Larger turnips, and those that will be grated or mashed, need to be peeled. You can use a sharp paring knife or vegetable peeler. Once peeled they can be cut into any shape you like. The French like to cut them into large squares and then pare (or "turn") them into small ovals before cooking them to serve with duck or other poultry. The parings can be used in stocks or soups.

If you are eating the turnips raw, as part of a vegetable salad or crudité platter, they can be crisped up by soaking the pieces in ice water for 30 minutes or so. Drain the pieces and dry well before serving.

Boiled Turnips

Some recipes call for parboiling turnips before continuing with the preparation. Plain boiled turnips are fine if the vegetable is ultra fresh. Serve them when they are still a little crisp, seasoned well with salt and pepper, and tossed with melted butter and chopped fresh parsley.

Place 1½ pounds very small trimmed whole or cut-up turnips in boiling salted water to cover. Simmer over medium heat until tender, about 10 to 15 minutes, and drain. If the turnips are going to be cooked further as part of another recipe, drain them when they are still slightly crisp.

For a slightly different taste, substitute well-flavored chicken stock for the water when you boil the turnips. When the vegetable is cooked, drain and reserve the cooking liquid for use as a soup base.

Steamed Turnips

Place 1½ pounds very small trimmed whole or cut-up turnips in a steamer basket or a colander. Steam, covered, over simmering water until tender, 15 to 20 minutes, depending on the size of the pieces.

Microwaved Turnips

Turnips are one vegetable that microwaves very well. Place up to 1 pound cut-up turnips in a microwaveable dish, add 2 tablespoons water. Cover with plastic microwave wrap, vent, and microwave on high 5 to 6 minutes. Let stand 5 minutes before uncovering.

Turnips and Carrots with Herb Butter

Serve this colorful dish, very hot, along with poached fish fillets, such as turbot or striped bass.

Makes 6 servings

4 tablespoons (½ stick) butter, softened
1 tablespoon minced green onion (scallions)
1 tablespoon snipped fresh chives
1 teaspoon chopped fresh thyme
2 tablespoons chopped fresh parsley
1 pound smallest firm turnips, peeled and sliced
2 large carrots, peeled and sliced on the diagonal
Salt and freshly ground black pepper to taste

Place the butter in a small bowl. Beat in the green onion, chives, thyme, and parsley. Set aside.

Simmer the turnip and carrot slices over medium heat, in salted water to cover, until crisply tender, about 15 minutes. Drain well. Season with salt and pepper. Stir in 2 tablespoons of the herbed butter, and heat through. Serve very hot, with the remaining herb butter in a separate bowl.

Two-Turnip Puree

Crisp roast duck, goose, or turkey will be greatly enhanced by this buttery puree. I also think it is excellent if you have thick slices of standing ribs of beef on the menu. Add it to any holiday dinner for some surprised and delighted comments.

Makes 6 to 8 servings

1 pound smallest firm turnips, peeled and cut into large chunks
1 medium-size rutabaga, peeled and cut into large chunks
3 cups well-flavored chicken stock, or more
2 tablespoons butter
2 tablespoons heavy cream
Salt and freshly ground black pepper to taste
1 tablespoon fresh chopped parsley

In a large saucepan, simmer the turnips and rutabaga in the stock until very tender, about 20 minutes or more. Drain very well, reserving the liquid to use as a stock or soup base. Mash well. Beat in the butter and cream. Season well with salt and pepper.

Return the puree to the saucepan and cook over low heat, stirring, until the puree is thick and fluffy, 3 to 5 minutes. Serve very hot, garnished with the parsley.

Variation: *Add 1 cup fluffy mashed potatoes to the turnips, and then beat in 1 cup very tender braised cabbage and 2 tablespoons butter. This everyday dish goes very well with smoked sausage, such as kielbasa.*

Turnip and Carrot Pancakes

Why not make these to serve with thick slices of spicy sauerbraten? A little horseradish cream to spoon on top will make them irresistible.

Makes 6 servings

1 pound small firm turnips, peeled, and grated
2 medium-size carrots, peeled, and grated
½ small onion, grated
3 tablespoons chopped fresh parsley
1 large egg
3 tablespoons all-purpose flour
Salt and freshly ground black pepper to taste
Olive oil or mild vegetable oil
Horseradish Sauce (recipe follows)

In a medium-size bowl, toss together the turnips, carrots, onion, and parsley. Beat in the egg and flour. Season well with salt and pepper.

Heat 1 tablespoon oil in a large heavy skillet over medium-high heat. When the oil is almost smoking, drop the turnip mixture by spoonfuls into the hot skillet, pressing down with a wide spatula to make thin, ragged pancakes. Fry until golden brown on the bottom, about 2 minutes. Turn with a spatula. Brown on the other side, adding a little more oil if needed, about 2 more minutes. Remove the pancakes to a heated platter, keep warm, and continue with the remaining vegetable mixture, adding a little more oil as needed. Serve very hot, sprinkled with a little salt. Pass the horseradish sauce on the side.

Horseradish Sauce

Makes about ⅔ cup sauce

3 tablespoons prepared horseradish (the red variety is fine, too)
½ cup light sour cream
Salt to taste

Beat together all the ingredients in a small bowl. Refrigerate several hours. Stir well before serving.

Veggie Hash

I like to top servings of this delicious hash with a poached egg, and pass a platter of hot Italian sausages on the side for an easy busy-night dinner. The vegetables can be prepared early in the day and finished at dinnertime.

Makes 6 to 8 servings

2 tablespoons butter
3 small firm turnips, peeled, cut into ¼-inch dice, simmered in salted water to cover until just tender, about 10 minutes, and drained
1 small rutabaga, peeled, cut into ¼-inch dice, simmered in salted water to cover until just tender, 10 to 15 minutes, and drained
2 waxy white potatoes, brown skinned, unpeeled, cut into ¼-inch dice, simmered in salted water to cover until just tender, 10 to 15 minutes, and drained
2 large carrots, peeled, cut into ¼-inch dice, simmered in salted water to cover until just tender, about 10 minutes, and drained
1 cup boiling onions, boiled in water to cover for 1 minute, drained, and peeled, then simmered in salted water to cover until tender, about 15 minutes, and drained
3 tablespoons heavy cream
1 teaspoon chopped fresh thyme
1 teaspoon chopped fresh oregano
Salt and freshly ground black pepper to taste
Hot pepper sauce to taste
1 tablespoon thinly sliced green onions (scallions)

Melt the butter in a large skillet over medium heat. Add the drained vegetables and cook, tossing, until well coated with butter. Stir in the cream and herbs. Season well with salt and pepper. Cook over medium heat until the vegetables begin to brown slightly, up to 10 minutes. Stir in the hot pepper sauce. Serve very hot, garnished with the green onions.

Variation: *To serve as a dinner entrée, spoon a generous amount on a heated dinner plate. Make a hollow in the top with the back of a large spoon. Slip a soft poached* *egg into the hollow. Season with salt and pepper. Serve with crisp grilled hot Italian sausages on the side.*

> Note: *For a slightly different, but more time-consuming, presentation, instead of dicing the vegetables, use a very small vegetable garnish baller to cut tiny balls out of the vegetables.*

Winter Vegetables in Cabbage Leaves

Prepare these lovely little winter packets in the morning, and then simmer in the stock and wine just before serving. Serve alongside generous portions of poached salmon, or with roast partridge or pheasant.

Makes 6 servings

2 tablespoons butter
1 small onion, cut into ¼-inch dice
1 large sweet potato, peeled, cut into ¼-inch dice, boiled in salted water to cover for 2 minutes, and drained
1 large Russet potato, peeled, cut into ¼-inch dice, boiled in salted water to cover for 2 minutes, and drained
2 small, firm turnips, peeled, cut into ¼-inch dice, boiled in salted water to cover for 2 minutes, and drained
2 medium-size carrots, peeled, cut into ¼-inch dice, boiled in salted water to cover for 2 minutes, and drained
6 large napa cabbage leaves, boiled in water to cover until pliable, about 2 minutes, and drained on kitchen towels
1 teaspoon grated fresh ginger
1 teaspoon dried marjoram
Salt and freshly ground black pepper to taste
⅓ cup chopped fresh parsley
½ cup well-flavored chicken stock
¼ cup dry white wine
1 cup blender Hollandaise sauce (page 20)

Melt the butter in a medium-size heavy skillet over medium heat. Add the onion and cook, stirring, until wilted, about 3 minutes. Add all the remaining vegetables, except the cabbage, and cook, tossing, until just tender, 6 to 8 minutes. Stir in the ginger and marjoram. Season well with salt and pepper, and stir in the parsley. Remove from the heat.

Spread out the cabbage leaves. Divide the vegetables among the leaves. Fold the edges of the cabbage leaves over the filling and roll up like a sausage. Arrange the packets, seam side down, in a skillet just large enough to hold them in one layer. Pour in the stock and wine. Cover and cook until heated through, about 5 minutes. Remove the packets from the stock. Drain and serve very hot with a little of the blender Hollandaise over them. Pass remaining Hollandaise in a separate dish.

Creamed Turnips

Grilled duck, or any game bird, goes well with this old-fashioned dish.

Makes 6 servings

1 tablespoon butter
1½ pounds small firm turnips, peeled, cut into ½-inch dice or sliced, simmered in salted water to until just tender, about 15 minutes, and drained
⅔ cup heavy cream
Pinch sugar
¼ teaspoon nutmeg
Salt and freshly ground black pepper to taste
2 tablespoons snipped fresh chives

Melt the butter in a heavy, medium-size saucepan over medium heat. Add the turnips and toss to coat. Pour in the cream and cook, uncovered, until the sauce is thick and the turnips are very tender, 15 to 20 minutes. Stir in the sugar and nutmeg. Season well with salt and pepper. Cook 5 minutes longer. Serve very hot, garnished with the chives.

Old-fashioned Buttered Turnips

Here is an inexpensive, late fall treat to serve with pot roast, Salisbury steak, or country-style pork ribs with sauerkraut.

Makes 6 servings

2 pounds small firm turnips, peeled, cut into 1-inch cubes, boiled in salted water to cover until tender, 10 to 15 minutes, and drained
2 tablespoons butter
Salt and freshly ground black pepper to taste
1 tablespoon chopped fresh parsley

Dry the turnips on a towel. Melt the butter in a small skillet over medium heat. Add the turnips, and cook, tossing, until they begin to turn light brown, 5 to 8 minutes. Season well with salt and pepper. Serve very hot, garnished with the parsley.

Cider-braised Turnips and Apples

Slice two grilled pork tenderloins, and arrange the slices on a heated serving platter. Ladle these turnips around the edges. Spoon a little of the apple cream sauce over the pork. Garnish the whole with more chervil.

Makes 6 servings

3 tablespoons butter
½ small onion, thinly sliced
2 pounds small firm turnips, peeled, boiled in salted water to cover for 3 minutes, drained, and sliced
1 medium-size Golden Delicious apple, peeled, cored, and finely chopped
½ cup fresh cider
¼ cup chicken stock
Salt and freshly ground black pepper to taste
¼ cup cream
Snipped fresh chervil

Melt the butter in a medium-size covered saucepan over medium heat. Add the onion and cook, stirring occasionally, until just wilted, about 5 minutes. Add the turnip slices and cook over medium heat, tossing, for 5 minutes. Add the apples, cider, and stock. Season well with salt and pepper. Cover and simmer over low heat until the turnips are very tender, and the apple slices have fallen into a puree, 20 to 30 minutes.

Stir in the cream. Stir gently to create a thick sauce of the apples and cream, without breaking up the turnips. Heat through. Serve the turnips very hot, with the sauce spooned over them, garnished with the chervil.

Glazed Turnips with Sliced Chestnuts

Turnips are a much maligned vegetable. The small ones are deliciously sweet and crisp, and with this sweet glaze they are even better. Serve these alongside herb-roasted racks of lamb or pork loin.

Makes 6 servings

2 tablespoons butter
½ cup well-flavored chicken stock
¼ cup dry white wine
6 small turnips, peeled and sliced
¼ pound chestnuts in the shell, peeled, and sliced
1 tablespoon sugar
Salt and freshly ground black pepper to taste
Chopped fresh parsley

Melt the butter in a medium-size heavy saucepan or skillet over medium heat. Stir in the stock and wine. Add the turnips and chestnuts. Cover and simmer over low heat until the turnips are just tender, about 15 minutes. Uncover and sprinkle with sugar. Cook over medium heat, tossing, until the sauce becomes a thick glaze, 3 to 5 minutes. Season with salt and pepper. Toss to coat the turnips and chestnuts with the glaze. Serve very hot, garnished with the parsley.

Zucchini

Zucchini belongs to the same *Cucurbita* genus as yellow squash, pattypan, and pumpkin. As this is one of home gardeners' favorite summer crops, and the abundance of the harvest often tries the minds of grower and recipient alike, I think it deserves a section of its own.

For some time the only variety available was the familiar long green, or green-striped zucchini, which was frequently allowed to grow to be a foot or more long. Today you can find a bright yellow zucchini, along with small round ones, no bigger than a tennis ball. Some markets will also feature tiny little finger-length zucchini, which are delicious butter-steamed whole, or trimmed and added as is to crudité platters or cold buffets.

Even though zucchini has been overwhelming the American market only for the last twenty-five to thirty years, it has been very popular in Europe for a long time, long enough to have garnered a number of different names. In France it is called courgette, in Italy it is zucchini, zuchetta, or cocozelle, in England you will find it as courgette, marrow, or vegetable marrow. No matter what it is called, it is an extremely versatile vegetable. Not only can it be baked, fried, stewed, stuffed, and eaten raw, among other ways, it is so delicately flavored that it can be incorporated in muffins, breads, desserts, and other sweet preparations.

Occasionally you hit on a particularly bitter batch of zucchini. Bitterness probably has to do with the soil rather than the season. Sometimes the zucchini in your pot throws off quantities of water, while other times, in the same recipe, you need to add a lid to the pot because the zucchini releases so little water. The amount of water seems to be determined by the variety of zucchini as well as the rainfall during growing. If it is too watery, it can be salted. Salting may remove some of the bitterness, too.

Like all squashes, zucchini is low in fat and calories, making it an ideal diet ingredient. It is a good source of beta-carotene—even though the flesh is pale green—which makes it one of those foods that may aid in the prevention of some types of cancer. Zucchini also provides moderate amounts of vitamin C and potassium.

While zucchini is not the only squash to produce edible blossoms, they are the ones we seem to eat most frequently. The colorful orange blooms of the zucchini plant are tender, moist, and slightly peppery. They can be eaten raw, in salads, like nasturtium and chive flowers, or stuffed with all manner of fillings and either baked, braised, or deep fried to enjoy as part of any meal.

Zucchini blossoms contain few calories, no fat or cholesterol, but do offer a good amount of beta-carotene and some vitamin C.

While the flowers are relatively delicate, they should be rinsed and dried (or spun in a salad spinner if eating uncooked) before eating, to ferret out any bugs that may be hiding inside. They will crisp up slightly if wrapped lightly in paper towels and refrigerated for an hour or two before adding to the salad bowl.

Selection: Like any other thin-skinned squash, zucchini is perishable and should be handled with care. Regardless of the color or shape, zucchini should be brightly colored, heavy in the hand, firm, and no longer than 6 to 8 inches in length. Larger squash tend to become fibrous and have mature, tough seeds that I find unpleasant in cooked dishes. Avoid any zucchini that have cuts, discolored patches or bruises, soft spots, or are limp and flaccid.

You will need about ¼ pound zucchini per person.

Storage and Preparation: Zucchini is best when eaten as soon as possible after being harvested. If it must be stored, place it, unwashed, in a perforated plastic vegetable bag, in the vegetable drawer of the refrigerator and plan to use it within two to three days. If you cook zucchini often, it is better to buy frequently in usable quantities than to stock up.

Since the entire squash is edible, zucchini requires little preparation. It should be well washed, dried, and the stem and blossom ends trimmed. Zucchini can be halved, sliced, cut into long ribbons with a vegetable peeler, diced, grated, or cut into all sorts of shapes. It can be eaten raw, in sticks, cut into salads, or cooked, and incorporated in hundreds of dishes.

> **Tip:** *Zucchini, like all squash, contains a great deal of moisture. Some recipes call for salting it to remove some of this liquid so that it does not water down the finished dish. To do this, salt the cut squash, tossing in a colander or large strainer. Let it drain over a bowl, or in the sink, for up to 30 minutes. Rinse thoroughly with cold running water to remove the excess salt. Then transfer to a kitchen towel and wring or press dry before continuing with the recipe.*

Stir-fry Medley

Make a big bowl of fluffy rice as an accompaniment to this wonderful mixture and serve with thick, rare slices of grilled flank steak.

Makes 6 to 8 servings

2 tablespoons olive oil
2 small zucchini, trimmed, thinly sliced
¼ pound full-flavored mushrooms, such as shiitake (stems discarded) or cloud ear, thickly sliced
1 green bell pepper, seeded and cut into strips
1 bunch (6 to 8) green onions (scallions), white and light green parts only, cut on the diagonal into 1-inch pieces
1 teaspoon curry powder
Salt and freshly ground black pepper to taste
1 medium-size, ripe tomato, coarsely chopped
1 cup sugar snap peas, strung
Chopped fresh parsley
Sour cream, regular or light, or plain yogurt

Heat the oil in a wok over high heat. Stir in the zucchini, mushrooms, bell pepper, and green onions. Season with curry powder, salt, and pepper. Fry over high heat, stirring, until the vegetables are crisply tender, 3 to 4 minutes. Stir in the tomatoes and peas. Cook, stirring and tossing until the vegetables are heated through, about 2 minutes longer.

Serve very hot, garnished with the parsley. Pass a bowl of sour cream or plain yogurt on the side.

Zucchini Soufflé

I do like soufflés. They are really much easier to deal with than most people think. The only thing to remember is that soufflés wait for no one. All the diners need to be at table when the soufflé is removed from the oven. Still, some soufflés, like this one, can have a life after heat. If you allow this soufflé to cool, it will collapse in on itself. Invert it onto a serving plate, cut into wedges like a flan, and serve with Raw Salsa (page 349) on the side. Served cold like this, it is wonderful with cold cuts and a salad. Hot and puffy, it goes well with broiled or grilled fish.

Makes 6 servings

6 tablespoons ($^3/_4$ stick) butter, plus additional
    for buttering
$^1/_4$ cup freshly grated Parmesan cheese, plus
    additional for sprinkling
1 very small onion, minced
2 medium-size zucchini, trimmed and grated
$^1/_4$ cup dry white wine
3 tablespoons all-purpose flour
1 cup milk, hot
4 large eggs, separated, whites beaten until stiff
Salt and freshly ground black pepper to taste

Preheat the oven to 375°F. Generously butter a $1^1/_2$-quart soufflé dish. Dust the inside of the dish with the cheese, knocking out any excess. Set aside.

Melt 3 tablespoons of the butter in a heavy skillet over medium heat. Add the onion and zucchini and cook, stirring occasionally, until translucent, 8 to 10 minutes. Stir in white wine and simmer 1 minute. Remove from the heat.

Melt the remaining 3 tablespoons of butter in a medium-size saucepan over medium heat. Stir in the flour and cook, stirring to keep from browning, about

3 minutes. Whisk in the milk all at once. Cook, whisking, until smooth and thickened, 3 to 4 minutes. Remove from the heat and cool. Beat in the egg yolks, one at a time. Beat in $^1/_4$ cup cheese. Stir in the cooked zucchini. Season well with salt and pepper. Turn the mixture into a medium-size bowl.

Stir in one-third of the egg whites to lighten the mixture. Gently fold in the remaining egg whites. Spoon the mixture into the prepared dish and bake until well puffed and golden brown on top, 30 to 35 minutes. Serve at once.

Summer Vegetable Bake

Serve this with a whole baked fish and a big green salad.

Makes 6 to 8 servings

$^1/_4$ cup pure olive oil
2 large onions, very thickly sliced
2 medium-size zucchini, trimmed, sliced about
    $^1/_4$-inch thick
2 cloves garlic, minced
2 large tomatoes, cut into wedges
2 green bell peppers, trimmed, seeded, and cut
    into large chunks
2 tablespoons chopped fresh oregano
1 teaspoon chopped fresh thyme
Salt and freshly ground black pepper to taste
$^1/_2$ cup grated Gruyère or fontina cheese

Preheat the oven to 450°F.

Heat the olive oil in a medium-size heavy skillet over medium heat. Cook the onions and zucchini, stirring occasionally, until the onions are just translucent, 6 to 8 minutes. Stir in the garlic and cook 1 minute longer.

Spoon the onions and zucchini into a medium-size gratin dish. Spread the tomatoes and bell peppers on top. Bake, uncovered, for 20 minutes. Sprinkle with the herbs. Season well with salt and pepper. Spread the cheese over all. Bake until the cheese is melted and beginning to turn golden brown, about 10 minutes longer. Serve very hot.

Fried Zucchini

Substitute these for regular French fries (which originated in Belgium, by the way) and pile them on the plate with hamburgers, foot-long hot dogs, or a thick grilled sirloin steak. Or serve as a snack with drinks.

Makes 6 to 8 servings

1 cup all-purpose flour
1 tablespoons seasoned pepper, such as
    Mrs. Dash
½ teaspoon salt
2 pounds smallest zucchini, trimmed and cut
    lengthwise into wedges
Oil for deep-frying

Mix the flour, pepper, and salt in a small plastic bag. Shake the zucchini wedges in the flour.

Heat the oil in a deep-fat fryer to 375°F. Fry the zucchini wedges, a few at a time, until golden brown, 2 to 3 minutes per batch. Remove the zucchini from the hot oil with a slotted spoon. Drain on paper towels and season with salt if needed. Serve very hot.

Zucchini Tian

This sort of vegetable dish has a definite North African accent. A tian is not only the dish but also the vessel it is cooked in. In any event, there are no extraneous ingredients to overpower the distinct, though delicate, flavors of the individual vegetables. I have served this in several different countries and have never had any left over, though I think it would be very good cold, especially with cold roast lamb. Serve this hot, with anything that comes from the grill, whether fish, fowl, or meat.

Makes 6 servings

2 to 3 tablespoons pure olive oil, plus additional
    for greasing
2 medium-size zucchini, trimmed, thinly
    sliced across

1 red onion, thinly sliced
Salt and freshly ground black pepper to taste
Pinch cumin
1 tablespoon chopped fresh thyme (or several
    whole sprigs thyme)
2 tablespoons chopped fresh parsley
Red wine vinegar

Preheat the oven to 375°F. Lightly grease a medium-size gratin dish, shallow baking dish, or earthenware *tian.*

Arrange the zucchini and onion slices in an overlapping pattern, one layer deep in the prepared pan. Season well with salt, pepper, and cumin. Sprinkle with the herbs. Drizzle with the olive oil.

Bake for 25 to 30 minutes. Serve hot, warm, or cold. If you have any left over to serve the next day, sprinkle the cold dish with a few drops red wine vinegar and drizzle with more olive oil.

Parmesan Zucchini Pancakes

Vegetable pancakes are surprisingly versatile. Children love them and I think they make an excellent way to introduce new vegetables to young eaters. If you make them extra small, they can be an elegant garnish for such delicate dishes as poached salmon or turbot or veal scaloppine.

Makes 6 servings

3 medium-size zucchini, trimmed and grated
½ small red onion, minced
1 large whole egg, beaten
⅓ cup all-purpose flour
1 tablespoon chopped fresh oregano
Salt and freshly ground black pepper to taste
3 tablespoons freshly grated Parmesan cheese
3 tablespoons olive oil

In a small bowl, toss the zucchini and onion together. Beat in the egg, flour, seasonings, and cheese.

Heat the olive oil in a large heavy skillet over medium-high heat. Drop the mixture by large tablespoonfuls in the skillet, pressing down with the back of a spoon to flatten the pancakes. Fry the cakes, turning once, until crisp and dark golden brown, 2 to 3 minutes per side. Serve hot.

Zucchini Vegetable Tartare

Cut very thin slices of pumpernickel bread, and spread them with an almost transparent layer of sweet butter. Arrange the bread around the bowl of vegetables. Serve thick chunks of garlic sausage, salami, or pepperoni; squares of feta cheese; and a bowl of plump black Greek olives along with the tartare for a perfect al fresco lunch beside the pool, or at the beach. This vegetable mixture is much less rich than the original dish traditionally made with finely chopped or ground raw steak.

Makes 6 to 8 servings

2 small zucchini, trimmed and finely chopped
1 small red onion, minced
1 large ripe tomato, peeled, seeded, and finely chopped
½ small green bell pepper, finely chopped
3 tablespoons capers, drained and chopped
¼ cup chopped fresh parsley
2 to 3 tablespoons mayonnaise, prepared or homemade (page 13)
1 teaspoon Dijon-style mustard
1 large hard-cooked egg yolk, mashed
2 tablespoons olive oil
2 tablespoons fresh lemon juice
¼ teaspoon Worcestershire sauce
Salt and freshly ground black pepper to taste
Hot pepper sauce to taste (optional)
Leaf lettuce
1 tablespoon chopped fresh chives

In a medium-size bowl, toss together the zucchini, onion, tomato, bell pepper, and capers. In a smaller bowl, beat together all the remaining ingredients, except the lettuce and chives, until thick and smooth. Stir this mixture into the vegetables. Taste for seasoning and add salt and pepper if needed. Add the

hot pepper sauce if using. Refrigerate 1 hour or more. To serve, mound the tartare on a bed of lettuce and garnish with the chives.

Vegetable-stuffed Zucchini

The Middle Eastern flavor of these tender stuffed zucchini makes for perfect pairing with a lemon-braised chicken.

Makes 6 servings

2 tablespoons olive oil, plus additional for greasing
1 bunch (6 to 8) green onions (scallions), white and light green parts only, thinly sliced
1 large tomato, peeled, seeded, and chopped
½ green bell pepper, seeded and finely chopped
¼ cup chopped fresh cilantro
3 tablespoons mayonnaise
Salt and freshly ground black pepper to taste
¼ to ⅓ cup plain dried bread crumbs
3 medium-size zucchini, trimmed, halved lengthwise, seeds removed with a sharp spoon
Freshly grated Parmesan cheese

Preheat the oven to 375°F. Lightly grease a medium-size gratin dish or a shallow baking dish large enough to hold the zucchini in a single layer.

Heat 1 tablespoon of the olive oil in a small skillet over medium heat. Add the green onions and cook 1 minute. Add the tomatoes and bell pepper. Cook over medium heat, stirring, for 2 minutes. Stir in the cilantro. Remove from the heat. Stir in the mayonnaise, and season well with salt and pepper. Add enough bread crumbs to hold the mixture together.

Fill the zucchini with this mixture, mounding it slightly. Arrange the filled halves in the prepared baking dish. Sprinkle the top of each zucchini lightly with some of the cheese.

Bake until very hot and the zucchini is tender when pierced with a knife, 20 to 25 minutes. Serve hot, or cool to room temperature. If serving at room temperature, drizzle a little olive oil over the top of each zucchini.

Vegetable Terrine

For the most part, I find vegetable terrines insipid, watery molds that are more good for you than good to eat. This one is not only colorful and easy on your diet, it tastes like something special as well. I like to serve it as a dinner party first course or as a luncheon dish on its own, with sun-ripened fresh tomatoes on the side, or as part of a cold buffet.

Makes 8 to 10 servings

Butter, softened
2 tablespoons olive oil
½ medium-size onion, finely minced
2 cloves garlic, minced
2 small zucchini, trimmed and grated
Salt and freshly ground black pepper to taste
3 tablespoons chopped fresh basil, plus leaves for garnishing
1 teaspoon grated fresh ginger
½ teaspoon ground ginger
2 medium-size carrots, sliced, steamed until very tender, and pureed in a food processor
1 teaspoon fresh lemon juice
1 pound spinach, stemmed, cooked in the water that clings to the leaves after washing until wilted, well drained, liquid squeezed out, and very finely chopped
¼ cup finely ground plain dried bread crumbs
1 cup low-fat ricotta cheese, beaten until very smooth
1 large whole egg, beaten
¼ teaspoon ground nutmeg
¼ teaspoon ground allspice
Raw Salsa (page 349)
Leaf lettuce (optional)

Preheat the oven to 350°F. Generously butter a standard loaf pan. Line the bottom of the pan with waxed paper or parchment. Butter the paper lining also.

Heat the olive oil in a medium-size heavy skillet over medium heat. Add the onion, garlic, and zucchini. Cook, stirring, until translucent and very tender, about 10 minutes. Season well with salt,

pepper, and basil. Puree the mixture in a food processor. Set aside.

Beat the grated and ground ginger into the pureed carrots. Season well with salt and pepper.

In a small bowl, stir the lemon juice into the spinach.

In a medium-size bowl, beat together the bread crumbs, ricotta, and egg. Beat one-third of this mixture into the zucchini, and one-third into the carrots. Beat one-third into the chopped spinach. Season well with salt and pepper. Stir in the nutmeg and allspice.

Spread the carrot mixture in the bottom of the prepared pan. Spread the spinach mixture on top of the carrots. Spread the zucchini mixture on top of the spinach. Press gently on the zucchini, to eliminate any air. Pick up the pan and slap it down on the counter to settle the terrine.

Cover the pan tightly with aluminum foil. Put the filled pan in a deep baking pan. Pour in enough boiling water to reach halfway up the sides of the pan. Bake for 1 hour.

Remove the baking pan from the oven and cool the terrine completely. Refrigerate overnight.

To serve, run a knife around the sides of the pan. Invert onto a serving plate that has been very lightly sprinkled with water. (This allows you to gently reposition the terrine without breaking it if it doesn't unmold in exactly the right place on the plate.) Lift off the pan. Gently peel off the paper.

Garnish the terrine with fresh basil leaves. Use a serrated knife to cut the terrine into slices. Serve each slice on a chilled serving plate, on a lettuce leaf if you like. Pass a bowl of raw salsa separately.

Spicy Roasted Zucchini

Roasted vegetables are all the rage right now. These are a little more interesting than the plain roasted variety. They can be served with almost anything that has flavor enough to stand up to the spices. I especially like to offer it with barbecued beef or pork ribs.

Makes 6 servings

4 medium-size zucchini, trimmed and cut into
2-inch sticks
2 tablespoons olive oil
1 teaspoon chili powder
1 teaspoon ground cumin
1 teaspoon all-purpose flour
$\frac{1}{2}$ teaspoon salt
Blue Cheese Dressing, prepared or homemade
(below), or prepared ranch dressing

Preheat the oven to 400°F.

Toss the zucchini in a medium-size bowl with the olive oil. Arrange the zucchini in one layer on a shallow baking sheet. In a small bowl, combine the chili powder, cumin, flour, and salt. Sprinkle the zucchini with a little of this mixture, tossing to coat well.

Roast, turning once or twice, for about 25 minutes. Sprinkle again with the chili powder mixture, and roast until crisp and golden brown, about 10 minutes longer. Serve the zucchini very hot, with the blue cheese dressing for dipping, if desired.

Blue Cheese Dressing

Makes about 1 cup

$\frac{1}{2}$ cup mayonnaise, preferably homemade
(page 13)
$\frac{1}{4}$ cup buttermilk
1 tablespoon white wine vinegar
$\frac{1}{4}$ cup crumbled blue cheese
$\frac{1}{4}$ cup chopped fresh parsley

In a small bowl, stir together all the ingredients. Chill at least 1 hour.

Stuffed Zucchini Blossoms

Some specialty markets sell zucchini blossoms, but your best bet would be either your own garden, or that of a neighbor. *Home gardeners usually will be delighted to share the blossoms, since each one you stuff to eat means one less to mature into a squash that must be dealt with. These are delicious as a substantial appetizer, but can be served alongside grilled fish as well. The best ones I ever ate were in an outdoor café on the quai at Saint-Juan-les-Pins in the south of France. These are as close as I have been able to come.*

Makes 6 to 8 servings

1 small zucchini, trimmed, and grated
$1\frac{1}{2}$ tablespoons minced onion
1 small clove garlic, minced (optional)
$\frac{1}{2}$ cup freshly grated Parmesan cheese
1 cup skim-milk ricotta cheese
3 tablespoons chopped fresh parsley
Salt and hot pepper sauce to taste
1 pound zucchini blossoms, 18 to 20 blossoms,
washed and carefully dried
1 cup unbleached all-purpose flour
1 teaspoon paprika (optional)
Pinch salt
1 cup light beer
Oil for deep-frying
Cooked Tomatillo Salsa (optional, page 341)

In a bowl, beat together the zucchini, onion, garlic (if using), Parmesan, ricotta, parsley, salt, and hot pepper sauce. Stuff each blossom with a spoonful of this mixture. Press the blossoms closed.

In a medium-size bowl, whisk together the flour, paprika, pinch salt, and beer.

Heat the oil to 375°F. in a deep-fat fryer. Dip the stuffed blossoms carefully into the batter, draining off any excess. Fry three or four at a time in the hot fat until golden brown, 3 to 4 minutes per batch. Remove with a slotted spoon. Drain on paper towels. Keep hot in a 350°F. oven until all the blossoms have been fried.

Serve hot, sprinkled with salt. Pass a little Cooked Tomatillo Salsa on the side if you like.

Index

T